# The Secret War in Mexico

Friedrich Katz

# The Secret War in Mexico

## Europe, The United States and the Mexican Revolution

With portions translated by
Loren Goldner

The University of Chicago Press

Chicago and London

The University of Chicago Press, Chicago 60637
The University of Chicago Press, Ltd., London
© 1981 by The University of Chicago
All rights reserved. Published 1981
Paperback edition 1983
Printed in the United States of America

00 99 98 97 96 95 94 93 92 91    4 5 6 7 8 9

Library of Congress Cataloging in Publication Data

Katz, Friedrich.
    The secret war in Mexico.

    Includes bibliographical references and index.
    1. Mexico—Politics and government—1910–1946.
2. Mexico—Foreign relations—1910–1946.   3. Mexico—
Politics and government—1867–1910.   4. Mexico—
Foreign relations—1867–1910.   I. Title.
F1234.K27        972.08        80-26607
ISBN 0-266-42588-6 (cloth)
        0-226-42589-4 (paper)

# Contents

# Acknowledgments

Parts of this book were published in 1964 in the German Democratic Republic as *Deutschland, Díaz, und die mexikanische Revolution* and were made possible by a grant from the Humboldt University in Berlin. The major part of the work is new, and the funds, time, and other means to carry it out were provided by the University of Chicago. I would like to express my thanks to the heads and collaborators of the following archives and libraries for allowing me to use their holdings.

| | |
|---|---|
| Austria | Haus, Hof u. Staatsarchiv, Wien |
| | Kriegsarchiv, Wien |
| | Verwaltungsarchiv, Wien |
| Cuba | Archivo Nacional de Cuba, Havana |
| France | Archives du Ministère des Affaires Etrangères, Paris |
| | Archives du Ministère de la Guerre, Vincennes |
| | Archives Nationales, Paris |
| German Democratic Republic | Deutsches Zentralarchiv, Abteilung Merseburg |
| | Deutsches Zentralarchiv, Abteilung Potsdam |
| | Sächsisches Landeschauptarchiv, Dresden |
| | Deutsches Wirtschaftsinstitut, Berlin |
| | Deutsche Buecherei, Leipzig |
| | Deutsche Staatsbibliothek, Berlin |
| | Universitätsbibliothek, Berlin |
| German Federal Republic | Archiv des Auswärtigen Amtes, Bonn |
| | Bundesarchiv, Koblenz |
| | Bundesarchiv, Abteilung Militärgeschichte Freiburg im Breisgau |
| | Staatsarchiv, Hamburg |
| | Staatsarchiv, Bremen |
| | Hauptstaatsarchiv, München |
| | Kommerzbibliothek, Hamburg |
| | Iberoamerikanisches Institut, Berlin |
| | Iberoamerikanisches Institut, Hamburg |
| | Bibliothek der Freien Universität, Berlin |

| | |
|---|---|
| Great Britain | Public Record Office, London |
| | British Science Museum, London |
| Mexico | Archivo General de la Nación |
| | Archivo de la Secretaría de Asuntos Exteriores |
| | Fundación Condumex |
| | Archivo del Departamento Agrario |
| | Biblioteca de Chihuahua, Chihuahua |
| | El Colegio de Mexico |
| | Archivo de la Palabra |
| Spain | Archivo del Ministerio de Relaciones Exteriores |
| United States | National Archives, Washington, D.C. |
| | Library of Congress, Washington, D.C. |
| | Regenstein Library, Chicago |
| | Lilly Library, Bloomington, Indiana |
| | Sterling Library, Yale, New Haven, Connecticut |
| | Library of Claremont Colleges, Claremont, California |
| | Bancroft Library, Berkeley, California |
| | Netty Lee Benson Collection, University of Texas at Austin |
| | Newberry Library, Chicago |

I want to thank the following people in Mexico who have given me access to their private papers: Lourdes González Garza for allowing me to see the papers of Roque González Garza; the family of Martín Luis Guzmán for allowing me to see his papers.

I would like to express my appreciation to Richard Estrada and William Meyers, who worked as research assistants for me; to Linda Greenberg and Carlos Rizawy, who translated parts of the sources in chapter 7; to Paul Liffman for his work correcting the text; and to Celia Wittenber for typing large portions of the manuscript.

I must also express my gratitude to my many colleagues and friends who read parts or all of the book and provided valuable help. Manfred Kossok and Walter Markow of the Karl Marx University, Leipzig, had read the manuscript of the German book and provided valuable suggestions. I owe a special debt of gratitude regarding the German book to Don Daniel Cosío Villegas and his collaborators at the Colegio de Mexico in the years 1962–67. Don Daniel made it possible for me to be one of the first foreigners to gain access to the archives of the Mexican Foreign Ministry. His collaborators, Luis González y González, Moïsés González Navarro, Luis Muro, Fernando Rosenzweig Hernández, Berta Ulloa, generously allowed me to consult the sources they had accumulated for the Historia Moderna de Mexico.

With respect to this publication, I received important criticisms and suggestions from Robert McCormick Adams, who read the first and last chapters; Paul Friedrich, who read the first chapter; Akira Iriye, who read my description of Mexico and Japan; and John Coatsworth and Hans Zeisel, who read the whole manuscript. Parts of this book were written in German and translated into English by Loren Goldner, and I wish to express my gratitude to him. I would like to express a special debt of gratitude to my son Leo for his untiring and valuable help in the completion of this book.

Chicago                                                                          Friedrich Katz
October 1980

# Introduction

My interest in various aspects of the Mexican Revolution is of long standing. It began during the years of emigration I spent in that country and bore its first fruits in 1964, when I published *Deutschland, Díaz und die mexikanische Revolution* in the DDR, where I served as Professor of Latin American History at the Humboldt University in Berlin. That book covered the history of German policies in Mexico from 1870 to 1920. It consisted of two distinctly different parts. The first was a study of what might be called old-fashioned nineteenth-century imperialism. It described Germany's efforts to gain a foothold in Mexico in both the economic and political fields and to utilize that country for its global aims. The second part analyzed the transition in German diplomacy to what might be called the more flexible stratagems of twentieth-century imperialism. It dealt with Germany's attempt to forge an alliance with Mexican revolutionaries; the aims were much the same, but the methods and instruments were new and, to say the least, unconventional.

In the 1970s, both American and Mexican publishers asked me to revise the book and to prepare English and Spanish language editions. At first, I intended merely to spruce it up with some sources that had not been previously available to me and to write a new postscript describing the research carried out since the book was first published in 1964. I felt that the main thesis developed there, the analysis of German policies toward Mexico, had held up well under the scrutiny of time and new sources. Nevertheless, as the process of revision proceeded, I found that I was writing a very different book. My growing awareness of the complex interplay of the great foreign powers with Mexico and among each other made it impossible to limit the narrative to the relationship between Germany and Mexico. The whole fabric of international policies, the interplay between business interests and their governments, and their role in the political and social turmoil of the emerging revolution would have to be told. I became more and more interested in the effect these outside forces had on the course of the Mexican Revolution and how they influenced not only the foreign policies but the internal social and economic programs and policies of the revolutionary factions. The integration of social and diplomatic history became the aim of this new work.

Its title, *The Secret War in Mexico,* conjures up images of cloak-and-dagger agents in hushed-up fights along dark alleys. The reader will find sufficient material in the latter part of this book for a number of espionage

ix

novels although, should they be written, no master spy would emerge in their pages. The term "secret war," however, refers to a new strategy of alliances and understandings that the great powers and the business interests linked to them developed early in the twentieth century as a response to the wave of revolutions that swept some of what are now called the developing countries. The United States applied this strategy with great success in Cuba in 1898, when it used elements of the Cuban independence movement to obtain the expulsion of Spain's forces from Cuba and to establish American supremacy in their place.

The new strategy of exploiting social conflicts and anticolonial struggles was not adopted by the European powers until World War I, when each side tried to aid revolutionary movements that were directed at its rivals. The Germans attempted to support revolutionary liberation movements against the British in Ireland and India; and they allowed Lenin to return to Russia through Germany. The British sent Lawrence to Arabia to lead an Arab revolt against Germany's ally, Turkey; and together with the United States, the British supported nationalist movements, above all the Czech nationalist movement led by Thomas Masaryk, against the Austro-Hungarian Empire.

What makes Mexico an especially interesting case in that international game is that so many of the great powers were involved and the methods they used embraced both classical nineteenth-century and more "modern," twentieth-century strategies in response to the revolutionary movements. Direct and indirect military intervention, diplomatic and economic pressures, destabilization, attempts to play off one faction against the other—all these tactics were used by at least one of the great powers in Mexico between 1910 and 1920.

The policies of the great powers were not uniform. In each of the countries, policy toward Mexico became the subject of bitter debate and conflict. These debates took place both within the governmental bureaucracy and between government ministries and various private institutions with interests in Mexico. After the outbreak of World War I, the military establishments in each country demanded a greater role in the formulation of the policy to be followed in Mexico. At the same time, policy conflicts arose between various business interests in Mexico as well as between some of those interests and their respective governments. The result was a complicated interplay involving many nations and many forces within each nation.

The turbulent setting in which these events took place makes Mexico a case study not only of how local rifts can be exploited for global ends, but of how global rifts can be exploited for local ends. It became clear in the course of my research that this study would be incomplete and one-sided without dedicating as much attention to Mexico's revolutionaries as to the great powers. Like the Russian, Czech, Indian, and Irish revolutionaries, the Mexicans attempted to use the rivalries of the great powers for their own ends. The favor of one or more of the great powers became a weapon used by contending revolutionary factions, but a weapon that necessarily altered the posture of its possessor. The core of this work is thus an assessment of the influence of external pressures on the programs and policies of Mexico's revolution.

What has emerged from the revisions of *Deutschland, Díaz und die mexikanische Revolution* is thus a new book. It contains extensive analysis of the internal development of the Mexican Revolution as well as new chapters dealing with the policies of Great Britain, France, and the United States. The parts of the former book dealing with Germany's policies toward the revolutionaries have been revised and broadened. Those dealing with Germany's economic policies and its political expansion into Mexico in the nineteenth century have been greatly abridged and condensed.

The United States had the greatest impact on Mexico's revolutionary movements. I have given more space and attention, however, to the policies of the European powers. United States policy toward the Mexican Revolution has been the subject of considerable research, while Europe's relations with Mexico have received less attention. I have tried to correct this imbalance. I have by no means neglected the American role. On the contrary, in some places I was able to update its history with the aid of hitherto unknown European and Mexican sources and some recently declassified American documents. Also, perhaps more than other authors, I have focused on the activities of U.S. business interests and intelligence agencies in Mexico. Above all, I have attempted to place United States policies within the broader context of European and Mexican developments.

This book is divided chronologically into four parts. The first part deals with the Porfirian period and the first phase of the revolution up to the fall of Madero in February 1913. The second comprises the Huerta period, 1913 to 1914. The third part deals with the years 1914 to the beginning of 1917, the period in which the revolutionary factions waged their civil war and in which the United States mounted its punitive expedition into Mexico. The fourth part of the book covers the period from the United States' entry into World War I until its end in 1918. An epilogue examines the period from the end of the war to the fall of Carranza. Each part is subdivided into chapters on the development, during that period, of the Mexican Revolution, and on the policies of the United States, Great Britain, France, and Germany.

The search for new sources has taken me to state and private archives in both German states, Austria, France, Great Britain, Mexico, the United States, Cuba, and to some extent Spain. I have also used some microfilms from Japanese archives photographed by the National Archives after World War II and translated for me by Mr. Shimomura.

**Part 1**

**From Díaz
to Madero,
1910–1913**

# 1 Origins, Outbreak, and Initial Phase of the Revolution of 1910

The advent of some revolutions can be seen from afar. The last French king to complete his reign peacefully prior to the French Revolution of 1789, Louis XV had clear forebodings of the troubles ahead. The mischievous joy with which he bequeathed these troubles to his successor is embodied in the phrase "après moi le déluge."

Few people in Porfirio Díaz's administration, least of all Díaz himself, had any such forebodings about the Mexican Revolution of 1910 just a few months before it actually broke out, and no one then could have sensed just how much of a deluge it would turn out to be. "I consider general revolution to be out of the question as does public opinion and the press,"[1] the German envoy in Mexico, Karl Bünz, had written to his government on the eve of the revolution, and he reiterated that opinion nearly a month after its outbreak. Undoubtedly he was still under the influence of the lavish celebration the Mexican government had just staged for Mexico's then one hundred years of independence, but his view was in fact shared by most other foreign and domestic observers. Even the small minority of dissenters who had hopes of overthrowing Díaz, including Francisco Madero, the leader of the coming revolution, did not know that they were bringing on a social revolution.

It cannot be said that they were all being obtuse. With very few exceptions, none of the innumerable "revolutions" which had come to epitomize Latin American politics to the outside world ever since that continent had gained its independence from Spain had represented genuine social upheavals. And even when it came to pass, the Mexican Revolution for many years remained an isolated instance of such a social upheaval in Latin America. What made for the unique and unforeseen developments in Mexico? Very generally it was the impact of certain developments in the late nineteenth century that changed the face of most of Latin America but were to have a special effect on the unique social landscape of Mexico.

During the final decades of the nineteenth century and the early years of the twentieth, the countries of Latin America were pulled increasingly into the frenetic development of world capitalism. By 1914, $7,567,000,000 worth of foreign capital had flooded the Latin American economies, and there appeared to be no end to this wave of investment.[2]

3

In no sense did this transform those nations into industrial societies on the model of the United States or Western Europe. On the contrary, it solidified foreign dependency and intensified the characteristics of underdevelopment that lingered on as the legacy of Spanish and Portuguese colonial rule. The export of cheap raw materials, the import of expensive industrial goods, the control of some of the most important sectors of the economy by foreign firms, enormous disparities in wealth, concentration of land in the hands of a small group of owners of large estates, an overall per capita income far lower than that of the industrialized countries, a backward educational system with resultant widespread illiteracy—all of these elements, to varying degrees, prevailed in most of Latin America.

One of the main transformations effected by integration into the world market was a strengthening of the centralized power of the state. The state now had sufficient revenues to organize, maintain, and buy the loyalty of a reinforced army and police, as well as a more efficient bureaucracy. State power was enhanced enormously by a communications revolution (construction of railroads and roads, installation of telephones and telegraph) and by the provision of modern equipment for the armed forces. The consequences of these transformations were particularly noticeable in those Latin American countries run by dictators, for they now had the means to maintain themselves in power for far longer spans of time than their predecessors had in the first half of the nineteenth century.

The most outstanding of these dictators, especially in terms of longevity, was Porfirio Díaz, who ruled Mexico for thirty-one years.[3] But, while lack of democracy, coupled with symptoms of underdevelopment and dependency, created profound dissatisfaction in many parts of Latin America, the Díaz regime was the only Latin American dictatorship to fall victim to a large-scale popular revolution in the years before the 1930s.

It would be a mistake to seek to explain this unusual situation in terms of greater underdevelopment in Mexico. In comparison with much of the rest of Latin America, its dependence on the export of raw materials was less overwhelming: Mexico, for instance, did not develop a monoculture and hence was less affected by the fluctuations and cycles of world market prices. Nor was Díaz any more unpopular than the common run of Latin American dictators; on the contrary, Don Porfirio could claim considerable popularity because of his widely touted bravery in the war against the Napoleonic invasion of Mexico.

What unique circumstance, then, apart from the symptoms of underdevelopment and dependency prevailing in most of Latin America, accounts for Mexico's unique historical experience?

The explanation that first springs to mind is that the Mexican Revolution was part of a more general trend occurring in the most rapidly developing nations of Latin America, a trend which in other countries of the continent only took on different forms. This trend, or movement, consisted in the rapid development of a middle class which began to seek more political and economic power as its size and economic importance increased.

In other Latin American countries of comparable size and growth rate, traditions of parliamentarism made it far easier for the middle classes to achieve their goals with a minimum of violence or none at all. In Argentina in 1916 the radical party led by Hipólito Yrigóyen, with a largely middle class constituency came to rule as a result of an electoral victory. In Brazil similar results were somewhat more difficult to achieve. It took a military coup staged by an army under largely middle class influence to transform the political structure of the country in a way more favorable to the middle classes. Nevertheless, traditions of parliamentarism and consensus politics were so strong in Brazil that the coup was achieved without violence and remained completely bloodless. Only in Mexico, as a result of its long tradition of violent upheavals, and because it was governed by an autocratic dictator, was a violent revolution necessary to obtain the incorporation of the middle classes into the political process.

While this explanation has some merits, it is not sufficient to explain the uniqueness of the Mexican Revolution. The victory of middle-class–inspired political forces introduced a relatively long period of political stability and parliamentarism both in Argentina and Brazil, but in Mexico it ushered in one of the most profound social revolutions in the history of Latin America. The motives for this outcome are to be found, I believe, in the convergence of three developments on the eve of the revolution, each initiated early in Díaz's reign and brought to near-completion toward its end: the expropriation of the free-village lands in central and southern Mexico; the transformation of the country's northern frontier into "the border," that is, its political and economic integration into the rest of the country, as well as into the U.S. sphere of influence; and the emergence of Mexico as the focal point of European-American rivalry in Latin America.

**The Expropriation of Free-Village Lands in Central and Southern Mexico**

Part of the legacy the Spanish colonial power bequeathed to all those regions of Latin America—Mexico, Peru, Bolivia, and Ecuador—in which there had been a concentrated and socially differentiated Indian population before the arrival of the Europeans was the so-called free villages. Even though much Indian land had been expropriated by the conquerors and transformed into large estates, a substantial portion remained under the direct control of the Spanish crown. The oppression of the peasants living in those villages often exceeded that of the peons on the haciendas. In contrast to the hacendados, the corregidores (the Spanish officials in charge of overseeing the Indians) were only temporary appointees and as a rule interested only in squeezing what they could from their "wards" for as long as their stay lasted. Nonetheless, the free villages were able to preserve some features of their traditional organization and a degree of internal autonomy never known by the peons on the large haciendas. The free villages outlasted the colonial power, and, in the aftermath of independence, with the weakening of the central government, even improved somewhat their economic and political position.[4]

With the strengthening of the state under Díaz and the construction of railroads, which drastically increased land values, however, the free villages soon came under attack. In its effort to "modernize" the country, the Díaz regime embarked on a radically new agrarian policy. Joining ranks with local hacendados, it launched a campaign of large-scale expropriation of village lands and political subordination.[5]

The regions most affected by this new policy were central and southern Mexico, first, because increased market production and new railroads had caused land values there to soar, and, second, of course, because most free villages were concentrated there. Initially, the campaign proved successful, for it left the villages in possession of only a minimal amount of land and a modicum of political autonomy. Some land was left them as a token of their former status as well as for a sound economic reason: to keep a large enough labor force in the vicinity of the plantations and to tide them over the seasons in which the planters had no need of them. Some political autonomy was left them as well, but only because they managed to cling to it with unyielding tenacity.

Ultimately, however, the campaign bred considerable discontent. At first, it had elicited only sporadic unrest in various parts of central and southern Mexico, which federal troops quelled with little effort. When the expropriations spilled over into Morelos and Guerrero, however, the foundation was laid for the largest peasant revolt in the history of independent Mexico. Many circumstances made those regions a hotbed of peasant unrest. One was their proximity to the capital city, which had prevented their succumbing to provincialism, with its attendant reduction in material expectations and its constriction of the cultural horizon. Another was the easy availability of arms. The mountain ranges favored guerrilla warfare and complicated the movement of the federal troops; the density of population prevented the fragmentation of peasant forces, which had often proved their undoing. Thus, the expropriations not only engendered unrest but did so in regions where the unrest was likely to become virulent.

Through its agrarian policies, then, the Díaz regime had managed to antagonize substantial segments of the population, but it is unlikely that such policies alone could have proved the undoing of the Díaz government; other Latin American countries were similarly afflicted without undergoing a national revolution as a consequence. The agrarian problem in Mexico was compounded, however, in an explosive way by two separate developments.

### The Transformation of the Northern Frontier into "the Border"

Prior to Díaz's assumption of power, the states of Sonora, Chihuahua, and Coahuila enjoyed a fair measure of autonomous existence. Remote and isolated, not just from the rest of Mexico but from the rest of the world as well, and well-nigh independent politically and self-sufficient economically, they formed the mainstay of Mexico's northern "frontier." In the last quarter of the nineteenth century, however, with the advent of Díaz and the influx of unprecedented amounts of foreign, especially American, capital into Mexico, the country's northern frontier underwent a radical change when Díaz and the United States, respectively, imposed their political and economic controls on the region. Railway construction, begun in the 1880s, offered the most dramatic piece of evidence of the degree to which the former enclave was to be integrated into the rest of Mexico and the American sphere of influence. The railways illustrated in the most palpable way possible that what had once been a frontier was being transformed into "the border" and that what had once been largely beyond the reach of any country was now within the reach of two countries at once.

The political transformation was launched when Díaz set out to demolish systematically the almost independent principalities that regional caudillos such as Ignacio Pesqueira in Sonora and Luis Terrazas in Chihuahua had established. Naturally enough, this proved easier in some states than in others. Much more aggressive intervention was required, for example, to establish Díaz's supremacy in Chihuahua and Sonora than in Coahuila, where some decades earlier Benito Juarez had severely undermined the power of the local oligarchy when he broke Santiago Vidaurri's iron-fisted hold on the region.[6]

The economic transformation was mainly the work of American investments that began pouring into all of Mexico at unprecedented rates during the 1880s. Northern Mexico had always had a large share of this investment. By 1902, for instance, more than 22 percent of all U.S. investment in Mexico had gone into these three northern states, 6.3 percent went to Chihuahua, 7.3 percent to Sonora, and 9.5 percent to Coahuila, primarily in mining, farming, and transportation.[7]

The repercussions of this dual transformation of the frontier, the political and the economic one, caught up most quickly and unkindly with the very people who had done the most to make the frontier habitable in the first place and who were its unique product: the military colonists. In the mid-eighteenth century, the Spanish crown had established military colonies along the northern frontier to fend off roaming bands of Apaches and other nomads. The method employed was always the same: land along this frontier was granted to anyone willing to take possession of it and defend it with his life. In the nineteenth century, Benito Juarez followed this example and established more such colonies.

The inhabitants of the colonies were privileged in many respects compared to the free villagers of central and southern Mexico. Unlike the villagers, they were not wards of the crown during the colonial period but enjoyed rights generally reserved for Spaniards and their descendants, the criollos. They owned their land individually and were allowed to sell it, or buy additional land.[8] They usually owned more land and more cattle than the free peasants of Mexico's other areas. Their communities were entitled to greater internal autonomy, and the military colonists had not only the right but the duty to bear arms.

By 1885 great changes took place in the Mexican frontier region. The Apaches were finally defeated, and the frontier became appreciably quieter. Neither the hacendados nor the government any longer needed the military support of the peasants, but what they felt they did need was the land the peasants had so assiduously reclaimed, and they felt no qualms about turning against their former allies.

After the first railways linked northern Mexico to the central parts of the country and to the United States in 1885, the increasing value of the peasants' land ushered in a wave of expropriation. First hit were the most recently established settlements, but even the oldest and most prestigious ones were not spared. Resentment was acute. "We are deeply concerned that lands we consider our own, since we have received them from our fathers and worked them with our own hands, are now passing into other hands," the inhabitants of the village of Namiquipa wrote to President Díaz in 1908 (without much success). "If you do not grant us your protection," they continued, "we will have to abandon our homes in order to subsist."[9] An emissary sent to Mexico City to represent the population of another of Chihuahua's oldest military colonies, Janos, bitterly (but also unsuccessfully) complained to Díaz: "The owners of the colony of Fernández Leal, located two leagues from Janos, are enjoying a comfortable life in the United States, while we who suffered from the invasion of barbarians whom our fathers fought cannot keep our lands."[10]

The northern military communities lost not only their lands but also their cherished political rights, the most precious among them their municipal autonomy. The right of a village to elect its own municipal authorities had been conferred on many settlements in the eighteenth century by the Spanish crown. The right was reconfirmed after independence and extended to newly founded settlements as well. The greatest guarantor of that autonomy, however, was not the official charter of any short-lived government but the atomized and isolated pattern of settlements that prevailed along the frontier until about the mid-nineteenth century. Because it was no longer a factor after Díaz came to power, state authorities were able to disregard with impunity those hallowed rights and traditions and to usurp for themselves the privilege of appointing such officials as the *jefes políticos* (district administrators) and *presidentes municipales* (mayors) at their own discretion.[11]

The loss of municipal autonomy aroused almost as much passion as the loss of land. On 16 November 1910, when the populace of the old frontier village of Cuchillo Parado shouldered their rifles and enlisted in the revolutionary forces, the removal of the mayor who had been imposed on them was the most burning issue.[12] And it was the removal of a popularly elected mayor by the state authorities and his replacement by a village usurer that drove the inhabitants of the mountain town of Bachíniva in Chihuahua to join the revolution in 1910.[13]

While peasant unrest did not assume revolutionary proportions until 1910, the expropriation of land and the suppression of traditional rights did precipitate sporadic uprisings long before the revolution began. In Chihuahua, for instance, the government lost more than five hundred men in a two-year struggle with about sixty insurgent peasants of the village of Tomochic, who, in 1892, declared themselves bound only by the law of God and revolted against the encroachments of the government.[14]

Repercussions of the frontier transformation affected another group of peasants, the Indian tribes that had managed to retain their lands and a measure of autonomy throughout the Spanish colonial period as well as during the first half-century of independence. Unlike the military colonists who were mainly concentrated in Chihuahua, the most militant Indian tribe came from the neighboring state of Sonora. They were the Yaqui Indians, who inhabited one of the most fertile regions of Sonora, the Yaqui Valley. Several abortive attempts to seize their lands had been made before, but it was not until Díaz came to power that a concentrated offensive was mounted to expel them from their lands. The offensive met with fierce resistance. Long and bloody battles took a heavy toll on both sides, and, although the federal troops finally succeeded in defeating the most formidable force among the Yaquis and in capturing its leader Cajeme, they never managed to root out all guerrilla resistance.[15]

Both of these traditional peasant groups—the frontiersmen and the Indians—thus found themselves helpless in the face of blatant assaults on their property and independence until the turn of the century. The only allies they found before 1900 were former caudillos, landowners who had been ousted from positions of political power. Luis Terrazas, the richest landowner in Chihuahua and formerly governor of that state, secretly encouraged the rebels of Tomochic in the justified hope that they could discredit his chief rival Lauro Carillo, then governor of Chihuahua and a Díaz protégé, and spell his political demise.[16] Similarly, José Maria Maytorena, a prosperous hacendado of southern Sonora, scion of a prominent hacendado dynasty, whose political aspirations also had been frustrated by the Díaz government, provided a haven for fugitive Yaqui rebels.[17]

The peasants, however, did not receive the support of any nonrural classes in these states before 1900. The simple reason was that the transformation of the frontier had beneficial effects for the middle classes and the industrial working class who therefore had little reason to support the fighting peasants. Foreign investment in such projects as railroad construction greatly multiplied the economic opportunities of these classes and, until 1900, brought about a significant rise in real wages.[18] Moreover, Díaz's overthrow of the old political oligarchies had created vacancies that the middle class was able to fill and from which it was able to exercise, for a time at least, some real power, until once more displaced by another emerging oligarchy.

Not until 1900–1910 was the favorable disposition of these groups toward the regime reversed, for, in those ten years, foreign investment began to show its ugly underside. It was accelerating at a breathtaking rate: between 1900 and 1910 investments in Mexico leaped to three times the amount invested between 1876 and 1900.[19] One of the results of this increase was a soaring inflation rate that cut deep into the real wages of the middle and industrial working classes and sharply curtailed the investment opportunities of middle class entrepreneurs by tightening available credit. The government added to the burden on these two groups when it sought to raise their taxes to make up for the reduced value of taxes paid by foreign investors and the local oligarchy. Another result of increased foreign investment was a heightened vulnerability to the business cycle of the United States, which manifested itself most painfully during the economic crisis of 1907. Again the burden on the middle and working classes was increased by an external factor—the return of thousands of Mexican workers discharged from American mines and factories during each recession.

For the middle classes, falling income and rising taxes constituted only two elements of a rapidly deteriorating social and economic situation. Between 1900 and 1910 their opportunities for upward mobility were dramatically reduced through new political structures implemented by Díaz in northern Mexico. In the last years of his regime Díaz gave up his attempts to divide political from economic power and to limit the political power of the regional oligarchies in their native states. As a result political positions and patronage jobs, which in Mexico had always been crucial to the survival of the middle classes, came under the exclusive control of the state's oligarchies. At the same time these powerful groups exercised an increasing degree of control over regional and local authorities, frequently a traditional fiefdom of the middle classes. Among the latter a profound resentment against the state's oligarchies began to emerge.

Discontent within the industrial working class and the middle classes manifested itself in an upsurge of nationalist sentiment and growing resentment toward foreign investors, who were largely held responsible for their plight, and toward the Díaz regime, which refused to curtail their advance. In the final account, then, despite an auspicious beginning, the transformation of the frontier eroded support for the Díaz regime among the nonrural population.

In this period manifestations of discontent also emerged among a rural group that until then had remained passive and docile to both the large landowners and the state and national governments. These were the traditional hacienda peons, a sector of the agrarian population that, since the colonial period, was proportionately much more prominently represented in the North than anywhere else in the country. Before the reasons for their discontent are explored further, a word of caution is needed to dispel the notion that the Mexican Revolution was a peons' revolution brought about by those who were poorest and fought by those who suffered most. Historical evidence does not bear this out. That revolution was not for the most part prosecuted by peons will become evident in the remainder of this book. With some notable exceptions, Pablo Martinez del Río, scion of one of Mexico's most distinguished hacendado families, probably was quite correct in observing: "The war against the hacendado was practically never carried out by the inhabitants of the hacienda (who in many cases remained loyal to it until the end) but by the inhabitants of neighboring villages (who wanted more land)."[20]

Nor does historical evidence support the notion that the revolution originated where the spiritual and material deprivations of the peons were the greatest. In fact, Mexico's "revolutionary" North offered its peons a markedly higher standard of living than the comparatively "unrevolutionary" South, where debt peonage had degenerated to the level of virtual slavery but where the strict isolation and supervision of the peons made revolution extremely difficult. Neither slavery nor serfdom reigned on the northern haciendas in the Díaz era. Debt peonage, still widespread in the mid-nineteenth century, had been widely eroded by the development of mining and industry in northern Mexico, as well as in the southwestern United States, which offered alternative opportunities for employment. It persisted on only a limited number of haciendas in Durango, Chihuahua, and Sonora. On most haciendas, the old breed of peon was replaced by a new hacienda resident, highly differentiated and stratified in terms of the rights he could exercise and the wages he could command. There evolved a social ladder that extended from the peons still remaining up to the affluent tenants on some haciendas in Chihuahua.[21]

On northern haciendas, an important role was played by yet another group, present in the South only to a limited extent—the vaqueros, or cowboys. Cattle raising, naturally enough, became the chief industry in those regions of northern Mexico where the lack of an adequate water supply had severely checked the spread of agriculture. The vaqueros were well armed and often owned their own horses; they were indeed a privileged class. They were better off than the peasants, many owned their own cattle, which grazed on the hacienda lands, and their opportunities for social mobility were greater than were those of the peasants. For every seven or eight vaqueros, there was a foreman who received twice the salary of a regular cowboy. Anyone who remained on the hacienda long enough had a good chance of rising to this position.[22] On the whole, then, the situation of resident workers on northern haciendas was better than that of their counterparts elsewhere in Mexico, and yet their relations with the hacendados often were more antagonistic.

This antagonism may be explained by the breakdown of the patriarchal relationship between the traditional peon (whose ancestors in most cases had lived on the hacienda for centuries) and the hacendado, a relationship that had characterized both northern and central Mexico for the greater part of the nineteenth century. It continued to characterize central Mexico even during the revolutionary period, for here many peons had become a kind of privileged retainer on haciendas where the bulk of the laborers consisted of expropriated peasants. In Santa Ana Tenango, for example, on a hacienda in Morelos that belonged to the richest land-owning family in the state, the Garcia Pimentels, the majority of the *peones acasillados,* "resident peons," refused to join revolutionary ranks or even to accept the land of the haciendas granted them in the course of the later agrarian reforms.[23] Such was not the case, however, in the North, for on the eve of the revolution, Luis Terrazas complained bitterly, "Since the beginning of the unrest, I have been trying to arm the peons of my haciendas, but, I must tell you honestly these workers are infected with ideas of revolution and only a few of them are loyal to me. Arming disloyal people, as you shall see, would be counterproductive because they will go over to the enemy with their weapons and equipment."[24] This breakdown of patriarchal bonds on northern estates was not due to a lack of effort on the part of the hacendados to maintain them. Luis Terrazas made it a point to visit each of his haciendas at least once a year. On those occasions a holiday was declared, and the peons lined up to receive him and the gifts he brought. He went to great pains to remember the name and history of each peon.[25]

But the transformation of the frontier tended to vitiate those efforts. First, the traditional patriarchal relationship was strained intolerably by the enormous growth of the estate holdings of Terrazas and other barons of the North, which made it more and more difficult for the landowners to establish personal relationships with their peons. Second, it was drained of much of its meaning with the defeat of the Apaches in 1884. Until then the hacendado, like the medieval lord of Europe, had been able to offer protection from attacks by furnishing his peons with a safe refuge in his thickly fortified *casco* (the central residence hall of the hacienda which in northern Mexico had been built as both a refuge and a fortress) and by sending out retainers to fight the wandering Indian bands. When the attacks ceased, that protection was no longer needed. Characteristically, the one region in northern Mexico where relations between peons and hacendados remained the closest—many hacendados even armed their peons and led them into the revolution—was southern Sonora, where the danger of attacks by rebellious Yaquis persisted.[26] Third, the patriarchal relationship was undermined by the peons' growing awareness of higher wages and better living conditions on ranches in the neighboring United States. Thousands of them, especially vaqueros, left to find work on the ranches of the American Southwest. Those who returned to Mexico did so with fresh doubts about the patriarchal goodness of the Mexican hacendados, who paid them a fraction of what they had earned in the United States.

One additional element of discontent seems to have been limited mainly to the peons on the huge Terrazas haciendas of Chihuahua. Here, in contrast to the great majority of all haciendas in the North, restrictions on the freedom of movement of many peons, such as debt peonage, had not disappeared. The old caudillo's unwillingness to break with traditional forms of servitude was combined with a unique capacity to avoid doing so. Because of his enormous economic and political power, Terrazas had the means, which few other northern hacendados possessed, to enforce an increasingly unpopular system of debt peonage among his largely recalcitrant laborers.

In contrast to the "traditional" peons found mainly in Chihuahua, and to a lesser degree in Sonora, a new kind of "modern" estate laborer emerged, especially in the third state that was to provide an important segment of the northern revolutionary movement—Coahuila.

The term "modern peon" is perhaps the most appropriate one to designate the thousands of migrants from central Mexico, many of them expropriated peasants, who streamed into the newly developed regions of northern Mexico. The majority settled in a small area where perhaps the most rapid economic growth of the Porfirian period took place, the Laguna area of Coahuila and Durango. In its cotton fields they earned the highest agricultural wages paid anywhere in Mexico. In addition, all forms of forced labor, such as debt servitude, had practically disappeared in that region. Even the *tienda de raya*, the ubiquitous company store, was different in the Laguna from that on most haciendas in Mexico. Workers were paid in cash rather than scrip and thus were not obliged to limit their purchases to the company store. The hacendados, who frequently charged lower prices in their shops than neighboring merchants, used the *tienda de raya* as a supplementary incentive to attract scarce laborers rather than as a means to increase their profits or to force workers to remain on their estates.[27]

In spite of these advantages the region where these immigrants had settled, especially the Laguna, became an inexhaustible reservoir of revolutionary troops in the years 1910–20.[28] The basic reason for this was not primarily opposition to the region's landowners. By comparing their situation with conditions in central and northern Mexico, from whence they had come, many migrants saw it in a favorable light. Only twenty years and one generation later would the Laguna's peasants (now born and bred in the North) turn against the region's estate owners.

In the 1910–20 revolution in fact many of the permanent resident peons on the haciendas revolted not against but together with their hacendados.[29] Like medieval lords in Europe, some of the landowners of Sonora and the Laguna even led their well-paid and well-treated peons into battle.

The links of the many nonresident laborers to the hacendados were obviously more tenuous than those of the permanent residents. They constituted a far more heterogeneous group in social and economic terms, but many of them also participated very actively in the revolution, at times with and at times against the hacendados. For most of them, though not for all, the prime determinant in their actions was not land hunger— which became the prime motive one generation later—but the need to survive. By Mexican standards, nonresident laborers earned very high wages but were subject to extreme insecurity. They found well-paid employment in the cotton fields part of the year, and the rest of the time they had to make do elsewhere. In the Laguna, some laborers, called *eventuales*, remained near the cotton estates to find odd jobs, sometimes in industry or mining, sometimes on estates that produced other crops.[30]

Others became permanent migrants alternating their work at cotton harvesting in the Laguna with agricultural and nonagricultural labor in other parts of Mexico and in the southwestern United States. It was a precarious existence, for each of these sources of employment was subject to constant cyclical fluctuations. On the average, every third year insufficient rainfall affected the flow of the Nazas and disrupted the cotton harvest in the Laguna,[31] while cyclical depressions at times affected not only mining in Mexico but work in industry and agriculture in the United States as well.[32] In such a recession the Mexican laborers were the first to be dismissed. One such crop failure or depression was difficult enough to bear for the migrant workers, but when all occurred simultaneously, as was the case between 1907 and 1910, the situation became catastrophic.[33] It was compounded by the fact that many of those migrants had no villages or extended family networks to fall back on, as the peasants of central and southern Mexico had. It was precisely this rootlessness that made them more prone than the traditional peasants to join revolutionary armies fighting far from their native soil.

By 1910 only one Mexican group finally benefited from the transformation of the frontier, the new caudillo class in Chihuahua and Sonora, which had begun to rise from the ashes of the old one in the last quarter of the nineteenth century.

The new class was an amalgam of "blue-blooded" and upstart caudillo dynasties. Some of the older ones who had been removed from power in the course of Díaz's transformation were able to make a comeback. Most prominent among them was the Terrazas clan, which made its peace with Díaz in 1903: Luis Terrazas was reappointed to the governorship of Chihuahua, to which he was succeeded by his son-in-law Enrique Creel and somewhat later by his son Alberto Terrazas.[34] Other members of the new caudillo class were recruited by Díaz from the lower end of the old ruling stratum in the course of his political revamping of the region. Most prominent of these were Luis and Lorenzo Torres, military men who headed Díaz's faction in Sonora during Díaz's successful revolt of 1876; they ousted Ignacio Pesqueira, who had dominated the state for many years.[35]

The economic gains of these groups were tremendous even before 1900. In addition to their traditional sources of income, they were able to take advantage of completely new ones that the influx of foreign capital had opened up: middleman functions for foreign companies moving into Mexico; sale and utilization of public lands considered worthless before the railroads were built; and, above all, control of the credit system in their home states.[36]

After 1900 their economic preeminence was coupled with political preeminence. Díaz gave the new caudillos almost unlimited control over their states and put many of them in important positions in the federal government. Their power now exceeded the wildest dreams of their predecessors in the pre-Díaz era. Anyone wishing to hold a government post, whether at the local or state level, had to go through the new power brokers. Anyone going to court had to appeal to judges appointed by them. Anyone needing credit had to turn to banks controlled by them. Anyone seeking employment with a foreign company probably had to depend on their mediation. Anyone losing his land to a *compañia deslindadora* (surveying company) could blame them. The new local oligarchy had not only gained unprecedented power, it also threw off the constraints and obligations its predecessors had borne. It did not respect municipal autonomy, nor did it have to provide protection against the assaults of the Apaches or the federal government. It is therefore not surprising that the oligarchies of Chihuahua and Sonora quickly became the prime target of an opposition that united the most diverse groups of the population, albeit by little more than their common hatred of the omnipotent caudillo oligarchy.[37]

The caudillos of Coahuila were an exception to all this. Unlike Sonora and Chihuahua, Coahuila saw no lasting alliance formed between the new oligarchy and the Díaz government. In fact, by the time the new century dawned, the two were in open conflict.

In 1885, Porfirio Díaz had sent a close confidant, General Bernardo Reyes, to the northeastern states of Nuevo León and Coahuila as military commander with the directive to break the hold of the local caudillos so that their power could be assumed by the central government. Reyes was successful at first, but after he was appointed governor of Nuevo León in 1887 he allied himself closely with the old oligarchic circles and became one of the most powerful caudillos in Mexico.[38] He was able to increase his already considerable support in the armed forces when he was given the post of minister of defense in 1900. He became the only new caudillo to call into question the power of Mexico's financial and political oligarchy, popularly called the Científicos because they espoused Auguste Comte's positivism and Herbert Spencer's social Darwinism.[39] The ambitions of Reyes and the northeastern groups tied to him soon aroused the mistrust of Díaz, who sent Reyes back to Nuevo León in 1903 and put an end to his role as minister of defense.

This relegation by no means induced Reyes to abandon his ambition to become the ruler of Mexico. In 1908 he let it be known that he hoped Díaz would include him in his ticket in the election of 1910 as candidate for vice-president. It was widely assumed that in view of Díaz's advanced age he would not outlive his term and that his vice-president would succeed him. Reyes hoped to force his candidacy upon a recalcitrant Díaz by mobilizing important sectors of the upper and middle classes to agitate in his favor.

The mounting enthusiasm that part of the northeast's upper classes (and to a lesser degree some Sonoran hacendados) manifested toward Reyes led to an increasing hostility toward them on the part of the Díaz administration. Unlike the elites of Chihuahua and Sonora, some of whose representatives Díaz had accepted into his administration, the wealthy and powerful merchants and landowners of the Laguna were excluded from representation in the federal government. Díaz took one further step by forcing Governor Miguel Cárdenas, who enjoyed the support of large groups of hacendados in Coahuila, to resign and by preventing the election of another landowner of the state, Venustiano Carranza, who was backed by most of the state's upper class.[40]

Díaz's opposition to this group of the northeastern elite as well as the latter's mounting bitterness may have been compounded by their increasing conflicts with foreign interests. The best-known, but by no means unique, conflict of this kind concerned the Laguna's (and probably all of Coahuila's) wealthiest family, the Maderos. (This family had never supported Reyes but one of its most prominent members, Francisco Madero, had for some years attempted to set up political opposition to the Díaz administration.) In contrast to the Torres and Terrazas families, the Madero clan, which was the wealthiest and most powerful family in Mexico's northeastern region, had never cooperated harmoniously with the U.S. companies and had become notorious among those companies for its ill-concealed confrontation tactics. At the turn of the twentieth century, Francisco Madero had formed and led a coalition of hacendados in the Laguna region to oppose attempts by the Anglo-American Tlahualilo Company to monopolize the water rights of that irrigation-dependent area. When the Maderos cultivated the rubber substitute guayule, they had clashed with the Continental Rubber Company. Another conflict developed because prior to 1910 the Maderos owned the only smelting oven in northern Mexico that was independent of the American Smelting and Refining Company.[41]

The Maderos were not alone in their fight. Many other members of the northeastern upper class were interested in water rights in the Laguna, in the cultivation of guayule, and in the operation of independent smelting ovens in northern Mexico.

These factors would not be sufficient, however, to explain why some of the northern hacendados finally decided to revolt. Northeastern Mexico was not the only region of the country where conflicts had emerged between landowners and the federal government. In Yucatán a similarly bitter conflict had erupted. In an attempt to raise the world market price of henequen (sisal), their staple crop, the hacendados of Yucatán had come to an agreement with the National Bank of Mexico to buy up large amounts of sisal which were to be kept off the market so that demand would outstrip supply and the price of henequen would rise. Instead of adhering to this agreement, the bank, strongly influenced by Mexico's economics minister, Olegario Molina, who maintained close ties to the largest sisal buyer in the country, the International Harvester Company, suddenly dumped all of its henequen on the market. The result was an unprecedented fall in the price of sisal and near ruin for many planters. Dissatisfied as they were with the policies of the Mexico City government, the planters would never even remotely have considered the option of calling on the peasants to rise against the federal government. They were mortally afraid that their peons, who lived in conditions of semislavery and who had lost much of their land to the hacendados, would make them the first target of their revolt.[42]

The revolutionary hacendados of Coahuila, the majority of whom were located in the Laguna area, entertained no such fears. Most of the Laguna had been unpopulated wasteland before the hacendados reclaimed it. Unlike their counterparts in Yucatán, they did not have to confront a mass of peasants whom they had expropriated. The fact that the peons on their estates received the highest wages and enjoyed the greatest freedom found anywhere in the Mexican countryside had created a new kind of paternalistic relation between these landowners and their peons. The hacendados attempted to strengthen this relationship by providing schools and medical care to their workers. Some enlightened landowners, such as Francisco Madero, even extended many of these services to nonresident peons, thus earning their loyalty.[43]

In the long run the hacendados' confidence in the passivity and loyalty of their peons proved to be completely unfounded. In the 1930s the second and third generation of Laguna peons set up the most militant peasant movement in Mexico. As a result the most radical agrarian reform that took place in Mexico in the thirties occurred in the Laguna. For the period 1910–20, however, with some significant exceptions, the hacendado's optimism was not unrealistic. Rather than rebel against the landowners, most of the peons of the Laguna preferred to join them in their fight against the federal government. Thus the northeast's hacendados, in addition to strong motivation to revolt, had a unique kind of mass support that allowed them to do so.

## The Characteristics of the Frontier

These uneven developments raise two obvious questions: Why did the North become the mainstay of the Mexican Revolution from which both its victorious leaders and armies emerged? And why, among the many frontier regions that developed on the American continent, was northern Mexico practically the only one where a large scale and successful revolutionary movement took place?

The answer to the first question is obviously linked to the rapid, largely foreign-induced, economic change in the North which led to large-scale economic and social dislocation. Northern Mexico, however, was not the only region so affected. Rapid growth linked to dislocations occurred elsewhere in Mexico, for example, in Morelos, Veracruz, and Yucatán. Radical social movements did emerge in all those regions, though not simultaneously; the Zapata revolt broke out in Morelos in 1910, but in Veracruz and Yucatán radical protest movements developed in the 1920s.

What distinguished the revolution in northern Mexico from these other movements was the diversity of social classes and strata that joined the revolution, on the one hand, and the access of the northern revolutionaries to arms, on the other.

What was unique to the North was that substantial portions from all classes of society participated in the revolution. It was the only part of Mexico, for example, with a relatively large stratum of revolutionary hacendados, whose support for anti-Díaz political movements threw them into alliance with middle classes and even the lower classes of society.

A dissatisfied middle class which resented the fact that it was excluded from political power, that it seemed to garner only the crumbs of Mexico's economic boom, and that foreigners were playing an increasingly important role in the country's economic and social structure existed in most parts of Mexico. Nowhere, however, had it grown as rapidly as in the North, and nowhere had it suffered such losses in so short a span of time. Not only was the northern middle class profoundly affected by the cyclical crises of 1907 that hit the North far more than any other part of Mexico, but it also suffered greater political losses. In the nineteenth century because of the isolation of the frontier states it had enjoyed a degree of municipal and regional autonomy which was equaled in no other part of the country. The absorption of the North by the central government cost this class most of these traditional rights.

Nevertheless these losses were at first compensated for by two advantages the Díaz regime brought them: one was rapid economic growth and the building of railroads from which many of them benefited. The other was what could be called the introduction of the two-party system into some of the northern states. In Chihuahua for instance, after he became president, Díaz removed the traditional oligarchy from power and imposed his own men on the state. The Mexican president was not strong enough, however, to prevent the old ruling group from forming its own political party and challenging the new rulers of the state. In the resulting conflict both sides sought the support of the state's middle classes which thus gained a certain degree of political and economic leverage.

When Díaz, in a profound political reversal at the turn of the century, gave political control of their states to the oligarchy, he put an end to the two-party system and completely excluded large segments of the middle classes from political power. At the same time their economic situation grew drastically worse. They were first hit by inflation and rising taxes and many of them were ruined by the crisis of 1907–10.

The same crisis affected the North's industrial working classes to a degree unprecedented in their experience and unparalleled in the rest of Mexico. With the possible exception of the city of Mexico it was in the North of the country that the greatest number of unemployed workers could be found on the eve of the revolution.

Also the agricultural population of northern Mexico exhibited a number of traits that distinguished them from their counterparts in the rest of the country.

Because of the Apache wars, they had a far greater fighting tradition and more arms than peasants in any other part of the country. Because so many of them were engaged in industry and mining, many more peasants in the North had links to the nonagricultural population than in any other part of Mexico. The migrants and the vaqueros who formed a large part of the population of the northern countryside had no deep-rooted traditional attachment to a specific community.

These three factors were obviously conducive to their joining revolutionary armies.

To all of these characteristics that distinguished most social classes in the North from their counterparts in the rest of Mexico must be added a tradition of cooperation among all classes of society which first emerged in the Apache wars and which reemerged in the course of the revolution. While uprisings of peasants, industrial workers, and members of the middle classes occurred in different parts of Mexico, only in the North were all of them able to unite among themselves and to join forces with a group of revolutionary hacendados.

The proximity to the United States was the last element that helped to transform the dissatisfaction of nearly all segments and classes of frontier society into revolutionary activity. The transformation of the frontier into the border did more than change many frontiersmen into revolutionaries. It also gave them the means for carrying out a revolution. Proximity to the United States provided them with an easy solution to the perennial problem facing all revolutionaries—access to arms. In spite of its neutrality laws, the United States was used as a sanctuary by revolutionaries preparing to launch a movement in Mexico. The ideological consequences of the economic symbiosis between Mexico's frontier and the American Southwest were as strange as the practical ones. A pronounced anti-

American nationalism was combined with the desire of the Mexican middle and working classes to obtain the rights and freedoms enjoyed by their counterparts in the United States.

All these elements provide an explanation of why the Mexican North played a role so different from the rest of the country during the revolution. It also helps to explain why the Mexican North was the only frontier region in Latin America which became a center of large-scale revolutionary activity.

None of the vast frontier regions of South America had the kind of easy access to arms and ammunition northern Mexico had. Because the Mexican frontier neighbored one of the most highly developed countries of the world, economic growth was more rapid and more one-sided and therefore produced more dislocations than in any other frontier region of Latin America.

There was also a very uncommon kind of influx by foreigners. Foreign immigrants were important to the development of many frontier regions in Latin America. Thus, Germans working mainly as farmers played an important role in the growth and development of southern Brazil and southern Chile. But they were always subordinated to native authorities. Because of northern Mexico's proximity to the United States, American immigrants were usually wealthier and far more privileged and powerful than immigrants to South American frontier regions. They brought with them the specter of annexation to the powerful neighbor to the north and thus evoked a degree of nationalist resentment far greater than in the South American frontier regions.

The rapid integration of northern Mexico into the political structure of the Díaz regime and into the economy of the United States and the resulting appropriation of its public lands by a domestic oligarchy and foreign investors suddenly closed off access of its vast land resources to its lower and middle classes. Their resentment was increased by the fact that many of these lands remained sparsely settled, were frequently not cultivated, and largely used for speculative purposes. These developments undermined whatever free peasantry had developed in northern Mexico in the days of the open frontier. The disappearance of the free peasants led to a concomitant disappearance of democratic political institutions that were the product of a century long evolution on the northern frontier. These political changes in turn affected all of the population whether they were peasants or not.

## The European-American Rivalry

The Díaz regime was toppled not simply because of the many forces it alienated inside Mexico, but because of the powerful forces it alienated outside the country—important interest groups within the United States.

In his effort to stem what he came to view as an onslaught of American investors, Díaz made increasingly friendly overtures toward European powers, inviting them to invest in his country and to challenge the American primacy there. When his invitation was heeded, Mexico emerged as a focal point of European-American rivalry in Latin America.

If Díaz expected to strengthen his own authority by challenging American influence, he miscalculated badly. Stung into action, American interest groups withdrew their support from him and began to search for a more congenial ally among his foes. By incurring American resentment before he had secured enough European support to counterbalance its ill effects, Díaz inaugurated yet another development that would eventually claim him as casualty.

Díaz's position toward the United States had not always been uncooperative. Following a sharp conflict over the right of U.S. forces to cross the Mexican border in pursuit of bandits and nomadic Indians at the beginning of his presidency, Díaz had been noticeably benevolent toward American investment in Mexico. His stance changed, however, with his growing awareness of the proprietary attitude the American business community, convinced of its "manifest destiny," had come to adopt toward his country. That attitude was most succinctly articulated by James Speyer, whose bank was one of the largest investors in Mexico, in a talk with the German minister in Mexico. "In the United States," Speyer said, "there is a pervasive feeling that Mexico is no longer anything but a dependency of the American economy, in the same way that the entire area from the Mexican border to the Panama Canal is seen as part of North America."[44]

Díaz's changing attitude was affected even more by the American victory in the Spanish-American War of 1898, the ensuing policy of the "big stick," and by the chain of American interventions in Panama, Haiti, and Cuba. What created the greatest change, however, was a difference in the character of the U.S. companies that began to move into Mexico. No longer middle-sized concerns whose influence had predominated up to the turn of the century, but rather, large trusts, as they had first surfaced in the United States, now came to carve out their place on the Mexican scene. Large enterprises such as the Mexican Petroleum Company, with close ties to Standard Oil, increasingly dominated the field.

Díaz himself showed his alarm over these trusts on several occasions. In 1908, for instance, he expressed to Edward Doheny, the head of Mexican Petroleum, his concern that that company might fall into the hands of Standard Oil, and made Doheny promise to give him advance notice if a merger with Standard was contemplated.[45] This was not the first time that Díaz had expressed such alarm. "The Mexican government has now formally taken a position against the trusts formed with American capital," the Austrian minister to Mexico reported to his superiors and continued:

"A series of articles appeared in semiofficial newspapers pointing to the growing dangers that the intensive activities of the trusts are presenting to the Mexican producers. The latter will soon be slaves of the North American money markets. The economic development in the country is creating a dependency on the powerful Union to the North, and the political consequences of such dependency are obvious."[46] The French envoy to Mexico indicated in a letter to his Foreign Minister Delcassé how patent and infectious the government's concern over American trusts was becoming: "We can as little afford to be indifferent toward such activity," he suggested, "as the Mexican leaders who are concerned for their country's independence."[47]

Alarm began to infect much of Mexico's ruling elite, the Científicos, who had never been happy with American domination of the investment drive. First, they traditionally had closer ties with European rather than with American financial circles. Second, and more important, the less well-established European companies were generally more accommodating in their dealings than the American ones, often acquiescing to a Científico business partner where Americans had balked. Third, and most important, American predominance was inimical to the Científicos' concept of what Mexico's economic development should be.

The German minister to Mexico, Freiherr von Wangenheim, made this quite clear in a report he submitted to his superiors on the aims and organization of the "cosmopolitan" (i.e., Científico) elite. He wrote:

> In their view, the political future of the country depends entirely on the development of the economy. To realize this, however, the country needs help from abroad, including the United States. Mexico is thus increasingly destined to become an area of activity for capitalist firms from all countries. The cosmopolitans, however, paradoxical as this may sound, see precisely in economic dependency the guarantee of political independence, insofar as they assume that the large European interests that have investments here constitute a counterweight to American annexationist appetites and that they will pave the way for the complete internationalization and neutralization of Mexico. Behind the scenes, but at the head of the cosmopolitan group, stands the Finance Minister, Señor Limantour. His allies are *haute finance,* as well as the top-level civil servants with interests in the domestic and foreign companies, senators and deputies, and, finally, the local representatives of European capital invested in Mexico.[48]

In an effort to ensure the neutrality and independence of the Mexican "arena," the elite turned with mixed success to France, Germany, Great Britain, and, after 1905, even to Japan. On 28 April 1901, the French minister reported a conversation with the president of the Mexican Chamber of Deputies, José López Portillo y Rojas:

> He [López Portillo] spoke at length of the serious efforts made over the

last few years by the United States to carry out a general invasion of Mexico with American capital, railways, and industry. "There can be no question that we cannot respond to this invasion in a radical fashion, as the United States has contributed to the development of our country in the past, continues to do so today, and will contribute further in the future. We must keep such a powerful neighbor in a good mood and we must do nothing to antagonize it. On the other hand, we have the right and also the duty to look elsewhere for a counterweight to the constantly growing influence of our powerful neighbor. We must turn to other circles, from which we can draw support under certain circumstances, in order to preserve our industrial and commercial independence. We can find such a counterweight only in European and particularly in French capital." Señor López Portillo thus summarized the outlook expressed to me by many leaders who are not hypnotized by American power and who are worried about the American's attempts at controlling Mexico's economic life.

And the envoy reminded his own foreign minister, "We must support with all our power the efforts of the Mexicans to have important firms financed by French capital, which would be taken over by the Americans without our help."[49]

French influence in Mexico, however, was never a significant counterweight to the United States. French capital investments were predominantly in public debt and the rest were in banking and industry. In these areas, French influence was indeed an obstacle to American expansion. But in the decisive areas of raw materials and the railway system, French influence was of little consequence and could in no way challenge the U.S. presence. Also the French share of trade was minimal.

With one significant difference the same can be said of Germany's economic role during the Porfirian period. The Germans had invested heavily in Mexico's public debt, only little in raw materials, somewhat more in railways. The one field where Germany had made important, even spectacular, inroads into the Mexican economy was trade. By 1910 German imports to Mexico were second in volume only to those from the United States, albeit a distant second; while 55 percent of all goods imported into Mexico came from the United States, only 12.3 percent originated in Germany.[50] The significance of Germany's economic presence derived not from any counterweight it created to U.S. influence but from the groundwork it laid for its later, more prominent involvement during the revolutionary period (see chap. 2).

Great Britain was the one power that seriously challenged U.S. predominance in Mexico. Its economic interest and involvement in the country was long-standing. Mexico's preeminent trading partner and investor for most of the nineteenth century, it had been displaced by the United States after the construction of the railroads that linked Mexico to its northern neighbor. For a time the British seemed resigned to this loss of influence, and the German minister passed on to his government rumors to the effect that Britain considered giving up its consulate in Mexico City and concentrating its efforts on retaining its supremacy in South America. This trend was reversed, however, at the turn of the century with the discovery of large petroleum deposits in Mexico and the related, virtually meteoric rise of one of Britain's largest Mexican companies, the Pearson Trust.[51]

Weetman Pearson, later Lord Cowdray, first went to Mexico in 1889 as head of a British construction firm. He carried out extensive drainage and harbor construction there and rose to prominence when his company acquired and rebuilt the Tehuantepec Railway, which, prior to the completion of the Panama Canal, represented a strategically and economically vital link between the two coasts of North America. But Pearson's real significance lies in the fact that he founded what became Mexico's largest petroleum producer, the El Aguila Oil Company, which by 1910 controlled 58 percent of the country's oil production.[52] Subsequently, this company became vitally important to the British empire for its fleet was just then making the change from coal to oil as its primary fuel and its own oil reserves were not sufficient. Pearson's company also became vitally important to Mexico when Díaz decided to make it the spearhead of his most drastic efforts to curb American influence by enhancing its European competitors.[53]

Díaz's efforts were focused primarily on the American railway monopoly, an instance of American domination particularly resented in Mexico. At the beginning of the twentieth century, most of the Mexican railway network was in the hands of two American companies, Standard Oil and the banking house of Speyer. In a conversation with the German minister Heyking in 1903, Díaz had already voiced his fear that "Mexico will find itself in the same situation as the United States, where the railway companies have repeatedly shown that they have more power than the government."[54] The German minister himself expressed similar fears: "Even from the strictly economic point of view, it would seem problematic to leave four of Mexico's links with the rest of the world in the hands of two American companies, where one has to reckon with the probability that these same companies, tiring of rivalry, would be able to unite or merge in order to exploit freight rates to monopolize all traffic." And he continued, "Already, the Standard Oil Company, after acquiring the line between Tampico and Monterrey, is charging such high freight rates that the petroleum recently discovered near Tampico cannot be transported by train. Since the steamship lines from New York and New Orleans to Veracruz also are controlled by Standard Oil, it must be feared that it, together with the Speyer consolidation, will attempt to divert all Mexican traffic to the

United States on the basis of the freight rates they have established and to cut off Mexico's trade with Europe."[55] His successor, Wangenheim, reported in a similar vein. "The Mexican railway freight rates are thus completely dependent on big American capital, and the actual consequence of this is that the freight rates are adjusted to American interests. As a result, to subsidize this arrangement, rates for all shipments within the republic are so much higher than the rates of imports that domestic products cannot compete with American goods because of transportation costs. In other words, the railways are indeed promoting trade, namely American trade, but are permitting no domestic industry to develop."[56] Complaints about the effect that the preferential treatment for American goods at the expense of European goods was having on Mexican railways were aired by the German consul in Chihuahua: "If it is already extremely difficult for the German businessman on the U.S. border to gain an edge for German goods, it will become virtually impossible for him to compete with American goods at the current railway freight rates."[57]

It became increasingly clear to the Mexican government that its desire for a trade policy oriented more toward Europe would never be successful until U.S. control of the railroads was broken. Through a series of financial manipulations, a new company, the Mexican National Railways, was formed in 1907–8, which gave control over the majority of rail lines to the Mexican government. The most important posts on the board of directors of this new company were given to some of the executives of the Pearson Trust.[58]

With Díaz's blessing, but probably at the instigation of the Pearson Trust, the newly formed railway system then took its most anti-American measure: it immediately canceled a contract its predecessors had signed with the American-owned Mexican Petroleum Company to supply it with oil.[59] In all other areas, however, the company proceeded with caution. Indeed, some measures designed to weaken U.S. influence on the railroads do not seem to have been implemented. In 1909 the company decided to dissolve the American monopoly in sales of railroad equipment, but, in practice, little changed.[60] In 1911, price changes favoring European goods were announced, but it cannot be ascertained whether they were actually introduced.[61] The board of directors of the new company requested that American employees learn the local language, but, after a protest by the U.S. ambassador, this regulation was essentially ignored.[62] Characteristically, the tremendous possibilities of consolidating Mexico's economic independence through "nationalization" of the railroads were never exploited by the Díaz government.

The foremost beneficiary of Mexico's assumption of control over its railroads was the Pearson Trust; the foremost loser was Standard Oil. While some American companies were scarcely affected by the new developments and others even profited from the fact that a sudden increase in freight rates had been avoided, Standard Oil had unequivocally lost out to the Pearson Trust. The latter was now given a distinct preference by the Mexican government over Standard and all other oil companies. It received major concessions of government lands in the states of Veracruz, San Luis Potosí, Chiapas, Tamaulipas, and Tabasco, to the exclusion of all other oil companies. As an initial consequence of these measures, Pearson obtained important supply contracts from the Mexican National Railroad. The founding of a new oil company, the Compañia Mexicana de Petroleos El Aguila, in 1908 was further evidence of the strong bond between Pearson and the Mexican government. Partners in this company, which controlled all of Pearson's oil assets, included both Pearson and some leading Científicos, such as Foreign Minister Enrique Creel and the son of Díaz himself.[63]

All this produced, quite predictably, mounting American resentment, exacerbated by the fact that, between 1905 and 1911, Mexico began to advance to the forefront of petroleum-producing nations. In 1910 it was the seventh largest producer in the world (3,352,807 barrels); in the following year, production more than quadrupled (14,051,643 barrels) and the country became the world's third largest oil producer. Some observers were convinced that the largest reserves in the world were in Mexico.[64] In the face of such vast opportunities, Mexican business interests in Mexico were less and less prepared to put up with the Díaz government's anti-American collaboration with the Pearson Trust, and soon the opinion became rife that the only way to end that collaboration was through a change of government in Mexico.

### The Weakness of the Mexican Army

A characteristic that differentiated Porfirian Mexico from most of the larger countries of South America, such as Brazil, Argentina, Chile, or Peru, and might help to explain not so much the outbreak as the victory of revolutionary movements was the relative weakness, even backwardness, of the Mexican army. The Porfirian armed forces constituted one of the few Latin American armies to be defeated in a conventional and guerrilla war by revolutionary troops.

In contrast to most countries in South America, Porfirian Mexico did very little to modernize its army. Although a modern military academy was set up to train officers, the soldiers were still recruited by the levy system, which consisted of forcibly impressing the poorest and most recalcitrant elements of society into the army where they were subjected to the worst possible conditions. Unlike the South American countries, Mexico called in no foreign instructors to implement modern techniques of organization and warfare. In fact Díaz constantly reduced the military's share of the national budget.[65] In view of Mexico's long history of military *pronunciamientos*, he obviously feared the army far more than popular uprisings (which except for the 1810 revolution of independence had never assumed national proportions in Mexico) and felt that the relatively weak army was strong enough to quell the local revolts.

Such fears were not limited to Mexico. Many countries of South America shared a similar history of military coups, but in contrast to Mexico these countries were faced with the possibility of wars with neighboring Latin American countries. Argentina, Brazil, and Uruguay had fought a long and bloody war against Paraguay, which lost a large part of its territory. In the war of the Pacific, Chile had annexed important parts of Bolivia and Peru. A perennial rivalry existed between Argentina and Brazil, and Chile and Argentina had conflicting territorial claims. Mexico had no fear of attack by any Latin American country, for its neighbors to the south, the Central American republics, were so small and divided that they could never present a threat to Mexico.

In the nineteenth century, Mexico had been the victim of two foreign aggressions: the Mexican-American War and Napoleon and Maximilian's ill-fated attempt to conquer Mexico. After the defeat of Maximilian and the establishment of excellent relations with the Continent, an attack from Europe was considered out of the question. This left only one potential danger: the United States.

As I have pointed out, there is no doubt that Porfirio Díaz and the Científicos were not only conscious of, but greatly worried about, that danger to Mexico's independence. Many of Mexico's leaders assumed that two eventualities could lead to a United States intervention in their country: internal turmoil which would endanger American investments or the potential threat to America if Mexico would involve itself too strongly with a foreign power.

Neither Díaz nor the ruling oligarchy believed that strengthening the army would counter that danger. A strong army might increase the risk of coups and internal conflict and thus precipitate rather than weaken the danger of a U.S. intervention.

The kind of modernization which a strong army needed would have required European instructors and strong links to European powers. Such military links could have provoked deep suspicions on the part of the United States.

Díaz and the Científicos thought the best way of limiting United States influence in Mexico and preventing American intervention in their country was through strengthening economic but not military ties with Europe. The European powers rather than the Mexican armed forces would constitute the most effective deterrent to United States intervention in Mexico.

If one adds to these considerations the fact that the only serious challenge to the ruling oligarchy in Mexico before the revolution came from the military, the deliberate neglect of the Mexican armed forces is not difficult to understand.

Díaz had tried to make up for the weakness of the army, and at the same time to set up a counterweight against it, by establishing a well-organized, professional, national police force, the rurales.

In contrast to the soldiers who were inducted in the army from the lowest classes of society and who were kept there for many years under abysmal conditions, the *rurales,* many of them former bandits, were well-paid professionals. They were Mexico's most efficient fighting force, but they numbered only a few thousand men and were too small a force to make up for the deficiencies of the whole army.[66]

### On the Eve of the Revolution

The increasing opposition to the Díaz regime that emerged across the entire social spectrum after the beginning of the twentieth century, particularly in the northern states, engendered opposition movements on a national scale for the first time since the establishment of the Díaz dictatorship. The most radical opposition came from the Liberal party, led by the Flores Magón brothers. It was created in 1902 by a group of intellectuals with strong anarcho-syndicalist tendencies. Persecuted by the authorities, the leading members were forced into hiding and eventually fled to the United States, where they set up a revolutionary junta in Saint Louis.[67]

The party called for the overthrow of Díaz and played an important role in organizing strikes and several abortive uprisings against the regime. It gained some influence among intellectuals, members of the middle class, and the industrial workers. Though its newspaper *Regeneración* was not allowed to circulate in Mexico, it had more than twenty-five thousand readers. The party's great weakness was that it never succeeded in gaining substantial influence among the peasantry.

The same held true for another opposition movement that emerged during this same period, the Democratic party. Unlike the Liberals, it did not seek to mobilize the peasants. It was essentially a party of the "outs" among Mexico's upper class, and had no desire to change the country's political structure. Its main objective was to replace the aging Díaz with its own leader, Bernardo Reyes, and to break the power monopoly of the Científicos, the oligarchy that had formed around Díaz. To this end they demanded more democracy and expanded participation in political life. Traces of anti-American nationalism were also evident. By means of these policies, the movement led by Reyes attempted to unify the opposition wing of the upper class with the discontented groups of the middle class.[68]

The emergence of these political parties was by no means the only sign of increasing opposition to the Díaz regime after the turn of the century. The most dramatic manifestations were two strikes, one at Río Blanco in 1906 and the other at Cananea in 1907; their fierce suppression by the government enormously intensified popular discontent.

At the Río Blanco textile factory in central Mexico, workers engaged in bloody clashes with the factory owners, who had issued regulations that provided new forms of control over the work force. The workers turned to Díaz for mediation; he agreed to intercede but supported the factory owners on almost every point. Refusing to accept the mediation proposals made by Díaz, the workers launched a strike. In describing the situation, the German minister in Mexico, Wangenheim, wrote: "To the delegation of factory owners from Orizaba, which had asked for federal aid to crush the workers, he [Díaz] replied, sobbing, 'Thank God, I can still kill.' The killing was already under way the day before yesterday, under the supervision of Commander Ruíz, who has a reputation for cruelty and ruthlessness and who has been appointed successor to the district chief wounded in the fighting."[69]

Wangenheim, who himself was anything but sympathetic toward the strikers, reported several days later: "More and more details are being divulged on the simply barbaric fashion in which Commander Ruiz has dealt with the insurgent workers in Río Blanco. One could hear constant shooting in the mountains from Orizaba as late as yesterday, as fugitive workers who had been found in their hideouts by the troops were killed. More than four hundred Indians have been shot. The Mexican Railway alone has brought nine cars piled high with corpses from Orizaba."[70]

At Cananea, in the northern border state of Sonora, the striking miners demanded compensation at the same level of American miners. This strike was crushed with similar ruthlessness.[71] These two strikes and their repression began to give a new quality to the anti-Díaz opposition forces in Mexico.

When the tense situation was exacerbated by the almost simultaneous start of an economic, political, and international crisis, the revolution was finally rife. Mexico's economic crisis was the result of the enormous growth in foreign investments after 1900, compounded by a crop failure that most acutely affected the northern states. The flood of foreign investments after 1900 had made the country more and more dependent on the advanced industrial nations; the adoption of the gold standard by Mexico in 1905 had slowed economic growth and the cyclical crisis that occurred in the United States during 1907–8 had a devastating effect on Mexico in general and the northern states in particular.

Chihuahua was one of the states hardest hit. The German consul there reported in 1909: "The economic situation has been particularly bad because of increases in the costs of necessary food and beans. Most food prices have doubled, and beans have gone from 6 to 15 pesos per hecto-liter. The purchasing power of the public has been seriously reduced.... The population's consumption has been reduced to the most essential foods. The earnings of the workers have been reduced still further, and wages have dropped to between .75 and 1 peso a day."[72] This means that price increases of between 200 and 300 percent were accompanied by wage cuts.

Although the working class was most acutely affected by the crisis, the middle class was not spared. The banks and state agencies that were controlled by the Científicos attempted to shift the burden of the crisis to the middle class as well as the working class. The banks called in their outstanding loans and gave credit almost exclusively to companies owned by the oligarchy. In the rare cases where other enterprises received credit, they were charged exorbitant interest rates averaging 12 percent. The German consul reported further: "Even though the banks have been somewhat more liberal in their loans, the cost of money has remained quite high and has made business difficult. Even first-rate companies have been unable to obtain funds at less than 10 percent, while the interest rates of the banks have been 12 percent per annum and the rates of the private moneylenders have ranged from 18 to 24 percent."[73]

The situation of the middle class was aggravated by the numerous scandals that rocked Mexico's most prestigious financial institutions, such as the Banco Minero in Chihuahua, owned by the Terrazas group. These scandals threatened the safety of whatever funds these banks had been able to accumulate in better times.[74] The government did nothing to alleviate the situation. Small- and middle-sized firms were granted no tax cuts; quite the contrary, they were often burdened with higher taxes at a time when they could least afford them. By contrast, the large landowners and foreign companies more often than not continued to enjoy the tax exemptions they had been granted during the preceding period of eco-nomic upswing.

What compounded the crisis in the northern states was, of course, the return of the thousands of Mexican workers laid off in the United States. At the frontier town of Ciudad Juarez alone, approximately two thousand workers, whose fare to the border was paid by U.S. companies, crossed the border on the way to their homeland in 1908.[75] The presence of these people tended to give a particularly militant edge to the unrest that was brewing.

Mexico's international crisis was the result of two mildly provocative gestures toward the United States in which the aging Díaz indulged him-self. The first was nothing more than his friendly reception of Jóse Santos Zelaya, former president of Nicaragua, who had been forced out of office by the United States because of his strong anti-American bent. The second, a slightly more serious gesture, was Díaz's refusal to extend the U.S. navy's lease on a coaling station in Baja California.[76] That these relatively insignificant incidents so irritated the United States only highlights the tensions building up as a result of the preferential treatment Mexico had accorded to America's European rivals during the preceding decade.

The political crisis was the result of Díaz's long hesitation to name a successor. The resulting confusion was to tip the scale in favor of the revolution. That confusion first began to manifest itself in 1908, when Bernardo Reyes, whose ambivalent relationship to the Científico elite has already been noted, and Ramón Corral, who enjoyed the full support of the Científicos, set out to compete for the vice-presidential nomination in the 1910 elections. The vice-president would succeed Díaz in the event of his death, which it was thought would occur during his next term.

Reyes promoted his own candidacy through rather novel tactics. To compensate for his less favorable position within the ruling group, he tried to gain support from the population as a whole and was successful in building a certain base of support in the middle class. In the opinion of the German minister, Reyes's supporters were in the main "youthful enthusiasts of the educated classes, younger officers, and lawyers."[77] Stormy meetings on his behalf were held in many parts of the country. One factor in his favor was that his party, except for the small anarcho-syndicalist Liberal party, was the only nationwide opposition party. Yet, while his movement fought against the Científicos, it did not attack the president or the system he had created.

In that same year, Díaz granted an interview to an American journalist, James Creelman, possibly with the aim of splitting the opposition. He stated that in his opinion Mexico was now ripe for democracy. He no longer intended to present himself as a presidential candidate in 1910 but wished to give this office to someone else. He assured Creelman that, henceforth, he would not only tolerate opposition parties but would give them every possible assistance.

Díaz's desire to split the opposition, and probably his underestimation of the discontent in the country, gave his antagonists some room to maneuver on the local and national levels during 1908–9. This margin of freedom did not offer the opposition an opportunity to win but allowed it to organize.

The Creelman interview and the measures that followed it resulted in a politicization of large parts of the population that had scarcely participated in political life in the past. The newly founded movement included not only discontented members of the middle class but also, for the first time, peasants, who had earlier used local movements to express their bitterness and despair. In the gubernatorial elections of 1909 and 1910, they voted on a massive scale in the state of Morelos and the southeastern state of Yucatán.[78]

The most important new group that arose at this point was one that rapidly acquired national significance, the Anti-Reelectionist party under the leadership of Francisco Madero, from the state of Coahuila and a member of one of the wealthiest families in Mexico. After studying law in France, he returned to Mexico in 1892 to take over one of his father's haciendas. A dreamer and a spiritualist, on the one hand, he combined, on the other, a practical economic outlook with explicit philanthropic ideas. At the outset, he raised the wages of his agricultural workers, had them undergo regular physical examinations, and introduced compulsory schooling, so that the living standards on his hacienda vastly exceeded those on neighboring estates. Madero coupled this attitude toward his workers with the introduction of new, more productive methods of culti-vation, which greatly increased profits and soon made his hacienda into a kind of model enterprise in both social and economic terms. Those years on the hacienda shaped his attitude toward the agrarian question; the condition of the peasants could be improved, not through land reform, but through the hacendado's enlightened, patriarchal attention to their prob-lems.

Some of the factors in the development of the Madero family's political role have already been presented: Díaz's failure to integrate the family into his political system and the growing conflict between the Maderos and American companies. It is difficult to measure the impact these factors had on Francisco Madero. Undoubtedly they did influence him. His hostility toward American attempts at monopoly were to be ex-pressed both in his writings and in his later activities as president of Mexico.

Madero became a national figure in 1908, when he published a book on the presidential succession. In it, he characterized Mexico's fundamental problem as that of absolutism and the unlimited power of one man. Only the introduction of parliamentary democracy, a system of free elections, and the independence of the press and of the courts could transform Mexico into a modern, democratic state. The book was very cautiously written. While harshly criticizing the Díaz system, he praised the dic-tator's personal qualities. He came out against excessive concessions to foreigners and reproached Díaz for being too soft toward the United States. Social questions, however, were barely dealt with. Madero did present arguments against certain by-products of the agricultural system—such as illiteracy, the landowners' promotion of alcoholism, and the deportation of rebellious Indians—but not against the system itself. Nor is there anything about land reform in his book. Although he touched upon the poor living conditions and the persecution of industrial workers,

Madero was more concrete and unambiguous in this area than he was with regard to the peasantry. This difference in approach to the two problems reflected the primarily agrarian character of the majority of the Mexican bourgeoisie.

Madero's book was more than a political analysis of the situation; it was a program calling for the formation of a new, Anti-Reelectionist party. The careful formulations, a certain easing of the censorship in the last years of the Díaz era, Madero's own social position, and the government's total underestimation of him made possible the appearance of the book. Its impact was considerable, for, in spite of its reticences, it was the first publication that openly attacked the political system. It enormously facilitated the formation of Madero's new party, which found most of its early members and supporters among the intellectuals and middle class.[79]

Although Madero's program essentially expressed the desires of the opposition bourgeoisie, its members at the beginning gathered around Reyes, who was more widely known than Madero and appeared to have a greater chance of political success. Madero's own family supported his views to some extent but considered his strategy hopeless and feared that they would lose their properties if they broke with Díaz.

In 1909 the new party announced its participation in the forthcoming election and selected Madero as its presidential candidate. Díaz did not take the movement seriously. Quite the contrary, as long as the Reyes party existed, the government welcomed Madero's appearance as a counterweight to Reyes, hoping it would split the opposition.

Madero's position suddenly changed at the end of 1909. There had been a big swing in favor of the Reyes movement at the beginning of that year. Large sympathy demonstrations for Reyes had taken place in many cities, and in Guadalajara and Monterrey there had been bloody clashes between his supporters and the police. It was then that Díaz decided to act. He made it clear to Reyes that he would oppose his candidacy and election to the office of vice-president with all the means at his disposal. Confronted with the choice of surrendering or of leading a revolutionary insurrection against Díaz, Reyes chose the first path. He allowed Díaz to send him off to Europe with the official explanation that he was making a study of military institutions there. After Reyes's banishment, the Madero movement took on dimensions that no one had expected. When Madero toured the country in the electoral year of 1910, he was welcomed in the city of Guadalajara by more than ten thousand people; almost as many participated in a rally by his party in Monterrey, in spite of hindrances by local authorities and the police. More than fifty thousand persons demonstrated for him in the capital.

The movement led by Madero gained a foothold in both the lower and upper strata of society and was, aside from the Liberal party, the only real opposition to Díaz. In contrast to Reyes, Madero had never exercised any functions in the Díaz administration, which contributed to his party's steadily increasing popularity among the industrial workers and peasants, in spite of its lack of a program for social and economic reform. The strength of the movement also brought a wing of the opposition bourgeoisie, after Reyes's withdrawal, over to Madero. The growing support for Madero prompted more and sharper reactions by the Díaz government. The persecution of Madero was intensified, meetings of his party were outlawed, and Madero himself was arrested shortly before the elections.

The elections were carried out in the usual fashion, and Díaz was declared the victor. The government considered its position to be so strong that it freed Madero on bail. Nonetheless, he fled to the United States, where he emerged with a program and addressed the Mexican people with a statement known as the San Luis Potosí plan. This plan, like his book and the electoral program of his party, essentially reflected the desires and aspirations of the wing of the Mexican bourgeoisie hostile to Díaz: broadening of political power, the introduction of parliamentary democracy, and limitation of rights of foreigners. In the plan, Madero declared Díaz deposed, made himself the provisional president of Mexico, elaborated the principle of no reelection of the president, and free, secret balloting.[80] Social questions again were barely mentioned, but the plan nevertheless contained an important contrast to all previous programs by Madero: it contained a paragraph promising the return of all unjustly expropriated lands to the peasant villages; nothing was said, however, about the implementation of such a procedure.

## The Madero Revolution

For some of Madero's supporters, especially the members of his family who had rallied to his cause when his movement began to show certain prospects of success, and after Díaz had moved against the family, his revolution was to be nothing more than a kind of coup d'etat by the ruling class and the army against the dictator Díaz. Madero's father stated in a press interview: "Twenty-six Mexican senators are participating in the revolution.... This is not a small uprising but a revolution in which Mexico's financial groups are actively taking part."[81] What unfolded, however, was something quite different. Madero's program, although it hardly mentioned social demands, became the crystallization point for the opposition movements of peasants, workers, and the middle class.

Madero's revolt on 20 November 1910 elicited only scattered uprisings on that date. The most spectacular one was staged in Puebla by Aquiles Serdan and his wife, along with a few followers, but it was crushed handily by government troops. But the veritable storm, the nationwide upheaval that broke loose soon after was no longer to be crushed. Revolutionary movements sprang up in the most unlikely places. Many, of course, remained without any larger repercussions or even resonance. Revolutionary movements of formidable proportions were generated only in the border states of the North and the southern state of Morelos.

Many of the movements that now arose had at first only limited contact, if any, with the national leadership of the Anti-Reelectionist party. Some local leaders, such as Toribio Ortega, who led the revolution in the Chihuahuan village of Cuchillo Parado, had been local chieftains of the Anti-Reelectionist party. Others, such as Pancho Villa, had no political affiliation but maintained personal ties to important Madero officials. Still others, of whom Emiliano Zapata was the best example, had neither political or personal ties to Madero.

Within a few months after Madero returned to Mexico, the leadership of his party managed to bring most of the revolutionaries (above all those from northern Mexico) under some kind of control.

The popularity of Madero and some of his regional leaders, as well as the arms and ammunition they were able to provide, contributed to their increasing domination of the revolutionary movements. Nevertheless, profound differences in their leadership and social composition became increasingly apparent. These movements were by no means all of the same type. In Coahuila what began as a popular movement soon came under the control of Díaz's old hacendado opposition, whose chief ambition was to achieve power at the national level. The leaders, Madero and such allies and former Reyes supporters as Venustiano Carranza and Felícitas Villareal, were anxious to steer the revolution into solely political channels and to forestall any extensive social reforms. Their supporters comprised a motley assemblage of other hacendados, members of the middle class, unemployed workers, dispossessed peasants, and hacienda peons (frequently loyal to their patrons!).

In Sonora the Maderist movement resembled, but did not replicate, that of Coahuila. It, too, was in the hands of hacendados, albeit a weaker group, whose ambition was confined to seizing control of their home state.[82] Like those of Coahuila, the hacendados of Sonora wanted political reform but opposed social reforms. They enjoyed the support of similar groups but with the major addition of one group—the Yaqui Indians of Sonora. The leader of the Maderist movement in Sonora, José Maria Maytorena, scion of an old hacendado dynastry that had been forced out of power by the Díaz-supported Torres-Corral group, was an old patron of the Yaquis. When, at the turn of the century, in order to crush their guerrilla movement, the Mexican authorities had decided to deport all Yaquis from Sonora to Yucatán and other remote provinces, Maytorena, who had employed many of them and had always assumed the role of protector with regard to Yaquis living near his haciendas, had opposed the deportation order. Sharp clashes ensued between him and the Sonora government, culminating in his temporary arrest. For that courageous stand, he was now able to count on the dedicated support from the Yaqui protégés.

In contrast to those of Coahuila and Sonora, the revolutionary movements in Morelos and Chihuahua did not come under the leadership of hacendados. In Morelos that was hardly surprising since it was purely a peasant movement to begin with. Unlike other states, moreover, the Morelos opposition had been organized long before Madero's candidacy for president, when it attempted to elect a propeasant candidate, Patricio Leyva, as governor of the state, in the hope that he would stave off the merciless onslaught of the sugar planters on free-village lands. When Leyva was defeated by the candidate of the Díaz "machine," the peasants threw their weight behind the next promising opposition candidate, the hacendado Madero. As their leader, however, they elected one of their own, a peasant from the village of Anenecuilco named Emiliano Zapata.[83]

The strongest revolutionary movement in the country developed in Chihuahua. It, too, was not under the leadership of hacendados, simply because there were almost no opposition hacendados in Chihuahua: Luis Terrazas and his dominant group had forged an alliance with all the large landowners in the state, through either marital or economic ties.[84] The revolutionary movement, a coalition of the middle class, the workers, and the peasantry recruited its military and political leaders almost exclusively from the middle class.

The head of the Anti-Reelectionist party in the state, Abraham González, was the descendant of one of the state's leading families and a one-time rancher who had been unable to hold out against the competition of the large haciendas, primarily those belonging to the Terrazas-Creel clan.[85] One of the military leaders of the Chihuahuan revolutionary movement, Pascual Orozco, was a muleteer who had become embittered with the state government for having given important concessions to a rival.[86] Chihuahua's leading intellectual pioneer and mentor of the revolution, Silvestre Terrazas, a distant relative of the Terrazas clan and obviously the black sheep of the family, had for years edited the most influential and, for a long time, the only opposition newspaper in the state, El Correo de Chihuahua, and had been imprisoned several times by the state government run by his relatives.[87]

One of the reasons why such middle-class leadership was accepted by the other groups in the revolutionary coalitions, that is, the peasants, was that relations between the urban middle class and the free peasants in Chihuahua probably were closer and better than almost anywhere else in

Mexico. Many of the former military colonists had, after all, belonged to what could be called an agrarian middle class and were wealthier than most free peasants of central and southern Mexico. That a majority of them were mestizos prevented the emergence of cultural or racial barriers that frequently provoked antagonism between the largely Indian peasants and the mestizo urban middle class in other parts of the country.

Nevertheless, the local leadership of the peasantry fell to its own men. Toribio Ortega, who led the residents of his village, Cuchillo Parado, when they revolted on 18 November, had functioned for years as the spokesman of those villagers.[88] Heliodoro Arías Olea, who was the spokesman for the peasants of Bachíniva, had been trying over a long period of time to have the corrupt state-appointed mayor removed from office. A peasant leader in the classical style, Arías Olea was able to lead his villagers into the struggle.[89]

There was only one major leader of the revolutionary movement in Chihuahua who can be said to have sprung from the ranks of this peasantry: Francisco "Pancho" Villa.[90] To be sure, his link to, or descent from, this group is by no means clear. His background was extremely varied—hacienda peon, miner, bandit, merchant—and much of it is shrouded in legend. The story of his becoming a bandit because he killed a hacendado who raped his sister is still disputed, but his record as a cattle rustler is not. Rustling was not considered a disreputable activity among a large segment of Chihuahua's prerevolutionary population, for, until 1885, everyone had access to large herds of unclaimed cattle that grazed on the state's immense public lands. After that year, when the Apache wars ceased and railroads linked this northern state to the United States and to the rest of Mexico, the hacendados began exporting cattle and appropriating public lands. The traditional right of the people to dispose of such "wild" cattle was abolished, but in the eyes of many Chihuahuan peasants Villa was simply reinstating a privilege that had once been theirs.[91]

Cattle rustling did not constitute the only link between Villa and those militant peasants. In the years just prior to the outbreak of the revolution, he had established headquarters near the town of San Andrés, a former military colony involved in a protracted land and tax dispute with the state's oligarchy and its government. In 1908 the village had revolted against the taxes imposed on it. The uprising (in which Villa did not participate) was put down but many of the insurgents joined Villa two years later when he took up arms for Madero.

Despite his links to the village community, unlike Zapata, Villa did not become a traditional peasant leader. Until his death, the Southern revolutionary remained a spokesman and advocate of his native village of Anenecuilco. There is no evidence that Villa showed similar interest in

San Andrés. In contrast to the peasants who fought with Zapata, many of the men who joined Villa—associates from his bandit days such as Tomas Urbina, hacienda administrators such as Nicholas Fernández, and foremen of cattle ranches such as Fidel Ávila, who later became governor of Chihuahua—can scarcely be described as peasants.

This heterogeneity was characteristic of a large segment of Chihuahua's revolutionary army, which consisted not only of peasants and members of the middle class but also of workers, mainly railway workers, miners, and a large number of unemployed, who often were the most easily recruited. It was this army, led by Pascual Orozco and Pancho Villa, that in 1911 won the decisive battle of the revolution which ended in the capture of the border city of Ciudad Juárez.[92]

Madero, who had gone from the United States to Chihuahua to direct the revolution, found his most important power base there. The weak Díaz army, whose generals had become old and whose human and material resources were far below their nominal levels of strength because of widespread corruption, was less and less capable of mastering the situation. At this state of the revolution, the consequences of the unique competition between the United States and Europe for the decisive foreign influence in Mexico became apparent. The U.S. government, and probably its business interests as well, presented the Díaz government with the bill for its efforts on behalf of the European powers. While officially neutral, the attitude of the United States was, in many respects, unfavorable toward Díaz. The U.S. administration had been a generous host to Madero and allowed him to make his preparations while residing in the United States and had created no important obstacles to the shipment of U.S. arms to the revolutionaries.

In March 1911, however, the United States concentrated large military units on the Mexican border and sent its warships into Mexican ports. These steps hurt Díaz. To some observers, they suggested that the U.S. government considered him no longer capable of controlling the country, to other observers they gave the feeling that Díaz desired U.S. intervention. There are also indications, though it cannot be clearly demonstrated at present, that the Standard Oil Company provided the Madero movement with important aid.

The U.S. attitude, the victory of Madero's forces at Ciudad Juárez, and the inability of the government to contain uprisings now bursting out in many parts of the country demonstrated the weakness of the Porfirian army and thereby the fragility of Díaz's hold over Mexico. At this point, the oligarchy showed itself ready to drop Díaz in order to maintain the system. It found a receptive ear among the conservative wing of Madero's movement, who increasingly feared an expansion of the revolution, and their willingness to compromise was indeed strengthened as the revolution spread. Their influence was a decisive factor in bringing about the Treaty of Ciudad Juárez in 1911.

By May 1911 the situation had become favorable for the revolutionaries. The entire country was in an uproar after Madero's troops captured Ciudad Juárez. The Díaz government could hold out for only a few weeks more—or a few months at best—before it totally collapsed. This, however, was not what Madero wanted. Instead of setting about to destroy the system once and for all, he began compromise negotiations with the Díaz supporters. The radical wing of the revolutionary movement urgently warned him against involving himself in any compromises. "Revolutions are always painful operations on the body of society," Luis Cabrera, one of the most prominent revolutionary intellectuals, wrote to Madero. "The surgeon has the duty, above all, not to sew up a wound before it has been completely cleaned out. The operation...has begun. You have opened the wound and you are obliged to close it. But woe unto you if, from fear of a bloodletting or from compassion from the pain besetting the country, you close the wound without having cleaned it and without having destroyed at its roots the evil you wanted to eradicate. The sacrifices will have been in vain, and history will curse your name." Cabrera called on Madero to solve the economic and social problems of Mexico, since, "at the bottom the political and democratic demands are nothing else but the expression of economic demands."[93]

Madero disregarded these warnings, and, on 21 May 1911, signed the Treaty of Ciudad Juárez. While the treaty did provide for the removal of Díaz and his vice-president Corral, it also accepted the perpetuation of essential institutions of the Díaz regime, principally the federal army, and left its supporters, not the revolutionaries, in key positions in the new provisional government. Francisco León de la Barra, Díaz's former ambassador to the United States, was named interim president. The revolutionary armies were to be demobilized. The provisional government's main task was to hold elections within the shortest feasible time.

Seen as a whole, the Treaty of Ciudad Juárez meant the end of Díaz but it preserved the old state apparatus, including the army, the judicial system, and the parliament. It said nothing of social changes of any kind, of land reform, or of the abolition of debt peonage. Many of Madero's supporters viewed the treaty as the beginning of the end of the revolutionary movement.

Madero obstinately continued to follow the path on which he had embarked. For five months, without raising the slightest objection, he allowed the provisional government of León de la Barra to do almost everything it could to destroy the revolution. The German minister, Paul von Hintze, who was close to León de la Barra, reported: "De la Barra wants to accommodate himself with dignity to the inevitable advance of the ex-revolutionary influence, while accelerating the widespread collapse of the Madero party and thus, over time, putting the authority of the legal government on a firmer footing. On the whole, his project has thus far been a success."[94]

## The First Months of Madero Rule

After the elections, which were an unequivocal victory for Madero, he assumed the presidency. He continued to use the old Díaz forces as his power base, leaving the state apparatus firmly in their hands and allowing them to retain crucial cabinet posts. He invited many members of his own family to join his cabinet: his uncle Ernesto became minister of finance; his cousin Rafael Hernandez, minister of economics; his relative-by-marriage, José González Salas, minister of war; and his brother Gustavo, his unofficial right hand and jack-of-all trades. He also invited to serve in his cabinet some prominent leaders of the revolutionary movement, such as Abraham González, whom he appointed minister of the interior, and Miguel Díaz Lombardo, whom he appointed minister of education. Such vital portfolios as those of the foreign minister, however, continued to be held by such inveterate Díaz supporters as Manuel Calero.

Many contemporary observers and, later, some historians have viewed Madero's policies as an expression of a naive estrangement from reality. His statement, "If we have freedom, then all our problems are solved," is said to show that, in actuality, he had no program for ensuring stability or for solving the social and economic ills that beset the country. If, however, one looks more closely at his policies and tries to trace their ancestry, it becomes clear that he was by no means a dreamer who, alien to this world, was moved by abstract spiritist influences, but rather a perfectly coherent politician who reflected in his world view the ideology of the landowning class, tinged with a good dose of philanthropy.

In his world view Madero shared two fundamental credos with the old-style Científicos: first, that only a continuous flow of new, foreign capital would enable Mexico to modernize, although, of course, that flow had to be better regulated than it had been under Porfirio Díaz in order to prevent the encroachment of American trusts; second, that only large landholdings would permit Mexican agriculture to modernize. The haciendas, of course, had to be managed by progressive, fair-minded, and generous hacendados, and such illiberal means of exploitation as debt peonage would have to be abolished. Thus, Madero essentially agreed with the Científicos that the existing socioeconomic system was the only rational one and needed to be preserved. Where he differed from them was in his belief that, in order to preserve the system, the middle class had to be integrated into the political process much more than it had been. The introduction of political democracy was a step in that direction. It allowed the middle class to share in the exercise of power at both the local and state levels, much less so at the national level. It also put an end to those economic measures, such as unequal taxation, that had proved most deleterious to the rising middle class. The preservation of the existing system also required that the various movements of the industrial workers be steered from revolutionary paths into evolutionary ones by legalizing strikes and unionization. But the preservation of the existing system required, as well, that radical peasant movements, pushing for immediate land reform, be stopped in their tracks. It appears that primarily out of this latter consideration, Madero decided to leave the old federal army intact.

This decision, however, was the one that most irritated even those members of the upper and middle classes who otherwise agreed with Madero. Many of his supporters came from the North and were not greatly affected or threatened by peasant demands; they could not understand the tenacity with which he clung to the federal army and warned him repeatedly of the grave danger its preservation would bring about. "To preserve the federal army at the very moment when still-lingering elements of the old regime are raising their heads," Roque Estrada, one of his former collaborators, wrote him, "and then to dissolve the revolutionary armies at the same time, means to pave the way for the triumph of reaction."[95] But Madero refused to heed the warning. Until his last day in office, when military officers murdered him, Madero considered the federal army a cornerstone of his regime. He had hoped it would help him in his two-front battle, against the radical revolutionaries demanding social changes, and against the conservatives attempting to regain the absolute power they had lost.

Madero's first and sharpest confrontation in this battle was with the revolutionary peasantry. His policy on the peasant question was expressed most clearly in his relations with the liberation army of the South under Emiliano Zapata. When he met with Madero for the first time on 7–8 June 1911, Zapata formulated three demands: the return of the expropriated lands to the peasants, the establishment of a new revolutionary administration in Morelos, and the withdrawal of the troops of the old Díaz army. Madero explained to him that the problem of returning the land required serious study and thorough investigation and could not be resolved instantaneously. He did agree to two concessions, however, if Zapata were willing to disband his army: a Maderista from outside Morelos to be appointed governor of the state—Zapata's nomination was not even considered—and federalized former revolutionary troops to garrison Morelos. The planters, the provisional government, and the federal army there were not willing to abide by even these limited concessions. Federal troops entered the state and soon engaged in hostilities with the Zapatistas. Madero, though he protested against the actions of the provisional government, could not, or would not, restrain the federal troops, so that full-scale war soon broke out again in the state. The fighting continued even after Madero assumed the presidency.[96]

Embittered and disappointed by the actions of the Madero government, Zapata rose against Madero on 25 November 1911 and proclaimed the Ayala plan. He demanded the return of all expropriated lands to the villages, the distribution of one-third of the hacienda lands among the landless peasants, and the expropriation and breakup of all haciendas whose owners had fought against the revolution. This plan became the program for the struggle of the revolutionary peasants in southern Mexico for the following decade.[97]

Despite the fact that Madero had carried out no significant social changes, he was compelled to deal with the daily mounting opposition of the Díaz forces, who hatched plot after plot against him. For the Díaz forces, the handful of new faces in the old state apparatus was already too numerous. They also considered Madero's campaign against Zapata to be far too lax and moderate. Madero himself had not proposed a single law on the question of agrarian reform, but the strong radical wing of his party, who called themselves the "Renovadores," enthusiastically advocated such reforms. In the widely discussed speech of Luis Cabrera, one of the leading Renovadores, before the parliament on 3 December 1912, he outlined the plight of the peasantry and energetically called for land reform.[98] The Díaz forces feared that Madero might be inclined to go along with this orientation.

The main objective of the Científicos, however, was to regain the omnipotence they had enjoyed throughout the country under Díaz. To this end, they waged an ever intensifying struggle against Madero, which they carried out in legal and illegal ways with the aid, in great measure, of the democracy Madero had fostered.

The press and parliament constituted the legal battleground. Madero had effectively brought full freedom of the press to Mexico. Neither Zapata nor the trade unions, however, were able to make use of this freedom, because they lacked the means to publish their own newspapers. The Madero party itself had only one newspaper, the *Nueva Era*. While the government had bought up a majority of the stock of *El Imparcial*, the propaganda sheet of the old Díaz regime, it had not reshuffled the editorial board.[99] All other papers remained in the hands of Díaz supporters and daily directed fierce attacks on the new president. But it was not enough that almost all the old newspapers were united in a common front against Madero; there then arose a flood of new publications subsidized by the

Díaz forces which far outdid the others in their hatred of and attacks on the new government.

The parliamentary system, which Madero introduced, also worked primarily to the benefit of the Díaz forces. Neither Zapata nor the trade unions were represented in the national congress. Although Madero's followers had the majority, only a small number of them, the Renovadores, were real revolutionaries demanding radical changes in the social structure. The other "Maderists" had strong ideological and social ties to the Díaz system. The balance of forces among the delegates facilitated the actions of the Díaz supporters, who made up roughly one-fifth of the delegates. In the parliament, they pursued essentially three objectives: (1) the complete discrediting, by means of hard-hitting propaganda speeches, of the Madero regime; (2) the prevention of any movement in the direction of social change; and (3) the paralysis of the government apparatus, thus further contributing to the triumph of the conspirators.

The conspiracies constituted the second, illegal terrain of operation for the opposition. These activities were facilitated mainly by the unaltered functioning of the old Díaz army and the gradual demobilization of the revolutionary armies.

The first conspiracy was the attempted coup in December 1911, in which General Bernardo Reyes attempted to seize power for himself. He crossed the Mexican–U.S. border on 13 December and called on the people to rise against Madero. His coup was a total failure. Madero's victory had not yet completely paled; his popular support was still strong enough to defeat the conspiracy. The old Díaz forces, moreover, had not yet recovered their strength and many of them did not trust Reyes. In addition, Madero still seemed to enjoy U.S. support. On 25 December, Reyes surrendered to the Mexican army and declared: "My call on the Mexican people and the army to liberate themselves from Madero was met with icy silence; when I personally set foot on the soil of the fatherland, no one rallied to me. I bow to the united will of the nation, which does not want a revolution."[100]

More serious was the insurrection of Pascual Orozco, the former revolutionary general in northern Mexico, whose ambitions Madero had painfully frustrated when he refused to support Orozco's candidacy for the governorship of Chihuahua. Orozco refused to be mollified when Madero appointed him head of the militia there and presented him with a generous settlement of one hundred thousand pesos for his services to the revolution. Instead, Orozco organized an army of his own, consisting of many of his own militiamen and other disillusioned Maderists. His was a revolutionary program that gained him the support of many former revolutionaries, especially Zapatista peasants who deeply resented Madero's moderate political stance. Curiously enough, his movement was financed by large American firms, as well as by the conservative landowners of Chihuahua.[101] Such an alliance between the most powerful landowners of the North and rebels demanding land reform was not without precedent. Twenty years earlier, in 1892, Luis Terrazas encouraged the inhabitants of the village of Tomochic in their struggle against the state government headed by his rival Lauro Carillo. When, in part because of this incident, Terrazas was able to oust and replace Carillo, he had no qualms about supporting the state action that resulted in wiping out almost all the inhabitants of Tomochic. Terrazas and the American firms probably hoped to use the Orozco uprising in a similar fashion as a means of destabilizing the government and gaining the upper hand in the resulting confusion.

The Orozco rebellion began on 3 March 1912 and managed to win a few victories; but, within four months, Orozco was decisively beaten by government troops and his army dispersed. The insurrection failed because important portions of the Díaz army, however much they sought to bring about the overthrow of Madero, did not want to allow former revolutionaries, however conservative they had become in the meantime, to seize power.

On 16 October, the Veracruz garrison, under the leadership of Felix Díaz, a nephew of Porfirio Díaz, rose against the Madero government. Felix Díaz called on the federal army to join him. Many generals and officers of the old Díaz army were prepared to do so, but they did not see Felix Díaz as the right man to lead a movement with any serious hope of success. Hintze, the German minister, who was on good terms with leading officers of the Mexican army, described the situation accurately:

> General Felix Díaz, by his own admission, built his revolution on the discontent within the army. It is his personal weakness that accounts for his total defeat once he actually engaged the troops of the government. Instead of seeking immediate negotiations with the handful of federales on the outskirts of Veracruz, he lingered in the city, putting on festivals and organizing processions. Even the smallest success in the period immediately after his revolt would have prompted important sections of the army to go over to him. I base this opinion on the confidential statements of many leading generals; it has now become a widely held view. The Díaz revolution has collapsed because of the incompetence of its leader.[102]

Madero displayed a fatal softness toward the leaders of these coup attempts. After Reyes gave his word of honor not to flee, he was promptly released. Later, he was put into the Santiago Tlatelolco prison, where he enjoyed special privileges and thus was effectively in a position to organize new conspiracies from his prison cell. Felix Díaz was condemned to death in the wake of his defeat but the Supreme Court, which was made up of judges appointed by Porfirio Díaz, annulled the sentence handed down by a military court, and Felix Díaz was transferred to the same prison as Reyes. As he now enjoyed the same privileges as Reyes, he, too, was able to involve himself in conspiracies almost without interruption. Madero said: "I would be willing to grant amnesty to those conspirators who, like Orozco and Díaz, could show they had acted for patriotic goals."[103]

A further setback for the Madero revolution was the complete reversal in the American policy toward Mexico. In its initial stages, the Madero movement had enjoyed both the sympathies of the American government and the support of some of the major American companies in Mexico. Rumor had it that Standard Oil rendered valuable services to the movement, and this rumor had not yet been put to rest.[104] But that good relationship began to go awry in March 1912, soured by a series of increasingly acrimonious confrontations between Madero and the American government and business interests.

Much of Madero's initial support in the United States came from those elements who hoped that he would perpetuate the Díaz system while favoring U.S. capital over European investors. Such views were quite clearly expressed by H. L. Wilson, the U.S. ambassador, who wrote, in the wake of Madero's victory: "I am now of the opinion that Mr. Madero will change his ideas of government, and that, as time passes he will be compelled by the forces of circumstances to revert more and more to the system implanted by General Díaz." He expressed the firm conviction that "Madero will do justice to American interests."[105]

By 1913 the change of U.S. attitude toward Madero was complete; it had shifted from veiled sympathy or at least tolerance to unremitting hostility. There is a widely held view today that U.S. hostility toward Madero can be attributed to the personality of Ambassador Wilson. It has been asserted that he had received bribes from Díaz and that Madero had refused to continue the practice. Other commentators point to Wilson's close financial ties to the Guggenheim concern, which participated vigorously in the struggle against Madero and also exerted an important influence on the Taft administration.[106] Still others have pointed to the deep-rooted differences in temperament and outlook of Wilson and Madero. Some of these factors undoubtedly played a role, but they were not decisive. In the last analysis, the large American companies in Mexico and the American government stood behind Ambassador Wilson, and it is there that the roots of the American opposition to Madero must be uncovered.

If one considers Madero's financial and foreign policies, the extremely intense U.S. opposition to him initially seems incomprehensible, for Madero implemented almost no anti-American measures. In foreign policy, he moved away from the pro-British orientation of the Díaz era. With respect to American companies, once again, anti-American actions undertaken by Madero were in fact minimal. He announced a small tax on crude oil and took steps to dismiss the American employees of the national railways who were unable to speak Spanish.[107] Like his predecessor, Madero also attempted to float loans, primarily in Europe, but was unsuccessful. The European banks refused to handle a Mexican bond in 1911–12, and it had to be entrusted to the Speyer bank in the United States.[108] The significance of these moves for the Americans lay less in their actual effect than in their potential to set a precedent for future actions.

More significant for the U.S. government and American companies was not what Madero did but what he failed to do. The German envoy, who maintained close relations with both the Mexican government and the U.S. embassy, wrote at the beginning of 1912:

The shift of America's Mexico policy from sympathy for Madero's government to virtually open hostility is due to several factors:

1. Madero's refusal to satisfy American demands that he provide compensation for loss of life and property outside the normal channels, that is, outside a legally defined investigation of the commission established for this purpose.

2. His demonstrated intention to encourage European immigration.

3. His steadfast refusal to yield to American pressure on the reciprocity treaty.

4. His effort to awaken and cultivate patriotic sentiment in the Mexican population, which has culminated in his intention to introduce universal military service. These are the motives that are generally known: hidden from view but, perhaps even more important, are the following factors:

5. Madero apparently gained the effective support of the U.S. for *his* revolution by promising to turn Mexico's oil industry over to the Standard Oil Company and to hand over the [English] isthmus railway to the Mexican [in reality, American] railways. I don't think that the current President made such commitments himself, as he is too honest and upright for such things. But the wheeler-dealers of his party and his family, namely, his brother, Gustavo Madero, may have handled this side of the revolution. It is nonetheless a fact that Francisco I. Madero has honored none of these commitments. He has, nevertheless, been warned repeatedly, and warned by the well-known [Sherburne] Hopkins, the professional attorney of the Latin American revolutions inspired by the United States. He has also—or so I have been told—been warned indirectly by Dawson, the promoter of these revolutions. Hopkins has been here for three weeks; he may have received the final refusal from the President. The shift in the attitude of the American embassy and the reversal in the attitude of the Washington administration dated effectively from the same time.[109]

The liberal hacendados, who were in power under Madero, and the middle class, which constituted his strongest layer of support, were even less willing than the Científicos under Díaz to grant the Americans unlimited hegemony in Mexico. But it was Madero's domestic policies that determined the final attitudes of both the U.S. firms and the U.S. government.

The legalization of trade unions and the great strike wave of 1911–12 had a tremendous impact on the American companies. The freedom of the press and freedom of speech that, by comparison with the Díaz period, were rather far-reaching, permitted the emergence, for the first time, of previously concealed anti-American currents. The Zapata movement in Morelos, of course, had very little effect on American firms, but Madero's inability to put it down was by many Americans interpreted as a lack of desire to do so, and therefore raised the specter of a general insurrection in the countryside. The existence of the radical wing of Madero's party openly calling for changes in the agricultural structure of the country gave substance to such fears. It was becoming increasingly obvious that Madero, in spite of his conservative tendencies, was not the man to "revert to the system implanted by General Díaz."

In Hintze's view, the full force of American opposition to Madero began in March 1912. It had essentially four aspects:

1. Increasingly hostile notes of protest to the Mexican government, in which every trivial incident was played up
2. The evacuation of Americans from many regions of Mexico and the arming of a section of the American colony in Mexico, whereby the U.S. Embassy attempted to whip. up an atmosphere of hysteria against the Madero government and to lay the basis for an American intervention in Mexico
3. An extensive press campaign in the U.S., in which Madero was portrayed as incapable of bringing about "law and order" in Mexico
4. Support of coup attempts against Madero

While the Reyes conspiracy (December 1911) took place at a time when the U.S. government was still placing its hopes in Madero, large American companies appear to have provided Orozco with arms several months later. According to the Austrian minister to Mexico, Orozco had received important aid from American mining and rubber companies, as well as from the Hearst trust.[110] Even more obvious, however, was the support of American businessmen and diplomats for Felix Díaz's attempted coup.

At the beginning of 1912, Felix Díaz had gone from Havana to Washington in an attempt to secure support for his anticipated insurrection. He took with him a letter of recommendation from the representative of the American Banknote Company in Cuba, Brooks, to General Leonard Wood, the head of the U.S. General Staff, which stated:

Díaz can be Mexico's "man on a white horse" if the U.S. helps him come to power. With the moral support of the U.S. he would be able to change the situation in Mexico in such a way that an intervention will not be necessary. Naturally, his prospects depend on the desires and actions of the U.S. Use this letter as you see fit. If I were in Washington, I would bring it to the attention of the State Department and would try to see that Díaz at least gets a hearing. I will advise Díaz to contact you, so that you can serve as a go-between.[111]

There are no records of Díaz's efforts in Washington. The stance of U.S. diplomacy during his insurrection, however, would indicate that they had not been in vain. Hintze reported:

With the outbreak of the Díaz revolution in Veracruz [16 October], the American embassy, without any notification of the other missions, officially informed the Mexican government that the American government would oppose a bombardment of Veracruz by government troops. Commander Hughes, of the cruiser *Des Moines*, which arrived in Veracruz on 20 October, communicated the same message. In his dealings with the Mexican authorities, this officer manifested an abruptness and a condescension that deeply insulted the Mexicans. Consequently, at the American embassy, people are saying, "He is the devil of a man."[112]

It is clear that such an attitude on the part of the U.S. government constituted direct involvement in the insurrection on the side of Felix Díaz. The U.S. chargé d'affaires, Hintze reported, "informed me of the Mexican authorities' reception of the above dispatch. President Madero had personally reminded him of Mexico's right, within the framework of international law, to do what it pleased. After a heated discussion of approximately one hour, Madero burst into tears, recognizing the unshakeability of the American stance and his own impotence."[113]

The failure of the insurrection did not discourage either the Americans or the Científicos. A new conspiracy was organized to overthrow Madero. The conspirators struck in February 1913. This time, U.S. support for the anti-Madero plotters assumed such massive proportions that it tipped the scale in favor of the conspirators.

# 2 Germany and Mexico

If in its origins the Mexican Revolution was closely bound up with international relations, in its dynamics it was almost inextricably tied to them. Germany's heavy-handed involvement in Mexico bears no minor responsibility for this. Its bold incorporation of Mexico into its global strategies, the most spectacular but certainly not the most audacious instance of which is the Zimmermann telegram, had a profound effect upon the course of the revolution. But even though Germany's involvement in Mexico did not assume any really overwhelming proportions until the final phase of the First World War, it dates back much further than that. The significance of Germany's bold initiatives in Mexico cannot, in fact, be fully grasped without an understanding of the stake Germany developed in Mexico as far back as the Porfirian era.

## Germany and Mexico in the Porfirian Period

Efforts of the Científicos to create a European counterweight to U.S. influence had centered on three countries: Great Britain, France, and Germany. On the eve of the revolution, Great Britain was by far the dominant European power in Mexico, the only one that constituted a serious challenge to U.S. economic domination. Germany's economic and political influence in Mexico was far more limited. Unlike Argentina, Chile, and Brazil, which had tens of thousands of German immigrants, Mexico had only 2500 German residents in 1910.[1] German investments were also limited in scope and, although estimates vary, at most they made up 6.5 percent of all foreign capital invested in Mexico in that same year.[2]

Insofar as foreign trade was concerned, Germany's role was somewhat more important, even though a great discrepancy existed in imports and exports between the two countries: in 1910–11, 12.9 percent of all Mexican imports came from Germany but only 3 percent of its exports were destined for that country.[3]

It would be erroneous to conclude from Germany's relatively weak economic influence in Mexico that, prior to 1910, no serious efforts had been undertaken by German merchants, capitalists, or politicians to gain a strong foothold in the country. The first such attempt was made early in the nineteenth century by merchants of the Hanseatic cities of Hamburg, Bremen, and Lübeck, who had become junior partners of English trading houses in Mexico. In the second half of the century, these merchants succeeded in breaking the English trade supremacy in Mexico and even assumed for themselves the hegemony their former British partners had exercised up to that point.

By 1878 Hanseatics controlled two-thirds of Mexico's foreign trade. "Forty years ago," wrote a German commentator in 1889, "there still existed no less than seventy-nine English import houses in Mexico, which had branches and corresponding influence in all the important parts of the interior. They played an important role in politics, influenced legislation in their interests, and were obediently served by the customs officials. Ten years ago, that is in 1879, their previous total had been reduced to three, active almost exclusively in banking, and no longer having any ties to English industry."[4]

The position of German businessmen, in spite of their success, was very precarious. Their trade supremacy was fortuitous and, in the last instance, was a passing affair. It derived neither from German political hegemony nor from economic hegemony but was the result of a temporary conflict between Mexico and the major powers that had supported Maximilian's ill-fated empire.

After the resolution of this conflict, serious attacks on the German trade monopoly were to be expected. German businessmen dealt primarily in manufactured goods, especially textiles, which, until 1876, made up almost 80 percent of Mexican imports.[5] Only a very small portion of these textiles were manufactured in Germany. Because German merchants obtained most of them from Great Britain and France, they were especially dependent on the textile producers of those two countries.

This dependence was ultimately their undoing. As soon as French and Mexican relations were normalized to some degree, the French textile manufacturers transferred the marketing of their products to merchants in southern France, who had established subsidiaries in Mexico—the so-called Barcelonettes (named for the southern French locale from which most of the merchants originated).[6] In the fierce trade war that ensued, the Barcelonettes pushed the Germans almost out of the textile business by the end of the 1880s. Bitterly, the magazine *Der Export* reported that, of the more than eighty "first-rank" German import houses that had dominated most of the Mexican trade twenty years earlier, two-thirds had been forced into liquidation or had liquidated voluntarily. "At the same time, however, many French import houses established themselves quite prosperously, as German houses had done initially throughout the country, with hundreds of branches, and these firms now monopolize almost the entire 'ropa,' or textile, trade. This wholesale retreat, its causes, and the inevitable consequences should serve as an example.''[7]

German businessmen did not leave Mexico but shifted to importing other goods, expecially hardware products, the manufacture of which was particularly well developed in Germany.[8] The share of these goods in Mexican imports, minimal in the 1860s and 1870s, increased rapidly during the Díaz period. It was during this same period that German banking capital entered Mexico. As a result, the position of German businessmen, which had been seriously shaken at the end of the 1880s, strengthened from year to year. They failed, however, to regain their earlier influence. In 1905 the German minister counted sixty German wholesale traders in Mexico,[9] and in 1911 the German trade expert Bruchhausen[10] estimated the value of German capital invested in Mexican trading houses at 41,675 million pesos (83,350 million marks).

In 1888 Germany made its second attempt to establish a dominant position in Mexico when the Díaz government approached various European powers with the request for a loan. Díaz had avoided the United States from the beginning because of his desire to use Europe as a counterweight to American influence in obtaining loans. The first major borrowing by the Díaz regime met with serious skepticism in both London and Paris because of the conflicts that had resulted during the Maximilian period. In Germany, however, circumstances were quite favorable: not only had Germany had no conflict with Mexico over Maximilian, but Russian securities had been dropped from the German stock exchanges in the same year, and therefore capitalists were seeking other investment opportunities.[11]

To Georg von Bleichröder, German Chancellor Otto von Bismarck's personal banker, Mexico seemed to present a unique possibility for combining rapid profits with the establishment of German financial supremacy. In 1888, under his leadership and with the participation of the British banking house of Anthony Gibbs and Sons, a syndicate handled a bond issue of 10.5 million pounds sterling for the Mexican government. The terms were extremely favorable for the group: interest was set at 6 percent, the banks received a commission of 1.25 percent, and the certificates were sold at 70 percent of their nominal value.[12] Most important, the agreement contained a secret clause in which the Mexican government committed itself to offering Bleichröder an option on any further bonds it might float. In the words of the German minister, Zedwitz, the purpose of this agreement was "to prevent the Mexican government from making use of the services of any foreign banking house other than the Bleichröder firm in the conclusion of future transactions and to assure Bleichröder of a monopoly in Mexico similar to the one enjoyed by the

Rothschild house in Brazil."[13] Bleichröder's profits from this transaction were large.

The Mexican government, however, had no intention of submitting to the financial control of Bleichröder. The success of this bond sale prompted British and French banks to change their attitudes toward Mexico, and, as early as 1889, the municipal government of Mexico City effortlessly floated a bond issue on the London exchange. Bleichröder naturally saw this as a threat to his monopolistic ambitions and a violation of the secret clause in his contract with the Díaz regime. He immediately sent a memorandum to Mexico "containing an unequivocal warning to the government here not to ignore the Bleichröder house in the future."[14]

These threats only served to strengthen Díaz's resolve to free himself from the threat of a German banking monopoly. Therefore, when the Mexican government tried to float yet another bond issue in 1889, it sought a new source. The U.S. attempts to step in were "rebuffed both politely and firmly," as the French minister in Mexico reported, "because Mexico fears the United States."[15] Díaz wanted to find a base of support not in the United States but in France. The French minister was told by Díaz that he "would be very pleased to find a counterweight to Herr Bleichröder in French finance."[16] The request received the warmest support from the French government, whose representatives in Mexico even conducted parts of the negotiations. "I will do my best, Monsieur le Ministre, to fight our hereditary enemy, but to do this I need help and cooperation in Paris,"[17] the French envoy wrote to the French foreign minister about his attempts to push Bleichröder out of the Mexican capital market. Spurred by the German's success in the previous year, a French consortium was formed to take over the new loan.[18]

Bleichröder, who had followed these proceedings very carefully, invoked the secret clause of his agreement[19] and requested that the bond issue be transferred to him. The Mexican government not only refused to comply but even offered to repay the outstanding debt on the 1888 bond issue in order to free itself fom the secret clause. Bleichröder refused out of hand and, at his bidding, Minister Zedwitz made a threatening visit to Mexico's Foreign Secretary Ignacio Mariscal, which, however, failed to bring about the desired results.[20] The French minister reported to the Foreign Office in Paris, "When Baron Zedwitz insisted on the application of the agreement between the Mexican government and the Berlin banker, and added that, if necessary, the German fleet would back up these demands in Veracruz harbor, Mariscal calmly replied to my young and hot-headed colleague that even before the appearance of his fleet in the Gulf of Mexico, ten thousand soldiers of the American army would occupy Mexico."[21]

Zedwitz's threats were ineffective and the secret clause was never mentioned again. The German banker maintained some influence over Mexico's finances—he was granted the bond issue of 1890[22] because of the exacting terms demanded by competing French bankers—but the ease with which Mexico discarded the secret agreement put an end to Bleichröder's dream of controlling the country's finances.

After the turn of the century, far more powerful German institutions than either Bleichröder or the textile merchants began to express interest in Mexico. Attracted by that country's wealth and stability, some of Germany's largest banks attempted to penetrate the Mexican market. Some tried to do this as partners, mostly in a junior capacity, of U.S. financial institutions; others attempted to go it alone. Although a few of the ventures were quite profitable, none succeeded in gaining a major foothold or making serious inroads into the Mexican economy.

Germany's largest banking house, the Deutsche Bank, was oriented toward cooperation with U.S. interests, whose supremacy it implicitly recognized. This attitude expressed itself in the close collaboration with the American-based Speyer banking house in Mexico. The latter, as a result of its ambitious economic expansion in that country, succeeded in bringing almost half of the Mexican railway network under its control and was attempting to gain influence over the financial system through loans to the government and through the founding of a bank there. But it was precisely in this area that Speyer lacked the necessary support of the Mexican government, which consistently gave preference to European over U.S. capital. To overcome this difficulty, Speyer made an offer of alliance to the Deutsche Bank. "Herr Speyer," wrote the German minister in Mexico, "seems to want to mix the star-spangled banner with the German colors in order to do business here under a hybrid flag."[23]

Speyer made it clear to the Deutsche Bank from the first moment of their collaboration that it would be limited to the role of junior partner. He explained to the German minister, Freiherr von Wangenheim, in telling him of his plans for a joint venture, that Mexico was viewed in the United States "solely as a dependency of the American economy" and that Germany "could in the future conduct major transactions in Mexico" only with the cooperation of the United States.

> The conversion of the old Mexican bonds on the agenda for 1909 will also be carried out under American auspices, and the Haus Bleichröder will have to get used to the idea that its leading role in Mexico is over. Europe cannot conduct a sentimental policy in North America. Roosevelt will be reelected, and the Monroe Doctrine, in its limited concept, or as a claim on absolute control of the North American hemisphere to the [Panama] canal to the exclusion of any foreign incursion, will become an unquestioned axiom for all Americans. Germany must draw

the logical conclusions by recognizing the doctrine as an unalterable fact, but, at the same time, it must make the legitimate demand that the United States guarantee all capital Germany has invested in the area affected by the Monroe Doctrine.[24]

The demands were accepted by the Deutsche Bank. In 1904, it helped Speyer push Bleichröder out of the Mexican bond market and jointly with Speyer founded the Banco de Comercio e Industria, whose management positions were reserved for Americans. This development met with a vehement protest from the German diplomats in Mexico, who saw it as a constraint on German economic power. In June 1906, the chargé d'affaires, Bressler, sent a warning to the German Foreign Office concerning the new bank. In it, he wrote that a German bank in Mexico must fulfill three functions: finance German businesses, facilitate the liquidity of Mexican purchases of German goods, and involve itself in transactions with the government. He cautioned that the new bank would not be able to meet the first two obligations, since its director was a confidant of Speyer. "The Germans will be outvoted and finally pushed out, as has already happened to the Deutsche Bank in Mexico once before."[25]

Nevertheless, the example of the Deutsche Bank served as a precedent for further collaboration with Americans. The Frankfurter Metallgesellschaft founded a mining company together with American financiers, the Compañía Minera de Peñoles, but the control of that company remained in the hands of the German partner.[26] Bleichröder invested substantial sums in the American-controlled Mexican Petroleum Company.[27] The Hamburg-American Shipping Line (Hapag) collaborated with U.S. shipping companies based on an agreement concluded in 1902 with the American-based Morgan bank.[28] Cartel agreements between German and American firms in the same period gave the Americans free rein in many sectors of the Mexican market:[29] August Thyssen, the German steel magnate, for example, worked out an agreement with an American company in which he promised not to supply railroad tracks to Mexico,[30] and in return a similar agreement was reached between German and American firms concerning the sale of pipeline.[31]

After 1907 the German and American cooperation of business interests in Mexico gave way to rivalry and confrontation. This was due, on the one hand, to mounting German-American competition in other parts of the world and, on the other, to the penetration into Mexico of new German financial groups with fewer links to U.S. capital than the Deutsche Bank had.

One of the most important of these was the Berliner Handelsgesellshaft, managed by Carl Fürstenberg. "For the last time prior to [the First World] war," he wrote in his memoirs, "Germany attempted to penetrate a new overseas economic sphere."[32] The Berliner Handelsgesellschaft participated in the most important anti-American measure ever undertaken by the Díaz regime: the attempt to gain control over the Mexican railways. With the aid of various other European and even U.S. banks, it succeeded in realizing this aim; and the German stockholders, represented by the Fürstenberg group, thus acquired control of 20 percent of the stock of the Mexican National Railways.

"Germany should be quite satisfied with the situation of both of the northern lines controlled by the state," Wangenheim commented on this development. "The German stockholders and noteholders of the Central Railway, which has been in financial difficulty for a long time, are improving their position and are becoming 20 percent co-owners of the Mexican National Railways. With such a proportion of holdings, they will also be represented on the board of directors, and the Mexico government will be obliged to take account of the German vote in its future railway policies."[33]

Conflict with American firms was the inevitable result of the influx of German capital into the Mexican railway system. The Berliner Handelsgesellschaft very quickly began to use its influence in an anti-American direction. At its instigation, the German representatives on the board of directors, together with the representatives of the Mexican government, succeeded in weakening the quasi monopoly that had existed for American suppliers, and to a lesser degree British, in the sale of equipment for the railroads prior to their nationalization.[34]

The consequences, however, were not as expected by the Berliner Handelsgesellschaft. The first contract that was diverted from an American or English firm went not to a Germany company but to a Russian one, which was to supply track for the railroads. The German minister assumed, probably correctly, that it was the British members of the board who had pushed through this contract.[35]

The Germans may have met with better success with regard to the change in the freight rates, which previously had been completely oriented toward American interests. In a letter to his Foreign Office of 31 March 1910, the German consul in Chihuahua wrote that, as a result of the railway rates dictated by the United States, European goods were at a disadvantage compared with American goods in northwestern Mexico.[36] The German companies did not remain passive, and, on 21 January 1911, they were advised by the Mexican National Railways that the rates in question would be revised.[37] Whether these revisions were in fact carried out has not been ascertained.

The Berliner Handelsgesellschaft had envisioned an expansion of its activities far beyond the railroads. Fürstenberg informed the German trade expert Bruchhausen that the Frankfurter Metallgesellschaft, which had close financial ties with the Berliner Handelsgesellschaft, had plans for investments in zinc and copper mines.[38] (These projects were never implemented because of the outbreak of the revolution.)

The Berliner Handelsgesellschaft was not the only German financial institution whose activities had taken an anti-American turn. In 1906–7, the Dresdner Bank had begun to show a serious interest in Mexico and developed plans for stepping into the country's production of raw materials. In 1907, the Deutsch-Südamerikanische Bank, which belonged to the Dresdner Bank and the Schaffhausener Bankverein, had opened in Mexico, and in 1909–10 had developed ties with the Madero family.[39] Previously, in 1906, the Dresdner Bank had established relations with the Pearson firm.[40] Both of these interests were in direct competition with the Americans.

The Deutsch-Südamerikanische Bank was not tied to any U.S. firm, and developed strong interest in Mexican raw materials, which had previously been the domain of U.S. interests. In 1910 it participated in a project to found a drilling company "for the systematic exploration and economic exploitation of the mineral wealth"[41] of the country. As Germany's minister to Mexico Karl Bünz wrote:

> I consider the success of this company to be an extremely important step in the direction of the economic domination of this country for German industry and German capital. . . . I see the significance of the above mentioned firm for our industry and our capital, assuming that it produces practical results, particularly in the fact that we would assure ourselves, once and for all, of a dominant position in this country so rich in economic opportunities. The concession involves the entire territory of the republic and includes not only water but also ore, coal, and oil discoveries. At the same time, this offers unbelievable prospects for our capital and machines. I am not hiding the fact that everything depends on a tremendous practical success. Nevertheless, I am certain that we have reached a stage that, from a national standpoint, we will never again give up.[42]

The Dresdner Bank developed even more ambitious plans. In June 1910, the bank's representatives informed Bruchhausen that it wished to invest 40 million marks into the development of ore discoveries in Tlaxiaco,[43] but, because of the Mexican Revolution, this plan was never carried out. The bank enjoyed great prestige with the German diplomats because of its aggressiveness and because it was free from American ties. Bruchhausen recommended that the Dresdner banking group be supported, as it "maintains closer, purely German ties through the work of German industrial firms that are allied to it in Mexico, through the new Mexican mortgage banks it has founded, and through its branch in Mexico City."[44] He compared it unfavorably with the Deutsche Bank, which, in his opinion, had done too little to obtain contracts for German firms, and wrote: "In the Dresdner banking group, the German industrial viewpoint will be more visible and will also be taken into account by the Mexican government for contracts in goods and services in return for loans."[45]

None of these ambitious plans involved oil. This German reticence was essentially due to the influence of the Standard Oil Company. In 1907, the Deutsche Bank had attempted to break the monopoly of petroleum sales held by Standard with large investments in Rumanian oil fields. It had been defeated by Standard and had had to commit itself to undertake no further actions against American oil interests. The commitment would be void only if Germany passed legislation for a state petroleum monopoly.

As long as no such law existed, the Deutsche Bank was unwilling to make investments in Mexican petroleum, investments that would have led to an immediate break with Standard Oil. After a talk with the head of the Deutsche Bank, Arthur von Gwinner, Bruchhausen reported: "Strangely enough, Herr von Gwinner's interest in Mexican petroleum was obviously quite negligible. He thought he had had enough of oil in the Steaua Romana and he would be quite content if no more petroleum were discovered anywhere. After the experiences the Deutsche bank has had with petroleum, his irritation is comprehensible, but not his complete lack of interest."[46] Nevertheless, the bank pushed strongly for a law that would create a Reich petroleum monopoly and, in 1910, had already sent a geologist to Mexico in search of oil fields. After a year this effort had not produced any conclusive results.

Another consideration that inhibited German oil investments was of a strategic nature. Unlike the British navy, which strongly supported Pearson's oil enterprises, the German navy gave no similar backing to the Deutsche Bank. It was no doubt convinced that, in case of war, the British navy could easily interrupt German access to Mexican oil fields.

In summary, it can be stated that in 1910–11 important sectors of German industry and banking were developing ambitious investment plans for Mexico. These plans had emerged after the economic crisis of 1907–9 but could not be realized because of the Mexican revolution of 1910 and the First World War. Therefore, the total direct German investment in Mexico was scarcely higher in 1911 than it had been in 1905. Bruchhausen's estimate of these investments, which he placed at 75 million pesos (150 million marks) for 1911, shows this clearly. Of this sum, there were investments of 42 million pesos in trade, 10 million pesos in industry, 13 million pesos in agricultural enterprises, and 10 million pesos in banking. The most significant change after 1905 was the increase in German capital invested in banks. Bruchhausen estimated the value of the Mexican public securities held by Germans at 30 million pesos (60 million marks).[47]

If one considers actual German investment in Mexico, it becomes clear that, in spite of increasing German-American rivalry there, the areas of friction between the two were not yet very great. A major portion of the German investments were in import and export trading and in state bonds, where American investments were minor and where common interests linked German and American companies. Even though rivalry had increased in the banking system, some German banks continued to cooperate with the Americans. In raw materials, where American interests were great, German involvement was minimal; only in the railway system were there sharp differences. Since the British investment structure was similar to that of the United States, the areas of conflict between German and British firms were also not very great. On the basis of investments actually made, Germany's main rival in Mexico was France, because it concentrated in the same areas: state loans, banking, foreign trade, and industry (in the latter the competition was the least intense).

The situation was quite different, of course, if one views it in relation to the plans of major German companies in Mexico. Had these plans been carried out, Germany's influence would have been greatly strengthened and would have become a serious threat to the United States.

## Germany's Trade with Mexico

In its economic relations with Mexico, Germany was most successful in the export field. By 1910–11, about 13 percent of all Mexican imports came from Germany.[48] But this success was very temporary since Germany had lost out on the product it was most interested in marketing—armaments. It was in this area that Germany had made significant inroads in other countries of Latin America between 1870–1914. Krupp, Germany's largest arms manufacturer, sold them cannons; the Mauser works sold them rifles; and German military instructors trained many a Latin American army.[49]

Germany's greatest rival in this field was France. The Germans won out in Argentina and Chile, the French in Brazil and Peru. Mexico, whose market Germany coveted, was the scene of its greatest defeat. While Mauser managed to obtain some contracts for rifles, Krupp was the principal loser—Mexico's army was equipped with artillery produced by the Saint Chamond works of France.

Krupp's defeat was due to a multiplicity of factors. He seems to have held Mexico in such contempt, despite his interest in capturing its arms sales, that much of the materiel he sent there was of inferior quality. In 1902 a competitive performance for artillery pieces was organized in Mexico among Krupp, Schneider-Creusot, and Saint Chamond. Krupp suffered a humiliating defeat: his cannon proved to be the worst, and it was on that basis that Saint Chamond was awarded the arms contract.[50]

Krupp's performance led both the German minister and the German military attaché in Mexico, who had done everything possible to further Krupp's cause, to send letters to Berlin highly critical of the German artillery pieces.[51]

Another factor contributing to Krupp's loss was that he was not always ready to pay the kind of bribe demanded by Mexican officials. In a letter to the German Foreign Office, Krupp wrote, "The Mexican delegate entrusted with the negotiations at that time requested that I calculate an additional cost of 25 percent on the materiel his government wished to order and that I pay him the difference, which, since such things are against my business principles, I refused to do."[52] If these "business principles" ever existed, they were to disappear rapidly in the following years. It was not the question of bribery but rather the amount of the bribe that repeatedly was the focus of Krupp's discussions and negotiations with various Mexican arms purchasers.

German armament manufacturers also suffered from the ambiguous attitude German bankers assumed toward their sales efforts in Mexico: In 1893 Bleichröder completely reversed the position he took in 1888, when he made his first loan to Mexico and presented the Mexican army with two Krupp cannons and introduced Krupp's representative to high Mexican officials;[53] both he and the Deutsche Bank manifested strong opposition to a deal the Mexican government was considering to purchase artillery pieces from the Gruson works, which belonged to Krupp. The German minister saw as the reason for this that both parties "were attempting to prevent the possibility that the [Mexican] government would undertake new acquisitions of war materiel, and to prevent even a penny of state revenue from being diverted from the servicing of their bonds."[54]

The most important cause, however, for the inability of the German arms manufacturers to gain a dominant position in Mexico was the close links between some of the Científicos and the French financiers. These links extended to the War Ministry, whose procurement officer, Manuel Mondragón, was a major investor in the Saint Chamond works.[55]

The Germans had attempted to offset their disadvantages by allying themselves with Bernardo Reyes, who was secretary of war between 1900 and 1903. Reyes secured a contract for the delivery of rifles by Mauser to the Mexican army. As a reward for his pro-German stance, the Germans showered him with decorations, such as the Order of the Red Eagle.[56]

When Reyes resigned his post on 1 January 1903, German arms producers were dealt their most crushing blow. Even an about-face by the German representative could not change the situation. The German minister to Mexico refused to deliver to the kaiser a sword that Reyes had given to the German monarch as a gift. It was delivered only after explicit assurances from the Mexican foreign minister that his government would take no offense if such a gift were accepted.[57]

Germany's position is best summarized by Minister Bünz, who wrote in 1909: "As far as we are concerned, there is not much to be hoped for from Mexico as long as Limantour and Mondragón control the country's finances and its army. Both are oriented toward France and not toward us."[58]

In spite of its severe loss in the area of arms sales, Germany managed, on the eve of the revolution, to outrank both Great Britain and France insofar as volume of exports to Mexico was concerned. Here, only the United States outranked Germany. If one takes an overview of German exports to Mexico, one finds that their greatest success was in the private Mexican market, that is, in consumer and investment goods intended for Mexican industry. The share of German goods used by foreign firms in Mexico was greater than the German share of foreign investments, but, conversely, in government purchases, the German share was smaller than indicated by its position in the Mexican financial system.

The rapid expansion of German industry during the first decade of the twentieth century and its intensive effort to adapt itself to new markets led, in most countries of the world, including those of Latin America, to an advance of German goods at the expense of older British and French industry. Very important for German exports to Mexico, moreover, was the control of a large part of Mexican foreign and domestic trade by German businessmen. Their position, following their defeat in the 1880s, had solidified at the beginning of the new century and was of decisive influence. Equally significant was the cooperation of German and American concerns in Mexico. Of lesser importance, but not without effect, were direct German investments and loans to Mexico.

These German advantages were partly offset by cartel agreements between German and American companies, which made the Mexican market the domain of the latter, as well as discriminatory freight tariffs for European goods on Mexican railroads, which were particularly effective in northern Mexico. Moreover, the greater transport distance separating Europe from Mexico meant a longer delivery time, giving the United States a decisive advantage.

What importance did exports to Mexico have for German industry and German trade in general? In 1910, exports to Mexico amounted to 1 percent of total German exports, and thus ranked twentieth among countries to which Germany exported goods.[59] In Latin America, Mexico ranked fourth in importance for German exports behind Argentina, Brazil, and Chile.

German industry's exports to Mexico showed a great fragmentation.

No sector of industry was involved in what could be considered major exports to that country. Germany's imports from Mexico were of no strategic importance, nor was German heavy industry dependent on them in any way. The obvious conclusion, then, is that the leading circles of German industry were far less interested in trade with Mexico than in trade with other countries with whom the total volume was often smaller but where important members of German industry were involved. Because of the structure of German-Mexican trade, commercial interests always played a subordinate role in the shaping of the German government's policy toward Mexico.

## Political Relations between Mexico and Germany, 1898–1910

Prior to 1898, Mexico played a very minor role in the diplomatic activities of Germany. Unlike Argentina and Brazil, which had been the recipients of mass migrations of Germans, there were only 1,800 Germans in Mexico at the turn of the century. Not only were German investments and trade there minimal, but those groups that were interested before 1898 were not, on the whole, very influential. This situation changed radically after 1898, and the country began to play a more important, though not a major, role in German foreign policy. In part, this was due to the Reich's most important bankers' becoming interested in Mexico; but, the protection of German interests in Mexico was less important for Germany than the utilization of that Latin American country in an increasingly complex game of international diplomacy. The basis of these maneuvers lay in the new importance German-American relations were assuming.

As the United States emerged as a world power after the Spanish-American War, Germany began to think in terms of either a conflict or an alliance with the former. These considerations were strengthened by two facts, that both countries seemed to have stood on the brink of war in Manila Bay in 1898, and that, in both, imperialist tendencies, overseas expansion, and the buildup of naval forces were developing at an accelerated pace.

In this context, Mexico assumed a new dimension in German eyes. Its strategic geographic location appeared to offer far-reaching possibilities for influencing U.S. policy in a wide variety of ways. These included attempts to establish military bases against the United States in Mexico, to strengthen the Mexican army for a possible struggle with its northern neighbor, to reinforce U.S.–Japanese and later U.S.–British tensions. The culmination of all these intrigues was the ill-fated Zimmermann telegram of January 1917. The total failure of these maneuvers was matched only by their clumsiness and vacillation, for German policy wavered constantly between the desire to use Mexico as an anti-American instrument and the fear of antagonizing the United States because of Mexico.

Germany's first intrigue in Mexico in the twentieth century took place in 1902 as part of a more general policy of expansion into Latin America. It was a year in which German-American tension reached a high point. Germany manifested its presence in Latin America in a very direct way in July 1902, when the German cruiser *Panther* sank a Haitian ship in the Caribbean. In that same year German, British, and Italian warships bombed and blockaded the Venezuelan port of La Guaira in order to collect outstanding debts from Venezuela. It was during this time of German expansionism that representatives of the kaiser made efforts to gain a foothold in Mexico. An American attorney working in London reported to the U.S. ambassador there that he had been approached by some Germans interested in purchasing Mexico's Baja California Peninsula. When the attorney inquired about the identity of the purchaser, he was told that the German kaiser was privately interested in the transaction. In response to his somewhat astonished question concerning the reason for such a purchase, he was told openly that Baja California was an excellent place for "naval operations." The attorney thereupon refused to have anything further to do with such a transaction.[60] Before Germany could resume its efforts, it suffered a stinging rebuke in Venezuela. In 1903 Theodore Roosevelt forced the European countries to withdraw their navies from Venezuela and to accept U.S. arbitration in their conflict with that South American nation. Probably as a result of the failure of its Venezuelan adventure and Roosevelt's hostile attitude, Germany abandoned its plans to set up a naval base in Mexico and became extremely wary of any move that could antagonize the United States. This came out very clearly at the beginning of 1904.

In February of that year, shortly before a planned visit to Mexico by Germany's Far Eastern Naval Squadron, the undersecretary of state of the Mexican Foreign Ministry told the Cuban minister to Mexico that "something very important for Mexico, for you, and for the other countries of Latin America" could emerge from the visit, "for our northern neighbor will begin to understand that we have friends and that we no longer live in the isolation of earlier times. I do not mean to say that anything concrete exists yet, for these things must be worked out in steps—you, of course, understand that we currently maintain the best of relations with the United States and that we must do so—but the day will come when everyone will follow the path most suitable for himself, and you will see that we have made our preparations for that moment."[61]

This position was encouraged by the German chargé d'affaires, Flöcker, who hoped to play up the visit of the fleet and obtain an agreement that would have German naval officers sent to train the Mexican navy.[62] Flöcker, however, was not supported by headquarters in Berlin, which had attempted to avoid friction with the United States after the U.S.–German tension over Venezuela. The chargé d'affaires was sharply called to task by the German secretary of state himself. "To my regret," the secretary wrote to him, "I feel obligated, on the basis of several events that have occurred during your tenure in Mexico, to inform you that it would be highly desirable if you could show much more reserve in your current position, since energetic activity by us in the direction of innovation will be far more appropriate at a time when a real minister has taken over. One of the first things to come to mind in this connection is the idea of commandeering German naval officers for the Mexican navy. Such a step, for reasons involving our relations with the United States, appears to us to be inopportune."[63]

When Germany's Far Eastern Squadron arrived in January 1904, the secretary of state gave Flöcker instructions to present the visit in such a way "that does not take on the character of a demonstration from which the the United States, and particularly the American press, can draw the wrong conclusions."[64] Flöcker thereupon did everything to keep the fleet's stay within this framework. He did not transmit the fleet commander's invitation to President Díaz to inspect the flagship.[65] After the fleet left, he stated with satisfaction that the outbreak of the Russo-Japanese war had prevented America from focusing on the visit.[66] The Mexicans did not understand that there had been a reversal of German policy in Latin America and did not abandon the hopes they had connected with this military demonstration. "We welcomed the visit of the German fleet for many different reasons. Now the Americans will see that we are not to be held in contempt,"[67] the undersecretary of state of the Mexican Foreign Ministry told the Cuban minister.

### Germany, Mexico, and Japan

In 1905 relations among the great powers underwent a profound change. In that year Japan defeated Russia and emerged as a world power. Soon afterward, strong U.S.–Japanese tensions began to manifest themselves. These tensions were due to the rivalry of both powers in the Far East and the restrictions imposed by California authorities on the rights of Japanese immigrants in that state. This situation led to multifarious German plans for penetration into Mexico in order to use that country as an instrument either to cement a German-American alliance or to exacerbate the U.S.–Japanese conflict.

Tensions between the United States and Japan exercised their first influence on German policies in Mexico in 1906. In December, President

Díaz and Landa y Escandón, the governor of the Federal District of Mexico, informed the German Minister Wangenheim of their intention to introduce universal military service. Landa y Escandón wanted to know if Germany would be willing to send military instructors. Wangenheim wrote home that, if they were successful, "Mexico would be obligated to us and, as a result, the equipment and weapons for the planned reserve units, except for the rapid-fire cannon, would be purchased from us. But, beyond all this, we will be a position to benefit from other commercial advantages deriving from our military friendship." Moreover, he saw in the strength of the Mexican army the possibility "that Mexico would evolve into a military power simply on the basis of universal military service, which could become a factor in military calculations involving the United States." He knew perfectly well that "the thrust of the military reform . . . is aimed at the United States," but he nourished the illusion that "American disgruntlement over our military support of Mexico will only reach the breaking point when Mexico begins to be a serious obstacle to U.S. plans for expansion. By that point, however, Mexico's military friendship will have clearly acquired a certain value for us."[68]

The kaiser's annotation to the last of these remarks was: "and in the growing threat of a conflict with Japan, for America as well." Wilhelm II welcomed Wangenheim's proposal and cultivated the even greater illusion that the United States would look favorably on a Mexican army strengthened by German instructors. "Very good! Agreed," he noted. "I believe that by the time Mexico becomes a military power worthy of attention, the clash between America and Japan will already be so near at hand that America will be pleased to have it as a powerful ally. I have nothing against fulfilling the wishes of the Mexicans if they approach us. What is right for Argentina and Chile is all right for Mexico."[69]

Within less than a year after he wrote his report, Wangenheim underwent a complete shift: He suddenly realized that sending German instructors to Mexico could indeed lead to a conflict with the United States, and decided that good German-American relations were more important than a German-Mexican rapprochement, although he continued to welcome the deepening of American-Mexican tensions. He felt that Germany should do all it can to avoid tension with the United States, but, "we must do our best to increase tension between the United States and other countries."[70] He also felt that a strengthened Mexico might be of real political and military use but thought that this hope was not worth the deterioration of relations with the United States. He thus opposed German military instructors for Mexico. In order to deal with the danger that Mexico would call on the French military if Germany refused, he suggested the Mexican government be encouraged to build up its army without foreign help.[71]

Equally important in Wangenheim's change of heart was the position of those of his countrymen who held Mexican government bonds. "Will . . . the introduction of universal military service be advantageous to German material interest in the long run?" he asked. "I cannot give a positive answer to this question. Expenditures for the army will be a burden for the Mexican budget and will therefore decrease the security of the Mexican government paper owned by Germans. The popularity of Mexican bonds depends on foreign confidence in the ongoing peaceful development of the country and on the belief that the United States will intervene in Mexico if domestic unrest should ever erupt here. Should Mexico extricate itself from American control with military armament, its credit will sink until there is proof that a corresponding improvement of the country has been achieved by militarization. For the time being, however, our interests in Mexico will be better served by the Limantour regime and modest American surveillance than by a reorganized Mexican army."[72]

Germany's Secretary of State Tschirsky shared Wangenheim's reservations and directed him to encourage the Mexican government to build up its army on its own. Should French instructors be brought in, however, he told Wangenheim to resume his efforts on behalf of German instructors.[73] These recommendations can undoubtedly be attributed to the Franco-German competition to equip and train Latin American armies. A French success in Mexico would, in all probability, have affected the military policies of other Latin American countries.

The beginning of 1907 saw yet another shift in the German stance against support for Mexican plans to reform its army, despite repeated warnings from the German ambassador to the United States, Speck von Sternburg. Thus, following thorough discussions with leading U.S. politicians, he had considered all German involvement in Mexico as a "risky venture," as Germany would "quickly lose the trust of the American people and their government." Should a conflict develop between the United States and a Mexican army strengthened by Germany, there could be a "tremendous uproar in the easily aroused American character and a demand for retribution and revenge." Even if a European country were to send instructors to Mexico "and we are able to gain advantages, which are not to be underestimated, in the sales of military materiel that would probably be involved, the disadvantages of such an undertaking, which I have the honor of pointing out, would nevertheless far outweigh any benefits."[74]

German diplomacy, however, once again advocated sending its military instructors to Mexico. Two factors were instrumental in bringing about this shift: on the one hand, the German minister had learned of Mexico's intention to invite military instructors from France,[75] and, on the other hand, in the opinion of German diplomats, U.S.–Japanese relations had deteriorated so badly and the situation had moved so much in favor of Japan that the United States would hardly be in a position to undertake any action against a German advance in Mexico.

Wangenheim wrote that, in the opinion of the Mexicans, the United States could not wage war against Japan "as long as the Panama Canal is not finished, while the Japanese must begin the struggle before the canal is open. Since Japan proved in its war against Russia that it does not let the proper moment pass it by, war will be at hand shortly. In such a war, the Americans will be defeated."[76] Kaiser Wilhelm obviously shared this opinion, since he annotated these remarks with "Good" and "Correct" and considered the entire report to be "well researched and well written."[77]

With the aid of a number of influential politicians, in particular the governor of the Federal District, German diplomacy once again attempted to persuade the Mexican government to request German instructors for its army.[78] These efforts seemed to promise a degree of success, but, at the beginning of 1908, the entire military reform project was dropped by the Mexican government.[79] Tensions between Japan and the United States abated, and, consequently, the American threat to Mexico increased. The economic crisis of 1907 created even greater difficulties for the plans for military reform.

In this period German diplomacy attempted to pursue simultaneously two completely opposite goals with regard to the United States. While trying to pressure the Mexican army into using German instructors, German diplomats were attempting to work out a joint action with the United States in the Far East in which Mexico once again would play an important role. Such an action was considered possible because an agreement on the delineation of spheres of interest in China had just been worked out among Japan, Russia, Great Britain, and France. This threatened the other two interested powers—Germany and the United States.[80] By joining the United States and China, Germany not only hoped to strengthen its position in China but also (as Wilhelm II stated in an interview, whose publication was blocked at the last minute by Reichskanzler Bülow) to bring the United States into opposition to Great Britain.[81]

The realization of such plans depended on the deepening antagonism between the United States and Japan. In the spring and summer of 1907, German diplomats thought that Mexico would be the arena for increasing tension. After the Japanese-American gentlemen's agreement of February 1907, which prohibited the emigration of Japanese workers to the United States, a flood of these immigrants began to pour into Mexico; during the summer of 1907, more than 12,000 were recorded.[82] In all probability, they hoped to slip into the United States illegally from Mexico despite the ban.

German diplomats saw in these immigrants the future shock troops of a Japanese invasion army aimed at the United States. In May 1907 Wangenheim reported that he had received a report from the president's entourage that 4,000 Japanese reservists and officers were aboard two Japanese merchant ships. The Japanese, of course, wore no uniforms but some of the officers wore insignia. Wangenheim reported that he had heard that "The Japanese are now spread throughout the country and are armed. In the state of Chihuahua there are currently 5,000 Japanese ready to bear arms and an additional 3,000 in the state of Jalisco."[83] While he doubted the veracity of this account and characterized it as "adventurist," he considered it possible "that Japan still wants to have the option, in the event of war with the United States, to form a large contingent from its reservists in Mexico."[84]

Replies by the German consuls in Guadalajara and Chihuahua to Wangenheim's inquiries revealed this report to be utterly groundless. The consul in Guadalajara wrote that there were, at the most, 300 Japanese in the state of Jalisco, and they showed no signs of being armed.[85] The consul in Chihuahua reported that between 2,000 and 3,000 Japanese in khaki uniforms were there at the moment; the Japanese minister to Mexico later explained this by saying that former soldiers in Japan had the right to keep their uniforms and to wear them in civilian life. Of arms they might be carrying, he knew nothing. He reported that most of them had crossed the border and entered the United States illegally.[86]

The increase in Japanese immigration to Mexico in June and July 1907 gave new life to rumors of an imminent Japanese invasion of the United States through Mexico. In July, Wangenheim reported that Japanese, wearing their uniforms, were distributed throughout Mexico in groups of six to ten men. "According to the survey made by the English consulate here, at least one thousand young Japanese per week have emigrated to Mexico over the last three months. The consulate also pretends to know the names of two Japanese generals who are alledgedly among the immigrants." Wangenheim went on to state that many observers "saw this maneuver as linked to belligerent plans by Japan against the United States," but that he personally considered this unlikely, "as I have to assume, based on the reports from Tokyo I have received, that Japan at least wants to delay its confrontation with the United States for a number of years. The increase of Japanese immigration may very well be linked to the difficulties it has encountered in the United States." Nonetheless, he added: "It is not completely out of the question that Japan might intend to make a landing in Mexico after repelling the American fleet, to use it as a base of operations for an attack on California."[87] He expressed the conviction that the Mexican army would be neither able nor willing to oppose the Japanese.

German diplomacy was further strengthened in their belief when several months later the Mexican ambassador in Japan expressed his hope to the German ambassador there "that there would be an armed conflict between the United States and Japan. Mexico could only gain from such a war, as some benefits would surely emerge for Mexico. My ideal would be the breakup of the United States as a result of such a war, in which the south and the west would break away from the northern states. Then Mexico would be able to breathe."[88]

Wangenheim's remarks, together with a report by the retired Prussian magistrate Kritzler,[89] who had observed the landing of Japanese immigrants in Salina Cruz and had asserted that most of those who were posing as agricultural workers belonged to the "educated classes," impressed both the kaiser and the German general staff. As Wangenheim told the Austrian minister to Mexico, the German staff had ordered him to study the role "that might be played by Mexico in the event of a Japanese-American conflict as a possible Japanese base of operations"[90] and had instructed employees of the legation to take a "pleasure trip" to the ports on the west coast of Mexico. Wangenheim came to the conclusion that, with the defeat of the American fleet, a Japanese landing in Mexico would be perfectly possible, although he did not consider it likely. He felt that, in such an eventuality, "a Japanese fleet would sail up the Gulf of California, which offers favorable landing spots, would disembark troops at one of these spots, and would strike a mortal blow at that state."[91]

Such reports and the rumor Wangenheim relayed that the Japanese in Mexico were undergoing military training ("apparently the Japanese always drill in groups of 6 to 10 men. As soon as work is over, they put on their uniforms, arm themselves with staffs, and go through military exercises under the command of the oldest man present"[92]) were the basis for German diplomacy's proposal to the U.S. government for a joint military action on the American continent. In a conversation with President Theodore Roosevelt in November 1907 the German ambassador to the United States, Speck von Sternburg, asked if a war between Japan and America would not also mean a land war. "Japan is apparently already preoccupied with the question of a military base in Mexico, and an attack from Canada also has not been ruled out. Wouldn't support from German troops be of considerable value to America?"[93]

A landing by German troops on the American continent with the permission of the United States would have meant the end of the Monroe Doctrine. It also would have allowed Germany to increase its influence in Mexico considerably. Roosevelt, who feared Germany no less than he feared Japan and did not want to see European troops on the American continent under any circumstances, was perfectly aware of these consequences and refused. The German diplomats, however, did not give up. Two months later, for example, the kaiser warned the U.S. ambassador in Berlin about the 10,000 Japanese in Mexico.[94]

Wilhelm II attempted to exploit these ''10,000 Japanese'' in still another fashion. The Russian-Japanese settlement of 1907 had deeply unsettled German diplomacy. In a letter to Czar Nicholas II on 28 December 1907, Kaiser Wilhelm warned him about the Japanese, underlining the example of Mexico. ''A German gentleman,'' he wrote, ''who has just returned from Mexico, told me that he personally counted 10,000 Japanese on the plantations in southern Mexico, all wearing military jackets with brass buttons. After work, at sundown, they assemble under sergeants and officers dressed as simple workers, in squads and divisions, drilling and working out with wooden staves. My source claims to have seen such workouts often when the Japanese thought themselves to be unobserved. These are Japanese reservists who carry clandestine weapons and are conceived of as an army corps that can seize the Panama Canal and cut off that connection to America.''[95]

In this way the kaiser had raised the rumors transmitted to him by Wangenheim to the status of undisputed fact. He had only added the information about the threat these Japanese posed for the Panama Canal, information that must have appeared completely unrealistic to the czar if he made the slightest use of his knowledge of geography. Thousands of kilometers separated Mexico from the canal, much of it impenetrable jungle, with not a rail or a road of any kind linking the two.

Speculation on the part of Germany about the Japanese role in Mexico came to a temporary end in February 1908. For whatever reasons and through whatever pressures, the United States had persuaded Japan to put a freeze on further emigration to Mexico.[96]

The ambivalent attitude of German diplomacy during 1906–8, particularly on the question of the Mexican army reform, clearly revealed for the first time the dilemma it faced in Mexico up to the outbreak of the First World War. For military reasons, Germany desired a strong anti-American Mexico under its own influence, but Mexico seemed too unimportant to risk a conflict with the United States. Although an offensive, anti-American policy was in accord with the interests of the German armament industry, the German holders of Mexican government paper feared any Mexican-American tension. These contradictions were at the bottom of German diplomacy's constant twists and turns prior to 1914.

On the whole, German activities during the Porfirian period constituted anything but an unbroken chain of successes. In the economic field, Germany had failed every time it had hoped to achieve supremacy in Mexico.

This was the case for the German merchants in the 1870s, for Bleichröder in the 1880s and 1890s, and for Krupp in the first ten years of the twentieth century. This was also the case for the German bankers who hoped to exercise decisive influence in the country. Most of these interests, nevertheless, though they had not achieved supremacy, had achieved a modicum of success.

The same cannot be said of Germany's political initiatives, which proved to be dismal failures; up to 1910, Germany was only marginally involved in the increasing struggle between European powers (mainly Britain and, to a lesser degree, France) and the United States for supremacy in Mexico.

Germany's limited economic successes basically were due to one objective cause: the country's unwillingness to carry out large-scale investment in Mexico's raw material production because of strategic considerations (the conviction that in time of war Mexico's raw materials would not be available) and because of cartel agreements between German and American interests.

The failure of all the European powers to assert their political leadership in Mexico also had a certain objective basis—Europe's weakness in comparison with the United States in Mexico. Moreover, the differences among the European powers were greater than their differences with the United States and, therefore, a united stand of the Old World in Mexico was an impossibility.

The failure of Germany's political initiatives also had an important subjective basis: Germany overestimated the seriousness of U.S.–Japanese tension and underestimated the strength and determination of the United States to put Europe in its place as far as Mexico was concerned.

## Germany and the Mexican Revolution

The outbreak of the Mexican Revolution, and even more its success, took German diplomacy completely by surprise. The German diplomats assigned to Mexico during the period of the revolution, and for that matter all diplomats in that country during that period, failed to understand the forces that had led to the revolution and were shaping its course. Most German diplomats were imbued not only with a conservative ideology but with one that was profoundly racist as well.

The views of Edmund von Heyking, German minister to Mexico from 1898 to 1902, were revealed by his wife Elizabeth, who shared his opinions completely, in her diaries, published after her death. Concerning Mexico, she wrote: "The teeming, bestial mass of humanity that one sees here or in China kills the last shred of any belief I might still have in immortality. But, confronted with this mass of people who are nauseating and scarcely more elevating than the lowest of beasts, the thought of a possible afterlife can only be the basis for renewed horror."[97] She described Foreign Minister Mariscal as "a little Indian apeman." Minister Bünz used similar terms, referring to the Mexican people as "beasts."[98]

Such attitude of European diplomats profoundly influenced their assessments of Mexico's internal situation: In their eyes the country was absolutely unfit for any type of democratic government and the people would never be capable of overthrowing the Díaz regime. Thus, on 17 September 1910, despite the major impact Madero's campaign had already produced in Mexico, Bünz wrote that an "expert" on the Mexican people had told him: "A mere attempt to loosen the hold of the police or to do away with the salutary effects of Don Porfirio's iron fist, and all hell would break loose. The people are as obedient as children as long as they are amused and kept under heel; but, at the same time, they are also as mindless, selfish, and ill-behaved as an uneducated child. If ever a people needed a strong hand to keep it in check and to educate it for its own good, it is the Mexican people." And Bünz added, "I am convinced that the man is right."[99]

Bünz did not expect a revolution but felt that local disturbances were possible. "I consider general revolution to be out of the question, as does public opinion and the press. The return of a period like the one that reigned in this country before Díaz, given the growth of railways and roads that make possible the rapid movement and use of military forces in almost every part of the country, is something I consider to be ruled out once and for all."[100]

For a relatively long time after the revolution had broken out German diplomats were unwilling to recognize or to acknowledge the fact that the Díaz regime was crumbling. When they finally realized that Porfirio Díaz would not be able to maintain himself in power, their half-blind confidence in his regime was replaced by a similar notion that the revolutionaries only wanted to replace Díaz by another personality while maintaining the most essential characteristics of his regime, especially as far as foreigners were concerned. This was the basis of the first serious German analysis of the revolution, which was compiled in 1911 by Bruchhausen, the commercial attaché of the German legation in Mexico.

The analysis was quite realistic as far as the causes of the revolution were concerned, but it was suffused with large doses of wishful thinking in its prediction of the course which it would take.

Bruchhausen correctly described the mixture of corruption, social injustice, and repression that characterized the Díaz regime.[101] Practically all Porfirian officials, both in the federal government and in state and local administrations demanded bribes as a matter of course. In many states judges could be bought. Peasants were persecuted. "Many families which had occupied lands for a century and a half have been deprived of them, the small farmer sees enormous stretches of uncultivated land which he is not allowed to cultivate, workers have been sold to haciendas for 3 pesos."

Bruchhausen characterized the Díaz regime with the remark that power in Mexico "is based less on the law clauses than on strong will" and that "this power is exercised less through the army than through the police (secret police and rural constabulary, a courageous, loyal, and well-paid organization with tremendous powers and primarily made up of bandits)." An extensive intelligence service enabled Díaz to "utilize his rapid and ruthless capacity for decision in such a way that every revolt against the existing order is nipped in the bud." These characteristics of the regime in no way moved Bruchhausen to condemn it in its entirety. On the contrary, "this principle, which was right for three-quarters of the population and which remains so today, is also extended to all advanced classes as soon as desires for power or attempts at change crop up." In other words, Díaz's main error was in having kept the ruling stratum too small and having given the non-Científico bourgeoisie and the middle class too few opportunities for development, not the dictatorial quality of his regime.

The rural middle class was, in Bruchhausen's opinion, the driving force of the revolution. "All serious revolutionaries come from the politically more liberal north and have their base of support in the people with land of their own (rancheros) and those who work land for half of the crop (medieros)." These revolutionaries he felt were in no sense hostile to foreigners. Quite the contrary: "It seems fairly clear that during thirty years of peaceful development it is not only the current regime that has learned to appreciate the work of foreigners but also generally those sections of the population that wield political power. The uprisings were not in the slightest way directed against foreigners and foreign property." He stated categorically that the revolutionaries did indeed wish to do away with certain injustices of the Díaz system, but in no way did they want to destroy the system itself. "Because the revolution is not being made by bandits but by honest citizens, a statesman will be found to guide economic progress in the same way as before but with less corruption and more understanding, particularly where the cooperation of foreigners is concerned."

This assessment was also expressed in the analytic guidelines that German Minister Paul von Hintze gave the German press after the fall of Ciudad Juárez and the ouster of Díaz. The press was to emphasize the Mexican dictator's virtues where favoritism toward foreign capital was concerned, but "the praise of the fallen president should stop short of casting any doubts on the goodwill, patriotism, and honest intentions of the revolutionaries."[102]

What developments had brought about this new attitude on the part of German diplomacy toward the Mexican Revolution? To a large degree it was due to the belief that Madero would govern as Díaz had governed because he came from one of the wealthiest families in Mexico. Germany even nourished the hope that Madero would actually place the Díaz system on a firmer footing after making a few minor changes. Bruchhausen had expressed this hope as early as 1911, and Hintze had held to the same view until mid-1912.

In all likelihood, an additional factor played no small role in Germany's initially positive attitude toward Madero: the close collaboration of the Deutsch-Südamerikanische Bank with the Maderos. This bank was among those that had moved into Mexico rather late and had not linked itself with the Científicos as the Deutsche Bank and Bleichröder had done. It set up close ties with an "outsider"—the Madero family. After the outbreak of the revolution, the Díaz police searched the offices of the Deutsch-Südamerikanische Bank, intercepted its correspondence, and even confiscated part of its assets. The Mexican government's actions, according to the German minister, "were caused by its suspicions . . . that the bank is supporting the Madero family for revolutionary ends."[103] While the bank initially denied the charges, it became obvious, after Madero's victory, that they had not been unfounded. "Prior to the revolution, the Deutsch-Südamerikanische Bank maintained business ties with the wealthy and enterprising Madero family and continued them during the revolution, as well, in spite of pressure from the Díaz government."[104]

It is quite possible that this bank was behind a shipment of German arms smuggled into the country for the revolutionaries. In December 1910, the Mexican consul in Hamburg had reported that sixty crates, whose contents were officially reported as machinery, actually contained arms and ammunition. The shipment had left for Galveston, Texas, on 13 December aboard the *Frankfurt*, to be shipped to Monterrey in Mexico.[105] Two days later, the consul reported a new shipment of arms in thirteen crates with false markings aboard the steamer *Eger*, which once again were to be smuggled into Mexico.[106]

In his memoirs, H. L. Wilson, the U.S. ambassador to Mexico, discussed German financial aid to Madero. The revolutionaries, he recalled, "received financial aid from certain sources in the United States and Europe, more specifically from Paris and Frankfurt am Main."[107] It is not clear that he meant the Deutsch-Südamerikanische Bank, which was based in Berlin, not Frankfurt.

The only major German firm with headquarters in Frankfurt that had important interests in Mexico was the Merton concern, that is, the

Frankfurter Metallgesellschaft. To what extent it maintained close ties with the Maderos at the time of the revolution cannot be ascertained. During World War I, in any case, the former Madero smelter was taken over by a company linked to the Frankfurter Metallgesellschaft. There are no further indications that the latter was involved in the Madero revolution.[108]

This orientation toward the Mexican Revolution by German businessmen, financiers, and diplomats was not shared initially by headquarters in Berlin. This became clear as a result of the intervention by Díaz's consul in Hamburg in March 1911. After he had heard of plans to smuggle arms to the revolutionaries, he approached Mayor Burghardt of Hamburg, and requested that the shipment be stopped or, at least, that he be provided with more detailed information about it. The mayor was quite reserved and told the consul that "There is no legal basis for stopping the shipment of arms, and I am hardly in a position to give you the information you desire."[109] He refused to intervene, stating that all he could do was "have the police authorities warn the suspected companies about the shipment and to indicate to them that they could face serious difficulties with the Mexican government for making such shipments." This response was indicative of both the altered attitude of many German businessmen toward Díaz and of the fact that the German arms industry and the Hamburg shipping business were both making substantial profits from shipments to Latin American revolutionaries and did not intend to give up this lucrative business.

The Mexican government thereupon ordered its minister to file a complaint with the German Foreign Office in Berlin. The Mexicans found a warmer reception there than they had in Hamburg. The Reichschancellor himself handled the affair and sent the following letter to the mayor of Hamburg: "In view of the vital commercial ties between Germany and Mexico, it is not in our interest to nourish the revolution in Mexico with shipments of arms. It is thus to be recommended that similar requests by the Mexican General Consul meet, where possible, with compliance and, when arms shipments to the Mexican insurgents are brought to the attention of the Senate, that as much pressure as possible be applied to the circles involved to keep such shipments from taking place."[110] The victory of the revolutionaries which occurred only a short time later put an end to this conflict.

The chancellor's personal intervention in this affair was only one manifestation of Germany's increasing interest in events in Mexico. An even clearer sign of the importance attributed to Mexico can be adduced by the appointment of one of Germany's most capable diplomats, Rear Admiral Paul von Hintze, as minister to Mexico. He had served in the Far Eastern Squadron of the German fleet as a young officer and had later been the kaiser's aide-de-camp and his personal representative at the court of Czar Nicholas II. He was one of the kaiser's confidants and very close to the Pan-Germanists. An important qualification, which undoubtedly contributed to his appointment, was his special expertise in Far Eastern affairs.[111]

## The Japanese Mirage

Even more than in the period preceding the revolution German aims in Mexico during the years 1911–13 were extremely complex, varied, and at times contradictory. One of the more important objectives was to use the events in Mexico to provoke further tension between the U.S. and Japan. A Japanese-American war that would neutralize two of its rivals was an old dream of German diplomacy, especially of the kaiser.[112]

To make this dream a reality, a rumor concerning the existence of a secret Mexican-Japanese treaty was circulated in Berlin and enthusiastically promoted by the German press. Although the German Foreign Office had received reports at the end of March from its representatives in Washington and Tokyo who considered such a treaty to be highly unlikely,[113] the semiofficial *Kölnische Zeitung*, in the wake of the mobilization of U.S. troops on the Mexican border, wrote: "One may have doubts about the details that have come to light concerning a secret treaty between Mexico and Japan against the United States. This treaty is nevertheless such a natural explanation for the United States' most recent military steps and, at the same time, a diplomatic move by one of the two rivals so closely tied to international relations in the Pacific that probability, at least, would indicate that such a treaty actually exists or, at least, did exist until the U.S. decision to intervene put an end to it."[114] On 9 April a sensational article appeared in the New York *Evening Sun,* asserting the existence of such a treaty and even claiming that the U.S. ambassador to Mexico, H. Lane Wilson, had seen it. The newspaper attributed the mobilization of American troops on the Mexican border to the treaty. The information had been placed in the paper by the German military attaché in the United States, Herwarth von Bittenfeld.[115]

This propaganda campaign was not without results and was enthusiastically welcomed by the kaiser. Bernstorff had reported from Washington as early as 4 April: "American public opinion is gradually approaching hysteria with regard to Japan, comparable to anti-German hysteria in England."[116] Wilhelm II annotated this with "No harm done!" Weeks earlier, he had already expressed his hopes concerning U.S.–Japanese–Mexican relations. On a report by Bernstorff, according to which President William H. Taft had told the Japanese ambassador to the United States that "relations between the United States and Japan are the best conceivable and that all rumors of Japanese-Mexican machinations are well-intended fabrications,'' the kaiser noted in the margin: "A dumb fellow, this comedian."[117]

There are even claims that the German secret service turned over to the U.S. government the text of the Mexican-Japanese secret treaty. In 1917, a former agent of the German secret service, Horst von der Goltz, who had gone over to the side of the Allies, published a book, which was to be the proof of his new outlook. He asserted that in 1911 he had stolen a copy of the treaty from Mexican Finance Minister Limantour on the orders of the German government and had brought it to the attention of the U.S. ambassador in Mexico.[118] The immediate result had been mobilization of U.S. troops on the Mexican border. While Goltz's assertions do indeed coincide with the general objectives of German policy during that period, there is no documentary evidence to support them.

It is quite improbable that such a treaty actually existed. In his report of 23 March 1911, the Mexican ambassador to Tokyo, Pacheco, wrote: "The report originating in Berlin that a treaty recently has been signed between Mexico and Japan, in which Japan, in exchange for certain rights on the Tehuantepec railway and for a coaling station on Mexico's west coast, agreed to aid Mexico with land and naval forces should it become involved in a war with a third party, caused a great sensation here—though even the slightest evidence of such a treaty was lacking—and was widely and lengthily discussed in the press and in public."[119] Neither Bernstorff[120] nor the German minister to Japan believed in the existence of such a treaty, and the latter reported from Tokyo: "In diplomatic circles, the report of a Japanese-Mexican alliance agreement is nowhere taken seriously."[121] H. Lane Wilson also wrote to the U.S. State Department that he had never heard of such a treaty.[122]

Still other factors tend to confirm that the German Foreign Office had no knowledge of a secret Japanese-Mexican treaty. On 5 March 1917, German Secretary of State Arthur Zimmermann, after the revelation of his alliance proposal to Mexico, made a long speech before the Budget Committee of the Reichstag.[123] In order to justify his offer to Mexico and the planned involvement of Japan, he quoted almost all the reports from German diplomats during the 1900–1917 period dealing with Mexican-Japanese rapprochement. Nothing would have better served his purpose at that moment than to be able to disclose that a secret Mexican-Japanese treaty did in fact exist as early as 1911. Of such a treaty he said not a word.

The origins and purposes of this propaganda about a Japanese-Mexican alliance were understood not only by American and Mexican diplomats but by Japanese diplomats as well. "One hears, for example, that this maneuver by American land and naval forces is aimed at restraining

Japanese intentions toward Mexico,'' the Japanese consul in Portland reported to his foreign minister,

> and that the government's real target is not so much Mexico as Japan. One hears that there are observers that have seen 50,000 Japanese currently carrying out military maneuvers on the Pacific Coast of Mexico. It has also been reported that two Japanese warships have left Japan for an unknown destination. They are, according to these reports, headed for Mexico. . . . One also hears that negotiations for an alliance are currently in progress between Japan and Mexico. Various people cite the view of German military expert Count Ernst von Leventow that Japan will begin a war with the United States before the completion of the Panama Canal, to solidify its control of the Pacific Ocean, which is vital to Japan's future, in the same way that Japan declared war against Russia for reasons of national security . . . . The reports cited above are to be understood as an attempt to whip up the local population's hostility to Japan and to use it for purposes of rearmament, although the necessity for rearmament . . . is not being pushed immediately. All this . . . can be attributed not so much to the activities of those elements who—as protagonists of imperialism, which literally has to be seen as the spirit of the age during the past few years in the United States—are agitating for rearmament, nor to those business circles in shipbuilding, who stand to gain from rearmament, as to the machinations of a third country, which hopes to take advantage of America's estrangement from Japan.[124]

The "third country" to which the consul referred obviously was Germany.

The attempts to exploit events in Mexico to stir up tension between the United States and Japan, which would facilitate German expansionary activities, were pursued throughout 1912. In February of that year, an anonymous article appeared in *Atlantic Monthly* under the title "A Letter to Uncle Sam." The author warned of the "yellow peril" emanating from Japan and argued that only "an alliance of the white race," in particular of the United States, Great Britain, and Germany, could put an end to this menace. For such an alliance to come about, the United States would have to recognize the world's real situation. This included a revision of the Monroe Doctrine, which should be applied only to those areas in which the United States actually exercised hegemony, or, more precisely, as far as the Panama Canal. With such an interpretation, the doctrine would be recognized immediately by all the other powers. "South of the Equator, the Monroe Doctrine is an anachronism, but not to the north of it. We will be completely occupied in enforcing it between the Equator and the Rio Grande. We may need Germany's prestige to assert our hegemony as far as the Equator." In view of an alleged Japanese-Mexican rapprochement, the author recommended American occupation of Mexico. "In spite of all denials, Japan is flirting with Mexico . . . . Japan would like to make Mexico into a base of supplies for the protection of its interests on this continent. . . . If Mexico actually responds to the Japanese siren song, then we must take over Mexico. It is more than likely that this will be our fate. We have preeminent interests there, and we must and we shall protect them."[125]

Herwarth von Bittenfeld, the German military attaché in the United States and Mexico, in a report to his Ministry of War hailed the article as the "first swallow" in an American maturation in the direction of Germany. He attributed such importance to the article that he sent part of his report, obviously with the approval of Berlin, as a letter to the editor of the New York *Sun,* which published it on 6 April under the name of "Germanicus." Herwarth fully identified with the viewpoint of the *Atlantic Monthly* author. The only way to fight the "yellow peril," he wrote, was an alliance of the white race, which he called "Pan-Teutonicism." "Should there be a closing of the ranks by the forces of white culture, this would be the equivalent of a Triple Alliance between Germany, England, and the United States. Everything else is a *quantité négligeable* and will have to submit to it. United, these three powers can still confidently divide the world among themselves and place a distance between themselves and the upward-striving colored peoples which will last forever."[126]

So that it could fulfill its functions in this alliance, Germany was to obtain, among other areas, part of the Dutch East Indies. According to Bittenfeld, the initiative for such an alliance would have to come from the United States. "Germany cannot set this movement into action as it would be accused of self-serving motives by its jealous enemies. England still imagines that it can do everything by itself and that it can reduce Germany to the rank of a second-rate power. But the United States could very well propagate the idea of a white racial alliance."

American diplomacy attempted to exploit for its own ends such clearly expressed intentions on the part of Germany. The Mexican government, which had already become distrustful as a result of the German press campaign over the alleged Mexican-Japanese alliance, was informed by the Americans that Germany tried to push the U.S. into an intervention in Mexico. This report so upset the Mexican foreign minister that he informed Hintze that he had "received word from well-informed circles that Germany is pushing the United States to intervene in Mexico in hopes of tying up the United States in a long-term war and thereby to make it an object of hatred for all of Latin America. While the United States is caught in this snare, Germany wants to emerge as the savior of the Latin American countries and to begin settlements and annexations there."[127]

Hintze immediately denied everything. "I characterized the story as the height of poor taste and said that it was unnecessary to waste time or words on it. As Herr Calero nevertheless wished to unburden himself, calling the contents of the report 'ultra-Machiavellianism,' I was forced to lecture him on history to prove that Germany's interests have always been congruent with or parallel to Mexico's. I think I succeeded in defusing the story."[128]

Calero had accused Germany of pursuing a policy that would be seriously implemented two years later and eventually reached its high point in the Zimmermann note. To what extent did this accusation correspond to reality in 1911–12?

The notations by Wilhelm II cited previously and Bittenfeld's activities indicate that the German general staff and the kaiser would not have been unhappy to see a U.S.–Japanese war involving Mexico. True to an old tactic of German diplomacy, to give away things that one has never possessed—one need only observe Bittenfeld's position on the *Atlantic Monthly* article—Germany was agreeable to an American occupation of Mexico in the event of an American-Japanese war or even in exchange for recognition of German spheres of influence in South America. Whether it wanted direct U.S. intervention in Mexico if such circumstances and elements played no role, of course, is another question. This appears quite unlikely, for the whole German tactic in 1912–14 was aimed at preventing an American intervention to the extent that this was possible. According to Bernstorff, in case of an occupation of Mexico, the Americans would thus have succeeded in "skimming off the cream."[129] The growing English-German antagonism, however, that overshadowed everything else would even, in the event of an American-Mexican war, have made a unilateral German intervention in South America quite improbable.

### German Efforts to Prevent U.S. Trade Expansion into Mexico

For all of German diplomacy's efforts to exploit the Mexican events for its broad purposes, the immediate interests of German businessmen and industrialists in German-Mexican trade were never forgotten. Madero's victory, which in their view had been achieved with the aid of American firms, conjured up the danger of a Mexican-American reciprocity treaty. As early as 20 March 1911, León de la Barra, at that time Mexican ambassador to the United States, told Germany's ambassador to the United States, Bernstorff, that the U.S. government was pushing for the conclusion of such an agreement.[130] Such a treaty would have gained preferential tariffs for American goods in Mexico and given Mexican goods preferential tariffs in the United States.

According to German legal opinion, no harm would be done to German trade because the German-Mexican trade agreement of 1883 contained a most-favored-nation clause for both sides; in the event of a U.S.–Mexican reciprocity treaty, German goods would enjoy the same advantages as U.S. goods. The American interpretation was that the conclusion of such a treaty would render the most-favored-nation clause illusory and that only American goods would enjoy preferential tariffs.[131]

It could thus be expected that, if an agreement of this kind were signed, the Americans would push through their conception. For this reason, Germany decided to prevent its conclusion. The most desirable path would have been a joint action by all European countries with interests in Mexican trade against the U.S. plans. This, however, proved impossible, for the rivalry of these countries among themselves was greater than their opposition to the United States. "The European countries all live with the fear of coming into open conflict with the policies of the United States," Hintze stated in ruling out, from the beginning, a joint European action on this question.[132]

In view of this situation, the German diplomatic service decided to act on its own. On 1 June 1911, Hintze asked Felix Sommerfeld, a German Associated Press correspondent living in Mexico and a close confidant of the Maderos (and later head of their secret service in the United States),[133] to explore Madero's intention concerning an American-Mexican treaty.[134] Madero, in a conversation with Sommerfeld, came out against any reciprocity treaty, especially because the Mexican fiscal system could not afford a cut in customs revenues. And his uncle and new finance minister, Ernesto Madero, informed Sommerfeld in an official letter that "This government neither intends to conclude any reciprocity treaty between Mexico and the United States, nor has it ever considered such an act."[135]

Initially, Hintze was calmed by this news. But, when Mexican Congressman Burleson proposed a Mexican–U.S. reciprocity treaty in the Mexican parliament, he once again became anxious. His attempt, however, to initiate a campaign against such a treaty in the Mexican press failed completely. He reported, "I had sometime ago attempted to get articles into the papers, through a middleman, on the disadvantages of the reciprocity treaty. A failure. The press here prints what it is paid to print and nothing else, or nothing at all."[136] He complained that the press was financed mainly by the Americans and proposed to the German Foreign Office that it urge German industrial and commercial circles to create the means necessary for influencing the Mexican press on its behalf in the struggle against a Mexican-American reciprocity treaty.

The Wilhelmstrasse, however, showed no willingness to move openly against the United States in Mexico. "For our policy concerning events in Mexico," the Secretary of State Alfred von Kiderlen-Wächter wrote to

Hintze, "our general guideline is to defend German interests energetically, but, aside from that, to do everything we can to keep a low profile.
We also hold to this policy on the question of the American efforts at a
reciprocity agreement. The means we use to fight against them must be
applied covertly wherever possible. Attracting attention would be all the
more inappropriate, as the current Mexican government has no intention
of meeting the American wishes for preference."[137] At Kiderlen's instructions, all plans for a crusade in the Mexican press against the treaty
were abandoned.

German diplomacy then sought other ways of keeping the alleged
agreement from becoming a reality. When, at the end of 1911, various
German financial institutions, including the Bleichröder group and the
Deutsche Bank, were negotiating a loan with the Mexican government,
the German diplomats saw an opportunity. Bruchhausen proposed to the
German Foreign Office that the banks use the negotiations to put pressure
on the Mexican government. The following was to be communicated to
the Mexicans:

> The repeated efforts of the United States over the past year to obtain
> special treatment for American goods on the Mexican market through a
> reciprocity treaty are beginning to disturb large numbers of people in
> Germany. German holders of Mexican state bonds fear that a significant
> reduction in customs revenues, as the necessary consequences of this
> treaty, would compromise the stability of their securities currently
> maintained by a 62 percent customs guarantee. The danger thus exists
> that these Mexican securities will be thrown onto the market and that
> new ones will not be purchased by banks . . . . Since we do not believe
> that Mexico is considering a cancellation of its most-favored-nation
> treaties and hence a rupture in all its economic relations with Europe to
> the advantage of North America, we are requesting an official statement
> with which the fears of the consequences of a reciprocity treaty be-
> tween Mexico and North America can be alleviated.

Bruchhausen was quite optimistic about the results of such a maneuver.

> While it cannot be predicted with certainty that Mexico will respond to
> our request with a statement committing it to conclude no unilateral
> reciprocity treaty with the United States for the duration of the loan,
> such a development is highly likely. Mexico currently finds itself in a
> difficult situation. The mood of the government and of the population is
> against a reciprocity treaty. The example of Canada's rejection of rec-
> iprocity is having an immediate effect, as are diplomatic relations with
> Germany. Finally, there is, of course, our request that bonds be
> guaranteed by keeping Mexican tariffs free of any limitations imposed
> by reciprocity, as it is from such tariffs that the Mexican debt must
> ultimately be serviced.[138]

In a positive answer from the Madero government, Bruchhausen saw, at the same time, a guarantee for the future, and the Mexican government could, perhaps through diplomatic channels, be held to it if a future government in Mexico should ever be favorably disposed to the reciprocity question.[139] He expected the Dresdner Bank, in particular, "to push the viewpoint of German industry more to the fore."

Bruchhausen's suggestion did not go unheard in the German Foreign Office. Paul H. von Schwabach, the director of the Bankhaus Bleichröder, and Jüdell, director of the Dresdner Bank and of the Deutsch-Südamerikanische Bank, were sought for discussion of possible measures to be taken. The former, however, decisively rejected the Foreign Office's outlook. He said it was "impossible to burden the German banks' future loan negotiations with conditions that are not of a purely financial nature."[140]

Jüdell was somewhat more receptive. He instructed the Mexican branch of the Deutsch-Südamerikanische Bank to discuss the question of a reciprocity treaty unofficially with the Mexican government. At the beginning of 1912, the branch manager reported to the directors in Berlin,

We have had occasion to discuss with the Ministry of Finance the possibility that the United States of America might be given some form of preferential tariffs in Mexico. We motivated our question by saying that a chamber of commerce in Germany, on the basis of stories in the press, had inquired about this possibility at one of our German branches. The minister told us, in all clarity, that the Mexican government, up to that time, had received no such request from the United States and that his government would under no circumstances agree to any preferential tariffs, as such tariffs could only have a negative effect on Mexico's general tariff policy.[141]

Jüdell, however, was not prepared to take any further steps, for precisely the same reasons that had prevented all German banks in Mexico, up to that time, from using their economic influence to the benefit of German industry. He told the Foreign Office expert Hans Arthur W. A. von Kemnitz, "Should a German bank such as the Deutsch-Südamerikanische Bank make the handling of a Mexican loan dependent on the nonprovision of preferential tariffs to the United States, it would be pushed into the background by the foreign competition that makes no such conditions."[142]

Bruchhausen's projects proved completely fruitless when, at the beginning of 1912, as a result of the growing weakness of the Madero government, the German-Mexican loan negotiations collapsed and the Mexican government was forced to conclude the deal with Speyer, the U.S. banking house.[143] The German banks thus lost any further possibility, even if they had wanted it, of putting pressure on the Mexican government.

Over time, it became clear that the German fears were exaggerated. There is no indication that the American government was putting pressure on Mexico on the reciprocity question. The U.S. government was far more interested in protecting American investments in raw materials and railways than in furthering exports to Mexico. Moreover, the Mexican government was hardly prepared to conclude a reciprocity treaty. In a country where customs fees were the major source of revenue for the government, such a treaty, particularly in a period of financial difficulties such as 1911–12, would have amounted to a financial catastrophe. Mexico would have profited very little from an American tariff reduction for Mexican goods, as the most important exporters to the United States were the large American companies themselves. Most important, such a treaty would have led to tensions between the Mexican government and the European countries at a time when Mexican–U.S. relations were steadily deteriorating and would have eliminated any possibility for Mexico to find support in Europe against the United States.

### Germany and the Mexican Army

The Madero revolution appears to have aroused the hopes of the German armaments industry that its long-cherished desire of acquiring influence over the Mexican army and related military supply contracts would finally be realized. When Madero entered the capital after his victory over Díaz, a German businessman named Mardus, who was living in Mexico City, petitioned Madero to introduce universal military service in the country. He wrote that the German army was the best in the world and noted that German instructors had trained the armies of Brazil, Chile, and Japan. In his opinion, however, a direct agreement to send German instructors to Mexico would not be appropriate because Great Britain would then incite the United States against Germany. "Since Germany must avoid a war with the United States, as long as the English bulldog is squatting at the German gates in the form of a larger fleet, Germany should not tempt the powerful Yankee, who speaks so lightly of war."[144] Mardus suggested that Madero obtain military instructors for the Mexican army from Chile, whose army was being trained by Germans. He also recommended that a commission be sent to Germany under the pretext of studying "universal military service" there. In reality, the members of this commission were to join the German army in secret to acquaint themselves with its organization. Mardus's petition appears to have interested Madero and to have been partly in line with Madero's own plan.

It is not clear if this petition was submitted with the knowledge and consent of the German Foreign Office. In any case, it was in keeping with the general efforts of both the German arms industry and of German government policy on this question, as it had already been expressed in the discussions on universal military service in the 1906–8 period. The implementation of Mardus's plan would have given the major share of military supply contracts for Mexico to Germany, since Chile had no arms industry of its own and its army received weapons from Germany. Imperial Germany's most dangerous enemies would thus be kept out of contact with the Mexican army, while, at the same time, the German government would have avoided an undesirable confrontation with the United States.

Such a "detour" had already proved successful years earlier with other Latin American countries. Thus, in 1905 Chile had sent military advisers to Colombia, Venezuela, Paraguay, and El Salvador, while other countries, such as Ecuador and Nicaragua, had sent their officers to be educated in Chile. In all this, the German armament industry had never come away empty-handed.

On 13 September 1912, the German minister in Santiago, Chile, reported that the Mexican military attaché there had been ordered to gather information "on how the German military system can be adopted by a Latin American country."[145] The fall of Madero at the beginning of 1913, however, prevented these plans from taking any concrete form. Similarly, an attempt to purchase rifles from Germany in 1911 had been unsuccessful: General Luna, who had been sent to Germany, was offered only older rifles at excessive prices and, in addition, was presented with such delays in delivery that he was compelled to buy the weapons elsewhere.[146] Despite these failures, the Mexican government appears to have attempted to orient itself toward the German armament industry. Hintze reported, after Krupp and Vulkan had made offers to Mexico for the delivery of two gunboats, that "their prospects, at the present time, to the extent that personal influence has anything to do with the matter, look good."[147] Before orders could be placed in Germany, however, Madero was overthrown and these efforts were interrupted.

### German Banks and the Madero Government

The Deutsch-Südamerikanische Bank had attempted to use its ties to the Maderos to gain a firm foothold in Mexico. In these efforts, it employed various tactics. Initially, it tried to penetrate the bank and mortgage system. Hintze, who reported on the collaboration of the bank with the Maderos during the revolution, stated: "It thereby imposed a certain obligation on the Maderos, which they, and particularly the current finance minister, Ernesto Madero, recognize. Thus, the new government calls primarily on the Deutsch-Südamerikanische Bank in its financial dealings and even—in cases where the government lacks competence—

asks it for advice. It was on this basis that the new mortgage bank for Mexico was established in Mexico, which De la Barra recently cited as proof of foreign confidence in Mexico's convalescence and in the inexhaustibility of its resources. The bank is the creation of the backers of the Deutsch-Südamerikanische Bank, of the de Barry family in Brussels and Antwerp, and, finally, of a Swiss banking house."[148]

In these activities, the bank had attempted to reduce its risks to a minimum. "The prospects of a newly founded bank," wrote the German consul in Antwerp, "are already being viewed reservedly in banking circles."[149] Its participation in the new enterprise was limited to twenty-five hundred of a total of twenty thousand shares.

In spite of the limited participation of the Deutsch-Südamerikanische Bank, its influence on the Maderos was so important that the new bank was given special privileges by the Mexican government. Hintze reported that the new bank would stay in Brussels and "is establishing no branches in Mexico. All its affairs here are being handled by the Deutsch-Südamerikanische Bank. The bank's *raison d'être* is to issue mortages on real estate."[150] As a result, the Deutsch-Südamerikanische Bank had to bear a relatively small risk and could record a double gain: its share in the new bank and its exclusive role as mediator in all the new bank's dealings.

During that time, the Deutsch-Südamerikanische Bank had tried to involve itself in the Mexican bond market; at the end of 1911, it began negotiating with the Mexican government with the aim of participating in a new bond issue to be floated in 1912. It also had attempted to set up new industrial firms, together with the Maderos. "The engineers Briede and Bach, who have ties to the Deutsch-Südamerikanische Bank here," Hintze reported, "today asked my opinion about an industrial enterprise planned for the Republic. This is a project that, using coal mines in the state of Nuevo Leon that belong to the Madero family, will attempt to provide the growing industrial cities of Monterrey and Saltillo with electric energy."[151] Because of the tensions in Mexico itself and those between the Madero government and the United States, none of these new plans were ever implemented.

After the new bank had made loans totaling 2,763,000 francs, it ended its activities in Mexico in 1913 "because of the unrest there" and transferred them to Argentina.[152] The projected loan failed as well. The European banks withdrew their option rights on an announced Mexican bond totaling 11 million pounds sterling because of the Mexican-American tensions and lack of confidence in the solidity of the Madero government.[153] What developed out of the joint industrial projects of the Maderos and the Deutsch-Südamerikanische Bank is not clear. Since no further reports are available, this project, as well, probably went unrealized.

## Germany and U.S. Policy toward Mexico, 1911–13

During the first phase of the Mexican Revolution, all these objectives of German diplomacy remained subordinate to the desire to avoid a confrontation with the United States, as was the case throughout the period prior to 1910. For this reason, the semiofficial German press recognized the validity of the Monroe Doctrine.

After the American troop mobilization on the Mexican border, a section of the American press stated that this step had been directed primarily at Germany. An Associated Press report was cited, according to which Germany, in the event its interests in Mexico were endangered, would resort to measures that were not elaborated. The *Washington Herald* stated on 10 March 1911, "Troops are being sent to the [Mexican] border after Germany's threat to act." In order to anticipate Germany, the United States was obliged to concentrate troops on the Mexican border. Germany, according to the paper, had "torn up the Monroe Doctrine and cast it to the winds." The *Washington Post* went even further. On the same day, it wrote: "The implicit refusal to entrust German subjects and interests in Mexico to our protection goes against the spirit of the Monroe Doctrine. The obvious consequence that Germany would not hesitate to invade Mexico is ground for serious concern, should such an action enter the realm of probability. A direct action of this kind would be a *casus belli*." This report obviously was attempting to present the U.S. troop mobilization on the border not primarily as protection of North American interests but also those of Latin America.

Very shortly thereafter, at the beginning of April, a reply appeared in the semiofficial *Kölnische Zeitung*, which was circulated in the U.S. press by Bernstorff.[154] The newspaper affirmed that the German attitude toward the Mexican events had been completely distorted by "our friends in the English yellow press" in order to discredit Germany. American troops would never find themselves in the position of defending the Monroe Doctrine against Germany.

Should unrest occur in the port cities of Mexico in which local authorities cannot sufficiently protect German citizens, Germany would have to consider making use of its clear right, and one unreservedly recognized by the United States as well, to send warships there. But from the use of an undisputed right to actual involvement in the internal affairs of Mexico is an enormous step that no reasonable person in Germany would advise us to take. Even if the current unrest should lead to a total revolution in Mexico, even if Mexico were to ask to be incorporated into the United States, even if the Americans were to attempt this incorporation against the will of the Mexicans, Germany would certainly not play Don Quixote and draw its sword. How the

American states conduct or do not conduct their affairs among themselves is their own affair, and, if even in Europe we do not feel compelled to play the role of universal peacemaker, this is all the more true in America. For our part, the Monroe Doctrine presents no danger, and, if it is left to age in the archives or is occasionally dragged out and dusted off, is of no importance to us.[155]

Hintze, at that time the new German minister to Mexico, was told that Germany had nothing but economic interests in Mexico. "If I understand the instructions properly," Hintze elaborated, "this means that Germany's relation to Mexico's political orientation is that of observation and waiting."[156] Accordingly, he showed no interest when President León de la Barra informed him that "Mexico's foreign policy will aim at reliance on Europe and especially on Germany."[157]

This statement by Mexico's provisional president probably was meant in all seriousness. Neither León de la Barra nor Madero after him could afford to subordinate himself fully to the United States. Drawing support from Great Britain and France, as Díaz had done, also was impossible, since the interests of both these powers were too closely tied with the interests of the Científicos. Only Germany and, to some extent, Japan could be considered as a base of support against the United States.

In the economic sphere, German firms were perfectly willing to take advantage of the Mexican government's attitude. Politically, however, Germany was unwilling to struggle against the United States in Mexico. Thus, Hintze proposed that it be made perfectly clear to León de la Barra that Germany had only economic interests in Mexico "to avoid any dangers raised by silence or even by ambiguity."[158]

In contrast to the American government and the American companies, the German government, German heavy industry, and the German banks had every reason to be satisfied with the foreign policy of the Madero government. Madero had not subordinated himself to the United States and had not signed a reciprocity treaty with the American government; he had granted the Deutsch-Südamerikanische Bank special treatment and had broken the French monopoly in sales of equipment to the Mexican army. In addition to all this, German-Mexican trade had reached a high point in the period 1911–12.[159] Nevertheless, German diplomacy began to take an increasingly hard stance toward Madero after 1912. This shift had its origins not in Madero's foreign policy, but in his domestic policies.

When Madero took office on 6 November 1911, Hintze was convinced that in domestic political matters he would essentially follow in the footsteps of Porfirio Díaz in crushing all popular movements. Hintze viewed the revolutionaries as people "to whom freedom means impunity and to whom justice means the property of one's neighbor." In his opinion, the most important thing Madero had to understand was that "the new regime must protect itself more from its supporters than from its enemies, assuming that it wishes to govern." Hintze felt that the new government had two choices: Madero could agree to accommodate his own principles to reality and govern like all his predecessors on the basis of attempting to achieve only what is possible for a period appropriate to Latin American conditions (his term was to expire on 1 December 1916), or he could continue with his plans to make the people happy and thereby usher in anarchy. "It appears likely," he concluded optimistically, "that Madero will be converted to the path of compromise; I have obtained information from the most highly placed sources that his intentions are moving in this direction as well."[160]

Madero made no fundamental changes in the social structure of Mexico, but the democratic freedoms he permitted were already too much for German diplomacy. Hintze expressed this clearly in a report overflowing with chauvinism. "The cardinal error lies in his...belief that he can rule the Mexican people as one would rule one of the more advanced Germanic nations. This raw people of half-savages without religion, with its small ruling stratum of superficially civilized mestizos can live with no regime other than enlightened despotism."[161] And Kaiser Wilhelm noted in the margin: "Right!"

This attitude led German diplomacy to support the American attacks against the Madero government. The American ambassador H. Lane Wilson had armed Americans living in Mexico[162] in order to produce a hysterical atmosphere in the United States which would finally bring about an intervention. Hintze followed his example and organized the German colony into a "German corps," an act for which his Austrian colleague, who was anything but a supporter of Madero, characterized him as an "alarmist."[163] Wilson had urged the Americans living in Mexico to leave the country[164] and requested that Hintze take similar steps. Hintze did not go that far but presented the Mexican government with threats of similar action. Finally the German government followed ultimately in yet another respect the American example and in October 1912 sent a warship, the *Victoria Luise*, to Mexico.[165]

Collaboration with the American government, however, was certainly not without its dangers for the German government and German firms. Not only would such an orientation cause Mexico to call into question its pro-German policies, but it could also discredit the German government in Latin America and even contribute to bringing about an American intervention in Mexico. Thus German support for American actions in Mexico was severely limited. Hintze received instructions to move with caution, for "an identification of our interests in Mexico with those of the United States, which would be in and of itself undesirable, would, given the current situation and the sensitivity of those in power there, have a particularly unfavorable impact on them. In view of this, please preserve complete freedom of action in the public eye and avoid any steps that could be interpreted as the influence of the American ambassador, who is obviously acting on a *pro domo* basis.''[166]

The danger of joint action with the U.S. government was clearly emphasized to German diplomats when, on 31 March 1912, the U.S. ambassador urged both the British minister, Stronge, and Hintze to wire requests to their respective countries that troops be sent to Mexico. Stronge and Hintze immediately held a meeting and agreed that Wilson's move was a clever American maneuver. ''International troops landing in Mexico City would stir up the population of the United States and make it possible for the government, as a result of such an atmosphere, to carry out its intervention, that is, to wage war against Mexico.''[167] The British minister also unhesitatingly rejected Wilson's request. He told Hintze, ''England is essentially working with the United States all over the world and is doing rather well by it; this, however, is a case in which we would be merely making ourselves into a tool of American interests while endangering British life and property.''[168]

British and German diplomacy had attempted to avoid an American intervention in Mexico at any price. ''The English minister,'' wrote Hintze, ''told me *confidentially* that he had told the American representative in plain words: England has important interests and has invested heavily in Mexico—mines, railways, property, oil wells, and the like, as well as important commercial interests. This property and this trade make it impossible for England to view with indifference an intervention by the United States. England will do everything in its power to avoid such an intervention.''[169]

While Hintze shared Stronge's view, he nonetheless expressed himself with somewhat more reserve. ''If the United States simply must assume an open hegemony here, expressed in the usual forms, it is my most humble opinion that our interests lie in delaying that moment and in doing nothing to bring it about, without, however, publicly opposing the United States or its representative here.''[170]

The objective pursued by German diplomacy was not the landing of foreign troops, which would inevitably have provoked an American occupation of Mexico, but a military coup to establish a dictatorship in the country. After the failure of the coup attempted by Felix Díaz, for whom he had no respect, Hintze regretfully noted that ''the coming man has not yet appeared,'' but added that ''the little conspirators, people who anywhere else would be known only as scoundrels—the De la Barras, the Flores Magóns, and so on—have neither the moral nor physical courage to strike. All that remains for a revolution having any hope of success is once again the army, naturally, under a leader of a higher caliber than the theatrical Felix Díaz.''[171]

Hintze had also begun to refer to a man whom he considered an appropriate candidate for the role of military dictator. This was none other than the former Díaz general, Victoriano Huerta, who was currently serving in the federal army and whom, according to Hintze, "many viewed as a strongman," a characterization with which Huerta, in his own statements, seemed to concur.[172] The hopes Hintze entertained for Huerta were the basis of the German diplomat's actions during the events of February 1913, which led to the overthrow of Madero and to Huerta's seizure of power.

# 3 The United States, Germany, and the Fall of Madero

## Internal and External Pressures on the Madero Government

A superficial observer in late 1912 or early 1913 might have had the impression that the Madero movement had essentially solidified its control over the country. The attempted coups of Bernardo Reyes and Felix Díaz were put down, and Orozco no longer represented a serious danger; the Zapata insurrection, while still developing in full force, had affected only a relatively small part of Mexico. In reality, however, the Madero regime was moving relentlessly toward its demise and had, to a very large extent, broken its ties with the forces that brought it to power.

As disillusionment with Madero increased among his former supporters, he began to rely more and more on the old Díaz bureaucracy and the federal army. But precisely these strata viewed Madero as a usurper and wanted to return to power in their own right. For a long time their effectiveness had been impaired by their divisions (Reyistas versus Científicos) and the reluctance of many conservatives to act without being assured of the firm backing of the United States. As American opposition to Madero increased, conservative opposition to Madero hardened and opposing factions sought to unite with the common aim of toppling the Mexican president. They considered the federal army as the main basis for any such coup. It was an opinion that many foreign observers, including the German minister to Mexico, shared. In October 1912 he expressed the conviction that it was only a matter of time until the army assumed power in Mexico.[1]

In late 1912 and early 1913, the radicals of the Madero movement, the Renovadores, who were quite aware of this danger, made a last attempt to change the course of the regime. In a memorandum to Madero they wrote: "The revolution is heading toward collapse and is pulling down with it the government to which it gave rise, for the simple reason that it has not ruled with revolutionaries. Compromises and concessions to the supporters of the old regime are the main causes of the unsettling situation in which the government that emerged from the revolution finds itself.... the regime appears relentlessly bent on suicide."[2]

Madero, however, rejected these arguments. To a group of radical deputies who warned him of the disastrous consequences of his policies, he replied that the people and the army stood behind him.[3]

The Madero regime, however, had to deal not only with its domestic opponents, but with the opposition of the American government and of American business in Mexico. On 15 September 1912, the American government had presented Mexico with its sharpest protest note to date, in which it accused the Mexican government of discrimination against American companies and citizens. As example, the United States cited the imposition of a tax on crude oil, the dismissal of several hundred American employees of the Mexican National Railways, and a government decision against an American cattle company. Moreover, the Mexican government was deemed incapable of protecting American lives and property. The note listed thirteen Americans who had allegedly been murdered during Madero's term in office.[4] In December 1912, the American ambassador to Mexico, according to his colleague Hintze, had had

> long conferences with President Taft and Secretary of State Knox about what was to be done in Mexico. After the American note of September 1912 had been answered in a fashion which was simultaneously evasive and negative, Washington saw the need to act. He—Wilson—proposed either to seize some of Mexico's territory and hold it, or to upset the Madero administration (literally). President Taft had been prepared to do both, but Knox had balked at the thought of occupying Mexico. Thus the three of them agreed to upset the Madero administration. As means to this end, they would utilize the threat of intervention, promises of offices and rank (which here are synonyms for income from bribes) and direct money bribes.[5]

In December 1912, the Mexican Foreign Minister Lascuráin went to Washington with the hope of arriving at an agreement with the American government. The proposals he made are not known in detail. In any case, he appears to have succeeded in obtaining a last breathing spell from the American government; at the same time he was threatened with an intervention in no uncertain terms. Lascuráin summarized his impressions on the matter to the German minister in Mexico: "The United States of America did not want an intervention in Mexico; nonetheless, the higher circles have made it clear to me that they would be compelled to intervene against their will if the ongoing killings of Americans and the destruction of American property did not stop. Donc, nous ferons un dernier effort supreme pour en finir. That is also the decision of the current council of ministers; troop movements have already begun."[6]

The State Department's attitude toward Lascuráin's proposals indicate a certain retreat on the part of the American government and continued attempts to reach an agreement with Madero. It was at this time that the first differences between H. L. Wilson and Knox came to the fore. In a memorandum, Lane Wilson asked for an unequivocal threat to intervene. The government of the United States, he wrote, "cannot commit itself to the principle that a cruel and devastating warfare, the sole object of which, as nearly as can be judged by an impartial opinion, is the gratification of the rival ambitions of aspiring chieftains, can be carried on in territories contiguous to it for an indefinite period."[7] These accounts made it clear that in its last month the Taft administration was buffeted by extremely contradictory aspirations. On the one hand, Taft was afraid that the newly elected President Woodrow Wilson, whom he profoundly distrusted, might give in to Mexican revolutionaries. He may very well have wanted to create a fait accompli before Woodrow Wilson was inaugurated. This would explain the fact that (if Hintze's report of Henry Lane Wilson's account is correct) Taft and Knox took the decision to topple Madero in December 1912, when they were in charge of a lame-duck administration. While I have found no direct confirmation of Lane Wilson's allegations concerning his plot with Taft and Knox in any other source (it must be emphasized that if his allegations were true, Taft and Knox would have done everything in their power to say as little as possible in writing about their participation in it), it is significant that at the same time that this plot was being hatched Taft wrote to Knox "I am getting to a point where I think we ought to put a little dynamite for the purpose of stirring up that dreamer who seems unfitted to meet the crisis in the country of which he is President."[8]

While the lame-duck character of the administration may explain Taft's enthusiasm for toppling Madero, it also offers an explanation for the reticence that Knox showed in acquiescing to his plot.

Knox's reticence was strengthened by Lascuráin's readiness during his visit to the United States, a readiness bolstered by American threats of intervention, to accommodate American wishes. It was also reinforced by increasing evidence that Ambassador Wilson was exaggerating by far the degree of insecurity and insurgency in Mexico. As Knox's confidence in the reliability of his ambassador decreased, he became more and more afraid of being drawn into a military intervention which neither he nor Taft wanted. This fear was indicated, though not spelled out, in a memorandum Knox sent Taft on 27 January, which may have constituted an attempt to get the president to abandon his support of Ambassador Wilson's plot. Knox stated that Henry Lane Wilson's reports revealed "an intention on the part of the ambassador to force this government's hands in its dealing with the Mexican situation as a whole, the apparent disagreement between the ambassador and the department being so fundamental and serious that the department feels it would err if it did not bring the matter pointedly to your notice."[9] It is not clear how Taft reacted to this memorandum. The policy of the administration in the crucial weeks that followed this exchange of notices, during which Henry Lane Wilson played a decisive role in toppling Madero, may be the best indication of Taft's real attitude. As will be shown, the administration refused Henry Lane Wilson's request for permission to threaten the Mexican government with intervention in order to secure his aims, but a few days later, after he had done it anyway, the administration countenanced his actions.

## The Decena Trágica

In January 1913, a new conspiracy was organized against the Madero government, a conspiracy in which rival conservative groups had for the first time managed to unite and to at least temporarily bury their differences. Its most prominent leaders were the Porfirian General Mondragón together with Felix Díaz and Bernardo Reyes, who participated in the preparations from prison. The conspirators had established contact with many officers in the army[10] and Ambassador Wilson also appears to have already known of these plans.

On 20 January, when the Cuban minister to Mexico, Marqués Sterling, asked Wilson, "Mr. Minister, do you think that the overthrow of the Madero government is imminent?" he replied, "Its overthrow will not be easy, but it is not impossible."[11] On the following day, H. Lane Wilson paid a call to the German minister. "I want help and hope to get it from you. The British Minister is a good fellow, but more than optimistic—to which he [H. L. Wilson] attached a request that we contribute to the 'enlightenment' of the diplomatic corps."[12] It would not be wrong to assume that Wilson wished to prepare the diplomatic corps for American support of the conspiracy against Madero.

The conspirators initially planned to strike on 11 February. Since, however, the regime was alerted to their plan, they moved into action on 9 February.[13]

The main contingent of rebels, which was recruited from sections of the capital garrison, first freed Felix Díaz and Bernardo Reyes from prison. Other rebels seized the National Palace and took the president's brother Gustavo Madero and the Minister of War Peña as prisoners. General Lauro Villar, who remained loyal to the regime, succeeded in retaking the National Palace. Once in the palace, he entrenched himself and awaited the main rebel contingent led by Reyes and Díaz. Both conspirators, assuming that the palace was in the hands of their supporters, approached it totally unaware of the actual situation. Villar gave the order to fire, and hundreds of rebels were killed, among them Bernardo Reyes. Díaz then retreated to a fortress in the city, the Ciudadela, with the remainder of his troops.[14]

Madero himself, along with his government, emerged unscathed from the events, but critical decisions were soon forced upon him. He could either gather the revolutionary forces still under arms around himself and announce that the demands of the revolution would be met; in so doing, he would have won back at least part of his popularity and would probably have been in a position to annihilate the Díaz forces. Or he could continue to use the federal army and the Díaz bureaucracy as his major base of support, and thus put his fate in their hands. Madero opted for the latter.

At first glance, the position of the regime appeared to be a strong one. With few exceptions, the uprising had found little support in the country; in the capital itself, Felix Díaz had only slightly more than fifteen hundred soldiers at his command.[15] It looked as if a decisive attack on the citadel would very quickly subdue the rebels, who were isolated and had lost the advantage of surprise. But the situation developed differently.

The commander of the government troops, General Lauro Villar, had been seriously wounded, and Madero appointed Díaz's former general Victoriano Huerta as his successor. It was a decision for which he would pay with his life. Madero took this resolve in spite of the fact that he had ample reason for distrusting Huerta. The latter had a consistent record of relentless opposition to revolutionaries and intrigues with Madero's enemies. In 1911 he had been instrumental in provoking a break between Emiliano Zapata and the federal government of interim President León de la Barra. In so doing Huerta had deliberately ignored instruction for moderation Madero had given him.[16] In 1912 while commanding the federal forces who were fighting in the North against the Orozco rebellion, Huerta attempted to eliminate another prominent revolutionary leader. In 1912 he accused Pancho Villa, who was fighting on his side against the rebels, of having stolen a horse, and without giving him the benefit of a trial attempted to have him shot. Only a last minute intervention by Madero saved Villa's life.[17] A short time later Huerta intrigued with the conservative oligarchy of the state of Chihuahua in order to oust its governor and most prominent revolutionary, Abraham González.[18] Madero finally began to doubt the general's loyalty and in October 1912 he removed him from his command.[19]

Felix Díaz and his co-conspirators had from the beginning attempted to draw Huerta into their plot. They had so strongly hoped for his participation that on two occasions, 1 January and 17 January 1913, they postponed their planned coup because Huerta was reluctant to take part in it.[20] It was not loyalty to Madero but the fact that he was not offered sufficient incentive that deterred Huerta from taking part in the revolt.[21]

On the eve of the attempted coup on 8 February an emissary of Huerta's General Delgado, according to a report a confidant of Felix Díaz gave a British diplomat, "was deputed to interview General Díaz with a view to arriving at some arrangement but the proposals put forward by either side were so divergent as to render any compromise impossible."[22]

But on 9 February, after having been put in a position of decisive power by Madero, Huerta was in a very different situation vis-à-vis the rebels and could now reopen negotiation on the basis of strength. A day after the fighting broke out, on 10 February 1913, he entered negotiations with them and met personally with Felix Díaz on the following day.[23] In those negotiations both sides arrived at an agreement to overthrow the Madero government and decided that Huerta must stage a "phony war" with the aim of eliminating as many troops loyal to Madero as possible before attempting a coup. For this purpose rurales loyal to the president were sent on suicidal attacks against the Ciudadela. "During the following week," Felix Díaz's confidant further reported, "officers of General Huerta's staff were constantly visiting the citadel and providing General Díaz with news. One officer named Del Villar actually furnished him with a plan of the present disposition of the National Palace, so that he might know which part to bombard."[24]

Madero obviously did not know these facts but in view of Huerta's antecedents, it is difficult to understand why the Mexican president had no compunctions about reinstating the general in February of 1913 to an even more important position than he had occupied before. Was it naiveté, a spur of the moment decision after the outbreak of the revolt which he later felt he could not revoke, or a calculated gamble to maintain the loyalty of the federal army by appointing one of its most popular and able generals as commander in chief? No satisfactory answer can yet be given to this question.

The ten days between the uprising and the end of the "phony war" are recorded in Mexican history under the name Decena Trágica, the "tragic ten days." The expression "phony war" is accurate only to the extent that Huerta was not fighting with the aim of defeating the Díaz movement. This war was absolutely real, however, and claimed many victims. Huerta had his cannon arranged in such a way that they could not possibly hit the rebel positions but bombarded the surrounding houses, instead. Countless civilians died in this fashion. Huerta sent many soldiers from units loyal to Madero to their death in hopeless frontal attacks, while he protected those troops he felt he could count on himself.[25]

Ambassador Wilson intervened decisively in these events, in part secretly and in part openly. His secret activity consisted in establishing contact with both Díaz and Huerta and in doing everything he could to achieve unity between them around the overthrow of Madero.

From the beginning, Wilson participated in the negotiations between Díaz and Huerta. On 10 February, he wrote to the American State Department of his knowledge that "negotiations with General Huerta are taking place."[26] On 16 February, he told the German minister, Hintze: "General Huerta has, since the beginning of the Díaz uprising, been in secret negotiations with Díaz; he would come out openly against Madero if he were not afraid that the foreign powers would deny him recognition. Ambassador, I have let him know that I am willing to recognize any government that is able to restore peace and order instead of Mr. Madero's Government, and that I shall strongly recommend to my government that it grant recognition to any such government."[27] H. L. Wilson thus implicitly stated his conviction that Huerta would never stage his coup without his encouragement.

The open side of H. Lane Wilson's activity aimed at discrediting the Madero government at home and abroad through threats and protests, at isolating Madero from his supporters, and finally at forcing him to resign. To these ends, Wilson needed the support of at least a part of the diplomatic corps. It was important for him to be able to address both the Mexican government and foreign opinion as well as the State Department in Washington in the name of the "diplomatic corps" and not merely in the name of the American government. This gave a particular vigor to his activities. Since he knew that he could not rely upon the support of all foreign diplomats—the representatives of several Latin American states were sympathetic to Madero[28]—he organized a committee of the representatives of the major powers including Germany, Spain, and Great Britain. In spite of his protests, the French chargé d'affaires was excluded from the activities of this committee at Wilson's behest for reasons which are not known in detail.[29] This "committee" thus made its decision unilaterally "in the name of the diplomatic corps"; repeatedly, however, Wilson failed even to consult the members of this body.[30]

It was the German minister to Mexico, Rear Admiral Paul von Hintze, on whom Wilson relied most and whom he praised most highly. "I formed a high opinion of Admiral Von Hintze from the first moment of our acquaintance and this opinion I had no occasion to modify subsequently. Through all the trying hours of the revolutions against Díaz and Madero, culminating in the bombardment of the City of Mexico, his sympathy and advice were of infinite value. While the bombardment was in progress he was especially active and supported me in every crisis with unswerving courage and absolute disregard of every consideration except the faithful performance of the duties pertaining to his high office."[31]

The basis of the collaboration between Wilson and Hintze was their common desire to overthrow Madero. At every step in the pursuit of this goal, Wilson could count on the support of Hintze.[32] But the ideas of the two diplomats on the question of Madero's successor diverged widely. Wilson saw Felix Díaz as the "coming man" in Mexico, whereas Hintze rejected him, judging him incompetent and, moreover, too pro-American.[33]

Wilson's open activity had already begun on the first day of the insurrection. His first objective was to depict the Mexican government as incompetent and unwilling to protect foreigners living in Mexico and to shoulder it with responsibility for the situation in a series of "protests." With the approval of the Spanish, British, and German ministers, Wilson had already called on the foreign minister on 9 February to pose to him "categorically" the question of whether the Mexican government was prepared to protect foreign lives.[34] In spite of assurances by the foreign minister that he would do everything in his power, Wilson characterized his reply as unsatisfactory.[35] Wilson also sent a letter to Felix Díaz, in which he requested protection for foreigners, thereby already placing the latter on a footing of equality with the Mexican government.

Wilson outlined the tactic he intended to use in a memorandum which he forwarded to Secretary of State Knox. He asked

> that the Government of the United States, in the interest of humanity and in the discharge of its political obligations, should send firm, drastic instructions, perhaps of a menacing character, to be transmitted personally to the Government of President Madero and to the leaders of the revolutionary movement.
>
> If I were in possession of instructions of this character or clothed with general powers in the name of the President, I might possibly be able to induce a cessation of hostilities and the initiation of negotiations having for their object definite pacific arrangements.[36]

These proposals nonetheless went too far for the American secretary of state. He wrote to Wilson that the president did not believe in the "advisability of such a manner of proceeding"[37] at the present time. He was above all afraid of being dragged into an intervention. Moreover, Knox probably did not wish to burden himself with the direct responsibility for a coup d'etat four weeks before Woodrow Wilson took office. H. Lane Wilson, however, who felt completely secure with the oral directives he had received in December 1912 from Taft and Knox, did not take the instructions of the secretary of state seriously, set into motion the tactic he had proposed, and was convinced—correctly, as it turned out—that the Taft administration would support him in spite of possible differences of opinion.

On 11 February, Wilson visited Madero in the company of Hintze and the Spanish minister to criticize him for the "inhumanity" of the fighting and simultaneously to threaten him with an action by American warships for the protection of foreigners.[38] This was the first in a long succession of threats which contributed significantly to Madero's overthrow. On the afternoon of the same day, Wilson and Hintze sought out Felix Díaz, allegedly to register their "complaints concerning the inhuman aspects of the war." Undoubtedly the most important reasons for this visit were simply Wilson's desire to assess the strength of Díaz, with whom he had already conducted secret negotiations, and Wilson's effort to present Díaz in the best light to the diplomats and to the American government.

Whereas the views of Hintze and Wilson had been in complete accord concerning the visit to Madero, the meeting with Díaz revealed a different assessment of his role and importance. Wilson launched into hymns of praise for Díaz and wrote, "My colleagues and I were pleased with the frankness as well as with the humane views expressed by General Díaz.... He received us with the honors of war."[39]

In contrast, Hintze reported: "Honor guards at the southeast entrance, people in grey field uniforms, a band of criminal types hailing us with raucous cries of Viva Felix Díaz.... Díaz does not give one the impression of being a very intelligent character, and seems more impulsive than strong; Mondragón looks suspicious. Relations between them are apparently not very good; Mondragón is attempting to dominate Díaz. Result of this visit: Díaz is in trouble, he talks about a thousand men who have rallied on his behalf in various states and who are en route to the capital, but will not say from where."[40]

On the following day, the situation in the capital became more critical. Madero had brought reinforcements from the federal states to Mexico City, but Huerta's phony war tactic rendered them ineffective. The Cuban minister described the situation in the city vividly: "Here and there in the plazas, a living soul moves about, creeping along the walls or slipping through gardens. And often corpses, scattered randomly along the street-car tracks or heaped in awful piles of rotting flesh: a mestiza who wanted to go shopping at a nearby store and who never arrived, a young man who was unaware of the dangers—and everywhere, puddles of blood, grenade fragments."[41]

This situation offered Wilson a welcome opportunity to move more sharply and openly against Madero. On 14 February, according to a report by Hintze, Wilson received Foreign Minister Lascuráin and explained to him that he would have three or four thousand American soldiers at his disposal within a few days and "that then *he* would restore order here." Should Lascuráin wish to avoid such a development, "there was only one way: tell the President to get out; in a legal way; make him and the Vice President hand over their powers to the Legislative Assemblies; don't you call the Chamber of Deputies, but call in the Senate.'' Lascuráin fully agreed, stating, ''I suppose you are right. I shall devote myself exclusively to that purpose to get the President out.''[42] Thus the American diplomat had achieved one of his most important goals, division within the government.

Wilson then went a step further. After Lascuráin's departure, he called together the key members of the committee of the diplomatic corps and informed them of his discussion with the Mexican foreign minister, making clear to them that he had only been bluffing about the American soldiers; he presented a proposal ''that the powers represented here—for the moment America, Spain, England, and Germany—support the President's resignation and call upon Madero to step down.'' Hintze agreed and made his own proposal that ''this be done as a suggestion in a friendly way, without mentioning any authorization or mandate from our governments.''[43] The committee decided to entrust the Spanish minister, Cólogan, with the task of ''communicating'' this ''suggestion'' to Mexico. Cólogan went to see Madero the next morning and asked him to resign. Madero indignantly rejected this request and stated that ''he did not recognize the right of diplomats to meddle in the internal affairs of Mexico.''[44]

Wilson's threats, however, were not without effect. That very day twenty-five members of the Mexican Senate went to the National Palace to ask Madero to resign.[45] Madero then turned directly to President Taft, informed him of Wilson's actions, and implored him to renounce any intervention in Mexico.[46]

On the afternoon of 15 February, Wilson and Hintze once again went to the presidential palace, this time with the intention of bringing about a cease-fire for the evacuation of foreigners from that part of the city in which the battle was raging. They had initially wished to speak to Huerta alone, but were simply escorted in to see the president. Wilson used this opportunity to make renewed, serious threats, for which he also indirectly invoked the names of the European states. He stated that the question of an intervention had never been raised by him with the White House, but that ''now Washington, acting on the request of the European powers and American public opinion, wished to take serious steps.'' This declaration, however, went too far for Hintze, for he was not prepared to share responsibility for an American intervention in Mexico; he told Madero, ''soothingly,'' that ''the German government has asked the American government to order its warships to provide help and support for the Germans living in the capital.'' He thereby distanced himself, if only slightly, from the declaration of the American ambassador.

Wilson's actions were provocative in the extreme. When he complained about the dangers the fighting created for the American embassy, Lascu-

ráin proposed that he move the embassy to the suburb of Tacubaya.
According to Hintze Wilson replied that it was indeed in his power to
relocate, but that he would not, even if he received the order to do so; "he
would abandon his embassy only as a dead man." He even stated quite
openly his sympathies for Felix Díaz, when he told President Madero to
his face that "Felix Díaz has always been pro-American."[47]

On 16 February, tensions developed for the first time between Wilson
and Hintze. The occasion was the cease-fire requested by the diplomatic
corps to allow foreigners to remove their property from the combat zone.
This cease-fire was actually concluded, and Wilson had played a decisive
role in arranging it. Nevertheless, he informed no member of the diplomatic corps of this development, for he obviously feared that the evacuation of the foreigners from the combat zone would weaken their desire for
an intervention in Mexico and would reduce the pressure they were
bringing to bear in favor of such a move. Thus he consciously issued
contradictory or false information about the cease-fire.

Hintze was taken aback by Wilson's actions. In his diary that day he
wrote about his meeting with the American ambassador:

> Visited the American ambassador to learn the results of negotiations for
> extension of the cease-fire. Ambassador: the armistice is off because
> the Federals have broken it. And to my formal and repeated question,
> "Is it a fact that the armistice is off and that all the negotiations are
> futile?" the ambassador repeatedly and expressedly replied "It *is* a
> fact," and added that the government troops had broken the cease-fire,
> as he had sent in American observers who became convinced that the
> Federals had dug trenches and filled them with dynamite. I was leaving
> as Schuyler happened by to tell Wilson that it would soon be seven
> o'clock—the time when the negotiators wanted to return for resumption
> of talks on the extension of the cease-fire. I turned angrily to the ambas-
> sador and reminded him that he had in fact assured me that the negotia-
> tions were off and that the cease-fire was over! He replied calmly that
> this was not true, and that he only doubted that the negotiators would
> return; somewhat embarrassed he asked me to return that evening. I
> replied that I had no reason for doing so. It is clear that the ambassador
> is simply ignoring his duties as *doyen;* he provides information to no
> one in the diplomatic corps, yet consistently acts in its name. The
> French chargé d'affaires requested admission to the meetings of the
> major powers; Wilson refused. Ambassador declares, Blanquet will *not*
> fight against Díaz, and that four hundred of his troops have gone over to
> Díaz; this is apparently one of the fabrications which had been released
> on behalf of Felix Díaz.

This confrontation was, however, only a symptom of the hostile attitude Hintze then adopted toward Wilson's activities. Until 16 February
he had supported all of Wilson's actions against the Madero government.

He had considered the victory of Felix Díaz to be almost an impossibility, and he was obviously assuming that Madero's departure would lead to a seizure of power by the "strong man" he had waited for so long—he was undoubtedly thinking of Huerta. Such a solution would have ended Madero's rule while rendering impossible a victory by Felix Díaz. His conversation with Henry Lane Wilson on 16 February in which the American ambassador told him that he was in constant communication with both Huerta and Felix Díaz and that he considered the overthrow of Madero to be imminent gave a shock to Hintze. The German minister had not been convinced by the American ambassador's allegation but nonetheless formed the impression that a complete or at least partial victory by Díaz with Wilson's help had become a distinct possibility. Such a victory by Díaz, who was assumed to be pro-American, would not only have harmed the interests of the German firms in Mexico, but also had the potential to cast Hintze himself in a bad light in Berlin, because of his previous collaboration with the American ambassador. It must have become clear to him that Wilson had used him and not vice versa, as he had believed. For these reasons he wired Berlin on 17 February: "American ambassador working openly for Díaz, told Madero in my presence he was doing so because Díaz is pro-American. This partisanship is making the activities of the diplomatic corps difficult. Government troops beginning to tire of fighting. Information coming from Washington to be viewed with skepticism, as colored in favor of Díaz. Am working with all energy solely for the protection of Germans, am *otherwise* distancing myself from other American requests without actual clashes."[48]

Hintze's change of attitude toward the American ambassador was not shared by his two other colleagues in the small group of diplomats which H. L. Wilson had dubbed "the diplomatic corps." Both the Spanish and British ministers, Bernardo de Cólogan and Sir Francis Stronge continued to support the American ambassador until the overthrow of Madero. Cólogan, in spite of a much vaunted private "friendship" for Madero, turned out to be the president's most virulent opponent with the exception of H. L. Wilson. Not only had he attempted to pressure Madero directly by asking him to resign, he had also attempted to secure the same aim in an indirect way. He had told officers of the Mexican army to tell the president they would refuse to fight for him. In a confidential note to H. L. Wilson his British colleague Stronge had urged the American ambassador to convince Taft to secure Madero's resignation by threats of intervention.

Cólogan's attitude is the easiest to understand. The Spanish colony in Mexico to a large degree consisted of merchants, hacendados and hacienda administrators. They were not worried at the prospect of American domination of Mexico. What they feared above all was the outbreak of a peasant uprising. Cólogan's main criticism of Madero was that he had been either unable or unwilling to suppress Zapata. He wrote his government that Madero's revolutionary pronouncements were responsible for "Zapatism, the rising of the Indian plebs with its attendant plunder, murder, burnings, rapes, and other barbarities, which continued to be encouraged by Mexico's executive authorities (at least such accusations were made) as a political reserve, so that it was generally assumed that Madero was incapable of restoring peace."[49]

Stronge's continued identification with H. L. Wilson is more difficult to understand. On the one hand Britain had maintained closer links than any other power (except France) with the Díaz regime and the British obviously hoped that a counterrevolution in Mexico might restore them to the preeminence they had formerly enjoyed. On the other hand Britain had more reason to fear U.S. domination of Mexico than any other power. For this reason Foreign Office officials were critical of their representative's role during the Decena Trágica. Sir Louis Mallet wrote Stronge:

> The situation is doubtless very critical and you are the best judge of how to deal with it but I am doubtful of wisdom of pressing resignation on Madero as the revolt is essentially a question of internal politics. I must however leave this more or less to your discretion. It would likewise be better to refrain from making any communication to the United States Ambassador which he might interpret as encouraging the military intervention of the United States Government—the sole responsibility of that must be left to the United States Government. Neither party in Mexico would presumably thank us for encouraging it.[50]

Hintze, on the other hand, had reversed himself early enough to prevent any such criticism from being leveled at him from Berlin.

His growing mistrust of Wilson and his desire to thwart Wilson's intentions regarding a takeover of the government by Felix Díaz led Hintze to the first step he took without Wilson's knowledge in the course of the Decena Trágica. On 17 February, the German minister, without confiding in his American colleague or seeking his opinion beforehand, made the following proposal to Lascuráin: "Installation of General Huerta as Governor General of Mexico, with full powers to end the revolution according to his own judgment."

Lascuráin thereupon called Hintze to the National Palace and presented his proposal to Madero. According to Hintze's account, Madero responded in the affirmative. "Lascuráin sees President," he wrote in his diary, "gives him my proposal—returning after a considerable amount of time he implies that suggestion essentially accepted. Whether it will be Huerta or someone else not yet decided. I point out: every minute counts, and that it seems to me Huerta is only man with sufficient prestige in the army. The selection of someone else—who is perhaps weaker—would be a serious mistake. Lascuráin intends to bring this up."[51] Hintze's goals are clearly expressed in these proposals. A seizure of power by Huerta with the aid of the Mexican government (it is not clear whether Hintze wanted to turn to Madero or whether Lascuráin gave him no alternative) that succeeded without a plot involving Wilson and Felix Díaz would undoubtedly have made Huerta less dependent on the American ambassador and would have made it easier for him to draw on the European powers for support.

If Madero ever had any intention of stepping down, he very quickly gave it up. He was reinforced by a telegram from President Taft, which stated that he did not wish to intervene in Mexico; moreover, new troops under the command of the former Díaz general Blanquet, whose loyalty Madero did not doubt, had arrived in Mexico City. Lascuráin informed Hintze that "the idea of appointing a Governor General was again discarded last night because of the good news."[52]

In the interim, Wilson's conspiracy with Huerta and Díaz had reached a decisive stage. On the morning of 18 February, Wilson told the German minister:

Since February 16, he [Wilson] has attempted to contact Huerta directly; General has nonetheless stated each time that he could not leave the palace. For two days, delegates from both camps have met with him [Wilson] at different times in the embassy, in order to arrive at a settlement. As a basis for negotiation, he [Wilson] has asserted that a government led by De La Barra, Huerta and Díaz would always have the support of the United States. Senator Obregón, one of the delegates, formally asked him [Wilson] whether, if such a government were formed, the United States would abandon its plans for intervention; he answered this question in the affirmative. General Blanquet's troops have evidently gone over to Díaz, but Blanquet is in the Palacio Nacional. After the negotiations, which took place yesterday—February 17—he thinks that the whole affair can be settled *today*—February 18.[53]

Although more and more news of the conspiracy filtered through, Madero's almost blind faith in the loyalty of the federal army and its commanders could not be shaken. During the night of 17 February, the president's brother, Gustavo Madero, who had learned about the meetings between Huerta and Díaz through a friend, arrested Huerta and brought him at 2 A.M. to the president. The general defended himself, invoking his loyalty and his services in the crushing of the Orozco uprising, and promised to take decisive measures against the insurgents on the following day. Madero reprimanded his brother, freed Huerta, and gave him 24 hours to prove his loyalty.[54]

When Hintze visited Madero at 11 A.M. the following day, he found him full of optimism. "President says that west side of citadel was intentionally given up to allow Díaz's numerous deserters an opportunity to escape, and while he did not wish to engage in prophecy, he feels the whole affair will be over in 3–4 days."[55]

While Madero was expressing his optimism to Hintze in this fashion, the conspiracy entered its final phase. On the morning of the same day, Huerta induced a group of senators to ask Madero to step down. When he refused to fulfill this request, Huerta had him arrested by troops from his army at 1:30 P.M.[56] An hour later, Hintze went to the American embassy at Wilson's request. "Had scarcely entered the embassy when door burst open, Licenciado Cepeda rushed in with a bleeding hand and announced: it is done, we have made him prisoner, I come from the room where the struggle took place. Unable to get anything further out of him, as he fainted while the wound was being bound."[57]

Huerta had in the meantime already received his first cash reward. "It is a small symptom," wrote Hintze, "but one worthy of mention, that on the day of the coup, the pockets of the new interim President, General Huerta, were stuffed with rolls of five-hundred-peso notes. He rather casually passed two or three of these notes to the head of the American cable company, whom I have to thank for this information, requesting him to send off news of the coup, presented naturally in a favorable light. Mexican generals do not usually circulate with rolls of five-hundred-peso notes. The source of the money? Partly from American interests, partly from the group of Científicos who were driven from office by Madero. The latter were Porfiristas who administered the extortion and exploitation of the nation in high style under Díaz."[58]

At 3:00 P.M. Wilson called the diplomatic corps together. Hintze gave the following account.

> As the group was slowly assembling, a letter arrives from General Huerta announcing the arrest of the President. Wilson proposed that the diplomatic corps (a) affirm its confidence in Huerta and in the army, (b) request Huerta to come to terms with Díaz and to rule jointly with him, and (c) to place himself and the army at the disposal of the legal authorities.
>
> Wilson turned first to me, asking for my vote. I agreed to a, but say that b and c appeared to exceed my authority and rights and that I would first have to request instructions on them. Wilson: Your government will never disavow you for supporting the unanimous opinion of the diplomatic corps. I: It does not seem to me that the opinion of the entire diplomatic corps is so evident. Whereupon the British minister, the Japanese envoy, the Chilean and Brazilian ministers and the Austrian envoy agree with me, as well as the Spanish minister. The diplomatic corps decides to respond *only* to the part of the note in which Huerta asks that the diplomatic corps be informed of the arrests of the

President and his ministers, and to let Wilson—to whom the note was *exclusively* addressed—do with the rest of it what he will. Wilson is drafting the note.[59]

This incident expressed both what drew Hintze and Wilson together and what kept them apart. Both of them wanted the overthrow of Madero, and neither of them hesitated to announce their confidence in Huerta and in the army immediately after the success of the coup. But Hintze sought to avoid everything that could facilitate Felix Díaz's coming to power; hence his refusal to request Huerta to come to terms with Díaz. Hintze and other European diplomats, who increasingly had the impression that the coup in Mexico represented a victory for the United States, did not wish to compromise themselves in any way. "Wilson appears to have informed Huerta and Díaz in the name of the diplomatic corps," wrote Hintze, "that this solution—arrests, etc.—will be welcomed by the diplomatic corps; Wilson claims to have informed me, the English and Spanish ministers as well as the Austrian chargé d'affaires of this. In reply, all four of us say: no, but we will make no formal protest."[60]

On the evening of 18 February, Wilson brought Huerta and Felix Díaz to the American embassy. There the two men, their advisers, and the American ambassador met for several hours. It was a long, difficult, and stormy meeting. As an eyewitness told a British diplomat, "General Huerta declared that he had no personal ambition and that he was prepared to go into private life in forty-eight hours, and that all he desired was to put an end to warfare and bloodshed in the country. But from the moment that it became a question of real facts, this disinterestedness rather sheered off. The main question for discussion was, of course, who should be President, and General Díaz claimed the post. General Huerta said he must have forty-eight hours to consider, and then he would suggest a name. At this point the discussion became so acrimonious that Ambassador Wilson suggested that Huerta and Felix Díaz should be left alone in the room to exchange views."[61]

This did not mean that Wilson intended to allow the two participants to negotiate without his interference. While favoring Felix Díaz the ambassador was convinced that the only solution for the time being was for Huerta to assume the presidency. As soon as Díaz's advisers had left the room where the negotiations were taking place, he approached one of them and said, "Doctor, can you not say something to persuade Díaz to yield and to allow Huerta to become interim President? Otherwise the real fighting will begin."[62]

The adviser agreed since Huerta had more soldiers than Díaz and since Huerta possessed "many trump cards in the possession of Madero, his family and his Cabinet."[63] Nevertheless the adviser's counseling did not suffice to influence Díaz. It took many threats and cajolements by the ambassador until an agreement known in Mexican history as the "Embassy Pact" was reached. It was decided, even before Madero had resigned, to form a new government with the heavy participation of the supporters of Felix Díaz.[64] Huerta was chosen as provisional president, but had to commit himself to holding quick elections and to supporting the candidacy of Felix Díaz. Wilson was so enthused by the results of these negotiations that in front of a large number of diplomats who had assembled on 21 February, Wilson greeted Díaz, saying, "Long live Felix Díaz, the savior of Mexico."[65] Wilson instructed all American consuls, "in the interest of Mexico," to "urge general submission and adhesion of the new government."[66]

The first problem confronting the new men in power was the fate of Madero. In order to give the new regime a legal veneer, Madero's resignation was necessary. To this end, he and Pino Suárez, his vice-president, were promised safe passage abroad if they would sign a formal statement of resignation. Trusting this promise, both signed such statements. In accordance with the Mexican constitution, Foreign Minister Lascuráin then automatically became provisional president, a post he promptly resigned while naming Huerta as his successor. The coup was thereby given a semblance of "legality."[67] The new regime nonetheless had no intention of fulfilling its promise to allow Madero and Suárez to leave the country. The two men posed far too great a danger to the regime; once in exile, they would have had the opportunity to advocate a new revolution and to call into question the legality of the new government.

The decision on Madero's fate depended in the last instance on the American ambassador. "The victory of the recent revolution is the work of American policy," Hintze stated. "Ambassador Wilson made the Blanquet-Huerta coup; he himself brags about it."[68] In these circumstances, an unequivocal warning by Wilson to the Mexican government would undoubtedly not have been without effect. Wilson, however, gave Huerta a free hand, making it clear to him that he would raise no objection to Madero's execution. When Huerta asked him if it would be better to "send the ex-President out of the country or to place him in a lunatic asylum," Wilson replied that "he should do that which was best for the peace of the country."[69]

A day later, Hintze intervened with Wilson on behalf of Madero's life. He had hoped for a coup d'etat through which a strong man would come to power with domestic policies fundamentally different from Madero's, but whose foreign policy would strengthen Mexico's orientation toward Europe. Hintze nonetheless had to admit with disappointment that as a result of the coup, "the American embassy, and *without much attempt to hide the fact,* rules through the provisional government, whose principal figures General Huerta and Minister de la Barra are morally and financially dependent upon U.S. support. I must therefore repeat that the American predominance, in whatever form, of which I have often spoken as the future of this country, has imposed itself with the consequences that were to be anticipated, such as reciprocal treaties." He now called Madero—whom he had characterized as "incompetent" only two weeks before and whom he himself had called upon to resign—an "independent patriot" who "did not wish to be a pliant tool of the Americans."[70] Thus he was interested in keeping Madero alive as a possible counterweight to the new regime which he considered completely pro-American.

On 20 February, Hintze visited Wilson and expressed his concern that the new regime would kill Madero. "Wilson replies: Taft and Knox have indicated their recognition of and their satisfaction with his actions, that he did not see why he should interfere with the regime, and that, moreover, he had no right to do so." Hintze remained stubborn and warned Wilson that Madero's execution "would represent a violation of the conscious agreement and, further, a blemish upon his activity in this revolution; if, on the other hand, he prevented the execution for these and for humanitarian reasons, he would add a page of honor to his country's history and to his own achievements."

Wilson was able to infer from these words that, in the event of Madero's execution, he might be accused by the Germans of complicity. After some hesitation, he stated his readiness to seek out Huerta together with Hintze and to discuss Madero's fate. "Drove to palace to see Huerta," wrote Hintze,

> Wilson tells him of our concern that Francisco Mädero might be executed. Huerta: such a decision is not for me to make, but will be taken up by the new cabinet, which is meeting this afternoon at 4:00 P.M. Wilson appears to be satisfied with this. I object that Francisco Madero is not the prisoner of the cabinet, but of the President of the Republic, and that he—Huerta—has control and responsibility for his fate, that it seems best to me for Francisco Madero to be sent to Europe, as was General Díaz in an earlier period, and that then the government will have its hands free and Francisco Madero will be politically a dead man.

Huerta rejected Hintze's request with a feeble reply. "He had," he explained, "previously been assigned to escorting General Díaz to Veracruz, and had fought a skirmish en route for the general's safety; he assured me that Francisco Madero would be exposed to assassination during transfer by any switchman or telegraph operator, and that he would not take responsibility for Madero's life in such a move." Pathetically, he added that "he gives his word of honor that F. Madero's life would be spared and protected, no matter what happens. I: That is a valuable assurance, but who will take responsibility for the zeal or excesses of some guard or watchman or some other subordinate? Huerta: I also take responsibility for that with my word of honor. I: We take your word, General, given as it is in the presence of the American ambassador and myself, as a complete guarantee. Huerta: short of an earthquake, he will be safe."[71]

It was revealing of Wilson's attitude that in his report on the conversation with Huerta, he played down his request and did not report on Huerta's promise, explaining that he had only "unofficially requested that the utmost precaution be taken to prevent the taking of his [Madero's] life or the vice president's life except by due process of law."[72] Such a move had to fail, in the last analysis, unless Wilson placed his full influence behind the request to save Madero. In fact, he had done the opposite and on the previous day had made it clear to Huerta that he was giving him a free hand. The conversation with Huerta was conducted mainly by Hintze, while Wilson remained silent for the most part. Numerous pleas, including those of Madero's mother and wife, could not move Wilson to change his mind. He told Madero's wife, as she later related, "the overthrow of your husband was due to the fact that he never wanted to consult with me."[73]

Wilson's attitude indicates that he not only wished to undertake no effective steps on Madero's behalf, but that he actually favored his execution. On this question, there was a certain antagonism between him and the American secretary of state, who just before his departure from office wished to avoid anything which might burden him with the responsibility for the murder of Madero. On 20 February, he wrote to Wilson: "General Huerta's consulting you as to the treatment of Madero tends to give you a certain responsibility in the matter. It moreover goes without saying that cruel treatment of the ex-President would injure, in the eyes of the world, the reputation of Mexican civilization, and this government earnestly hopes to hear of no such treatment but on the contrary that he has been dealt with in a manner consistent with peace and humanity. Without assuming responsibility, you may in your discretion make use of these ideas in your conversations with General Huerta."[74] Wilson nonetheless took little account of this directive. He was obviously quite untroubled by any thoughts that noncompliance might create difficulties for him with the State Department.

On 22 February, Madero and Pino Suárez were taken from their cells, told they were to be transferred to another prison, and assassinated on the way. It was officially announced that the president and the vice-president had been killed during their transfer from the National Palace to prison during an attempt by supporters to free them.

The identities of the murderers of Madero and Pino Suárez are well known. They were two members of the federal army, Francisco Cárdenas and Rafael Pimienta. What is hotly disputed is whether they acted on orders from Huerta, and whether Henry Lane Wilson was in any way involved or at least shared some responsibility for the murders.[75]

According to Ernesto Fernández y Arteaga,[76] one of the few Mexican officials who ever spoke to Francisco Cárdenas, Madero's executioner, both questions can be answered affirmatively. Fernández, son of a high Porfirian official, Ramón Fernández, who was governor of the federal district and long-term minister to France, had joined Madero in 1909. After Madero became president, Fernández played an important role in the Mexican diplomatic service. During the Decena Trágica he sought refuge in the British legation in Mexico City. On 20 February he spoke briefly to León de la Barra, whom he had known before. "You would not know," de la Barra told him, "how much we labored to save Mr. Madero's life." León de la Barra gave no further explanation and Fernández concluded from this conversation "logically it can be deduced from this that if de la Barra worked to save Madero's life, someone wanted to take it." Two years later he felt that he could clearly establish the identity of the person who had ordered the killing. Fernández had joined Carranza in 1913 and, after the split between the first chief and Pancho Villa, became consul of the Conventionist faction in El Paso. In the first months of 1915 he received a letter from Madero's widow informing him that the Mexican president's assassin, Francisco Cárdenas, was in Guatemala. After he had shown this letter to the leaders of the Conventionist faction, Pancho Villa and Miguel Díaz Lombardo sent Fernández to Guatemala in order to obtain the arrest and extradition of Cárdenas. "Both aims were achieved," Fernández later wrote, "Cárdenas confessed to having killed President Madero, but excused his actions by stating that he was only carrying out orders from his superiors and if he had not done so they would have killed him."

In the declaration of Cárdenas, Fernández reported, "There is a very important aspect and that is a statement that on February 22 he was in the office of Aureliano Blanquet and that the latter told him to await the return to the Palace of the 'Señor Presidente' who would have to ratify the order [to kill Mr. Madero]." At this moment, Fernández wrote, "Huerta was at a reception of the American embassy held to commemorate Washington's birthday. Ambassador Henry Lane Wilson neglected his visitors during the reception and spent over one hour alone with Huerta. A person who accompanied Huerta at the time and was still alive and now resides in Mexico reported this fact to me. What did Huerta and Wilson speak about during this meeting behind closed doors? Did Blanquet know about the proposed meeting and what would be discussed there? It is probable that Blanquet knew of everything and for that reason told Cárdenas he would have to wait for the return of the 'Señor Presidente' to the

Palace to ratify the order.'' While this testimony strongly implicates Huerta in the murder of Madero, it is less conclusive as far as Henry Lane Wilson's role is concerned. The fact that Huerta conferred with Wilson before ratifying the decision to kill Madero does not necessarily imply that he spoke about this with the American ambassador.

The most damaging evidence against the American ambassador is the attitude that he assumed when speaking to Huerta about Madero's fate. On 17 February, he had given Huerta to understand that he did not care about what happened to the imprisoned Mexican leader. Many historians feel that Wilson dispelled this impression by going with Hintze to see Huerta on 20 February and by joining Hintze in asking that Madero's life be spared.[77] Hintze's account of this meeting reveals that Wilson had no wish to accompany him in the first place and only did so under pressure. When Huerta attempted to disclaim responsibility for Madero's fate by referring the matter to the cabinet, Wilson immediately agreed and again had to be pressured to secure a pledge from Huerta to save Madero's life. It is also significant that he considerably weakened the import of this pledge in his report to the State Department.

Henry Lane Wilson's attitude could not fail to impress Huerta and convince him that the administration in Washington would not greatly object if he had Madero killed. It was probably this attitude of Wilson's that led Schuyler, the first secretary of the U.S. embassy, to tell Chief of Staff Leonard Wood that Wilson was "responsible for Madero's death."[78]

There is widespread agreement among historians regarding Henry Lane Wilson's role in the coup against Madero. Such, however, is not the case where the role of the Taft administration is concerned. One school of thought argues in this regard that no direct involvement of the U.S. government in Wilson's plan for the coup can be proven by any existing documents. They emphasize the differences of opinion between Ambassador Wilson and Secretary of State Knox in January 1913 and the negative reactions of the latter to the proposals made by Wilson on the first day of the Díaz uprising; they largely absolve both the American president and secretary of state from any responsibility for the event in Mexico in February 1913. Another school of thought asserts that Wilson's tactic was nothing new but was essentially a logical conclusion of his two years' tenure in office. They emphasize that while some differences of opinion at times emerged especially in January 1913 with the State Department, his policies were never disavowed by his superiors.

Henry Lane Wilson's remarks to Hintze concerning his discussions with Taft and Knox on their decision to overthrow Madero are important insofar as they are a first indication that the American president and his secretary of state were informed of Wilson's plan for a coup and that they shared responsibility for it. While these remarks are not conclusive, they were sufficient to convince the German ambassador in Washington, Bernstorff, one of the most informed and perspicacious observers of events in the United States, of the responsibility of the administration for the fall of Madero; "one can conclude from the contradictions between Taft's and Wilson's pronouncements," Bernstorff wrote his superiors, "that they are pursuing the usual American policy of replacing hostile regimes with pliable ones through revolutions without taking official responsibility for it."[79]

Contemporary observers and later historians have frequently attributed Madero's rise as well as his fall to one common characteristic: his naiveté. He was naive enough, it was assumed, to take Porfirio Díaz's promise that this time there would be an honest election in Mexico seriously. He was so naive in fact that Díaz did not take him seriously until it was too late and allowed him to campaign freely, thus setting in motion a train of events that finally led to the 1910–11 revolution. Madero's naiveté made him accept a compromise whereby the federal army was retained in power while the revolutionary troops were disbanded and it was this same naiveté that led him to name Huerta as commander-in-chief of his army during the tragic ten days.

Nothing could be more wrong than to consider Madero's political and revolutionary activities between 1908–10 naive. On the contrary he based his strategy on the fact that the prerequisite for a successful revolution was the political mobilization of the population. To be allowed to carry out such a mobilization in turn required that the government consider him harmless. It was a masterful strategy which, as he outlined in an interview he gave to Hearst in 1911, had been his aim from the moment that he entered national politics. "At the beginning of the political campaign," Madero said, "the majority of our nation's inhabitants believed in the absolute effectiveness of the public vote as a means of fighting against General Díaz. Nevertheless, I understood that General Díaz could only have been toppled by armed force. But in order to carry out the revolution the democratic campaign was indispensable because it would prepare public opinion and justify an armed uprising. We carried out the democratic campaign as if we had no intention of resorting to an armed uprising. We used all legal means and when it became clear that General Díaz would not respect the national will . . . we carried out an armed uprising."

In the same interview Madero stated that Díaz "respected me because since I was not a military man he never believed that I was capable of taking up arms against him. I understood that this was my only defense and without resorting to hypocrisy I succeeded in strengthening this concept in his mind."[80]

The maintenance of the federal army, which Madero agreed to in the peace negotiations that took place in 1911, was the basic cause for his fall. No government in Latin American history which sought to carry out social transformation managed to do so without destroying the existing army. This was the experience of both Arbenz in Guatemala and Allende in Chile. But Madero did not want to carry out social transformations. He hoped to maintain the social and economic status quo and only transform the political structure. He was thoroughly convinced that the interests of the class of which he was a member and which he represented, the liberal landowners and industrialists of the North, were the interests of all of Mexico. In order to maintain prosperity and stability, both the hacienda system and the steady stream of foreign investments would have to be maintained. He felt that replacing the federal army by a revolutionary army which in spite of its heterogeneous composition to a large degree consisted of revolutionary peasants would mean violence in the country-side and could put an end to the hacienda system. The federal army, he believed, would be the best guarantor for the kind of stability he wanted if only it could be kept in line. To do this he practiced a policy of carrot and stick. The carrot was the maintenance of all federal officers in their position and the invariable partiality he showed to the federal army whenever any kind of conflict between it and former revolutionaries erupted. The stick was the fact that in spite of the promise he had made in 1911 to dissolve the revolutionary army he had recruited a substantial number of former revolutionaries into the rural police force thus setting up a counterweight to the federal army. His plans for establishing universal military service, had they been realized, would also have created such a counterweight since conscripts would have been far less susceptible to the political ambitions of their officers than professional soldiers were. Thus, the maintenance of the federal army, which caused his downfall and death, was the almost inevitable product of his upbringing and social concepts. The one case where the term naiveté might be in order was in relation to his naming Huerta as commander-in-chief of his troops after the beginning of the coup. Even in this case it is not clear whether Madero was really naive or was taking a calculated risk, like the firefighters who attempt to prevent the spread of a brush fire by setting small fires of their own. He may have been very worried that large segments of the army might join the attempted coup. By naming a popular commander, such as Huerta was, who since he had not participated in the coup did not seem to be involved in it, Madero might have believed he could successfully retain the loyalty of the army and defeat the conspiracy.

In the final account Madero's failure represented the failure of the social class to which he belonged and whose interests he considered to be identical to those of Mexico: the liberal hacendados.

Not only Madero but all the national revolutionary leaders who came from this class, such as Sonoran governor José María Maytorena and Venustiano Carranza, ultimately went down to defeat for similar reasons. All of them had called on the peasants to revolt in their favor and all of them turned on their erstwhile allies when they demanded the implementation of large-scale agrarian reform. None of these leaders was toppled by the peasantry, but indirectly all of them owed their overthrow to the agrarian problem. It was primarily his fear of peasant demands that led Madero to keep the federal army intact. Both Maytorena and Carranza were toppled with relative ease by rivals after they had lost peasant support.

**Part 2**

**The Huerta Dictatorship
and the European-American
Confrontation, 1913–14**

# 4 Huerta and His Internal Opposition

The assessment by Germany's representative in Mexico, Paul von Hintze, that Mexico's traditional ruling classes were behind the Huerta coup was confirmed by the attitude these classes assumed toward the new regime. Huerta enjoyed fulsome praise from both conservative newspapers and conservative deputies. In the countryside, many hacendados set up armed contingents, generally known as Defensas Sociales, to fight for the new regime. The archbishop of Mexico offered a Te Deum for the new president.

Some of the main characteristics of the Díaz period reappeared, intensified many times over, in the Huerta dictatorship. No one has described this better than one of Huerta's most enthusiastic supporters, Hintze himself: "The government displays a corruptibility and depravity that exceeds anything known in the past. Everyone seems to want to steal as fast as he can, because he knows that he does not have much time for it. A contract that was presented to me for a shipment of rapid-fire cannon, for example, totaled approximately 10 million marks, of which 7.5 million marks are for bribes and 2.5 million represent the value of the cannon. (One of the worst is the eldest son of the president, Captain Huerta.) Unfortunately, the army is not free of this corruption."[1]

Huerta, though, was a very different personality from Don Porfirio, who always had a very pronounced sense of dignity. The new dictator frequently acted like an oriental despot. In conversations with foreign diplomats, he referred to his ministers as "pigs I would just as soon spit upon,"[2] and treated them accordingly. On 23 March, for example, according to Hintze, he ordered five of his ministers

> by telephone, to go to the Country Club, a public place about twelve kilometers from the city.... These are Huerta's habits; he holds his cabinet meetings primarily in taverns and restaurants. Since no one really knows where he is, this protects him to some extent against assassination. The ministers rushed to meet him; Huerta, however, after a quick glance, ordered them to drive to the National Palace and to await him there. The ministers—quite upset—everybody here is always ready for anything—drove to the National Palace. Arriving there, they were taken into custody, on orders of the president, by a general and

several adjutants and placed under arrest. At two o'clock that afternoon, a second order from the president released the frightened men and also explained the reason for their arrest: the ministers had not worn the buttonhole emblems and the silk sashes that are prescribed for major generals in civilian clothing.[3]

Diplomats and civil servants who wished to confer with Huerta had to go from one travern to another to meet with the alcoholic president.[4]

These unattractive idiosyncracies were combined with a strong cynicism and tremendous cruelty. "The honest and respectable people don't come to me, so I must rule with the scoundrels,"[5] Huerta was quoted by Hintze. His terrorism against any opposition quickly took on such forms that even Hintze, who favored a "firm-handed" policy, wrote: "This terrorism is not that of an enlightened autocrat but is currently assuming the form of a senseless rage."[6] And, elsewhere,

> The phantoms of those executed each night are stalking Huerta. The former governor of the Federal District and Huerta's collaborator was taken in February 1913 from the president's chambers, after making some careless remarks, to the suburb of Tlalpam and was killed without ceremony. The leader of the Catholic Party, Somellera, was first detained in San Juan de Ulua, then freed, but was forced, under threat of death, to hand over a considerable sum of money and to leave immediately for Europe. The methods of the government correspond roughly to those employed in Venice in the early Middle Ages, and we could look upon them with equanimity were they not occasionally extended to foreigners.[7]

It would nevertheless be erroneous to view Huerta as an incompetent or as an inefficient drunkard. Beneath the frequently drunken exterior lurked a very clever and adept politician. The best evidence for this is that, despite mounting revolutionary unrest, increasing pressure by the United States, and splits within the ranks of his supporters, Huerta managed to stay in power for seventeen months—and then to leave Mexico alive.[8]

The new regime, however, was not just a replica of the Díaz dictatorship. Unlike its Porfirian predecessor, which had been dominated by a financial oligarchy, the military played a far greater role under Huerta. Initially, it was made up of representatives of various military cliques: that of Huerta, the Felix Díaz-Mondragón group, and the Orozco group, which had already rebelled against Madero. In addition, the Huerta regime had taken on several leading politicians of the Díaz period, including the former foreign minister and provisional president, León de la Barra.

According to the agreement that had been signed in the U.S. embassy, Huerta was to be only the provisional president, he was to hold elections soon, and he was to support the presidential candidacy of Felix Díaz. He did not stand by this agreement, however, but remained in power and quickly succeeded in forcing out of his government the representatives of the other cliques. Felix Díaz was shunted off to Japan as a special ambassador and most of his supporters were pushed out of the government.[9] This infighting, on the whole, had little bearing on the domestic policies of the Huerta government.

There is little doubt that the Huerta regime represented a conservative restoration, but the discontinuities with the Madero regime frequently have been exaggerated. No profound social transformation (above all, not in the landholding pattern) had taken place under Madero, so that Huerta had to carry out few changes in order to return to the conditions that existed during the time of Porfirio Díaz. Only insofar as political liberties were concerned had there been a clean break between the Madero regime and its prerevolutionary predecessor. Under Madero elections were freer and more honest than ever before. Congress became a real forum for opposing views. The press was free and some groups calling for social reform were tolerated. This tolerance had its limits, as in the case of Emiliano Zapata and his adherents in Morelos. It was greatest, perhaps, where labor was concerned: unions and strikes had been legalized.

These freedoms were abolished by Huerta—some immediately, others gradually. Those revolutionaries considered "radical" were murdered (for example, Abraham González, the revolutionary governor of Chihuahua) or forced to flee. In other fields, Huerta proceeded with more caution. Trade unions, at first, were permitted, and even some strikes were tolerated. On 1 May 1913, the anarchosyndicalist Casa del Obrero Mundial was allowed to hold a May Day parade, but, a few weeks later, in June, some of its leaders were arrested and union meetings were banned. The organization itself was declared illegal at the beginning of 1914.[10]

Madero's most important legacy to the Huerta era was Congress. Initially, Huerta did not dissolve Congress, for he anticipated its support and, moreover, had attempted to preserve the fiction of his legality both at home and abroad. Congress had also cooperated with the new president in the early months. But, as opposition to Huerta intensified and the revolutionary movement against him grew, the opposition to him in Congress also grew.

On 23 September, Belisario Domínguez, the representative from the state of Chiapas, delivered the most vehement attack on Huerta heard in Congress since the coup. Given the terror then reigning in Mexico, it was an act requiring enormous courage. Domínguez specified Huerta as Madero's murderer and called on the Senate to depose him. Two days after making this speech, Domínguez disappeared and his corpse was not discovered for many days.[11] The Chamber of Deputies then adopted a resolution on 9 October "which established a commission of inquiry into this ominous disappearance, called on the Senate to take the same steps, declared President Huerta personally liable for the safety of the people's representatives, and threatened that, if the Congress did not feel protected in the capital, it would move its meetings to another, more secure location."[12]

With this decisive move, Congress threw down a challenge to Huerta, which he attempted to settle by means of a second coup—this time directed at Congress. On the evening of 10 October, he sent his minister of the interior to Congress with his reply: "The government declares the resolution to be unacceptable and requests Congress to reconsider it." Hintze reported that

> This produced tremendous agitation and the usual battle of words, which ended in a rejection of the government's proposal. The president of the chamber attempted to save the situation by suggesting that the proposal be referred to committee. The government insisted on an immediate decision. The president terminated the meeting amidst a tremendous uproar, and the deputies attempted to leave the chamber when the general inspector of the police appeared with a large detachment of his men, read off a list of roughly one hundred deputies, and declared them under arrest. Some deputies attempted to defend themselves, whereupon the police drew their guns. The parliament was surrounded by troops who fended off the crowd. Eighty-four deputies were taken to prison under military escort and incarcerated and the rest were released.[13]

Huerta, thereupon, called for new elections, which took place on 26 October. Hintze once again provided an informative account of these events. "The elections took place with widespread absenteeism and were seen as a big hoax . . . . Of course, the Mexican government made no effort to hide the fact of such a hoax. The vast majority of senators and deputies simply were appointed or elected on orders of the government or through falsified ballots."[14] Various foreign diplomats, including Hintze, obtained the electoral instructions Huerta had sent to the governor of Puebla. They read, in part:

> In those places where the election is actually held, white ballots are to be used, in order to create an absolute majority for the following persons: President: Division General Victoriano Huerta; Vice-President: Division General Aureliano Blanquet . . . . If the chief of police finds, upon inspection of the ballots, that the election results do not correspond to the guidelines established here, he is to make the appropriate changes prior to submitting the ballots, so that the ballots and the electoral procedures comply rigorously to regulations.[15]

In spite of the support of the old Díaz army and the Díaz bureaucracy and in spite of all its recourse to terror, the Huerta regime had to struggle from the first days of its existence against an armed opposition, which daily became stronger and, by the end of 1913, already controlled a large part of the country. The centers of this movement were the areas that had already played a decisive role during the Madero revolution: the Morelos region, where the "Liberation Army of the South" had taken the field under Emiliano Zapata, and the northern states of Chihuahua, Coahuila, and Sonora, where the movements of Francisco Villa and Venustiano Carranza had their bases.

## The Zapata Movement

After taking power, Huerta attempted to win Zapata's support by offering him the governorship of Morelos. But Zapata refused to make any deal with a man he detested as "opposed to every norm of legality, justice, law, and morality and much worse than Madero." Instead, in a manifesto to the Mexican people promulgated on 30 May 1911 he announced the firm resolve of the Liberation Army of the South that "The revolution will be continued until the fall of the so-called president."[16]

In its composition Zapata's was the most homogeneous of all revolutionary movements. Its constituents shared virtually the same background: the great majority of them were free peasants, some of whom had been employed for several months as agricultural workers; a minority consisted of hacienda peons. They also shared the same enemies: the hacendados who had appropriated the landholdings of the free villages. And they shared as well the same demands: the return of expropriated lands, and the expropriation of a major portion of the large landholdings. Note that the constituency of the Zapata movement included only a few industrial workers (there was no industry or mining in Morelos) and no middle classes (who remained mostly tied to the landowners); note also that the enemies of the movement did not include foreign landowners (they had hardly penetrated into the region). And note further that as a consequence of the demands the movement at least in its core areas did not consider the interests of anyone apart from peasant and hacendado.

The leadership of the movement did not, however, reflect this homogeneity. While Emiliano Zapata (and to a lesser degree his brother Eufemio) and subordinates like Genovevo de la O were peasant leaders in the classic mold—they had been spokesmen for their villages in the Díaz period and had fought hacendado encroachment of peasant lands—other leaders were of different origins. Felipe Neri was a kiln operator from a Chinameca hacienda, José Trinidad Ruíz, a Protestant preacher from Tlaltizapán, Fortino Ayaquica, a textile worker from Atlixco, Puebla, Jesús Morales, a saloon keeper from Ayutla.

As the movement grew stronger the number of its intellectual supporters increased. In its early stages the most prominent and influential of the intellectuals, who for a time became an ideologue of the revolt, was Otilio

Montaño, a schoolteacher from Ayala. He was later joined by radicals from Mexico City, the most prominent of whom were Gildardo Magaña, son of a wealthy merchant who had studied business administration in Philadelphia, and Antonio Díaz Soto y Gama, a lawyer. While Magaña worked above all as organizer and diplomat, Soto y Gama soon emerged as the main ideologue of the movement. Both men had impeccable credentials in Zapata's eyes. They had been linked to the Liberal party opposition in the Díaz period and implicitly recognized Zapata's leadership.

In its organization Zapata's was a guerrilla movement, divided into groups of two hundred to three hundred men, whose leaders referred to themselves as "generals." For much of the year the soldiers lived in their home villages, but they banded together when an important battle was to be fought, and, after the fighting was over, withdrew to their villages once more.

The homogeneous composition and the guerrillalike organization of Zapata's movement made for both its strengths and weaknesses. Its strengths were its unity, its consistency, and its resilience. The unity of the movement is evidenced by the fact that a conservative opposition never developed within its ranks. Its consistency is evidenced by the boldness of its reforms. Zapata was the sole revolutionary leader in Mexico who carried out land distribution in the areas under his control during the insurrection. In so doing, he went beyond even his own Ayala plan, which, aside from the return of the stolen lands, had provided for only partial expropriation with compensation of the hacienda lands. Now, all hacienda land was expropriated without compensation; it was not, for the most part, handed over to individual peasants but was given to the village communities, which, in keeping with their old customs, put it at the disposal of their members. The resilience of the movement is evidenced by the fact that, despite several occupations of Morelos cities by enemy troops, the countryside always remained in the hands of Zapata. Given the guerrillalike organization of the army, the movement was virtually unbeatable at its center.

The weaknesses of the movement were two: the narrowness of its interests and the immobility of its army. The narrowness of its interests is evidenced especially by Zapata's lack of understanding for the problems of the working class, especially in the early years of the revolution. While he would occasionally denounce the "bourgeois, who in his insatiable greed robs the industrial and agricultural worker of the fruits of their labor,"[17] he did not achieve any concrete appreciation of the demands and interests of the latter group prior to 1917. The immobility of the army is evidenced by the difficulty with which the Zapata movement expanded into the neighboring states of Guerrero, Mexico, and Puebla in 1913–15.

The peasants were simply unwilling to leave their local terrain for any length of time; what happened outside hardly concerned them.

On balance then, the Zapata movement tended to be well-nigh invincible at its center, but virtually ineffectual beyond its confines. With the support of the peasants, it was able to resist every attack successfully, but was scarcely capable of waging an offensive war. Both these tendencies were further affected by Morelos' logistic position. Morelos did not, for one thing, have any arms factories. Nor was there money to pay for smuggled weapons. The sugar haciendas, for the most part, had been shut down, their lands distributed to the peasants and used mainly now for subsistence agriculture to feed the movement. The area had no points of contact with the world beyond Mexico, and, as no ports had been occupied, it was not possible to sell sugar abroad to raise funds. Zapata was limited to seizing arms from the enemy and to alleviating his lack of money to some extent through attacks on haciendas, trains, and enemy troops.

## The Revolutionary Movement in the North: Background

Both the revolutionary movements of northern Mexico and the armies they generated were of a completely different nature from those of the South. The movements themselves were far more heterogeneous, and the armies were far more "professionalized" than those of the South. That heterogeneity, as I have already suggested, simply reflected the heterogeneity of northern society in general as well as the dissatisfaction that had seized most segments of that society in the course of Díaz's regime. The kind of exclusively "peasant" revolution that characterized southern Mexico was unthinkable in the North. The free villagers, who made up 80 percent of Morelos' rural population and a similarly high percentage of its revolutionary forces, represented a much smaller part of the rural population of the North.[18]

The tendency toward professionalization had begun to manifest itself after Madero's victory in 1911. Until then the revolutionary forces, in the North as well as in the rest of Mexico, were essentially the result of a popular uprising. No professional soldiers, with the exception of a few mercenaries recruited in the United States, participated in the revolution. After his victory, Francisco Madero had dissolved most of the army that had brought him to power. At the insistence of the revolutionary governors of northern Mexico and under pressure from many of his former soldiers, Madero had retained some of the revolutionary troops as rurales (federal police).[19] The social composition of these rurales has never been studied, but it can be assumed that a high percentage of them was constituted of people who found no occupation or were at the bottom of the social ladder in civilian life, that is, landless laborers and unemployed workers.

The Orozco rebellion of 1912 had at first weakened, then strengthened those contingents. At first Orozco had weaned many of the North's rurales from Madero's banner and organized them into an army of his own. As a result the governors who had assumed control of the states of Chihuahua, Sonora, and Coahuila after the victory of the revolution suddenly were confronted by a twofold danger. On the one hand the Orozco rebellion represented a substantial threat to their control of their respective states, but on the other hand the governors suddenly had to rely mainly on the old federal army which only recently they had been fighting and which they did not trust. To counter both dangers, revolutionary militias were either built up from scratch or former Maderist units were reactivated. In Coahuila, Pablo González took command of the units assembled by Governor Carranza. In Sonora, the municipal president of Huatabampo, Alvaro Obregón, led the most extensive militia unit that the state organized against Orozco. Pancho Villa assumed the leadership of the largest militia units fighting Orozco in Chihuahua.

The federal army viewed with the greatest hostility the formation of these state militias, which threatened their exclusive control of the armed forces in Mexico. With Madero's support, the army leadership attempted to bring these new militias under its control or to disperse them. Carranza conducted an agitated correspondence with Madero, who had tried to subordinate the state militias of Coahuila directly to the federal army.[20]

When Maytorena, who was commanding the state militias of Sonora, attacked Orozco's troops at La Dura, nearby units of the federal army refused to support him.[21] The most serious blow leveled at the new state militias undoubtedly was Huerta's attempt to have Pancho Villa shot on the pretext that he had stolen a horse. This effort was frustrated by Madero's intervention, but Villa's arrest and subsequent imprisonment in Mexico City contributed significantly to the disorganization of the state militia in Chihuahua.

In its actions, the federal army was perfectly conscious of one fact: the state militias would be the nucleus of a new revolutionary army should the federal army attempt to carry out a coup d'etat. This, in fact, did occur. The most important commanders of these units, Pancho Villa, Alvaro Obregón, and Pablo González, became the military leaders of the new revolutionary movement that swept Mexico after the murder of Madero.

The existence of these state troops as the nucleus of the revolutionary armies (especially in Coahuila and Sonora) was not the only element that tended to "professionalize" them. This tendency was further enhanced by the existence of four social groups in northern Mexico only weakly represented in the South.

There were a great many migrants from other states of Mexico who constituted an extremely mobile labor force. They worked as agricultural laborers during the harvest season and at other times labored in the mines or across the border in the United States. Unlike the free peasants of southern Mexico or the military colonists of the North, their links and attachment to specific localities and villages were smaller. They constituted a group of men of great potential mobility who would far more easily become professional soldiers than would peasants with deep roots in their native villages animated by the hope of regaining their lost lands.

There was a large stratum of unemployed miners and industrial workers for whom the army soon became the main means of livelihood. To a lesser degree the same was the case for many of the cowboys who joined the revolution. They had ties to the land less strong than those of the peasants and, as the herds they were tending became depleted in the course of the revolution, many of them had no choice but to join the army.

In addition to these groups and partially intertwined with them was yet another—outlaws that separated the northern army even more from the civilian population. The proximity of the United States, presenting tremendous opportunities for smugglers and bandits, contributed to the creation of a larger lumpen proletariat than elsewhere in Mexico. Many of these outlaws joined the northern armies and influenced their development.

The professional armies could only be maintained because in the North the revolutionary leaders had the opportunity either to tax or to confiscate cattle herds and cotton crops of hacendados and sell them either legally or illegally—notwithstanding American vigilance—in the United States.

As a result of these differences, the strengths and weaknesses of the revolutionary movements of the North present an obverse image of those in the South. Where the South was weak, the North was strong; where the South was limited by the narrowness of the interests it represented, the North had the broadest imaginable social base; not a class in Mexico did not find representation here. Where the army of the South was characterized by immobility, that of the North, made up to a larger degree of nonpeasants, was prepared to fight anywhere.

But the strengths of the South were the weaknesses of the North. Where there was unity in the South, there was diversity in the North: there did not exist a movement that was not sooner or later divided into a radical and a conservative wing. Where there was consistency in the South, there was ambivalence in the North: no movement could firmly hew a certain line in the face of so many conflicting interests that made up its constituency. Where there was loyalty in the South, there was less dependability in the North. Once the funds ran out, many officers and soldiers in the North refused to fight on.

In the North, unlike the South, an external circumstance deepened the

relief of the picture: the neighboring United States. Every northern revolutionary movement was to a certain degree dependent economically on
the United States; each maintained agents in the United States and was
obliged to work closely with American businessmen. But each movement
was faced as well with a strong anti-American attitude on the part of large
segments of the population. This attitude was reinforced by the fact that
demands for the annexation of the northern part of Mexico were repeatedly heard in the United States, and Mexicans in the United States
frequently were treated as second-class citizens. These two opposing
tendencies—dependence on the United States and particularly strong
anti-American currents—led to a constant flux in the attitude of the northern revolutionaries toward the neighbor to the north. The proximity of the
United States both broadened the northern revolutionary's base of support and put at its disposal invaluable resources. But it also increased the
diversity of an already disunited front, the ambivalence of already uncertain reformist efforts, and the unreliability of an army in which pay
frequently played a determining role in ensuring loyalty.[22]

### The Carranza Movement

The differences between the revolutionary movement in Chihuahua and
those in Sonora and Coahuila in 1910 and 1912 emerged more sharply after
1913. The histories of most great social revolutions reveal various common elements. In its first phase, a revolution is led by rebellious members
of the ruling stratum who desire political change but not socioeconomic
transformations that would endanger the power of their class. In this
respect, there are striking similarities between Madero in Mexico and men
such as Mirabeau in Paris in 1789–90 or Prince Lvov in Russia in February
1917.

The leadership of these men of the first phase of a revolution is quickly
called into question by forces demanding radical social reforms. The rise
of these new movements is facilitated in every case by attempts of
counterrevolutionary forces to seize power for themselves, which effectively accelerates the radicalization not merely of the poorest strata of the
population but of the middle classes as well. There were important links
between the attempted flight of Louis XVI of France and the accession to
power of the Girondists, between the war of the European states to restore the power of the king and the rule of the Jacobins, and between the
Kornilov putsch and the October Revolution in Russia.

In Mexico, as well, the revolution entered a new, more radical phase,
though it was far less radical than those in France in 1793 and in Russia in
October 1917. While men such as Pancho Villa in Chihuahua, Emiliano
Zapata in Morelos, and Alvaro Obregón in Sonora were far more radical

than Madero had been, the same cannot be said for Venustiano Carranza, the man who claimed for himself the leadership of the revolution after March 1913.[23]

After a few weeks' preparation he became the first and, for a time, the only Mexican governor to fight against Huerta actively. On 26 March he issued his plan of Guadalupe, which called for the overthrow of Huerta, free elections, and the reestablishment of legality. This plan became the official program of the northern revolutionaries. Unlike Madero's previous plan of San Luis Potosí, it contained absolutely no demands for any kind of social reform. No mention at all was made of the land issue.

Carranza, like Madero, was a hacendado from Coahuila, though far less wealthy than Madero. On the whole, he had been closer to the Porfirian regime than Madero had. In contrast to Madero, he had held important, though not top-level, positions during the Díaz period. For example, he had been a senator without ever having distinguished himself through any particular opposition to the Díaz regime. He had joined Bernardo Reyes in 1909 and, after the latter had submitted to Díaz and left Mexico, Carranza had rallied to Madero, participated in the 1910 revolution, and become governor of Coahuila.

In most respects, Carranza was even more conservative than Madero. He shared little of Madero's pronounced faith in parliamentary democracy, freedom of the press, tolerance of the opposition, or free elections. Nonetheless, he distinguished himself from his former chief in several important ways which allowed him to play a leading role in the Mexican revolution up to 1920.

Unlike Madero, Carranza was convinced that the only way the revolutionaries would ever be able to maintain themselves in power was by destroying the old federal army. He manifested a far more explicit nationalism than Madero, both in the economic and political realms. Ultimately, he was much more a demagogue than Madero. In contrast to his former leader, he did not hesitate, when faced with no other choice, to promise extensive social changes that he had no intention of carrying out. He did have one thing in common with Madero, however; he did not want to destroy the hacienda system.

Carranza was determined not to wage the struggle against Huerta as a social revolution. His Guadalupe plan was even more conservative in social terms than Madero's San Luis Potosí plan. While Madero mentioned the agrarian question, however briefly and vaguely, Carranza made no social demands whatsoever. To his more radical supporters, who demanded the inclusion of more far-reaching reforms—land distribution, labor legislation, and the like—he stated, "Do you want the war to last for five years? The less resistance there is, the shorter the war will be. The large landowners, the clergy, and the industrialists are stronger than the federal government. We must first defeat the government before we can take on the questions you rightly wish to solve."[24]

Carranza obviously had the example of the Madero revolution in mind. With a single, generalized demand, Madero had succeeded in opening the ruling classes to compromise and in winning over the peasantry to his cause. But the two years of the Madero period had made a deep impression upon both the ruling classes and the peasants. The former were convinced that even the slightest concession to the revolutionaries could endanger their power; the peasants were no longer willing to go into battle merely for general demands that did not express their specific interests.

Carranza's refusal to engage in what might be called revolutionary warfare contributed significantly to his defeat in his home state. He had limited himself to strengthening the state militia by levying new taxes and waging a conventional war against Huerta. He made no attempt to win a mass base for the revolutionary movement in Coahuila by means of reforms or even promises of reforms. Nor did he try to build a significant guerrilla force. The better-equipped and more numerous Huerta troops could easily defeat the state militia in a conventional war—and this is precisely what happened. In 1913, Carranza's army was beaten three times in Coahuila—at Anhelo, Saltillo, and Monclova—and Carranza decided to leave the state, which was now largely controlled by Huerta's troops, and to seek refuge in Sonora, where large sections were controlled by the revolutionaries.

The situation Carranza encountered in that northwestern state was somewhat different from that of his home state. José María Maytorena, the governor, was a man whose background—he too was a hacendado—and social ideas were very similar to those of Carranza. Unlike his Coahuilan colleague, however, Maytorena did not feel that he would be able to funnel the revolution into conservative channels and preferred leaving the state rather than take radical social measures. He wrote that, on 24 February 1913, the decision was made by the civilian and military leaders of Sonora "to defy General Huerta . . . . I could not countenance the methods that were advocated nor the measures that I would be forced to take . . . . They included a general confiscation of property, which would include the properties of people who had no political interests and had not participated in the events in Mexico City . . . forced loans . . . detentions and executions of peaceful citizens whose only crime was their wealth and the fact that they did not adhere to our cause."[25] Maytorena had requested a leave of absence and had gone to the United States. He had been replaced by a provisional governor, Ignacio Pesqueira.

The military leaders of the revolution in Sonora, and later in other states—whose importance was increasing from day to day—were of more radical persuasion. Most of these men were by no means agrarian revolutionaries. The state legislature of Sonora, in which they exercised decisive influence, had shelved an agrarian law that the socially most radical leader in Sonora, Juan Cabral, had introduced and that called for an immediate, extensive land reform.[26]

The social and economic measures taken by these men nevertheless went far beyond what either Carranza or Maytorena considered admissible. They had confiscated many estates of hostile landowners, which they were administering, and were using the proceeds to finance the revolution. They had made broad promises of agrarian reform (most of which, as was later shown, they were unwilling to keep), and their official declarations were increasingly tinged with radical ideas, some of which (especially in relation to workers' rights) they wished to implement.

When Carranza arrived in Sonora, his power was quite limited in scope. He had lost most of his immediate constituency in Coahuila. In contrast to Madero, who, as a result of his book and his electoral campaign, was a recognized national leader, Carranza was essentially unknown outside his home state. He was thus far more vulnerable to pressures from local leaders than Madero had been. As a result of these pressures in Sonora, Carranza was forced to broaden the leadership of his movement.

In Coahuila, Carranza's movement had significant upper class backing. In Sonora and in other states where his movement began to develop, men of more modest origins, mainly from the middle class, became important in directing the movement. This is not to say that there were no links between the leadership of the Carranza faction in Sonora and large landowners. Both the interim governor, Ignacio Pesqueira, and his relative, Roberto Pesqueira, who was responsible for arms purchases in the United States, belonged to a hacendado family, and Alvaro Obregón and Plutarco Elias Calles also had family ties to wealthy hacendados. In addition, Calles, as well as Adolfo de la Huerta, had been hacienda administrators during the Porfirian era. It is worth noting, however, that, except for the Pesqueiras, none of the important leaders of the revolution outside Coahuila who were close to Carranza were hacendados. Obregón had worked as a mechanic, schoolteacher, and tenant farmer before acquiring a middle-sized ranch, which he owned at the time the revolution broke out.

Calles also had led a varied existence as schoolteacher, municipal employee (he was dismissed for alleged fraud), and hotel supervisor before becoming the administrator of a small hacienda, as well as a flour mill.[27]

Benjamin Hill, Obregón's nephew, belonged to a wealthy family in Navojoa, Sonora. As a young man, he was sent by his parents to study in Italy. A biographer claims that he studied military science at an Italian officers' school; the English minister to Mexico wrote in a report that Hill had joined the Mafia while in Italy. At the time of the beginning of the Mexican revolution, he was a shopkeeper in his home town.[28]

In contrast to these leaders, a number of others who also occupied high posts in the military were self-made men of far humbler beginnings. Salvador Alvarado had pursued many occupations, among them pharmacist, shopkeeper, tenant farmer on a ranch in the Yaqui Valley and innkeeper.[29] Francisco Murguía had been a street photographer.[30] Depending on which of his biographers one trusts, Cándido Aguilar, leader of the Carranzist revolutionaries in Veracruz, had been either the administrator of a small estate for fifteen years or had run a dairy business in his home town.[31]

A relatively large number of generals of the Carranza movement came from the working class. Pablo González had been a mill worker. The Carranzist generals in Durango, the brothers Domingo and Mariano Arrieta, had been miners. Manuel Diéguez, from Sonora, had worked as a copper miner in Cananea. Heriberto Jara, one of the leaders in Veracruz, was a former textile worker in the large mills in Río Blanco, and Jesus Agustin Castro was a former miner and later a streetcar operator from Torreón.

Some of these generals had been active in political life prior to the revolution. Jara was one of the leaders of the textile workers' strike in Río Blanco in 1907, and Diéguez of the copper miners' strike in Cananea in 1906. These were among the most important and bloodiest strikes of the Díaz period, and, in their aftermath, both Jara and Diéguez were imprisoned by the Díaz administration. Pablo González and Salvador Alvarado had fought against the Díaz regime as members of groups organized by the Liberal party. Obregón's revolutionary career, in contrast, only began in 1912, when he mobilized a large contingent of volunteers against Orozco in his home town of Huatabampo.

Most of the civilians close to Carranza, however, were intellectuals. The most outstanding was Luis Cabrera, a former schoolteacher and journalist. Isidro Fabela was a lawyer and Pastor Rouaix, an agricultural engineer. These men had taken an active part in the Madero revolution and had belonged to the more radical wing of the Madero movement during 1910–13.

Notable in the composition of the Carranzist leadership was the weak representation of the peasantry and the nearly complete absence of hacienda peons or inhabitants of free villages. Although Obregón, who came from a once-powerful family in Sonora, had worked at different times as a schoolteacher and shopkeeper and had temporarily made ends meet as a small farmer, it would be ironic to consider him representative of the Mexican peasantry. Absent from the ranks were such "classic" peasant leaders as Calixto Contreras from Durango, who, since 1905, had led the peasants from San Pedro Ocuila in their fight to regain lands appropriated by a neighboring hacienda, or Toribio Ortega, who had led the peasants of Cuchillo Parado in a similar fight. Both were Villista generals. Only after the defeat of the convention in 1915 did some peasant leaders, such as Domingo Arenas from Tlaxcala or Severiano Ceniceros from Durango (the first a former Zapatista, the other a former Villista general), join Carranza's forces.

Some of Carranza's military leaders, nevertheless, maintained special relations with the peasantry, though more in their functions as patrons and protectors than as leaders and spokesmen. Thus, Adolfo de la Huerta, as the administrator of a hacienda, had won the goodwill and confidence of the neighboring Yaqui Indians by hiding them from the federal troops among his agricultural workers.[32] The Obregón family appears to have played a similar role as protector for the Mayo Indians, which made it relatively easy for Obregón to win them over and mobilize them.[33] Cándido Aguilar had treated the peons on the hacienda he administered so well that many of them joined him when he became a revolutionary. The extent to which the Carranza movement lacked peasant leaders was already evident from the fact that the principal advocates of peasant interests and reform in the countryside came from the ranks of the working class and the intelligentsia. This was, perhaps, best reflected in the composition of the delegation Carranza chose to negotiate with Zapata in 1914. He made a conscious effort to include some of the most outspoken advocates of agrarian reform in his organization, but significantly, not a single one of the three men—Luis Cabrera, Juan Sarabia, or Antonio Villarreal, who later broke with Carranza—was a peasant.

Can definitive conclusions be drawn from the composition of the Carranza leadership with regard to its social base and its support? There rarely has been a revolutionary movement whose leadership faithfully reflected its base of support. Nevertheless, the heavy participation of members of the middle class in the civilian and military leadership of the Carranza movement is evidence of the extensive influence they wielded in that movement, not least because the revolution led by Carranza offered the Mexican middle class access to the elite political, military, and financial positions of the country. His nationalism particularly reflected middle class fears of growing foreign domination.

It was above all the pressure of the more radical leaders from Sonora that forced Carranza to do what he had refused to do in Coahuila, to promise social change. In a speech in September 1913, he declared that

at the moment when the armed struggle called for in the Guadalupe plan has ended, the social struggle, the class struggle in all its power and its grandeur must begin. Whether they want it to happen or not, the new social ideas must win out among the masses against all opposition. It is not merely a question of dividing up the land and the natural resources, not merely a question of honest elections, not merely a question of opening new schools or of the equal distribution of the wealth of the land. Something much greater and much more sacred is at stake: the creation of justice, the pursuit of equality, the disappearance of the powerful, and the creation of an equilibrium in our national economy.[34]

At the time he was announcing such deeds, Carranza was doing everything in his power to preserve the hacienda system. He had been unable to prevent or reverse the confiscation of hacienda lands carried out by his military commanders, but he did all he could to keep the temporary expropriations from becoming permanent. He informed the commanders that they could indeed control the revenues from the estates that had been seized but the haciendas as such were to be left intact. When one revolutionary general, Lucio Blanco, distributed the land of the de los Borregos hacienda, in the northeastern state of Tamaulipas, among the peasants, he was censured by Carranza and transferred from his post.[35]

Carranza was successful in insuring that nowhere in the declaration by his government was the temporary seizure of the haciendas viewed as the preliminary stage of a land distribution. His unmistakable objective was to return the vast majority of the estates to their former owners before the question of agrarian reform was raised at all. As we shall see, in 1915–18 he attained this goal, which he pursued with iron determination.

The second stage of the Mexican Revolution, 1913–14, lasted much longer than the initial Maderist phase. It affected a larger number of people and required much greater resources. If Carranza wished to finance the revolution without resorting to expropriation, he had to find an alternative source of revenue, and only one proved to be available to him—the large foreign companies. To a great extent the costs and burdens of the revolution were shifted to foreign capital; this was compatible with both Carranza's own views and those of the nationalist wing of the northern agricultural and industrial bourgeoisie. The latter was pursuing the double objective of securing greater revenues for the country from its natural resources and preserving the hacienda system with those revenues.

There was an additional basis for this policy. Since Carranza wanted little social change and, in contrast to Madero, was not prepared to allow broad parliamentary democracy, nationalism was the sole factor that could secure a mass base for him.

In 1913, however, the idea of putting nationalist pressure on foreign capital was still far in the future. Carranza's forces controlled only a few areas of northern Mexico and had to rely on American arms shipments. Cooperation and promises—not pressure and nationalistic declarations—were the sole means by which he could obtain financial support from foreign capital. This policy, naturally, was not likely to win him mass support and remained strictly secret. It was used primarily to gain support among the American companies that were making efforts to push the British out of Mexico. In view of this, Carranza appears to have made secret agreements with both of the oil companies closely linked to Standard Oil: the Mexican Petroleum Company and the Waters Pierce Oil Company.

The Mexican Petroleum Company, according to the account of the chairman of the board, Edward L. Doheny, in 1913 began to divert money to Carranza in the form of advance tax payments long before his troops occupied the oil fields of Tampico.[36] There is no evidence to indicate whether Doheny's "generosity" was based on any promises made to him by Carranza or solely on the hope that, once in power, the Constitutionalists would take reprisals against Cowdray, who was supporting Huerta. One indication that some kind of negotiation and, perhaps, agreement between the two had taken place is that evidence does exist substantiating negotiations between the Mexican leader and another oil executive, Henry Clay Pierce, who was also linked to the Standard Oil Company.

The central question in the dealings with Pierce was not petroleum, but railroads. Some evidence indicates that Pierce had supported the Madero movement in 1911 in the hope that, after his victory, Madero would remove the Cowdray people from management positions in the railways. These ties between Pierce and Madero seem obvious from the fact, for example, that both men employed the same attorney, Sherburne G. Hopkins, to represent their interests in the United States. He was characterized by the German minister to Mexico as the "professional attorney of the 'Latin American revolutions' fabricated by conspiracies in the United States."[37]

After Madero became president, Hopkins had actually attempted to persuade him to dismiss the railway directors close to Cowdray. Madero, however, had not cooperated, possibly out of fear of becoming completely dependent on Standard Oil. Pierce then hoped that, through the mediation of Carranza, he would be able to resume his former controlling position in the Mexican railway system. To this end, he retained Hopkins. Carranza, too, appointed Hopkins as his representative in the United States, even though he was aware of his real role, which had come to light in a public session of a U.S. congressional committee in 1912,[38] and of the fact that the lawyer also worked for Pierce.

Documents stolen from Hopkins's New York office during a break-in in April 1914 were turned over to the *New York Herald*, which published them in sensational form. These documents, as Hopkins told one of

Villa's representatives in the United States,[39] were quite authentic. They included an extensive project, submitted by Pierce via Hopkins to Carranza, that proposed the establishment of a separate administration for the railways of northern Mexico, independent of the board of directors headquartered in Mexico City. In Pierce's view, the board was controlled by supporters of Cowdray, and the purpose of the proposal, as Hopkins wrote to Pierce, was to "reach a settlement whereby you could profitably move back into northern Mexico."[40]

Carranza did not unambiguously support these proposals, but, nonetheless, appointed as director of the railways Alberto J. Pani, who enjoyed Pierce's confidence and appeared to have special ties with the oil companies.[41] In return, Pierce promised to promote a benevolent attitude toward the Carranza government among U.S. financiers with interests in the Mexican railroads.[42]

His collaboration with the more radical leaders of Sonora and the northeastern part of Mexico; his promises of social reform, however moderate; and the funds he received from the oil companies permitted Carranza and his movement to capitalize on the dissatisfaction with the Huerta regime in many parts of the North and to acquire increasing importance. Until the end of 1913, units close to Carranza controlled the major part of Sonora and parts of the states of Coahuila, Nuevo Leon, and Tamaulipas.

### The Villa Movement

The second large revolutionary movement in northern Mexico, which officially recognized Carranza's leadership but had developed extensive autonomy, had its stronghold in the state of Chihuahua, as it had in 1910. The differences that existed in 1910 between that state and the neighboring states of Sonora and Coahuila—an absence of hacendados in the leadership, with a consequent far stronger popular base—became even more pronounced in 1913.

These differences were linked partly to the lack of continuity between the "moderate" leadership of the state during the Madero period and the leadership of the Constitutionalist revolution. In Coahuila and Sonora, the state bureaucracy, from the beginning, had organized the Constitutionalist movement and thus kept it under control. It mobilized troops, furnished them with resources, named many of the leaders of the armed forces, and coordinated their activities. Insofar as the leadership of the state was concerned, Carranza provided a clear continuity between the Madero period and the Constitutionalist years in Coahuila.

In Sonora, despite the fact that the Maderist Governor Maytorena had left for several months (he returned to office in August 1913), the state legislature and the bureaucracy provided a wide measure of continuity. As the replacement for Maytorena, they named another hacendado, Ignacio Pesqueira, whose social ideas were scarcely different from those of his predecessor.

By contrast, no such smooth and controlled transition between the Madero and Constitutionalist periods occurred in Chihuahua. Large segments of the state bureaucracy and state legislature had joined the Orozco rising in 1912 and had rallied to Huerta after his coup in 1913. As a result, the revolution in Chihuahua could not be organized by the state government as in Coahuila and Sonora, and assumed many more characteristics of a popular uprising than was the case with its neighbors. The break with the past and the radical tendencies in the state were further strengthened by the murder of Chihuahua's moderate revolutionary leader, Abraham González, who was thrown under a moving train by Huerta's emissaries.

A very different type of leader soon assumed control of the revolutionary movement in the state—Francisco "Pancho" Villa. He had crossed the Rio Grande from Texas with eight men in March 1913, had taken control of the major part of the state, and had become the unquestioned head of the revolutionary movement there. By his origins—he had been a tenant farmer on a hacienda and a bandit—and his more radical social ideas, he was definitely of a breed far removed from the leaders of the Constitutionalists in the two neighboring states.[43]

The local and regional leaders who joined him at first were also far different from their counterparts in Coahuila and Sonora. In the early stages of the Villa revolution hacendados played no role in its leadership while peasant leaders were far more strongly represented than in the two neighboring states. Toribio Ortega, who for many years had been the spokesman of the peasants of Cuchillo Parado and had led practically all the men of his village into the revolution on 16 November 1910, had become a leading general in Villa's army.[44] Calixto Contreras, who spent years in Porfirian jails for having led the people of San Pedro Ocuila in their protest against the usurpation of their lands by the hacienda of Sombreretillo, was another of Villa's leading generals. John Reed has given an unforgettable description of Ortega, "a lean dark Mexican who is called the honorable and the most brave by his soldiers. He is by far the most simplehearted and disinterested soldier in Mexico. He never kills his prisoners. He has refused to take a cent from the Revolution beyond his meager salary. Villa respects and trusts him perhaps beyond all his generals."[45] Porfirio Talamantes, whom Porfirian Governor Creel had called "a dangerous agitator" because he had become a spokesman for the villagers of the old military colony Janos, whose lands were being expropriated by the Chihuahuan oligarchy, had become a colonel in Villa's army.[46] Fidel Ávila, whom Villa appointed as governor of Chihuahua to succeed Manuel Chao in 1914, was once a foreman on a hacienda who led many of its cowboys and peons into the revolution.

Such men were by no means the only leaders of influence in the Villa movement. Tomas Urbina, a crony of Villa's from his bandit days, remained a bandit and in the course of the revolution attempted to set up a cattle empire closely modeled after that of the legendary Luis Terrazas, one of Mexico's wealthiest hacendados. Rodolfo Fierro, a railwayman who soon assumed important administrative and military functions in the Villa movement, was Villa's executioner, a man feared for his cruelty by friend and foe alike.[47]

There were fewer intellectuals in Villa's entourage than in Carranza's. In the first months when Villa ruled Chihuahua, the two who acquired the greatest influence upon his movement were Silvestre Terrazas and Federico Gonzalez Garza.

Silvestre Terrazas had been editor of an opposition newspaper, *El Correo de Chihuahua,* during the Porfirian era and had been repeatedly jailed for his opposition to the state government. For Villa he represented the most important link to the Chihuahuan middle class and the northern leader gave him responsible positions in the new state administration. Terrazas became secretary of state, temporary governor, and administrator of confiscated estates. In this function he seems to have exercised a strong influence on the way his native state was governed. He seems to have been one of the instigators of the extensive confiscations Villa carried out and one of the main advocates and defenders of this program. Although he wrote extensively before and after he became a Villista official, he abandoned all writing and ideological efforts in the crucial years 1913–15. He very rarely dealt with problems extending beyond his native state.[48]

In contrast to Terrazas, Federico González Garza, who also occupied important positions in the Chihuahuan government, came from outside the state and had occupied important positions in the Madero administration, such as subsecretary in the Ministry of Justice and governor of the Federal District. Federico González Garza was one of the first high officials of the Madero administration who joined Villa and one of the few who advocated radical agrarian reforms. Unlike Silvestre Terrazas, Federico González Garza became one of the most influential ideologues of the Villa movement and drafted some of its most important pronouncements.[49]

As Villa's movement extended into other states, its leadership, like that of the Carranza movement, changed and became far greater in scope. As will be shown further on, this broadening had an opposite effect from

Carranza's case. More conservative men, such as Felipe Angeles, members of the Madero family, and Sonoran Governor José Maria Maytorena began to exercise an increasing influence over Villa. In December 1913, though, when Villa assumed control of Chihuahua, these men had not yet joined his movement.

At that point Villa and his leadership carried out social and economic policies different by far from those implemented by Carranza. Even if he had shared the more conservative ideology of Carranza, Maytorena, and Pesqueira, however, the situation in Chihuahua would have forced him to take far more radical measures than the other northern leaders had taken.

A purely political revolution with a minimum of social content, such as Carranza was attempting to bring about, would have been impossible in Chihuahua in 1913. In Coahuila and Sonora, a considerable number of the hacendados had either joined the revolution or had remained neutral. In Chihuahua, almost all of the large landowners initially had given active support to Orozco and later to Huerta. At the same time, Orozco, even after he joined with Huerta, could still count on important support from disillusioned Maderist revolutionaries. In order to break the power of the hacendados and at the same time undermine the popular support for Orozco, the Chihuahuan revolutionary movement had to effect radical changes.

The necessity for such change was caused by an economic situation that was significantly worse in Chihuahua than in the other northern states. The crisis of 1907–10 had hit that state harder. One piece of evidence of this severity was the greater loss, in 1907, of retail sales, as compared with the other states of the North.[50] More intensive fighting and destruction had occurred in this state during 1910 than in any other part of the North; from February 1912 through the end of 1913, bitter struggles had taken place. Many business operations, particularly mines, had ceased activity. Agricultural production had decreased significantly. This state of affairs, in addition to his social origins and his unabashed hatred of the hacendado class that had ruled Chihuahua for so long, impelled Villa to resort to more radical measures in his region than Carranza and regional leaders in Coahuila and Sonora had implemented.

On 21 December 1913, Villa, who had recently been elected governor of his state by the generals of the Division of the North, issued a decree that was to have profound consequences. He announced the expropriation, without compensation, of the holdings of the Mexican oligarchy in Chihuahua. In addition, in all areas occupied by his troops, many Spaniards were expropriated and expelled. Villa not only distinguished himself radically from Carranza in this approach to the agrarian question but also from Zapata. Whereas, in the areas administered by the latter, such lands were almost immediately distributed among the peasants, the decree issued by Villa stated that the lands were to be placed, initially, under state control. Revenues from these lands were to be used to finance revolutionary struggles until the final victory of the revolution and, at the same time, support the widows and orphans of revolutionary fighters.

Once the revolution had triumphed, this property was to serve four purposes: to finance pensions for widows and orphans of revolutionary soldiers, to compensate veterans of the revolution, to restore to all villages the lands that had been expropriated by the hacendados, and to cover taxes not paid by the hacendados. In these objectives, a second difference between Villa and Zapata in their approaches to the agrarian question became apparent: Villa's decree limited the land reform to two groups—the participants in the revolution and their surviving relatives and the expropriated peasants.[51] The decree was silent on the question of a more extensive land reform on behalf of landless peasants, peons, and similar groups.

How are these different approaches in the North and South to be explained? In contrast to the sugar fields in the South, it was hardly possible, when dealing with some of the expropriated lands of the North, especially the large cattle-raising haciendas, to redistribute them among individual peasants. Cattle raising required large economic units that had to be administered either individually by the state or on a cooperative basis. In addition, the revenues from these haciendas were the financial basis of the Villa movement. Zapata, who was almost unable to market sugar as long as the fighting continued, was in a better position to allow a subsistence economy (which many peasants who received land in Morelos practiced) than Villa, who was obtaining money for arms purchases through the sale of cattle.

Military considerations played an important role in still other respects in the two leaders' approaches to the agrarian question. Zapata's immediate distribution had created a peasantry that was prepared to fight to the last to defend its lands. They were hardly prepared, however, to mount an offensive war from their home territory even though only an offensive war could destroy Huerta's army. Villa was in fact planning this type of military action. An immediate land reform would have tied the peasants to the soil; the promise of land reform after the end of the war constituted an incentive to join the revolutionary army.

Land reform during the absence of the soldiers was unthinkable for Villa. This was stated with utmost clarity by a northern delegate to the Revolutionary Convention in 1915: "The soldiers now engaged in combat will hardly be pleased if the land is turned over to peaceful peasants who are not fighting for it, who would undoubtedly get the best land, while the soldiers have legitimate hopes of being able to get the best sections for themselves because of their participation in the revolutionary struggle."[52]

The structure of the northern revolutionary army also explains Villa's reluctance to distribute immediately the largest of the expropriated estates. The revolution of 1910 had been organized by a political party with a recognized national leader, Francisco Madero. In 1913 such a political organization was lacking, and, in the early phases of the revolutionary movement, the authority of the national leaders was quite limited. Local leaders arose in different parts of Mexico and led the struggle against Huerta. Their ideological, military, and geographic ties to other groups and to the national leaders were often quite loose. If Villa wished to weld these individual groups into a national army and subordinate it to his control, the appeal of his charismatic personality was not sufficient. He had to be in a position to provide them with arms and ammunition and, simultaneously, take account of the desires of the local revolutionaries to control the property of the hacendados.

Revenues from expropriated estates were thus essential to Villa and were administered in light of these objectives. For the most part, the old administrators remained at their posts, and existing tenant-farming agreements initially were taken over unchanged. While roughly a third of the haciendas were placed under the control of individual revolutionary leaders, the Chihuahuan state government took over the administration of the remaining two-thirds.[53]

Villa's administration of the expropriated estates was determined not merely by military considerations but also by the catastrophic supply situation in Chihuahua. Whereas in Zapata's home state of Morelos more than 80 percent of the population was active in agriculture and a considerable number of the inhabitants of the cities had fled, a much smaller percentage of Chihuahua's population was engaged in cultivating the soil. Wherever the revolutionaries went, they distributed significant quantities of food to the urban unemployed and the hungry. The *El Paso Times* reported in January 1914: "Unemployed Mexicans from the devastated lumber and mining operations are being provided with daily rations.... Madera, Pearson, and Casas Grandes are daily being provided with food rations by the Constitutionalist army. Inhabitants of these cities, who cannot obtain work because the industries are no longer functioning due to the revolution, are turning to the Constitutionalist army and are obtaining food on the basis of decrees by Villa and the army."[54] It was characteristic of Villa that the supplies to orphanages and childrens' homes were particularly generous.[55] The price of meat was also drastically reduced in the large cities, and the markets were stocked with beef from the expropriated haciendas. A decree in December 1913 reduced meat prices to a fraction of their previous levels.[56]

While these factors undoubtedly explain certain aspects of the different methods used by Villa and Zapata in dealing with the agrarian problem, they do not explain everything. It would hardly have been possible for

Villa to postpone land reform if pressures for such reform were as great in Chihuahua as they were in Morelos. One obvious reason was the far smaller percentage of peasants. A significant part of the rural population consisted of cowboys far less interested in agrarian reform than the peasants, and the urban population cared still less.

The main pressure for land reform came from the former military colonists. Villa had placated this group by promising to make its members the principal beneficiaries of his proposed land distribution plan. He stipulated that they were not only to regain their expropriated lands but each of their inhabitants who fought in the ranks of the revolutionary army would have the right to additional hacienda land as well. In addition, part of the revenues from the confiscated haciendas was set aside to finance low-interest credit to poor peasants.[57]

The fact that Villa had confiscated the large estates from their former owners constituted clear proof for the Chihuahuan peasants that Villa was serious when he promised agrarian reform. Since a disproportionate number of the inhabitants of the former military colonies were fighting in the ranks of Villa's army, far from their native land, they were more than willing to have land distribution delayed until their return from the war.

Villa's position on land reform was the result not only of pragmatic considerations but also of his ideology with regard to agrarian questions. This was most clearly expressed in a conversation with John Reed in which Villa told the American journalist:

> When the new Republic is established there will never be any more army in Mexico. Armies are the greatest support of tyranny. There can be no dictator without an army.
>
> We will put the army to work. In all parts of the Republic we will establish military colonies composed of the veterans of the Revolution. The State will give them grants of agricultural lands and establish big industrial enterprises to give them work. Three days a week they will work and work hard, because honest work is more important than fighting, and only honest work makes good citizens. And the other three days they will receive military instruction and go out and teach all the people how to fight. Then, when the *patria* is invaded, we will just have to telephone from the palace at Mexico City, and in half a day all the Mexican people will rise from their fields and factories, fully armed, equipped and organized to defend their children and their homes.
>
> My ambition is to live my life in one of those military colonies among my *compañeros* whom I love, who have suffered so long and so deeply with me.[58]

It is questionable to what extent Villa actually wanted to live in such a military colony. In 1920, when he made peace with the government, he did not enter a colony but settled on a hacienda the government placed at his disposal. Yet the life he led there was not altogether unlike the life of a military colonist. What is significant in Villa's remarks is his identification with one of the oldest and most imporant traditional forms of organization of the Chihuahuan peasantry. His attitude was due in part to the enormous prestige these colonists enjoyed among the peasantry of northern Mexico. Even after the end of the Apache wars, the rising of the mountaineers of Tomochic, in which sixty men kept more than a thousand federal soldiers at bay, maintained and enhanced this prestige.[59]

Villa's attitude was also due to very concrete links he had established with the inhabitants of such former colonies. On the eve of the revolution, he set up his base of operations near San Andrés, one of the oldest and most assertive military colonies in Chihuahua. Its riflemen had played a decisive role in defeating the Apache in the 1880s and their descendants had staged an uprising against the state government in 1908 to protest a tax increase.[60] It was from San Andrés that Villa drew much of his support when he began to participate in the revolution of 1910.

The ideology of the peasants from military colonies displays a set of special characteristics reflected impressively in Villa himself. These people had fought for over a century against the Apache—a struggle waged with great severity and merciless cruelty. Prisoners were never taken and every possible means of warfare was used. This same tradition of struggle lived on into the days of the revolution, with the result that those who maintained it saw themselves as a fighting elite. "We defended civilization against the attacks of the barbarians,"[61] the inhabitants of Namiquipa proudly wrote to Porfirio Díaz. They held in contempt those who did not fight.

The right to the land did not derive merely from inheritance but had to be constantly reaffirmed and defended in battle. Only the man who fulfilled his duty in battle had the right to acquire a piece of land. The inhabitants of these military colonies had special contempt for the peons on the haciendas. Their attitude toward the large landowners was different from that of many peasants in southern and central Mexico. In the central regions, the inhabitants of the free villages had been involved in long-standing conflicts with the neighboring haciendas. This often led to armed conflict. But such clashes were much rarer in the North prior to 1885. There was sufficient land and cattle and the common struggle against the Indians united large landowners and military colonists, the one dependent upon the other. Only after the defeat of the Apache and the construction of railroads did this situation change radically, and then the hacendados undertook massive expropriations of land.

This conflict, however, was relatively new, not all hacendados were involved in it, and an ambiguous attitude toward hacendados in many villages was the result. Actions were taken against the "bad" hacendados, but cooperation continued with the "good" ones, those who did not threaten the property of the peasants. Had these "good" hacendados not fought side by side with the peasants against the Apache for more than a century? The northern peasants lacked the centuries-old hostility toward the hacendados that had made it impossible for the peasants of Morelos to form a common front with the large landowners there.

The peasants of the northern colonies had been more independent and more prosperous than the peasants of the free villages in the South. In contrast to the latter, the northerners enjoyed complete municipal autonomy under Spanish colonial rule and were not directly subject to control by the state. Not only had they obtained more land, cattle, and tax advantages, but they also lacked the egalitarianism that characterized the social organization of the village communities of southern and central Mexico. Within the village community, each man was free, in contrast to the South, to buy or sell his land as he pleased.[62] As a result, a far larger agrarian middle class had developed in Chihuahua than in central Mexico, and its influence was felt throughout the revolution.

Much of the mode of thought and action of these Mexican pioneers was reflected in Villa's ideology. This was clearly expressed in 1913, when Villa announced that it would be primarily veterans of the revolutionary army who had to some extent "earned" their land who would be allowed to keep it. Villa's frequent cruelty, for example, his relentless execution of prisoners, was part of a long and savage tradition of frontier warfare in which no quarter was given and none was sought.

Villa's distinction between "good" and "bad" hacendados and his readiness not only to protect the property of but also to cooperate with members of this first group, such as Madero and Maytorena, were also linked to these traditions of the northern frontiersmen. Finally, this same tradition was the source of Villa's goal, in his agrarian law of 1915: the creation of a stratum of prosperous small peasants—not members of egalitarian village communities—who, as articulated in Villa's remarks to John Reed, would occupy a central place in the political and economic life of Mexico.

Can Villa in the final account be designated as an agrarian revolutionary similar to Emiliano Zapata in the South? Contemporary analysts and politicians as well as later historians have tended to view him either as a reformer or as a bandit, but neither label aptly describes him. Although there is little doubt that he had been a bandit before 1910, there is no reason to term his later activities banditry. If the word "bandit" is used to describe someone with no consistent ideology, whose primary aim is to secure riches for himself, it did not apply to Villa. As I have attempted to show, he had a clear-cut ideology to which he held fast. His interest in money was limited. While literally millions of dollars passed through his hands, he kept very little. Money to him was a means of achieving power, of strengthening his army, of securing the loyalty of his subordinates, and of achieving social transformations. Some of the methods he used—the execution of prisoners and the imposition of forced loans upon the wealthy—have frequently been cited as characteristic of a bandit. In fact these same methods were utilized by practically all leaders and factions in the Mexican Revolution, though usually with some attempt at dissimulation.

Neither does the term "agrarian revolutionary" suffice to describe Villa. Athough he was greatly interested in the peasantry, he showed equal interest in the urban poor. In fact, while in the long run the peasantry would have benefited most from his triumph if his land reform had been implemented, in the short run the main beneficiaries of his rule were the urban poor of Chihuahua, those saved through his distribution of food and his supply of cheap meat to city markets.

On the whole Villa was a complex mixture of social revolutionary and nineteenth-century caudillo. His aims (at least in the regions of Chihuahua, Durango, and Coahuila, where his main interest lay) were those of a social revolutionary, though his methods of ruling were similar to those of a classic Mexican caudillo of the nineteenth century.

Unlike the municipal councils of Zapata's core region in Morelos, popularly elected bodies played an insignificant role in Villa's decision making and, unlike most leaders of agrarian revolutions in other countries in the twentieth century, he had set up no political organization to constitute the basis of his power. Like the nineteenth-century caudillos, he ruled through his army and through a complex patron-client relationship with his subordinates. What he had in common with some popular leaders of the third world in the twentieth century was the charismatic appeal of his personality. No other leader of the Mexican Revolution became such a legend in his lifetime, or remained so even after his death, as Pancho Villa. No other leader of the revolution, even Zapata, could win the kind of mass appeal and authority that Villa had. Villa's popularity was one factor, but by no means the only one, that led to conflicts with Carranza.

### The Differing Social Policies of Villa and Carranza

Villa's social policies differentiated more and more the zones he controlled from those under Carranza's rule. Although Carranza had permitted the temporary confiscation of haciendas, Villa's policies were fundamentally different from his. Villa's expropriations not only were far more extensive than those carried out by Carranza, but they were also meant to be final and irreversible. Whereas Carranza tenaciously refused, in all his speeches, decrees, and proclamations, to make any connection between the "intervention" of haciendas (the official expression that was used to refer to the temporary character of the occupation of these estates) and agrarian reform, such a connection was clearly articulated by Villa in his decree of December 1913. Carranza also had attempted to emphasize the limited and temporary character of such hacienda occupations by leaving their administration in the hands of the local authorities. (When Carranza did set up a central administration for confiscated estates in late 1914, its main aim was not to administer those properties but to return them to their former owners.) Villa, however, created his own central authority for the administration of confiscated estates—the Administracion General de Bienes Confiscados.[63]

These differing approaches contributed significantly to increasing tension between Villa and Carranza. The latter did not dare initially to make a frontal attack on Villa's policy. He did, however, have Villa appoint one of his generals, Manuel Chao, as military governor of Chihuahua at the beginning of 1914. Under Chao, the expropriations were not reversed, but the tempo of the reforms was significantly slowed.

In mid-1914, Carranza asked Villa to turn over control of all expropriated lands.[64] He conceived this move, as he explained later (in 1917), as the first step toward the return of these estates to their former owners.[65] Villa's refusal to comply, in the opinion of one of his closest collaborators, Silvestre Terrazas, secretary of state of Chihuahua and the administrator of the expropriated estates, contributed greatly to the eruption of open conflict between the two leaders.[66] Villa's policy of massive expropriations without land reform was to have important consequences for his movement and for the entire development of the Mexican Revolution. It laid the basis for the destruction of the Huerta regime and for the break with Carranza, but also for Villa's defeat in the civil war that followed.

The large resources accruing to Villa from the expropriated lands made it possible for him to assemble the best equipped and most effective revolutionary army. Massive arms purchases were made in the United States and brought into Mexico, initially by smugglers and later quite legally. No less significant was the fact that Villa now had the means to build a semiprofessional army. In contrast to Zapata's peasant army, this one was paid not in land but in money. Consequently, Villa's troops were free from the constraints that kept Zapata's troops from fighting far from their own region. Villa's soldiers were better suited for waging an offensive war than their future southern allies. The danger of such a professional army, of course, is that, when no more money is available to pay them, a considerable part of their ranks can easily change sides. This, to a large extent, was to be the case after Villa's defeat in 1915.

In 1913 and 1914, the Division of the North was the main striking force of the revolution and was primarily responsible for Huerta's defeat.

The revenues from the expropriated haciendas was a powerful link that contributed to holding together the heterogeneous classes and groups in Chihuahua. Another factor that strengthened the revolutionary leadership in Chihuahua was that there appears to have been an increase in the standard of living, particularly in 1914. The two years of Villa's rule were the only ones during 1910–20 when peace reigned in that state. The great battles and struggles of the revolution were settled outside its borders. While the prices of vital necessities fell, thanks to Villa's subsidies, unemployment disappeared. At the same time that the developing economy was on the upturn and in need of new labor power, many thousands of men were under arms. Thus, as a result of the labor shortage, higher wages were paid in many branches of industry and mining. The expropriated estates attempted to attract tenant farmers by waiving rent for the first year of their activity.

This prosperity, the opportunity for social mobility in the new Chihuahua administration and, to some extent, in Villa's army, and, above all, the hope of participating in a national government influenced by Villa tied important parts of the middle class in Chihuahua to the Villa movement.

The increase in the standard of living, which contributed substantially to a mass base in Villa's home state, nevertheless lasted only a short period. In the second half of 1914, war expenditures increased so substantially that Villa and all other revolutionary leaders printed increasingly large amounts of paper money to finance the revolution. The result was a mounting inflation and a shortage of goods, and, after 1915 in particular, increasing discontent among the population.

One of the main consequences of Villa's social and economic policies was the emergence of a new bourgeoisie within his movement with increasingly conservative leanings. It had a twofold origin. The first of these was the group initially recruited from among the generals and leading revolutionaries who had received the land of the expropriated haciendas for purposes of administration in order to supply the revolutionary armed forces.

In 1914, John Reed visited the hacienda of Canutillo, which had been given to Tomás Urbina, a Villista general who had been a crony of Villa's in his bandit days. "I went out at dawn and walked around Las Nieves. The town belongs to General Urbina—people, houses, animals and immortal souls. At Las Nieves he and he alone wields the high justice and the low. The town's only store is in his house."[67]

The second category of the new bourgeoisie consisted of the agents who controlled the export of agricultural products to the United States and the import of American arms into Mexico. They were, for the most part, intimately tied to large American companies. This group included men such as Felix Sommerfeld and Lázaro de la Garza. Sommerfeld, previously head of Madero's secret service in the United States, had a monopoly on the import of dynamite into the area controlled by Villa and also maintained close ties with the Standard Oil Company.[68] De la Garza, a businessman from Torreón, was another of Villa's financial agents in the United States.[69] Both men made large amounts of money during the revolution and betrayed Villa in the process.

Villa himself appears to have viewed many of these deals as an inevitable but necessary evil for supplying his troops. Insofar as is known, he neither took part in them nor enriched himself personally from them. The same cannot be said of Villa's brother Hipólito, who became financial agent for the Division of the North and profited from his dealings.

This conservative bourgeoisie was strengthened by two other social groups within the Villa movement. The first was the state bureaucracy. Whereas in the areas controlled by Zapata hardly any administrative apparatus was set up, the situation was different in the regions administered by Villa's armies. The presence of cities and larger towns, the extensive development of the money economy in the region, the numerous foreigners and foreign companies, and, finally, the long border with the United States—all this required the construction and maintenance of an extensive bureaucracy.

Where was the personnel for such a bureaucracy to be found? The old Díaz bureaucracy, a large segment of which had sided with Huerta, was for the most part unwilling to enter the revolutionary administration, and Villa had little inclination to take them on. He thus resorted to the only people he trusted, the Madero family and their collaborators. This explains, for example, the rapid rise of Felix Sommerfeld, Madero's former secretary, to Villa's representative in the United States.

The influence of these mainly conservative forces was reinforced by hacendados from Coahuila and Sonora who had rallied to the revolution but who had tense relations with Carranza and were seeking an alliance with Villa. The Madero family's antagonistic relations with Carranza were not based on serious ideological differences but on deep rivalry. The same was true of the Sonoran hacendado Maytorena, who returned to his home state in August 1913 and reassumed the office of governor.

Carranza sensed a competitor in Maytorena, the only other Maderist governor besides himself then holding office, and preferred the more radical middle class revolutionaries, Alvaro Obregón, Plutarco Elias Calles, Salvador Alvarado, and Benjamin Hill, who presented a less immediate threat to him. Villa's old loyalty to Madero and the increasing rivalry with Carranza had the effect of tying him more and more closely to those whose ideology differed greatly from his own. This alliance with a section of the hacendados was an important difference between the Zapata and Villa movements.

The most influential spokesman for the conservative wing within the Villa movement was one of Mexico's most prominent military men, General Felipe Ángeles.[70] Of all the personalities who participated in the Mexican Revolution after 1913, he was probably the most authentic disciple of Madero's ideas. He was one of the few professional soldiers who had served in the Porfirian army before 1910 and had joined Madero and remained loyal to him in 1913. At Madero's command, he had fought against both Zapata in 1912 and against Felix Díaz in the uprising in Mexico City in 1913. Several months after the outbreak of Carranza's revolution, Ángeles joined forces with him and was appointed undersecretary of war in his cabinet.

The new generals who emerged from Sonora's revolution, particularly Obregón, protested this appointment and, under pressure from them, Carranza removed Ángeles from his responsible post. Deeply resentful about his demotion, Ángeles asked to be transferred to Villa's staff. Villa was more than happy to welcome this brilliant artillery officer to his army.

Like his mentor Madero, Ángeles was a supporter of free elections but an enemy of radical social change. He opposed the expropriation of the large estates. Above all, he advocated closer relations with the United States, which he greatly admired.[71] Villa, however, was only moderately influenced by his views. He stated in a confidential discussion with Duval West, Woodrow Wilson's representative in Mexico, that foreigners should not be permitted to own land in Mexico. West reported to Wilson his conversation with Villa: "In the same conversation, he stated that Mexican industry should be primarily developed by Mexican capital. I received the impression that he held to the popular demand of 'Mexico for the Mexicans' and that he saw an open door for foreign investors as a danger for the country." In West's opinion, the Villa movement believed that "the wealth of the rich should be administered by the government to benefit the popular masses.... The socialist idea, even if it is not clearly articulated, appears to predominate throughout this movement."[72]

These ideas of Villa's deserve all the more attention since they were expressed not in a propagandistic speech but in a confidential discussion with President Wilson's special representative in Mexico. Far from being mere rhetoric, they greatly shaped Villa's practical attitude toward the Americans. His massive expropriation of Mexican property in his home state of Chihuahua prevented the Mexican landowners there from doing what they did in other states to protect themselves from this action—selling their land, either in appearance or in actuality, to foreigners, especially Americans. Such measures to prevent American penetration into Mexico were never adopted by Carranza during this period.

Villa, nevertheless, was regarded with genuine sympathy by the Wilson administration, by a section of the U.S. armed forces, by the general American public, and, finally, by American companies. The reasons for this sympathy are complex and can hardly be reduced to a common denominator. For many American politicians and some of the American companies, Villa was, above all, a strong man who would create order in Mexico. In contrast to Carranza, he appeared to have the authority and power to control the revolutionary groups, which were often isolated from one another or caught up in rivalry among themselves, and to bring them under a central authority. In January 1914 a leading U.S. official made this clear to the French ambassador in Washington, who reported,

> In contrast to what is generally said, my interlocutor told me, Villa is hardly a man of no property. His parents had a ranch and enjoyed a certain affluence. His education was limited to grammar school, but he at least got that far; he is not the illiterate the newspapers describe; his letters are even well formulated.
>
> He is, like Huerta, of Indian origins, an excellent horseman, and a crack shot. Without fear of physical danger or the law, he already led the life of a "rancher" at a very early age. It is the same life many of us led until recently in the distant areas of the west, in areas that lie outside of the power of the authorities, where every man was his own master and sometimes controlled others, sometimes had followers and created his own law. . . .
>
> Villa wins popularity easily and makes sure his popularity lasts. He takes care of his soldiers, he helps them, he sees to their needs and is quite popular among them. The romantic story of the marriage that he supposedly had with a young girl from Chihuahua during the occupation of that city is not true. He is married and is not separated from his wife.
>
> He would be unable to rule but could create order quite nicely if he wanted to. If I were the president of Mexico, I would entrust him with this task; I am completely convinced that he would do it masterfully; he would also compel all the rebels to remain peaceful. In Mexico's current situation, I see no one besides him who could successfully handle this task.[73]

During a conversation with the French military attaché in Washington, Woodrow Wilson voiced similar thoughts. "Speaking of Villa," the attaché reported in December 1913, Wilson "expressed his admiration that this highwayman has gradually succeeded in instilling sufficient discipline into his troops to convert them into an army. Perhaps, he added, this man today represents the only instrument of civilization in Mexico. His firm authority allows him to create order and to educate the turbulent mass of peons so prone to pillage."[74]

The impression of authority grew out of the fact that Villa was more successful than most other revolutionary generals in limiting or preventing looting and excesses following the capture of cities and towns. He was careful to see that, with the exception of Spanish estates, no property of foreigners was touched or confiscated.

For President Wilson and Secretary of State William Jennings Bryan, there were still other reasons behind their sympathies for Villa. Both were part of a long list of American liberal politicians searching for a type of Latin American revolutionary that had scarcely ever existed—one who would, for example, carry out a certain modernization and various reforms in order to stabilize the country and protect it from more profound revolutionary unrest, but would leave U.S. interests absolutely untouched. Wilson was quite clear on this point. "We should let every one who assumes to exercise authority in any part of Mexico know in the most unequivocal way that we shall vigilantly watch the fortunes of those Americans who can not get away, and shall hold those responsible for their sufferings and losses to a definite reckoning. That can be and will be made plain beyond the possibility of a misunderstanding."[75]

John Lind, Wilson's representative in Mexico, gave the clearest expression to this view. In a report to the president, he characterized the revolution as essentially a movement that had attempted to make conditions in Mexico more like those in the United States. About the goal of U.S. policy toward the revolution, he wrote, "we must be the 'pillar of cloud by day and the pillar of fire by night and compel decent administration . . . . From this necessity there is no escape, unless revolution and anarchy are to continue the order of the day in Mexico.' . . . Let this housecleaning be done by home talent. It will be a little rough and we must see to it that the walls are left intact, but I should not worry if some of the verandas and French windows were demolished. General Villa, for instance, would do the job satisfactorily."[76] This idea of a revolution guided by the United States inspired Wilson, and Lind explained that Villa was the man to lead such a revolution. Ángeles contributed to this impression when he joined Villa. Ángeles, in both public and confidential discussions with American representatives, repeatedly emphasized his opposition to radical social change.[77] His views were quite well known, and, for a long time, Wilson considered him the best presidential candidate for Mexico.[78]

An additional factor that kept conflict between Villa and the United States to a minimum in 1913 and the first half of 1914 was that none of the really wealthy landowners in Chihuahua whose property Villa had expropriated had sold their holdings to United States interests. Luis Terrazas, in particular, in spite of offers by American buyers, refused to sell his property to them.[79] His refusal was no doubt inspired by the firm conviction that, sooner or later, the revolutionaries would be defeated. If he had agreed to such a sale and the Americans had then requested that his property be handed over to them, a conflict could easily have erupted. Since this did not happen, conflicts of this kind, which might have resulted from Villa's legislation, were avoided.

The essential economic difference in the relationships between the two leaders and the Americans was in the degree of their independence from the United States. In 1913–15, both obtained their weapons from the United States and, in this respect, were quite dependent on the Americans. The financial relations of both to American firms were nonetheless quite different, and this difference had an important impact on their policy toward the United States. Villa, as a result of his massive expropriations of Mexican property in Chihuahua and in the Laguna area of Coahuila and Durango, was in a financially secure position. Until the latter part of 1914 he had adequate means at his disposal to finance his military campaigns. Carranza, however, who opposed expropriation of Mexican property, was far more dependent on contributions and taxes from foreign companies, and he obtained these funds, at first, though secret agreements and, later, by imposing taxes on the foreign companies operating in his zone.

Paradoxically, Villa's greater financial independence from the Americans permitted him to maintain better relations in 1914 with the United States than Carranza. Because of adequate resources, Villa at first saw no reason to increase the tax burden on U.S. companies as did Carranza in his zone.[80] Equally important was that Carranza, on the basis of his secret agreements with American firms, had reason to cultivate a verbal radicalism and nationalism. In practice, however, Villa, by his drastic restrictions on the opportunities and rights of local oligarchies to sell their property to foreigners, did far more to curtail the influence of American companies.

### Relations among the Revolutionary Factions

The profound differences that increased in scope as the revolutionaries grew stronger and controlled more territory did not lead to any overt conflict or even to public confrontation during the year 1913. Huerta was still far too powerful, and the wish to overthrow his regime remained the paramount aim of all the revolutionary factions.

Zapata never overtly criticized the northern revolutionaries during the year 1913, but he refused to recognize their leadership. He would not sign the plan of Guadalupe, which proclaimed Carranza the head of the revolutionary government, and in a modification of his own plan de Ayala proclaimed himself the supreme leader of the revolution. Nevertheless, he was fully conscious of the fact that his own movement would never be able to achieve supremacy in Mexico and thus attempted to establish relations with the more radical of the northern factions. In the latter part of 1913 he sent one of his close intellectual advisers, Gildardo Magaña, who for a time had been in prison with Pancho Villa, to establish closer relations with that leader in Chihuahua. As a result of that visit Zapata became convinced that Villa was an advocate of agrarian reform and in a long letter praising the northern leader he suggested that he apply the principles of the plan de Ayala in implementing his agrarian reforms.[81] Villa did not do so but his confiscation of the estates of the oligarchy was sufficient to convince Zapata that he was the only prominent northern leader who would support his agrarian program. It was in this early period that the basis for the later alliance between the revolutionary leaders was established.

Zapata's refusal to establish any organizational links with the northern revolutionary movements had no practical consequences for the military course of the revolution since the region he operated in was separated by hundreds of miles from the North and common military actions between them were scarcely possible.

For the two northern movements, however, some kind of military and political cooperation was essential to their success. The fact that they operated in adjacent regions made military coordination imperative. A common wish to secure U.S. recognition was a powerful element driving them together. Early in 1913 Villa recognized the plan of Guadalupe and Carranza's leadership. In return the "First Chief" supplied him with some arms and money and recognized him as military commander of the Division of the North operating in Chihuahua.

Differences between the two leaders and their respective movements soon emerged. When Villa resigned his governorship of Chihuahua after only a few days in office in order to concentrate all his efforts on organizing and leading his army, Carranza, deeply incensed at Villa's reforms in Chihuahua, foisted on Villa a successor he did not want.[82] During the tenure of the new governor, one of the generals of the Division of the North, Manuel Chao, the tempo of reforms in Chihuahua slowed significantly.

At the same time Villa began to throw his support behind revolutionary politicians who were disgruntled with or opposed to Carranza. Frequently their opposition to Carranza was based on personal conflicts for power rather than on ideological considerations. This was certainly the case for José María Maytorena, who returned to assume the governorship of Sonora in August 1914.[83] Maytorena was in some respects even more conservative than Carranza, but Carranza feared him because he was the only other constitutionally elected governor from the Madero period who fought against Huerta and could thus eventually be considered a rival to the First Chief. It seems precisely for this reason and in spite of the latter's conservatism that Villa did everything he could to bolster his power.

In spite of these emerging rivalries the Constitutionalist movement managed to gain control of nearly half of Mexico by the end of 1913.

## The Civilians and the Military in the Revolutionary Movement

Two essential characteristics differentiated the Mexican revolution of 1913/14 from its 1910/11 phase as well as from other revolutions in the twentieth century.

With the conspicuous exception of the Zapatistas, the fighting was primarily conventional; guerrilla warfare played a subordinate role. The federal army in the North had withdrawn to highly fortified cities and railway crossings where it was attacked by well-organized and frequently better-armed revolutionary troops. Except in Morelos and its surroundings, where guerrilla warfare predominated, guerrilla movements had sprung up only in limited parts of the country, and they were not strong enough to immobilize significant parts of the federal army.

Another characteristic of this period of the Mexican Revolution was the lack of a political organization, like the 26 of July movement in Cuba or even the Anti-Reelectionist Party in the first phase of the Mexican Revolution. The latter had been transformed from a mass political party into an electoral machine after Madero's victory and for all practical purposes had ceased to exist.

Some political legacies of the Madero period survived during the first months of Huerta's coup in Mexico City. Unions continued to operate and some radical deputies continued to voice their opinions in Congress. After Huerta's second coup, by which he dissolved Congress in October 1913, legal opposition all but ceased. In the cities sympathizers of the revolution did not set up underground organizations but went north to join Carranza and sometimes Villa. A few radical intellectuals went to Morelos and threw their support behind Zapata.

In the territories controlled by the northern revolutionaries there was also little political activity. No political party was organized and with few exceptions no elections at either the local or regional level were held. The civilian authorities were for the most part identical with those elected during the Madero period. New authorities on the whole were more likely to be appointed than elected. This situation was due largely to the fears of revolutionary leaders that political controversy could undercut their not yet fully established or recognized authority. They were perhaps even more worried at the prospect that latent divisions and tensions between them, which at this stage of the revolution they were attempting to suppress, could emerge into the open if elections were held.

As a result of this impasse in the political arena, there was only one organization that carried out a process of mass mobilization and gave ambitious and talented individuals a chance for a rapid rise in their social status. This was the army. It was an institution that both committed revolutionaries and ambitious men hoping to profit from the revolution saw as the main instrument for carrying out their objectives. The first group considered the army as the institution least dominated by the upper and middle class leadership of the Madero period and the one with the most power to destroy the resistance of civilian authorities to reform. To many others the army represented a unique instrument of social mobility. Anyone who mustered a sufficient number of volunteers could present himself to revolutionary authorities and obtain recognition as an officer. He could then frequently confiscate an adjoining hacienda, the proceeds of which would be destined to supply his troops but which would at times also flow into his pockets. To individual soldiers who joined his army Villa held out promises of grants of land. Most other revolutionary leaders had made no such promises. To many soldiers who joined their forces the army provided at the very least a steady income and at best an opportunity for advancement and at times (though most leaders attempted to prevent it) possibilities of plunder.

The passivity and immobility of the civilian structure led to the ever increasing influence of the military in all walks of life in the North. It was a process that Carranza fiercely opposed, partly because he was a civilian who had no direct control over a military force of his own and partly because he considered the army too radical in social terms and too sympathetic with social transformations. In contrast, Villa, though all his proclamations were opposed to military rule, in fact favored this tendency. As Silvestre Terrazas, Villa's highest civilian official, described it in his memoirs, the military began to assume more and more prerogatives.[84]

On the whole, in spite of divisions and internal contradictions, the revolutionary armies proved to be far superior to their federal opponents. Their morale was much higher, for they were volunteers, very different from their unwilling counterparts whom Huerta had impressed into his army. Many were ideologically motivated and even those who were not were buoyed by the enormous popular support they enjoyed in the years 1913–14. Their generals were younger and in fact militarily far superior to those of Huerta. This was particularly true for Villa and Obregón. At the time the second phase of the revolution set in, early in 1913, there was only one way in which the revolutionaries were inferior to their opponents—in access to money and arms. This inferiority was drastically reversed once the revolutionaries received help from what in early 1913 was considered an extremely unlikely source: the United States.

# 5 The United States, Great Britain, and Huerta

Immediately after Huerta's accession to power, the Huerta government appeared to observers both in Mexico and abroad as an instrument of U.S. policy. Hintze, for example, spoke of it as the "government of the American embassy."[1] But several months later the United States was waging an extremely sharp battle against the Huerta government, and one of the main reasons for the break between Huerta and the United States was the implementation of a new Mexican policy by Woodrow Wilson, who was inaugurated on 4 March 1913. Wilson had been elected as a result of growing opposition to the large corporations among the American middle classes by making himself the spokesman of these groups during the electoral campaign. "The government of the United States is currently the darling of the big companies,"[2] he had announced, and he promised a domestic and foreign policy independent of the large corporations. Those who had elected him were now awaiting practical proof of his liberalism. It quickly became apparent that the situation in Mexico, which was the first foreign policy question he confronted, offered him a rare opportunity for fulfilling campaign promises.

The driving forces and motivations behind Wilson's Mexico policy remain to this day one of the most disputed questions in American history. In the view of many European diplomats of the time, many of his political opponents, and some historians, Wilson was an agent of the large American companies whose interests he wished to promote. In the eyes of his supporters and other historians, he appeared to be attempting to push through an idealist policy against the will of all U.S. business interests involved in Mexico.

The reality is far more complex than these two views would have it. In a recent study, Robert Freeman Smith presented Wilson's attitude toward "backward" countries.[3] The basis of Wilson's thinking was that the underdeveloped countries had to be brought to accept as their own the social order and norms of the more advanced industrial countries. As early as 1901, he had written: "The East is to be opened and transformed. The standards of the West are to be imposed on it; nations and people who have stood still the centuries through are to be quickened and to be made part of the Universal world of commerce and of ideas which has so steadily been a-making by the advance of European power from age to age. It is our peculiar duty to moderate the process in the interests of liberty: to impart to the peoples thus driven out upon the road of change our own principles of self-help; to teach them order and self-control in the midst of change."

Among the most important norms of Western society, as Wilson defended it and wished to spread it, was the concept of free enterprise. "If America is not to have free enterprise, then she can have freedom of no sort whatever," he stated. The underdeveloped countries would have to maintain the norms of an industrial society based on the idea of the free enterprise system, which meant undertaking no expropriations and permitting no confiscations. With regard to Mexico, not only did he oppose any expropriation of American property throughout his term of office, but he also fought any limitation of the tremendous privileges enjoyed by American companies in the Díaz era.

Wilson was an outspoken opponent of European companies operating in Latin America, which he saw as harmful and imperialistic. Where American companies were concerned, he distinguished between "bad businessmen" and "good businessmen." "He was firmly convinced that some bad businessmen stirred up revolutions and exploited people through dishonest practices. In addition, bad businessmen were those who called for an all-out invasion of Mexico. Those who wanted limited intervention were not necessarily classified as bad."[4]

Wilson's opposition to English firms in Mexico and his attempt to steer the Mexican revolution in such a way that the "legitimate rights" of foreign companies would not be violated and the system of free enterprise would not be endangered conformed completely with the desires of most American representatives of big business in Mexico. Wilson's Mexico policy was distinguished from that of some American companies by his rejection of any annexation or establishment of a direct American protectorate over Mexico. Many American businessmen active in Mexico also rejected the methods Wilson wanted to use to create a stable Mexico based on the principles of the free enterprise system. Not a dictatorship, which was what the majority of foreign businessmen in Mexico preferred, but a parliamentary democracy was the sole means, in Wilson's view, of creating a stable situation and averting revolution, not in Mexico alone but throughout Latin America. As a solution to the problems of Latin America, he once stated: "I will teach the Latin American republics to elect good men."[5] As a prototype of such Latin American politicians, Wilson was thinking of Madero, who, like himself, had believed that the introduction of a parliamentary system would constitute the most important means of solving Mexico's problems and bringing stability to the country. The overthrow of Madero was, in Wilson's view, a heavy blow against the solution to Mexico's problems that he envisioned.

Another element must be added to the forces that shaped American policy—the historical experience of the United States with the countries of Latin America prior to 1913. With the possible exception of Chile, where in 1892 President Balmaceda, despite U.S. support, was defeated by his opponents, the United States could point to a long series of successes in Latin America. In 1898, American troops had landed in Cuba and, without much difficulty, had brought the developing social revolutionary movement under control, so that in 1902 they had turned Cuba into a de facto protectorate of the United States. The uprising organized by the United States in Panama against Colombia had also proceeded without serious problems. In February 1913, American diplomacy in Mexico also appeared to have scored an easy victory against Madero. Wilson considered his objectives to be of a completely different nature, but previous U.S. experiences in Latin America probably convinced him that he had the power to impose any solution he considered right on the United States' southern neighbors. The Undersecretary of the Foreign Office Sir William Tyrrell, a close collaborator of British Foreign Secretary Grey and, according to French diplomats, the head of a pro-Wilson group in the British Foreign Office,[6] described Wilson's ideas and the discrepancy between his subjective hopes and the objective consequences of his policies already visible in 1913:

> With the opening of the Panama Canal it is becoming increasingly important that the Governments of the Central American Republics should improve, as they will become more and more a field for European and American enterprise: bad government may lead to friction and to such incidents as the Venezuela affair under Castro. The President is very anxious to provide for contingencies by insisting that those Republics should have fairly decent rulers and that men like Castro and Huerta should be barred. With this object in view, the President made up his mind to teach these countries a lesson by insisting on the removal of Huerta . . . . The President did not seem to realize that his policy will lead to a "de facto" American protectorate over the Central American Republics; but there are others here who do, and who intend to achieve that object.[7]

Without naming them, Tyrrell was undoubtedly referring to certain large American corporations, whose policies in Mexico have been studied far less than those of the Wilson administration have.

## U.S. Business Interests and Mexico

If one considers the activities of the large American companies in Mexico in the period 1910–14, they seem initially to be extremely contradictory. American capital had worked closely with Díaz and at the same time had contributed to his downfall. American capital had had a hand in Madero's seizure of power and at the same time had played a decisive role in his overthrow. American interests had helped Huerta come to power, and American interests had worked against him with the same resoluteness.

One can only understand these phenomena when one realizes that American business interests in Mexico by no means possessed a monolithic policy. At times the interests of most groups moved in the same direction, but at other times were quite opposed to each other. This reality had already struck the Austrian minister to Mexico in 1912:

> While the petroleum trust [i.e., Rockefeller], which a few days ago bought up the most prestigious independent newspaper in Mexico, *El Imparcial,* with the approval of the ruling party here, has every reason to support Madero's government, which it helped to power in 1910, there are other interests in American high finance, such as those involved in the Mexican railroads, in rubber, in chewing gum and mining, along with Mr. Hearst's newspapers, which are hoping to benefit from Madero's overthrow and which are therefore supporting Orozco's people with money, arms and good advice in El Paso, San Antonio, and Douglas [Arizona].[8]

One group was made up essentially of Americans with interests in agriculture, those with investments in small- and medium-sized businesses, and others holding Mexican securities. Their business activity was based largely on the peonage system and the privileged position of foreigners, two pillars of the Díaz regime. Every dislocation of that system was a hard blow for these elements, and therefore they had always been hostile to the Madero government. Huerta, however, reestablished the Díaz system, and was hailed by the same group.[9] They repeatedly called on the American government to recognize Huerta. This group included the American financiers holding securities and investments in state bonds and railways, who were therefore interested in a strong, solvent Mexican government. One should mention in this connection the banking house Speyer and Company and the president of the Mexican National Railways, E. N. Brown, who also called on Wilson to recognize Huerta.[10]

The second group, including the large American raw materials producers in Mexico, was headed by the oil companies. These companies had helped Madero come to power and had initially supported him, but as a result had come into sharp conflict with other groups of American businessmen. When Madero did not comply with their demands, they pulled away from him and joined the other Americans who were hostile to Madero.

After Huerta's coup d'etat, these companies initially adopted the same stance as the other American firms. On 6 May, the chairman of the board of the Southern Pacific Railroad, Julius Kruttschnitt, sent to President Wilson a memorandum worked out by Delbert D. Haff, who had worked for years as an attorney for American companies in Mexico and was retained by the largest American companies in the country, including Doheny's Mexican Petroleum Company. In this memorandum there was reference to the real danger which European capital represented for American interests:

> In addition to that fact, foreign nations are becoming restive and are seeking to undermine the influence of the United States in Mexico. The British Government has already recognized Huerta in a most marked manner by autograph letter from the King due to the efforts of Lord Cowdray (Sir Weetman Pearson) who has the largest interests outside of American interests in the Mexican Republic. He is using his efforts to obtain a large loan in England, and I am informed that he has succeeded on condition that the English Government would recognize Huerta, which has been done. If Mexico is helped out of her trouble by British and German influence, American prestige in that country and the commerce of the United States will suffer great damage.[11]

The companies requested that the American government arrange a cease-fire between Huerta and the Constitutionalists and then recognize Huerta on the condition that he hold elections as soon as possible. The United States definitely was not to push for Huerta's resignation; quite the contrary, the companies expressed their admiration for Huerta. "He is the de facto president at the present time, and is a man of energy and executive ability, is in command of the army, and is, better than any other person, able to carry out such an agreement."[12]

Twenty days later, on 26 May, the same companies addressed a new memorandum to the American government. This memorandum no longer recommended the recognition of Huerta, but called on Woodrow Wilson to mediate between the Constitutionalists and Huerta and to persuade the general to hold elections. The United States would then be prepared to recognize the new president, if in its opinion the elections had actually been fair.[13] Within twenty days, therefore, a total turnabout had occurred in the Mexican policies of these American companies. Whereas on 6 May they had been promoting the recognition of Huerta, pointing to the danger of pushing Huerta into the arms of European capital, and particularly of British capital in the shape of Lord Cowdray, on 26 May they were calling for steps that would necessarily lead either to Huerta's departure or to further extension of the civil war in Mexico.

From this point onward, the large raw material producers, led by the American oil companies, supported the struggle against Huerta with all the means at their disposal. "As far as we know," the chairman of the board of the Mexican Petroleum Company, Doheny, stated before a United States Senate commission of inquiry in 1920, "every American company with interests in Mexico expressed its sympathy for Carranza and also helped him—as in our case—from the moment that President Wilson turned against Huerta."[14] The Mexican Petroleum Company refused to pay taxes to Huerta and paid them to Carranza instead. Carranza apparently received a total of $685,000 in the period 1913–14 from Mexican Petroleum, according to its chairman.[15]

If one wishes to understand this sudden and total shift in the attitude of the American companies, it is necessary first of all to analyze the position of the oil companies. In the period 1910–13, Mexican oil production had undergone significant growth. It had increased from 3.5 million barrels in 1910 to 16.5 million barrels in 1912. On a world scale, Mexico had advanced from seventh to third place and in 1912 accounted for 4.07 percent of world oil production.[16]

From 1910 to 1913, American investment in Mexican petroleum had surpassed British investment, which, however, was still extremely important and amounted to over 40 percent of the capital invested in Mexican petroleum.[17] Politically and economically, Cowdray had been greatly strengthened by the British fleet's transition from coal to oil. To cover its increasing oil needs, the British admiralty had concluded a comprehensive supplier's contract with Cowdray.[18]

The American-British competition took on a completely new character. Prior to 1910, the objective of this competition was rather limited: the conquest of the Mexican market for refined petroleum, whose value was estimated at $300,000. After 1911, however, the struggle was for sources of oil. On the basis of the rapid increase in oil production, it was assumed that Mexico would soon occupy the first place in world oil production.[19] The strong position of British investors in Mexico might mean the loss of the monopoly held by Standard Oil in a large part of the world. In a conversation with the German military attaché in the United States, Herwarth von Bittenfeld, the chief of the American general staff, Leonard Wood, stated, "The petroleum wealth of Cowdray's concession alone thus exceeds that of Russia, while the oil wealth of Mexico as a whole in all probability exceeds that of the United States."[20]

As early as 1911, after Madero's victory, the Standard Oil Company had hoped that the new Mexican government's hostile attitude toward Cowdray would make it impossible for him to obtain new concessions and that a conflict with the Mexican government might push Cowdray to sell his Mexican holdings. When, in the same year, Madero announced an investigation of the Cowdray enterprise, the British oil magnate sought a rapprochement with his American competition, which led to the signing of a supplier's contract between them.[21] This agreement in no way prevented the American oil companies from hoping, after Huerta's coup d'etat, that because the latter had come to power with American aid, he would push through the measures that Madero had not taken.

Huerta, however, had no such plans. He continued Díaz's policy and allied himself with European, and particularly British capital against the American companies. This shift had already become apparent in May 1913. The German chargé d'affaires in Mexico reported as early as 3 May that the Mexican government "would like to take a firm attitude, both politically and economically, with regard to America."[22] Some months later, Huerta defined the policy he was already pursuing in a letter to the German businessman Holste. "As you know," he wrote, "it is my intention and the goal of my efforts and those of my collaborators to reduce the influence of American capital in this country and to interest European capital in Mexico, all the more so because Europe has on many occasions expressed its friendship for us and its sense of justice."[23] The reasons for Huerta's rapprochement with European capital were in part the same ones that had also been decisive for Díaz: the far greater willingness of European businessmen to give Mexican politicians a share of their profits, a willingness which was a result of the relative weakness of the European countries in Mexico, and the leading Mexican politicians' fear of being completely controlled by the United States. Woodrow Wilson's refusal to recognize Huerta and his increasing hostility toward his regime doubtless strengthened those tendencies.

The American president's policies nevertheless were not the primary cause of Huerta's favorable disposition toward European capital. It was also due to a policy of intensive wooing of the new regime by Lord Cowdray's British oil interests. Only one day after the cessation of hostilities J. B. Body, Cowdray's main representative in Mexico, called on Felix Díaz, who was still considered the strong man of the regime. "He requested me to send you his best regards," Body reported to Cowdray.[24] Body felt that these "regards" were so important that he sent a corresponding cable to his chief in London. Cowdray immediately sent back a telegram of congratulations to Felix Díaz, which his representative personally delivered to the Mexican politician.[25] There is little doubt that these congratulations were sincere. Cowdray and his representative felt that they had every reason to be satisfied with the outcome of the coup which had toppled Madero.

Only two days after Madero's arrest by the conspirators, Body reported to his chief, "The new cabinet of which undoubtedly you have been advised by the newspapers, is, we think, satisfactory on the whole . . . so far as Riba and I know all of the members of the new cabinet have very kindly feelings towards us as a firm." What above all enthused the Cowdray people was the "impression that General Huerta and his cabinet would now act with an iron hand to quell any further uprisings and to suppress such revolutionary parties as do not immediately lay down their arms. In business circles there is a marked feeling that we shall soon have better times again.''[26]

These initial formal steps were followed only six days later by much more concrete offers by the Cowdray interests to help bolster the new government. On 27 February, only a few days after the coup, Body called on the new minister of finance, Toribio Esquivel Obregón, and ''offered our services to him and the government. He received me most cordially and told me that he had known about our firm for many years and had formed a very high opinion of us.''[27]

Esquivel Obregón had taken note of Body's offer, but had as yet made no concrete demands on the British oil company for help. The next cabinet minister whom Body looked up, Rodolfo Reyes, was far less reticent in this respect. Rodolfo Reyes, the son of Bernardo Reyes, who had hoped to assume the leadership of the revolt but had been killed on the first day of the coup, had actively conspired against Madero and was now minister of justice. When Body called on him ''to offer our services,'' Reyes immediately set out to utilize them. He first asked the British oil man to assist him ''by obtaining certain information which he desired regarding the Huasteca Petroleum Company,'' but what Reyes wanted above all was to obtain the British oil company's help in securing recognition of his administration by the British government. He was by no means acting on his own but on instructions of the whole cabinet which had heard that the British minister to Mexico Sir Francis Stronge had sent negative reports to London about the murder of Madero and Pino Suarez. Both Reyes and Foreign Minister León de la Barra, whom Body had visited one day before, urgently asked the British oil man to request his chief, Lord Cowdray, ''to smooth over or assist in smoothing over the complications which they fear might result.''[28] Body not only agreed to their request by immediately cabling his chief in London for assistance, but he also shared the Huerta cabinet's resentment at the doubts the British representative in Mexico had expressed concerning the Mexican government's role in the murder of Madero. ''I have reason to know,'' he wrote Cowdray, ''that the British minister has not been at all clear in his reports to the Foreign Office; he has rather left it to them to decide whether they should acknowledge the present government on account of the unfortunate manner in which the ex-president and the ex-vice president lost their lives. Of course, I have not mentioned to the British minister the request I have received from the Government, nor to the Mexican Government that I know of our minister's reports.''[29]

Immediately after receiving the cable from the representative in Mexico, Cowdray went to the Foreign Office with the aim, as he put it, ''of getting a definite expression of opinion from them about recognizing the new government."[30] There is no exact report of what went on at this meeting, but indications are that it proceeded according to Cowdray's wishes. A high official of the Foreign Office wrote that he had assured Cowdray "as far as I know, his Majesty's Government would pursue the usual course and recognize as Head of the Mexican State whoever was constitutionally elected."[31] Immediately after this meeting the British oil magnate sent a corresponding cable to his representative in Mexico and the latter now felt strong enough to confront and pressure the British minister into revising his views.

There was nothing subtle or restrained about the way Body treated the highest representative of his country in Mexico. He bluntly "told the minister we had several important negotiations pending with the Mexican Government, and I have received indications that they would not look upon them with such favor as they might do while the British Government withheld recognition of the present legally constituted administration."[32] Body persuaded the British minister to go with him to the American embassy in order to find out what the American ambassador thought about the new administration in Mexico. Henry Lane Wilson's opinion about the Huerta government was a foregone conclusion. He told his British colleague "that he had advised his Government that the present Administration was perfectly legal and constitutional." Henry Lane Wilson, who in contrast to President Woodrow Wilson favored the recognition of Huerta, also began to pressure his British colleague, "He said to Stronge that in view of this advice to Washington he presumed that he [Stronge] would make a similar announcement to his Government." The hapless British minister attempted to defend himself by concealing his reservations about Huerta and stating that "he had cabled his foreign office fully." Body continued to pressure the British envoy, "I told him I thought his messages could not be as clear as the ambassador's else the Foreign Office would not be awaiting definite news from him as you informed me they were." The British minister now caved in and agreed to show Body the confidential reports he had sent to London. "We returned to the legation and I was shown the cable dispatches which our minister had sent London and as I knew they were not all definite or clear."

Stronge now fully capitulated. He not only agreed to tell the Foreign Office "that the present government of Mexico was legal and constitutional," but even agreed that the American "Ambassador should inform Washington of our Minister's actions." A few days later a favorable report by Stronge on the stability of the Huerta regime arrived in London.[33]

The Huerta administration very soon showed how much it appreciated Cowdray's intervention in its behalf. "I had an interesting talk with the Governor of the Federal District this morning," Body reported on 6

March to his chief. "He told me that General Huerta wished to see me in order to personally express his regret at the manner in which we had been treated by the late administration and to assure me that the present government was disposed to make amends as far as possible by granting any reasonable favor that we might ask."[34] Thus it comes as no surprise that Pearson was granted substantial concessions by the Huerta regime.[35]

Cowdray was greatly enthused by these reports from his subordinate in Mexico. He found that the relationship between the Mexican government and his companies was "gratifying." He must have felt even more gratified a short time later when he was informed by Body that the Waters Pierce Oil Company headed by his long-time rival, U.S. oil man Henry Clay Pierce, who maintained close links to Standard Oil, "is not looked upon with favor by the present and probable future Administration. They do not seem to be able to get close to the ruling powers and do not know how to make themselves sympathetic."[36]

It is thus not surprising that this close cooperation of the Huerta administration with European interests in general and Cowdray in particular produced increasing hostility among many U.S. business interests in Mexico and particularly among the oil and raw material producing companies.

The objectives which these companies pursued by supporting Wilson's anti-Huerta policies were varied. Their first and simplest objective was to replace a government considered hostile to U.S. interests by one they assumed would be more favorably disposed toward them. There are indications that Carranza had made promises to Edward Doheny and Henry Clay Pierce to improve their situation at the expense of British interests.

Some American businessmen hoped that the fighting in Mexico would lead to a separation of northern Mexico from the South and its annexation by the United States. In mid-1913, Emeterio de la Garza, a close collaborator of Huerta's, traveled to the United States to persuade the American government and American businessmen to avoid an intervention in Mexico. In New York, he made a speech to American bankers in which he pointed out the serious dangers for the United States of an armed intervention in Mexico. "Emeterio de la Garza," wrote Hintze,

> now feels that he was attentively listened to; he thinks he has made an impression, and perhaps convinced some people. On the following day, one of the heads of Speyer and Co. . . . invited him to a visit, at which he also met John Hammond. Both men began by telling him: "You had a great, magnetic influence on the meeting (this is a Spanish phrase), but you have not been initiated (no está Usted en el secreto). Your notion of our desires is completely wrong. We want, and need no intervention. We want nothing more than Baja California and the entire area north of the line running from the southern tip of Baja California to Matamoros

(Tamaulipas). This area will either come under our control of itself, or we will occupy it; then you can come and try to take it away from us. That is what we want, and we will get it without firing a shot, since you are incapable of resisting, because of your advanced internal collapse.[37]

Is this a truthful presentation or a fabrication of Emeterio de la Garza, one of Huerta's supporters, intended to stir up fears of American annexationist intentions in Germany? In his diary, Woodrow Wilson's confidant, Colonel House, reports a visit paid to him about the same time, on 24 October 1913, by Otto Kahn, one of the most important bankers in the United States and a partner of Morgan and Speyer. Kahn told House that he "was considering a possible solution to the Mexican question." He thought that

> our government could inform the northern states of Mexico, which are currently in a state of insurrection, that if they desire to hold an election to determine if they should secede from the rest of the republic, our government was prepared to send a cordon of troops to the dividing line with the remainder of Mexico to prevent any interference from those quarters and to make it possible for them [the northern states of Mexico] to hold a free election to decide this question. He thought that if a separate republic were set up by these northern states, it would form a buffer zone between the United States and the insurgent part of Mexico.[38]

House rejected this proposal, indicating that it would be tantamount to a U.S. declaration of war on Mexico.

Other forces, including the railway companies, finally placed their hopes on an armed American intervention. In a letter to the American government in March 1913, the railway companies had initially called for the recognition of the Huerta government. They were, however, far too closely tied to the large raw material producing companies to oppose them and thus changed their position on July 1913. At that time, a conference of bankers from various countries with interests in the Mexican railways took place in Paris, and the representatives of the American, British, French, and German banks agreed that "the American government should intervene and restore order."[39]

The railway companies were not alone in calling for an armed intervention in Mexico.[40] They were joined by William Randolph Hearst, who owned important property in Mexico and obtained additional properties at extremely low prices. A similar position was quickly adopted by the American oil companies, whose spokesman Senator Albert Fall was making increasingly open calls in the Senate for an armed American intervention in Mexico.[41]

Although there were indeed differences, often of a substantial nature, between Wilson and individual American companies in Mexico, particularly those pushing for an extended military intervention, there was no head-on clash between Wilson and most American business interests in Mexico during this period.

## Woodrow Wilson's Policies in Mexico, 1913/14

Wilson's policy toward Mexico consisted of two stages: the first phase lasted from March to October 1913 and the second from 11 October 1913 until the overthrow of Huerta in July 1914. In the first phase the American government attempted to force Huerta to resign, while essentially preserving his army and his administration. His successor was not to be one of the revolutionaries, but a conservative politician from the ruling circles of Mexico. Wilson hoped to gain the support of the European powers for his policies.

Early in 1913 Wilson suggested to Great Britain and the other European powers that Huerta not be recognized. When these countries ignored his proposal and recognized Huerta anyway, Wilson did not follow suit but attacked Huerta even more strongly. On 14 July, he called on Huerta to announce elections and not to present himself as a candidate; should he fail to comply, Wilson would not be willing to mediate between Huerta and his opponents. When these demands were rejected, Wilson recalled the American ambassador and sent John Lind as his personal representative to Mexico.

On 12 August 1913, Lind made the following set of new proposals to the Mexican government: immediate cease-fire in Mexico, followed by free elections with the participation of all parties at the earliest possible date; all parties would accept the results of the elections and would support the elected government. In return, Wilson stated his willingness to mediate between the Huerta government and the revolutionaries.

These proposals were rejected by the Huerta government, and Lind presented it with a new note on 22 August, in which the demand for prompt elections and Huerta's nonparticipation as a presidential candidate were repeated. Lind clearly threatened a military intervention by the United States in case the demands were rejected but promised an American loan to Mexico in the event that the Mexican government accepted his proposals.[42] When, on the morning of 27 August, Lind's note remained unanswered, Wilson went before Congress to elaborate a Mexican policy which he characterized as a policy of "watchful waiting." Americans were asked to leave Mexico; in addition, the United States imposed an arms embargo. This embargo had the most severe impact on the Huerta government, since previously it had been able to purchase arms freely in the United States, whereas the revolutionaries, whom the American government had not recognized as a belligerent party, had not had this privilege.

The tensions between the United States and the Huerta government abated somewhat on the evening of the same day, when Wilson received the reply to Lind's note, in which the Huerta government showed its first concession to Wilson's demands. Although it reaffirmed that Mexico did not recognize the right of the United States to interfere in its internal affairs, it also stated that Huerta was already disqualified as a candidate by the constitution itself.

Three weeks later, on 16 September, Huerta told the assembled diplomatic corps that he would not permit himself to be nominated. When, on 24 September, Huerta's foreign minister, Federico Gamboa, was nominated as the presidential candidate of the Catholic Party, this nomination received the full support of the American State Department, which announced publicly that a Gamboa government could count on the recognition and support of the United States. The Americans were so pleased with this turn of events that they asked Huerta to send a personal representative. "I feel that we have nearly reached the end of our trouble,"[43] Secretary of State Bryan wrote to Wilson on 25 September.

With their support of Gamboa's candidacy, the administration in Washington had not recognized Huerta, but it had clearly recognized his regime. Gamboa had been one of Huerta's closest collaborators, and the Catholic Party, which had presented him as its presidential candidate, was an important element in the old Díaz oligarchy. American diplomacy was now confronted with the question of how the revolutionaries, who already controlled over a third of Mexico, would react to an assumption of power by Gamboa.

The American government's relations with the revolutionaries were contradictory. On the one hand, the United States had been the only great power to send representatives to the revolutionaries for negotiations, while on the other hand it had not recognized them as a belligerent party and had made it impossible for them to purchase weapons legally in the United States, though the Huerta government was free to purchase weapons prior to 27 August. It would not be wrong to suppose that American diplomats, prior to October 1913, had attempted to use the revolutionaries as a lever against Huerta, but that they feared an excessive growth of their power.

After the announcement of Gamboa's candidacy, the U.S. government did everything it could to get the revolutionaries to recognize a potential Gamboa government. On 1–2 October 1913, William Bayard Hale, as Wilson's personal representative, met with the Constitutionalist representative in Washington and told him that the American president "would morally support Gamboa or any other man who won legal elections on

October 26." At the same time, Carranza was asked to wage the struggle "with the ballot and not with the gun." This request was made along with unmistakable threats. On 26 September, the U.S. State Department had already declared that it would recognize the Gamboa government even if the revolutionaries opposed it. And Hale told Carranza on 2 October that President Wilson "would not recognize a government which was produced by a revolution."[44] In this way, it was made absolutely clear to the Constitutionalists that the American government would fully support Gamboa and that the revolutionaries, even if they were to defeat a Gamboa government, could never expect to be recognized by the United States.

It is clear that these proposals were completely unacceptable to the Constitutionalists. A recognition of the Gamboa government would have represented a capitulation to the Huerta system, and a struggle "with the ballot and not the gun" against a regime that had overthrown the only Mexican government ever chosen in free elections was unthinkable for revolutionaries of all shadings. Thus the negotiations between the American government and the Constitutionalists were destined to fail in the initial stages. Another factor contributing to this failure was that several days after the beginning of the negotiations the situation in Mexico changed completely: Huerta dissolved parliament on 10 October, held "elections" on 26 October, and in spite of all promises had himself named as president.

How can this move, which represented an open challenge to Wilson, be explained? The sudden shifts in Huerta's attitude toward the American demands for his resignation—stubbornness prior to 27 August, then flexibility, and once again stubbornness after 11 October—were in no way the results of an accident or of Huerta's problems with alcohol. In addition to the pressure and threats of the American government, two factors in particular had prompted Huerta to make concessions on 27 August.

First, there was the pressure of the not unimportant section of the ruling class which was not linked to Great Britain and which feared that conflict with the United States would lead to an extension of the revolution; if a war should break out, its property might be destroyed. "The propertied classes," Hintze accurately reported on 16 September, "who have stuck by him [Huerta] are beginning to bolt, fearing that their property would be endangered in a clash with the United States."[45] These were the groups that had nominated Gamboa, and every victory of the revolutionaries strengthened their pressure on Huerta to give in to the United States.

Much more important, however, was a second factor, the attitude of the European powers and Japan toward the Huerta government. In his policies toward the United States, Huerta had counted on the support of Japan, Germany, and particularly Great Britain. In the period between the end of August and the middle of September, however, it appeared that these powers were no longer willing to support Huerta.

On 10 September 1913, Hintze wrote to Berlin: "The foreign minister, Señor Gamboa, has expressed himself quite acidly on the vainly awaited support from Japan: the Japanese have neither money nor courage; we cannot rely on them."[46] Gamboa's opinion was the result of the behavior of the newly arrived Japanese minister to Mexico, Adatchi. The Huerta government had organized for his arrival large sympathy rallies having an explicitly anti-American character. The Japanese legation immediately lodged a protest with the Mexican government. As the Japanese chargé d'affaires in Mexico, Tanabe, reported to his foreign minister, the Japanese had protested the attempts to link the welcoming ceremonies for the new Japanese minister "with demonstrations against a foreign country."[47] Adatchi himself commented along similar lines: "The undersigned made an effort not to respond to the anti-American mood of the population in various cities, and repeatedly emphasized that the friendship between Japan and Mexico resided primarily in the development of commercial and industrial relations."[48]

There was also a certain change in the attitude of German diplomats in Mexico. Whereas Kardorff, the German chargé d'affaires, had encouraged Huerta to resist Wilson with promises of German support, Hintze, who resumed his duties on 5 September, reversed this line.[49]

The most important factor for Huerta was the stance of British diplomacy. From the time Huerta assumed power until the end of 1913, British policy in Mexico had moved along two contradictory lines. On the one hand, Great Britain had attempted, in view of its growing antagonisms with Germany, to avoid a clash with the United States; on the other hand, it sought to promote the important petroleum interests of Lord Cowdray, who had the closest ties to the Huerta government. Behind this policy, there stood not only the economic and political pressure of the Cowdray trust, but strategic interests as well, for the British admiralty had concluded an important supplier's contract with this company.[50]

Shortly after Huerta's accession to power, the British government had at first responded positively to an American request not to recognize Huerta for the moment and to take no steps without consultation with the United States. As Huerta's position became increasingly clear, however, the British recognized him within three weeks and without informing the American ambassador beforehand.[51]

On 4 July, the British minister in Mexico took the initiative and called a conference of the European diplomats in Mexico to put pressure on the United States over the question of recognition for Huerta. "Participants in the conference included the envoys of England, France, Italy, Spain,

Belgium, and Norway, as well as the German chargé d'affaires and myself," the Austrian minister to Mexico reported. The English minister, Mr. Stronge, explained that the increasing anarchy could only be controlled by strengthening the current government. He proposed that the heads of the local missions wire their governments to work through their Washington embassies for U.S. recognition of President Huerta.[52] Shortly thereafter, the British ambassador in Washington, Sir Cecil Spring Rice, intervened with the American government along similar lines.

When these steps produced no change in the American attitude toward Huerta but did inject tensions into British-American relations, British diplomacy appears to have made a temporary retreat. On 11 September, Hintze reported: "The English minister has recently been firmly opposed to any attempts by the diplomatic corps to pressure their governments for collective moves against American policy.... He even told me that he was doing this on explicit instructions, and that England did not want to emerge here in any way which might appear to be in opposition to American policy."[53]

This attitude by Japan, Germany, and Great Britain makes Huerta's willingness to give ground on 16 September understandable. The consequences, however, were much more serious than British diplomacy had desired. Thus it is no surprise that there was a new, complete turn in British policy. Sir Francis Stronge was recalled and Sir Lionel Carden was appointed as the new minister.

Carden was one of the most outspoken exponents and representatives of British imperialism in Latin America. During the Díaz period, he had served for more than fifteen years as British consul general in Mexico.[54] He had been important in persuading the Mexican government to abolish a series of subsidies to French, German, and American companies. The French Minister to Mexico Couthouly, quite beside himself, had written of this "chargé d'affaires of a new and previously unknown kind," who "could only be described as a businessman, rather than the queen's chargé d'affaires."[55] In the opinion of the French envoy, Carden had used his position for his own personal enrichment. In September 1885, after Carden's plans seemed a bit slow in coming to maturity, Minister Couthouly gloated: "The unfortunate British minister is now contemplating the collapse of his plans to become rich which he worked out with the help of Mr. Romero Rubio; Mr. Carden has sold his horses."[56]

After fifteen years of service in Mexico, Carden had been sent to other Latin American countries, where he represented British interests with the same intensity and pushed anti-American policies. According to a report which the German minister sent to Berlin, he told Hintze "that in Cuba,

Guatemala and other Latin American countries, he had always encountered the same foe: the Americans. He had always considered them to be people of *mala fides,* as unscrupulous intriguers and as confidence men . . . . Behind all their talk of civilization, justice, humanity and morality, they were nothing but ruthless businessmen. He had often attempted to reach an understanding with Americans: they had always broken their word.''[57] Carden's anti-American stance in Cuba was so aggressive that Secretary of State Knox had asked the British Foreign Office to recall him from Cuba.[58]

Carden had business ties with the Cowdray concern; he held stock in various companies, including a land company on the isthmus of Tehuantepec, in which Cowdray was also involved.[59] According to a report by Hintze, Carden told the German minister that he had been sent to Mexico ''to propose a 'line of conduct' to the Foreign Office; Sir Edward Grey values his judgment. His latest view: the Huerta government should be supported . . . . He will propose that the Huerta government be supported even *against* the United States.''[60] Shortly after his arrival in Mexico, he became one of the closest advisors to Huerta, who ''made no decision on any important matter without having consulted Sir Lionel Carden.''[61]

Woodrow Wilson, Secretary of State Bryan, and their representative in Mexico John Lind were convinced that it was London who persuaded Huerta to carry out his coup against the Mexican parliament and thereby take the step that annulled all previously concluded agreements between his government and the United States; this act signified a clear break with the United States. There is no evidence in the Foreign Office files to support these suspicions. Nevertheless, the reports by Carden's German colleague Hintze,[62] which are quoted extensively in these pages, suggest that American suspicions of Carden may have been far more correct than many historians have assumed. Carden's hatred for Americans was only matched by his boundless admiration for Huerta.

One of Carden's principal aims, as he repeatedly stated to his German colleague, was to force his own government to take a hard anti-American line not only in Mexico but in all of Latin America. Carden's aim was not merely to keep the pro-British Huerta in power and to introduce greater tension into relations between Mexico and the United States, but, as the U.S. chief of staff told the German military attaché in Washington, also to obtain important petroleum concessions for British companies which the Mexican parliament would never have ratified. The British minister ostentatiously expressed his support for Huerta's actions, presenting his credentials on the day after the dissolution of parliament.

Huerta's coup provoked an extremely sharp reaction from the American government. Wilson accused Huerta of ''bad faith'' in a note and announced that he would recognize no elections held under Huerta's auspices. From that moment, Wilson did everything he could to topple Huerta.[63]

The American government's first steps were aimed at Great Britain. Wilson and Bryan were firmly convinced that the interests of British oil companies formed the basis of British policy in Mexico. Colonel House recounted conversations with Bryan and Wilson on this question in a letter to the American ambassador in London: "I found that he [Bryan] was negatively disposed to the British government, that its Mexican policy was dictated by financial motives, that they were supporting Huerta at the instigation of Lord Cowdray and that not only had Cowdray already obtained concessions from the Huerta government, but was also anticipating further concessions. He saw Sir Lionel Carden in a very bad light. I met the president, and his views were not very different from those of Mr. Bryan."[64]

The American government then attempted to get the British government to withdraw its support from Huerta and to put an end to the grants of oil concessions to British companies in Mexico. Wilson had initially wanted to address a sharp note to the British government accusing it of bearing responsibility for Huerta's remaining in power. When it was pointed out to him that such a note would be disputable in terms of international law and might arouse opposition to the United States both in Latin America and in Europe, Wilson took another course of action: on 27 October 1913, he made a militant speech in Mobile, Alabama, in which he denounced foreign interests in Latin America. Describing Latin America, he spoke of "states that are obliged, because their territory does not lie within the main field of modern enterprise and action, to grant concessions are in this condition—that foreign interests are apt to dominate their domestic affairs: a condition of affairs always dangerous and apt to become intolerable. What these states are going to see, therefore, is an emancipation from the subordination, which has been inevitable, to foreign enterprise and an assertion of the splendid character which, in spite of these difficulties, they have again and again been able to demonstrate."[65] According to Link, Wilson obviously meant Great Britain when he spoke of foreign interests and it was Mexico which he referred to as "Latin America."[66] With this speech Wilson was making an open challenge to British imperialism in Mexico.

In November 1913, the British government finally gave in. The undersecretary of state in the British Foreign Office, Sir William Tyrrell, traveled to Washington, where he had lengthy discussions with Wilson and Bryan.[67] In these discussions, Bryan accused Britain of being interested in only one thing in Mexico—petroleum—and of subordinating its

Mexican policies to the objectives of the "oil barons." In these negotiations Tyrrell disclosed the British government's willingness to give up
support for Huerta and to cede leadership in Mexican policy completely
to the United States.[68]

The origins and objectives of British policy in Mexico were already the
subject of controversy in 1913 and 1914 and remain so among historians
today. In 1913 and 1914, British government spokesmen vehemently denied that their policy in any way signified support for Huerta. According
to them, the recognition of Huerta was only a routine diplomatic affair in
which the government, in keeping with British and international custom,
recognized a de facto government in power. The British government, they
said, was in no way pursuing anti-American objectives in this case, and
never thought of doing so. Misunderstandings had arisen because the
British government, at the time of Huerta's recognition, had not been
aware of the extent of American opposition to Huerta. At this time,
Woodrow Wilson had not yet shown how repugnant Huerta was to him.
There was absolutely no question of any influence on British policy by
Lord Cowdray, and this was affirmed both by spokesmen of the British
government and by Cowdray himself.[69] Cowdray had, of course, been
consulted, but the British government had made its decision quite independently of his opinion. Carden had never had an anti-American attitude, and interviews with him were falsely reported in the press. Access
to the archives of the British and French foreign offices made possible an
examination of these statements.

There is no question that the recognition of Huerta was anything but a
routine affair. In 1913, a member of the British Parliament had already
pointed out that the recognition of Huerta was in contradiction to certain
traditional principles of British diplomacy, which prescribed that official
recognition be withheld from any head of state who came to power by
assassinating his predecessor, and that if recognition were in fact granted,
this should occur only after a certain period of time. The member invoked
a precedent involving Serbia. In 1903, the Serbian king Alexander Ob-
renovich was murdered by Peter Karageorgevich, who succeeded him.
The British government refused to recognize Peter and gave as the reason
for its attitude the murder of his predecessor.[70] Although the British government had received from its envoy in Mexico the report that Huerta was
in all probability responsible for the murder of Madero, recognition was
quickly granted to him. Sir Louis Mallet of the Foreign Office had written
to Grey: "I personally agree with Mr. Spicer that we should be guided by
our major interests, independently of the murder of Madero."[71] In other
respects, too, the recognition of Huerta contradicted previous British
procedure in such cases. Provisional presidents were not as a rule recog-

nized by an official letter of the king. The British government, however, decided to break this tradition in Huerta's case and to answer his announcement that he had taken power in Mexico with an official letter of the king.[72]

To what extent was British policy in Mexico directed against the United States?

The American government had made it clear to the British Foreign Office that it would be quite pleased if both governments could discuss their viewpoints prior to recognition of Huerta. Along these lines, Sir Harold Nicholson argued in the Foreign Office for consultations with the governments of other major powers, particularly the United States, France, and Germany, prior to any recognition of Huerta. But Grey, the British foreign secretary, reacted to this proposal with the words: "Our interests in Mexico are so big that I think we should take our own line, without making it dependent upon that of other governments,"[73] and he ordered the recognition of Huerta. British government spokesmen later asserted that this step was taken in part because the true extent of the United States' opposition to Huerta was still not known to the English government. In fact, President Wilson had not yet made his attitude toward Huerta absolutely clear at that time. In the summer and fall of 1913, however, there could no longer be any doubt of Wilson's deep opposition to Huerta. The British reaction was not to attempt a rapprochement with American policy, but to appoint one of the British Foreign Office's most vehement opponents of the United States, Sir Lionel Carden, as minister to Mexico. Carden was hardly eager to have this post, for he had hoped to be appointed British ambassador to Brazil. Prior to his departure from London on 1 September 1913, Carden wrote a memorandum to Grey, in which he proposed a series of guidelines for British policy in Mexico with the aim of putting a damper on American influence, not only in Mexico but throughout Latin America, and of setting clear limits on the Monroe Doctrine.[74]

Carden introduced his memorandum with a history of the expansion of American influence in Latin America over the past twenty-five years and with a representation of what were in his opinion the devastating consequences of this expansion for Britain's position in Latin America:

> The history of the period mentioned shows that the intervention of the United States Government in the domestic affairs of their weaker neighbors has only been effected by force of arms, whether by open war as in the case of Cuba, or by promoting or aiding revolutions, as in Panama, Nicaragua, Honduras and Mexico. In all these cases British interests have suffered severely through the destruction of property and the interference with trade and industry. Nor can it be shown that such

interventions have had any effect which is likely to prove permanent in bringing about improved political conditions or removing the causes which have produced unrest in the past.

Moreover, the United States Government has given repeated proof that, far from favouring the principle of the open door in Latin America, they view with jealousy the competition of European nations for the trade of those Republics: and all their influence has been and is being directed towards obtaining such special advantages for their citizens, by reciprocity conventions and otherwise, as will ensure for them in course of time a great preponderance if not a virtual monopoly in all matters connected with finance, commerce or public works.

Carden accused the United States of responsibility for all those uprisings that had broken out in 1910/11 and in 1913 and for all the damage or danger to English property they had caused. Carden proposed that the British government unambiguously inform the American government that it did not support its policy toward Huerta.

By adopting such a line we should avoid for the future being drawn into acquiescing in lines of policy of which we do not approve or about which we have not been consulted: we should leave ourselves free to afford effective protection to the great interests we have at stake which are being constantly imperiled by the ill considered or interested action of the United States: and we should regain the influence we used to have in Latin America and with it a considerable part of the trade which we have lost and are still losing.

As regards the present crisis in Mexico it would seem to be madness at such a juncture to contemplate substituting a new and untried man, for the present Provisional President, who from all reports is proving himself thoroughly competent to dominate the situation—and the interests of British and all other foreign investors would appear therefore to demand that he be given a free hand and be offered all possible moral and financial support.

What Carden demanded from the British government was a frontal attack on American policy in Mexico aimed not merely at promoting British interests there, but at placing limits once and for all on the Monroe Doctrine. Prime Minister Asquith, to whom Carden's memorandum was presented, had no objections to its proposals, but merely noted: "Sir Lionel Carden's description of American policy and methods in Mexico does not seem at all overcoloured."[75] Carden's chief, Foreign Secretary Grey, was nonetheless hardly inclined to let the situation develop into an outright confrontation with the Americans in Mexico, even if he had no intention of reversing British recognition of the Huerta government. He did not want to take a hard line toward the United States: "I do not dispute the inconvenience and poor results of United States policy but while I am prepared to keep free hand, His Majesty's Government cannot with any prospect of success embark upon an active counter-policy to that of the United States or constitute themselves the champions of Mexico or any of these Republics against the United States.''[76]

These remarks show that there were different opinions in the British government with respect to the policy to be pursued in Mexico. When the question of Huerta's recognition was being discussed, Nicholson, in contrast to Grey, argued for prior consultation with the American government. Carden's anti-American memorandum had evoked no objection from Prime Minister Asquith, but was nonetheless in part rejected by Grey. What was the significance of these differences of opinion? Did they perhaps represent differences within British financial circles? In the opinion of the Foreign Ministry of France, the great power most closely allied with England, they did. On 20 April 1914, the heads of the political-commercial division of the French Foreign Ministry drafted a memorandum for the French foreign minister on the English policy in Mexico, stating that England's policy in Mexico could be divided into three phases: (1) from February to November 1913, England adopted a pro-Huerta orientation; (2) from November 1913 to February 1914, premonitions of an Anglo-American rapprochement came to the surface; and (3) from February to April 1914, England fell in line behind the United States. ''England's policy orientation,'' wrote the French diplomats,

during the Mexican crisis, which is in some respects a policy of retreat, can partially be explained by the existence of two contradictory tendencies in the Foreign Office: one, which is favorably disposed to Huerta, and the other, which is inclined toward President Woodrow Wilson. The policy can also be explained by the parallel action of powerful economic groups that represent English interests in Mexico. At the beginning, these groups were convinced that Huerta was the only man capable of restoring order in the country. This analysis is held by a certain number of the colleagues of Sir Edward Grey, who believe that the defense of British interests actually required the support of President Huerta. Thus, England was also the first power to recognize him as President ad interim in April 1913.[77]

In the view of the French Foreign Ministry, the goals of the pro-Huerta groups in the British Foreign Office went much further than mere support for their preferred candidate in Mexico. ''At that time,'' wrote the French Foreign Ministry, ''it was not without a certain pleasure that London viewed the possibility of a conflict between the two republics [the United States and Mexico]; the British are quite happy to live with Mexico's old hostility toward the United States and do not even shrink from the perspective of a war which would occupy the government of the United States for years.''[78] This interpretation of French diplomacy, which was quite well informed on the motives of English policy, is largely in keeping with Carden's statement to Hintze in November 1913 that he would welcome a war between the United States and Mexico, because such a war could lead to the destruction of the Monroe Doctrine. Carden's views were obviously not merely those of some strongly anti-American diplomats, but also those of powerful groupings in British high finance and in the British government.

### The Reason for the Vascillations in British Policy

On the instructions of his government in December 1913, Carden told the Huerta regime that it could count on no support from England in a conflict with the United States.[79] Great Britain's retreat is generally attributed to the following causes:

1. Antagonisms between Britain and Germany were becoming increasingly strong and far overshadowed the British-American rivalry in Mexico. Great Britain was more and more dependent on American support, which it valued more than Mexican oil concessions.[80]
2. The United States had declared itself willing to accede to British desires on the question of Panama Canal fees. Contrary to existing treaties, the American Congress had voted a reduction in Panama Canal fees for American coastal shipping and had thus given substantial advantages to American trade. In the discussion between Tyrrell and Wilson, the American president promised to come out for the abolition of this law;[81] the resulting proposal was approved by the U.S. Congress in April 1914.
3. The United States had committed itself to do everything it could to guarantee British concessions in the event of Huerta's defeat. On 13 November 1913, President Wilson wrote to Sir William Tyrrell: "I beg that you will assure Sir Edward Grey that the U.S. government intends not merely to force Huerta from power, but also to exert every influence it can to secure for Mexico a better government, under which all contracts and business and concessions will be safer than they have been."[82]

In addition, however, two other factors seem to have played a special role. On the one hand, it seemed that the petroleum of Pearson's oil fields was not suitable for the British navy. On 19 January 1914, the British ambassador in Washington, Sir Cecil Spring Rice, told his Austrian colleague: "The British admiralty initially considered Pearson's oil; its material inferiority and quite relative utility for the fueling of ships, however, have become apparent, so that the admiralty is no longer counting on the Mexican oil wells. There is thus no longer any reason to fear a clash with the United States."[83]

The poor quality of the oil supplied by Pearson actually led to the annulment of his supplier's contract with the Admiralty. "In view of the quality of the oil, which does not conform to the conditions of the suppliers' contract, the British Admiralty has declared the suppliers' contract with the Cia Mexicana de Petroleo 'El Aguila' S.A. or Pearson (Lord Cowdray) concern to be null and void."[84] The British Admiralty then attempted to compensate for the deficiency of the Cowdray shipments with contracts with American oil companies in Mexico, and succeeded in concluding a contract with Doheny's company. On 2 June 1915, the German consul in Tampico reported:

> Shortly after the disclosure of the differences which have developed between the Cia Mexicana "El Aguila," Lord Cowdray concern, and the English Admiralty over the quality of the former's oil supplies, the Huasteca Petroleum Company (Doheny's), the large American firm located here, contacted the English government and apparently worked out a larger contract for oil shipments. This contract will apparently run for twenty years, providing for daily shipments of fifty thousand barrels of heating oil and oil for the Admiralty, and will be signed by the Huasteca Petroleum Company and the British Admiralty on one hand, and the two large English steamship companies Cunard and White Star on the other.... This contract for an American company is to be seen as a major blow to the Lord Cowdray interests, and all the more so because the "El Aguila" Company made its large investments, which cost an enormous amount of money, strictly in anticipation of the profitable business it expected to conduct with the English Admiralty.[85]

This development doubly strengthened the U.S. position with regard to Great Britain. On the one hand, the British Admiralty was dependent on the shipments of American oil companies to meet its needs, and on the other, the Pearson company was dependent on the Standard Oil Company for at least part of its petroleum supplies to the British navy.

Finally, Great Britain's policy retreat was due in no small part to the fact that in British financial circles, just as with the American companies, there were serious differences of opinion on the policy to be pursued in Mexico. While the raw materials producers around Cowdray were calling for British support of Huerta, those groups with interests in railway stocks and securities feared that tensions with the United States could compromise Mexico's ability to pay. The British companies with interests in the Mexican railways actually went so far as to call openly for American intervention in Mexico. In July 1913, the British bankers Edgar Speyer—who had close ties with the Speyer banking house of New York—and Tiarks told the director of the Berliner Handelsgesellschaft, Beheim-Schwarzbach, "that the only hope was an American intervention and that extremely important interests were at stake."[86]

At the beginning of January 1914, British bankers sought out the British Foreign Secretary Sir Edward Grey and told him

> that Huerta would in all probability step down if England, Germany and France propose that he resign, and in any case leave no doubt in his mind that Mexico will receive no support from any of those powers as long as he remains at his post. They thus suggested to Sir Edward that he embark on such a policy, which in their opinion would give a loophole both to President Wilson and to Huerta, and to consult with the German and French governments on these questions. They were convinced that the United States government would welcome the proposed solution with great relief and would contribute unselfishly to the restoration of law and order in Mexico after Huerta steps down.[87]

This conversation did in fact take place several weeks after Tyrrell's trip to Washington, but it is quite probable that these circles were already advocating such perspectives in November and December.

The successes of the revolutionaries had contributed further to this shift in attitude among many British companies. "The spread of the unrest, the successes of the revolutionaries, and the increasingly large damages suffered by foreigners in Mexico as a result of the revolution," high-level analysts in the French Foreign Ministry reported, "are changing the attitudes of economic circles in London. People there fear that they overestimated Huerta's capabilities and that they may have supported him too unthinkingly. At the same time that this attitude is spreading in business circles, the position of the secretary of Sir Edward Grey, Sir William Tyrrell, who is strongly pro-American and who just returned from the United States, is rapidly improving in the Foreign Office."[88]

American diplomacy did not limit its efforts to depriving Huerta of British support. It simultaneously waged a fight to restrict British investments in Mexico as well as in the rest of Latin America. Wilson had made this aim clear in his speech at Mobile, and it was again stressed by Walter Page, the American ambassador to Britain, in a speech to British businessmen on 19 March 1914. The United States, he said, "will warmly welcome your investments in all parts of the Americas on the condition that these investments do not give you control of the country in question. The Monroe Doctrine, as you know, means only one thing—that the United States would prefer that no European government annex any further countries in the new world. In those days, there was only one way for a foreign government to acquire territory, and that was to actually conquer the country. Today there are much more refined ways of conquering countries."[89]

The struggle initially began on 13 September 1913, when the U.S. State Department delivered a note in Brussels to all governments who had recognized Huerta: "The President regards all contracts as illegal and void since Huerta assumed despotic authority and all laws passed by the Mexican Congress as non-existent, and that it seems advisable to so inform the would-be concessionaires."[90]

Success was not long in coming. On 12 November 1913, Sir William Tyrrell assured the American ambassador in London that Cowdray had obtained no new concessions in Mexico and that, in any case, Great Britain would refuse to recognize such concessions if they were granted.[91]

The offensive against Cowdray was now extended to other Latin American countries, and particularly to Colombia, Costa Rica, and Nicaragua. Full of bitterness, Cowdray wrote on 24 November 1913: "the American Government did not scruple to bring diplomatic pressure to bear upon Colombia to such an extent as to prevent the Colombian Government ratifying the contract it had made with us for the exploration of oil in that country . . . . They have brought similar pressure . . . to bear on two other American countries in which we were prospectively interested."[92] When the American ambassador in London learned of this, he congratulated Cowdray. "He [Lord Cowdray] told me this morning that he (through Lord Murray) had withdrawn the request for any concession in Colombia. I congratulated him. 'That, Lord Cowdray, will save you as well as some other people I know a good deal of possible trouble.'"[93]

Inspired by these successes, Ambassador Page wrote to Wilson several months later: "I believe that if Taft (let us say) had had another four years, Cowdray would have owned Mexico, Ecuador and Colombia, or so much of them as he cared for, with such a grip on their Governments as would have amounted to a mortgage. He could have controlled them at any time and in any essential way he chose. The more I see and hear and learn, the surer I become that these countries owe their freedom from this dictatorship to you—for which release you will never get the credit or the thanks you deserve . . . . The British Government will not risk displeasing us for them."[94]

The substance of this "freedom" was that the concession in Colombia was granted to the Latin America Petroleum Company, a subsidiary of the Standard Oil Company.[95] In view of such an American policy, it is no surprise that Sir Edward Tyrrell had already told Bryan in November 1913: "Mr. Secretary, you are talking just like a Standard Oil man. The ideas that you hold are the ones which the Standard Oil is disseminating. You are pursuing the policy which they have decided on. Without knowing it, you are promoting the interest of Standard Oil."[96]

Huerta's dissolution of the Mexican parliament had not only demonstrated to Wilson Great Britain's influence on the Huerta regime, but had also shown him how weak Gamboa and the Catholic Party—the forces he had counted on—actually were. American policy thus underwent a complete turn. In the first weeks after Huerta's coup, the American government attempted to exploit the revolution to exercise a large degree of control over Mexico. On 30 October, Wilson asked Carranza's approval for an American intervention in Mexico. American warships were to blockade the Mexican ports and American troops "would occupy the Mexican cities to protect the lives and property of foreigners,"[97] while the revolutionaries carried on the struggle against Huerta. This plan failed because Carranza opposed it and broke off negotiations with Wilson's representative, Hale, when it was proposed.[98]

At the same time, representatives of the American general staff approached Carranza with a proposal to decree the separation of northern Mexico from the rest of the country, but this, too, he rejected. On 19 January 1914, the Austrian ambassador in Washington reported:

> The German military attaché, Major von Herwarth, who is departing from here today, was good enough to allow me to peruse all reports of any relevance. Major von Herwarth enjoyed the special confidence of the general chief of staff, Major Gen. L. Wood, with whom he had on repeated occasions over the past months conducted discussions of the overall military and political situation in Mexico; moreover, he was confirmed in his assessment of the seriousness of the situation by all high-ranking officers of the War Department.... I learned first of all that Gen. Wood had already secretly contacted Carranza through emissaries in October of last year to sound him out on his probable reaction to a declaration of independence by the northern section of Mexico between the Rio Grande and the 26th parallel. It seems that Carranza, who necesarily saw the secession of the northern provinces merely as a prelude to their annexation by the northern neighbor, acted as a patriot and rejected this suggestion.[99]

It became clear that the American government had made a completely false estimation of Carranza. He was in no way willing to subordinate himself to the United States, but on the contrary made it clear that he would oppose an American intervention with all the means at his disposal. Recognition of this led to a new shift in American policy. Carranza's unreliability, in the eyes of the Americans, led to a new attempt to preserve the Huerta system, but without Huerta. Hintze reported that on 14 November the American government demanded of Huerta: "*(a)* the congress shall never assemble; *(b)* General Huerta must eliminate himself from the situation. Should these conditions be met, the United States will assume full responsibility for Huerta's life and well-being, and will not only recognize the new interim president, but will fully support him and promote a reconciliation with the rebels."[100]

The rationale for the first of these demands can probably be found in a statement Lind made to Hintze shortly before: "Carden supports Huerta and wants this Congress, that is elected by fraud and on order, to convene in order to pass laws on his or Cowdray's concessions.... we cannot allow this Congress to act as the legally constituted parliament, but the English want it just to carry through some laws and concessions in their favor."[101] It was an attempt to restore the status quo. Huerta, however, showed no inclination whatever to step down; he was still convinced that he could count on British aid and hardly paid attention to the American proposals. This led to a new rupture in the negotiations between him and the American government.[102]

Wilson then adopted a wait-and-see attitude toward Mexico, which he maintained until early 1914. He may have wanted to eliminate all British support for Huerta prior to any further action, or perhaps he nourished the hope that Lieutenant Berthold, of the American naval formation anchored off Mazatlan, expressed to the captain of the German warship *Nürnberg:* "In November, there were plans for an intervention; these plans, however, were given up in the hope that both sides would be weakened to such an extent that they would have to ask the United States for help."[103]

### The United States and Mexico Early in 1914

In the first weeks of 1914, a new shift in the American attitude toward Mexico took place. The revolutionaries had continued their advance and already controlled more than half of Mexico by the end of January. Wilson now faced four options for his Mexico policies.

1. He could intervene militarily. The proposals he made to Carranza for joint military action at the end of 1913, his later, repeated interventions in Mexico as well as the American interventions in Haiti and Santo Domingo all indicate that in principle he did not shrink from military intervention as a means to achieve his goals. Such a step would nonetheless have tied the United States down in Mexico for years just at the time when tensions were increasing in Europe and when Japan had to be reckoned with. For this reason, an intervention was seen only as a last resort.

2. Wilson could recognize Huerta. This would have been a capitulation by the American president which he could never have countenanced. There were, moreover, no forces pushing him to take such a step: the European powers had given him a free hand in Mexico, and the large American interests there were for most part backing Carranza.

3. He could try to bring about the appointment of another representative of Mexico's ruling class to replace Huerta as president. As in the past, this was the solution that probably would have been most welcome to

the majority in the American government and to the American interests, despite their temporary collaboration with Carranza, because the old Díaz regime would essentially be preserved in such a move. Both Huerta's stubbornness and the new balance of forces in Mexico, however, worked against such a solution. In a discussion with Hintze, who had repeatedly proposed a solution similar to that attempted with Gamboa, Lind, Wilson's representative in Mexico, declared that "the rebels have won so much territory and are so sure of their final victory that they cannot be pushed aside but must be taken into account in the negotiations."[104]

4. The American president could at least partially recognize the Constitutionalists. Since the three other options could not be exercised, Wilson had no choice but to take this path. This step was made easier for him by the fact that many large American interests, especially the oil companies, were collaborating with Carranza and that Carranza's representative had pledged to the American government that American concessions would be respected under all circumstances.[105]

On 3 February 1914, Wilson lifted the arms embargo on Mexico and recognized the revolutionaries as a belligerent party, thereby allowing them to purchase arms legally in the United States.[106] Wilson had thus placed himself clearly behind the insurgents, but they very quickly dashed the hopes the American government had placed in them, for they were in no way prepared to subordinate themselves to the American government, as the "Benton affair" demonstrated.

William Benton was a British landowner who held an important hacienda in northern Mexico. Benton had a long history of conflict with peasants living on lands adjacent to his estate. Villa, after his victory in Chihuahua, had allowed the inhabitants of a village close to Benton's hacienda to graze their cattle there. When Benton learned of this, he became furious and went to see Villa. There was an altercation, and Benton was killed. Of course, reports of what happened are contradictory. When Benton's death produced an international uproar, Villa stated officially that Benton had attempted to draw a pistol against him and that he was brought before a court martial, sentenced to death, and executed.[107] It was a version very few people believed and in a conversation with the British consul in Torreón Villa himself conceded that events had been quite different. The consul, Cunard Cummins, reported to the Foreign Office,

> In Gomez Palacio some years ago at the time when I had to exert almost daily a restraining influence on Villa, he more than once endeavoured to clear himself of responsibility for the death of Benton. At a later period when he was in this City as the chief leader of the triumphant movement

of that day he again mentioned his defense when I reminded him that this charge against him was not withdrawn.

His version of what occurred is briefly as follows: He was with difficulty dominating a large force of armed men composed of criminals and desperados, men from whom he could not permit a disrespectful word and hold his position as commander. A foreigner entered his head-quarters and in loud unmeasured terms upbraided and defied him. Suddenly the foreigner on whose head the perspiration was visible passed rapidly his hand to his hip pocket and Fierro, the man who acted as Villa's bodyguard, believing Benton was about to draw a pistol, immediately shot him. It then appeared that the victim had reached for his handkerchief. Villa admits anger had arisen and high words were being exchanged.

It seems that Villa expressed regret to the widow, a Mexican woman, and promised to ensure that she is not defrauded of her husband's property.[108]

Benton's execution provoked strong reaction in Great Britain, and the British government asked the American government to investigate the affair. With this step, the British wanted to document their support of Huerta and their nonrecognition of Carranza and to make clear that they viewed the insurgents strictly as U.S. agents, and at the same time to make the United States responsible for every attack on British property in Mexico.[109]

The American government was pleased with the British maneuver, for it was interpreted as a recognition of the Monroe Doctrine in its most explicit form, that is, of the United States as a mediator in all quarrels between European and Latin American states. Bryan immediately demanded that Villa send Benton's body to the United States for the investigation. Villa, for his part, was prepared to do so, but Carranza, his superior, to whom Bryan also addressed himself, quite simply refused to fulfill this demand. He stated that he would involve himself with the Benton affair only if the British government sent him a request to that effect.[110] He was influenced in this stance by three considerations: first, he wished to force Great Britain into a de facto recognition of his government; second, he was afraid of being seen as an American agent by many Mexicans if he bowed to the American demands; and, finally, he wanted to avoid any, even implicit recognition of the Monroe Doctrine.

Carranza's attitude provoked an intensified interventionist campaign in the United States, and the demand for armed American intervention in Mexico grew increasingly loud both in the press and in the U.S. Senate. The relations between the American government and the Mexican revolutionaries again cooled, and the American government therefore renewed steps to bring about an agreement with the Huerta government on the basis of a Gamboa-style settlement. The foreign minister of the Huerta government, López Portillo, told Hintze that at the end of March Lind had proposed to him "making Gamboa's second note, in which the latter asserts the impossibility of the current president's candidacy in new elections as provided by the constitution, as the point of departure for new negotiations based on a temporary vacating of office by Huerta with his simultaneous candidacy for the next election."[111]

The lifting of the American weapons embargo made it possible for the revolutionaries to continue their advance with greater force. In April 1914, they captured the extremely important railway center of Torreón. New revolts erupted in many parts of the country. The bankers and the governments who had initially supported Huerta financially and diplomatically for the most part withdrew their support under pressure from the United States. In spite of the extremely difficult situation in which the Huerta regime found itself at the end of 1913 and the beginning of 1914, it was able, surprisingly enough, to hold out until July 1914.

If one seeks the cause of this fact, the question arises, above all, of why the Huerta government showed such solidity, in contrast to the Díaz government, which had capitulated after relatively insignificant victories by the revolutionaries. When Díaz announced his resignation in 1911, his troops controlled a larger part of the country than did Huerta's troops at the beginning of 1914. The United States, while not favorably disposed toward Díaz, had not openly turned against him, as it did later against Huerta. Where, then, are the causes of the relative tenacity and stability of the Huerta government, by comparison with the Díaz dictatorship, to be found? The answer lies essentially in the attitude of the old ruling strata of Mexico, that is the large landowners, the clergy, and the army.

Díaz's resignation in 1911 did not signify a definite defeat for the old ruling strata. They had in fact accepted Madero as president, but in no way consented to any social changes; they succeeded primarily in preserving the Díaz bureaucracy and the old army at the same time that the revolutionary armed forces were dismantled. A settlement on such a basis with the revolutionaries of 1913/14, who had come to see the consequences of the treaty of Ciudad Juárez in the form of Huerta's takeover, was no longer possible. While Zapata and Villa simply refused any agreement with the ruling strata, Carranza inclined more willingly toward compromise. His refusal to accept social demands in the Guadalupe Plan because he did not want to antagonize the ruling classes was intended as a sign of this willingness. But he lacked the authority Madero possessed in 1913, and above all he could not and did not want to comply with the most important demands of the ruling strata: preservation of the old federal army and dissolution of the revolutionary armies.

The impossibility of a compromise and the fear that their property would be expropriated and the army dismantled made the struggle against the revolutionaries a question of life or death for the old ruling strata and for the officer caste of the old army. This explains their stubborn and relentless resistance to the revolution and their willingness to give financial support to Huerta after the European sources of money had begun to dry up.

The struggle against the United States, however, was in no way in the interest of the entire ruling stratum of Mexico, for a majority of its members were not tied to British capital and feared total defeat in a simultaneous struggle against the revolution and the United States. These circles had put up Gamboa as presidential candidate in the summer of 1913 and were seeking a compromise with Wilson. Huerta's final break with the United States confronted them with tremendous problems. While they wholeheartedly repudiated Huerta's anti-American policy, they nonetheless had no possibility of imposing their objectives. They could not unleash an insurrection, for to do so would only have aided the revolutionaries. Moreover, Huerta had been able to bring the officer corps of the army over to his side by making concessions to them and by offering them possibilities for enrichment that were unparalleled in Mexican history. Hintze, who sympathized with Huerta, provided a lucid analysis of the situation:

> The army, consisting of the most dubious elements . . . without capable leaders, with corrupt generals at its head, marches from defeat to defeat. For the most part, of course, it does nothing. Like General Velasco, for example, who has been on the march from Hipólito to Torreón since the 22d of last month, with the alleged aim of retaking this important place from the rebels. Huerta knows all about the knavery and sins of his generals, but he does not dare move against them: "If I forbid the army to steal, it will revolt against me." Nor does he dare call to task the leaders who have been guilty of the shameful surrender of places entrusted to them, or of ignominious flight. Munguía, who gave up Torreón without resistance, and Escudero, who abandoned Durango without firing a shot, were brought for appearance's sake before a military court, which disqualified itself, and then rewarded with new posts; Munguía has even been recently promoted to division general, the highest military honor! Rubio Navarrete, who a few weeks ago was not only abysmally defeated—he lost every cannon—but was decimated on the retreat, is now leading a new column in the north. The criterion for generals in Huerta's eyes is not whether they are capable or honest, but whether they are loyal to him.[112]

The tenacity of the Huerta government, however, cannot be explained solely by the support of Mexico's ruling strata. It was based at least as much on the hidden but nonetheless effective diplomatic and economic support of the Carden-Cowdray group in Mexico.

Carden's attitude after British diplomacy's retreat from Mexico was characterized in Hintze's words: "On the questions that concern the countries with the largest interests here, the British minister has publicly, since November 13, done a complete about-face—in favor of American policy. He has even asked me to decline the—quite customary—invitation to the opening of the new congress on November 20, 'because the American press had sharply criticized his audience with the government immediately following the dissolution of the old congress.' Privately, however, he is working in the same fashion as before."[113]

Carden was active in three areas. First, with the promise of British support, he encouraged Huerta to remain in power and functioned throughout as his closest advisor and confidant. The extent and the nature of their collaboration is characterized in Hintze's report of 3 February 1914: "On January 23, a larger conspiracy was discovered, on January 30 another. On January 24, twenty suspects had already been summarily executed, half of them military, half civilian. Since then, five or six suspects have nightly been dragged from their beds, taken to the outskirts of the city and hanged or shot, after which they are covered with gasoline and burned. I get the details on the disclosure of these conspiracies from the British minister, who as Huerta's confidant is initiated into all mysteries of his governments."[114]

Second, Carden attempted to incite French and German diplomats to a decisive move against American policy in Mexico. He thereby wished on the one hand to bolster Huerta and on the other to put pressure on British diplomacy. At the beginning of December 1913, shortly before the British-American agreement on Mexico, he proposed to the French and German ministers that the European powers jointly land troops in Mexico, and in so doing asserted that Huerta had given his approval to such a project. Carden probably had no directives of this kind from London, but wished only to suggest such a venture to the French and Germans so that they in turn would put pressure on British policy. His plan failed, however, since both the German and French diplomats rejected it.[115]

Roughly seven weeks later, at the end of January 1914, Carden made another attempt. He showed to the French minister Lefaivre an excerpt of a telegram from Grey in which Grey, on the basis of a discussion with British bankers, suggested a joint venture by the European powers to force Huerta's resignation. Carden at this point wanted to convince the European diplomats that the telegram contained the exact opposite and that Grey had proposed an armed intervention by the European powers in Mexico. He urged Hintze and Lefaivre to win over their governments for a military intervention in Mexico, at the same time seeking to toughen his proposal: "He [Carden] knows the United States from the activities and experiences of a long life and is convinced that however much the United States might bully and blast, they would live with a fait accompli; in fact, they would be scared to death by an intervention of the three powers."[116]

Finally, Carden attempted to win over the Foreign Office. He told Hintze one of the most important arguments he used in this effort: "Very few people in England grasp the real goal of American policy; they and public opinion do not understand that it is not Mexico but the entire continent which is at stake. The United States may have told them that they want to stop at the Panama Canal; they will never do so. Once they have gotten that far, they will of necessity take Colombia, since there are places there which are convenient for the construction of another canal. Then comes Brazil; the Northern regions have always had a certain inclination to break away from the country, and the United States would help them to do so, and from there it's on to Cape Horn."[117] And, he claimed, all the undersecretaries of state in the Foreign Office as well as Foreign Secretary Grey agreed with this view.[118]

In order to reach his goal, Carden attempted to win over the British navy and army, which were then to put pressure on the Foreign Office. After the British minister had invited Admiral Craddock, who was commanding the British fleet in Mexican waters, to visit Mexico City, Hintze reported on a conversation he had had with his British colleague: "He [Carden] wants to influence the Admiralty through Craddock, and beyond that the War Office, through the military attaché he has requested from Washington (First Lieutenant Gage); when the same complaint arrives in London from three different places, Sir Edward Grey will really have to think about what his policy of 'a free hand for the United States' is provoking here."[119]

The Foreign Office was, however, no longer prepared to undertake an anti-American venture in Mexico. Grey's sole move was a proposal made at the beginning of 1914 to replace Huerta with a candidate from his entourage who was acceptable to the Americans.[120] The British foreign secretary had thereby embraced the same orientation that the Germans had. In his proposal to the State Department, Grey indicated that he was basing his calculations on the support of Germany and France on this question.[121] The American government, however, had in the meantime backed the revolutionaries and refused this proposal. The United States knew that England, which in November had announced its withdrawal from Mexico, would take no steps to implement Grey's proposal.

In 1914, when Benton was executed by Villa's troops, it seemed for a moment as if Carden's hopes had better prospects of fulfillment. With unconcealed cynicism, he told Hintze that Benton's execution "was a lucky incident'' and said: ''We shall make the most of it.''[122] In both the British press and in Parliament, a storm of outrage erupted. The newspapers sharply condemned the policy of withdrawal from Mexico and demanded an energetic British response, in which an armed intervention was not ruled out.[123] Similar calls were heard in Parliament, both from Conservative and Liberal quarters. On 26 February Grey praised the United States ''which has concerned itself with the Benton affair as if he were an American citizen,''[124] but only a week later, on 3 March, he stated that the British government, if it received no amends from the revolutionaries, would unilaterally take the steps it considered necessary.[125]

The British circles that had mounted the campaign around the Benton affair were not all pursuing the same ends. For the Cowdray group, it was a means of bringing about an anti-American and pro-Huerta shift in British policy. But for the groups around Grey it was to be a means of pressuring the United States to take steps in implementing Wilson's still unfulfilled promise to review the tolls for the Panama Canal. Wilson in fact asked the Senate on 5 March 1914 for a review of the Panama Canal fees with the remark that he could not otherwise see ''how the questions of a much more delicate nature and of greater importance could be dealt with.''[126] The issue of ''greater importance'' was Mexico. It did in fact appear to be a ''delicate'' question, for as early as 31 March, the law on Panama Canal tolls was approved by the American Congress.

After Wilson's appearance before the Senate, the British campaign around the Benton affair came to an end. Grey also rejected a resolution of the British colony in Mexico City calling for strong British action in the wake of the Benton affair.[127] The British government indicated that it was yielding to the United States by recalling Carden to Great Britain for a briefing. Thomas Hohler was nominated to replace him as chargé d'affaires; as he told Hintze, ''to maintain agreement with the American representative and to work jointly with him was the sole instruction which Sir Edward Grey had given him in the course of a one-hour discussion of the Mexican problem; [Grey] spent the rest of the time complaining about the misunderstandings that had arisen with the United States.''[128]

For Carden, in contrast to his chief, the foreign secretary, the Benton affair was a means of pursuing the same policy he had attempted to implement from the first day he had set foot on Mexican soil—to prevent U.S. intervention and/or a victory of the revolutionaries. He had hoped that the Benton case would force Grey to revise his policy and give up what Carden considered the foreign secretary's surrender to American policy in Mexico.

Was Carden alone in pursuing such a policy? Was it the last and lonely stand of an old and embittered diplomat consumed by his hatred for both the Americans and the Mexican revolutionaries?

There is strong evidence that Cowdray's policies proceeded along similar lines to those of the British minister and that both shared the same basic aim of preventing a unilateral American intervention and resulting U.S. supremacy as well as a victory of the constitutionalists.

It was along these lines that in January 1914, Cowdray seriously attempted to convince the American ambassador in Britain, Walter H. Page, who until then had been his most ardent opponent, of the necessity of a joint U.S.-European intervention in Mexico. It was a grandiose scheme whose implementation could have led to U.S. control of northern Mexico while the Europeans (and especially the British) would have assumed control of Mexico's oil fields.

Cowdray first attempted to show the ambassador that the Mexican people were incapable of being ruled by democratic means and that the revolutionaries were really unprincipled bandits. "I stated," Cowdray wrote in a memorandum on his conversation with Page, "that there was no patriotism in the country . . . that everybody knowing Mexico realized that every man taking an active part in Mexico, at the present time, was out for himself and himself alone."

This led Cowdray to arrive at the conclusion "the country must be ruled by a strong hand or by a semi-constitutional one, supported by foreign troops."

Above all, the British oil magnate wished to impress on the American representative that a unilateral U.S. intervention in Mexico would be "a very long and troublesome affair. . . . Their commissariate would be subject to daily attack while the Mexican easily carried a week's supply of food on his back."

Cowdray told Page that there was one way to restore order in Mexico, to prevent the United States from getting bogged down there, and to achieve results with a minimum amount of fighting. "I feel that if there were international intervention the probabilities were that no armed intervention would be necessary, although, of course, such an intervention would be abortive unless it were understood it would become active in case of necessity."

Cowdray intimated that both Huerta and Mexico's upper classes would welcome such international intervention and that U.S. prestige would be bolstered by it and then stated what to him was certainly the most important project: British control of the oil region. He told Page that

those nations who had recognized Huerta would naturally explain to him that as the position in Mexico is considerably worse today than what it was when he took over the government some nine or ten months ago, they felt now that it was time that they joined hands with the U.S. to bring about peace.

That the whole of the Mexicans would feel thankful for international intervention as it would avoid the active intervention of the United

States alone which it was felt must come sooner or later if settled conditions were going to prevail. While the better class of Mexican might refrain from giving outward support to such international intervention they would nevertheless welcome it. That such intervention would save the face of everybody. That the U.S. could look after the rebels of the north, while the European nations could be looking after the country tributary to Tampico, Veracruz and Puerto Mexico. That owing to it having been fully expected that Washington was going to actively intervene, and which never came off, that it might be necessary for the international intervention to actually land a few troops to show they really meant business, but that in my opinion, there would be no real fighting or trouble.

The American ambassador, who in all his public utterances in Great Britain was constantly expounding on the Wilsonian concept that foreign nations or interests should not be able to exercise any decisive power in Latin America, on the whole agreed with Cowdray's suggestions. "He appeared to be most personally favorable to the idea." His only reservation according to Cowdray was that the U.S. image might suffer "as the American nations would think it would be considered to be shirking its own responsibilities" if it asked for assistance. He was also worried about the financial cost of such an intervention.

Ideologically, Page had no reservations at all about Cowdray's subsequent suggestions which would have practically converted Mexico into a protectorate of the great powers. Cowdray had proposed that "an international commission would have to be responsible for a time for the administration; to do this it would be necessary to effectively control the army, finances and justice."[129]

One of the reasons why Page responded so positively to Cowdray's suggestions was that only a short while before, he himself had made a proposal along similar lines to Colonel House.[130] Both Page and Cowdray were wary of anything becoming known about their project:

it was understood that our talks were strictly confidential, that my name had not to be mentioned in connection with it in any shape or form...and that he had merely been speaking as a private individual and not as a representative of a nation.

When I asked him if I might mention what we had talked about to our Foreign Office he said of course he could not prevent me but I must make it perfectly clear that he had not either as an individual or as the ambassador suggested that the assistance of England and other nations was required or asked for. At the same time if England cared to move, its suggestions would be gladly listened to.[131]

When Cowdray and Page discussed these options, they may have known that similar proposals had been put forth by Germany a short while before (chap. 6). This may have been one of the reasons why both men agreed that Germany would have to participate in such a joint intervention.

These proposals nevertheless did not have the least chance of ever being implemented, for Woodrow Wilson remained adamantly opposed to any European military presence in Mexico.

There are indications that the failure of this proposal did not prevent Cowdray from refusing to accept Grey's capitulation to Wilson or keep him from looking for new ways of preventing U.S. intervention or victory of the revolutionaries. He was infused with a strong sense of optimism about events in Mexico when Carden returned to Britain for a brief stay in March 1914. In a letter to his representative in Mexico Cowdray wrote on 14 March

> Carden arrived some three or four days ago. He is emphatic in his opinion that the President will pull through, and referred to the conditions of the army; he explains that Blanquet advised him that they had 110,000 men in the field, in addition to 40,000 rurales. He pointed out that the government controls that part of the country holding about four-fifths of the population of the republic, thus having unlimited sources of recruiting for the army, and of carrying on the government of the country without foreign assistance; that the Constitutionalists have their maximum strength now, without further recruiting grounds, and control nothing but a devastated country devoid of resources.

Cowdray fully agreed with this assessment of the British minister. "His optimism is very comforting; in fact, Limantour, who was in London and whom he saw, left feeling happier about the prospects of Mexico than he had felt for many a long day.... The position today may therefore be summarized with the conclusion that the Constitutionalists, without further resources of men or money must be whipped and dispersed in small banded gangs; that intervention will not take place, and that the conditions generally will gradually improve."[132]

Other British enterprises in Mexico may not have shared Lord Cowdray's optimism about the prospect for Huerta victory but in view of the experiences of British interests in the territories controlled by the revolutionaries, they were no less worried than the British oil magnate about the possibilities of either U.S. intervention or victory of the Constitutionalists.

In the region controlled by Villa, a syndicate had formed under the leadership of the American newspaper baron Hearst for the purchase of mines, haciendas, and goods in Mexico; the syndicate's representative was the American special agent to Villa, Carothers. When Villa captured the city of Torreón, he confiscated $800,000 worth of cotton warehoused at British haciendas and turned it over to the syndicate, which shipped it through the United States for sale in Canada. The British ambassador to the United States, Sir Cecil Spring Rice, thereupon lodged an energetic protest with the State Department. "In response to Spring Rice's request that the cotton be confiscated in El Paso, where the landowners had taken refuge and where they could have made their claims stick, they were referred instead to the courts," reported the Austrian ambassador in Washington. "The State Department knows this and nonetheless refuses to replace Carothers with a new special agent, because it would have to request an exequatur for him from Huerta or Carranza. This cheap legalism and the increasing indifference to the loss of human life and property in northern Mexico prompted Sir Cecil Spring Rice to compare the American government with the government in Timbuktu."[133]

When the financial situation of the Mexican government became desperate in March and April 1914, Cowdray and the British financiers around him decided to help Huerta.

In spite of his optimism and his desire to support Huerta, Cowdray, and other British interests in Mexico probably as well, realized that such help could be very costly. "The other side of the picture," Cowdray wrote, "is that Huerta is wanting money and will have it from the sources most easily available. In consequence, foreign corporations of Mexican industries have before them a very hard, trying, and ruinous time, until the Mexican Government's expenditure can be reduced, or until the country is in such a condition as will justify foreign bankers advancing the Government further sums."[134]

Overt British financial help could also easily lead to renewed British-American frictions. With some reluctance Cowdray and other British enterprises in Mexico now decided to help the Mexican dictator out financially. Such aid could only be provided, however, in indirect and camouflaged form if a British-American rupture were to be averted.

One of the first steps toward financial aid for the Huerta regime was a loan of 45 million pesos. It was not the big European banks but their branches in Mexico which provided the loan. They claimed to have taken such a step under compulsion, for Huerta had threatened them with creation of a state bank and the imposition of a 1 percent capital tax; moreover, a portion of the proceeds of this loan were to help in the payment of foreign loans.[135]

Nevertheless, Cowdray had no intention of single-handedly or even principally financing Huerta. As he had indicated in his letter to his representative in Mexico, his main hope was that bankers would relieve him of this burden by extending a loan to the Mexican president. In the first months of 1914, Huerta did receive a large surreptitious loan from British bankers in order to enable him to buy arms (see chap. 6). While there is no direct evidence linking Cowdray to this loan, his stated interest in securing it and the primary role of his companies in Mexico as far as British investments in that country were concerned, all point to some involvement of his in an affair—the massive shipments of arms to Huerta—that nearly brought on a Mexican-American war.

## The Landing in Veracruz

The developments in Mexico from February through April 1914 corresponded less and less to the desires and ideas of the American president and his government. On the one hand, Huerta, with the support of Mexico's ruling classes and the financial aid of European banks, was holding out much longer than Wilson had expected. On the other hand, Woodrow Wilson felt more and more uneasy about his relationship with the revolutionaries. What he had envisaged from the first day when his administration had gotten in touch with the Constitutionalists was a paternalistic relationship with them. It would be up to the American president to decide what was good not only for Mexico but also for the revolutionaries. Until October 1913, Wilson had attempted to use the Constitutionalists to secure aims they themselves fiercely opposed: under the combined pressure of the United States and the revolutionaries Wilson had hoped that Huerta would resign and be replaced by Gamboa or another associate. The result of such a "solution" would have been the maintenance of the federal army whose elimination was one of the main aims of the revolutionaries.

Carranza had unequivocally told Wilson's representative that he would not accept such a solution.[136] After Huerta's dissolution of Parliament in October and his election as president, Wilson had decided to throw his full support to the revolutionaries. At this point he felt even more strongly the need to be able to exercise control over his allies. With this aim in mind he had proposed to Carranza in October 1913 that United States troops occupy a large part of Mexico while the Constitutionalists did the actual fighting against Huerta. Carranza again refused to accept the American president's proposal.[137] Wilson at that time felt that he had no choice but to comply with the Mexican leader's wishes and to withdraw his plan for massive U.S. intervention in Mexico. He now gave increasing support to the revolutionaries by both diplomatic means and arms supplies, hoping thus to ensure his control over them. But this aid did not make the Mexican leader more pliable. Carranza's refusal to accept Wilson's proposals after Benton's death showed the American president that he would need to utilize more direct means if he wished to exercise any greater degree of influence on the course of the Mexican revolution.

These developments aroused in Wilson an increasing desire for direct intervention in Mexico, which would secure for the United States a key position in the country and thereby permit it the opportunity of exercising great influence over Mexico's future development. In April 1914, in fact, Wilson appears to have decided to undertake an armed action in Mexico. He was provided with the necessary pretext by a minor incident that occurred on 9 April.

An officer and seven crew members of the American cruiser *Dolphin*, anchored in the Mexican harbor of Tampico, were sent ashore to purchase fuel. When they landed, they were arrested by Huerta's troops on the pretext that the port was in a state of emergency and that no unauthorized persons were allowed on shore. When Huerta's general in command in Tampico learned of the arrests—exactly two hours had elapsed—he immediately had them freed and expressed his regret over the incident.

This was not enough for the American admiral, Henry T. Mayo. He demanded a formal apology from Mexico and assurance that the Mexican officer responsible for the arrests, Colonel Ramón Hinojosa, himself be placed under arrest; in addition, the Mexicans were to atone for this incident by raising the American flag and honoring it with a twenty-one-gun salute. The ultimatum was to expire at 6 P.M.

The commander of the Tampico garrison sent an official apology and had the responsible officer arrested, but requested an extension of the deadline with regard to the twenty-one-gun salute because the question could only be decided by the president himself. Huerta, for his part, saw in the refusal of this American demand a possibility for giving his collapsing regime a patriotic hue, and he rejected it.

There then ensued an exchange of notes between Huerta and the American government which would have been comic had its consequences not been tragic and bloody. Huerta responded to renewed American demands for a cannon salute by declaring himself willing to order such a salvo if the United States would salute the Mexican flag in the same fashion. He simultaneously proposed to bring the entire affair before the international court of arbitration in The Hague. The American government, however, rejected these proposals. Since Huerta continued to refuse to meet the American demands, on 20 April Wilson requested from both houses of Congress full powers for an armed intervention in Mexico. These powers were granted to him by a vote of 323 to 29.

Wilson had worked out plans for an occupation of Veracruz, Tampico, and Mexico City. All preparations were completed and almost the entire American fleet had been sent to Mexican waters. Wilson initially wanted to attack at the end of April, but a report that arrived in the interim prompted him to advance the date. On the night of 21 April, more precisely, he learned that the German steamer *Ypiranga* was en route to Veracruz with a large shipment of weapons for Huerta on board. To prevent Huerta from receiving these weapons, Wilson on the same night ordered the American fleet to occupy the customs house in Veracruz. He was further encouraged in this action by the report of the local American consul that Huerta's troops would offer no resistance.

On 21 April, American marines landed in Veracruz. Huerta's General Maas withdrew his troops from the city, but, against his orders, the cadets of the naval academy as well as individual soldiers and volunteers fought back against the Americans. The fighting lasted more than twelve hours. The fire power of the American naval artillery and the absence of any support from the Huerta government forced the defenders to retreat. On 22 April, after 126 Mexicans and 19 Americans had been killed, Veracruz was firmly in American hands.[138]

Reaction to this attack both in Mexico and in the United States was far more negative than Wilson had anticipated. Throughout Mexico, large anti-American demonstrations took place, and thousands of Mexicans offered themselves as volunteers for Huerta's army in the belief they would be used against the American troops.

Wilson had told Carranza nothing of his plans for an attack on Veracruz. The conference at Nogales in November 1913 had shown Wilson that Carranza would never agree to joint action with the Americans, but Wilson was hoping for benevolent neutrality from him. Carranza, however, had quite a different view of the matter. In a sharply worded note to the American government, Carranza demanded the withdrawal of American troops from Veracruz and stated: "The invasion of our territory, the stationing of American troops in the port of Veracruz, the violation of our rights as a sovereign, free, and independent state could provoke us to an unequal but just war, which we wish to avoid."[139]

It is not clear that Carranza seriously contemplated a confrontation with the United States. In any case, such a project, to the extent it was actually considered, was averted by a declaration by Villa in which he distanced himself from Carranza and refused to condemn the American occupation of Veracruz. On 28 April, Villa and Carranza decided to offer no resistance to the Americans if they did not attack the areas controlled by the revolutionaries.[140] Nevertheless, a further advance by the Americans could have forced them to change their minds. Wilson was perfectly aware of this danger of a general Mexican-American war.

In the United States there arose powerful opposition to further action in Mexico. Thousands of members of trade unions, peace organizations, church associations, and other groups sent telegrams of protest to Wilson.[141] This widespread opposition to U.S. intervention in Mexico was matched at the other end of the political spectrum by groups demanding an extension of U.S. intervention.

Leading American military figures came out in favor of an occupation of a large part of Mexico. As early as November 1913, the American chief of staff Leonard Wood had emphasized the significance of Mexico's oil to the German military attaché Herwarth von Bittenfeld. According to the German official's report, Wood had stated: "These oil reserves, as well as the fact that Lord Cowdray, could, because of the Pearson concessions, still develop very lucrative wells from south of the capital right up to the border, present the danger that a large maritime petroleum station could develop inside the Canal Zone which would be primarily at the disposal of the British Admiralty. The United States could not tolerate this; it would be better to play it safe and to secure the necessary stations for the American naval and merchant fleet through an active intervention."[142] Some American military leaders viewed with condescension Wilson's "idealistic" justifications for his policy and wanted clear language. Thus, according to a report by Bittenfeld, General MacIntyre, of the Insular Bureau of the War Department, stated:

> We want to have public opinion on our side, but how are we attempting to bring that about? We preach to the crowd that we must guarantee legal elections and order in our sister republic, knowing full well that in the half-civilized Latin American countries almost every change of government is achieved not through elections but through revolutions: what then is the point of this hypocrisy? Why don't we use our press to make it clear to the entire country that vital interests related to the Panama Canal are at stake here which are infinitely more important for the future of the nation and the world power status of the United States than the murder of Madero, a bloodthirsty Huerta or any other usurper in the president's office?[143]

After the seizure of Veracruz, Secretary Garrison, of the War Department, advocated an attack on Mexico City. American settlers in Mexico, the railway companies, and the oil concerns called for the occupation of the capital. The spokesmen for the oil companies, Senator Fall of New Mexico and Senator Lodge of Massachusetts, introduced a resolution in the Senate that would empower President Wilson to dispatch troops throughout Mexico "to protect American life and property." It is probable that this group had the support of Doheny. The resolution was, nonetheless, defeated in the U.S. Senate.[144]

The pressure from opponents of further American intervention in Mexico and the fear of being tied down in Mexico at a moment when international tensions were on the increase finally caused the American government to give up its plans. The Austrian minister in Mexico reported that Admirals Badger and Fletcher, who commanded the American naval squadron in Veracruz, explained Wilson's attitude to American officers who were pressuring for an advance on Mexico City by the fact "that the

President wanted to avoid an engagement of American military forces that might last for years. Should American troops, more precisely, press on to Mexico City, the United States would then be obligated to oversee the complete pacification of the country, which would, given the enormous expanse of Mexico and the well-known nature of the terrain, require years."[145] The renunciation of the plans for an extension of the American intervention in Mexico, however, in no way signified the abandonment of the American government's intentions of imposing on the country a government acceptable to itself. On the contrary. With Veracruz occupied and therefore already available as a pressure point, the American government undertook a large-scale action for the realization of its plans.

On the suggestion of the Secretary of State, the representatives of Argentina, Brazil, and Chile offered their mediation in the Mexican-American conflict on 25 April 1914. The purpose of such mediation, however, was not limited to the settlement of the differences, but aimed primarily at the creation of a new government satisfactory to the Americans. Washington submitted essentially four points to the mediating countries: (1) the dismissal of Huerta; (2) the appointment of a provisional president acceptable to both sides in Mexico from the ranks of the "neutrals" or the revolutionaries, while excluding Carranza and Villa from that office; (3) the appointment of a provisional government in which all groups, including Huerta's supporters, would be represented; and (4) the declaration of a cease-fire between the two contending sides.[146]

Reflected in these proposals was the American government's mistrust of the revolutionaries, which had been constantly increasing since the Benton incident and particularly since Carranza's protest against the American occupation of Veracruz. The Americans no longer doubted that a revolutionary victory was inevitable. The only way of preventing it would have been by further armed intervention, already rejected by the United States for the reasons cited previously. The purpose of its proposals was to weaken the revolutionaries and to bring the new government as much as possible into the American sphere. It was the attainment of this goal that dictated Carranza's exclusion from the planned provisional government, since he had come out most unambiguously against U.S. hegemony. The new president, even if he were to come from the ranks of the revolutionaries, would owe his power primarily to the American government, which would have a decisive say over his nomination, and he would thus attempt to orient himself to the United States. The inclusion of a pro-Huerta figure in the provisional government would also have weakened the power of the revolutionaries, while a cease-fire would preserve part of the old federal army and thereby provide a countervailing power against the revolutionary forces.

The plans for mediation encountered resistance both in the Huerta government and among the revolutionaries. While the obstacles thrown up by the Huerta government were cast aside as a result of U.S. pressures, the opposition of the revolutionaries brought about the complete failure of the plans for mediation.

The conference was opened on 22 April 1914, at Niagara Falls, on the Canadian-American border. Participants included delegates from the United States and the three mediating countries, Argentina, Brazil, and Chile, and representatives of Huerta. Carranza's delegates had refused to attend the conference. On the following day, Huerta announced through his delegate Emilio Rabasa that he was willing to step down "if a stable government is created which is in a position to include the necessary representatives of public opinion."[147] His attitude hardened, however, under the influence of Sir Lionel Carden.

Carden had been called to London early in 1914 for a briefing, and the British government had let it be known confidentially in Washington that it would recall Carden from Mexico and send him to Brazil. As a result of indiscretions in the American State Department, these plans became known before their execution. The British government therefore allowed Carden to remain at his post in order to avert the criticism that it was ceding to American pressure.[148]

Carden returned to Mexico in April 1914. Shortly after the beginning of the mediation conference, he had called for Huerta's ouster on the condition that "all his acts in office be legalized."[149] Hintze noted in this regard: "That simply means the legalization of all the favors and concessions Carden has won for the English with his rabid support for Huerta."[150] When his proposals proved unacceptable, Carden did another turnabout and encouraged Huerta to remain in power. At the same time, Cowdray's Light and Power Company and his El Aguila Oil Company provided Huerta with money.[151] It seems that Carden and Cowdray wanted to support Huerta until the United States recognized the concessions he had granted to Great Britain.

While this move by Carden served the interests of Cowdray, the continuation of the fighting which it brought about was extremely damaging for other British interests. "The stubbornness and passion with which this man [Carden], so close to his own demise, is able to activate his hatred of the United States, even to the detriment of his country and his compatriots, is striking."[152]

Carden's efforts were not without effect. The American secretary of state, after the appropriate feeler to Great Britain, proposed on 2 June 1914 that the governments of both countries regard the state of the oil concessions of 20 April 1914 as final and recognize no changes which any Mexican authorities might undertake.[153] The Americans thereby legalized all the concessions granted to British oil companies up to that date, renouncing in advance recognition of any expropriation of British oil fields on behalf of American firms. At the end of June 1914, this agreement was extended to mining rights.[154]

This settlement stood in contrast to Wilson's earlier statements that he would never recognize the concessions granted by Huerta. It is improbable that this American attitude was the result of British activity alone, for in May and June 1914 the British position in Mexico was weaker than ever. Not the least of the factors influencing such a policy was the increasing dissension between the American government and Carranza. It was quite possible that after his victory, Carranza would orient himself toward Great Britain just as Huerta had done, and the American government hoped to preclude this possibility in advance with such an agreement. In the wake of this agreement, Huerta appears to have received no further support from Cowdray. Similarly, Carden was instructed to offer no obstacles to American policy.

As his regime became weaker, as he lost the support of Europe, and as his troops retreated in growing disarray under the blows of the advancing revolutionaries, Huerta became more and more compliant. He was finally willing to grant every request of the Americans, in order to save at least some vestige of his regime. The enmity of the revolutionaries, however, destroyed any such hopes.

Carranza had initially agreed in principle to participate in the mediation discussions. When it became obvious, however, that it was not American-Mexican differences, but the internal situation in Mexico which was to be discussed there, he recalled his delegates with the explanation that those problems could be "solved only by Mexicans."[155] The American negotiators characterized this attitude: "They refuse to accept anything from the mediators...even when it is something they want.... They wouldn't even accept it if it were offered to them on a golden platter."[156]

Carranza rejected the mediators' demand for a cease-fire with Huerta and continued his advance on the capital. The American government then attempted to pressure him through a renewed arms embargo which it imposed on Mexico on 1 June.[157] The advance of the revolutionaries was to be stalled by closing off the supply of arms, until they yielded to American desires.

Carranza, however, was not impressed by this maneuver. In the middle of June, he had his delegates in Niagara Falls once again assert that the revolutionaries were at no price willing to negotiate the internal order of Mexico before an international forum. Carranza's stance finally caused the collapse of the entire mediation conference, and it ended on 5 July 1914, having achieved nothing.[158]

On 15 July 1914, when Huerta's military position was completely hopeless and he considered himself to be in immediate danger, he stepped down and appointed the Supreme Court member Francisco Carbajal as his successor. "I am," he declared on that occasion, "depositing the honor of a private man in the bank known as the conscience of the world."[159]

# 6 Germany and Huerta

## German Business Interests and the Huerta Regime

In 1913, the German financial circles involved in Mexico were in disarray, even if this disarray was less pronounced than that of the British and American financial groups.

Like their British and American colleagues, German businessmen and plantation owners were among the most enthusiastic supporters of the dictator, for they hoped that the Huerta regime would bring back the privileges and benefits of the Díaz era: legal favoritism for foreigners, prohibition of trade unions and strikes, and unlimited support for the system of indebted servitude in the countryside. This last benefit was primarily of interest to the German coffee planters in Chiapas though many German businessmen in other parts of the country had, over time, acquired haciendas. Since the German consuls in Mexico, with the exception of the consul general, were all businessmen or plantation owners who functioned as honorary consuls the mood in these circles was clearly expressed in their official reports.[1]

Other supporters of Huerta included the banks. Under Díaz these were known as the "German group" and were more closely associated with the Científicos: the Deutsche Bank, Bleichröder, and the Dresdner Bank. They provided 19 percent of a loan totaling 16 million pounds sterling for Huerta, which was signed in Paris on 8 June 1913 by an international bank consortium including the Banque de Paris et des Pays-Bas, J. P. Morgan and Company, and Kuhn Loeb and Company.[2] The conditions under which this loan was provided were particularly favorable. The banks purchased the paper for the loan at 90 percent of its nominal value and sold it at 96 percent. The Huerta regime had to commit itself to undertake no further borrowing without approval of this bank consortium, thereby allowing these banks effective control over the financial life of Mexico.[3]

The banks had not been prompted to extend this loan to Huerta for financial considerations alone. With it they hoped to reconquer the central position in the Mexican financial world that they had enjoyed under Díaz. Moreover, the largest and most important of the banks, the Deutsche Bank, undertook in the first months of the Huerta dictatorship the first serious German effort to penetrate Mexican petroleum production and to gain a foothold there.

Several years before, in 1907, the Deutsche Bank had been bested in competition with Standard Oil to supply the German petroleum market through an agreement in which Standard Oil had been granted a virtual monopoly in this domain. It had, nevertheless, been specified that passage in Germany of a law creating a monopoly on petroleum by the Reich would nullify entire sections of the agreement. The efforts of the Deutsche Bank to obtain such a law in 1912–13 seemed about to succeed, and the bank thereupon began to look at Mexico as one of the most important countries whose oil reserves had not yet been developed.

In November 1912, Hintze wired the Foreign Office in Berlin: "Local German firm Bach, Krupps German munitions representative has conducted search for oil with expert geologist Angermann under contract with Batavian oil company in the Hague, has discovered 200 hectares of best accessible oil fields in states of Tamaulipas and Veracruz, claims these fields would cover Germany's total consumption, can secure them immediately with option agreement. Informed of planned monopoly law, firm proposing to break ties to Dutch if German experts are sent to the oil fields.... Cable report that experts are coming would prompt firm to suspend relations with Dutch. Request reply by wire."[4] The Bach firm had explained its proposal to the German legation in the following fashion: "German capital has not up to now participated in this tremendous development in any notable way, and it is the purpose of these lines to illuminate the current opportunities for a German company. An enormous opportunity is in fact presenting itself at this moment, but one which can be exploited only by the most rapid and energetic intervention."[5] The proposal was submitted by the Foreign Office to the Deutsche Bank and to its subsidiary Deutsche Petroleum AG.

The German navy also appears to have shown a temporary interest in Mexican oil, for the Austrian minister to Mexico reported on 12 September 1913: "In the immediately preceding period Germany as well has turned up in Mexico to secure for itself the possession of larger oil fields. As the German minister, Rear Admiral von Hintze, has told me, the naval command has manifested a serious interest in Mexican oil, and it is mainly through its efforts that a German financial group has now seriously taken up the question of the acquisition of oil fields in Mexico."[6]

In spite of the interest of the Foreign Office and the navy, the negotiations, which were mainly carried on through the German legation, dragged on slowly. The Deutsche Petroleum AG showed no real interest and decided only after several months to send a geologist, Dr. Wunstorff, to Mexico.[7] Wunstorff, who worked for the state geology division in Berlin, was given a leave of absence for the duration of his trip on request of the

Deutsche Petroleum AG; the minister for commerce and trade wrote to the Foreign Office: "In view of the national interest at stake in this trip, I wish to waive the usual deduction of the leave of absence from seniority, in accord with the Minister of Finance."[8]

After extensive investigation, Wunstorff recommended to the Deutsche Petroleum AG the purchase of large oil properties in Mexico. On 11 September 1913, Hintze reported: "Dr. Wunstorff said he had submitted favorable reports and had made various proposals by wire to buy. Nonetheless, he had continuously received negative replies on the question of purchase."[9] The Deutsche Petroleum AG, in fact, never actually acquired oil properties in Mexico, but constantly gave evasive replies to queries by the Foreign Office in this domain. Thus it was stated, for example, in a letter to the Foreign Office on 6 March 1914: "Dr. W. Wunstorff returned from America in the fall of last year, but has since that time been so involved with other pressing tasks, that a definitive discussion with him on the results of his trip could not take place."[10]

In view of the fact that Wunstorff had traveled to Mexico under contract with the Deutsche Petroleum AG and that half a year had already elapsed since his return, this reply sounds somewhat peculiar. The real reason for the negative attitude of Deutsche Petroleum AG was identified by the Austrian minister in Mexico in a report to his foreign ministry: "To conclude this report, I would like to point out that interested German parties had sent an expert to Mexico to study the oil fields, but that German finance has until now declined to make any investment in the Mexican petroleum industry. Apparently decisive in this matter were the wishes of the Standard Oil Company, which had strong ties with a section of the Berlin banking community."[11]

The Deutsche Bank's attention to the wishes of Standard Oil was also partly a result of the failure of the anticipated law for a Reich petroleum monopoly. The interest of the German navy in Mexican oil may also not have been very strong in view of the fact that in the event of a war with England, Germany would hardly have had access to Mexican oil.

The failed attempt to move into Mexican oil production greatly diminished the interest of the German banks in Huerta. The attitude of the banks changed completely when, at the beginning of 1914, Huerta confiscated the customs fees that were designated for the payment of foreign debts. On 20 January 1914, representatives of the international banking groups that issued the loans of 1899, 1910, and 1913, which had been guaranteed by customs fees, met in Paris. According to the report of Paul von Schwabach, director of the Bleichröder banking house, a protest against the confiscation of the customs fees on behalf of all the banks was lodged with the Mexican government.[12]

In view of this meeting and after a discussion with the former finance minister of Díaz, Limantour, Schwabach came to the conclusion that the best solution would be the removal of Huerta imposed by the European powers:

> I asked: could General Huerta not be prompted to declare, in view of the current precedence of the military question over all others, his desire to place himself at the head of the troops and to renounce the presidency? Mr. Limantour thought that such a development would indeed be very nice, but pointed out that Huerta was suffering from an eye infection. I thereupon proposed that Huerta take leave of the capital for at least a few weeks to recover from his eye infection, and after the recognition of a new president by Washington, return well rested to Mexico City. Mr. Limantour thought such a solution possible, insofar as it was not imposed by America.
>
> There are, as far as I can see, only two ways to present such a proposal to Huerta; either through the representatives of the European powers with the greatest interest in the matter, namely, Germany, France, and England, whose counsel, even if stated energetically, would be less bitterly received than anything coming from Washington, or else through private channels.... [In exchange for European support of the United States in this question, Schwabach hoped] that the insurrection would be put down in the foreseeable future, after a president recognized by the United States took over, and particularly after America, as a gesture of loyalty, gives up all support for the rebels, to the extent that it has not already decided to help the regime in Mexico City.[13]

The purpose of Huerta's resignation was to save his system from a victory of the revolution. A victory of the Constitutionalists would have had the gravest consequences for the German banking group since Carranza had declared from the first day of his revolution that he would not recognize the debts of the Huerta regime. Therefore, the banks were threatened with the complete loss of the loan floated in June 1913. A new regime based on Huerta's voluntary resignation, which would fight against the revolutionaries, would legally succeed Huerta and would assume his debts.

Unlike the German banks, German shipping interests seem to have been consistent in maintaining a good relationship with the Huerta regime from its beginning until its end. The Hapag (Hamburg American Shipping Line) was one of the German firms with the closest ties to the Huerta regime. These ties were strengthened in early and mid-1914, when all other firms and German diplomacy were beginning to distance themselves from Huerta, by important arms shipments for the Huerta regime. It is not improbable that Hapag's close ties to Cowdray and their common holdings in the Tehuantepec line contributed to this orientation.

The Huerta government had attempted to attract German heavy industry through a series of important construction contracts. On 18 June 1913, the German chargé d'affaires, Rudolf von Kardorff, submitted an offer by the Huerta regime to German firms for a contract for the expansion of the port of Mazatlán. "According to general opinion at this end," he stated, the offer "was quite commendable and lucrative for German capital."[14] The contract, however, never materialized; the precise reasons for this are not known. Contributing factors were probably the revolutionaries' advance on Mazatlán, which was already underway at that time, and the ever increasing financial difficulties of the Huerta government.

The German arms industry appears to have practiced complete "neutrality," for it supplied both sides with weapons at the same time. At the end of 1913, when Huerta was no longer able to make purchases in the United States because of the arms embargo, he relied increasingly on German producers. In November 1913, the Deutsche Waffen- und Munitionsfabriken signed a contract with Huerta for the delivery of one hundred thousand Mauser rifles and 20 million rounds of ammunition worth a total of 2.48 million marks. Since the Deutsche Waffen- und Munitionsfabriken were themselves strained beyond capacity, part of this contract was given to the Austrian Steyrer-Werke.[15] At the end of December, a Mexican contract for eighty thousand rifles and 100 million rounds of ammunition went out: three-eighths to the Deutsche Waffen- und Munitionsfabriken, three-eighths to Hirtenberg (a factory located in Austria), and the remaining one-fourth to the Fabriques Nationales d'Armes de Guerre Henstal.[16]

In March 1914, the German armaments industry received its biggest contract to date from the Mexican government. Krupp, which had attempted in vain in September 1913 to sell cannons to the Mexican government, was also involved in this deal.[17] After a large bribe had been paid to Huerta's finance minister, De la Lama, contracts were given to Krupp for a battery of mountain cannon, to the Deutsche Waffen- und Munitionsfabriken and their Austrian and Belgian syndicate partners for 200 million rounds of rifle ammunition, and to Bergmann for one hundred machine guns.[18]

The same German firms attempted to produce German weapons for the Constitutionalists as well. In February 1914, Bernstorff wrote to the Foreign Office: "New York representative of Krupp and Deutsche Waffenfabriken informed me that he had received orders from Mexican Constitutionalists and that he had passed them on to German firms. He is afraid that the fulfillment of these contracts, desirable as they are from a business point of view, might be cancelled by the Kaiser's government for political reasons. Money to pay for the deliveries is available, and American producers are not in a position to fulfill the needs of the Constitutionalists. Seen from here, there are no objections to be raised to above-mentioned arms shipments."[19]

The Foreign Office was not opposed and wanted only not to assume responsibility. "A ban on arms shipments by German firms to the Mexican insurgents," the Foreign Office advisor Kemnitz stated in this regard, "does not seem appropriate in light of the situation. Nonetheless, such shipments cannot be given any official approval, and the firms in question will be given notice, should they turn to us in this matter, that any unsettled claims resulting from such shipments will receive no official support."[20] These contracts, too, were probably fulfilled. In any case, more precise information on this question is not available.

The Berliner Handelsgesellschaft, in contrast to the banks of the so-called German group, was among the outspoken opponents of the Huerta government and an advocate of American intervention in Mexico. This firm had been involved in 1907 in the "nationalization" of the Mexican railways and had issued certificates totaling $40 million on the Berlin stock exchange, of which a large portion still remained in its control.

The railroad interests were the first to be affected by the revolution and by the policies of the Huerta government. In July and August 1913, representatives of the international bank consortium involved in the Mexican railways met in Paris. The director of the Berliner Handelsgesellschaft, Dr. Beheim-Schwarzbach, reported on this meeting. "The state of affairs in Mexico," the chairman of the board of the Mexican National Railways, an American, E. N. Brown, informed the participants in the meeting, "exceeds anything previously experienced. Anarchy appears to be total." Brown denounced in particularly sharp terms the corruption of the Huerta regime, which was costing the railway owners dearly. "Thus, for example," Brown continued, "there are now 27 appointed operations managers as opposed to the previous figure of 18, even though barely 50 percent of the lines are operable, which thus means a tripling of personnel for this area of activity alone. Most of the operations managers are completely ignorant; they are there because they have influence in the relevant locales and because the regime needs them as allies."[21] Brown's explanation for this state of affairs had typically racist overtones: "Out of a population of 15 million, 13 million are Indians, mestizos and other riffraff, who have undoubtedly no sense of moral obligation."[22]

The participants in the conference decided to ask the American government to intervene. Beheim-Schwarzbach gave the warmest support to this proposal. He stated in a report to Secretary of State Jagow: "Here it must be noted that while such a decision may not conform to the views of the Foreign Office, since the Americans will thereby take even more *pleinpouvoir* for themselves, it nonetheless appears to be the only practical solution.''[23]

If one views the attitudes of British and German financial interests and businesses toward an American intervention in Mexico, there emerge profound differences, both qualitative and quantitative. In quantitative terms, the British investments in Mexico were much more important than German investments: their total value was four times as great. The value of German and British exports to Mexico was, however, almost identical.

Weighing more heavily on the scales were the qualitative differences between the German and British investments in Mexico. Among British investments, raw material production, especially oil, occupied a prominent place. The interests of powerful groups in Britain were tied up in this sphere, and the strategic importance of raw materials increased still more the influence of their producers. For these groups, an American occupation of Mexico or the victory of a pro-American government would have been a catastrophe, for it would have resulted in their expulsion from Mexico or at least it would have put severe limits on their expansion. Of all the investors with interests in Mexico, the raw material producers, particularly the owners of oil wells, were the group least affected by the civil war. In spite of the fact that from 1910 to 1920, almost uninterrupted fighting took place in Mexico, oil production in this period quadrupled. Thus the British and American oil producers had less to lose than any other business interest by a continuation of the armed conflicts.

The situation was quite different for German financial and business interests. The heaviest burden fell on the bondholders, which meant primarily the large banks. What concerned these circles most was not so much the pro-German or anti-American moods as the solvency of a Mexican government that would be willing and able to pay the interest on its bonds. Naturally these banks preferred a government independent of the United States, one willing to grant them advantages on loans. This desire was nonetheless subordinate to their interest in the maintenance of the solvency of the Mexican government.

After the Deutsche Bank failed to gain a foothold in Mexican oil production, the interest of German high finance in Mexican raw material production remained minimal. The few German firms that had made investments in Mexican raw materials had done so in partnerships with American companies, as, for example, the Frankfurter Metallgesellschaft. These firms, too, would have had little to fear from an American occupation of Mexico or from U.S. hegemony. The plans drawn up in 1911 for greater German investments in Mexican raw materials had been abandoned in the wake of the fighting in Mexico and probably in view of the increasing tension in Europe as well.

For the subsidiaries of German banks in Mexico as well, an American intervention would have had no catastrophic consequences. The most important of these subsidiaries, the Banco de Comercio e Industria, was a joint venture of the Deutsche Bank and the American Speyer banking house. This convergence of interest would have offered a certain guarantee that even under American occupation the bank would not have had to suffer unduly. Nor did German merchants in Mexico have fundamental objections to an American hegemony or an occupation of the country, for they acquired two-thirds of their goods in the United States. As early as 1912, under the impact of the fighting in Mexico, they had pronounced themselves in favor of such an intervention. Their initial support for Huerta was based less on his anti-American attitude than on his social policies and his re-creation of the old Díaz order.

American hegemony in Mexico would have had its most important impact on German exports to Mexico. It has already been mentioned that the fear of a Mexican-American reciprocity treaty was affecting German diplomacy in Mexico. Nonetheless, the interests of the German firms exporting to Mexico were subordinated, for reasons already shown, to the interests of the German holders of Mexican bonds and securities, that is, the major banks, and were never decisive for German policy in Mexico.

### The German Government and the Huerta Regime

The policy of the German government in 1913 was ambivalent. On the one hand, there was an attempt to support Huerta. Such a policy in 1913 was in keeping with the demands of the majority of German banks, German businessmen in Mexico, and the German commercial and shipping interests. Moreover, Mexico played a specific role in the strategic plans of Germany. As early as 1907, the kaiser was contemplating the possibility of a Japanese-American conflict, in which Mexico would have real significance as a launching ground for an attack on the United States. Such a war would have neutralized two enemies of Germany. It is possible that Mexico was already being considered for use in the event of a German-American war.

German diplomats, on the other hand, had attempted to avoid all friction between Germany and the United States concerning Mexico. At a time when Germany's opposition to England, France, and Russia was coming increasingly to the fore, German interests in Mexico were hardly sufficient to create an additional confrontation with the United States. The desire to avoid conflict with the United States nonetheless had certain limits. If Great Britain or France were prepared to take the lead in an anti-American action in Mexico, and thereby to bear the brunt of American opposition, Germany was disposed to follow them under certain circumstances. But Germany under no circumstances wished to oppose the United States alone.

There was one course of action that Germany never attempted until June 1914: cooperation with the United States in Mexico. Through such cooperation, Germany could have put pressure on Britain's petroleum supplies, with a resulting direct military impact. But the price of such a move—a weakening of its position in Mexico and a decisive loss of prestige in Latin America—was much too high for Germany ever to have considered it.

German policy in Mexico in 1913 passed through four distinct phases. In the first phase, which lasted from Huerta's seizure of power until the beginning of April 1913, German diplomacy exercised the greatest caution toward him. The fear that he might be working for the Americans, initially advanced by Hintze, and the question of his ability to win out in Mexico, led to this reserve. The secretary of state declared in a note to the Reichskanzler on 27 March 1913: "For the moment General Huerta is running a de facto government. He has not yet been able to achieve a general pacification of the country.... We therefore have reservations at this time about recognizing General Huerta formally."[24]

Like British diplomacy earlier, German diplomacy embraced the position of Lane Wilson, who made the recognition of the Huerta government contingent on its willingness to make good on foreign demands for indemnification arising from alleged damages incurred during the Madero revolution.

The initial reserve of German diplomacy was quickly modified when Huerta's efforts to reestablish the situation of the Díaz era became apparent and his anti-American stancě became clear. German diplomacy then shifted to a phase of full support for the Huerta government with openly anti-American overtones.

This policy was facilitated by the attitude of the German chargé d'affaires in Mexico. Shortly after Huerta's seizure of power, Hintze fell seriously ill and was replaced by Rudolf von Kardorff as chargé d'affaires. In contrast to the extremely adept and agile Hintze, who was masterfully capable of conducting an anti-American policy behind the scenes while preserving a pro-American stance in public, Kardorff was a gruff diplomat who thought in the most primitive categories and who emerged as the spokesman of the most extreme followers of Huerta and the anti-American forces. Precisely these qualities elicited the approval of the kaiser, who consistently underlined the anti-American passages in Kardorff's reports as well as those discussing Huerta's dictatorial tendencies. In the margins he penned such notations as "good," "good observation," "wire my approval," and the like. Kardorff developed a childish enthusiasm for Huerta. On 2 April he submitted a report on the opening of the Mexican Congress:

A storm of applause, rare even in countries of Roman impulsiveness, followed the ringing words of the old general . . . . Huerta had done what no one else had been able to do for months. He had instilled confidence. Confidence together with respect. The old soldier, who may not have asked his Savior for counsel too often in the past, had spoken of God, had implored the higher powers and taken them over as his own. He had spoken plainly and simply to his countrymen of their duties and of love for the fatherland . . . . But in addition, the strong and intimidating undertone—an important thing in this situation—had come through in an imposing way to everyone.[25]

The kaiser noted on this report: "Bravo—things are the same everywhere and the same success will be had wherever people have the courage to confront parliament in such a fashion." The kaiser annotated the passage on the "strong and intimidating undertone" with the word "essential." Kardorff closed his report with the sentence: "In one's heart the conviction took hold: in the breast of this old soldier there resides both will and love for the fatherland, a clear instinct for what is useful in the moment and capacity for imagination, cleverness, and no overbearing scruples," which Wilhelm II marked with the words: "Bravo! Such a man has our sympathies."[26]

Huerta must have had the sympathies of the kaiser all the more when Kardorff characterized the overthrown Madero as an "ambitious man, capable of serving as an effective tool for a hundred selfish goals, and who did so. But this tenacity, which made him appear at times energetic, at times fearless, was in one case blind persistence, in another case caprice combined with fanaticism."[27] Here Wilhelm wrote "Bebel" in the margin. In the victory of Madero the kaiser saw a victory of the socialists, and Madero's failure only confirmed for Wilhelm the necessity of a strong, absolutist regime.

As early as 26 March, Kardorff advocated the recognition of Huerta.[28] The most important obstacle to recognition up to that time besides uncertainty about Huerta's attitude toward the United States, was the desire to obtain a commitment from the Huerta government on indemnifications through the combined pressure of the great powers. The British government had in the meantime changed its attitude and was no longer willing to delay recognition. Several weeks later Kardorff delivered a blunt rebuff to the American ambassador, who on the basis of previous conversations with Hintze was anticipating collaboration of the American and German governments on the question of recognition. "I treated with the appropriate contempt the astounding statement from the ambassador to a diplomat, to the effect that Germany would quite simply follow the lead of the United States and recognize Mexico no sooner and no later than America did, and asserted what Mr. Wilson had blithely overlooked, namely, that the kaiser's government would make its decisions on this question strictly according to its own calculations.''[29] Kardorff saw support for the Huerta government as the sole means of saving European interests from the grip of the United States. ''Should England grant recognition immediately, and should other governments—as I've heard Spain, for example, intends to do—follow suit, Germany would achieve nothing with a recognition separate from that of the International Commission, but would only reap a certain unpopularity in Mexico as the alleged underling of the United States.''[30] And one month later he wrote:

> The European states having interests in Mexico must at this time grasp the particular interest they have in the preservation and strengthening of the current government. In the struggle for the suppression of the unscrupulous and unpatriotic spirit of part of the Mexican population, a spirit perverted by the basest materialism and once again current as it was before the old dictator, the Mexican government is left to its own resources. It can solve the financial crisis only with help from abroad. Europe will have to choose, for its economic interests, between the extension of state and private credits to a country with much future potential, albeit currently quite agitated, or the probability of being merely tolerated—and perhaps not even tolerated—for the foreseeable future in one of the richest countries of the world.[31]

In spite of the repeated recommendations and exhortations of Kardorff, the Foreign Office nonetheless continued to delay recognition of Huerta. Germany held firm to the strategy of pushing Great Britain to the fore in every question where it found itself in opposition to the United States. Only on 15 May, after the British government had officially announced the recognition of Huerta, did the German Foreign Office also resolve to take the same step.[32]

In June 1913, the first, though relatively minor, clash with the United States came. On the advice of Kardorff, who had wired Berlin that a ''show of German flags important in current situation,''[33] the German battleship *Bremen* was sent to Veracruz. This step angered the commander of the American fleet stationed there. ''I had the impression,'' reported the *Bremen*'s commander to the kaiser,

> that the appearance of Your Majesty's Ship *Bremen* did not entirely please the American admiral in charge off of Veracruz. He of course wired a welcome to Your Majesty's Ship *Bremen* and was personally very cordial; nonetheless, he cooled considerably at the end of the first week when I was able to give him no departure date for Your Majesty's Ship *Bremen* . . . . My statement that I had come to calm the local German population of course became less believable every day, since the papers happened to be running almost daily accounts of the German colony's festivities in the capital.[34]

The anti-American activity of German diplomats reached a high point with Kardorff's participation in a joint decision of all European diplomats in Mexico to request their governments to pressure the United States for the recognition of Huerta. Kardorff moved on this decision one day later, when he wired the Foreign Office: "Only Huerta capable of difficult task of achieving peace in Mexico; nonetheless narrrowly self-interested countermoves by United States, already visible in various domains, can paralyze him and create crisis; consequences for European interests unforeseeable."[35]

The growing tensions between Huerta and the American government brought the possibility of an armed American intervention in Mexico increasingly to the fore and confronted German diplomacy with serious decisions. It was clear that an armed venture conducted jointly with the other European powers against the United States was unthinkable. Thus Kardorff considered the possibility, in the event of an American intervention, "that once again, America's special position requires that we, in order to exercise at least some control over its actions and to save for Europe what is to be saved, take the *parti du feu* and conduct a joint action in Mexico, making the best of it, instead of impotently protesting unilateral American actions."[36]

For a time, German diplomats consoled themselves with the hope that Japan could thwart an American intervention in Mexico. "Japan is the only power in the East which can protect Mexico against rape by the colossus from the north, and yet Mexico, as the neighboring country of a possible future enemy of Japan, is of an importance for the latter which should not be underestimated."[37] But as early as September, Germany recognized that this hope was unrealistic.[38] The maintenance of the Huerta regime was for Japan in no way worth a conflict with the United States.

The Japanese minister in Mexico defined Japanese policy to his German colleague, who reported as follows:

Japan's policy is to concentrate all its efforts to win the friendship of the United States. This is the goal: Mexico is only an object to be utilized in this policy. Japan has for an extended period played nothing but a spectator's role and left America a free hand here in the hope that—with or without intervention—Japan could use the rift between the two countries in its negotiations of friendship with the United States. The Mexican foreign minister, Moheno, apparently approached him enthusiastically about collaboration, but it is quite impossible to negotiate with this man. And the president of the republic, Huerta, expressed similar ideas to him which are, from the Japanese standpoint, simply insane.[39]

Hintze himself considered an armed venture by Japan in Mexico quite impossible.

In a war for an objective on the American continent, Japan is risking its power position in Asia. From my experience, I have every reason to suppose that Russia will seize the opportunity to settle accounts for Tsushima and Mukden. Germany, England, and France would be sorely tempted to lay claim to a China in chaos, in the absence of their most dangerous rival. And Germany would have to come to terms with one of the few chances still left to it to seize and hold, in this redivision of the world, its fair share and a share that was usable. Japan would have to stand by during a decisive attack by the other Asian powers; even with a retreat from the American war, if the others acted promptly, it would be too late.[40]

Japan's attitude during the Huerta period confirmed this interpretation. Aside from the weapons it sold to Huerta, and occasional visits by the fleet to Mexico, Japanese diplomacy showed the greatest reserve where support of Huerta against the United States was concerned.[41]

In July 1913, German diplomats still nourished the hope, through joint pressure by the European powers on the American government, of bringing about American recognition of Huerta. After the Foreign Office had learned that Great Britain had proceeded along the same lines, Bernstorff intervened in Washington in mid-August 1913 to obtain American recognition of Huerta.[42]

This move was not only a complete failure, but the American government responded for its own part with a diplomatic offensive. It delivered within the same month identical notes to Great Britain and Germany, in which it announced American proposals for the settlement of the Mexican question. In addition, it urged the German government to have its representatives advise Huerta "to give the most serious attention to all proposals of the American government and to consider the consequences it might bring upon itself by a refusal of the kind offices of this government."[43]

This was a clever maneuver. The American proposals had not even been announced, nor had the European powers been requested to support them. The Europeans were only to urge the Mexican government to give its attention to the proposals. The Americans thereby brought additional pressures to bear on Huerta and gave the impression that the other powers at least partially approved of the American orientation in Mexico. In keeping with this, Kardorff commented: "United States obviously attempting to use Europe for its own ends."[44]

The matter was nonetheless too small to risk offending the United States, and thus Kardorff was instructed to bring up "appropriate friendly suggestions" with the Mexican government. In this effort, he was to add that "we naturally do not identify with proposals which are completely unknown"[45] and simultaneously to avoid everything "which could be interpreted by the Mexicans as a German mandate to the United States or encouragement of an invasion."[46] Kardorff, also acting on instructions, advised the Huerta government not to reject the American proposals "unexamined and unread."[47] He weakened the effect of this move, however, through a simultaneous attack on the American policy. "I have mentioned to the American chargé d'affaires that the ban on arms shipments to Huerta is a measure threatening the stability of the Mexican government, and thereby directly endangering German lives, about which I am obligated to inform the German government by wire."[48] The kaiser noted this protest with the remark: "Correct!"

The American proposals of July 1913 attempting to bring about Huerta's departure drew sharp opposition from the German diplomatic office as soon as they were made public. "We have refused our support," declared Jagow.[49] "As we have often stated," explained Kardorff,

> Huerta is currently the only man in the position to overcome the difficulties and put Mexico back on a new, firm, and healthy basis. Does Mr. Wilson not see that his policy of opposition to the general is the reason that in the northern part of the country, foreign lives and property are still endangered and that safety and order have not been restored? Does he not see that he, the declared enemy of the big syndicates, is serving quite well the interests of the trusts in Mexico, which are using the collapse of values to grab up mines and land at low prices? Does he not know that, on the other hand, with the paralysis of Huerta's government, thousands of American middle-sized and small capitalists are being stripped of their existence and driven to ruin?[50]

With tremendous satisfaction Kardorff conveyed an anti-American resolution of the European colonies in Mexico, who therein thanked their governments for the recognition of the Huerta regime and simultaneously condemned American policy.[51] The resolution was greeted by the kaiser with the words: "Good. Finally unity against the Yankee."[52]

Kardorff made it known quite bluntly to other diplomats and to the Mexican government that the German government was prepared to play a leading role in supporting Huerta in his struggle against the United States. Huerta acknowledged the stance of German diplomacy with expressions of gratitude and with the assurance "that the Germans would always be received by him with open arms in every aspect of their activity in Mexico."[53]

At the beginning of September 1913, Kardorff returned to Berlin, and Hintze, who had recovered in the meantime, once again assumed his tasks. At a farewell banquet given for him by the Mexican government, Kardorff had no compunctions about openly stating both his sympathy for Huerta and his contempt for the Mexican people. He asserted, "I believe in a great future for Mexico, when domestic peace is restored and, in keeping with the intentions and plans of the president, based as they are on intelligence and experience, that this still-childlike people, in need of firm leadership and control, will be lifted not immediately but gradually to an ever higher cultural level. It gives me pleasure to be able to inform Your Excellency that the Germans in Mexico have complete confidence in the president's ability to reestablish domestic peace."[54] The results of German diplomacy in Mexico went well beyond the goal it had set for itself. A disconcerted Hintze declared ten days after resuming his duties that

> the English minister informs me that Mr. John Lind, the well-known advisor of the American embassy, has complained to him that the German chargé d'affaires was encouraging the Mexican government to resist American policy. The English minister (who, as we have often reported, is quite sympathetic to Germany) attempted to allay the American's fears by ascribing German moves merely to the sympathies which evolve from a long stay in a country, and which occur unconsciously.... But Mr. Lind persisted, and emphasized his impression that the German chargé d'affaires was acting advisedly. The American representative repeatedly made similar allusions to me.[55]

The Mexican question was threatening to lead to a serious clash between Germany and the United States. Berlin immediately sounded a retreat. On 7 October 1913, Hintze was advised by Montgelas, "Please avoid any further opposition to the United States and counter any such interpretations of our policy. Sole German interest rapid reestablishment of order and of normal relations between United States and Mexico."[56] The alarm was obviously so great that a passage initially included, "without upsetting the Mexicans," was deleted. A similar directive was also sent to Bernstorff in Washington.[57]

The second phase of German policy in Mexico, from 13 September 1913 until Huerta's dissolution of the Mexican parliament on 11 October 1913, was a phase of retreat. Its fundamental aim was to avoid anything that could lead to conflict with the United States. Hintze wrote about his policy in this period: "With regard to this, I am encountering in diplomatic circles (including the American embassy), in public opinion, and with the government a notion that Germany is taking a leading role in such a policy [directed against the United States]. In accordance with Your Excellency's previous general instructions I will carefully and explicitly attempt to calm such tense expectations and fears, without upsetting the Mexicans."[58] Not the least of the reasons for this retreat were indications that the Huerta regime was yielding to the United States on the question of Huerta's presidential candidacy and of Gamboa's nomination. Hintze hailed Gamboa's nomination and saw in it the possibility of maintaining the Huerta system without Huerta and thereby avoiding both an American intervention and a victory of the revolutionaries.[59] After Huerta's second coup, German diplomacy in Mexico entered a new phase of activity.

For the first time since Huerta's seizure of power in February 1913, there arose great differences of opinion between Germany and Great Britain on the Mexican question.

Hintze had hailed the dissolution of the Mexican parliament, just as British diplomats had, since he interpreted it as a weakening of the position of the revolutionaries. "I must stick to my opinion that a military dictatorship is the government appropriate to the situation and the one which serves us best, and that Huerta, in spite of his alcoholism and his forays into the state treasury, is the best dictator."[60] After the final break between Huerta and the American government, however, the paths of British and German diplomats separated. British diplomacy placed itself squarely behind Huerta and encouraged him in his anti-American policy. The goal of British efforts after the coup was the maintenance of Huerta's power, for important concessions to British firms were bound up with his willingness to subordinate himself to British policy. British diplomacy was also temporarily willing to tolerate serious differences with the United States.

The main goal of German diplomacy was, however, the maintenance of the system of Huerta and Díaz, if necessary by sacrificing Huerta personally to avoid conflict with the United States. The reason for this attitude was quite simple; in October 1913, all plans for investing German capital in the Mexican petroleum industry had been abandoned and hence there was little interest in concessions. Moreover, German diplomacy's enthusiasm for Huerta diminished to the extent that British influence in Mexico grew, although German diplomats never took very seriously the possibility of a strictly British hegemony in Mexico.

Moreover, Hintze had come to the view, after the victories of the revolutionaries, that the Huerta regime could be saved only with the support of the United States. Thus he sharply criticized the attitude of the British minister, Sir Lionel Carden:

> He derives the basis of his assessment of what is and what will be from his familiarity with the Mexico of President Porfirio Díaz.... Based upon this period, he considers the ruthless despotism of a clever...unscrupulous Indian to be the appropriate form of government for Mexico. He overlooks the fact that in the last years of Porfirio Díaz a socialist revolution has been set into motion under the slogan "land" and that he collapsed because of it. Behind the dominating personality of Díaz, he thought he perceived a unified nation, and he refuses to see that under the great shadow there was only the grey multitude from which a nation will one day be forged. He considers the economic resources of the Mexican people to be inexhaustible and ignores the fact that the major resource—minerals—has passed and continues to pass increasingly into the hands of foreigners. He counts on the person of Huerta in the same way that everyone previously clung to Díaz and

does not see that Díaz ruled *with* the United States of America and that Huerta is attempting to rule *against* them.[61]

These almost revolutionary-sounding words of Hintze's naturally refer in no way to the necessity of land reforms or the nationalization of foreign property, but on the contrary affirm that it was all the more necessary for the Huerta government to cooperate with the United States in view of these problems. The attitude of German diplomacy was finally determined by the belief that a settlement between Huerta and the United States would be principally at the expense of Great Britain.

To the same extent that German diplomacy was little inclined to adopt the British attitude in Mexico, it had little inclination to support the American policy, which appeared to Germany to be heading toward armed intervention. "The current situation, from the standpoint of our economic interests, is certainly not very favorable," Bernstorff declared. "It is nonetheless preferable, in my humble opinion, to the possibility of an American intervention. Even if President Wilson were to remain firm and carry out his program of treating Mexico exactly as Cuba was treated, the Americans would still pick up all the pieces in Mexico after the intervention."[62] Germany hoped to use the British-American antagonism to win a decisive position for itself in Mexico. After the break between Huerta and the American government, the United States turned to the German government with the suggestion that it withdraw recognition of Huerta. Jagow refused, though his answer was evasive, and requested Hintze to "make a concrete proposal, confirmed by wire, for further action."[63]

Hintze's answer was a proposal which under the name of "friendly cooperation" in fact envisaged a kind of American-British-German protectorate in Mexico. "Mexico, left to itself," he wired,

will be mired in its revolutions for years. The powers with interests here, given their losses in life, property, and profits, as well as their capital investment, cannot sit idly by for such a time . . . . No European power can attempt to influence American policy toward Mexico by itself, for such an attempt would have serious consequences and would be hopeless in the long term. But a parallel effort by the major European powers, in which England would have to participate, can have an effect, and precisely in the direction of friendly cooperation with the United States, for which the latter has already laid the foundation with its various suggestions to European powers. This European project (Germany and England are sufficient) would have to begin by offering support to the union in the demands which are essential to the United States, and which are comparatively unimportant to Europe. Huerta is the first stepping stone in the attack; he could be persuaded by friendly cooperation to have one of his people elected president and to remove himself temporarily from the scene. Further policy would be determined as the case arose. The essential is not to allow the union to fend for itself, but to influence it through ongoing friendly cooperation.

This cooperation would have to provide Mexico with a loan under joint financial control, and finally would have to envision joint police actions, should Mexico show itself further incapable of defending life, property, and profit.[64]

The execution of such a plan would have brought the greatest benefits for German imperialism. The Huerta system would be maintained, and Germany would have achieved a position in Mexico all the more important on account of Germany's limited assets in Mexico. A unilateral British or American domination of the country would have been avoided, and Germany would constantly have had the possibility, as the force able to tip the scales, of playing Great Britain and the United States off against one another.

Collaboration of the European powers in Mexico was the prerequisite for the realization of such a plan. It nonetheless never came about. French diplomacy had indeed made general allusions to the necessity of a collaboration in Mexico, and the French minister to Mexico had declared himself in agreement with Hintze's plan, but concrete steps were not proposed.[65]

The British government at first showed absolutely no interest. It had attempted initially to support Huerta and to share power in Mexico with no other power. Carden stated to Hintze: "Europe is an old woman—a joint action by Europe is nonsense. That is an idea of Lefaivre [the French minister to Mexico], who is dreaming of a 'proportional intervention of the United States and the European powers,' as well as of 'financial control.' Mexico needs no financial control, since it can maintain itself through taxation."[66] Hintze summarized Carden's opinion with the words: "England will act alone and will reap the benefits alone."[67]

As British-American tensions reached their high point, British diplomacy appears temporarily to have considered cooperation with Germany, though hardly with the goal of joint intervention in Mexico as Hintze conceived it, but most probably only as a means of exerting more pressure on the negotiations which were already in progress with the United States. In November 1913, British Foreign Secretary Grey, in order to probe German intentions, suggested to the German Foreign Office a "joint course of action," which in the words of the German undersecretary of state were "thus far vague" and "without precise proposals."[68]

After the British-American agreement on Mexico, a collaboration with Germany lost all interest for the British government. It was an attitude that was not shared by Lord Cowdray, who had formulated proposals along lines very similar to those of Hintze in his conversation with the American ambassador in London. He may very well have known of Hintze's views, for he and Page had arrived at the conclusion that it would be impossible to exclude Germany from an eventual international intervention. In spite of Cowdray's influence, the British government was not willing to subordinate its overall strategic concepts to the interests of Cowdray's companies. The main reason for the British government's failure to accept Hintze's plan was that at a time when Germany was Great Britain's most important global rival and British diplomacy was oriented toward an alliance with the United States against Germany, a German-British collaboration directed against the United States was unthinkable. German diplomats, on the contrary, seized upon the idea of a collaboration of the European powers on the Mexican question with great interest, around the goal of "friendly cooperation," as Hintze put it. The German ambassador in Paris was instructed to inform the French government that a collaboration with France in Mexico would "not be unwelcome" to the German government.[69] The circumstances under which the German government would have been prepared for such an action can be gleaned from the answer given to Hintze's proposal by the German undersecretary of state: "Friendly cooperation depends on England, which is currently temporizing."[70] He made this attitude more precise in his response to Grey's vague proposal: "I have declared myself to be largely in agreement with this suggestion. We are not inclined in any sense to take the lead in this affair."[71] Such a move under British leadership would have brought double benefits for German diplomacy. On the one hand, the Huerta government would have been stabilized in Mexico, the German position would have been strengthened, both a unilateral control by the United States and a victory of the revolutionaries would have been avoided; on the other hand, in the event of possible American opposition Great Britain would have borne the brunt of it. German diplomacy definitely hoped for such an eventuality. When Bernstorff communicated from Washington Tyrrell's fear "that American public opinion would hold England responsible if intervention becomes inevitable," Kaiser Wilhelm annotated this point in the report with the remark: "That would be wonderful."[72]

It is not unlikely that Germany's willingness to cooperate with Great Britain was prompted by the desire of German diplomats in the years 1912–14 to preserve England's neutrality in the event of a conflict with France and Russia. In the discussions between Lord Haldane and the leaders of the German Reich, including the kaiser, which took place at the end of 1912, England's major demand, aimed at a limitation of the German fleet expansion, was rejected, but German diplomacy nonetheless attempted to attain its goal through cooperation in other questions of less importance with Great Britain. Mexico probably constituted one of the questions in which Germany hoped to achieve a rapprochement with Great Britain, and thereby to increase the possibility of British neutrality in the event of a European war.

Even if the European powers had agreed on a joint venture in Mexico or on Hintze's proposals for a protectorate, such a project probably would never have received the approval of the American government, even though some important American politicians had come out for a joint intervention in Mexico. In 1912, President Taft had discussed with the British ambassador the possibility of a joint American-British invasion of Mexico with the possible participation of Germany. Important officials of the Foreign Office were horrified at such ideas, which they rejected as a "mad enterprise."[73]

In 1913, Walter Page, U.S. ambassador to Great Britain, a political foe of Taft and a supporter of Wilson, was also considering a joint European-American intervention in Mexico that would include Germany. He cited as a precedent, in a memorandum which he presented to Wilson's collaborator Colonel House, the joint American-European intervention against the Boxer Rebellion in China. In contrast to Taft, he mentioned as a precondition for such an intervention a commitment by all participants not to take advantage of the incursion into Mexico for their own purposes.[74]

Such a joint action would have had certain advantages for the American government. Domestically, the anticipated opposition movement could have been countered with the argument that the United States had invaded only to avoid a unilateral European action. It was also possible that the Americans anticipated less resistance from the Mexican population to an international intervention force than a purely American army would have met.

Such an international intervention, however, would have represented a serious blow to the prestige of the United States and its hegemony in Latin America and would have been a de facto violation of the Monroe Doctrine. The United States would have been admitting that it simply was not in a position to assure "law and order" in Mexico. American claims to hegemony in South America would have been very difficult to maintain after such an admission.

Woodrow Wilson's unambiguous rejection of a joint intervention in Mexico by the great powers had still other motives. He was firmly convinced that there was a fundamental difference between the objectives of the European powers in Mexico, which he viewed as imperialist, and his own objectives, which he viewed as selfless.

The European powers had no way to compel the United States to act in concert with them in Mexico. Bernstorff stated realistically: "Unfortunately Europe can in no way influence American policy, because it does not have the power to counter it."[75] Wilhelm II nonetheless rejoined: "It would indeed have such power if England made common cause with the continent."[76] The kaiser took England's concessions in Mexico very unkindly. When Hintze reported from Mexico on 26 November that British warships had been dispatched to the oil-producing region of Mexico, but would not land troops there out of consideration for the United States, the kaiser remarked: "These are strictly English oil fields. That's how afraid they are of America. Oh Disraeli, what has become of your spirit."[77]

In spite of the British concessions to the United States and the obvious unfeasibility of his plan, Hintze clung to it.

> Mexico is in the long run incapable of ruling itself. The way out of this situation is the intervention of foreign powers. The United States would now like to reserve such an option for itself alone, but cannot do so at present and does not want to, as intervention is quite unpopular. From here it does not appear impossible that the psychological moment has come when the United States would not be unwilling to accord the right to an influence of European powers, couched in the friendliest form, to collaborate in the pacification of Mexico through its counsel and even through actions such as, for example, police measures and financial control. The Huerta government would, as it had repeatedly intimated in confidential talks, be agreeable to such a perspective.[78]

The advisor in the Foreign Office, Kemnitz, commented realistically on this suggestion of "friendly cooperation": "I'm afraid the moment is long past, if indeed it ever was at hand."[79]

Along with these efforts at "friendly cooperation," Hintze had attempted, after Huerta's coup and his break with the United States, to negotiate between the two parties on the basis of the maintenance of the Huerta system. For an extended period after the coup, Hintze had placed his hopes on "an energetic conduct of the war." "I have not stopped—as a private individual—confronting the current holders of power with their mistakes and telling them that, if they were to make themselves masters of the country through real war, that recognition would either be accorded to them as a matter of course, or would become superfluous."[80] Only a month later he had to admit: "Huerta's government is too weak to put down the revolution, and no one here can think otherwise today."[81]

In the middle of October, the Huerta government approached Hintze, urgently requesting him to mediate between it and the American government. Hintze refused an official mediation, since he feared that "it would expose us more than is desirable."[82] Unofficially, however, he acted enthusiastically as a mediator. His goal was an agreement between the Huerta government and the United States for Huerta to depart and to be replaced by another member of the ruling classes.

Hintze's first initiative was made on 7 November 1913. On that day, he proposed to the American chargé d'affaires in Mexico, O'Shaughnessy, the appointment to the office of president of Huerta's brother-in-law, General Maas, who was of German origin and who had particularly good relations with Hintze.[83] O'Shaughnessy proved willing enough, but the proposal was not further discussed, since Huerta, feeling the strength of British support for him, showed no inclination to step down. Disappointed, Hintze wired Berlin on 13 November: "Have from discussion and observation impression that English minister would be quite pleased to see a belligerent entanglement of United States of America with Mexico and that he is propping up Huerta."[84] Hintze stated to opponents of a Huerta-Wilson agreement in Berlin: "Lind confirms my calculation that the United States will if possible wage only half a war; consider that in view of the inevitable dangers of such a conduct of the war, we must tolerate consequences, partially unfavorable to us, of an agreement."[85] What Hintze meant by "half a war" he underscored with the words: "Given the military weakness of the union, nothing is to be expected of it, prior to the mobilization of adequate forces, except the closing of the northern border and all the ports. For the moment it will allow the rebels to wage war in the interior, since the rallying of the rebels to Huerta in the event of an American military adventure against him is unlikely. Such a half-war is more dangerous to our interests in the long run than a real war."[86] A victory of the revolutionaries was what Hintze feared the most and was something to which, judging from his communiqué, he even preferred an American occupation.

Hintze was heavily involved in the new attempt at negotiation between Huerta and the American government in the middle of November 1913. He traveled to Veracruz, where Lind was staying, and communicated to him the proposals of the Mexican government.[87] These attempts at mediation received the full approval of the Foreign Office and the kaiser. Bernstorff was instructed to support Hintze's efforts and to give expression to the German government's willingness to press Huerta to step down, if the American government would agree to Maas as his replacement.[88]

Even after the failure of these negotiations, Hintze did not give up his efforts to save the Huerta regime through an agreement with the United States. In every discussion with American representatives, he affirmed the necessity of still coming to an agreement with Huerta. At the beginning of December 1913, he suggested to the American chargé d'affaires that the Mexican question be brought before The Hague Court of Arbitration, but despite O'Shaughnessy's support, the American government rejected the proposal.[89] His unsuccessful effort led Hintze to an assessment of the situation which was extremely pessimistic from the point of view of the German government: "Domestically, the weakening of the Huerta government unfortunately continues. I regret it, as I cannot yet see what will follow it, and I would not be justified in expecting anything better."[90]

The German attempts to save the Huerta regime through a joint action by the European powers or by mediation between Huerta and the American government had failed. It could point to a certain success only in one area: it had been able to avoid a direct confrontation with American diplomacy in spite of the resentment U.S. policy was promoting in Germany.

The American actions in Mexico had not only given rise to the sharpest reaction in most of the ruling circles in Germany but had also provoked the German press to sharp attacks. Thus the *Leipziger Neueste Nachrichten* saw in the American actions in Mexico nothing but a policy aimed exclusively at the exploitation of Mexican petroleum supplies, and the *Rheinisch-Westfälische Zeitung* warned the Latin American states against United States aggression.[91] The kaiser himself used expressions like "quite unheard-of interventions in foreign affairs," "swinishness," and so on and called Wilson's representative in Mexico, Lind, an "agent of Rockefeller."[92] Nonetheless, this attitude was subordinated to the desire to avoid a clash with the United States. On 16 October 1913, five days after Huerta's second coup, Bryan sought out Bernstorff and asked Germany to revoke its recognition of Huerta.[93] While the Foreign Office had no intention of taking such a step, it nonetheless gave an answer which, in contrast to Great Britain's negative response, was, in the words of Secretary of State Jagow, "evasive."[94] America's ambassador was repeatedly informed that Germany "had no political interest in Mexico."[95] This orientation did not fail to have its effect. Bryan thanked Bernstorff for German restraint in Mexico, and the American ambassador in Berlin, Gerard, even stated on 27 November 1913 his belief "that a possibility exists of convincing the German government to withdraw its recognition of Huerta."[96] Hintze showed the same caution as the Foreign Office in Berlin toward the United States in Mexico. He himself defined his attitude: "Our policy falls between opposition and a laissez-faire attitude. We in no way support American policy, but we also do not openly oppose it, as we energetically protect German citizens and their interests. Such a policy has of course only limited aims and perhaps cannot be very popular in any country; it is nonetheless the sole policy possible for an individual European power here."[97]

This was the sense of Hintze's action when he dissuaded the European diplomats in Mexico from sending a telegram of protest by the diplomatic corps to the United States over its attitude in Mexico. At the end of November 1913, the French and Belgian ministers had proposed to the European diplomats in Mexico that they send a collective telegram to their governments protesting both a possible American intervention and the refusal of the United States to recognize Huerta,[98] in addition to calling on the European powers to send troops to Mexico for the protection of their citizens. Hintze, who still believed in the possibility of "friendly cooperation" and who knew that the dispatch of German troops to Mexico was out of the question, was anything but enthusiastic about this proposal. "I am afraid," he wired to Berlin, "that joint telegrams will arouse the ire of the United States, giving the appearance of organized opposition among the diplomatic corps here, and would interfere with friendly influence on Washington."[99]

The affair put German diplomacy in a difficult position. An agreement to cosign the telegram could have led to tensions with the United States, whereas refusal to sign or an abstention might have elicited very negative reactions from the Huerta government and moreover created the impression of Germany's subordination to the United States. Hintze was thus instructed "to avoid difficulties with the United States under any circumstances" but was simultaneously requested to "stop short of open opposition to a collective telegram."[100]

With the indication that new proposals by the United States were forthcoming, Hintze actually was able to influence the diplomatic corps and to persuade a majority of diplomats to withdraw the proposal, so that the issue was never put to a vote. It was revealed that the British and Japanese ministers were confronted with the same dilemma as Hintze. They immediately seized upon his argument and came out against a protest telegram.[101]

In one question, nonetheless, Hintze's "reserve" had its limits: in his attitude toward the revolutionaries. When the rumor surfaced in October 1913 that the American government intended to recognize the revolutionaries as a belligerent party, Hintze proposed to the Foreign Office "that it be made known in a friendly fashion that a considerable number of the rebels were murderers and robbers" and that "to grant these bandits the rights of a belligerent party contradicts every basis of humanity and morality."[102] At the same time he reported that the British, the French, and the Spanish ministers had sent similar communiqués to their governments. Bernstorff received appropriate instructions on the matter. But as neither Great Britain nor France lodged complaints in Washington, Bernstorff did nothing.[103]

In this entire affair, the general attitude of European diplomats in Mexico gives the impression that everyone was playing a kind of double game.

They knew perfectly well that their governments would never move alone against the United States. Underlying their public stance of aggressiveness toward the United States was the hope that their colleagues would interpret such a stance as real and encourage their governments to anti-American actions.

One question which might have led to a diplomatic conflict between Germany and the United States was the dispatch of German warships to Mexico. After Huerta's coup, Hintze had wired Berlin: "Request warships sent to east coast to calm colony provided other European powers do same; if not, transfer protection to American warships."[104] The kaiser agreed to send warships to Mexico, but remarked disdainfully "Of course! A ship is indeed needed! And none is there!"[105] To the second half of Hintze's telegram, he responded with a categoric "No!" With the kaiser's agreement, the naval staff immediately ordered the warships *Hertha* and *Bremen* to the east coast of Mexico, without awaiting similar moves by other European powers and without notifying the Americans in advance. The *Nürnberg* was also ordered to head for the Mexican coast.[106] With the dispatch of the *Hertha,* Germany's previously observed principle of following Britain's lead in all undertakings in Mexico was broken for the first time.

The American press underscored the fact that the first non-American ship to visit Mexico was German. The *New York Sun* and the *Journal of Commerce* reported that, according to Bernstorff, "there is astonishment in official circles here that the American government was not informed in advance of this move."[107]

The *New York Tribune* wrote that "there has previously been no doubt about Germany's peaceful and pro-American intentions. Thus such a step might create embarrassment for the American government, if this example is followed by other nations and if the Mexican question, whose settlement is the exclusive affair of the United States, is transposed to an international arena."[108] American diplomacy nonetheless held back from a protest. The dispatch of foreign warships to the American continent prior to that time had not been considered a violation of the Monroe Doctrine, and the American government was not prepared to strengthen the opposition of the European powers to its Mexican policy by such an extension of the Monroe Doctrine. The United States moreover still hoped to enlist the support of German diplomats in its struggle against the Huerta government. The attacks by the American press were in fact ignored by German diplomacy, but they nonetheless prompted it to certain precautionary measures. Thus Bernstorff was instructed to inform the American government of the dispatch of the *Nürnberg.*[109] The naval staff, which had planned the visit to Mexico and to South America of a fleet formation made up of two battleships and a light cruiser, was advised by

Zimmermann in a letter to the head of the German Admiralty, Tirpitz: "A visit to Mexican ports would best be avoided for the moment, since such a show of force in the Gulf of Mexico, where His Majesty's Ships *Hertha* and *Bremen* have already been sent, seems neither called for nor politically useful at this moment."[110] The captain of the *Hertha* received instructions from Hintze "to cultivate good relations with the Mexican authorities and to establish a positive relationship with the American naval forces."[111] During the visit of the *Hertha*'s captain to Mexico City, a visit to Huerta was expressly ruled out, since the visit to the president of the British Admiral Craddock had shortly before prompted a serious reaction by the Americans.[112]

In spite of all these precautions, the presence of German warships in Mexican waters aroused the suspicion of the Americans. The captain of the *Bremen* therefore suggested that the ships be withdrawn as quickly as possible. Otherwise "conflicts could easily arise with the Americans, who as matters stand have the largest interests here and who already consider themselves masters here."[113]

Similar efforts to avoid a conflict with the United States were also expressed in the realm of propaganda. On the subject of the attacks on American policy in Mexico appearing in a number of newspapers controlled by German heavy industry, the semiofficial *Norddeutsche Allgemeine Zeitung* wrote, for example: "The press of our country must in general write much more carefully and guardedly in its commentaries on the diplomacy and statesmanship of President Wilson and Secretary of State Bryan. It is unfair, and moreover senseless to state, as many of our editors have done, that the Americans are seeking to seize Mexico in order thereby to harm German interests."[114]

The German government's attempts to avoid antagonizing the United States were on the whole successful until April 1914. In the first month of 1914 Germany seemed to deal with the vacillation of Woodrow Wilson's Mexican policy without provoking his antagonism, but it was forced to recognize that its plans for the rescue of the Huerta regime with a compromise between Huerta and the United States and for "friendly cooperation" that would secure significant influence for Germany in Mexico had definitely failed.

Hintze, suggesting that "European interests in this struggle with neither end nor solution had been routed," approached Lind one more time at the end of January 1914 with a proposal to resume negotiations with Huerta. Lind stated that the revolutionaries had become so strong that they could no longer be ignored. Even though Hintze had to agree, he still clung to the hope "that the fortunes of war could still take another turn."[115]

At the beginning of February, Hintze found himself forced to report to the Reichskanzler: "It must be admitted at this time that the promotion of negotiations between the United States and Mexico in the foreseeable future appears from here to be virtually hopeless."[116] A short time later the tensions between the United States and Carranza resulting from the Benton affair and the attitude of the American chargé d'affaires O'Shaughnessy, who was attempting to bring about a compromise between Huerta and the United States, gave him new hopes for such an agreement.

At the end of March 1914, the situation appeared favorable to Hintze for a renewed attempt at mediation. Through middlemen, he contacted Huerta, who also indicated his willingness to negotiate with the Americans.[117] The United States, however, refused once again, so that Hintze had to record an additional failure. The more he recognized that every attempt to bring about an agreement between Huerta and the United States was condemned to failure, the more he fell back on his proposal for "friendly cooperation," that is, for a joint intervention and a resulting joint rule of Mexico by Europe and the United States.

Hintze's commitment to this resolution was not only in keeping with his desire to facilitate German penetration in Mexico, but was also related most intimately to his whole conception of the Mexican revolution. This conception, which he articulated thoroughly in this period, was based on an overt racism. He was, of course, compelled to recognize certain socioeconomic causes of the Mexican revolution—one of those causes being "the revolt of the Indians against a centuries-old exploitation"—but the revolution was for him above all an expression of the "inferiority" of the Mexican race, of its "incapacity" to rule itself. The "so-called Mexican people," he wrote, "is made up of an aggregation of Indian tribes, themselves to some extent hostile to one another, of various ethnological origins, roughly 12 million, a dreary, dull, sluggish mass uninterested in work or activity; in addition, Spanish and Indian mestizos, some with considerable black admixture, roughly 3 million. There are practically no purely white Mexicans, aside from some naturalized Germans and declining numbers of other Europeans. The mestizos have inherited, as is typical with bastard races, the vices but not the virtues of the races which produced them, which is particularly apparent here because of the addition of black blood."[118]

This outlook brought Hintze to the conclusion "that Mexico, left to itself, would remain mired in its revolutionary period for years, and that foreign aid must help it through."[119] He naturally did not want to concede such "aid" and hence the control of Mexico to the United States, and he was thus left with only one conclusion: "foreign aid, and that naturally means by all the powers having interests here."[120]

As late as mid-March 1914, Hintze considered "friendly cooperation" to be a possibility. The United States, however, did not have the slightest thought of giving the European powers any position in Mexico, particularly after the British withdrawal. This was shown with complete clarity by one American conception of a joint European-American intervention in Mexico; had such an intervention come about, then the United States would have assured exclusive control for itself and would have reduced the European states to a purely secondary role. After his visit to Washington, the British chargé d'affaires in Mexico, Hohler, told Hintze that "the American chief of staff, Leonard Wood, had immediately broached this question, and had in fact proposed a joint military intervention in Mexico by all powers with interests there, in a form that would have given the United States the lion's share of troop commitments and command of operations, with the other countries represented to some extent by 'military delegations' of lesser strength."[121] Hintze naturally refused such "friendly cooperation" categorically: "I don't take Wood's proposal seriously; it assures the Americans of all the advantages and gives the other participating countries more than their share of the blame and the disadvantages."[122]

Bernstorff saw much more clearly the impossibility of "cooperation" with the United States as proposed by his colleague in Mexico. After a visit by Hohler in Washington, Bernstorff wrote, Hohler "seems moreover to be convinced that all such attempts at mediation are based on false premises. President Wilson, more precisely, will hear nothing of foreign help. He wants only a free hand, and his entire policy is oriented to that. Any step taken by foreign powers in Washington would only play into Mr. Wilson's hands. He would then be able immediately to stir up the atmosphere in public opinion here which he needs to impose his will in Mexico through force."[123]

In view of the increasing tensions in Europe, German diplomacy was attempting even more than in the past to avoid conflict with the United States over the Mexican question. In December 1913 and January 1914, the Foreign Office rejected the proposals of the British and French ambassadors for joint landings of European troops in Mexico. Jagow as well, in his statement on the Mexican question before the Reichstag on 17 February, after the announcement that the American arms embargo on Mexico had been lifted, limited himself to a mere echoing of the American viewpoint and consciously avoided any criticism of American policy.[124]

The desire to rekindle British-American antagonism, however, came more and more to the fore. At the beginning of March 1914, the director of the Deutsch-Südamerikanische Bank, Trug, informed the Foreign Office "that in Hamburg, London, and Paris, a statement of protest against the weakness and disunity of Europe with regard to America in the Mexican question is being contemplated. The protagonists of the movement in Hamburg are the small and medium-sized firms that have interests in

Mexico. The banks have until now maintained their distance." Somewhat disconcerted, he asked "if the attempt should be made to avert such a statement in Hamburg." The answer of the Foreign Office was unequivocal. "After consultation with the undersecretary of state," wrote Kemnitz, "I have assured Mr. Trug that the interested parties should above all make sure that loud protests are made in London. If that takes place, a similar statement in Hamburg cannot hurt anything."[125]

To the extent that American hegemony appeared to be solidifying itself in Mexico and that Germany was being pushed into the role of an impotent spectator, the kaiser's anger against the United States increased, as well as against Great Britain and France, which in his eyes had betrayed European interests in Mexico. His anger in this regard was directed above all at Great Britain. When, on 28 January 1914, the German ambassador in London, Lichnowsky, reported that British bankers had proposed to the foreign minister a joint venture by Great Britain, France, and Germany to force Huerta's departure, in which their representatives in Mexico would inform Huerta "that none of the three powers would support Mexico as long as he remained in power," Wilhelm II erupted: "Absolutely not! Huerta is the only man who can keep order in Mexico—he has to stay."[126] To the bankers' statement that such a move would "build an excellent bridge" for both Wilson and Huerta, the kaiser remarked: "That means that instead of Huerta leaving under American pressure, we Europeans have to pressure him for the Americans, so that they can have a free hand! What rubbish! But Huerta will stay, as far as I'm concerned!"[127] He underlined this opinion once again at the end of the report: "I am of the opinion that Huerta must remain and be supported as long as it is possible."

The kaiser harshly condemned the British withdrawal from Mexico in the Benton affair. At the end of March, he received a report from Bernstorff, in which Bernstorff predicted a European withdrawal from Mexico and explained that Wilson's policy had demonstrated "that Europe is not sufficiently united and strong to resist American policy in the Western hemisphere."[128] To this, Wilhelm II noted in the margin: "England has left Europe brilliantly in the lurch and brought it into general discredit. It should have united with the *continent* in order to defend *Europe's* interests *jointly* in Mexico, and thereby break the Monroe Doctrine. Wilson would have been forced to action and would have come off with a bloodied hand in Mexico." On a report arriving almost simultaneously from London, which said "People here are also saying that the European powers are completely lacking in the means necessary to make the rebels pay for harm to the life and property of European citizens," he noted: "if they do not work together." And he added, finally, with contempt: "How far John Bull has fallen!"[129]

The German kaiser viewed French policy in Mexico with the deepest contempt. He bitingly annotated the report from Paris that the French government had no intention of moving against the United States in Mexico with the remark "How docile la France has become!"[130] Wilson's policy, too, continued to draw his wrathful commentary. On a report from Bernstorff, according to which Wilson had stated before the U.S. Senate that it was necessary "to move energetically in Mexico and to win over England's ally, Japan, as well as the rest of Europe with concessions on the question of canal fees," he noted: "It won't win me over, I won't be bribed!"[131] He characterized the rebels as "bands of robbers,"[132] while asserting again and again that Huerta was the only man who could bring about "law and order" in Mexico.

### The *Ypiranga* Case

German diplomacy had failed in all its attempts to bring about either an agreement between the Huerta regime and the United States, or "friendly cooperation" giving Germany a decisive influence in Mexico. The only "success" it could record for itself was the avoidance of conflict with the United States over Mexico.[133]

This success was not least of all attributable to Hintze, who masterfully practiced the art of the diplomatic game. He had the capacity for cleverly keeping his own real views to himself in discussion and for giving others the impression, through allusions and remarks saying nothing and committing him to nothing, that he agreed with them completely. He had succeeded in winning simultaneously the friendship and confidence of Madero and Henry Lane Wilson. He achieved his master stroke in the Huerta period. During that time, not only was he the confidant of both Carden and Lind, but he was also seen as an ally by Huerta himself, while the revolutionaries regarded him throughout as a friend of Madero.

The American intervention in Mexico and the related affair of the German ship *Ypiranga* seemed to call into question the "success" which was the source of such pride, if not simply to make a mockery of it.

The beginning of the Mexican-American disputes after the Tampico incident had already confronted German diplomats with an embarrassing situation. If Germany opposed the United States, such an attitude would lead to tensions with that country which Germany wished to avoid. If, however, Germany allowed American policy to go completely unopposed, this would be interpreted both in Mexico and throughout Latin America, where the American venture had evoked the sharpest protest, as a recognition of the Monroe Doctrine and of U.S. hegemony everywhere in Latin America.

While the Foreign Office took no position on the Mexican-American conflict and only continued to reaffirm its hopes for an early settlement, most of the German press launched extremely sharp attacks on the United States. The extent of the attacks was reflected in Bernstorff's telegram from Washington on 18 April. "The American press," he wired, "is beginning to complain about the attitude of the German papers, which are allegedly taking sides against the United States in the Mexican conflict. If pressure is possible, it would in my opinion be highly desirable to prevent a repetition of the battle of the press which took place during the Spanish war. The effect of such a battle would now be even more harmful than the previous one, because there appears to be nothing more for us to win from Mexico in the future."[134] The semiofficial *Norddeutsche Allgemeine Zeitung* thereupon had to attempt to curb the German press.

The attacks in the press had nevertheless not been unwelcome in the Foreign Office. On the same day that Bernstorff's telegram on the American complaints about the German press arrived in Berlin, the Foreign Office received a report from the German minister in Chile, Eckert, in which the opposite danger was underlined. "American press dispatches for several days showing tendency to alienate Latin American countries from us by implications that we are explicitly supporting U.S. policy toward Mexico. Request energetic countereffort through wire service, in careful form, taking Washington into account."[135] The Foreign Office now had an easy time of it and could make use of the German press. They instructed the minister to play up in Chilean newspapers the American attacks on the German press over the Mexican question.[136]

This careful game of strategy was suddenly and roughly upset by the *Ypiranga* affair.

In late February and early March 1914, a number of English and French banks had decided to support Huerta, whose position was becoming increasingly difficult, with money and arms shipments. An official loan, such as the one provided as recently as January 1914, was not considered, because the British government, which had already undertaken its withdrawal from Mexico at the end of 1913, and the French government, which did not wish to bring about any conflict with the United States over the Mexican question, had come out under American pressure against any loan to Huerta.[137] An official loan would thus have brought the banks into conflict not only with the United States, but with their own governments. They avoided this obstacle by negotiating, not with an official representative of the Huerta government, but with a private intermediary. This straw man was the American businessman DeKay, a confidant of Huerta. It was said that Huerta characterized him with the cynical words: "Respectable people don't come to me, and hence I must rule with the *canaille*."[138]

DeKay sold 51 percent of the shares of his almost completely bankrupt

National Packing Company[139] to the Mexican government and received in return bonds still unspent from the loan of June 1913 worth 3.5 million pounds sterling, of which 2 million were to have been spent on armaments.[140] These bonds were officially worthless, since the English and French banks, under American pressure, had not officially taken them over and issued them. In reality, though, they had secretly taken them over and deposited them in a Swiss bank, in order to divert all suspicion from themselves and also to avoid any taxes in their countries. The chief of the Swiss general staff who reported these facts to the German ambassador in Bern, had the impression "that the deal had been especially promoted by the English and that England was thereby rendering the Huerta government a tremendous service."[141] The representative of the English financial group that pushed through this deal was Neville Chamberlain.[142]

The bulk of the weapons were purchased in France from the Cartoucheries Françaises and from Saint Chamond. But since they did not completely meet the Mexican requirements, the French government helped out with weapons and ammunition for Huerta. The English firm Vickers and Armstrong also obtained a contract, and arms purchases were made in Switzerland and even in the United States. In Germany, however, no weapons whatsoever appear to have been purchased.[143]

These weapons and ammunition were combined with another arms shipment whose provenience was very different but which was shrouded in the same kind of secrecy. In the fall of 1913, Woodrow Wilson had embargoed all shipments of arms to Mexico. In order to circumvent this embargo, Huerta in the latter part of 1913 named a foreign intermediary to carry out arms purchases for him in the United States. Leon Rast, Russia's vice-consul in Mexico, was hired by Huerta, provided with ample funds, and sent to the United States. There he purchased large amounts of arms for the Mexican president but in order to hide their destination had them sent to the Russian port of Odessa. From there they were sent on another ship to Hamburg, where they were again transshipped and placed on board a German ship bound for Mexico, the *Ypiranga,* which belonged to Germany's largest shipping company, the Hamburg Amerika line, generally known as Hapag.[144]

It is difficult to fully ascertain why a German shipping line was chosen for this purpose. In 1917, DeKay told a German diplomat that the Hapag had been chosen because of its convenient connections with Mexico.[145] There may have been another cause which DeKay would, for obvious reasons, have preferred not to communicate to a German representative.

It was clear to English and French banks that an arms shipment for the Huerta government, however well disguised, could provoke a conflict with the United States, which their own governments wanted to avoid at all costs because of the mounting tensions in Europe. The arms suppliers thus took an extremely clever step by contracting a German shipping company, the Hapag, for the delivery of the arms to Mexico. They assumed quite correctly that the German government could thus be quite easily dragged into a dispute between the shipping company and the Americans and that finally German imperialism would appear in American eyes as the major guilty party for arms shipments to Huerta.

The Hapag ships *Ypiranga* and *Dania* took on the weapons in Hamburg and departed for Mexico. The *Ypiranga* was scheduled to arrive first in Mexico. Perhaps learning that, in the event of a conflict with the United States, the first ship would be very carefully searched, the *Ypiranga* had been loaded as a special precaution almost exclusively with American weapons.[146]

Wilson was informed of the imminent arrival of the *Ypiranga* on the night of 21 April 1914. He thereupon issued the order to move immediately to occupy the customs house in Veracruz to prevent the unloading of the weapons. After the *Ypiranga* had arrived in Veracruz, its captain immediately received from the Americans instructions not to unload his cargo and to remain in Veracruz until further notice.

The German cruiser *Dresden* was at that moment at anchor in Veracruz harbor. Her commander, who feared a seizure of the *Ypiranga* by the Americans, commandeered the ship to transport refugees under the auspices of the Reich. It thereby became part of the German fleet and protected from American seizure. The captain of the *Dresden* informed Admiral Fletcher of this measure and at the same time explained "that the captain of the *Ypiranga* has orders to unload no cargo."[147] Nothing else, moreover, was possible, as long as the ship was in the service of the Reich, for otherwise the German government would have had to bear the official responsibility for such a step.

A day later Bernstorff visited the State Department and there lodged a protest against the temporary seizure of the *Ypiranga*.[148] He considered this a violation of international law, since the United States and Mexico were not at war and no blockade had been imposed. Bryan thereupon officially told him "that Admiral Fletcher today overstepped his orders due to a misunderstanding and by instructing the captain of a German merchant ship not to leave the port of Veracruz with armaments destined for General Huerta."[149] Bernstorff was told that Fletcher had been instructed to apologize to the captain of the *Ypiranga*. Bryan declared at the same time that the American government did indeed hope that the arms would be unloaded in Veracruz, where they would be under American control, but that it was not arrogating to itself the right to take control of the arms.

This apology arrived at the Foreign Office several days before an analysis by its legal division stated that from the viewpoint of international law, the American position was unassailable and that any protest by the Germans would be unjustified.[150]

The strikingly polite and conciliatory American attitude toward German diplomacy was undoubtedly based on the desire to prevent Huerta from getting hold of the arms carried by the German ships. Since the American government did not wish to occupy all of Mexico and, moreover, wished to avoid an official state of war with Mexico, which would have been brought about by the imposition of a blockade, it needed the German government's agreement not to deliver weapons to Huerta. The official apology and the statement that the United States could not prevent the unloading of the armaments were intended to make it easier for the German government to take such steps without loss of prestige.[151]

On the day after the Americans had issued their apology, Bryan visited Bernstorff and requested the assurance of the German government that the arms on the *Ypiranga* would not be delivered to Huerta. In Berlin, however, no steps were undertaken to this end; an inquiry was merely sent to the Hapag director, Albert Ballin. The latter was clearly expecting an expansion of the Mexican-American war and replied to the government "that the arms and ammunition cargo of the *Ypiranga* would probably be shipped back to Germany."[152] The Foreign Office passed this information on to Washington. Since, however, it did not mention that this was merely a decision of the management of Hapag, the State Department presumed that it was a governmental decision. Wilson officially expressed his thanks to the German government,[153] and the American government even went so far, after the *Ypiranga*'s arrival in Tampico, as to prevent the seizure of the arms by the revolutionaries,[154] who had just occupied that city.

Hintze had initially raised objections against the delivery of arms to Huerta with the Hapag management after the American occupation of Veracruz. He specifically feared that the unloading of the arms would lead to an intensification of the war. "For some time," he reported, "there has been a de facto cease-fire between the Federales and the rebels, because the latter since the end of April (due to the reimposition of the embargo) are no longer receiving ammunition from the United States and because the former have exhausted their supplies: we have an overriding interest in the preservation of this cease-fire because of the Germans living in the country, who are gravely threatened by the hostilities between both parties. The desire and need of the Germans living here is not to prolong the agony of the current regime."[155] Still, Hintze predicted that the unloading of the arms would lead to tensions with the United States. "Our rivals would not hesitate to portray the delivery of the arms and ammunition from the *Bavaria* and the *Ypiranga* as a violation of previously correct behavior and to exploit it in Washington as 'ambiguity' and 'hypocrisy.' I am particularly thinking of England in this regard, which has reason to wish to turn attention away from the multiple fiascos of its policy here. The English minister here has already spoken to others in a vein which justifies the above fears."[156]

After the Martin Schröder firm, which had officially taken over the weapons shipments, and the Hapag had been offered larger fees by the Huerta government, both began pressing for a delivery of the arms to Huerta.[157] On 17 May, the Hapag representative in Mexico, Heynen, approached Hintze and requested approval to unload the weapons in Puerto Mexico, a port which was still under Huerta's control.[158]

Hintze then consulted Berlin, but avoided expressing his own reservations. The reply of the Foreign Office as well was ambiguous. The government wished to permit the unloading of the arms, but not to approve it explicitly. Hintze was informed that the Hapag had made no request to the Foreign Office and that hence no decision could be made in this matter.[159]

Hintze properly interpreted this reply, as his letter of 3 June to the Reichskanzler shows: "Your Excellency's decision referred the settlement of the question of the unloading of the *Ypiranga* to the Hamburg-America Line. I have understood from this that Your Excellency regards the further handling of this problem to be a private affair."[160] In spite of his reservations, he then did everything to see that the arms arrived smoothly in Puerto Mexico. On almost the same day that he wrote in his diary concerning the plans to unload the arms shipment, "This seems to me to satisfy the aims of the M. Schröder firm and of the other arms suppliers, but hardly those of the Hamburg-America Line or of the Germans here—because it prolongs the agony of the Huerta government,"[161] he staged a maneuver to get the arms out of Veracruz.

The Americans knew that the *Ypiranga* would under no circumstances be unloaded as long as it remained in the service of the Reich. Hintze used this to his own ends. "When on 17 May I released the *Ypiranga* from Reich service as unnecessary for the transportation of refugees," he elaborated, "I instructed the kaiser's consul in Veracruz to keep this release a secret from the Americans and from the other authorities to spare the ship and ourselves the unpleasantries which might arise from its cargo . . . . The Reich service flag was lowered when the ship left Veracruz for Puerto Mexico on 25 May."[162] This procedure was, however, too much even for the Foreign Office, whose advisor in the matter, Kemnitz, criticized Hintze's orders to keep the release of the *Ypiranga* from Reich service a secret with the words: "Such orders should best have been avoided." Concerning the lowering of the Reich service flag on 25 May, moreover, he noted: "should have been done earlier."[163]

The precise causes of the actions of the German authorities and the

Hapag over the unloading of the arms in Puerto Mexico are not clear. Why, in his telegram of 17 May, in which he requested the Foreign Office to take a position on the unloading of arms from the *Ypiranga*, did Hintze not express his own doubts on the question? The Foreign Office knew, both from press dispatches and a report from the naval attaché in Washington, the reasons for the attack on Veracruz, and the role played by the *Ypiranga*'s cargo in that attack; why did it leave such an important decision to the Hapag? Why, moreover, did the shipping company endanger its major interests in the United States to deliver a shipment of arms to Huerta?

It is possible that both Hintze and the Foreign Office wished to avoid a conflict with the powerful Hapag, particularly insofar as they were convinced that the shipping company would do nothing to endanger its position in the United States. As for Hapag itself, its judgment may have been impaired by the prospect of a handsome profit. It made no attempt to sound out the attitude of the American government with either its representatives in the United States or with the Foreign Office, but relied completely on the Hapag representative in Veracruz, Heynen. On 23 May, Hapag's management had wired Heynen to express its hopes that there would be no difficulties in unloading the arms in Puerto Mexico and that the Americans would create no obstacles. Only on 29 May, after most of the arms had been unloaded, did Hapag ask Heynen for his own assessment: "Please wire confirmation that the minister and the American authorities in Veracruz have withdrawn opposition before discharging ammunition in Puerto Mexico."[164] Heynen replied that the Americans had not informed him that they were opposed to an unloading of the arms in Puerto Mexico.

These actions by the German authorities, as well as by the Hapag, may have resulted from a mistaken assessment of American policy. When Ballin, who was the head of Hapag, expressed the view that the *Ypiranga*'s arms would be sent back to Berlin, and when Bernstorff passed this along to Bryan, Bryan had taken this as a binding commitment by the German government.[165] Thus, partly because of this assumed commitment and partly because Mexico and the United States were not at war, Bryan had not instructed the American authorities in Veracruz to prevent the *Ypiranga* from taking its cargo out of that port city,[166] although the American authorities had suggested to the Hapag that the arms be unloaded in Veracruz, where they would have been under American control. Some German diplomats and businessmen may even have assumed that the United States now wanted the arms delivered to Huerta in view of mounting tensions with the revolutionaries after the American occupation of Veracruz. Hintze explained the fact that American authorities had not prevented the *Ypiranga* from leaving Veracruz with its cargo of arms by a reversal of U.S. policy. He assumed that Carranza's sharp protest against the American occupation of Veracruz "had somewhat strengthened Huerta's position in the United States, for it is not naturally in America's interest to have a strong Carranza in Mexico in place of Huerta."[167] The Hapag also told Bülow, former German Reichschancellor and the Reich government's representative in Hamburg, "that Washington, which in April was disappointed with the activities of the rebel leaders Villa and Carranza, intends to leave Huerta somewhat more firmly in the saddle for a while."[168]

The cargo of the *Ypiranga* was unloaded on 28 May in Puerto Mexico. The Hapag steamers *Bavaria* and *Dania*, both carrying weapons for Huerta, arrived there at the same time. The Huerta government received a total of 20,000 rifles and 15,000 boxes of ammunition.[169] German diplomacy had failed in all its efforts with regard to Mexico. The sole exception was its effort to avoid conflict with the United States. The delivery of arms to Huerta now threatened to destroy even this "achievement" of German diplomacy.

Hintze's pessimistic predictions were immediately and completely fulfilled. A storm of outrage erupted in the United States against the German government, which together with the Hapag was attacked in the sharpest fashion by the American press. The *New Evening Post* spoke directly of a "breach of faith" by the German Reich. "All the local papers I have seen last night and this morning," reported the disconcerted German consul in New York, "are up in arms about the fact that the Hamburg-American Line steamers *Ypiranga* and *Bavaria* have in the last few days apparently landed weapons destined for General Huerta in the port of Puerto Mexico."[170]

The Austrian and British ministers in Mexico, "the latter not without malicious pleasure," showed Hintze telegrams from their colleagues in Washington reporting that the American government was "enraged over delivery of arms and the like to Huerta from the *Ypiranga* and the *Bavaria*."[171] "It seems doubtful," wrote Boy Edd, the German naval attaché in Washington, "that such a step was desirable from the standpoint of German interests. Not only the American government circles but public opinion as well are taking a very dim view of the action of the German steamship line. The army and the navy are particularly disturbed by the *Ypiranga* affair."[172] Bryan expressed to Bernstorff his particular annoyance at the conduct of Hapag, "because he had taken it for granted that the weapons would not be landed." The *Ypiranga* had also called at Tampico, and the Constitutionalists were prevented from confiscating its cargo only by the American government. Finally, this episode was particularly displeasing to Bryan because "it will now be difficult to withhold arms from the Constitutionalists."[173]

The Germans attempted to shift the blame to the Hapag representatives in Veracruz. Bernstorff told Bryan that "exclusive responsibility for the delivery of the *Ypiranga* cargo belongs to the shipper's representative in Veracruz, who thought that in view of the changing circumstances that the Americans had no objections to delivery."[174] It was simultaneously affirmed in a communiqué for the semiofficial German press "that if the American authorities had made it known that they were opposed to the delivery to Puerto Mexico, it is obvious that the Hamburg-American Line, in view of its large holdings in the United States, would have taken such a request into account."[175]

The *Ypiranga* affair threatened to have very unpleasant consequences for the Hapag. When its two ships returned to Veracruz, they were given customs fines of 118,000 marks by the American authorities there.[176] At the same time, a representative of the Constitutionalists told the German naval attaché in Washington "that the Hamburg-America line would find itself beset with tremendous complications in its commercial and shipping activities under a Constitutionalist regime."[177]

German concerns about the consequences of the *Ypiranga* affair soon proved to be exaggerated. In spite of the extremely sharp initial reaction by the Americans, the affair had no further consequences and was quickly forgotten. Not the least of the reasons for this initially surprising attitude of the American government was German policy in Mexico, whose aims in May and June 1914 were for the first time since the overthrow of Madero to a large extent congruent with American aims.

## Germany's Attempts to Use and to Oust Huerta

There was no longer any doubt among German diplomats that Huerta and his government were finished. Huerta was beaten militarily, and moreover the growing danger of war in Europe—the outbreak of the First World War was only weeks away—made any support of Huerta by the European powers, which had already been ruled out earlier, quite out of the question.

Huerta, who had hoped, after the unloading of the *Ypiranga*, that he would be able to rely on Germany against the United States, was also obliged to recognize this. On 29 May Huerta sent for Hintze, who reported, "England had initially treated him very well, but had then abandoned him; the French are a great people, but had done nothing for him. Germany was confined within too small a territory; it would have to incorporate Austria and Denmark; Germany's natural enemies are England and Russia. Germany wants to colonize and needs oil; he is offering Germany 150,000 square kilometers of land and the oil fields around Tampico, which would be legally taken away from the Americans."[178] It is not unlikely that Huerta's hopes were based at least in part on the proposals

Hintze had made two months before to Minister of Education García Naranjo.

García Naranjo reports in his memoirs that Hintze had invited him to a long discussion in late March or early April.[179] At this time Huerta's delegates in the Mexican parliament, probably as a means of pressure against Great Britain and in order to give the government a "national hue" in the eyes of the population, had proposed a project (which in reality was never meant seriously) to nationalize the Mexican oil fields. In his discussion with García Naranjo, Hintze opposed a nationalization of the oil fields, which he considered unrealizable. He urged the Mexican government to nationalize the oil transport system instead, that is, the pipelines and tankers, and to found a corresponding joint stock company with a capital of 400 million marks. "The government could keep 51 percent of the stock for itself and offer 49 percent for sale. I am firmly convinced that His Majesty Wilhelm II would be the first to buy up a large share of the stock."[180] Hintze stated further that, according to García Naranjo, the Mexican government would not only acquire a large source of revenue through such a step, but that it would also have the ability to control the sources of income of the large oil companies.

These proposals by Hintze are mentioned neither in his diary nor in his reports. This, of course, does not preclude the possibility that he actually made them. It is possible that by presenting such proposals he was acting directly on behalf of Wilhelm II; this could be inferred by the reference to the purchase of stock by the kaiser and by the fact that the kaiser twice took a direct hand in Mexican affairs in the period up to 1914. It could, however, have been a personal initiative which, because it failed, he did not report to Berlin. García Naranjo's report appears to be true, however, because this project was in keeping with both Hintze's economic and political aims. As a member of the imperial navy, Hintze was particularly interested in questions of oil. He had expressed his conviction to the Austrian minister in Mexico that because of the German navy's initiative extensive German investments in Mexican oil production were to be expected;[181] he had also energetically promoted the Mexican mission of the petroleum engineer Wunstorff. It is quite possible that after the Deutsche Bank's withdrawal from the Mexican oil industry, he was looking for new ways of assuring a greater influence for Germany in this domain.

Had the Mexican government taken up Hintze's proposals, then many possibilities for action would have been opened up for Germany in Mexico. Germany would have achieved, without large capital investments and without a direct attack on American holdings in Mexico (only a small pipe line and no oil fields were to be expropriated with compensation, and the Mexican government would hold, as it did with the railroads, the majority of shares) decisive gains at the expense of both Great Britain and the

United States. The German position in the "friendly cooperation" sought by Hintze would have been greatly strengthened even before he had articulated the project. In the event of too strong an American or British resistance, Germany would still have the opportunity of withdrawing in exchange for appropriate American or British compensations in Mexico or elsewhere.

García Naranjo passed on Hintze's proposals to Huerta and to the ministers José María Lozano and Querido Moheno. Huerta showed great interest in the project, but insisted on including England. "I would not like it," he apparently said, "if the German Reich were Mexico's sole partner in such an important project. In my opinion we must give French and British capital the opportunity to acquire shares. Above all, it should not be forgotten that the State Department in Washington has an unjustifiably hostile attitude toward us. England has given us many proofs of its friendship. It would thus be an error to bypass British interests and not invite the English to participate in the planned projects. In short, the shares for the transport project should be sold not only in Berlin, but on the Paris and London markets as well."[182]

Lozano, Moheno, and García Naranjo considered the entire project to be dangerous. "Lozano, Moheno, and I," García Naranjo reported, "agreed that Mexico had nothing to gain from a possible clash among the European powers; what interested us was the attitude of these powers toward the United States. If we embark on an anti-British adventure, we would then be courting the danger of the British Empire's intervention on the side of Woodrow Wilson."[183] Although Moheno was entrusted with further exploration of the project, he never conducted the appropriate negotiations with Hintze. It is not improbable that the Mexican government was in touch with British representatives who had naturally rejected out of hand a project that would have curtailed the rights of their companies in Mexico and opened the oil industry to their German rivals.

Hintze's proposals undoubtedly revealed to Huerta Germany's potential interest in Mexican oil. When, after the American attack on Veracruz, it became obvious to him that he could no longer rely on the English, he then offered Germany the American oil fields in Mexico to gain Germany as an ally against the United States. The offer made on 25 May in the discussion with Hintze was, however, completely unacceptable, for Germany would never have dared contemplate a unilateral, frontal attack against the United States in Mexico. And in May 1914, when Huerta's position had become untenable and when, above all, the danger of war in Europe was becoming more and more threatening, such a move was quite unthinkable.

Hintze made this unmistakably clear to Huerta in his reply to the latter's offer.

The interests of Germany as well as of many other European powers are in a happy and prosperous Mexico, for with such a Mexico the European trading and commercial interests would prosper as well. The representation of these economic interests are nevertheless constrained by the present political conjuncture so that while it may be expressed in energetic diplomatic action or in amicable favors, it must call a halt before more active steps. The reasons for this are the antagonisms in Europe, the ceaseless European arms race, the political dynamite in various parts of Europe, all of which are material for an imminent and explosive war in which the very existence of nations would be at stake. In such circumstances, every country has reservations about over-extending itself around the world. Should this occur, whichever country did it, it would be the signal for another country to attack. Not out of hostility to Mexico, but because it would want to exploit the momentary weakness of its rival, and would be obliged to do so. As far as I can tell—and I am speaking not as the German minister but as one old soldier to another—Huerta has nothing to hope for from Europe, except discreet diplomatic help.[184]

German diplomacy, exactly like its American counterpart, sought an agreement between the Huerta government and Carranza under U.S. auspices as the best solution. Hintze saw in such a solution, just as the Americans did, the only means of at least bringing the victorious revolution to a halt, and saw it as the only way of saving some elements from the general collapse of the Huerta regime and of preventing the most radical revolutionaries, Villa and Zapata, from entering Mexico City. Such an agreement would have to be concluded as rapidly as possible, Hintze told Huerta's foreign minister, Esteva Ruiz, "or we will be overrun by the supporters of Villa and Zapata."[185]

The prerequisite for the conclusion of such an agreement was Huerta's departure. Hintze worked incessantly to bring this about and had in his efforts the complete support of the American State Department. He first attempted to convince Huerta of the necessity of resigning. As early as 28 May, he had asked him to come to terms with the revolutionaries "without regard for himself."[186] Huerta, who did not want to break with Hintze and who was counting on his help if it became necessary to flee, gave Hintze the impression that he agreed but privately had no thought of stepping down. Carden's encouragement and above all the arrival of the weapons from the *Ypiranga, Bavaria,* and *Dania* gave him hope of still being able to remain in power.

Hintze nevertheless did not abandon his efforts to influence Huerta, but on the contrary became increasingly direct and explicit. On 9 June, he visited the dictator and told him

that his game was up and that the question was now to find a solution which would assure him or the nation of a future . . . . the nation and the army are exhausted and sick of war; I am astounded that a man of your intelligence cannot recognize this; you must give the nation time to catch its breath. Your violent means have failed; you have at your disposal many other methods which are at least as effective. Your preoccupation with showing no weakness and with placing honor above everything is untenable. What is at stake here is neither weakness, nor egoism, nor honor, but the existence of the Mexican nation and your own existence. What you must do at this time is *reculer pour mieux sauter,* which I would translate as *ceder para saltar mejor.*[187]

Huerta continued to entertain illusions. He hoped that the Americans would finally come to his aid as a counterweight to the revolutionaries. "I wish to tell you, as a friend, the secret of my policies: the end of the conference and its resolutions will be the eruption of chaos here, and everyone will call me back to my post; I don't tell my ministers that, but I'm telling you, that complete anarchy will set in and people will be pleading for me."[188] Hintze finally succeeded in getting Huerta to declare in principle his willingness to step down if the revolutionaries and the United States could agree on a presidential candidate acceptable to him. He was still vehemently opposed at this time to unconditional resignation.

Hintze had not merely attempted to influence Huerta directly. He also carried on intrigues with Huerta's ministers and attempted to incite them to push Huerta aside with or without violence. Together with the Brazilian representative in Mexico City, Cardoso, who had been handling U.S. affairs since the break in Mexican-American relations, Hintze visited Minister of War Blanquet, who had previously played a decisive role in the overthrow of Madero. Hintze recorded this discussion in his diary. According to this entry, both diplomats told the minister

that every man has his time. We then documented the impossibility for Mexico to wage war: no soldiers, no officers, no weapons, no ammunition, no money. We make it clear that America's first demand for a settlement *in all probability* will be Huerta's departure.... Blanquet literally says: *la guerra no nos conviene,* the war does not sit well with us, and agrees with us that Huerta *would have* to go before the United States made the same demand. Reminding him of his past as Huerta's comrade-in-arms, we tell him that *he*—Blanquet—would be the right man to convince Huerta of this. Blanquet immediately rehearses the sentences he wants to say to Huerta, in a loud voice as old people do, consistently using the familiar "tu." ... We take our leave amidst assurances of discretion and friendship. Blanquet repeats: Huerta will have to step down *por el bien publico.*[189]

This meeting took place prior to the arrival of the *Ypiranga* and the *Bavaria.* When the ships had unloaded their cargo, Blanquet reversed his decision: he thought that he was now strong enough to beat the revolutionaries.[190] But even before the conspiracy with Blanquet had definitely failed, Hintze had attempted to win over another minister of the Huerta government, Foreign Minister López Portillo, to similar plans.

On the morning of 1 May, Hintze spoke with López Portillo. In this meeting, he gave the following analysis of the situation: "I am considering the situation carefully. On one side of the scale is the impossibility for Mexico to wage war, and should it lose such a war, the existence of the Mexican nation and the Mexican state would be placed in jeopardy. On the other side, the personal interests of a single man, who has done his best to bring peace to the country, and who has been shipwrecked in the process. López Portillo said enthusiastically: that is the situation, yes, precisely."[191]

Following this discussion, López Portillo set about mobilizing the cabinet for a conspiracy against Huerta. Minister of Commerce Lozano, however, communicated the details of the plot to Huerta, who struck back immediately. "López Portillo arrived at the Foreign Office and was working then, when at 5 P.M. ministers De la Lama, Alcocer (Interior), and Lozano (Commerce) arrived and in the name of the president requested him to submit his resignation."[192] At this late hour of his rule, Huerta was in no position to execute the minister and limited himself to sending him into exile.[193] Hintze's next collaborators were the new Foreign Minister Esteva Ruiz and Finance Minister De la Lama.

One of the biggest obstacles with which Hintze had to deal in his efforts to bring about Huerta's departure was Carden's activity in Mexico. According to Hintze, the latter was "motivated solely by a burning hatred for the United States and thus by the desire to land one single blow through the vehicle of Huerta. He has told Huerta to 'play his card well,' for the United States would fall into his trap. There could be no doubt that President Wilson was extremely dissatisfied with Fletcher's coup in Veracruz and was looking for an occasion to extricate himself from the situation which had developed there. Public opinion in America was turning more and more against Wilson. Each day of irresolution was a gain for Huerta and a loss for the United States."[194] Characteristic of Carden's attitude was his reaction when Hintze told him of the delivery of the weapons from the *Ypiranga* and the *Bavaria*. "Carden jumps up and exclaims triumphantly: 'Then Huerta will stick.'"[195]

Hintze reported that when Carden could no longer count on any support from the Foreign Office, he said bitterly: "The British Government has given up on Mexico; he [Carden] now wants to launch a press campaign through powerful Englishmen here so that the British people can see what is being sacrificed here: not only Mexico, but all of South America."[196] Carden then attempted to bring about a change in British policy through German diplomacy. On 4 May, he visited Hintze and proposed to him: "Germany should suggest to England, and in any case help bring about in Washington an effective constraint on the shipment of arms and ammunition to the rebels."[197] He explained his proposal with the remark: "I want to scare London and they will do nothing without being scared."[198] Hintze, more far-sighted than Carden, understood that such a step would only help the Americans. "I pointed out to him that if such ideas were taken up by London and Berlin, the American government would perhaps have the occasion it is seeking to go before Congress and public opinion and to say: Europe wants intervention, we cannot help it."[199]

After all his plans had failed, Carden made his last attempt to influence the further development of the situation in Mexico. He proposed to Hintze as the solution to the Mexican question: "a completely neutral person as president; complete freedom for the individual states to choose their governors and to govern themselves internally as it suits them, thus giving the northern states to the rebels, even Morelos and Guerrero to the Zapatistas—and then see how things develop."[200] The execution of this plan would have prevented further advance by the revolutionaries and by the Americans, who in Carden's eyes stood behind the revolutionaries, and would above all have protected large regions where Cowdray's concessions were located from their control. "The goal of his project is to keep the Americans out of the country and to minimize their influence."[201] But Hintze had no interest in collaborating in a plan whose most important aim was the rescue of British oil interests, and thus he did everything to frustrate it. He persuaded Cardoso, to whom Carden had proposed that he present the plan to the mediators in Niagara Falls, to abandon such a project.

The impending collapse of the mediation conference and the relentless advance of the revolutionaries once again reduced Carden's and Hintze's viewpoints to a common denominator. Both of them considered the formation of a provisional government by the diplomatic corps, in order to save at least something of the Huerta regime. "Carden laughingly said of such a plan: 'I say, wouldn't it be glorious if we got behind the back of the Americans after all?'"[202] The further advance of the revolutionaries reduced all these plans to nothing, and at the beginning of July Carden lost all influence on Huerta. What had initially brought them together later drove them apart: the oil question.

Carden had approached Huerta and had requested permission for the shipment of oil out of Veracruz, which was occupied by the Americans. Huerta rejected this request. He wanted to give his government a "national hue" in its last days, to facilitate a possible return to power. He hardly had anything further to hope for from Cowdray; moreover, Carden had told him "that in an emergency Huerta's family could *not* seek refuge in the legation."²⁰³ It was Germany he turned to upon his resignation.

## The Departure of Huerta

Huerta asked the German government to get him out of Mexico in one of its warships. The reaction to this request in Berlin was anything but enthusiastic. There was a general desire not to be any more encumbered in the eyes of the new government than was already the case, and Hintze attempted to persuade Huerta to ask the British for a ship. Huerta absolutely rejected such a proposal, ostensibly because of his falling out with Carden. That was not the sole reason, however. Huerta, who had not given up the hope of returning to Mexico, wanted to appear as the national leader of the country. It was therefore necessary to allow his relations with Great Britain to sink as far as possible into oblivion and not to reassert them by departing on a British ship. On 15 July, Hintze wired Berlin: "Have given up my attempts to palm off Huerta onto an English warship, as his escape was being imperiled by his refusal."²⁰⁴

The German government had no choice. A refusal to get Huerta out of Mexico would have exposed it at home and in Latin America to the charge that it had subordinated itself to the United States. But the American government was itself pressing for Huerta's removal from the country. It was specifically concerned that Huerta might be pushed to acts of despair against Americans in Veracruz or against American property generally if he were deprived of the possibility of escape. "United States of America considers removal of Huerta service to be rendered to them but authorities are not informed,"²⁰⁵ Hintze cabled to the commander of the warship *Dresden*, which had been requisitioned for that purpose.

The report on Huerta's refusal to use an English warship was transmitted by Secretary of State Jagow to the kaiser with a recommendation to grant Huerta's request.²⁰⁶ Wilhelm II agreed with the words: "Then he can of course use our ship."²⁰⁷ In Jagow's opinion, however, Great Britain should in some way be involved in the evacuation of Huerta and his family.²⁰⁸ Hintze succeeded in reaching an agreement with Carden whereby the *Dresden* would take charge of the evacuation of Huerta and Blanquet, while Huerta's family and inner circle would depart on a British warship.²⁰⁹

After his arrival in Puerto Mexico, Huerta attempted to overturn these arrangements, asking the commander of the *Dresden* to take on part of his staff. The captain agreed, but was overruled by Hintze. "Accepting the most legally compromised of Huerta's sons and friends would be harmful to our interests. Have thus . . . explicitly limited my requisition to Huerta and Blanquet and in my telegram No. 81 explicitly repeated that only these two are designated to be received on board the *Dresden*,"[210] he wired to the *Dresden*'s commander. The evacuation of these individuals was to be undertaken by Great Britain, in order for the British to be as compromised as possible.

On 17 July 1914, Huerta and Blanquet boarded the *Dresden* with their wives and four daughters; they were taken to Kingston, the major port of the British crown colony of Jamaica. The "poor" refugees were prepared for this emergency: "Huerta and General Blanquet were well supplied with traveling money, and the women similarly with jewelry. Huerta had roughly half a million marks in gold with him. In addition, he had a much greater amount in checks and other paper,"[211] reported the commander of the *Dresden*.

The defeat of Huerta seemed finally to have shattered the plan and hopes of German diplomats for Mexico. Bernstorff noted with resignation: "There are now only two possibilities of solving the Mexican question, and both of them bear a frightening resemblance to Scylla and Charybdis. Power in Mexico must either pass into the hands of the Constitutionalists or the Americans must take charge of the pacification of the country."[212]

Bernstorff thus saw his belief confirmed that a German move against the United States in Latin America was impossible. Did the leaders of the German government, and especially the kaiser, share this prognosis? Certain indications speak against such a view. In 1917, the American publicist James Kelly published a report from London, according to which British diplomats had assured him that in July 1914, a joint British-German action in Mexico had been proposed by a representative of the kaiser to the Foreign Office, in order to prevent an American conquest of the country. "I am prepared to give you the greatest assurance," he was to have said, "that your country and mine would have no difficulties in delineating our respective spheres of influence in Mexico."[213]

Was this one of the numerous fabrications of war propaganda? On first approach, it might appear to be so. This mission was not recorded in the German documents. In July 1914, the events that constituted the prelude to the First World War, which broke out in August 1914, were playing themselves out. Could a venture in such a distant place as Mexico have been considered? Upon closer examination, Kelly's presentation appears increasingly probable, for the German proposals on Mexico could not be considered apart from the world events of those days.

German diplomacy, which on the fundamental question of fleet construction and imperialist expansion was moving on a course hostile to England, was already attempting, in 1913–14, to arrive at an understanding with Great Britain on secondary questions, in order to keep England out of a European war. In the July crisis of 1914, these efforts attained their high point with the mission of the Hapag director and personal friend of the kaiser Albert Ballin to England. It is not improbable, as Barbara Tuchman presumes, that it was Ballin who delivered the proposals concerning Mexico to the Foreign Office.[214]

A joint German-English action in July 1914 would have been a direct attack on the Monroe Doctrine and would have led to tremendous tensions between Britain and the United States. In addition, England's participation in a European war would have become much more difficult, to say nothing of the fact that the German government hoped to achieve a greater influence in Mexico through such a venture and to avoid the "Scylla and Charybdis" Bernstorff had painted in such grim colors.

The Foreign Office, according to Kelly's account, rejected these plans, without any elaboration. In the midst of the July 1914 crisis, the plan appears so unreal and so out of touch with reality that one is initially inclined to dismiss it as false. But were the hopes the German leaders entertained about England's neutrality in the event of a European war not just as unreal, though documented? The fact that German diplomacy showed particular aggressiveness elsewhere in Latin America precisely in July 1914 further confirms these suppositions.

In July 1914, when Haiti, because of internal conflicts, could no longer pay its foreign debts, the German minister there proposed to the United States a joint American-European trusteeship over the island nation's finances. Just as in the case of the plans for Mexico, this would have signified a break with the Monroe Doctrine. The American government also rejected this proposal, noting that it had for years consistently held to the view that no foreign commercial or other interests "which come from outside the American hemisphere can become so extensive as to represent a complete or partial control of the government and administration of an independent state."[215]

The outbreak of the First World War initially put an end to German hopes for a joint action by European states in Latin America against the will of the United States. The idea, however, was not abandoned. Germany merely sought out new partners, this time in Japan and in Latin America itself.

**Part 3**

**Fragmentation from Within,
Intervention from Without,
1914–17**

# 7 The Split among the Revolutionary Factions

Huerta's coup d'etat and the temporary victory it signified for the traditional ruling class had momentarily overshadowed the disunity and dissension within the revolutionary camp. The weakening of Huerta and the advance of the revolutionary army, however, revived the old contradictions that already existed under Madero and new ones were soon to be added. These were intimately linked with rapid and important transformations that occurred in the social composition and leadership of the revolutionary movements during 1913–15.

### The New Carranza Bourgeoisie

Within a portion of the Carranza movement as early as 1913 a new leadership arose for which the revolution became an important source of personal enrichment and from whose ranks a new bourgeoisie would soon develop. Very little is as yet known about this process of self-enrichment. Still less is known about the uses to which this new bourgeoisie put the newly accumulated wealth. The answers to these questions would shed light on the composition, modes of thought, and aspirations of these important spokesmen of the new Carranzist leadership.

There appear to be two distinct periods in the development of this new bourgeoisie. Until 1915, there occurred a sort of simple take over of the wealth of a part of the old oligarchy by this new group. It took place, for the most part, wherever haciendas belonging to the old ruling group were occupied by "revolutionary" generals and then frequently stripped of every movable object of wealth. At a session of the Revolutionary Convention in Cuernavaca, a speaker bitterly denounced such occupations by both Carranzist and anti-Carranzist generals.

It was in the state of San Luis and in parts of the state of Tamaulipas, where I witnessed this, each one of the interventions made did not benefit the people: not a piece of land was given to the people, nor did the proletariat benefit in anything; not even a grain of corn was given to the hungry nor to the disinherited. Although to say this causes disgrace, shame, and sadness, it is necessary to do so, for the interventions greatly enriched those who made them; it provided capital to those who, before the revolution, did not even have a cent . . . and today

253

they proudly and vainly ride through the streets of Mexico's metropolis, and through the streets of the capitals in vehicles whose origin they would not honestly be able to justify.[1]

While Carranza strictly forbade his generals to distribute the estate lands they occupied among the peasants, he gave them a free hand insofar as the revenues of these estates were concerned. Some generals used this income primarily to feed and arm their troops, but others spent most of it on themselves. The possibilities for self-enrichment evolved from their political and military power. Many provided "protection" against army confiscation and bandit attacks, primarily to foreign companies (which were not to be expropriated) but also to some Mexican hacendados and factory owners, and also "protection" against their own peasants and workers, for which the factory and hacienda owners then paid appropriate sums in return. A typical example was the case of Sewell Emery, the American owner of a sugar plantation in the state of Veracruz. Forms of debt peonage similar to slavery had developed in "classic" fashion on his hacienda. Woodrow Wilson's representative in Mexico, John Lind, who visited this hacienda in the company of Admiral Frank F. Fletcher in 1914, told of peasants who were driven to work by overseers with whips and who were supervised by armed guards. Shaken by this experience, he told a U.S. Senate committee in 1920: "Both Admiral Fletcher and I were astonished that such conditions still existed anywhere, but they undoubtedly did."[2] One could have expected major revolutionary upheavals on such a hacienda; but, in 1920, when Emery told the Senate committee of the conditions on his hacienda, he seemed quite satisfied with the development of the revolution in the region where his estate was located. In 1914 and 1916, a "revolutionary" general who supported Carranza established himself near the hacienda and in return for payments from Emery, protected the plantation owner not only from army confiscations but also from possible peon uprisings on his estate.[3]

In a confidential report to his government, Cunard Cummins, the British chargé d'affaires and former consul in Torreón, named other ways in which these revolutionary generals added to their own fortunes.[4] It is difficult to know whether all of his assertions were true, but there is little doubt about the methods he described. He wrote that General Benjamin Hill often had innocent people locked up in order to extort money from them. General Francisco Robelo, the temporary governor of the Federal District of Mexico, apparently ordered "the looting of many houses of prominent families." He also reported that Colonel Meza Prieto, the temporary chief of police of Mexico City, had "reorganized the well-known band of thieves known as *La Mano que Aprieta* ('The Hand That Grasps'). He arrested persons known to possess money and accused them of being political enemies of the Government; on the following day he would send one of his agents to offer the prisoner liberty on condition that he paid him from $1,000 up.'' General Ortiz Rubio, then governor of the state of Michoacan, "In order to abduct a respectable lady of the City of Morelia and to exact money, . . . sent some of his soldiers disguised with the cry of 'Viva Villa' to take prisoner the husband among the frequenters of a gambling house. Meanwhile, the wife was carried by force to the Governor's residence. The sum of $30,000 was obtained as ransom for the man besides $20,000 seized on the table when he was arrested.''

When the Carranza army began to wield power over increasingly large parts of Mexico after 1915, these sample ''methods'' of self-enrichment gave way to more complex, more indirect, and more effective forms of capital expropriation and accumulation in which the new bourgeoisie began to utilize its control of the state. Thus, as Cummins continued, ''Having gained dominion over the State of Sonora, Obregón seized the railways and employed the trains to foment exclusively his business enterprises, especially the harvesting and sale of the chick peas in the Yaqui River district; by control of the railways he was able to prevent the producers sending their crops to the market and to oblige them to sell them to him at ridiculous prices. In the chick pea business he has thus amassed a capital of some millions of pesos.'' Cummins made similar observations about generals Murguía and Dieguez, who used their control of the railway networks to acquire business monopolies.

Carranza himself is not mentioned in these reports by Cummins, and he was rarely accused of self-enrichment. The same is true for the most radical supporters of his movement. While Cummins did accuse Jara of being a ''dangerous Bolshevik,'' he never accused him of pursuing personal gain. Cummins barely mentions most of the radicals in this connection.

It would be a crude simplification to attempt to draw serious conclusions about the economic and sociopolitical views of the new upper class solely on the basis of its pursuit of private gain. Such an analysis would require thorough studies on the nature of capital investment, if indeed there was any, and on the ties—or lack of them—of this group with foreign capital and with the old ruling oligarchy. Between the interests of a man like Obregón, who founded an economic empire in Sonora,[5] and Murguía,[6] who deposited most of his money in U.S. banks, there are differences that cannot be overlooked.

## The Carranza Movement and the Domestic and Foreign Ruling Groups in Mexico

In contrast to Madero and his advisers, all the factions of the Carranza movement agreed on the importance of stripping the old Díaz oligarchy of its political and military power. For the new "Carranza bourgeoisie," this was the only way of securing their newly acquired wealth. For Carranza's radical supporters, the dismantling of the old Díaz army was the prerequisite for the implementation of social reforms in Mexico.

Carranza and his followers, in contrast to Madero, agreed on the importance of limiting the power of the foreign, predominantly American, companies, as well as that of the old Díaz oligarchy, and demanded action against foreign capital. Some of the Carranza leadership limited their demands to higher taxation and more state control of foreign interests, others called for total expropriation.

The opposition to foreign, primarily American, companies by the new upper class within the Carranza movement had its base in the natural antagonism of a rising bourgeoisie against the hegemony of large foreign concerns in its own country. In addition, the calls for annexation of northern Mexico, widely propagated in the United States, were registered with close attention by the revolutionaries, particularly those from the North. Financial motives also determined the attitude of the northern revolutionaries to foreign capital.

In the Mexican states controlled by Carranza, the highest revenue-producing plantations, mines, and oil wells were owned by Americans. As the production of Mexican industries and haciendas fell because of the civil war, the Carranzist authorities were forced, sooner or later, to impose higher royalties on foreign firms, which previously had paid virtually none.

While the Carranza movement and the earlier Madero movement differed in their respective attitudes toward the political and military power of the old Porfirian oligarchy, there were great similarities in their views concerning the economic power of the old ruling class.

Though the Carranza movement was vocally far more radical in its social policies, it nonetheless had made no serious break with Madero's economic conservatism. In his proclamations Carranza had repeatedly underlined the necessity for radical agrarian reform, which was to expropriate the large landholdings of the old Porfirian hacendados; but, as in the case of Madero, he took few practical steps in this direction. In fact, his actual policy went into the opposite direction. From 1915 on, he ordered the return of the confiscated haciendas to their former owners. By 1917, he was in a position to inform the Constituent Assembly of the successful implementation of such measures in most of the parts of Mexico under his control. There were a few notable exceptions, such as Tlaxcala, where a former Zapata ally, Domingo Arenas, had joined with Carranza. In return, the First Chief allowed some of his peasant followers to keep lands they had occupied.[7] In Sonora, some generals became owners of haciendas they had confiscated from Porfirian landowners.[8] Unfortunately the development and causes of this massive return of land, which distinguishes the Mexican Revolution from other great social revolutions, has never been studied.[9] It is therefore not easy to analyze the modes of action and the reactions of those affected by it and those who carried it out. Carranza's own motivations are relatively easy to explain, since his actions were quite in keeping with his conservative ideology; in addition, however, economic and political factors played an important role.

Carranza wanted to revive agricultural production, which had been seriously curtailed by revolutionary events, as quickly as possible. He was convinced that only the hacendados, and not the peasants, were capable of such a task. Political motives too may have influenced Carranza. In July 1914, when Huerta's hold over the country collapsed completely, the political power of the Porfirian hacendados suffered a setback but was not totally destroyed. There is no proof that in southern or central Mexico, outside of the area controlled by Zapata, major peasant uprisings resulting in the dispersion or departure of the hacendados had taken place. In many of the major regions of Mexico, on the contrary, the hacendados continued to control their property. Many of them such as those in Guanajuato, assembled or were subsidizing private armies, which officially called themselves "revolutionary."[10] Carranza, who wished to weaken and destroy, wherever possible, the most radical wing of the revolution, openly welcomed the cooperation of sections of the old oligarchy. The return of the occupied haciendas was both a compromise and a gesture of goodwill.

In contrast, it is much more difficult to explain why many of the Carranzist bourgeoisie gave up, with so little resistance, the estates they had occupied mainly for their own benefit. Even more difficult to explain is why the most radical leaders among the Carranzists, with a similar lack of resistance, tolerated the return of the expropriated estates to their former owners. It is however possible to formulate certain hypotheses. The bourgeoisie seems to have viewed its control of the state as a less demanding, less risky, less costly, and more profitable source of revenue than the administration of the haciendas. Rosalie Evans, the English owner of a hacienda near Puebla, described in a letter her return in 1917 to the hacienda she and her husband had abandoned years earlier, in the midst of the revolution. After their departure, a peasant village had taken control of the estate. Mrs. Evans called on the Carranzist general in charge and asked that he help her get her land back. The general said he was willing to move against the village on the condition that she give him part of her annual harvest. He also requested the same sort of pay from all the hacendados in the area.[11] Such a procedure was obviously far less risky for the general than the personal take over of an administration of the haciendas.

The acquiescence of the radicals in the Carranza camp to this massive return of expropriated estates requires a different explanation. It is striking that, at the same time that Carranza was ordering the return of those estates, he issued a series of decrees that provided for extensive agrarian reforms. It is quite possible that the most radical leaders among the Carranzists were convinced that it would be easier to push through an agrarian reform at the expense of the Porfirian hacendados than of the Carranzist military leaders. The radicals may have thought that once the haciendas had been extricated from the direct control of military personnel, the latter would have less reason to oppose a radical land reform.

In many respects, the new Carranzist bourgeoisie can be compared with the Thermidorians in France after the Jacobin dictatorship. The new French ruling group feared attack from both radical revolutionaries and representatives of the old oligarchy. From the former they feared a revival of the power of the Jacobins and from the latter a counterrevolution by the royalists or an invasion by the foreign powers allied with them. The Carranzist bourgeoisie also felt the pressure of both radicals and conservatives. On the one hand, its position was threatened by all the forces demanding an immediate and radical land reform, which would have endangered its newly acquired property and source of income. From the conservative forces, Carranzists feared the resurrection of the political power of the old oligarchy and, perhaps to an even greater extent, an increase in the foreign, predominantly American, influence on Mexico.

These considerations forced the Carranzist bourgeoisie into a constant see-saw policy between radicals and conservatives, just as their Thermidorian predecessors had done in France. To fight those radical forces within the revolution, demanding immediate and complete expropriation of the large haciendas, the Carranza bourgeoisie needed the support of allies from the old hacendado class. In order to keep the upper hand in this alliance, however, and not be swallowed up or dominated by his own allies, Carranza needed a certain amount of mass support.

## Carranza and His Opposition: The Break with Zapata

The opposition to Carranza was focused in those regions where the Maderist revolution had enjoyed its widest popular base and where the demand for more extensive social reforms had been expressed most vehemently: Morelos and Chihuahua. The most important and prominent leaders of the opposition were Emiliano Zapata and Francisco Villa.

The break between Carranza and Zapata is easier to explain, because it had a fairly marked class character. Zapata was the only revolutionary leader who initially carried out an extensive redistribution of land among the peasants of his region. The conflict between his movement and that of

Carranza grew out of the natural antagonism between a peasantry demanding immediate, radical land reform and a movement that, controlled as it was by both an old and a new bourgeoisie, opposed such radical changes. Until Huerta's defeat, Zapata had never recognized Carranza's authority, but, in the interests of the general struggle against Huerta, also had never made any statement against him. Shortly before Huerta's collapse, however, the Army of the South announced a supplement to the Ayala plan, which designated Zapata as the supreme leader of the revolution. At this point, Zapata came into open opposition to Carranza, whom he and his followers deeply mistrusted. They saw in him a man who was as unwilling as Madero to carry out the land reform. The proof of this, in their eyes, was the absence of any social demands in Carranza's Guadalupe plan and the composition of his government.

This distrust was increased by Obregón's actions at the time of the capture of Mexico City. Of all the revolutionary armies, Zapata's was the closest to the city. It was thus a matter of course that, after the defeat of the government that had succeeded Huerta, the Zapatistas would be the first to enter the capital. To prevent this from happening, Obregón concluded an agreement in Teoloyúcan with the chief of the Huerta police and the commander of the federal army in which both promised to hold the city against Zapata until Obregón could enter it.

After the occupation of the capital, Carranza attempted to conclude an agreement with Zapata. His main objective was to secure his southern flank against attack, in the event that the increasing menace of conflict with Villa became reality. In August 1914, he appointed a delegation that was to open communication with Zapata; its most prominent member was Luis Cabrera, who had called for land reform as early as 1912. To the extent that it can be ascertained, Carranza was prepared to recognize Zapatist control over the region they had occupied and accept some of their demands for land reform.[12]

The factor that made a temporary pact with Zapata desirable for Carranza, namely, his desire to have a free hand in his clash with Villa, had precisely the opposite significance for Zapata. He felt that Carranza would probably turn against him after defeating Villa. Therefore Zapata was not disposed to compromise and requested conditions from Carranza that were obviously unacceptable. He demanded full recognition for the Ayala plan, and thus for his own leadership of the revolution, as well as Carranza's resignation or the inclusion in the government of a Zapatist who would have veto power over all decisions of the Carranza government. As expected, the conditions were rejected.

After negotiations broke off, Zapata made one of his most impressive calls to the Mexican people. "The country would like something more," his proclamation (probably drafted by his adviser, Soto y Gama) read, "than Mr. Fabela's vague declarations which are supported by Mr. Carranza's silence. The country wishes to destroy feudalism once and for all." What, then, did Carranza and his followers offer the people? "Administrative reform...complete honesty in the handling of public monies...freedom of the press for those who cannot read; free elections for those who do not know the candidates; proper legal proceedings for those who have never had anything to do with an attorney. All those beautiful democratic principles, all those great words that gave such joy to our fathers and grandfathers have lost their magic for the people." The Mexican people had learned, the proclamation continued, that "with or without elections, with or without an effective electoral law, with the Porfirian dictatorship or with Madero's democracy, with a controlled or a free press, its fate remains as bitter as ever. The people continue to suffer from poverty and endless disappointments." And the question is raised: Are those who present themselves as the new liberators really better than the old ones? The answer is unambiguous: The men of the South will continue the struggle for the people's cause until victory.[13]

## Carranza and His Opposition: Background to the Break with Villa

While most scholars agree on the nature of the conflict between Zapata and Carranza, the cause of the break between Villa and Carranza is one of the most controversial problems of the Mexican Revolution, involving three radically opposed interpretations.

In two of these interpretations the conflict is seen essentially as a class struggle, while in the third it is merely a power struggle between rival caudillos, so frequent in Latin American history. Among the supporters of the class struggle theory, there are two strongly opposing schools. One views the differences between Villa and Carranza as it does the differences between Zapata and Carranza. According to its proponents, Villa had distributed the lands of the haciendas among the peasants and, thus, had engendered the animosity of the more conservative wing of the revolutionary movement.[14] The second school holds precisely the opposite view, namely that Villa, and not Carranza, was the embodiment of reaction. He had failed to carry out any land reform. He had given important positions to conservatives such as Ángeles and Maytorena. This school also asserts that Villa's agrarian program was more conservative than Carranza's and that he maintained closer relations with the United States than Carranza.[15]

The third school acknowledges absolutely no difference worth mentioning between the social character of the Villa and Carranza movements. In this view, the conflict is seen as nothing but a power struggle of two competing cliques. Both groups had articulated similar agrarian programs and similar support for the revolution and for democratic freedoms in their proclamations, while neither movement had realized the programs they had drafted.

What gives this problem such a difficult configuration is that none of these interpretations can claim the whole truth for itself because the reality presents a more complex mixture of the elements emphasized by each of these hypotheses and formulations.

There can be little doubt that Villa, unlike Zapata, had failed to carry out a massive land reform program in the territories under his control (for the reasons, see chap. 3). But there also is little doubt that profound differences concerning agrarian issues existed between the Villa and Carranza forces and that they were by no means only of a theoretical nature.

The First Chief was determined to return most confiscated estates to their former owners while Villa adamantly opposed this step and repeatedly stated that these haciendas should be given to the peasants (at different times Villa specified varying groups of beneficiaries) after the victory of the revolution. Silvestre Terrazas, Villa's secretary of state and temporary governor of Chihuahua, and administrator of expropriated haciendas and properties, stated the differences most clearly when he defined the conflict between Villa and Carranza: "One of the leaders wants to act very radically, confiscating the properties of the enemy and expelling the corrupt elements; the other disapproves of his conduct, proposes the return of some of the confiscated properties and allows himself to be influenced by an infinite number of enemies, who day after day estrange him from the aims, principles, and goals of the revolution."[16]

Roque González Garza, one of Villa's close collaborators, who for a time was to head the government of the revolutionary convention, expressed the conviction that differences of opinion over the issue of the expropriated estates had been crucial in bringing about a break between Carranza and Villa.[17] Yet it is an issue that has been essentially ignored by most historians. On the whole this neglect is not due to any conscious desire to obscure this problem but to the fact that in its manifestos and documents the Villa faction too downplayed or completely ignored this issue. As I attempt to show in another part of this chapter, this was no oversight. It was linked to the fact that Villa allowed such conservatives as Felipe Ángeles to articulate his ideology though he never permitted them to determine his policies. This attitude of Villa was due both to his lack of interest in (and perhaps contempt for) ideological questions as well as to his fear of antagonizing the United States by too radical pronouncements.

A second important social difference between the Villa and Carranza movements is that only in the areas administered by Villa did a significant share of the revenues of the expropriated estates filter down to the poorest classes of the population. His far-reaching social measures to lower meat prices in Chihuahua and to support unemployed miners and lumberjacks and his attempt (though not implemented) to provide credit to the poorest sections of the peasantry have already been outlined above. This socially oriented policy was one of the defining characteristics of Villa's ideology.[18] When Duval West, Woodrow Wilson's special envoy to Mexico, had a long discussion with Villa and his colleagues in 1915, he came away with the impression that the basis of Villa's ideology was that the property of the rich ought to be administered by the government for the benefit of the masses, and even if not clearly articulated, the socialist ideal appeared to dominate the movement.[19]

It is significant that, with few exceptions, all peasant leaders or peasant movements in northern Mexico sided with Villa. This appears to have been the case not only in Chihuahua but to a considerable extent also in Coahuila, Durango, and Sonora. Toribio Ortega and the peasants of Cuchillo Parado, who had been leading a struggle since 1903 against a neighboring hacendado and later against the mayor appointed by the state government of Chihuahua, were in Villa's ranks. The same was true for the leaders and for the large majority of the inhabitants of the villages of Namiquípa and Janos, who had been fighting against the state government in order to keep their lands since the beginning of the twentieth century. In Sonora, the vast majority of Yaqui Indians stood on the side of Villa. Another of his supporters was the most important peasant leader from the Laguna region of Coahuila and Durango, Calixto Contreras, who had led the resistance of the peasants of San Pedro Ocuila in 1905 against the expropriation of their lands by the hacienda of Sombreretillo.[20]

Unlike the Zapatista revolutionaries in southern Mexico, peasants constituted only one element in Villa's extremely heterogeneous movement.

For the conservative wing of Villa's movement, the conflict was mainly a power struggle, since its members did not object at all to Carranza's social policies. On the contrary, many upper class supporters of Villa, such as Ángeles and Maytorena, came out strongly against radical social reforms. Maytorena, the governor of Sonora and Villa's most important ally there, did everything possible to prevent a radical agrarian reform in his home state. He unhesitatingly thwarted the passage of an agrarian law that a revolutionary general, Juan Cabrál, introduced in the Sonora state parliament in 1914. Just as Carranza had done, Maytorena, in 1914, began returning many of the expropriated haciendas to their original owners.[21] Ángeles repeatedly came out against radical expropriation of haciendas.

These men expressed the outlook of the old bourgeoisie, which had grouped around Villa, and the new bourgeoisie, which had arisen within his movement. The "Villa bourgeoisie," although not so numerous and influential as the "Carranza bourgeoisie," fought no less energetically than the latter for the power to control Mexico. They wished to achieve this with Villa's aid, and hoped to push him off the political stage as soon as he had done his duty and their seizure of power was secured.

The antagonism of this group toward the Carranza bourgeoisie, with which it had an ideological affinity, did not stem only from considerations of power politics but from a far more friendly attitude toward the United States. One of the more important reasons for this attitude was that the cotton fields of the Laguna region around Torreón and the cattle herds of Chihuahua constituted two of this group's most important sources of revenue. Neither of these industries provided a basis for friction with the Americans. The cotton plantations of Laguna belonged primarily to British or Spanish owners, while most of the cattle-raising haciendas of Chihuahua were in the hands of Mexicans. Villa, moreover, needed the help of American companies in order to find buyers for those cattle. Thus, a wide network of quickly developed commercial relations soon became indispensable to Villa for supplying his army, even though he himself was never involved in any deals. In any event, the Villa emissaries who made the purchases and sales rapidly established quite intimate economic relations and ties with American companies.

This new Villa bourgeoisie saw in the equally new Carranza bourgeoisie a dangerous rival in the struggle to control Mexico. The makeup of their armies was an additional factor that spurred the antagonism between the two. The armies had largely developed into professional armies, and many of their leaders were motivated not by ideological but by purely opportunist considerations. They joined the side that offered them the most weapons, money, and chances for success. Characteristic of the northern army, in contrast to Zapata's, was the frequency with which units changed sides, depending on the military situation.

There were also regional factors. In a country such as Mexico, which was still undergoing a process of integration and formation as a nation, regional differences played an important role. The Villa movement had its center in Chihuahua, while the Carranza movement has its main origins in Coahuila and Sonora. This factor, however, should not be overestimated, either; Carranza had some followers in Chihuahua and Villa found supporters in Sonora and Coahuila.

Finally, there was yet another difference between the two movements that only became visible at a later stage of their development. The difference went back all the way to the nineteenth century and to the long drawn-out conflict between centralism and federalism. That controversy emerged after Mexico had gained its independence from Spain. The centralists, who attempted to impose a strong government on the country, consisted primarily of the Catholic Church and of members of the upper class of Mexico's central region. The federalists were a more heterogeneous group, comprising as they did both members of the middle and lower classes as well as a large segment of the upper classes, mainly of the peripheral states, who rejected the hegemony of central Mexico.

During the regime of Porfirio Díaz, the nature of both centralism and federalism changed radically. For the first time in Mexican history Díaz had effectively established the control of the central government over all of Mexico. Initially he had alienated members of the upper classes of the peripheral states in the process. In the last years of his regime, however, he managed to gain their widespread support by such means as allowing them generous opportunities for self-enrichment and placing members of the regional oligarchies in charge of their native states. The result was that, with the exception of some local industrialists and landowners, the middle and lower classes now became the main supporters of federalism in Mexico. For them federalism did not so much mean a strong state and a weak central government as a return to local autonomy and the elimination of the system of *jefes políticos* and other institutions which were considered instruments of outside control.

During the revolution still another form of federalism began to emerge. As the power of the central government grew weaker, regional strong men emerged and assumed control of regions or whole states. Some were revolutionaries, others landowners or would-be landowners, while some were acknowledged bandits who assumed control over their regions and saw no reason to relinquish it when a new central government was established in Mexico. At first it seemed to many observers that only Villa and not Carranza would be capable of establishing a strong centralized administration in Mexico. Carranza, on the one hand, had no constituency and no army of his own and was dependent upon the loyalty of his generals. Villa, on the other hand, was a charismatic personality in direct control of the strongest military force in Mexico.

Nevertheless, once Villa's army went beyond the borders of Chihuahua and its surrounding states, few attempts were made to implement a unified policy in the new regions where his army took control. Local and regional leaders, whose social and economic attitudes were often diametrically opposed to those of Villa, were allowed to remain in power as long as they remained loyal to the northern Mexican leader and supplied him with troops. In the few cases in which Zapata's troops occupied regions beyond the confines of Morelos and its surrounding areas, they carried out a similar policy. The provincialism of both Villa and Zapata reached a high point after they occupied Mexico City and proved unwilling and unable to establish a strong and effective central government for the whole country.

By contrast, once his troops consolidated their hold on large parts of Mexico, Carranza began to implement a unified national policy and attempted to consolidate the rule of his government for the whole of the country.

It was thus not surprising that federalists, regionalists, and localists, frequently of opposed backgrounds and political persuasions, tended to support Villa and not Carranza. They were convinced that both Villa and Zapata were mainly interested in their own regions and that for these leaders control of the central government only represented a means of securing resources for their states and of neutralizing potential opposition by the Mexico City administration.

## The Split in the Revolutionary Movement

The antagonism between Villa and Carranza was already becoming apparent at the beginning of 1914, although to the extent that Huerta's power remained unbroken, an extensive, if not always smooth, cooperation existed between them. The more Huerta's position deteriorated, however, the more the difference between them came to the fore.

On the agrarian question, Villa repeatedly demanded from Carranza a clear statement in favor of land reform and criticized his equivocation. With regard to the United States, however, Villa was more accommodating than Carranza. The Benton affair, in which Villa gave his assent to a foreign commission of inquiry under pressure from the United States (and against Carranza's wishes), and the U.S. occupation of Veracruz, to which Villa responded more favorably than Carranza, led to real tensions.

In June 1914, when the revolutionary armies were advancing continuously and Huerta's position seemed hopeless, it came to an open break between Villa and Carranza. Each wanted to be the first to reach the capital. Hoping to slow Villa's advance, Carranza requested of him five thousand men to reinforce the revolutionaries who had been vainly attacking the city of Zacatecas. Villa, whose distrust of Carranza was steadily growing, refused to split his army but said he was willing to move against Zacatecas with his entire army. When Carranza insisted, Villa offered his resignation, which Carranza immediately accepted—with pleasure.

Villa's army, however, opposed the resignation of its commander, and his generals, who had asked Carranza to select a new leader, urged Villa to remain at his post. Carranza then stopped deliveries of coal and arms to Villa. This was indeed a serious blow, for natural catastrophes had cut off Villa's direct supply lines from the United States and he therefore depended completely on supplies from his rival. Villa, thus, was unable to continue his advance on the capital.[22]

Carranza's moves against Villa elicited sharp protests within his own army. Since Huerta had not yet been definitely beaten and the United States seemed to be attempting, through negotiation, to save at least part of his regime, Carranza's generals were perfectly aware of the potentially devastating consequences of an open confrontation with Villa. A fight against Villa also was thoroughly unpopular among the troops. This opposition forced Carranza to allow a delegation from one of his armies, the Army of the Northeast led by Pablo González, to open negotiations with Villa.

On 8 July, an agreement was signed by representatives of both armies in the city of Torreón. It confirmed Villa in his position as commander of the Northern Division (as his army was called) and the administrative officials he had appointed. The coal and arms embargo was to be lifted. Moreover, it was recommended to Carranza that he form a cabinet with half of its members proposed by Villa. A convention of the revolutionary army leaders was to decide the future of the revolution; a ratio of one delegate for each thousand soldiers was established. None of the revolutionary leaders, including Carranza, were to stand as candidates for the presidency in future elections. Finally, at the behest of Villa's delegates, it was stipulated that the revolution "is a struggle of the oppressed against the encroachments of the powerful . . . . [The signers] commit themselves to fight against the federal army until it is annihilated, to create a democratic regime in the country, to bring prosperity to the workers, and to liberate the peasants economically with a just distribution of the land or with another solution to the agrarian question."[23]

Despite this agreement, Villa's distrust of Carranza grew steadily. This distrust was confirmed mainly by the unilateral occupation of the capital by Carranza's troops. Huerta's successor, Francisco Carbajal, initially attempted, with the support of the U.S. government, to bring about a compromise with Carranza. After these efforts failed, Carbajal resigned at the beginning of August and transferred his authority to Eduardo Iturbide, the chief of police of Mexico City. On 13 August, Iturbide and Huerta's army commander handed over the city to General Obregón, who commanded Carranza's largest army.

This unilateral action was not the sole reason for Villa's increasing distrust. It was fueled by other steps that Carranza took, such as closing railway service between Mexico City and Chihuahua. This maneuver so enraged Villa that he threatened to shoot Obregón, who had gone to Chihuahua to negotiate with Villa, and, on 22 September, he withdrew his recognition of Carranza's authority as leader of the revolution. Initially, there was no armed conflict, since all parties were placing their hopes on the convention of revolutionary leaders set for Mexico City but transferred to Aguascalientes on 10 October.

The convention opened as scheduled and was the last attempt to create unity among the revolutionaries. Four parties confronted each other. First there was the group around Carranza. He was not prepared to give up his claim as leader of the revolution at any price. His claim drew support from an important section of the traditional upper class, which had temporarily supported Huerta, but was now backing him against Villa and Zapata. With this support, Carranza had tried to preempt the Aguascalientes convention by calling his own convention of revolutionary generals in Mexico, which was to ratify his leadership. In a dramatic gesture, he had offered his resignation to the delegates, most of whom he had chosen himself, and it was promptly refused. Nevertheless, under pressure from the radical wing of the Carranza movement, a resolution was passed to go to Aguascalientes and to participate in the convention there.[24]

Then there was the Villa group, later joined by Zapatists, who arrived in Aguascalientes 16 days after the beginning of the convention. These groups were as little disposed to compromise as Carranza. They felt strong enough to take over the leadership of the revolution themselves. That the convention took place at all under these conditions and even conducted business for several weeks was due mainly to a fourth group, which was attempting to bring about the only real compromise.[25]

In contrast to the others this group was characterized by no firm political, geographical, or organizational unity. The common objective of its members was the elimination of Villa, Carranza, and, if possible, Zapata from the leadership of the revolution. Beyond that, the members of this group held widely divergent views on what the next step should be. In ideological and social terms, they occupied an intermediate position between Carranza and Villa. Most of its members, particularly its spokesmen, came from the middle class: Alvaro Obregón, the former rancher and public official who commanded the Army of the Northwest; Eulalio Gutiérrez, the most important revolutionary leader in the state of San Luis Potosí; Lucio Blanco, the revolutionary leader from northeastern Mexico. For most of them, Carranza was too conservative, Villa and Zapata too radical. They wished to reduce the power of the old ruling group far more than did Carranza, but, with few exceptions, they were opposed to the kind of radical social transformation Zapata and, to a lesser extent, Villa advocated. Some envisioned a system of parliamentary democracy, which neither Carranza nor the Villa and Zapata groups could establish. Others had set up what amounted to independent fiefdoms in their home states and feared Mexico's return to a strong central authority. By eliminating the three leaders, they hoped to attain these often heterogeneous goals. They actually succeeded in having

Gutiérrez elected provisional president, with the support of all parties at the convention, calling simultaneously for the removal of Villa and Carranza.

This compromise quickly proved to be untenable. The fourth group was too weak, too heterogeneous, and too divided to impose its will.

Carranza ignored the decisions of the convention and, on 8 November, recalled all his generals from Aguascalientes. Villa continued to recognize Gutiérrez as nominal president, with no intention, however, of giving up his own position. Villa and Carranza blamed one another for failure to reach a compromise, but continued to advance "proposals" to bring about unity among the revolutionaries. Villa proposed that both he and Carranza commit suicide simultaneously. Carranza suggested that they both withdraw to Havana, after Villa had placed his power in the hands of Gutiérrez and he had placed his in the hands of his general, Pablo González, who, in turn, would call a new convention in the capital. Since Gutiérrez was not a direct subordinate of Villa, while González was closely linked to Carranza, the implementation of this proposal would have eliminated Villa, but not Carranza.

In November 1914, there were armed clashes in Sonora between Carranza supporters and those of Villa's ally, Maytorena, whereupon the fourth group collapsed. Under Gutiérrez's leadership, a small section rallied to Villa and Zapata. The majority, under Obregón, went to Carranza.

This decision by Obregón and the Sonoran generals and contingents who supported him was probably based on two considerations—one regional, one national. In regional terms Obregón and his Sonoran allies were deeply incensed by Villa's unwillingness to grant them control of their home state and by his support of their rival for state power, Governor José María Maytorena. In national terms they calculated that they would be able to exercise more influence on Carranza's relatively weaker movement than over Villa and Zapata if they emerged as leaders.

**Victors and Vanquished in the Third Phase of the Revolution**

At the beginning of November 1914, when the break between Carranza, and Villa and Zapata, had become irreparable, the situation looked serious for Carranza. Many of his former supporters had abandoned him, and on 22 November he was compelled to evacuate the capital. He withdrew, first to Puebla and later to Orizaba. Whereas Villa and Zapata now controlled the center and the south—the greater part of Mexico—Carranza was pushed back to the periphery of the country. Most domestic and foreign observers expected his rapid defeat.

A few months later, however, the situation had changed completely.

Obregón, who proved to be the most important military leader of the Mexican Revolution, inflicted a series of crushing defeats on Villa's forces, from which they never recovered. Villa, perhaps out of fear of extending his line of communication too far, failed to follow up on his initial momentum by pursuing Carranza and his army into Veracruz. Obregón secured enough time and supplies to reorganize his army effectively and in April 1915 managed to defeat Villa in two decisive battles. Obregón concentrated his forces in the town of Celaya in central Mexico, following the strategy that had been so successfully used by the armies of the great European powers in World War I. His troops, heavily supplied with machine guns, were entrenched behind barbed wire. When Villa's cavalry tried the same strategy—a frontal charge—against Obregón that had secured a victory against Huerta, their ranks were decimated by machine gun fire.

Two weeks later, in the second battle of Celaya, Villa tried the same strategy again. This time defeat turned into rout. He lost most of his artillery and a substantial part of his troops. Neither Villa nor Obregón altered their basic methods and a similar battle, with equally disastrous results for Villa, took place in June 1915 in the city of León. At this point, an ever increasing number of Villa's supporters abandoned him and his weakened and partially demoralized army retreated to the North.

In a desperate gamble during September and October, Villa tried to recoup his losses and stave off imminent defeat by assembling most of his remaining troops in Chihuahua and, with enormous difficulty and great sacrifice, he marched them across the mountains of the Sierra Madre into the neighboring state of Sonora. His supporters controlled the major part of that state, and with their help he hoped to wipe out the remaining garrison of Carranza's troops. Control of Sonora would have given Villa at the very least a new lease on life—large foreign companies on which to impose taxes to resupply his army; the extension of the border with the United States, which would have made it far more difficult for the Americans to control the supply of arms to his territory; support of the militant Yaqui Indians, with whose help Villa hoped to march south again, join forces with Zapata, and regain control of central Mexico. The core of Villa's strategy was the destruction of Carranza's troops in the state, whose most important contingent was stationed in the border town of Agua Prieta, isolated from the rest of Carranza-controlled territory. But, again, he was dealt a crushing defeat, this time because Woodrow Wilson had already recognized Carranza on 19 October 1915 and had subsequently allowed the latter's troops to cross U.S. territory in order to reinforce his garrison at Agua Prieta.

When, after suffering enormous hardships, Villa returned to Chihuahua in December 1915, he found his former supporters surrendering in droves and Carranza's forces relentlessly advancing on his last strongholds. Had Villa been a Latin American caudillo in the "classical" mold, he could have done what most of these men did when confronted with defeat: take whatever riches they had accumulated and seek refuge outside of Mexico. The United States had declared its willingness to grant him asylum; instead, he retreated into the countryside and from there he was to wage five long and bloody years of guerrilla warfare.

After defeating Villa, Carranza turned on Zapata, who had to abandon Mexico City. He later lost most of the cities in Morelos, and he, too, retreated into the countryside to carry on a guerrilla war against Carranza. At the end of 1915, Carranza's troops controlled most of Mexico.

This turn of events, unanticipated as it was by most observers, often is explained by purely military factors and by Obregón's strategic superiority over Villa. It was undoubtedly Obregón's greater military skill that made it possible for him to lead his outnumbered army to victory over Villa; but the revolutionaries had often been defeated in the struggles against Díaz and Huerta, and yet they had always recovered. The Villa movement's inability to do this, the ring relentlessly closing in on the convention, and the latter's steadily disappearing power, which it soon would be able to wield only in the areas controlled by Zapata, must be explained primarily by the social composition of the contending sides and their respective political and socioeconomic problems.

### Carranza's Victorious Strategy

The civil war into which Mexico was once again plunged at the end of 1914 found Carranza in a situation that, militarily and politically, was dire. The armies of the convention far outnumbered his own and his support among the civilian population was wavering. Villa and Zapata enjoyed far greater support among the peasantry than he did, and considerable sections of the middle class, which ideologically tended toward Carranza, felt that Villa would be the probable victor in the revolutionary struggle and rallied to the convention partly for opportunistic reasons.

Carranza's only hope was his solid economic support; in this domain he had a certain advantage over his opponents. Control of the oil regions and the ports of Tampico and Veracruz provided him with important sources of foreign exchange and enabled him to equip a powerful army. To compensate for his military and political disadvantages with regard to the convention, he had, at the same time, attempted to win over two classes—the hacendados and the peasants—whose political and economic interests seem quite irreconcilable. To achieve this ambitious objective, Carranza did not hesitate, in some cases without apparent embarrassment, to promise the same land to both sides. To the hacendados he proposed to return the haciendas that had been confiscated by the revolutionary authorities; to the peasants he proposed to return or distribute land from the estates of the large landowners.

Carranza's promises to the hacendados were made sub rosa and were acknowledged publicly only late in the struggle and with a minimum of fanfare, but for the most part they were carried out in the end. The promises to the peasants were proclaimed in January 1915 in the form of a sweeping law, emphasized and promoted on every occasion and propagated among the population with the aid of all available mass media. The law envisioned the return of the expropriated land to the former village communities and effectively recognized the right of every peasant to a piece of land. To implement this very ambitious program, an agrarian commission was to be established, and, until it could be set up, governors and local military commanders were instructed to carry out the provisional land distribution. The proclamations made with such pomp and circumstance, however, resulted in little of what was promised; in 1915–20, only 173,000 hectares of land were given to a mere 44,000 peasants.[26]

But how successful was Carranza's tour de force of simultaneously wooing the peasants and the hacendados? His efforts proved quite fruitful among many hacendados in the northern and central regions of the country. Numerous large landowners, who had repossessed their land or who were expecting its return, began to aid the Carranza movement both in word and deed. In 1916, Carranza's General Diéguez was able to persuade the hacendados in Jalisco to assemble armed contingents against the armies of the convention.[27] Carranza was also successful among the peasants. Many historians believe that Carranza's agrarian law of 6 January 1915 had a real effect on the peasants. By being the first to issue an agrarian law, according to this view, he won over the peasants and thereby decided the civil war. The exact effects of this law, however, are very difficult to assess. The fact that few peasants other than Zapata's and Villa's immediate followers undertook guerrilla action to defend the convention following Villa's military defeat tends to confirm the idea that this law had at least some impact. But what was the basis of this impact? What prompted many peasants to place *more* trust in the promises of a landowner who had never intervened on their behalf, whose entourage did not include a single peasant, who returned the expropriated land of the haciendas to its previous owners than they placed in the statements of Villa and Zapata, who supported the Ayala plan, who had expropriated the lands of the hacendados, and who, in the case of Zapata at least, had distributed it to the peasants? Does the answer lie primarily in the time factor, in that Carranza was the first politician to issue a general agrarian law, as is often supposed? Much more important may have been the fact that Carranza's law led to the first political mobilization of the peasantry outside of Villa's and Zapata's home regions.

In contrast to the Maderist revolution of 1910 and 1911, in which political mobilization in the form of a mass movement took place simultaneously with military uprisings, the 1913–14 movement was primarily of a military nature. Neither Villa nor Carranza had formed political parties or attempted to organize the civilian population outside the army. Carranza's agrarian law for the first time required meetings of village communities, the election of representatives where they did not exist, and the activation of village committees in the countryside to formulate demands. Thus began a process of political mobilization which was in fact successful, particularly in the period 1915–17, when many peasants had not yet understood that Carranza was playing a two-sided game that prevented the implementation of his reform plans.

But Carranza's influence among the peasantry was strengthened not merely by the agrarian law but by other reforms as well. Even if little land was distributed, the Carranza authorities did generally abolish debt peonage and attempted to introduce the rudiments of social legislation in the countryside. The activities of Salvador Alvarado, who at that time belonged to the radical wing of the Carranza movement, show clearly its achievements and its limitations.[28]

Yucatán was one of the areas of Mexico where debt peonage was most widespread. In 1915, the large landowners, together with the American International Harvester Corporation, attempted to have Yucatán secede from Mexico, hoping in this way to prevent the spread of the revolution to the peninsula. Under Alvarado's leadership, Carranzist troops landed on the peninsula and subdued it within a few weeks. Alvarado then began to introduce far-reaching social measures. Debt peonage was abolished, and thousands of peasants left the haciendas. On the plantations themselves, minimum wages were imposed, the rudiments of health insurance created, and the hacendados were compelled to establish schools. The teachers employed in these schools, appointed by Alvarado, reinforced the peons in their resistance to the hacendados. Land reform, however, was not introduced. The large landowners were allowed to keep their haciendas but were forced to sell their main product, sisal, to the state-owned purchasing company, Compania Reguladora del Henequen. Part of the profits of this company went to the government treasury in Mexico City, while another portion was used for investments; the peasants, however, derived scarcely any benefit from them.

Reforms of the kind pushed through in Yucatán had no effect in regions like Morelos, where the peasants had gone much further on their own. In the areas that had not yet been touched by the revolution, their effect was considerable. The peasants saw the Carranzists as liberators who had freed them from debt peonage. All these measures won a certain mass base among the peasantry for Carranza. By itself, however, it was not enough to achieve victory over Villa and Zapata. For this, Carranza still needed the support of the urban working class.

In a dependent country such as Mexico in this period, in which the majority of the workers were employed in foreign factories, nationalism played a special role. Carranza's attitude in the wake of the American occupation of Veracruz had won him no small popularity among the workers. A lack of understanding on the part of Villa and Zapata and a series of clever measures enabled Carranza to win decisive influence among those workers organized in trade unions.

In all the towns the Carranzists occupied, they promoted the formation of trade unions, which in many cases were given the most elegant locales, previously reserved for the Díaz aristocracy. Thus the trade unions in Mexico City occupied the Jockey Club, formerly the most exclusive club in the country. The Carranzists' energetic measures to relieve the hunger in the capital stood in sharp contrast to the hesitant attitude of the Convention. While the Convention seemed helpless in the fact of demonstrations by hungry women, Obregón imposed emergency taxes on the church and business community, which were used in part to relieve hunger.

These factors were decisive in creating a situation in which, by February 1915, sections of the working class allied themselves with Carranza. The anarchosyndicalist Casa del Obrero Mundial concluded an agreement with Carranza. They stated their willingness to form "Red Battalions" in his support, while Carranza promised "to improve the situation of the working class with the appropriate laws and to issue all laws necessary to this end in the course of the struggle itself." Carranza's stance, along with the hunger and unemployment in the cities, drove thousands of workers into the Carranza movement. Six Red Battalions were formed, who took the field against the peasants "in the name of the struggle against reaction."[29]

### The Internal Weaknesses of the Convention Movement

To the extent that Carranza took the political offensive, the convention lost the initiative; a progressive paralysis and stagnation became generally visible to all. Not all segments of the convention movement fell victim to this process. In the area controlled by Zapata, Morelos and the surrounding region, the movement continued with uninterrupted elan to give living shape to the land reform that had been initiated. Agrarian commissions were appointed, haciendas were distributed to the peasants, and new political structures were created.[30]

Outside of Morelos and the nearby areas, however, enthusiasm for reform was not so extensive. Until mid-1915, after its military defeat, the convention movement proved incapable of working out a program for the social and economic transformation of Mexico. This inability to develop theoretical concepts and to give them reality, to the extent they existed at all, particularly on the agrarian question, was fatal to the convention.

A delegate warned the revolutionary convention in February 1915 that Carranza was anticipating their efforts by dealing in a demagogic way with the agrarian problem. The delegate expressed his anguish over the fact that the convention was only giving limited and piecemeal attention to the agrarian problem without propounding a clear-cut national solution to it. Above all he expressed his disagreement with the position of some delegates, particularly from the North, that any solution to the agrarian question should be postponed until a legislative assembly was elected.

"Venustiano Carranza," the delegate stated,

> for better or for worse, but undoubtedly for worse, understood that he could acquire some prestige only by solving the land issue; he thus occupied himself more than we the agrarians did with the resolution of this problem. I have read some articles and it is clear that he wants everything for himself; thus I attach no importance to that document, but I have come to say that they, in order to gain the people's sympathy, concern themselves with the truth more than we, the defenders of the people, do and if instead of completely and fully dealing with the agrarian problem we limit ourselves to Tepic and tomorrow to Zacatecas, and the day after tomorrow to Durango and then postpone a solution until the assembly becomes legislative, then we will have effectively circumnavigated the essential problem.[31]

The main cause for this sort of paralysis of the convention movement has often been seen as the inability of peasant movements to develop a national perspective. This weakness was undoubtedly a contributing factor to the convention movement's inability to win support among the working class. Thus on 7 November 1915, Zapata issued a proposal for a labor law. He proposed that "until the creation of the socialist state, which we all desire and which will be based on justice, some steps will have to be taken to improve the lot of the workers in today's inhuman capitalist system." Envisioned here were:

1. A series of social measures, including the eight-hour workday and the prohibition of nighttime labor for women and children under fourteen years of age

2. Formation of worker cooperatives to take over all firms and factories whose owners had abandoned them

3. Development of industries by the village communities in order to eliminate unemployment

4. Fixing of a minimum wage as a floor for the cost of labor.

The limits of this program are obvious. It fails to respond to some of the most important demands the Mexican labor movement made in the wake of the strikes of Cananea and Río Blanco: more control of foreign property, equal payment and treatment for foreign and Mexican workers, an extensive and clearly defined right to strike, and a guarantee of the status of trade unions.[32] But even the limited measures of 1914–15 do not seem to have been put into practice. Nothing is known of the extent to which the Zapatists realized any of these points during their occupation of the capital. Typical of the almost total helplessness of the convention in face of this problem was its reaction, when, on 20 May 1915, thousands of hungry women demonstrated in front of the building where it was meeting. The delegates collected money—each one gave 50 pesos—which was then distributed to the women.[33] No other measures to end famine were undertaken. Equally typical was the fact that no closer collaboration was achieved between the Zapatists and the anarchosyndicalist Casa del Obrero Mundial, although one of the Zapatists' leading spokesmen, the attorney Díaz Soto y Gama, belonged to that organization. The failure to consider any measure against foreign companies also helped to isolate the Zapata movement from the workers.

The peasants' incapacity to understand the problems of other classes or to develop a national perspective may partially explain why the convention failed to win the support of the workers and the middle class; it does not explain why the convention movement took no actions in the domain that most affected the peasants: the elaboration of an agrarian law and the implementation of land reform. In the last analysis, it was the composition of the leadership of the convention movement which, in contrast to the Carranza movement, made it impossible to establish coherent social and economic programs and actually give them shape. Both the Carranza movement and the convention were coalitions of regionally, socially, and politically distinct currents, groups, and classes. The convention, however, represented a far more heterogeneous complex of interests than the elements around Carranza, and, in contrast to the latter's movement, contained fundamentally irreconcilable factions.

In fact, there may have been almost no agreement on the agrarian question between Carranza and the radical intellectuals, bureaucrats, and workers in his movement; nevertheless, they were able to work out a modus vivendi, especially since the radicals, who were neither peasants nor peasant leaders, were willing to tolerate Carranza's passivity on this question as long as his policies in other areas—particularly foreign policy and the labor question—conformed to their ideas. Between 1914 and 1916, Carranza developed a close collaboration with members of the group that, at the Aguascalientes convention, had attempted to depose both Villa and Carranza but had ultimately fallen in with the latter. In this collaboration, he granted to Obregón a large measure of influence over policy and even accepted the broad outlines of his program.

The conflicting interests within the convention movement were much harder to reconcile. In theory, the members of that fourth group that had acted against both leaders at the convention and had split after the open break between the two, should have had greater influence in the convention movement than in Carranza's. Whereas Gutiérrez, one of its most important spokesmen, had been appointed president of the convention, his counterpart in the Carranza faction, Obregón, remained merely one of Carranza's military commanders. In practice, however, the situation was reversed. While the influence of Obregón and his group was constantly increasing between 1914 and 1916, that of Gutiérrez was steadily declining.

The convention government, the result of a compromise between the Villa and Zapata movements and the radical wing of the Carranza movement, was condemned to an illusory existence from its first day. After the Carranza supporters had left the convention, Gutiérrez no longer represented a real force. He had rallied to Villa and Zapata in the hope of controlling their movement, but they, in turn, wanted to use him only as a spokesman for the convention and thereby increase their influence. Neither Villa nor Zapata ever considered subordinating themselves to his leadership; in fact, they deeply distrusted him. Gutiérrez contacted Obregón, with whose aid he hoped to depose Villa and Carranza, but Obregón was not willing to play the game. When Villa uncovered the intrigues of Gutiérrez, he fled from Mexico City, which at the time was being occupied by Villa's and Zapata's troops.

## The Conservative Wing of the Convention

The conflict between Gutiérrez and his middle class adherents, on the one hand, and Villa and Zapata, on the other, was by no means the only contradiction that emerged in the ranks of the conventionist faction. The antagonisms between the peasant leaders of the convention, represented by Zapata, and its conservative wing, led by Maytorena and Felipe Ángeles, became increasingly sharp, menacing, and in the end irreparable.

Maytorena, after his return to Sonora in mid-1914, had ordered the return of confiscated property to the original owners;[34] Ángeles emerged as the most important representative and ideologue of the conservative group within the convention movement.

If there was any one politician in the period 1910–20 who, in every respect, could claim to be the spiritual heir of Madero, it was Felipe Ángeles—not Carranza. With his political perspective of preserving the old federal army, moving toward rapprochement with the United States, and using parliamentary democracy as a system and not merely as a facade, he was a veritable replica of Madero and, like him, Ángeles had a philanthropic disposition and a warm empathy with the poor from whom he received surprising support. However, although he saw it as the moral duty of the prosperous to help the less endowed, he categorically rejected any kind of land reform or transformation of the existing social order. In his view, the convention should have moved to Carranza's right instead of to his left and should have taken a stance that was unambiguously more conservative.

He articulated this viewpoint clearly and emphatically in a conversation with Villa's secretary of state, Federico González Garza, in mid-1915, as the latter recounts: "When General Ángeles and Lic. Díaz Lombardo were here they stated that in their opinion the main difference between us and the Carranzistas was that the latter wish to or promise to implement the revolutionary reform in the so-called preconstitutional period while we desired primarily to reestablish the Constitutional order before carrying out the reforms. In reality this was not the original motive for our break with Carranza and when I left Chihuahua no one even mentioned this difference."[35]

Ángeles summarized his social philosophy: "In the class struggle, I am with the exploited and against the exploiters; but I do not forget that the movement of social fraternity ought to be slow, especially in the countries where the masses lack education and the administrators lack honesty. However, we must do the utmost possible to diminish the injustices of the present capitalist society. To oppose the rich blindly means opposing the intelligent forces of the country. The rich are the men who within the present legal and social organization have the necessary intelligence to triumph in the selfish struggle of the existing systems."[36]

After the outbreak of the civil war in Mexico in 1914, the conservative wing around Ángeles attempted to limit the radicalization of the convention movement and to create, where possible, an opening to the traditional oligarchy. In this way, Ángeles, Maytorena, and their supporters hoped to win a controlling influence in Mexico after the defeat of Carranza. The conservatives initially attempted to win support for this opening to the right by recruiting numerous soldiers and officers of the old Huerta army into the ranks of the convention army. Ángeles issued a call in which he urged the members of the old federal army to rally to the convention. He may have been hoping to be able to mobilize this group, not merely against Carranza but also possibly for a coming struggle against Zapata and Villa. By returning the expropriated haciendas to their previous owners, this group hoped to win the favor of the large landowners. Through alliances with regional caudillos who were hostile to reform, such as the former Huerta officer Esteban Cantú in Baja California, the landowner Pelaez in the oil-producing region, and some hacendados of Chiapas, the conservative group hoped to reinforce its ranks further.

The greatest hopes of the men around Ángeles, however, turned on a closer collaboration with the United States. Ángeles repeatedly stated in public:

> To oppose foreigners, who bring us science, who know how to exploit the natural resources, and who provide the indispensable capital for this exploitation, is dishonest and shows a lack of respect for our international responsibilities and collective wills, our laws, under whose protection the foreigners came to develop the prosperity of our country.
>
> I am going to confess a very big sin: we Mexicans are the enemies of the Americans, simply because we do not know them. We know the Americans of the borders, but not the northerners who make this great nation progress, we do not know these great people who are analogous to the people of Rome during its flourishing. The United States of America is a great nation, with whom I would always like to be friends.... One of the reasons for my aggravation with Villa, which caused my estrangement from him, is his hatred of the Americans.[37]

Ángeles made it quite clear to Woodrow Wilson's adviser in Mexico, Duval West, that he was the politician in whom the respect and regard for property of all kinds was most deeply rooted. Duval West reported on his conversation with Ángeles, over conditions in Monterrey: "Since taking over the city, he appears to have attempted to leave the private property of all private citizens untouched. No confiscations or expropriations of private property belonging to any person have been undertaken or approved. He says that he has already been sharply criticized for this stance by Villa's supporters."[38]

Ángeles, Maytorena, and their supporters hoped that collaboration with the United States would attract even more conservative elements to the convention, would strengthen their economic and military dependency on the United States, and would thus prevent social upheavals. Ángeles actually succeeded, for a period, in winning Wilson's favor, and becoming his preferred candidate for the Mexican presidency. This rapprochement with the United States is certainly one of the reasons why the conservative wing of the convention, which, like the conservatives within the Carranza movement, rejected any radical reform, was never willing, in contrast to the Carranzists, to indulge in pseudo-radical rhetoric. Such rhetoric even without serious intent would clearly have raised eyebrows in America. Accordingly, the conservative conventionists not only rejected radical changes and programs but also attempted to play down what had already been achieved. In the manifestos of the northern revolutionaries, which were drafted primarily by Ángeles, there was barely any mention of the confiscation of haciendas by Villa and of the distribution of their revenues to the poor. As a result, there was a strange contrast between the rhetorical style of the two movements. With Carranza, the radical demagoguery far exceeded the actual extent of the reforms, while in the calls and programs put forward by Ángeles the ideological utterances of the northern revolutionary movement were quite modest by comparison with the changes actually implemented by the northern revolutionaries.

## The Convention and Land Reform

These circumstances explain why the conservative wing sharply opposed immediate land reform. In 1914 and particularly in 1915, this led to heated exchanges between the northern and southern constituencies at the convention, which in the 1914–16 period functioned as a kind of parliament of the movement associated with it.

In February 1915, General Buelna, who commanded the convention troops in the Tepic region of northern Mexico, asked the convention what was to be done with a number of haciendas that had been expropriated and were becoming a financial burden on the state. Should the revolutionary administration return them to their former owners in order to save administrative costs?[39] This problem prompted the southern delegates to the convention to formulate a plan for the immediate distribution of the hacienda lands in the area controlled by the convention. The agrarian commission of the convention, which consisted mainly of Zapatist delegates, proposed the village communal authorities as the principal agencies of such a reform. These local governments were to return all previously expropriated lands to the villages immediately and begin the distribution of the confiscated estates among the peasants in the territories where the convention ruled.[40] The execution of this unprecedented proposal would have made irreversible social changes that would definitely have ended the hacienda system and at the same time would have resulted in a massive political activation of the peasantry.

The northern delegates were unambiguously against the proposal. One reason after another was invoked: such extensive and far-reaching reforms ought to be thoroughly weighed prior to their implementation; the expropriation of foreign property would lead to conflict with the United States; the local governments were not the appropriate organs for the implementation of such measures; an immediate land reform would leave out the soldiers still at the front.[41]

This problem, as well as other socially important issues such as the rights of industrial workers and the convention's stand on private prop-

erty, led to constant conflicts between the northern and southern delegates. As a result, the convention was unable to draft a comprehensive
program of socioeconomic reforms before the beginning of 1916, by which
time many of the northern delegates had left. When such a program was
finally adopted, it was in practical terms irrelevant. The armies of the
convention had been defeated or dispersed, except in Morelos, and the
program of the now powerless body was forgotten in the toll of defeat.

## Villa and the Agrarian Question

In this conflict between radicals and conservatives within his movement,
Villa avoided taking sides. He probably felt that maintaining the unity
among all factions was not only essential to the rapid military victory he
hoped for but, above all, necessary to secure recognition by the United
States, which he saw as a key to his definitive triumph, as well. According
to his close collaborator and former secretary of state in Chihuahua,
Federico González Garza, Villa's sympathies definitely rested with the
radicals insofar as agrarian reform was concerned.[42]

In a letter to his brother, Roque González Garza, Federico reported an
altercation he had with Ángeles, who wished to postpone reform until a
newly elected government could draft the appropriate law. He wrote that
the Villa administration did not share this point of view but did attempt to
implement agrarian reform as soon as possible.

"This is clearly shown by the fact that the Agrarian Commission,
headed by Bonilla when I was there, had studied the problem and elaborated a law whose application in Chihuahua was delayed, not because of
the nonexistence of a constitutional government but because of our not
being able to find agricultural engineers capable of carrying out the land
division. If this difference did indeed exist, we would have to return to our
enemies all the properties which we confiscated from them without being
authorized to do so by any congress."[43] Federico González Garza then
went on to state that the final decision on such confiscation would have to
be subjected to ratification by a newly elected congress.

At a historic meeting with Zapata prior to their joint march into Mexico
City, Villa emphasized his commitment to land reform. "It is my wish,"
he told Zapata, "that we divide up the lands of the rich . . . . It is for the
people that we want land."[44] In the memoirs he dictated to his secretary
Bauche Alcalde at about the same time, Villa elaborated on the vision of a
Mexico peopled by free peasants, concentrated in military colonies, of
which he had spoken to John Reed several months before. There is an
almost poetic quality to this vision:

> And I see that orderly grouping of little houses in which our
> soldiers/farmers live: clean and white, smiling and hygienic, the true

homes for which one really fights with courage and for whose defense one would die.

I see these luxurious fruit orchards, these abundant vegetable gardens, these sown fields, these corn fields, these alfalfa fields which not only a *large landowner harvests* and *accrues* benefits from but rather an entire family *cultivates* and *gathers, cares for, and harvests*.

And I see that the school is the tallest building in the hamlet and the teacher is the most respected man; and that the one who studies and knows the most is the most appreciated youth; and that the happiest father is he who will leave his land, animals, and house to his learned, good, and honest child, so that new, healthy, learned, good, hardworking children will arise from this sanctified home, who will dignify the country and honor the race.

Oh, if life will only permit me to live long enough to see this dream realized! . . . The true army of the people, which I loved so much, dispersed through the entire land, plowing the soil, making it respectable and respected! Fifteen years! twenty years, perhaps! And the sons of my soldiers, who will bring this ideal to fruition will know with what tenderness I caressed this dream of my soul. And they will not suffer, they will not have the threat of suffering, which I endured in the fullest years of my life, which formed my youth and my entire maturity.[45]

At the same time, extensive preparations were being made for a land reform in Chihuahua. A land reform law was worked out and engineers from the agricultural college at Chapingo were called in to work on the planned land distribution.[46] Until Villa's first military defeat, however, no attempt was made to implement these measures. Some of the motives are doubtless the same ones that had prevented him from carrying out the agrarian reform immediately after taking power in Chihuahua in December 1913: the fear that many of his soldiers would leave the army in order to receive their share of the land and then work it. An immediate distribution of land moreover to the peasants would have critically undermined the revenue of the Villa government. The revenues from the expropriated estates were needed to support the nonagrarian sections of the population and to finance the war effort. Financing the war had become even more pressing after the outbreak of the civil war with Carranza, since the economic position of the Villa movement was steadily deteriorating. Foreign-currency revenues were declining precipitously, because cattle and cotton sales to the United States, which were the source of these limited revenues, dried up after a considerable part of the cattle had been sold and cotton production in the Laguna region had declined to an alarming extent. Prices for American arms and ammunition, however, had risen steadily since August 1914 as a result of the outbreak of the First World War.

In the period immediately following the break with Carranza, political motives, at first, also made Villa carry out a restrained policy on the agrarian question. Prior to the final victory over Carranza, which, in mid-1915, Villa was expecting in short order, he wanted to avoid at any price splitting or weakening his movement. Early land reform could easily have meant a break with the conservative wing. Also radical social reforms might have made the United States reluctant to recognize him. Villa expected and was hoping for rapid recognition by the United States, after which he would have a monopoly on American arms shipments.

Villa also may have shared some of his followers' fears that immediate land reform could intensify an already existing food shortage, which would have been extremely dangerous for his movement. All these considerations explain his caution and "moderation" insofar as immediate action was concerned. Villa's "caution," however, would have been to no avail if the pressure for land reform within his movement had been as urgent and powerful as it was in Zapata's army. Some of the reasons for this difference have already been indicated: the smaller number of peasants in the Chihuahuan population and the army of well-paid professionals with no ties to its home region.

The professional army became even stronger during the 1914–15 period. The Villa administration's confiscation of the largest cattle haciendas in the state had resulted in the sale or slaughter of most of the herds. Many unemployed vaqueros had immediately joined Villa's army and increasingly pushed the peasant element in the army into the background. These cowboys were naturally less interested in land reform than the peasants.

The leadership of the Villa army also had undergone an important process of transformation. Many of the original peasant leaders of the revolution from 1910 to 1911, such as Toribio Ortega, were dead and had been replaced by men like Rodolfo Fierro, who was not a peasant, or Martin and Pablo López, who had risen through the ranks and had never been spokesmen or leaders of their communities.[47]

### The New Turn in Villa's Policy

After his decisive defeat at Celaya in 1915, Villa's social policy changed. He had now become the underdog and, just like Carranza, was under pressure to expand his social base. Although recognized by everyone in his movement, this necessity produced no consensus about the direction in which the expansion should move. Ángeles and Maytorena hoped that Carranza's radical social promises would make it possible for Villa to enlist the more conservative element in the country and, more important, to win support from the United States. It was hoped that the United States would support the convention movement in spite of its military defeat, in order to prevent Carranza's exclusive military hegemony.

Villa's strategy to "widen the base" of his movement was diametrically opposed to the strategy of the conservative wing of the conventionists. He now attempted to put agrarian reform into practice and to give it a legislative basis. An emissary was sent to Sonora to implement land reform in that state.[48] And, in Chihuahua in August 1915, Villa congratulated the governor, Fidel Avila, who had signed an agrarian law, and instructed him to begin at once to apply it but to except from it the Terrazas haciendas, which were to be given to Villa's soldiers. "Regarding requests for land distribution, I wish to tell you that because soldiers and members of the army cannot go to Chihuahua to make their requests, please reserve all the Terrazas haciendas for them and distribute the rest."[49]

In May 1915, Villa had issued a comprehensive land reform law. All estates above a certain size were to be divided among the peasants. The owners would receive some form of indemnity and the peasants would have to pay in small installments. The state governments, not the federal government, were to implement the law. The communal property of the villages was not mentioned. The law reflected the heterogeneous and divergent character of the conventionist movement. In order to maintain the unity of the factions that supported him, Villa allowed the states wide leeway in the application of agrarian reform.

The law also reflected the wishes and desires of the northern peasants, the majority of whom had never been organized in communal villages, in contrast to those of southern and central Mexico. One of the main provisions of the law was best defined by Antonio Díaz Soto y Gama, one of Zapata's closest intellectual advisers:

When one compares the northerners' and southerners' opinions regarding agrarian problems, one sees that they were and are very different.

The restitution and settlement of communal lands to the people was the main preoccupation for the South. The plan of Ayala, a true reflection of southern thought, confirms this.

For the northerners—from San Luis Potosí, Jalisco, and Zacatecas northward, the solution lay in the division of the enormous latifundia and in the creation of a great many small properties, large enough to support the costs of good agricultural development, achieved with enough resources to guarantee abundant production and future prosperity.

One aspired, therefore, not for a poor parcel from the ejidos but rather for the possession of an agricultural unit deserving the name rancho—highest aspiration of all men of the fields.

The northerner was more individualistic, more removed from the old concept of the communal *calpulli*, more desirous of fully exercising the role of an independent proprietor, demanding for himself a portion of regular sized land which would be totally his and under his complete control, without the restrictions or taxes that the traditional indigenous communal structure imposed; therefore, instead of asking for the revival of this traditional structure, as the southerners desired, he aspired to be able to exploit and extensively cultivate the lot of land assigned to him in the land distribution, including the right to sell, to transfer, to impose taxes for the acquisition of funds, or to contract loans as required.

The law of Villismo, which is far from being well-studied and correctly understood, reflects this aspiration to acquire the most freedom for the owner.[50]

Despite some efforts at conciliation, such as the states' rights provision of the agrarian law, Villa's increasing social radicalism eventually led to a break with the conservative wing of his movement. Ángeles broke with Villa in August 1915.[51] Maytorena had prevented Villa's emissary in Sonora from carrying out any agrarian reform.[52] When Villa's army went to Sonora to help Maytorena in September 1915, he preferred to flee rather than face Villa.[53]

Maytorena's social conservatism played a major role in this decision. While he gave no public explanation for his departure, he later explained that one of the main reasons for his decision was Villa's desire to impose forced loans on wealthy merchants in Sonora and his own refusal to accede to such demands. According to Maytorena, Villa was becoming more and more convinced that the Sonoran leader's links to the upper class were discrediting the revolution.[54]

While Maytorena issued no public declaration against his erstwhile ally and continued to campaign against the recognition of Carranza by the U.S. government, he secretly dealt a crippling blow to Villa. In a confidential letter he instructed his two most loyal subordinates in Sonora, the Yaqui generals Francisco Urbalejo and José María Acosta, to limit their support of Villa to their native state. If Villa should ask them to push southward, they were to tell him that their troops did not want to be too far removed from their families. Should Villa insist, Maytorena wrote, "you should tell him that you will do everything in your power to convince your troops. Instead of doing this, you should disperse them, telling them to keep their arms and ammunition and await my instructions." Urbalejo and Acosta were then to go to the United States, where they would receive financial assistance from Maytorena.[55] After Villa's defeat at Hermosillo, a few weeks after this letter had been sent, most of his Yaqui troops abandoned him and refused to go with him to Chihuahua. It is not clear to what degree Maytorena's instructions or Villa's military disasters caused this.

The agrarian reform Villa planned in the last months of his rule over most of Mexico were never implemented. This was only partly due to resistance by conservatives within his own ranks. At least as important was the fact that it came too late. In August 1915, when the first large-scale land division was to take place in Chihuahua, the Villa administration was already in a state of dissolution. It was incapable of carrying out such an undertaking. It is also doubtful that many peasants, now that it was becoming increasingly clear that Villa had suffered crippling defeats, wanted to receive land from him. This would have constituted a declaration of allegiance to a loser and probably would have precluded their obtaining any land from Carranza, whose victory was becoming more and more probable.

Another reason for Villa's failures to win a wider and more solid mass base after 1915 was the specter of inflation, for which he himself was responsible. Like Carranza and other revolutionaries, Villa had never hesitated to print paper money to finance the revolution. This was not true for Zapata, in whose territory the money economy had been largely replaced by a subsistence economy. Such an economy was possible in rural Morelos but not in the North, with its mining industries and its long border with the United States. The value of the Villa currency depreciated rapidly after increasing quantities of paper money were thrown onto the market.[56]

Prior to Villa's military defeats, his money depreciated less than might have been expected considering the huge amounts his printing presses turned out. The main reason for this was the fact that, in a certain sense, Villa himself was living on credit. Many American and Mexican businessmen and speculators had acquired large amounts of his currency. They hoped that after his expected victory he would redeem his money (or at least accept it as tax payment) at the official rate of exchange, which was far higher than the black market rate at which they had bought it. After Villa's military losses, they dumped on the market all the currency they had previously acquired. This caused such catastrophic depreciation, that businesses, even in Villa's heartland of Chihuahua, refused to exchange goods for Villa money.

No one has described the ensuing situation, or Villa's helplessness in controlling it, better than a Spanish special agent sent to Chihuahua in 1915 by his government to negotiate with Villa for the return of confiscated Spanish property:

And if all of these motives are sufficient causes for determining the exhaustion and weakness of "Villismo," the scarcity and devaluation of money worsened the situation which was further exacerbated by the violent measures adopted by General Villa in order to remedy it; in effect, he attributes the blame for the high cost of living on an unjustified, unjust, and disproportionate rise in prices caused by the merchants' avarice. And in order to reestablish normal conditions and punish those who were responsible, he simultaneously ordered the confiscation of all the stores and warehouses, and the imprisonment of all Mexican merchants for 48 hours with no food so that they might learn the meaning of suffering from hunger. He also provided a special train for foreigners so that they could "go find gold on the other side." Although it is true that this last order was subsequently rescinded, these measures, instead of resolving the conflict inevitably intensified it. Because the merchants were afraid of infuriating General Villa and were unable to sell at their desired price, they refused to sell. Thus for several days it was difficult to find food to eat. These measures also constituted an untenable situation for the future because once today's commodities are exhausted certainly there will be no other merchant who would risk bringing in new products.[57]

A food shortage developed which could not be stemmed by Villa's draconian decrees aimed at forcing merchants to sell their goods. Hunger demonstrations and looting of food stores repeatedly occurred in the area controlled by Villa.[58] As a result his popular support dwindled even further.

By the end of 1915, both the conventionist government and Villa's regional administration for northern Mexico disintegrated. Zapata and Villa continued to wage guerrilla warfare in their respective regions, but the convention ceased to exist as a national movement. Its armies had dominated most of Mexico for only a brief period and outside of its core area had left barely a trace on the social structure of the country. Federico González Garza, perhaps the most intelligent of the intellectuals who had joined Villa, stated this most clearly. In September 1915, as defeat loomed on the horizon, he incisively described the basic weaknesses of the conventionist movement in a letter to his brother, Roque, who had headed the conventionist government in Mexico City for a time. The letter can be read as a kind of epitaph for the Villa government:

Since Huerta was ousted, we have to agree, that from a practical point of view, if we had known how to conduct an orderly confiscation subject to strict rules, and if we had had a distribution of land guided by an intelligent plan and without violence, we would by now have created new interests which would have helped to sustain the new regime.

This is how the constitutional assembly proceeded during the first period of the French Revolution, seizing the land of the nobles and immediately redistributing it, and this constituted the basis for the resistance of the Republican Regime. Despite all the horrors that accompanied the convention, neither the directory nor the succeeding consulate dared to undo the work of the First Assembly; they did not dare to decree the restitution of the confiscated estates. Napoleon, himself converted a while later to a monarch, understood that in order to secure his power he could not meddle with the Republican's work, but on the contrary he had to ratify, confirm, and incorporate into laws the institutions that had been created and implemented during the violent period of the revolution. If we want to create a solid structure, we must not forget the lessons of history.[59]

## Carranza in Power, 1915/1916

Two men from the city of Aguascalientes, Librado González and José Torres, sent a petition to President Venustiano Carranza soon after he had become president of the republic. They stated that they were writing with the full agreement

> of our brothers...on the haciendas, in view of the sad situation in which we find ourselves. We are poor, naked, and hungry; the work is hard; and on some haciendas no wages are paid at all—only two liters of corn on some and three on others are given us. It seems that you have won, although nothing of what was promised in this revolution has been granted.... We humbly request you to order the hacendados to pay some wages, even if it be little, at least three liters of corn and twelve centavos per day more than now. If you do this, it will be a great thing for this nation and all Mexicans will be grateful to you. [They also requested Carranza to bring about price reductions of industrial goods in view of the extreme circumstances in which the poor were living.] If you agree to this request, all of the poor people will be grateful to you and, if a counterrevolution should break out, we would help by signing manifestos to the country and, if possible, by taking up arms so that justice and mutual respect can prevail. When there were floods in Leon, Guanajuato, and Monterrey, there was charity, gifts were collected for the victims. Now, there is no charity and no compassion. As poor people, we hope that the first magistrate of this country will grant us his help.[60]

Carranza sent the petition to the mayor of Aguascalientes, who replied in agreement with the governor of the state that he was in touch with the "señores hacendados" and that the information contained in the petition was "entirely wrong." The hacendados, he claimed, were paying good wages, and, in the few cases where they did not have sufficient corn, the laborers were given wheat instead. The major had been unable to locate and identify the authors of the petition, so he assumed that the signatures were pseudonyms. He would consult with the "señores hacendados" about the affair.[61] This was the end of the matter.

The petition, by its tone and much of its content, as well as by the reaction of the authorities, could have been written in the time of Porfirio Díaz. It clearly illustrated the tremendous restorative powers of the hacendados (both old and new)—a restoration that was taking place in much of Mexico during the Carranza period, while land distribution was just a trickle.

The basis of that restoration, though, was the return of expropriated estates at an increasing rate as the Carranza regime consolidated its hold over most of Mexico. This process was unique to the Mexican revolution and distinguished it from comparable social upheavals. The process has never been described and studied. One reason for that omission is that it contradicts so strongly much of the official doctrine about the Carranza government. The other reason is that only very recently (1978) have scholars obtained access to the archival files which document this massive return of confiscated estates.[62]

As early as 1914 and 1915 hacendados whose estates had been confiscated by "revolutionary" leaders had turned to Carranza for redress. He was quite sympathetic to their demands, but until his victory at the end of 1915 he could satisfy them in a very limited way, because most of the confiscations had occurred in territories dominated by his rivals Villa and Zapata, over which he had no control. As to confiscations in Carranza's own bailiwick, his generals were very unhappy about returning any confiscated properties as long as the civil war lasted.

By the end of 1915 and in 1916, the situation changed. After his victory Carranza removed the confiscated estates from the jurisdiction of the state, local, or military governments and placed them under his direct control. For this purpose the administration of these intervened properties was given to a special agency created by Carranza, the *Administración de bienes intervenidos* ("administration of confiscated properties").[63] This was a clever political move. On the one hand, as long as the estates continued to be administered by the government, each provided Carranza with supplementary revenues for his treasuries. On the other hand, it clearly established that only the central government and not the local governments would be empowered to return estates to their former owners. This meant that the hacendados would have to make their peace not with local military commanders but with Carranza himself. Their loyalties, Carranza obviously hoped, would go the same way.

This restoration involved a long and complex bureaucratic procedure. The hacendado or his lawyer would begin by petitioning Carranza asking for the return of his confiscated properties. If the intervention (this was the official term for confiscations) had been carried out by Villa or other generals hostile to Carranza, the hacendado would insist that these actions had been an act of banditry characteristic of Carranza's enemies. If generals close to the First Chief had carried out the expropriation, the hacendado would state that obviously a misunderstanding had occurred. In practically all cases they insisted that they had never been involved in politics and had only tended to their business, that they were now on the brink of starvation, and their numerous families had no other means of support but the estates that they wanted returned to their control.[64]

Carranza then sent the petitions to the local authorities asking them to explain why the hacienda had been confiscated in the first place.

In the early stages of the movement, while Carranza still attempted to portray himself as a social revolutionary on the verge of carrying out radical reforms, he might receive radical pronouncements from some of his local officials objecting to any return of properties on grounds of principle. Thus in August of 1914 the hacendados Jesús and Joaquin Antonio Ruíz Espinosa y Parra, owners of the Hacienda del Peñasco in the state of San Luis Potosí asked for the return of their estate, which had been expropriated by revolutionary authorities. Major Escobar of the office of confiscated property in San Luis Potosí firmly objected to this request in that same month stating that

> the Espinosa y Parra are part of the group of hacendados from San Luis Potosí whose fortunes cannot be considered legitimately acquired capital, in other words it cannot be considered capital resulting from legitimate profit which the hacendados acquired after having paid their workers just salaries, but on the contrary the fortune of these individuals as that of the majority of the hacendados in the central part of our country which they call capital is in my humble opinion nothing but the salary that these same hacendados should have paid their workers. It is these workers who produced the merchandise which has made the hacendados rich and which has allowed them to have palaces in the capital, to have beautiful automobiles while the humble workers on their haciendas, as all of us who had the honor of being their guests could clearly see, don't even have pants to cover their nakedness nor do they have shoes to wear and they are the main producers of national wealth.[65]

Major Escobar continued "that there is not a single hacienda in San Luis Potosí where the worker is fairly treated and the hacendados occupy the position of feudal lords of older times while the peons are the modern serfs. The situation is now worse than it was, since the old serfs at least had beds to sleep in and clothing to wear while the new serfs of the so-called hacendados of San Luis Potosí do not even have enough to eat, not to speak of having anything to dress in or a bed to sleep on." In Escobar's opinion such hacendados "cannot be friends of a revolution which is attempting to put an end to their privileges. A universal law of self-preservation decrees that they will have to remain what they now are: enemies of the revolution. These are the basic reasons why this office of confiscated property intervened in the estates of the Espinosa y Parra family."

In the later years of the Carranza regime, few documents of this kind were forwarded. If the hacendado had been a blatant enemy of constitutionalism such a fact might be voiced, but even those instances were rare. Thus in May 1916, Guillermo Muñoz, a hacendado from Chihuahua, asked for the return of his properties which Pancho Villa had expropriated, insisting that "my humble personality is well known in the whole state of Chihuahua and the honorable persons in that same state can certainly give you any necessary information concerning my person and attest to the fact that I have never intervened in political affairs."[66] When Carranza asked the state governor for his opinion, he answered that "These properties should not be returned since Mr. Muñoz can be considered an enemy of the constitutionalist cause since he helped the Orozco and Huertista movements and besides belongs to the Creel and Terrazas families, maintaining close links to them."[67]

Such objections became rarer and rarer as time went by. In the regions where Carranza's enemies, especially Villa, had carried out confiscations, the local authorities would report that they lacked the necessary documentation to explain why the confiscation had occurred and would generally insist that they knew nothing derogatory about the hacendado who was asking for the return of his property. Frequently the local authorities went one step further and gave him a clean bill of health.

One of the reasons for this change among local administrators, as Rodolfo Cruz, a hacendado from Chihuahua and probably one of the few who really was not involved in politics, wrote to Carranza, was that "there are persons who offer to arrange the return of goods if they receive a certain sum of money."[68] The return of haciendas offered many opportunities for bribes of local officials or even national officials. From 1915 on, an increasing number of reports like that by J. G. Nava from the state of San Luis Potosí were sent to Carranza. Nava reported that a high official of Carranza's regime, Rafael Nieto, and his henchman, Julian Ramirez, would receive "20,000 pesos from the owner of the Hacienda del Jabali in the state of San Luis Potosí if his estates were returned to him."[69]

Neither negative advice from his officials nor instances of corruption could deter Carranza from his basic purpose of returning the estates to their former owners. Thus, in spite of the fact that Muñoz was identified by the provisional governor of Chihuahua as an enemy of the revolution, Carranza decreed in 1919 that restitution of all his properties was to be made to him.[70] The only condition the hacendados had to comply with in order to obtain his property was to waive any claims for alleged losses during the years of government control.

Carranza was prepared to consider only three kinds of exceptions to his rule of returning confiscated estates to their former owners. The first one was that any property discovered to belong to the clergy remained confiscated. Thus in the state of Puebla in 1917 more than 90 percent of the estates still under government control were considered to be church property.[71] The second exception in which Carranza showed a similar rigidity were the properties of former conventionists. Thus the estate of José María Maytorena, the former governor of Sonora who had sided with Villa, and part of the estates of the Madero family remained confiscated throughout the Carranza period.[72] Finally, in a few cases of very flagrant supporters of Huerta Carranza showed a certain reticence to return them their former properties. But in this last respect he was much more flexible than in the case of the clergy or former Villistas and by 1919 he was clearly ready to woo even the most conservative hacendados to his side by returning them their confiscated estates.

One factor did not prevent Carranza from returning estates to hacendados, the competing claims of peasants or even the fact that his own generals might have distributed some of the lands of these estates to peasants in accordance with Carranza's own agrarian laws. In the state of San Luis Potosí Carranza's governor General Gavira had returned to the peasants of the village of Villa de Reyes the lands which the neighboring Hacienda del Gogorrón had taken from them. But, according to a report sent to Carranza, the owners had bribed an agent of the new governor General Dávila and he returned these lands to the hacienda.[73] Carranza made no effort to check this practice but on the contrary intervened himself when some of his governors attempted to implement his own agrarian law. The most controversial such case occurred in the state of Tabasco in southeastern Mexico. It was the one state in Mexico, with the possible exception of Yucatán, where conditions of debt peonage akin to slavery were most prevalent in Mexico. When by the end of 1915 one of Carranza's most radical supporters, General Francisco Múgica, became governor of the state, he immediately set out to transform its social structure profoundly. He forced the hacendados to abolish debt peonage, raise wages, and set up schools and hospitals.[74] Carranza fully backed these measures but turned against his governor when he attempted to carry out agrarian reform. In early 1916 Múgica returned the lands belonging to a large corporation owned jointly by Spaniards and Americans, the Compañia Agricola Tabasqueña, to four hundred peasants of the village of Jonuta. In a solemn ceremony presided over by Múgica the peasants were returned their land in the name of Venustiano Carranza, whom they continually applauded. But as soon as he heard of that event through complaints by the owners, Carranza wired Múgica to return the lands to the corporation. At this point Múgica put his whole prestige on the line; he wired Carranza that if the lands were returned, he would immediately resign and intimated that uprisings might then break out in Tabasco. Not even this enormous pressure was sufficient to convince Carranza to ratify

Múgica's decree but at least it convinced him to allow the peasants for the time being to continue in the possession of their lands while the national agrarian commission in Mexico would review their claims. Múgica soon lost his position as governor and his successor imposed such high taxes on the peasants that the corporation hoped, though this hope proved unfounded, that the peasants would soon leave their new lands and allow the old owners to return.[75]

Among a number of radical supporters of Carranza such as Múgica, these measures led to an increasing feeling of despair and hopelessness. In a letter to another supporter of Carranza's who was also his superior, General Salvador Alvarado, Múgica wrote in August 1916, "I do not agree with the general policy that is being carried out . . . . a great agrarian commission has been created to watch over the functioning of this law. It has ended in a complete fiasco; in spite of the fact that the first steps are only being taken to solve the agrarian problem, measures are already being taken to put an end to these first steps before they have been undertaken . . . . When I was in the capital of Mexico in February and March of this year I saw that the Villistas, Zapatistas, and members of the convention were persecuted far more than the supporters of Huerta . . . . Where does all this lead us to, my dear General?"[76]

Múgica's evaluation of Carranza was echoed at the other side of the political spectrum. In November 1915 José Yves Limantour, who had been the most influential member of Porfirio Díaz's cabinet and had headed the Científicos, expressed his apprehension to Lord Cowdray's representative in Mexico J. B. Body that his properties might not be returned to him in spite of Carranza's victory, "I believe as you, in view of the new seizures that have been made upon the property of persons, who, like the Iturbes, Hilario Elguero and others who have never any interference with politics, that surely my town properties must be still in the possession of that canaille which persecutes us and has all the goodwill and support of Mr. Wilson. I am very much afraid that the letter I sent to Carranza through your good offices will not bring any good results."

Nevertheless Limantour remained basically optimistic about the policies of the Carranza government. He was convinced that the measures the Mexican president had taken against some of the landowners and members of the upper classes were of a temporary nature and that he could get his properties back by putting "the matter in the hands of some person who may have some chances of being heard by those people; and in order to do it with some chances of success I should require to know the right man 'under the circumstances.'"[77]

Limantour had obviously found this right man and his optimism over Carranza's policies proved to be entirely justified. This was the gist of a report by one of Cowdray's representatives, A. E. Worswick, written nearly two years later:

> A tendency to conservatism is observable now that the government is well established and is not so dependent on the radical military element. Undoubtedly Carranza is doing his utmost to free himself from the extremists, and the most hopeful sign is, that he is commencing to take into the government offices, some of the old regime. Pesqueira told me that this is their defined policy, and when the hatreds engendered by the revolution die out, they propose to utilize the services of as many of the best of the old government as possible, thus consolidating their position and placating, what they call, the "Reaccionarios" . . . .
>
> You probably know that they have returned Don José Limantour's properties, also Ignacio de la Torre's, and an amnesty law is promised in July which will bring back hundreds of the "emigrés," and we hope will make the City take on more of its old time appearance.[78]

At the same time, Carranza turned against another social group he had assiduously courted in 1915—the industrial workers. By late 1915 and early 1916, whatever enthusiasm the workers had shown toward him began to fade as their situation steadily deteriorated. There were serious food shortages caused by a drastic reduction in agricultural production during the civil war that engulfed Mexico in 1914–15 and speculation in foodstuffs by Carranzist officials. There was increasing inflation resulting from the devaluation of Carranza's paper money, as the printing presses turned out more and more of it, and there was serious unemployment resulting from the paralysis and eventual closing of many factories.

In late 1915 and early 1916, strikes erupted in many parts of the country. The dockworkers of Veracruz and Tampico, the electricians and streetcar operators of Guadalajara, the miners of El Oro, and the bakers and streetcar operators of the capital, went on strike. They demanded payment of their wages in gold and not in depreciated paper currency.[79] At the beginning of 1916, the "Red Battalions" were dissolved. When the railroad workers went on strike in 1916, the government announced their "mobilization"; one trade union office after another was shut down. Demonstrations of striking workers were even fired upon. The repression reached a high point in mid-1916. Because of the large price increases, the trade unions had called a general strike for 27 May. It was delayed, however, when the government promised an early wage increase. When it failed to materialize, thirty-six thousand workers struck on 31 July. Carranza immediately concentrated troops in the capital, seized the trade union offices and outlawed the Casa del Obrero Mundial. Draconian orders were issued, based on an 1862 ordinance which demanded the death penalty for advocating a strike.

These measures created sharp opposition in Carranza's own army. On 11 August, the strike leaders were brought before a military court and charged with high treason. The court acquitted them. Two weeks later, Carranza had them brought before a military court, and they were once again acquitted (only the leader of the electricians' union, Velazco, was condemned to death, but was later pardoned). Though Carranza did have the strike leaders rearrested, he was forced to free them several months later.[80] With malicious pleasure, the Austrian minister to Mexico wrote of Carranza's labor policy.

The industrial and agricultural workers are disappointed, because the promises that were made to them have not been kept. In the beginning, they were enthusiastically courted. They were given the splendid building belonging to the Jockey Club, the employers were forced to grant a wage increase of more than 100 percent, and the 8-hour workday was introduced. The proletariat became arrogant, and then the workers from the railroads and from other state companies also revolted. This had naturally not been the intention of the government, which then turned against its former protégés, ejected them from their palaces, and banned all meetings that did not have prior approval from the authorities. The factory workers' enthusiasm for the Carranza government is naturally over.[81]

At the same time that he turned against the radicals in his own movement, Carranza did everything possible to destroy finally what was left of Zapata's and Villa's movements.

In mid-1916, General Pablo González had organized his troops for a crusade of annihilation against Zapata. In a decree to the inhabitants of Morelos on 1 November 1916, he announced that all Zapatists and those suspected of being Zapatists would be shot. The offensive by the Carranza troops was successful initially and, within a few months, Zapata was forced to give up the cities he held in Morelos. He now fell back on guerrilla warfare.[82] The commanding staff and a small section of the army retreated into the mountains, while most of the remaining soldiers returned to the villages. During the day, they worked as peasants, and, by night, they attacked González's troops. González made no attempt to win over the peasantry. A cruel and brutal war was waged against them. As a result, even those peasants who might have wanted to abandon the struggle took up arms once again.

The destruction of Villa seemed even easier to accomplish. Only a few hundred men of what was once the mighty Division of the North had followed Villa into the mountains of Chihuahua. The great majority of his former commanders and soldiers either had fled across the border to the United States or surrendered to Carranza, who granted them amnesty and even accepted many of them into his army. This policy of directing his energies mainly against the radicals, both inside and outside of his movement, was feasible for Carranza as long as he could count on the support or, at least, the neutrality of Mexico's upper classes and on the support of the United States.

The upper classes had supported Carranza against the Convention and were profiting both from the return of their confiscated properties and from his repression of peasant movements. But to a large degree they were far less enthusiastic about having to share their revenues with him, his generals, and the Carranzist bourgeoisie. Nevertheless, they had learned the hard way in 1913–14 that it was senseless to oppose the United States. As long as Carranza seemed to enjoy U.S. support, most of the traditional upper class did not turn against him.

On the whole Carranza's efforts to restore the status quo of the Porfirian period were more successful than his attempts to rebuild the strong centralized state that Díaz had erected.

The revolution had essentially destroyed the Porfirian army and large parts of the Díaz bureaucracy and had replaced them by a motley array of divergent regional caudillos, mostly leaders of Carranza's army. What most of them had in common was that they would brook as little interference as possible from the central government in Mexico City. Beyond this common trait their policies showed wide divergences.

In the states that had made up the core of the Constitutionalist revolt of 1913, and whose main leaders had sided with Carranza in his struggle against Villa, members of the new bourgeoisie, who were also military men, such as Calles in Sonora, Espinosa Mireles in Coahuila, and the Arrieta brothers in Durango, became the governors.

They were conservative as far as the agrarian problem was concerned, liberal toward labor, and nationalistic with regard to foreign enterprise. Very little land was distributed and emerging peasant movements, for example, the Yaquis in Sonora or radicalized peasants from the Laguna region led by one of Villa's former generals, Calixto Contreras, were ruthlessly suppressed. Nevertheless, miners and industrial workers were encouraged to set up unions and the strikes they proclaimed frequently enjoyed the backing of the regional leaders. At times they contradicted the policies of the national government.

New pressures were applied to foreign enterprises, however, to increase their taxes and grant more benefits to their workers.

In Morelos and Chihuahua, where the most radical revolutionary movements had emerged and where Emiliano Zapata and Pancho Villa continued to resist, very different tactics were applied by the Carranzists.

Morelos was treated like a foreign occupied territory, and Pablo González applied a scorched earth tactic against the state's peasants.

In Chihuahua a more differentiated policy was carried out. Carranza gave political power to his middle and upper class supporters and allowed them to form militia units recruited in the state. At the same time the Mexican president sent troops from outside Chihuahua to combat Villa. This led to nearly five more years of tension, conflict, and occasional outbreaks, between Chihuahua's Carranzists and their ostensible outside allies.[83] These internal conflicts seriously impeded the struggle against Villa.

What Carranza's policies in both states had in common was that no attempt was made to win over the peasantry by even the most limited kind of agrarian reform. A strict tactic of relentless repression was the only coherent measure applied in the countryside.

This policy was in marked contrast to the one practiced by the Carranzist leadership in the southeastern states of Tabasco and Yucatán, where no radical social movements had emerged and where the power of the hacendados seemed practically unbroken. It was to these regions that Carranza sent his most radical supporters, such as Salvador Alvarado to Yucatán and Francisco Múgica to Tabasco, to organize and mobilize the peons on the estates as a counterweight to the hacendados.

Finally there was a fourth category of states in which Carranza applied yet another kind of policy. It consisted of those states of central and north central Mexico where no peasant uprising of the Zapata type had occurred. Not all of these states were firmly under Carranzist control but in those that were, the Mexican president tended to appoint outsiders, mainly from the North, as governors. Unlike their counterparts in southeastern Mexico most of these governors were not radicals nor were their social policies revolutionary. In contrast to Mexico's southeast, large parts of the country's center had, at least for brief periods of time, been controlled by Villa's army. As a result many haciendas had been confiscated. Even in those regions the Villistas had not controlled, Carranzist units, whom the First Chief was not yet powerful enough to restrain, had carried out confiscations.

As a result the hacendados of the central states had been greatly weakened by the revolution. In addition secessionist movements, which hacendados had sponsored or supported in Yucatán, Oaxaca, and Chiapas were far more difficult to implement in central Mexico. As a result the hacendados of the central states were far more willing than their counterparts in the southeast to reach an accommodation with Carranza's officials if their lands were returned to them. Many governors of central Mexico thus received large and continued payments by the hacendados and in return were quite willing to utilize their military forces to suppress emerging demands for hacienda lands. The fact that they and most of their troops were generally outsiders and not local revolutionaries made it easier to implement such a policy.

To many contemporary observers, the task of welding these regional principalities into a new and powerful national state constituted the most difficult—perhaps intractable—problem that Carranza faced.

The "national" force to emerge from the revolution, the revolutionary army, was not "national" at all but was largely a composite of the armed forces' regional leaders.

No national political party capable of even remotely balancing the army's influence had been formed in the course of the revolution. The only civilian organizations to emerge and acquire new strength in this period, such as labor unions and a few local peasant organizations which post-Carranza revolutionary governments and some governors success-fully mobilized in their favor, were rejected with a few exceptions after a brief period of collaboration with Carranza, for he feared their radicalism.

If the Mexican president wished to be more than a mediator between powerful local caudillos, and if he wanted to recreate a strong Mexican state, only two completely divergent options remained.

The first was the option advocated by conservatives both inside and outside the Carranza movement. It consisted of accepting Woodrow Wilson's offer of alliance and giving it a solid basis by accepting a large loan from American bankers.

This, it was hoped, would allow the Mexican president to replicate the policy practiced by Porfiro Díaz to build up a strong Mexican state with revenues derived from foreign sources.

The second option was a policy favored by the most radical and nationalistic elements within the Carranza movement. They advocated increased taxation of foreign holdings and restrictions on foreign invest-ment, as well as on the political influence of foreigners. Such a policy would have strengthened the state by increasing its revenues and have allowed it to rally its divergent supporters around a nationalistic platform.

While Carranza had made some concessions to the nationalists by im-posing taxes on foreign companies in late 1915 and early 1916, there are some indications, at least until March 1916, that he basically favored the first option and hoped to secure a loan from the United States.

These hopes of Carranza's and any prospect of the first option were shattered on the night of 8 March 1916 when Pancho Villa, with five hundred men, attacked the town of Columbus, New Mexico.

# 8 The United States and Mexico

## The Wilson Administration and the Revolutionary Factions

In contrast to the expectations of the Wilson administration, Huerta's defeat and the victory of the revolutionaries increased rather than decreased the problems the United States faced in Mexico. During this period one event decisively influenced United States policy in Mexico: the outbreak of the First World War in Europe. On one hand, the war strengthened the desire of American politicians and businessmen for armed intervention in Mexico. The war effort and the economic boom fueled by arms production had greatly increased the importance of Mexican raw materials and the profits to be derived from them. To exploit Mexican resources fully, peace and a pro-American government were required, but since no stable pro-American government had emerged from Huerta's defeat, American businessmen and politicians became increasingly shrill in their calls for armed intervention. On the other hand, the outbreak of the world war had greatly increased American fears of the consequences of armed intervention. Such a step would have limited United States possibilities of intervening elsewhere and would have committed the country to years of turmoil in Mexico. These considerations weighed heavily in Wilson's decisions.

The objectives of American policy were often at odds. For example, the Americans wanted to restore "law and order" in Mexico as quickly as possible, and the best way to accomplish this appeared to be by supporting one of the contending parties. But the Wilson administration also wanted a Mexican government willing to accept United States preeminence. Short of intervention, this could most easily be accomplished by playing off the contending sides against each other, by preventing any side from suffering excessive losses, and by working for a coalition government in which all groups would be represented. American policy was buffeted by all these contradictory tendencies in 1914–15. At first the Wilson administration supported Villa and expected him to triumph quickly.[1] Nevertheless, probably animated by the desire to allow no side to enjoy total victory, the Americans evacuated Veracruz in December 1914 and turned it over to Carranza's troops stationed nearby. Obviously Washington was hoping for a compromise among the various movements in Mexico, but when the fighting continued, the United States changed its tactics.

Washington adopted another policy, one of open threats to force the "restoration of order" and the formation of a Mexican government under United States auspices. On 2 June 1915 Wilson dispatched a sharply worded note to the belligerent parties calling on them to come to terms as quickly as possible. Otherwise the American government would be "constrained to decide what means should be employed to help Mexico save herself."[2] Needless to say, a settlement made under American pressure would naturally have assured the United States of a determining influence in the new Mexican government.

Wilson's note was icily rejected by both Carranza and Zapata. Zapata's brother Eufemio stated: "We are not afraid to defend our country . . . even if they [the Americans] send millions of soldiers. We will fight them, one man against hundreds. We may have no army and no ammunition, but we have men who will face their bullets."[3] Soto y Gama, Zapata's representative in the convention, sharply attacked Wilson, calling him an agent of Wall Street.[4] Villa, however, welcomed the note and stated his willingness to negotiate with Carranza.[5] His positive response reflected both his relatively friendly attitude toward the United States and his precarious military position—he had just suffered another painful defeat and his army was beginning to dissolve.

When it became apparent that Wilson's note had not had the desired effect, the United States considered other tactics. Wilson appears initially to have considered a military intervention in Mexico. He was, however, dissuaded from such a course by the deep tensions with Germany over the U-boat question. The State Department also considered "solving" the Mexican question by means of a military coup which would eliminate all the Mexican revolutionary leaders—Carranza, Villa, and Zapata. It was finally decided to convene a pan-American conference.[6] In so doing, the Americans hoped to accomplish two goals: to dispel the suspicion that the United States had aggressive intentions and to advance their own interests by giving them a pan-American coloring.

Secretary of State Robert Lansing envisioned a conference of representatives of the United States, Argentina, Brazil, and Chile, the stated aim of which would be to bring about a meeting of lesser chiefs in Mexico who would in turn create a new government. This new government would then be recognized by the United States and the ABC countries and provided with arms; simultaneously arms shipments to the other parties would be cut off. The lesser chiefs alone, however, were not to choose the new president and his cabinet: in its proposals for the conference, the United States claimed for itself extensive codetermination rights. In fact it appears that the Wilson administration had no intention of leaving such a momentous choice to the Mexican revolutionaries. It began to consider one candidate after another for the Mexican presidency who could then be proposed to and perhaps imposed upon the planned conference.[7]

The pan-American conference met on 5 August 1915 in Washington to establish concrete procedures for the appointment of a provisional Mexican government, but in the meantime, the situation had changed again. Villa was being pushed back still farther, and by August 1915 Carranza controlled roughly four-fifths of the country. The American government had done everything it could to prevent Carranza's victory. When Villa, whose situation was continuously worsening, began in July to make extensive requisitions from American companies and to impose heavy taxes on them, the American authorities manifested a tolerance they would not have shown in other circumstances. Lansing even proposed that Villa be offered better opportunities in the United States to sell goods from the regions he still controlled so that he would not find it necessary to resort to the taxation of American companies. "We do not wish the Carranza faction to be the only one to deal with in Mexico," he wrote. "Carranza seems so impossible that an appearance, at least, of opposition to him will give us the opportunity to invite a compromise of factions. I think, therefore, it is politic for the time to allow Villa to obtain sufficient financial resources to allow his faction to remain in arms until a compromise can be effected."[8]

By the end of August, it was clear that the imbalance of forces precluded the establishment of a Mexican government by the lesser chiefs. Such a result could only have been obtained by an American military intervention, a move which would have severely curtailed U.S. possibilities of influencing events in Europe, where World War I was raging, or in the Far East, where Japan was attempting to increase its influence in China.

It was at this time that American sympathies for Villa rapidly dwindled as the northern revolutionary leader began exacting ever increasing financial contributions from U.S. companies. Carranza, by contrast, had committed himself in a memorandum sent to the State Department "to protect the lives and property of foreigners, to grant general amnesty for Mexicans and foreigners, to guarantee freedom of religion, and to solve the agrarian question without expropriations."[9]

By the beginning of October 1915, both Lansing and Wilson felt that recognition of Carranza was the best option they had. A leading Mexican politician, Porfirio Díaz's former finance minister José Yves Limantour, expressed the view that oil interests were behind this reversal of U.S. policy: "I am told in the most confidential manner," he wrote Lord Cowdray's representative in Mexico, J. B. Body,

that Wilson's change of policy in favor of Carranza is due exclusively to the Texas Oil Company, which was able to enlist the cooperation of Col. House by some unknown means, but which must be highly important because it appeared that only a little while back Col. House was inclined to view the situation from a very different standpoint. It was Col. House who conceived the idea of having the A.B.C. intervene in order to facilitate Wilson's change of policy, and to this end he took advantage of someone named Lawrence, a young man who was a pupil of Wilson's and is in constant contact with the latter's secretary Tumulty, to make the suggestion to Naon the Argentine ambassador and a very fatuous gentleman, the whole plan which was carried out and for which he had taken so much credit, just as if it were completely his own. Once again the Texans have contributed to Mexico's disgrace.[10]

The "someone named Lawrence" referred to by Limantour was David Lawrence, who in the 1930s was to become publisher of *U.S. News and World Report*. He had met Wilson at Princeton and in 1914–15 had been sent by the president on a factfinding mission to Mexico. Upon his return he had recommended organizing a conference of lesser chiefs (a recommendation Wilson accepted) and sometime later had suggested unilaterally recognizing Carranza (a recommendation Wilson rejected in August 1915, when it was first made).[11] What links Lawrence may have had to the Texas Oil Company and whether the company favored recognition of Carranza could not be substantiated from any other source. If this oil company did indeed support the first chief, its policies would have been at odds with those of most major U.S. and British oil companies.

The British companies had never supported Carranza, while most U.S. companies lost their initial enthusiasm for him early in 1915 when his administration attempted to increase their taxes. In 1915 most American oil companies were supporting the conspiracy, to which we will turn in a moment, of the State Department official in charge of Mexican affairs, Leon Canova, and Mexican exiles to impose a conservative candidate as president of Mexico.[12]

When they learned that Wilson was contemplating recognition of Carranza, they went so far as to send a representative to talk with Britain's ambassador to the U.S., Cecil Spring Rice, requesting him "to use his influence with his government to the end that recognition of Carranza might be withheld until he had promised to respect duly and legally correct compromises, etc. entered into by preceding administrations."[13]

British oil interests were of like mind. A representative of the Cowdray interests told Maurice de Bunsen, an official of the British Foreign Office, "that we emphatically felt that His Majesty's government should advise our ambassador that they would not sympathetically assist in the recognition of the Carranza Government unless the Carranza party would pledge that contracts and concessions entered into with British investors and previously constituted governments would be validated."[14]

These views were shared by the British foreign secretary Edward Grey and as a result, Britain's representative to Mexico, Thomas Hohler, attempted to persuade Secretary of State Lansing to delay recognition of Carranza. But Lansing and Wilson refused to alter their views.[15] Strategic considerations were prominent in their minds. On 10 October, Lansing wrote in his diary

> Looking at the general situation I have come to the following conclusion: Germany desires to keep up the turmoil in Mexico until the United States is forced to intervene; therefore we must not intervene.
> Germany does not wish to have any one faction dominant in Mexico; therefore we must recognize one faction as dominant in Mexico.
> When we recognize a faction as the government, Germany will undoubtedly seek to cause a quarrel between that government and ours; therefore we must avoid a quarrel regardless of criticism and complaint in Congress and the press.
> It comes down to this: Our possible relations with Germany must be our first consideration; and all our intercourse with Mexico must be regulated accordingly.[16]

This was a view Woodrow Wilson fully shared.

As a gesture of goodwill to Carranza, it was decided that Villa, who had no idea of what was transpiring, would be sacrificed. On 1 November 1915, Villa waged what would prove to be his last decisive battle against Carranza at Agua Prieta on the Mexican-American border with the ten thousand men who remained with him. The battle was still undecided when, on the night of 2 November, three thousand of Carranza's troops who had been allowed by the American government to cross United States territory took Villa by surprise and inflicted a disastrous defeat on his forces. This battle marked the end of the Division of the North as a regular army. A few weeks after this defeat Villa was reduced to waging a guerrilla war.

After his recognition by the Wilson administration in October 1915, Carranza's relations with the United States gradually began to improve, though substantial areas of conflict remained, largely because of Carranza's efforts to alleviate Mexico's disastrous economic situation by exacting higher taxes from American companies.

Three years of uninterrupted civil war and the ongoing fighting with the guerrilla groups of Villa and Zapata had exhausted the country. A large portion of the arable land lay fallow. Both agricultural and industrial production had fallen off sharply since 1913. There was only one source that could provide the Mexican government with the means for rebuilding the country: the large foreign companies—most of them American—which had previously paid almost no taxes. The world war and the boom it brought on had generated a heavy demand for raw materials and thus led to an increase in oil production. On 6 December 1915, Carranza announced substantial tax increases for oil produced in Mexico. His justification for this move was that "the exported oil benefits only foreign industries and brings the country nothing except a tax. This export represents a depletion of our natural resources, and thus the oil, which is exported from the country and does not benefit its inhabitants, must be taxed in order to compensate this loss to the country."[17]

The Mexican government also pursued an anti-American policy with regard to the main export product of Yucatán, sisal. Until 1912, the International Harvester Company had enjoyed a monopoly on the sale of sisal and had kept the prices down. When Carranza's troops occupied Yucatán in 1915, they set up a state purchase and sales monopoly to counterbalance this situation. The state company succeeded in increasing the price of sisal. Whereas a pound of sisal cost only 4.5 cents in 1911, the price in 1917 was 19.5.[18] This increase was due not merely to the establishment of a state monopoly, but also to the fact that the war had made the import of sisal from Africa to the United States impossible.

In the hope of alleviating these tensions and of enabling the Mexican government to obtain new revenues without taxing U.S. companies, the Wilson administration attempted to help Carranza arrange a large loan in the United States. These efforts came to naught, however, for on the night of 9 March 1916 a Mexican raiding force of five hundred men attacked the town of Columbus, New Mexico, to cries of "Viva Villa" and "Viva Mexico." According to all available evidence, the leader of the attack was Francisco "Pancho" Villa. The raiders were repulsed by units of the 13th U.S. Cavalry, garrisoned in Columbus, after a six-hour battle. More than one hundred Mexicans and seventeen Americans died in the fighting. The response of the United States to this attack came quickly.[19] Within a week a punitive expedition, initially composed of 5,800 men and later increased to 10,000, under the command of General John J. Pershing, invaded the Mexican state of Chihuahua under orders from President Woodrow Wilson to destroy Villa's forces.[20]

The roots of Villa's decision to attack Columbus go back well before Wilson's recognition of Carranza and his decision to help the First Chief. In the spring and summer of 1915, Wilson was looking for a Mexican presidential candidate other than Carranza or Villa that his administration could back. Mexican conservatives closely linked to the old Porfirian elite, U.S. business interests, and high officials of the Wilson administration attempted to obtain U.S. government help in order to stage a counter-revolution in Mexico. Their spokesman was Leon Canova, head of the State Department's Mexican desk. Canova proposed to a number of cabinet members that the United States throw its support to a conservative group headed by Eduardo Iturbide, a descendant of Mexico's first emperor and the chief of police of Mexico City during the Huerta regime. Canova suggested a form of support that the United States used successfully in later years. It would supply the Iturbide group with stocks of food which it could then distribute among the population. These gestures, it was hoped, would secure for Iturbide the popularity he lacked. In return for such help and in exchange for a large loan—$500 million was mentioned—from U.S. banks, the conservatives were to grant wideranging rights to the U.S. government and to U.S. bankers, including "American supervision of customs collection." The conservatives were also to accept the appointment by the United States of an "unofficial administrative advisor" with unspecified powers to "oversee the necessary reforms." In his memorandum to Secretary of State Bryan, Canova did not explain what he meant by "necessary reforms."[21] He did, however, stipulate in another memorandum sent to Chandler Anderson, who frequently served as intermediary between the administration and business interests, that "all Church and other real property confiscated by revolutionary bands or others without proper or due process of law since February 13, 1913 shall be reoccupied by their legal owners."[22]

Canova's plot was far more than an attempt by a high State Department official and a few Mexican and American associates to secure advantages in Mexico. The plan was backed by important segments of Mexico's prerevolutionary oligarchy, of whom Manuel Calero was a representative, and by U.S. business interests, for whom Chandler Anderson was spokesman.[23] Its purpose was to exploit disunity within the revolutionary camp by reestablishing a Díaz style regime that, unlike its predecessor, would be dominated by the United States.

In all probability this plan was complemented by a secret agreement between the Mexican conservatives and the relevant American business interests (among which the oil companies played a dominant role), an agreement which Canova did not reveal to the administration officials to whom he submitted his project. According to this secret pact, U.S. interests were to have decisive influence in selecting Mexico's secretary of foreign relations and secretary of finance. The United States was to grant a large loan to Mexico and to supervise its finances in turn. The United States was to be given naval bases in the Pacific, mainly in Magdalena Bay. U.S. business interests were to share control of the Tehuantepec railroad, which hitherto had been under British control.[24]

The plan Canova submitted gained important support within the Wilson administration; most outspoken was Secretary of the Interior Franklin K. Lane, who in later years became closely identified with oil interests.[25] On his initiative the plan was discussed at a cabinet meeting, but Bryan dismissed the plan, declaring that the United States "should not take up a man who would probably play in with the reactionaries."[26] Although

Wilson did not voice any opinion at these meetings, he later expressed agreement with Bryan's position, and Canova's plan was discarded.[27]

Before drafting this plan Canova had attempted to obtain Villa's support for similar concessions to U.S. business interests in November 1914. Villa rejected these proposals and after Canova had worked out his secret agreement with the conservatives, he attempted to sidestep Villa and directly enlist the support of his army. In the project outline he submitted to Bryan, Canova wrote: "I'm assured that 20,000 men, mostly trained soldiers of the old Federal Army coming largely from Villa's ranks would adhere to it; but in all probability, Villa's entire army will join the movement."[28]

Villa heard about these intrigues and when Wilson did a sudden about-face in his Mexican policy by recognizing and then actively supporting Carranza, Villa became extremely suspicious of the real motivation for Wilson's policy reversal.[29] Villa's suspicions were fanned by a report he received from his representative in the United States, Roque González Garza, the former head of the government of the Revolutionary Convention. On 29 October Gonzáles Garza wrote Villa a long description and analysis of the events leading up to the recognition of his enemy:

> It was a great blow to me to see that you have always been miserably deceived; possibly this took place in good faith but you were always deceived. I was also deceived.... After arriving in Torreón...I was clearly told that, from the point of view of international political relations, our situation was very good; we were one step from recognition by the United States.... A few days went by and you received the clearest assurances that, from the point of view of international politics, everything was proceeding in your favor; that only a small effort on our part was required for the U.S. government to take us into consideration and that the original plan of the participants at the conference would be implemented with satisfactory results for us.

González Garza did not mention the name of the person who had given these assurances to Villa. That he left open the possibility that the intermediary had acted in good faith suggests that he was probably referring to George Carothers, the U.S. special agent in the Villa camp with whom Villa had especially good relations.

Bitterly, González Garza went on to describe how Villa's delegates at the Washington peace conference were treated by their American hosts:

> Our situation was depressing. Everything turned out to have been a lie; we were very badly off; we were not even listened to... The 19th of October arrived and the participants at the conference decided to recognize Carranza.... This decision, communicated *ex abrupto* to the four winds, was an enormous humiliation for us since we were delegates to the peace conference. We were not told anything and the

solemn declarations made by Wilson at an earlier date were simply discarded. All historical precedents were ignored. Even common sense was not respected, since we had come to the conference ready to make peace but in an honorable way. This resolution was approved and we suffered a great blow . . . . I have seen many injustices, but I have never thought that Carranza would triumph in the international political field after he played the comedy of being the most nationalistic of all Mexicans and after he provoked the United States two or three times. I do not entirely know what has been decided concretely, but I am convinced that something very dark has been agreed on; for I have no other explanation for the sudden change in U.S. policy against our group and in favor of Carranza.[30]

In another part of this letter, he stated, "God knows how many secret pacts" Carranza has signed with the United States.

Villa now became convinced that Carranza had bought recognition from Wilson by agreeing to Canova's plan to convert Mexico into a U.S. protectorate. Since Canova had submitted his plans to Villa, the latter had reason to assume that similar proposals had been presented to his rival. In view of Canova's important position within the State Department Villa naturally assumed that he acted on Wilson's instructions. He had no way of knowing that the cabinet had rejected Canova's plan.

As a result, on 5 November 1915 Villa issued a manifesto in Naco, Sonora, containing strong accusations against both Wilson and Carranza. The manifesto asked why Carranza—who "had never given guarantees to Americans, who had plundered them, who had deprived foreigners as often as he could of the lands they owned in the eastern and southern parts of the republic, and who had always aroused the repugnance of the United States"—had suddenly obtained not only the recognition but also the active support of the United States. According to Villa, U.S. support to Carranza entailed nothing less than a $500 million loan and permission for Carranza's troops to cross into U.S. territory. The manifesto bluntly answered its own question: "The price for these favors was simply the sale of our country by the traitor Carranza."[31]

The manifesto further charged that Carranza had agreed to eight conditions imposed by the United States: (1) amnesty to all political prisoners; (2) a 99-year concession granting the United States rights over Magdalena Bay, Tehuantepec, and an unnamed region in the oil zone; (3) an agreement that the ministries of the interior, foreign affairs, and finance would be filled by individuals enjoying the support of the Washington government; (4) all paper money issued by the revolution would be consolidated after consultation with a representative named by the White House; (5) all just claims by foreigners for damages caused by the revolution would be paid and all confiscated property returned; (6) the Mexican National Railways would be controlled by the governing board in

New York until the debts to this board were repaid; (7) the United States, through Wall Street bankers, would grant a $500 million loan to the Mexican government to be guaranteed by a lien on the entire income of the Mexican treasury, with a representative of the U.S. government to have supervision over Mexico's compliance with this provision; and (8) General Pablo González would be named provisional president and would call for elections within six months.

Villa's policies in the next months were clearly presaged by this manifesto. "Can foreigners, especially the Yanquis," he asked, "harbor the illusion that they can exploit 'peacefully while thanking God' the riches of Mexican soil?" As relations between the United States and Carranza seemed to become closer, Villa became more and more firmly convinced "that the sale of this country is complete." He now considered it his overriding task to safeguard Mexico's independence and to break what he conceived as an American stranglehold over his country. On 16 December he sent a letter to the commanders of Carranza's forces who were advancing on his last strongholds in Chihuahua. After describing the secret pact he assumed Carranza had signed with Wilson, Villa stated that, because of this new development, his troops had stopped fighting Carranzists "so as not to shed Mexican blood."[32] To the Carranza generals he proposed an alliance "that would unite all of us against the Yanqui who, because of racial antagonisms and commercial and economic ambitions, is the natural enemy of our race and of all Latin countries." In the event such an alliance was signed, he wrote, "he would give up command of his troops."

A few weeks later he wrote Emiliano Zapata in a similar vein; "we have decided not to fire a bullet more against Mexicans, our brothers, and to prepare and organize ourselves to attack the Americans in their own dens and make them know that Mexico is a land for the free and a tomb for thrones, crowns, and traitors."[33] By attacking the United States and inviting possible reprisals, Villa hoped to create an insoluble dilemma for Carranza. If Carranza allowed U.S. troops to penetrate into Mexico without offering resistance, Villa hoped to expose him as a tool of the Americans. If Carranza ignored the original agreement and resisted the Americans, so much the better. The tie between him and the Wilson administration would have been ruptured and his position severely shaken. Max Weber, the German vice-consul in Ciudad Juárez, wrote to a business partner in the United States in December 1916, "Villa wants intervention and stated in public in Chihuahua that, as long as the washerwoman in Washington is at the head, he will continue to burn and loot until America intervenes in Mexico and brings about the downfall of Carranza."[34]

Villa's attack on Columbus provoked a storm of protest in the United States and strengthened interventionist demands for the occupation of Mexico. It was a unique opportunity: in the eyes of the world—and especially in Latin America—an armed intervention would have as its target not the Mexican government, but merely Villa's "bandits." At the same time, the Americans hoped to gain the support or at least the passivity of Carranza, who stood to benefit from the elimination of one of his major opponents.

On 13 March 1916, the American government sent a note to Carranza, requesting permission for an American punitive expedition to pursue Villa on Mexican territory. Although the Mexican president granted no such permission, an expeditionary force under the command of General John J. Pershing crossed the Mexican border on 15 March and penetrated into the state of Chihuahua.[35]

The primary aim of the punitive expedition, according to statements by President Woodrow Wilson, was to capture Villa. The instructions actually given Pershing were of a more limited nature. If he brought about the destruction of Villa's forces, the expedition would have fulfilled its aim. Pershing managed to do neither. The Americans never succeeded in capturing the north Mexican leader (though without knowing it they once came very close when an American patrol passed within a few feet of a cave in which Villa, who had been wounded, was hiding). And his forces not only were not decisively defeated or disbanded by the Pershing expedition, they grew in size at a phenomenal rate as long as the Americans stayed in Mexico. In March 1916, at the time he attacked Columbus, Villa had about five hundred men. Several months before, most of the soldiers of his once powerful Division of the North had either surrendered to the Carranza faction or simply gone home. Villa had lost much of his popular support. Chihuahua's middle class had turned against him. Many of his former soldiers who had considered him invincible were disillusioned by his defeat. Others were simply weary of years of revolution and war. The punitive expedition changed all that. Villa became a symbol of national resistance against foreign invaders and his popularity soared. Such sentiments even emerged within Carranza's forces. "The general sentiment among the rank and file of the revolutionary (Carrancista) forces is one of sympathy with Villa. They openly express their admiration for his adventure, and their regret for not having been with him,"[36] one of Cowdray's representatives wrote the British oil magnate in April 1916 from Mexico.

This fact was noted with bitterness and fear by the Carranza leadership. "I have just heard . . . that some soldiers of this area have shouted 'viva Villa' and that they want to provoke a conflict with American troops," Obregón wrote his commander in Chihuahua. He added, "in case there are really soldiers who at this moment shout 'viva Villa' you must immediately have them shot."[37] These threats were obviously not very effective, for a few months later, in October 1916, Luis Cabrera reported to Carranza: "reliable information that arrives here indicates that in the state of Chihuahua there is more sympathy for Villa than we might assume and there are many desertions from our army which are the result both of the labor of our enemies and of the economic conditions of our soldiers."[38] Cabrera suggested that troops from the neighboring state of Sonora should replace soldiers from Chihuahua who still admired Villa. "These strong sympathies for Villa are the result of the penetration of American troops and they are certainly due to the fact that Villa is seen as being the enemy of the Americans."

By the end of 1916, Villa's army was reported to number over ten thousand men.[39] In late 1916 he captured and briefly held some of the largest cities in northern Mexico, such as Chihuahua City, and Torreón. This allowed him to seize large quantities of supplies and thereby to make up for the loss of access to arms and ammunition he had suffered when the United States recognized his rival, Carranza, in October 1915.

Because of the popular support he enjoyed, Villa managed not only to elude the Americans but to develop a highly effective strategy of hit-and-run guerrilla tactics. It was a strategy he was forced to develop largely in the field since his prior experience in this type of warfare had been very limited. Except for brief periods during the 1910–11 revolution against Díaz and the 1913 revolution against Huerta, he had led large and well-equipped conventional armies against his foes. Nevertheless, he soon became a master at the art of guerrilla warfare and the Americans proved virtually impotent to do anything against him. This fact was registered with great bitterness by the officers of the punitive expedition. "I feel just a little bit like a man looking for a needle in a haystack,"[40] Pershing wrote, and he went on to urge the United States Government to agree to the occupation of the whole of the state of Chihuahua by American troops. A short time later he went a step further and advocated the occupation of all of Mexico. These views were enthusiastically shared by one of his lieutenants, George S. Patton. "Intervention will be useless; we must take the country and keep it,"[41] he wrote to his father in September 1916. The basis for his opinion was expressed in another letter by Patton: "you have no idea of the utter degradation of the inhabitants. One must be a fool indeed to think that people half savaged and wholly ignorant will ever form a republic. It is a joke. A despot is all they know or want."[42]

While harrying the Americans, Villa concentrated his main energies against the Carranzists. His strategy was aimed at defeating Carranza's troops, rallying them to his cause, and then attacking the U.S. forces in Mexico. His successes were facilitated by the fact that the farther the punitive expedition penetrated into Mexico, the less disposed many of Carranza's soldiers and officers were to fight Villa. As war with the United States came to seem more and more imminent, they wanted to concentrate on repelling the foreign invaders.

This attitude was based on the very real fact that for many months

Mexico and the United States had been on the brink of war as tensions between Wilson and Carranza increased from day to day. On 16 March, Wilson had advised Carranza that he intended to send an expedition to pursue Villa into Mexico. Carranza had not agreed to his proposal, but instead had suggested reviving an old arrangement, designed to secure the border against Apache and bandit attacks, that had existed between the United States and Mexico in the 1880s. Under this agreement both sides were to be allowed to pursue marauders and bandits across the border. Carranza's proposal was specifically aimed at future attacks. Wilson chose to interpret it as an agreement on the Mexican leader's part to allow the punitive expedition into Mexico.[43] Carranza at first refrained from any sharp protest. He may have expected that Wilson would only stage a brief foray into Mexico and withdraw after a few days. He may also have hoped that the Americans would relieve him of the task of defeating and destroying Villa. But as the punitive expedition penetrated ever more deeply into Mexico—its size and its armaments constantly on the increase—Carranza formulated a sharp protest against the U.S. presence in Mexico.

Faced with an imminent threat of war, the United States and the Mexican governments instructed their respective chiefs of staff, Hugh Scott for the Americans and Alvaro Obregón representing Mexico, to enter into negotiations. After long and arduous talks the two generals reached a compromise. A joint protocol was signed by both. It stated that the Americans would not penetrate any deeper into Mexico since their main aim of weakening Villa's forces had been accomplished. They would first concentrate in the north of Chihuahua and then eventually leave Mexico. In the protocol no date was mentioned for U.S. withdrawal.

In spite of the fact that Obregón had signed it, Carranza refused to ratify the protocol. In his eyes ratification would have legalized the presence of U.S. troops in Mexico without establishing a specific time for their departure. Carranza's reservations were confirmed a short time after the signing of the protocol when the Americans in his eyes violated it. After unidentified Mexican raiders had attacked the town of Glenn Springs, Texas, new American forces had entered Mexico. Carranza responded by instructing his commanders to resist by force any further American penetration into his country.[44] An armed confrontation in the town of Carrizal a few days later seemed to signify the impending outbreak of a Mexican-American war.

On 20 June, a cavalry detachment of the punitive expedition attempted to pass through Carrizal. The American commander, Lieutenant Charles T. Boyd, had requested General Felix U. Gómez, who commanded the Mexican garrison in Carrizal, to allow his troops to pass through the town. Gómez, who had been instructed by his commander to resist any American penetration, refused. When Boyd attempted to enter Carrizal in spite of the refusal, hostilities broke out between the two sides. In the ensuing fight both Boyd and Gómez were killed. The Americans were defeated and most of Boyd's soldiers were killed or taken prisoner.

The first garbled version of this incident to reach President Wilson stated that the Mexicans had been the first to attack, Wilson responded by preparing a message to be delivered to a joint session of Congress in which he requested permission for American troops to occupy all of northern Mexico. Full-scale war between Mexico and the United States now seemed imminent.

Wilson never delivered his planned message to Congress. The possibility of a Mexican-American war aroused tremendous opposition in the United States. When news reached Wilson that it had not been the Mexicans but the Americans who had initiated the hostilities at Carrizal and when Carranza made a gesture of conciliation by freeing the American prisoners taken in that combat, Wilson decided to make a new attempt to find a compromise solution with Mexico.[45] Because of mounting tensions with Germany, the American president became more and more afraid of getting entangled in Mexico. As he told his secretary Tumulty,

someday the people of America will know why I hesitated to intervene in Mexico. I cannot tell them now for we are at peace with the great power whose poisonous propaganda is responsible for the present terrible conditions in Mexico. German propagandists are there now, fomenting strife and trouble between our countries. Germany is anxious to have us at war with Mexico, so that our minds and our energies will be taken off the great war across the sea. She wishes an uninterrupted opportunity to carry on her submarine warfare and believes that war with Mexico will keep our hands off her and thus give her the liberty of action to do as she pleases on the high seas. It begins to look as if war with Germany is inevitable. If it should come, I pray God it may not, I do not wish America's energies and forces divided for we will need every ounce of reserve we have to lick Germany.[46]

The governments of the United States and Mexico agreed to set up a joint Mexican-American commission composed of three representatives from each side. The head of the American commission was Secretary of the Interior Franklin K. Lane, a conservative Democrat who later became closely linked with U.S. oil interests. Among the Mexican commissioners the most important figure was Luis Cabrera, Carranza's most outstanding intellectual supporter.

The "compromise" the American side had in mind represented the greatest concession to American business interests in Mexico in the history of Wilsonian diplomacy, for the American commissioners demanded from the Mexican negotiators that, besides the problems of troop withdrawal and the related question of border security, completely unrelated matters pertaining to Mexico's internal affairs be considered.

The cornerstone of the American position was a proposal that in effect would have "cubanized" Mexico by imposing something very close to the Platt amendment, which allowed U.S. troops to enter Cuba unilaterally when the U.S. government considered such intervention justified. The U.S. commissioners wanted Mexico to accept a clause which stated "the Government of Mexico solemnly agrees to afford full and adequate protection to the lives and property of citizens of the United States, or other foreigners, and this protection shall be adequate to enable such citizens of the United States . . . (to operate) industries in which they might be interested. The United States reserves the right to re-enter Mexico and to afford such protection by its military forces, in the event of the Mexican Government failing to do so."[47]

Protection of the property of foreigners was a broad term that was by no means restricted to confiscations or depredations. As both U.S. business interests and the State Department were to make abundantly clear in days to come, taxes imposed on foreign business could be labeled as "confiscatory" and thus fall under the proposed plan. In fact in the years 1917–18 any Mexican decree which restricted the rights enjoyed by foreigners during the Díaz era was likely to be labeled "confiscatory."

The proposals not only enjoyed the backing of American oil companies, they may in fact have been inspired by them. On 30 August 1916, two of the three American members of the joint Mexican-American Commission, its head Franklin K. Lane and Judge Gray, had long conversations with two representatives of the Doheny oil interests, their lawyer Frederick R. Kellogg and State Department counselor John Bassett Moore, whose services Doheny had retained since 1914.[48]

Carranza refused even to consider these demands of the U.S. Commissioners. On 2 October 1916 at a commission meeting at Atlantic City his representatives presented Mexican counterproposals. As a prerequisite for any further negotiations the commission should first agree to a definite date for the unconditional withdrawal of the punitive expedition, the Mexican proposals stated. Both sides should then come to an agreement which would allow each to pursue marauders across the border but to do so only under strict limitations. Restrictions were set on the size of pursuing detachments and the time they could spend in the other country (not to exceed 5 days). Nor could the pursuit extend more than a hundred miles from the border. Only after the signing of an agreement on these issues would the Mexican government agree to discuss other questions, and the discussion would not deal with Mexico's internal problems but only with international affairs.

Wilson obviously considered this position a slap in the face. On 21 November, after conferring extensively with the president, the U.S. members of the commission presented Mexico with what was virtually an ultimatum. The commissioners demanded that the question of U.S. withdrawal be linked to a discussion of the protection of the rights of foreigners. "I must inform you in all solemnity," the head of the U.S. delegation informed his Mexican counterparts, "that the President's patience is at an end, that he regards present conditions in Mexico as intolerable."[49] Lane called on the Mexicans to accept U.S. conditions for troop withdrawals:

Nothing short of this will satisfy either the government or the people of the United States and it is well for you to know this clearly and definitely at the present moment. We do not wish to do anything that will either hurt your pride or diminish your sovereignty. We have no designs on the integrity of your territory or your freedom of action in the determination of your national policy but we are deeply and vitally interested in the fulfillment of your obligations to protect the lives and property of foreigners who have cast their lot with you, and in the satisfactory adjustment of every question which affects the cordial relations between the United States and your country.

Lane coupled these demands with a thinly veiled threat: "if, however, you have reached the conclusion that you do not desire the cooperation of the United States, if you feel that you want to cut yourself off completely, it is well for us to know this as soon as possible, as it will vitally affect our policy with reference to Mexico." In a subsequent discussion Lane elaborated on what the consequences of a Mexican refusal to accept the U.S. proposals would be: "it is up to you three gentlemen to determine whether Mexico is to have the benefit of such cooperation, or whether she desires to pursue a policy of isolation. This latter policy can lead to but one result, namely the downfall of the Carranza government with all the consequences that this will involve."[50]

Clearly intimidated by the threats from the United States the Mexican commissioners, including Luis Cabrera, signed the protocol the American side wanted them to sign. When it was presented to Carranza, the Mexican president refused to be intimidated and did not agree.

On 28 December Mexico's delegate Alberto J. Pani in a discussion with the head of the U.S. delegation reiterated Carranza's stand that the prerequisite for any American-Mexican negotiations was U.S. agreement to withdraw its troops from Mexico unconditionally. Only then could further problems be discussed. These would include international matters but not Mexico's internal affairs.

Wilson was now faced with two options. He could have U.S. forces remain in Mexico and risk a Mexican-American war, or he could withdraw unconditionally. In view of the mounting tensions with Germany, he chose the latter course and provided Carranza with one of the greatest triumphs of his career. On 28 January 1917 the punitive expedition was instructed to begin its withdrawal from Mexico, and on 5 February that withdrawal was completed.

Like the earlier U.S. intervention in Veracruz, the punitive expedition had profound consequences for U.S.–Mexican relations, for Mexico's foreign policy, and for its domestic developments. In fact the two interventions had much in common. Both interventions officially had very limited goals. In 1914 Wilson ostensibly wanted only to protest the arrest of U.S. soldiers by Huerta's troops and to prevent the arms of the *Ypiranga* from landing in Mexico. He declared that his intervention was not directed against the revolutionaries. Similarly the 1916 intervention was officially directed at the limited aim of capturing or destroying Villa's forces, and the U.S. emphasized that it only wished to help Carranza.

In both cases Wilson repeatedly declared that he had no intention of infringing upon Mexican sovereignty and in both cases this is precisely what he attempted to do.

In 1914 the American president had tried to mold the government of Mexico, and in 1916 he attempted to influence and set limits upon its policies.

In both cases the ostensible beneficiary of Wilson's actions protested against the U.S. presence in Mexico and threatened to resist by all possible means. In both cases Carranza's stubbornness won out, and the American troops had to withdraw from Mexico without achieving their main goals.

The 1914 invasion had seriously weakened what until then had been a tacit alliance between the Wilson administration and the Mexican revolutionaries. The punitive expedition destroyed this alliance.

It was the punitive expedition and in all likelihood the growing U.S. threats against Mexico in November that induced Carranza to send a memorandum to Germany that same month, proposing close cooperation in economic and military fields (see chap. 9). This memorandum in turn triggered Germany's fateful decision to send the Zimmermann telegram to Mexico.

The punitive expedition marked the end of Wilson's effort to find allies in Mexico, though he did continue to cooperate in very limited ways with the Carranza government. According to two members of the American-Mexican Commission, the president's whole attitude toward Mexico had changed as a result of the expedition. They "felt that the president really did not now represent the same spirit towards Mexico that he did when he wrote his article for the *Ladies Home Journal*"—an article in which he emphasized his complete respect for Mexico's independence and for the right of the Mexicans to conduct their own revolution. "In short," they concluded, "the generosity was lacking."[51]

### The Policies of Carranza, 1916–18

By attacking Columbus and bringing on the punitive expedition, Pancho Villa had not succeeded in provoking a complete break between the Carranza government and the Wilson administration. War between the two countries had been averted and the United States continued to maintain official relations with Carranza, even transforming de facto recognition of October 1915 into de jure recognition late in 1917.

In certain essential ways, however, Villa had been successful. He had permanently impaired the relationship between Carranza and the United States, which would never be the same as it was between October 1915 and March 1916. Carranza had lost the two great advantages he had hoped to secure by gaining American recognition: unlimited access to U.S. arms and the possibility of obtaining a loan in the United States. After the punitive expedition entered Mexico, the United States imposed a ban on arms sales to the Mexican government which remained in effect with some interruptions until Carranza's fall in 1920; and American loans to the Mexican government were offered on terms the Mexican president would not and probably could not have accepted. These blows were all the harder for Carranza to bear since there was no other country capable of supplying him with arms or money as long as the world war lasted.

As it became clear that unlimited American support for Carranza had ceased, armed opposition movements by radical, conservative, or simply localist opponents gained new strength and momentum.

Pancho Villa was by no means the only beneficiary of Carranza's difficulties. In the first months of 1916 Carranza's General Pablo González launched a full-scale offensive against Zapata, and wrested control of the cities and parts of the Morelos countryside from him. By the end of 1916, however, Zapata had begun a counteroffensive, which González's troops were unable to repel because Carranza was concentrating more and more troops in northern Mexico, both to repel Villa and in anticipation of a possible conflict with the United States. In February 1917 with the exception of the largest cities, Zapata again controlled the whole of Morelos.

Carranza's conservative opponents, who had been quiet or had failed to gain support as long as the Mexican president seemed to enjoy American backing, now took up arms again and assumed control of important parts of Veracruz, Oaxaca, and Chiapas. Fortunately for Carranza, the main leader of the conservatives was Porfirio Díaz's nephew Felix Díaz, a perennial loser. His 1912 uprising had been so badly organized that Hintze called him a theatrical personality incapable of organization. After the fall of Madero in 1913 not Felix Díaz, but Huerta reaped the fruits of the coup and Díaz was shunted off to the Far East. In 1914 he sought refuge in the United States and in February 1916 he attempted to return to Mexico from New Orleans. His lack of success continued to stalk him. The ship on which he and several companions were traveling became lost and when the navigators finally landed in Matamoros, Mexico, they fell into the hands of Pablo González's troops. An uncharacteristic stroke of good luck saved Díaz. González, who headed a court investigating the identity of the intruders, did not recognize him, and Díaz was freed. His escape did not, however, bring him a change of fortune. After González freed him, he went to Oaxaca where he attempted with the help of local supporters to capture the capital city of the state. When his supporters began fighting among themselves, he retreated with three thousand men into the southeastern state of Chiapas. When he finally arrived there, he had no more than a hundred men left.[52]

However mediocre his capacities for intrigue, organization, and military leadership, there was one area where Felix Díaz was always successful. Again and again he managed to secure American support. During his 1912 coup, the commander of the American warship *Des Moines* stationed in Veracruz had given him strong and undisguised support. During the tragic ten days he was the favorite of Ambassador Henry Lane Wilson under whose auspices the famous embassy pact was signed in which Huerta agreed to support the candidacy of Díaz for the Mexican presidency.

In 1916–17 he did not enjoy similar backing from the U.S. government, but important American business interests and some U.S. officials continued to bank on his future. In 1916 a high Justice Department official reported that the Felix Díaz movement was part of a grandiose scheme for economic control of Mexico elaborated without the consent of his superiors by the ubiquitous head of the State Department's Mexican Division, Leon Canova, and some associates. The official stated that a "well-placed informant" expressed the "belief that Canova and his associates and Haskell (an American businessman) and his friends are working together to get control of both the sisal and oil industry in Mexico and that they believe that, should they be successful, they can control the political parties of that country and place the Díaz faction in control."[53] Throughout his campaign Felix Díaz was supplied with money and arms from the United States. With the help of these resources he managed to rally increasing conservative support. Former officers of the federal army such as Higínio Aguilar, who had joined the forces of the convention after Huerta's defeat, now rallied to him. By 1917 Felix Díaz had abandoned his Chiapas retreat and advanced into Veracruz, where he managed to control substantial parts of the state.[54]

Apart from Díaz, various other conservative leaders at times linked to Felix Díaz and at times independent of him also obtained substantial help from U.S. corporations and not infrequently the tacit approval of U.S. officials. Manuel Pelaez, the regional caudillo who by 1915 had assumed control of the oil fields around Tampico, obtained substantial funds from the oil companies and managed to buy arms in the United States. Esteban Cantú, a former federal officer who had joined the conventionist forces in 1914, set up a quasi-independent principality in Baja California and maintained close relations with U.S. authorities across the border.

As the strength of the federal government ebbed, much of Mexico returned to conditions akin to those of the nineteenth century. Many regions were controlled by bandits, while others fell under the sway of regional caudillos who offered "protection" from outside interference of any kind, in return for recognition by the inhabitants of their authority.

The former conventionists, the emerging conservatives, local caudillos, or bandits by no means constituted the only opposition Carranza had to contend with. For dissension had increased within the ranks of his own movement as well. At times this dissension arose between radical supporters demanding social reforms and more conservative elements sharing Carranza's social views. Increasingly the policy of divide and conquer that Carranza had used to amass his own power now worked against him.

In many states the rival Carranzist candidates for state offices took up arms against each other and when Carranza threw his support to one faction the other revolted against his administration. This was the case in the state of Tamaulipas where Luis Caballero, who had been a supporter of Carranza's in the civil war, revolted against his erstwhile chief when he was not elected governor.

In addition to all this, popular dissatisfaction with the Carranza administration was on the increase. This was due to Carranza's unfulfilled promises of reform and to a dramatic decrease in the standard of living, as well as to general insecurity. Poor harvests resulting from bad weather and unstable conditions in the countryside were compounded by large-scale official corruption and speculation. As a result widespread starvation ensued. Industrial production had not reached prerevolutionary levels, and serious unemployment had developed.

Within the Carranza movement three different strategies for overcoming this enormous opposition were advocated. The least popular of these called for complete reconciliation with the U.S. government and U.S. business interests. All attempts to control or restrict activities of these business interests, it was argued, should cease, and internationally Mexico should align itself completely with the United States. After the United States entered World War I, this group advocated that Mexico follow the example of its northern neighbor by breaking with—and even declaring war on—Germany. The main advocates of this strategy were Alfredo Robles Domínguez,[55] a high civilian official in the administrations of both Madero and Carranza, and Felix Palavincini, a journalist and close associate of Carranza. They asserted that only an alliance with the United States would enable the Mexican government to obtain the arms, food, and money it needed in order to destroy internal opposition and increase the standard of living. They also argued that such an alliance would preclude the danger of an American intervention and would enable the country to profit fully from the economic boom occasioned by World War I.

This strategy had enjoyed some support within Carranza's ranks before the Pershing expedition entered Mexico. The most popular strategy among the victorious revolutionaries, however, was of a completely opposite nature. It was advocated by the radical wing of the Carranza movement and called for new efforts to regain the support of those social groups—the peasants and industrial workers—whom Carranza had wooed in 1915 and discarded in 1916.

The radical leadership was comprised of both new converts and old-line radicals. Among the former Alvaro Obregón was probably the most outstanding spokesman. The most outspoken and influential old-line radicals were Francisco Múgica, a former schoolteacher from Michoacán, Heriberto Jara, a textile worker who had taken part in the strike of Río Blanco in 1907, and Esteban Baca Calderón, one of the leaders of the other great strike movement that had shaken Porfirian Mexico: the miner's strike at Cananea in 1906. All three had cooperated with the Liberal Party and had been influenced by the social ideas of the Flores Magón brothers.

The radicals were most successful in the field of ideology and law. They succeeded in molding the new constitution elaborated between November 1916 and February 1917 by a constitutional convention in the city of Querétaro. In contrast to a draft proposal by Carranza that provided for few social reforms, the constitution as adopted in February 1917 contained provisions for far-reaching social and economic transformations. It guaranteed the right of every landless peasant to acquire free land, and stated that the haciendas were to be divided up to provide this land. The same article also contained tough measures directed at foreign companies in Mexico. These clauses essentially stated that: (a) the government could at any time carry out expropriations for the welfare of the nation; and (b) the owner of a piece of land was not the owner of the minerals found on that piece of land.

This signified a return to the old Spanish legislation which had been abandoned in 1884 by the Díaz government. In addition to these provisions, Article 123 established the right of workers to trade union organization, strikes, and the eight-hour workday and included far-reaching provisions for their social security.

In practical terms, however, the radicals were far less successful. They did manage to limit Carranza's persecution of labor leaders. And by the end of 1916 many of the leaders who had been arrested or even sentenced to death for their participation in strikes were freed by the government. But with respect to the peasantry the radicals had little success. Carranza refused to accelerate the pace of agrarian reform but instead returned the haciendas to their former owners or granted them to his generals. There is little reason to doubt the bitter indictment Zapata set forth in an open letter to Carranza. "The haciendas," he wrote his erstwhile ally, "are being given or leased to your favorite generals; the former members of the bourgeoisie have in many cases been replaced by modern landowners, complete with helmet, ammunition belt, and pistol."[56]

Only in exceptional cases where agrarian reform could serve to seriously weaken his enemies was Carranza ready to make significant concessions to the peasantry. This was the case in the Tlaxcala region. Zapata's most important adherent in this area, Domingo Arenas, stated his readiness to join Carranza if the latter agreed to recognize the land reform he had implemented. The First Chief acceded to his request,[57] and significant land reform was carried out in this area. But these events remained an exception and were not characteristic of Carranza's agrarian policy.

Carranza's own strategy for gaining support for his movement differed from those of the pro-American conservatives and of the radicals. It was not predicated upon reforms but upon two other bases: the growing war-weariness of the Mexican people and their nationalism.

After seven years of upheavals, fighting, hunger, and deprivation, many people were ready to follow anyone who offered them sufficient food to subsist and protection from pillaging armies of whatever faction.

By returning the haciendas to their former owners, Carranza hoped to bring food production up to prerevolutionary levels. But until 1919 he was unsuccessful in this. Food production remained far below 1910 levels. The economy was in shambles. Because of fighting, pillage, and large-scale flight from the countryside, no crops had been sown in many parts of Mexico. The country's once bounteous cattle herds had been depleted by being sold across the border to buy arms and by being slaughtered for food. Many people were ruined because the paper money they held had been issued by the vanquished conventionist faction and was not honored by the Carranzists, but even the victorious faction's paper money was not considered much better and merchants and producers largely refused to honor it. Most mines and industries were closed.[58]

All these difficulties were compounded by large-scale destruction of and interruptions in Mexico's not too highly developed transportation system. Only 16 percent of the rolling stock of the railroads was still in operation.[59] Large parts of the railway were preempted by the military. and interruptions in train service due to attacks by rival factions or by bandits occurred almost daily.

Apart from his largely unsuccessful attempts to stabilize Mexico by extending his control over the whole of the country, Carranza's economic strategy was two-tiered. On the one hand, in relation to Mexican hacendados and entrepreneurs he sought to encourage a resumption of economic activity largely by reestablishing prerevolutionary Porfirian conditions. The cornerstone of this strategy was the return of the haciendas to their former owners. In order to give the owners sufficient incentives to plant and sell their crops and to provide new stimuli to the economy, Carranza at the end of 1916 began replacing his paper currency with gold and silver coins. At the same time he attempted to shield the hacendados and entrepreneurs from the demands of the lower classes by largely banning strikes and by drastically limiting agrarian reform. There is no evidence, except from a few regions where the economy prospered, such as Yucatán, that Carranza attempted to impose large tax increases on Mexico's domestic upper classes. On the other hand, in relation to foreign enterprise such as the oil companies, which were prospering in spite of the revolution (and whose tax rate had been negligible in the Porfirian era), Carranza implemented a new strategy which constituted a departure from traditional Porfirian approaches. Their taxes were now increased while the traditional policy of laissez-faire practiced by Mexico's prerevolutionary government, was abandoned with respect to those foreign enterprises, above all mines, which had interrupted their activities. They were threatened with fines and confiscations unless they resumed production.[60]

It is difficult to assess the results of all these policies since statistical data from the revolutionary period is sparse and little research has been done on this subject until now.

One of the most salient characteristics of the Mexican economy in the years 1916–18 was its unevenness. Some export sectors developed at an extremely rapid pace. This was above all true of oil production, which increased without interruption throughout the revolutionary period. These increases, however, had nothing to do with Carranza's policies. The oil fields, almost all of which were located near the gulf coast, practically constituted an extraterritorial enclave protected by foreign warships, U.S. threats of intervention and "the revolutionary" forces of General Manuel Pelaez which were largely financed by the oil companies.

The production of mines, which enjoyed no such extraterritorial status and were scattered throughout Mexico, increased at a far slower pace, but it did increase. Rising mineral prices as a result of U.S. participation in the world war constituted a great incentive to mining companies to resume production. Resumption of production was also encouraged by a policy reversal on the part of Pancho Villa. In January 1916 his men had shot American mining engineers on their way to reopen a mine in northern Mexico. Villa had wanted to show Woodrow Wilson as well as U.S. businessmen that without his help they could not operate in Mexico. By 1917 he had become convinced that the only means by which he could finance his movement was by taxing U.S. mining companies. The obvious prerequisite for obtaining such taxes was to allow the mines to operate. There are no reports of shootings or executions of foreign miners or mining engineers by Villa's troops from 1917 onward.

The increasing prices paid in the U.S. for some agricultural products stimulated some types of export production in Mexico. There was a large increase in the sale of sisal from Yucatán and chickpeas from Sonora.

Production of manufactured goods and especially food for the domestic market rose far more slowly during Carranza's presidency, if at all. Insecurity in the countryside due to continued warfare and banditry, exactions by government officials and troops, and speculation by both hacendados and bureaucrats contributed to price increases and scarcity. The troubles caused by frequent breakdowns of railroads and other transportation facilities were compounded by U.S. restrictions on exports, including food, to Mexico. The result was widespread hunger and starvation in the years 1917–18. Patrick O'Hea, Britain's vice-consul in Torreón, vividly described the situation in what was generally considered a relatively well-to-do area, the cotton-producing Laguna Basin. In November 1917 he reported

> in regard to the conditions prevalent among the poorer classes, there is no doubt but what in the coming winter they will face worse conditions than have existed in the memory of the present generation.
>
> Wages are still based more or less upon the scale of prerevolutionary 1913, while the cost of necessities of life has increased to three times as much on the average, as the value of the same indispensable articles four years ago.
>
> Even so the laborer within the Laguna district enjoys a privileged condition over most of his fellows outside of it, for though wages be inadequate, and though there be much unemployment, at least there is not the sheer misery and almost complete lack of sustenance that is causing sickness and death all over the country.[61]

There was nothing very revolutionary about Carranza's domestic economic policies. What he basically attempted to do was to reestablish Porfirian conditions for the benefit of large segments of Mexico's traditional upper class as well as for its new bourgeoisie. These groups were to be cultivated at the expense of both foreign business interests and the lower classes of society on whom the burden of paying for the expenses of revolution were to fall. For obvious reasons Carranza had far less difficulties in imposing these burdens on the poor than on the foreign interests.

The Mexican president hoped that as economic recovery progressed the burden imposed on the poor would subside and he would then be able to gain their support. On the whole his strategy paid off though economic recovery was far slower than he had hoped. With significant exceptions, particularly in southeast Mexico, the bulk of the country's traditional hacendados as well as its new bourgeoisie remained loyal to the Mexican president until 1920.

The effects of Carranza's policies on the lower classes of society are far more difficult to assess. There were links but by no means automatic correlation between living standards and loyalty to the Carranza regime. That these links were of a complex nature can be seen from the situation in Yucatán, Veracruz, and the Laguna. In these areas economic recovery had proceeded at a more rapid pace than in most other parts of the country. As a result the traditional upper class had regained much of its wealth and power. This had begun to worry Carranza's military commanders who encouraged hacienda peons in Yucatán and the Laguna and industrial workers in Veracruz to organize and secure better conditions. These peons did meet Carranza's expectations by not joining rebels against him before 1920. But they became increasingly radicalized and tended to become more and more independent of the Mexico City government.

Conversely, in such states as Aguascalientes, where conditions remained very bad, many peons tended to rally behind the hacendados whom they considered to be the only group capable of assuring their sustenance and survival.

Often an even more important factor in determining the attitude of large groups of the population toward Carranza was whether he was capable of granting protection from pillage and depredations. Providing protection seemed in many respects an even more difficult problem for the Mexican president than effecting economic recovery, since the armies most people sought protection from were his own.

In a bitter letter to Carranza from Chihuahua, Francisco Murguía, the general whom the Mexican president had sent to combat Villa, stated that many people joined Pancho Villa out of bitterness over the exactions and pillage committed by government troops.[62]

Even if he wanted to, Carranza did not have the power to change his armies or to curb his own generals. Thus a vicious circle had sprung up; whenever a rebel group appeared, Carranza sent his army to fight them. The army by its behavior generated so much opposition that hitherto uninvolved civilians joined rebel ranks. The government then took reprisals and the ranks of the rebels swelled even more.

A British landowner, Charles K. Furber, who was kidnapped in 1918 by rebels in the state of Guanajuato and freed only after he agreed to pay a large ransom, had ample opportunity to talk to his captors and describe why they had risen against the Carranza government.

During my stay with the bandits, I endeavoured to inform myself as to their reasons for being up in arms, and I found that they seem to have been driven to it by the action of the Government. The region is largely composed of little villages and surrounding holdings of land. At the beginning of the revolution, the inhabitants lived in comparative comfort in their own houses and owned cattle and animals and tilled each his piece of ground. The villages had their little shops and their church and the people lived contented and happy. The Government troops went up there and began stealing animals, goods and chattels, the owners resisting were called bandits, their houses were burnt, everything was stolen and many were killed. These that were left took to the hills, got a rifle, and did their best to defend about all that was left to defend, their lives. When they finally banded together and became too strong for the Government, they were offered an armistice. A few accepted, were disarmed and shot. The present situation of these people today is one of extreme difficulty, they cannot surrender because the Government kills them, they cannot work in the hills as they have no guarantees nor money, and if they come down to the plains and find work they would soon be denounced and killed. The great majority of them are tired of the life that they lead with all its privations and dangers and would gladly lay down their arms and go to work if only the Government would afford them some protection and means of working. Instead of doing this, the Government is trying to fight them and I do not see any prospect of success for such a proceeding.[63]

The bitterness of the local population was further exacerbated by the fact that Carranza's troops were frequently outsiders from other parts of Mexico while the rebels were local men.

In a bold and largely successful move to break this cycle, Carranza attempted to arm large sectors of the civilian population. As central power broke down and armed bands roamed the countryside, local militias, called *defensas sociales,* had sprung up in many parts of Mexico. They attempted to keep intruders—which frequently meant all outsiders—away from their towns or villages. Carranza recognized many of these militias, supplied them with government arms, organized new *defensas sociales* and at the same time attempted to bring them under some kind of government control.

In those parts of the country where the land issue was the prime motive for guerrilla activity, Carranza's strategy did not meet with much success. He was unable to set up an effective network of *defensas sociales* in Morelos against Zapata or of gaining popular support in this way.

The situation was entirely different, however, in those parts of the country where resentment at the exactions of government troops was a prime motive for rebellion. Carranza armed substantial groups of the civilians and indicated to them that, if they kept rebel troops out of their villages and towns, his own troops would not enter them either. In addition, their arms gave the civilian population additional protection in case the government troops broke Carranza's implicit pledge and began pillaging towns and villages.

Carranza's efforts gained in popularity when he refused in some cases to subordinate the *defensas sociales* to the military and instead set up a separate command for them. In his eyes the *defensas sociales* were not only an instrument to defeat his opponents but also a means of counteracting the increasing power of his own army over which he exercised only a limited control.

This strategy was perhaps most successful in Chihuahua, where Carranza used it to fight Villa after the departure of the punitive expedition. After seven years of war and revolution, interrupted by only two years of peace (1914 until the end of 1915), a large part of the population was weary of war, disillusioned, and ready to accept anyone who guaranteed peace and quiet. As a result, thousands of men, many of them ex-Villistas, joined the *defensas sociales*. Carranza named an astute politician, Ignacio Enríquez, to head these forces. Enríquez was basically a conservative, but he had two qualities that won him many followers: he had long experience in mobilizing civilians for Carranza's aims—in 1914–15 he had headed one of the famous Red Battalions of industrial workers Carranza set up to fight the convention—and he was on bad terms with Carranza's military commanders in Chihuahua, a fact which enhanced his popularity among the members of the *defensas sociales* even more.[64]

The effectiveness of these state militias is attested to by a desperate appeal Villa addressed to them in December 1918. Villa accused Carranza of having set up a government of the rich, of betraying the ideals of the Mexican revolution of 1910, and of putting the country in jeopardy by following international policies which could easily encourage an invasion of Mexico by the United States. Villa's strongest accusations, though, were of a local nature. He accused Carranza and his commanders of stealing much of Chihuahua's wealth and taking it outside the state. He also accused them of bringing soldiers "from outside, men who are pressed into the army or who have been recruited from the jails in order to steal our wealth officially and destroy our wellbeing."[65]

Villa's appeal was strongly mixed with threats. He stressed that until 1918 he had always spared all prisoners captured from the *defensas sociales*, freeing them after their capture. Should the *defensas sociales* continue to fight him, he warned, he would be forced to take far stronger measures than he had in the past. Villa indicated that these measures would consist essentially of the extermination of the local militias. Villa appealed to the *defensas sociales* to join him in the fight against Carranza, with the stated aim of safeguarding the sovereignty of Chihuahua. While Villa still enjoyed substantial support in the state, which allowed him to continue fighting until he made his peace with the government in 1920, his appeal to the *defensas sociales* fell on deaf ears, not only because of the war-weariness of large parts of Chihuahua's population, but also because the middle class in the state had turned against Villa after his defeat in 1915. They had joined him only reluctantly in the first place when he seemed to be the obvious victor and seemed capable of offering them important positions both in the national administration and in the state administration of Chihuahua. His defeat had put an end to this hope, and the inflation his paper currency brought had ruined many of them. They had become, together with the state's upper class, Villa's most outspoken opponents in Chihuahua. By arming them and thus giving them the possibility of resisting the exactions of federal troops, Carranza had removed the one motive for opposition against his regime that Chihuahua's middle class still held.

In Mexico as a whole Carranza's most important means of gaining popular support, however, was not the creation of civilian militias but the manipulation of Mexico's nationalism. While the Pershing expedition was in Mexico, Carranza's prestige suffered as long as he was unable—and seemed, to many, unwilling—to expel the Americans from the country. After the battle of El Carrizal and even more after the punitive expedition left Mexico in February 1917, his prestige rose again. After the departure of the Americans, he capitalized on nationalist attitudes and policies, and in contrast to his social pronouncements there was widespread consensus that this was an aspect of his declared policy that he seriously wanted to implement.

It was a policy that allowed Carranza to profit from nationalist sentiment in the country and to weaken the traditional feeling of "geographic determinism." As long as World War I lasted and Germany was not defeated, many Mexicans felt that the alignment with Germany offered the one effective means of bringing to an end the decisive influence the United States had wielded and was still wielding in Mexico.

It would nevertheless be erroneous to view Carranza's nationalism solely as a means of distracting attention from unfulfilled social promises. It was genuine. Carranza hoped to achieve concrete aims with his policies, though they fell far short of the principles and rights enunciated in the 1917 constitution.

In the years 1934–40 during the presidency of Lázaro Cárdenas, Mexico's constitution was both the judicial and ideological basis for the expropriation and nationalization of the foreign-owned oil companies and for the division among the peasantry of foreign-owned haciendas and plantations.

There is not the slightest evidence that Carranza ever desired to use the constitution, whose most radical parts he had opposed, to implement such measures. His nationalistic policies were far more modest, had more limited aims, and were still strongly imbued with Porfirian traditions. Like his Porfirian predecessors, Carranza hoped to counteract U.S. economic and political influence by an increased European presence in Mexico. For Carranza (as for Reyes, whose party he had supported, though not for the Científicos), Europe ceased to mean Great Britain and France and now referred primarily to Germany.

Unlike his Porfirian predecessors, Carranza sought to increase the taxes paid by foreigners, to exercise some measure of control over their acquisition of Mexican property, and to force them to forfeit the right to appeal for protection to their respective governments.

It was this policy above all that the oil companies vigorously opposed, as did the U.S. government. But, unlike the oil companies, the Wilson administration did not believe that it constituted sufficient grounds for U.S. military intervention in Mexico.

One of the main reasons for this attitude was the increasing probability that the United States would become actively involved in World War I on the side of the Allies. It was precisely this prospect that led Germany to activate its Mexican policy to an unprecedented degree in the hope that the United States would become so embroiled there that it would not intervene in Europe.

# 9 Germany and the Revolutionary Factions

After the outbreak of the First World War, some of the leading figures in the German armed forces, among them Moltke, the chief of the General Staff, had nourished the illusion that the United States would enter the war on the side of Germany. On 5 August 1914 Moltke optimistically told the Foreign Office: "The mood in America is favorable to Germany.... Perhaps the United States could be induced into a naval action against England, with Canada as the victory prize."[1]

This illusion was soon dashed by the development of increasingly intimate British-American relations. At the same time that American commercial relations with Germany were interrupted by the British blockade, American industry was becoming more important as a supplier of weapons and materiel to the Allies. The major aims of German policy toward the United States were to cut off these supplies and to prevent the United States from entering the war on the side of the Allies. These aims could, under the best of circumstances, be reconciled only with difficulty.

Germany used a variety of methods to prevent American deliveries of war materiel to the Western powers. The primary means of achieving this aim was U-boat warfare. The German Admiralty planned to declare the waters surrounding Great Britain and France a blockade zone and to sink all ships entering these waters regardless of whether they belonged to a belligerent or a neutral state. Only if England declared its willingness to suspend the blockade of German ports were the naval leaders willing to give up this plan. In practice, however, the project ran up against significant obstacles. Attempts to put it into effect brought Germany to the brink of war with the United States in 1915 and 1916, and each time the German government retreated.

In addition to the U-boat war, Germany attempted to bring about a halt in U.S. arms shipments to the Allies by means of a propaganda campaign. This campaign prompted Representative McLemore to submit to the U.S. Congress a bill that would have imposed a weapons embargo on the belligerent nations. American high finance and heavy industry, which had major interests in weapons production, as well as the Wilson administration, which sympathized with the Allies, were instrumental in defeating this proposed legislation.

## Early German Plots with Anti-Carranza Forces in Mexico

Various covert actions were taken by the German government to prevent the supply of U.S. arms; the most "harmless" of these was the attempt made shortly after the outbreak of the war by German agents, including the military attaché to the United States, Franz von Papen, to buy up important plants of the American armaments industry and thus to render deliveries to the Allies impossible.[2] From the beginning this was a hopeless enterprise. Germany was in fact able to interrupt briefly the delivery of some arms shipments by the purchase of a factory in Bridgeport, but in general the supply of American war materiel was not to be stopped by such methods. Thus Germany turned increasingly to sabotage.

German and Austrian agents attempted to provoke strikes in the American armaments industry and even tried to plant bombs in factories and on ships. Some of these efforts were successful—one of the largest American shipyards, the Black Tom Shipyard in New Jersey, was set afire on 29/30 July 1916 by German saboteurs[3]—but on the whole the German secret operations in the United States, especially in the first two years of the war, proved extremely inept. The officer sent to the United States by General Falkenhayn to take charge of sabotage activities, Franz von Rintelen, conducted himself in such a clumsy fashion that very soon he was being shadowed by British and American agents and was finally arrested by the English on his return trip to Germany. Thorough reports on his activities appeared shortly thereafter in all American newspapers.[4] In a New York subway Heinrich Albert, the official in charge of finance at the German embassy in Washington, was relieved of an attaché case containing important documents on German conspiracies. The Austro-Hungarian ambassador to the United States, Dumba, had no better luck. He entrusted an agent with a letter on his sabotage activities which was confiscated by the English and given to the press; the American government immediately requested his recall. The German military attaché, Franz von Papen, who had also been declared persona non grata because of the discovery of all these conspiracies and had to leave the United States, was carrying a checkbook with accounts for sabotage contracts which fell into the hands of the English during a search of his ship in a British port. Because of the incompetence of German intelligence, it was not difficult for the defense authorities of the Allies and the United States to discover, publicize, and prevent many German intrigues and sabotage attempts, and thereby to influence public opinion in favor of U.S. entry into the war on the side of the Allies.

Mexico came to play an increasingly large role in the German plans to cut off American arms shipments to the Allies and to prevent American entry into the war on the Allied side. The Germans vigorously sought to provoke a Mexican-American war, for such a war would not only have interrupted the export of American arms, but would also have tied the United States down in Mexico and hence greatly complicated intervention in Europe. Moreover, the Mexican oil fields would probably have been destroyed, thereby denying the British fleet its extremely important supplies of Mexican oil.

German hopes of an American intervention in Mexico seemed to have a better chance of being realized than had the efforts to implement an arms embargo. The proposed ban on exports of war materiel was supported by the German-Americans, the Irish and some isolationists, but it encountered massive opposition on the part of American finance capital. By contrast, influential American interests which had important investments in Mexico, particularly the Standard Oil Company, came out in favor of American intervention there. In this effort, these interests could rely on such confirmed supporters of a hard line toward Germany as Theodore Roosevelt and saw their demand supported in the realm of public opinion by the Hearst and McCormick newspapers.

German efforts to provoke a Mexican-American war were also directed at the Mexican side of the border. In Mexico the Germans approached the widest possible spectrum of politicians and parties; they attempted to incite both extreme reactionaries such as Huerta and Felix Díaz and revolutionaries such as Carranza and Villa against the United States.

Until mid-1915, these conspiracies were organized by German military personnel in the United States. This was largely due to the fact that until March of that year the German legation in Mexico was being run by a minor official, Magnus, who limited himself to sending rueful letters on the situation in Mexico to the Foreign Office. Hintze had been sent to China as ambassador shortly after the outbreak of the war, and the German minister to Cuba, Heinrich von Eckardt, who had been appointed to succeed him, did not take his post until 1915. At the request of Bryan, who may already have feared German meddling in Mexico, Eckardt remained away from his post for several months.[5] Then in March 1915—against the will of the U.S. State Department—he assumed his post and soon became the center of the local German intrigues.

The first and best-known German conspiracy aimed at triggering a Mexican-American war was organized with the help of Papen and the naval attaché Boy Edd by Franz von Rintelen, a former representative of the Deutsche Bank in Mexico, who had been sent to the United States by the German General Staff.

Rintelen arrived in New York on 3 April 1915 and immediately began an extensive sabotage operation. But it quickly became clear to him that American arms shipments to the Allies could never be prevented by sabotage alone. This gave even greater importance to his plans for a

Mexican-American war. "I had studied the foreign policy situation of the United States and understood that the only country which the United States had to fear was Mexico," he wrote in his memoirs. "Should Mexico attack the United States, the United States would need all the arms it can produce and would not be in a position to export arms to Europe."[6]

By February Rintelen had already contacted Huerta, who was then in Spain, and promised him money and weapons if he would commit himself to wage war against the United States in the event of a victory by his party. He subsequently had a discussion with Huerta in New York, and arrived at the following agreement: Germany would land arms on the Mexican coast with U-boats, would provide Huerta with further funds for the purchase of arms, and would give him moral support. In exchange, Huerta committed himself to taking up the struggle against the United States. The German government had provided $12 million for this plan, $800,000 of which had been deposited in Huerta's name in Cuban and Mexican banks as an advance.[7]

Rintelen was confronted with the question of what guarantees Huerta could give him that he would keep his promise to attack the United States, particularly since Huerta had not exhibited great fidelity to his word. Rintelen probably assumed that the Americans would attempt with all means at their disposal, including military intervention, to topple Huerta, so that, regardless of Huerta's wishes, a Mexican-American war would take place if the former president returned to power.

Rintelen left the execution of the plan he had set in motion to Papen and Boy Edd. The conspiracy, however, was discovered by American and British intelligence officers who followed every move Huerta made and who had eavesdropped on the discussion between him and Rintelen. Huerta, who planned to go to Mexico, where Orozco and others had made preparations for an insurrection, was arrested by the American police before he could cross the border.[8] He then contacted Bernstorff and asked him to look after his family. Bernstorff, who did not wish to be connected to Huerta, passed his letter on to the American government, ostensibly without having looked at it or answered it. "That is really amazing," remarked Wilson.[9]

Because of their participation in this conspiracy and other intrigues, both Papen and Boy Edd were expelled from the United States at the end of December 1915. Prior to his expulsion, however, Papen had contacted a representative of the forces close to Huerta. This was Gonzalo Enrile, who was passing himself off as a colonel in the Mexican army and who had played an important role in Orozco's uprising against Madero in 1912. With his aid Papen hoped to win over Felix Díaz, who had made it known that he was prepared to collaborate with the Germans.[10] The project failed. The precise reasons are not known; it can, however, be assumed that Díaz was prompted by the collapse of Huerta's conspiracy to have no further dealings with Germany. Papen nonetheless maintained his ties to Enrile; he gave him a letter of recommendation and invited him to Berlin.[11]

At the beginning of 1916, Enrile, who was leading a somewhat down-at-heels existence as an emigré in Havana, decided to travel to Berlin and to seek aid for the organization of a new insurrection in Mexico. Prior to his departure, however, he made allusions to the purpose of his trip in Havana which came to the attention of Carranza's consul. The consul immediately reported to his government that Enrile and a Spaniard had gathered $5,000 in New Orleans and wanted to travel to Germany "in order to acquire money and support there for the purpose of disrupting at any price the existing relations between Mexico and the United States."[12]

In February 1916, Enrile arrived in Madrid and presented himself at the German embassy with Papen's letter of recommendation. The ambassador contacted the Foreign Office in Berlin and received the answer that the German government had no interest in Enrile.[13] Nevertheless, Enrile traveled to Berlin. He called on the Foreign Office, where he once again presented Papen's letter. The Foreign Office then contacted Papen, who recommended that Enrile "be kept on call,"[14] as he might one day be of use; he could not, however, provide more specific information about him. Enrile was then received by the Mexican adviser in the Foreign Office, Montgelas, to whom he introduced himself as the representative of all the forces opposing Carranza. He claimed to be representing Felix Díaz and all former Díaz politicians living in exile, such as former President De la Barra and Huerta's former minister of war, Blanquet, as well as the revolutionaries Villa and Zapata. He asked the German government for $300 million for the purchase of arms for a force of two hundred thousand soldiers—the "National Guard"—that he claimed to have at his command for the purpose of overthrowing Carranza. In exchange, Enrile promised a secret treaty between a government formed by the forces he represented and Germany, which would offer Germany, among other things:

1. A Mexican policy favorable to Germany and aimed against the interests of the United States
2. The creation of a strong army, which would invade American territory at a time propitious for Germany and Mexico
3. The expulsion of American capital through legal measures
4. Railroad, petroleum, mining, and trade concessions for Germany
5. Support for the separatist movements existing in several southwestern states (Texas, Arizona, New Mexico) and in California
6. Guarantees to Germany for loans and for deliveries of ammunition and weapons in the form desired by Germany.[15]

It is unlikely that there was any truth to Enrile's assertions about the forces he claimed to represent. The reactionaries were hardly as strong as he claimed, and Zapata would never have considered an alliance with

Germany or with the Díaz forces. Even if Enrile's assertions about the forces he represented had corresponded to reality, the German government in April 1916 was not interested in financing an insurrection against Carranza. Only a short time before the Americans had entered Mexico, and a Mexican-American war was becoming increasingly probable. The more inevitable it appeared, however, the more Carranza showed pro-German inclinations. Enrile's plans were thus completely at odds with the intentions and interests of the German government and hence were flatly rejected. This was, however, done in a very polite fashion, for Germany wanted to keep Enrile "on call." "Germany's relations with the United States," it was explained to him, "are at this time completely normal, and interference in Mexican-American differences is currently out of the question.... We were not pursuing political objectives there, but we want an open door and equal treatment. To the extent that the new 'National Guard' is able to work in this direction, and to unify the quarreling elements in Mexico, that will also be welcomed in Germany."[16]

The Foreign Office referred Enrile to the General Staff, which considered "possibly using him for intelligence work in France."[17] For reasons which were not made clear, but probably because he was suspected of being an Allied spy, all plans to use him as a spy were dropped at that point. Enrile was constantly under surveillance by the police during the rest of his stay in Berlin. Although his room was searched and his entire correspondence was confiscated, no compromising evidence against him could be found.[18] When he left Germany shortly thereafter, he attempted to obtain some compensation for his travel expenses. The Foreign Office, which had not invited him, refused, but indicated the possibility of repayment by the military authorities who had extended the invitation. The authorities consulted Papen, whose reputation had apparently suffered from such unproductive expenditures, and he responded that Enrile had only been invited (by the military attaché!) to "economic discussions" and that Germany should therefore refuse any reimbursement.[19]

The assertion of the Foreign Office that Germany had no political interest in Mexico and that it sought to provoke no conflict between Mexico and the United States might give the impression that the German intrigues and conspiracies had been conducted without the knowledge or at any rate without the approval of the Foreign Office. This, of course, was not the case. That the Foreign Office was just as involved in such activities as the military is shown by another plot, which was also aimed at provoking a Mexican-American war. This plot was set in motion at the same time as the conspiracy with Huerta, except that in this case Germany attempted to involve Villa.

In May 1915, the German propaganda chief in the United States, Bernhard Dernburg, gave the future chief of the Admiralty, Admiral Henning von Holtzendorff, a thorough report on American shipments of war materiel to the Allies. He also reported in his letter a conversation he had had with Felix Sommerfeld, Villa's representative in the United States. About this conversation, he made the following remarks:

> All the arms producers' contracts contain a clause which renders them null and void should the United States be pulled into a conflict. The policy of the United States toward Mexico is known to everyone, and we can be assured that the United States government will do anything to avoid an intervention in Mexico. The military authorities of the United States, on the other hand, are for an intervention, and so are the governments of Texas and Arizona, which lie directly on the Mexican border. Roughly two months ago, there was an incident on the Arizona border, which almost provoked an intervention. At that time, the chief of the American general staff was sent to the border by President Wilson, on the advice of Secretary of War Garrison to negotiate with Villa. These negotiations took place with the mediation of Felix A. Sommerfeld, and at that moment, as he had repeatedly told me, it would have been easy for him to provoke an intervention. Such a development at this time would have the following consequences for Germany:
>
> An embargo on all ammunition to the Allies, and since it is well known that the Allies are dependent on the United States for ammunition and war materiel, a rapid success for Germany, as well as a limitation on credit to the Allies and furthermore a shift in United States policy which would also be to Germany's advantage. On the other hand, Felix A. Sommerfeld also had hesitations about forcing an intervention with Villa because he does not know Germany's intentions with regard to the United States and does not know what Germany's desires for the future in its policy toward the Americans is and does not wish to run the risk of working counter to German policy or of worsening the situation through a hasty move instead of improving it. This opportunity appears to be presenting itself again in the immediate future, and Felix A. Sommerfeld has discussed it with me. He is quite convinced that an intervention in Mexico by the United States can be brought about. The Allies had ordered 400,000 rifles here, of which two factories, Winchester and Remington, are delivering 200,000 each: shipments of 14,000 to 18,000 every month, beginning in the fall. In addition, the Allies had ordered a shipment of 100,000 French military rifles. Various other factories, which previously were producing no war materiel, are now beginning to do so.
>
> Aside from Mr. Sommerfeld, who is the source of this idea, I am the only one who knows his plans. We have both declined to discuss this affair with the German ambassador here, since we are convinced that the less which is known the better, and moreover, that this delicate affair can only be decided directly at the appropriate level. After this report has been considered, I request that Felix A. Sommerfeld be given a "yes" or a "no" in whatever way, through me directly. In

conclusion, I would moreover like to mention that both Felix A. Sommerfeld and I give our word of honor as citizens of Germany that we will discuss this with no one, regardless of the decision that is made.[20]

Admiral Henning von Holtzendorff delivered this report to the secretary of state in the Foreign Office, Jagow, for an assessment and a decision. His reply leaves no room for ambiguity: "In my opinion, the answer is absolutely 'yes.' Even if the shipments of munitions cannot be stopped, and I am not sure they can, it would be highly desirable for America to become involved in a war and be diverted from Europe, where it is clearly more sympathetic to England. The Americans are not intervening in the Chinese situation, however, and hence an intervention made necessary by the developments in Mexico would be the only possible diversion for the American government. Moreover, since we can at this time do nothing in the Mexican situation, an American intervention would also be the best thing possible for our interests there."[21]

On 10 March 1916, Villa attacked the city of Columbus on the southern border of the United States. Was this attack the result of the plot between Sommerfeld and the German government? The German documents give no answer to this question. Nonetheless, one can draw certain conclusions from American reports, even if final confirmation is not to be found.

The key figure in the plot was Felix A. Sommerfeld, one of the most interesting members of the shadowy army of agents, double agents, and lobbyists who swarmed like locusts over Mexico once the revolution had begun. Sommerfeld was one of the ablest—and one of the strangest—of these men. He was, as Justice Department officials who interviewed him in 1918 put it, "a soldier of fortune."[22] Born in Germany in 1879, of a middle class family, he began studying mining and engineering in 1896 at the University of Berlin but soon became bored with his studies and in 1896, without telling any member of his family about it, he abruptly decided to go to the United States. Two years after he arrived, the Spanish American war broke out and Sommerfeld joined the army in order to go to Cuba and fight. A short time later, he changed his mind and decided that he wanted to return to Germany, allegedly as he later stated, because his father had become very ill. He easily overcame obstacles that others might not have found so easy to surmount: his membership in the American army and the fact that he had no money for the return trip. As far as the army was concerned, he simply took a furlough and then deserted. His solution for his second problem was no less simple. He had been living with a man named Zimmerman, a friend of his brother's, and he simply stole $250 from him, thus paying for the return trip. One year later, in 1899, he joined the special German contingent sent to China to put down the Boxer Rebellion. He fought for one year against the Chinese revolutionaries, returned to Germany, and seems to have completed his studies there as a mining engineer. At the beginning of the twentieth century he again immigrated to the United States, where he worked as a mining engineer and as a speculator in mining properties in the southwest.[23] From there he moved on to northern Mexico and made his home in Chihuahua, where he worked as an assayer in mining property. He was obviously not very successful at this and attempted to supplement his earnings by working as a stringer for the Associated Press correspondent in northern Mexico once the Mexican Revolution broke out. It was in this capacity that he first established contact with Madero and very soon gained his confidence. This was in large part due to the fact, as the U.S. consul in Chihuahua who knew him well stated, that he was a brilliant demagogue. "He relied on Madero's gullibility, inexperience, and pliability," consul Letcher wrote about him, "and quickly exercised a decisive influence on Madero which continued until the latter's murder."[24] Sommerfeld was so trusted by Madero that he was appointed head of the latter's secret police in the Mexican capital and later in the United States. In this capacity he constantly traveled to the border to forestall uprisings by Madero's enemies against him.[25] Sommerfeld cemented his relationship with the Mexican president by posing as a revolutionary and a democrat, which, according to U.S. consul Letcher, he definitely was not. As Letcher related, he could talk "with eloquence and earnestness about democracy in Mexico. Deep in his heart, however, as confidential discussions with him indicate, he is a convinced monarchist and absolutist, who firmly believes that monarchs and absolutist governments are the only ones which make any sense."[26] He probably saw the Mexican revolutionaries in much the same light as he had seen the Boxers in China, whom he had helped to exterminate.

While serving Madero, Sommerfeld established close relations with two groups with whom he was to maintain even closer contact in the years to come, the German government and U.S. business interests. His relations with the Germans were so close that German minister Hintze used him as an intermediary in 1912, when he wanted to find out whether the Mexican government was planning to sign a reciprocity treaty with the United States. During the Tragic Ten Days Hintze granted him asylum in the German legation and saw to it that he was able to leave the country. Sommerfeld then went to Washington,[27] where he renewed and strengthened a relationship he had already established in the Madero period with a figure even more shadowy than Sommerfeld himself, Sherbourne G. Hopkins. Hopkins was one of the most influential lobbyists for American business interests in the United States, and, according to Hintze, was also the organizer of Latin American revolts financed by U.S.

interests.[28] Hopkins gave Sommerfeld money and instructed him to put himself at Carranza's disposal.[29] With his gift for rhetoric he soon succeeded in doing this and became the intermediary who arranged negotiations between Carranza and Wilson's special representative, William Bayard Hale. Carranza had so much confidence in Sommerfeld that he sent him to Chihuahua to work with Villa and spy on his activities.[30] Sommerfeld did spy on Villa, but not for Carranza. He seems to have sent reports of the situation in Mexico both to the German naval attaché in the United States, Boy Edd, and to Hopkins.[31] At the same time he gained Villa's confidence and became one of his main agents in the United States and an intermediary with the American military and especially General Hugh Scott.[32] The connection to the Mexican revolutionaries proved quite lucrative for Sommerfeld. He had an exclusive concession for importing dynamite into the country which brought him a profit of $5,000 per month, and became one of the main ammunition buyers for Villa.[33]

The question arises as to what motives prompted Sommerfeld to approach German agents in May 1915 and to offer them his services. It could hardly be a question of "idealism," since he had generally shown himself to be unscrupulous and above all out for himself. But a war between Villa and the United States, such as he wished to help trigger, would have brought his lucrative contracts to an end. One explanation for his actions might be that he had other contractors besides the German secret service. His connection with Hopkins had grown so close that on 1 August 1914 a representative of the U.S. Treasury who worked at the Mexican border, Zachary Cobb, made a report on the relations between Hopkins and Sommerfeld in which he stated that the latter was obviously serving large U.S. business interests and especially Henry Clay Pierce, the head of Waters Pierce Corporation,[34] who had already come out for an American intervention in Mexico as early as 1913 at the meeting of the companies with interests in the Mexican railways. It is quite possible that Hopkins had given Sommerfeld instructions similar to those of the German secret service, although naturally for different reasons.

Was Sommerfeld in any way involved in Villa's attack on Columbus, New Mexico? What can be established is that through 1915 and early 1916, Sommerfeld maintained ever closer ties to the German secret service, and that at the same time he maintained his close links to Villa. Agents of the Justice Department stated that from April until August 1915 a total of $340,000 had been deposited in Sommerfeld's account in a St. Louis bank. Though it could not be precisely ascertained who in New York had deposited the money, the Justice Department agents nevertheless learned that on the same day money had been deposited by the same New York bank in a second account at the St. Louis bank where Sommerfeld's account had been opened. The second account belonged to the German embassy in the United States. Both accounts were closed on the same day. U.S. government agents concluded from this that certain ties must have existed between the two accounts, and they showed that all the money from the Sommerfeld account had been paid to the Western Cartridge Company for weapons shipments to Villa.[35]

Sommerfeld told the Justice Department that he had severed all links to Villa after Carranza had been recognized by the United States, and he attempted to enhance his credibility with U.S. military authorities by sending a long protest telegram to Villa after the shooting of American mining engineers in Santa Isabel. In this telegram he characterized this shooting as "the greatest crime which has been committed in Mexico." He asked Villa to condemn this act of violence to the American government and simultaneously to declare that he "would not permit a tax on foreigners or their rights."[36] Nonetheless, according to Carranza's agents in the United States, Sommerfeld continued to buy arms for Villa.[37] On the basis of this limited evidence it could be assumed, though not proven, that after Villa's defeat and U.S. recognition of Carranza Sommerfeld was pressuring the Mexican leader to attack the United States and that he had held out to Villa the prospect of German aid. But if Villa did indeed accept such aid, it implied no obligation whatever nor his enlistment in the service of Germany, as his later actions were to show, but merely utilization of the conflicts between major powers for the realization of his own goals. This was an attitude taken by many revolutionaries during the First World War.

While the possibility of German participation in the attack on Columbus cannot be ruled out, neither can it be documented, and there is much circumstantial evidence to the contrary.

The documents of the Foreign Office do not show that the attack occurred on the initiative of Germany; quite the contrary. On 28 March 1916, the German ambassador to the United States, Bernstorff, who knew nothing of the Dernburg-Sommerfeld conspiracy, wrote in a report to the Reichskanzler: "It cannot be a surprise that the attempt has been made to link Villa's attack to German intrigues and to present Germany as the true fomenter of trouble. Naturally, no proof of such a false assertion was produced."[38] In the Foreign Office, next to the words "false assertion," the marginal notation "unfortunately" was made, probably by the head of the Mexican section of the German Foreign Office, Montgelas. This would indicate the Foreign Office's regret that Germany had nothing to do with the attack.[39] It can further be assumed that the navy, on whose behalf Sommerfeld was working, would have endeavored to inform other agencies of the German government of its initiative in the attack, had it in fact been involved. In 1916–17, the navy had become increasingly embroiled in a conflict with the civilian leadership of the Reich, and other forces in Germany, over the question of unlimited U-boat warfare. The navy's prestige with the top civilian and military leadership of Germany would have been greatly enhanced by a successful action, particularly a provocation by Villa on the southern border of the United States, which also had the blessing of the Foreign Office. In no relevant German archive, however, can one find such a report or claim by the navy.

Most important, as described above, one can construct a perfectly rational explanation for Villa's attack on the United States without reference to Germany.

Villa's attack on Columbus and the subsequent American intervention in Mexico were in any case welcomed with enthusiasm by German and Austrian diplomats. "As long as the Mexican question remains at this stage," Bernstorff wrote on 4 April 1916 to the Reichskanzler, "we are, I believe, fairly safe from aggressive attack by the American government."[40] Every ebb in the tensions between Mexico and the United States, every possibility that the situation would be settled without war, created renewed malaise among the diplomats of the Central Powers. "Unfortunately," wrote the Austrian ambassador in Washington to his foreign minister, "the hope is disappearing that the United States will be forced actually to intervene militarily in Mexico and that the administration would therefore be prompted to drop its pretensions toward the Central Powers."[41]

The American intervention in Mexico was to have facilitated the launching of the unlimited U-boat warfare so much desired by the German army and naval commands. "If intending reopening of U-boat war in old forms," Bernstorff wired on 24 June 1916, "please delay beginning until America really tied up in Mexico. Otherwise to be expected that president will immediately settle with Mexico and will use war with Germany to win elections with help of Roosevelt people."[42]

The German government, however, did not merely limit itself to endorsing the American intervention, but did everything to increase it. At the same time the Germans were making efforts to intensify the anti-Mexican mood in the United States, they were also providing Villa with arms and other equipment.[43] As early as 23 March 1916, Montgelas wrote: "There is little point, in my opinion, in sending *money* to Mexico. To the extent that anything can be achieved there with money, the Americans will always be able to outbid us easily, since they simply have more money and because, moreover, they have infinitely more channels at their disposal than we do, since the Americans have been working in this way for a long time in Mexico. It would be something quite different if we could get arms and ammunition to Villa and his bands surreptitiously. This is, however, complicated by the fact that communications with northern Mexico from Veracruz are currently very poor."[44]

It was not difficult for the German secret service to get American weapons to Mexico. Plans for the German-owned arms factory in Bridgeport had failed, and the arms had since then been stored in Bridgeport.[45] There is therefore no reason to doubt the reports of British secret agents that these weapons were smuggled out of the United States to Villa in Mexico in coffins and oil tankers.[46] According to American sources, the German consulate in San Francisco appears to have been heavily involved in these arms shipments.

When it became increasingly clear that in spite of the American intervention in Mexico, there would be no war between the two countries, the German authorities looked for new possibilities to provoke an armed conflict through Villa. What had not been achieved by border violations might perhaps be brought about by an attack on the Mexican oil fields. According to Villa's former general, Vargas, the German consul in Torreón, which Villa had temporarily taken, made a proposal of this kind in December 1916. The consul, whom Villa had known from an earlier period, attended a victory banquet given in Villa's honor. After great hymns of praise for Villa's military achievements and capabilities, the consul proposed to Villa an attack on the oil fields, pointing out that there were no large garrisons between Torreón and Tampico. He promised him that in the event of the capture of Tampico, German ships would be waiting for him there with money and arms. The consul apparently even declared himself willing to accompany Villa, in order to function as a hostage should the action fail.

According to Vargas's account, Villa seemed impressed and even undertook preparations for the march to Tampico. At the last minute, however, he changed his mind and moved in the direction of Chihuahua. Vargas assumed that Villa was afraid of an international conflict which might prove very costly for Mexico. It is quite possible that after the American intervention of March, Villa wished to give the United States no further cause for an even larger intervention. Moreover, Villa, who was after all conducting a guerrilla war, probably wanted to remain on his home territory.[47]

One of the most intriguing conspiracies that contemporary U.S. politicians and some later American historians have associated Germany with is the conspiracy generally known as the plan of San Diego.[48]

The plan, signed by nine Mexican-Americans and purportedly drafted on 6 January 1915 in San Diego, Texas, called for an uprising of Mexican-Americans and blacks against Anglo-American domination in Texas, New Mexico, Arizona, Colorado, and California. All Anglo males over the age of sixteen were to be killed. After victory each state would first constitute an independent republic which would then have the option of joining Mexico. Although the plan had set the target date of 10 February

1915 for the uprising, nothing happened on that date. A few months later, however, violence did erupt in connection with this movement. Two Mexican-Americans, Luis de la Rosa, a former deputy sheriff of Cameron County, Texas, and Aniceto Pizaña, who came from a ranching family near Brownsville, Texas, staged a series of raids in south Texas (without resorting to the kind of massacre of all Anglo males the original plan had called for) and then retreated across the Mexican border. Shortly thereafter large-scale reprisals took place against Mexican-Americans in the lower Rio Grande Valley on the part of both U.S. authorities and individual Anglo-Americans. As a result, many Mexican-Americans left their homes to flee either northward or south across the Mexican-American border.

The movement subsided shortly after Carranza was recognized by the U.S. in October 1915 but erupted again after the punitive expedition entered Mexico in 1916. It seemed to have reached its high point when raiders at times labeled as Mexicans and at other times as Mexican-Americans attacked Glenn Springs, Texas, on 5 May 1916. The raids subsided again after the punitive expedition left Mexico.

One of the problems that intrigued both U.S. authorities at the time and later historians who dealt with this movement is whether it was essentially Mexican-American in character with at best limited support by Mexican factions or whether it constituted an attempt by outsiders to exploit for their own purposes the conflicts and problems in the United States southwest. Were these outsiders Mexican factions, Germans, or both? Recent research seems to indicate that this movement, while based on genuine Mexican-American grievances, was being utilized by Mexican factions[49] in a way not dissimilar to the way in which Americans were attempting to use Mexican revolutionaries for their own ends.

According to the testimony of one of the first organizers of the movement, Basilio Ramos, its first Mexican sponsors had been sympathizers of former President Victoriano Huerta, who in early 1915 was plotting a comeback. When the movement passed from the stage of manifestos to that of guerrilla raids, it seems to have passed from Huertista to Carranzista control.

According to historians L. Sadler and Charles Harris, the Carranza faction attempted to utilize the San Diego plan to pressure the United States into recognition of Carranza as the sole legal authority in Mexico. Harris and Sadler based their conclusion largely on the fact that a few days after the Wilson administration gave de facto recognition to Carranza the border raids did, in fact, cease. They resumed after U.S.–Mexican tensions flared up again as a result of the punitive expedition's invasion of Mexico and subsided once more after it left the country.

Were the Germans involved as well? Contemporary U.S. observers repeatedly expressed their firm conviction that this was the case but could offer no conclusive proof. There is no evidence for this in German archives, but that fact is hardly conclusive since not all plots of this kind were recorded in the documents preserved in German archives. It certainly is the type of plot the Germans would have liked to be involved in. If, indeed, it began as a conspiracy by Huerta supporters at a time when the former Mexican president was receiving German financial help and promising the Germans to start a war against the United States, then Germany's participation at this stage of the plot is quite plausible. Nevertheless, the man who masterminded the plot with Huerta, Rintelen, never mentions it in his memoirs nor is it among the accusations leveled by U.S. authorities in Rintelen's trial.

It is on the whole extremely unlikely that the Germans were in any way involved in the movement when it was taken over by Carranza between February and October 1915. Relations between the Germans and the First Chief were so bad during this period that cooperation of this kind would have been unthinkable. It was only after the punitive expedition had entered Mexico that joint sponsorship by Carranza and the Germans was at least conceivable. For relations between both sides had greatly improved as the threat of a U.S.–Mexican war increased. Hoping for German help in case of war, Carranza actively sought a rapprochement with Germany.

One indication that Germany might have been involved in the San Diego plan was the testimony of J. Knake Forsek, an American who had gone to Mexico where in 1916 Carranzista officials, who according to him were sponsoring the movement, tried to recruit him.[50] One of those sponsors was Mario Méndez, Carranza's minister of communication and from 1917 onward (and perhaps already in 1916) Germany's main agent within the Mexican government.[51]

If German agents did indeed participate in the organization of the San Diego plan, did this take place with the consent of Carranza? If so, what could have induced the Mexican leader to share sponsorship and perhaps control of such a delicate operation with a foreign power with which relations were improving but were yet far from close.

The answer could be provided by a letter that the Mexican secret agent José Flores sent to Carranza in February 1917. In it, he stated that in case of a German-American war he hoped that 200,000 German-Americans would join with Mexican-Americans in an uprising against the U.S. government.[52] As long as the punitive expedition was in Mexico, Carranza considered a Mexican-American war not only as possible but at times imminent. The one possibility he thought he had of distracting the U.S. from carrying out a full-scale invasion of Mexico was to provoke an uprising in the United States. Such a revolt would have taken on far greater proportions if not only Mexican-Americans and blacks but also German-Americans had participated in it. This is the promise the Germans may have held out. Nevertheless, it must be said that on the whole German participation in the San Diego plan remains unproven and circumstantial.

The most convincing argument to be made against German participation in the San Diego plan is the fact that the United States after the end of World War I never officially accused German agents of having organized and sponsored the movement. The peace treaty between the United States and Germany signed at the end of World War I specified that Germany would be liable for any damages caused to American interests by the activities of German agents in the United States in the period of America's neutrality. For this purpose a German-American claims commission was set up, and U.S. representatives made extensive investigations of every possible German intrigue against the United States originating in the United States and Mexico. No mention at all is made by the American representative to the commission of any German involvement in the San Diego plan.

From 1914 to 1917 the Reich government sharply denied any involvement in all these conspiracies and characterized American charges to that effect as "English provocations." Pan-German circles seized on these claims by the government and attacked it for not waging the war energetically enough. In July 1916, Attorney Pudor, supported by Falkenhayn, Tirpitz, Kapp, and Class, accused Reichskanzler Bethmann-Hollweg of pursuing an antinational war policy because he would not make full use of the opportunity to involve Mexico in a war with the United States. The Reichskanzler, charged Pudor, had pursued "a conciliatory policy benefiting Jewish commercial interests."[53]

In addition to the efforts to draw Mexico into an armed conflict with the United States, the German conspirators in Mexico pursued other plans, whose execution was entrusted to the new German minister Heinrich von Eckardt. The purpose of these activities is revealed by a report that Eckardt sent to the Reichskanzler at the end of July 1915.

First, the naval attaché suggested to me through the intermediary of the Kaiser's ambassador that we have the oil wells in Tampico destroyed. He further proposed that we help return to Germany men liable for military service who could not get to Europe from New York, and who had returned to Mexico. The Kaiser's ambassador and the military attaché told me expressly that the creation of travel possibilities for the reserve officers and aspiring officers *currently in the United States* would be very worthwhile. To achieve both ends, Herr Rau, at my behest, negotiated with intermediaries with whom I, for obvious reasons, could not have personal contact, following thorough discussions with the naval and military attachés.[54]

After Eckardt had already "concluded the negotiations on the Tampico affair in Galveston on February 22 and in New Orleans on February 24 and agreed on the plans," the action to destroy the Tampico oil wells was given up by the navy. On 11 March, the Admiralty wired Boy Edd: "Significant military damage to England through closing of Mexican oil resources not possible. Thus no money for such action available." Boy Edd immediately informed Eckardt, who thereupon cancelled all further preparations.[55]

Franz von Papen, at that time military attaché in the United States, initially appeared to have been of a different opinion. On 17 March he reported: "In view of the great importance of the Tampico (Mexico) oil wells for the English fleet and the large English investments there, I have sent Herr v. Petersdorf there in order to create the greatest possible damage through extensive sabotage of tanks and pipelines. Given the current situation in Mexico, I am expecting large successes from relatively small resources. Sabotage against factories here contributes little, since all factories are under the surveillance of hundreds of secret agents and all German-American and Irish workers have been laid off."[56]

As far as it can be determined, no acts of sabotage were carried out in Tampico in 1915–16. It is not clear whether Petersdorf failed—the Allies had many secret agents in and around Tampico—or whether Papen and the Ministry of War had accepted the views of the navy. Until the end of 1915, in any case, no new efforts appear to have been undertaken to conduct sabotage in Tampico.

It is not out of the question that the shift in the navy's attitude was based on its hope that this goal could be achieved more easily through other means. Roughly four weeks before the Admiralty decided to give up sabotage activity in Tampico, the German ambassador in Madrid reported that the former Mexican minister Reyes, who was negotiating the delivery of American oil from Mexico with the Allies, had just canceled oil deliveries at the behest of Standard Oil. In the Foreign Office, this was interpreted as a sign that Standard Oil wanted "to show itself favorable to us."[57]

This attitude on the part of Standard Oil was no accident. Whereas prior to the outbreak of the war the company had been in the sharpest competition with English firms, it now had a virtual monopoly on the German market. Nevertheless, it was not prepared to give up the large profits from deliveries to England on a long-term basis for the sake of a "friendship" with Germany. As it became more and more clear that the war was going to be a long one and that deliveries to Germany were not possible, the Mexican Petroleum Company (which had financial ties to Standard Oil) concluded a supply contract with the British Admiralty.[58]

Eckardt's other mission proved easier to perform. He was able to arrange for many German reservists to reach Germany through Italy during the first half of 1915. When this route was closed off by Italy's declaration of war, Eckardt did not give up, but attempted to channel reservists to Germany through other countries.[59] Unfortunately, it cannot be established to what extent he actually succeeded in this and to what extent German reservists, who came from the United States to Mexico in the years 1915–16, made use of this arrangement.

The German conspiracies in Mexico had one thing in common until 1916: they sought to employ the opponents of Carranza, whether they stood to his right, as in the case of Huerta, or to his left, as in the case of Villa. Only in 1916 did German diplomacy recognize that these forces were not sufficient to launch a Mexican-American war and begin to concern itself with Carranza.

### First German Attempts to Involve Carranza in Their Plots

German diplomacy had initially had an extremely negative attitude toward Carranza and had conceived of his regime in very critical terms. Thus the German chargé.d'affaires Magnus had called the Carranzists "a horde of Huns calling themselves Constitutionalists."[60] The same Magnus wrote elsewhere: "It is obvious that Mr. Carranza and his followers have condemned themselves in the eyes of the world by their past conduct, and that particularly Carranza himself has shown himself unworthy to cloak himself in the pretensions of a constitutional president."[61] The new envoy, Eckardt, who traveled to the area ruled by Carranza, was even sharper in his remarks: "Carranza's governmental bodies are prototypes of vulgarity and depravity, which wheel, deal, extort, and steal, just like the military commanders in the cities and in the countryside."[62]

In the conflict between the government of the revolutionary convention and Carranza, German diplomacy initially entered on the side of the former. "The government of the revolutionary convention has always been far more obliging to foreigners than Carranza has, thus thoroughly desirable to leave the capital in its hands,"[63] wrote Magnus to Bernstorff. The state of Chiapas, however, where most of the German coffee plantations were located, was in the area controlled by Carranza. For this reason Eckardt considered it "absolutely necessary, however fatal it may be in and of itself, to take up with the ruler of Veracruz the official relations he has been seeking."[64] On 4 June, Eckardt presented himself to Carranza as an agent with special powers, and on 10 November the German government, following the American example, gave de facto recognition to the Carranza government.[65] In spite of this recognition, the relations between the two countries remained cool until the invasion of Mexico by the American punitive expedition.

After Huerta's defeat, Carranza initially took a hard anti-German attitude. One of his most prominent supporters, the painter Gerardo Murillo, told Magnus that Mexico would never forget that a German warship had taken Huerta out of the country.[66] With the outbreak of the world war, Carranza declared his neutrality, but his initial sympathies were unambiguously with the Allies. His anti-German attitude was further strengthened when the German conspiracies with Huerta became known, conspiracies whose discovery, according to American reports, was apparently made in part by Carranza's secret agents.[67]

In the course of the year 1915, a transformation gradually occurred in Carranza's attitudes on foreign policy questions. After the battle of Agua Prieta, his victory over his domestic opponents was secure; the only power which could still overthrow his government was the United States. Thus Carranza sought, as all Mexican governments since 1900 had, a countervailing force against the United States. Prior to 1914, Mexican governments had turned first to England. This was no longer possible in 1915, and in any case it was improbable that Carranza would have moved in this direction. For the substantial support that Huerta had received from the English had created a powerful anti-British mood among Huerta's opponents. Moreover, England, which was completely involved in the war and dependent on American supplies, was hardly in a position to take an anti-American position in Mexico. The only major powers from whom the Mexican government could draw support against the United States were Japan and Germany.

Carranza appears initially to have approached Japan. This is not surprising: Japanese diplomats, in contrast to German, had engaged in no conspiracies with Carranza's opponents. On 9 September 1915, a Japanese resident in Mexico, Fukutaro Terasawa, wrote to an associate of the former Japanese Foreign Minister Kato:

I am active here behind the scenes with Carranza's government, and in fact am currently an adviser to the foreign minister: moreover, I have some additional secret secondary functions. But for the moment the most important thing is the policy toward Japan of the Mexican government. As the U.S. government has resorted to the use of force, it is now absolutely necessary to approach Japan. If you have any friends in Japanese government circles, could you do me a favor and explain something about Mexico to them? If the Japanese government is willing to take up close relations with Mexico, either openly or secretly, I will attempt to bring about an agreement that will be advantageous for

Japan. Concessions of all kinds can be provided. If ports are desired, I will secretly take steps.[68]

Terasawa's letter was given to Japan's former foreign minister, Kato, who passed it on to the head of the Political Division in the Japanese Foreign Ministry. The latter promptly contacted the Japanese envoy in Mexico with a request for further information. "Mr. Fukutaro Terasawa," replied the Japanese minister,

has apparently known the minister of the interior and foreign minister, who is the mind behind Carranza, for years, and is also well paid as an adviser or something of the sort. It is not, however, in keeping with the facts, as he states in his letter, that he has any access to political secrets. The foreign minister is actually of pro-Japanese persuasion and wishes to begin relations with the emperor's government. The sending of Commander Romero to Japan was also the result of his initiative. It might be supposed that he is toying with the thought of using Mr. Terasawa on occasion. The latter, however, is not satisfactorily educated and to all appearances does not have the capacity to be up to such a task.[69]

Carranza attempted on several other occasions to achieve a rapprochement with the Japanese. The Japanese, however, were prepared only to sell weapons to Mexico; there was no desire to develop any deeper ties. Japan was intent, during the First World War, on solidifying and extending its position in China. Mexico was viewed by Japan only as a means of putting pressure on the United States and as a possible means to be utilized should a war break out with the United States because of Japanese advances in China.

Carranza seems to have recognized this, for he turned increasingly toward Germany (see chap. 11). The growing German-American tensions and the discovery of the German conspiracies appear to have awakened in Carranza the hope that the German government, in the event of a Mexican-American war, would aid Mexico in one way or another. Thus, even though Mexican-American relations were relatively relaxed in late 1915 and early 1916, a slow rapprochement with Germany was brought about by Carranza.

The first expression of the gradual transformation of Mexican-German relations was the "solution" of the labor question on the German coffee plantations in Chiapas. The working conditions and the indebted servitude on the German coffee plantations were among the harshest in all of Mexico during the Díaz period. After the extension of the revolution to Chiapas, the agricultural workers had fled from the plantations, and their owners had been unable to bring in the coffee harvest. Eckardt asked for help from Carranza, who promised "to make sure that the plantation owners would be helped to circumvent the shortage of laborers, and to give the necessary recommendations to Mr. Rau, who will manage this affair with all necessary energies in the state of Chiapas. Thanks to the extensive personal contacts of Mr. Rau, there is also hope for success."[70] Unfortunately, the exact nature of this "solution" is not known. Two paths were available: either the agricultural workers were forced to return to the plantations as debt peons or free laborers were used.

Carranza took another step toward rapprochement by influencing his press in a pro-German direction. The German minister to Mexico triumphantly wrote, "On November 10, the final recognition of the Kaiser's government, which again as in May 1915 precedes the other powers, is announced here. Carranza, who has up till now been inclined toward the Allies, orders the press to withhold anti-German publications and to publish our war telegrams in unfalsified fashion."[71]

This slow shift in Carranza's attitude did not initially move Eckardt to change his attitude toward the Carranza government. In a thorough analysis of the situation in Mexico, Eckardt wrote on 24 January 1916: "The Mexico of today, under the regime of the 'Constitutionalistas' presents a picture of *unspeakable devastation, wretched ruins*. There was undoubtedly stealing in the Díaz era as well, but there was a state power which guaranteed the safety of life and property."[72] Of Carranza himself, he spoke with condescending irony:

> Don Venustiano is the generalissimo now recognized as the de facto ruler of the republic, the 'triumphant,' proclaimer of freedom, equality, and justice. Fantasy conjures up the image of a daring warrior on a fiery charger. But Don Venustiano rides no charger, and stays away from the battlefield. This former small landowner, who raised dairy cows, has the appearance of a *portly civil servant*. He can claim for himself the talents of neither a statesman, a military leader, nor an organizer; his only strength is a *hard head*, the obstinacy which does not allow itself to be diverted from the path leading to the ambitious goal. He has his pedantic mediocrity to thank for his success. In him, Woodrow Wilson may have found the man who would in the last analysis allow the railroad, oil, and mine concessions to be squeezed out of him, if his ambitious plans could only be fulfilled under such conditions. *History will call both Wilson and Carranza dishonest*, dishonest in the medieval sense.[73]

At this point Eckardt obviously had little sympathy for the revolution, which he attributed not to social ills but to the failure of the Catholic Church, whose avarice had prevented it from fulfilling its "mission" of isolating the Indians from the revolution. "The hoarding policy of the heads of the church, the for the most part uneducated Mexican-Spanish priesthood, which gave itself over to an immoral and easy way of life, instead of working to raise the intellectual level of the Indians with schools, are, as honest members of the clergy will concede, the reason for the horrible developments."[74] In Eckardt's view, the only solution was a "joint intervention of all powers to restore order."[75]

The deployment of the American punitive expedition in Mexico and the resulting danger of war created a completely new situation. The Mexican government now manifested, to a far greater extent than before, its desire to move closer to Germany. Germany became and was to remain for the duration of World War I the one country on which Carranza pinned his hopes of finding support against the United States. Carranza instructed the press to go still farther than he had in 1915. "The largest Mexican newspapers," reported Eckardt,

> have received orders to write favorably about Germany and to carry all reports which I will submit to them. I attribute the change to the tremendous demonstrations of power which have been thrust confidently and without self-glorification before everyone with eyes to see by our army and navy in the military sphere and by our people in financial and economic terms. The beacons of Germanic confidence in final victory casts its glow over the skies of the Southern Cross as well. The conclusion has been reached here, after calm calculation, that after the war, Mexico will be able to expect more of an economic and perhaps even financial nature from Germany than from an already exhausted France and a transformed Britain. The news from Skagerrak consigns England's unchallenged rule of the seas to the realm of legend.[76]

Eckardt's real judgment on Mexico is expressed very clearly at the end of his report: "In the German whose hatred for his enemies he shares, the Mexican sees a friend for the days of a—quite illusory—national future."[77]

At the time of the German-American U-boat crisis in 1916, according to the Austrian minister in Mexico, the Mexican foreign minister somewhat naively asked the German envoy "if he could ask Berlin to keep the United States permanently under the pressure of the danger of war with Germany."[78] At the beginning of 1916, Carranza appointed the Mexican Arnoldo Krumm Heller, who was known to be particularly pro-German, to be the Mexican military attaché in Berlin. This was undoubtedly considered to be a gesture of unusual friendship toward Germany. And in October 1916, Mexico again approached the German government "seeking from Germany a declaration in Washington according to which an armed intervention in Mexico would not be viewed with favor. In return, the Mexicans offered extensive support for the German U-boats, should they desire to attack English oil tankers leaving the port of Tampico."[79]

All these attempts at rapprochement by the Mexican government reached their peak when, in November 1916, the Mexican envoy in Berlin delivered a memorandum to Secretary of State Zimmermann, envisioning close German-Mexican cooperation. After an introduction affirming the friendly sentiments of the Mexican people toward the German people and noting that German trade with Mexico had always been fairer than that of the other countries, the Mexican government made the following proposals:

1. The elaboration of a new friendship, commercial and maritime treaty, or an improvement of the treaty of 5 December 1882, as the latter no longer corresponded to the demands of the current period;
2. the employment by the Mexican government, which wished to provide its army with the most modern technology, of German instructors;
3. the decision by the Mexican government to request Germany to build arms and munitions factories and provide the necessary specialists;
4. the Mexican government's plan to acquire German submarines, since Mexico's fleet consisted of only five or six gunboats;
5. in order to extricate itself from foreign, especially English control, the construction of an efficient radio station for a direct link between Mexico and Germany.[80]

Carranza's primary concern was thus to strengthen his military capacities—a perfectly comprehensible desire, in view of the Mexican-American tensions at the time. The German authorities reacted extremely cautiously. Open support for Carranza was in no way in the interest of German diplomacy. Bernstorff's and Eckardt's reports were constantly feeding the hope of the Foreign Office that there would soon be a real Mexican-American war. An identification of Germany with Carranza would have increased tensions with the United States, without essentially increasing the possibilities of a Mexican-American war. Thus Eckardt characterized his behavior in June 1916 as "extremely neutral,"[81] and for the same reason Bernstorff demanded: "Please treat the [Mexican] affair with caution, for it is constantly asserted that German money and influence are behind Villa."[82]

It appears that Eckardt simply did not forward the Mexican request for diplomatic support of June–July and October 1916 to Berlin. The only report in this regard to be found in the German documents is the following dispatch from Eckardt dated 8 November 1916: "At Carranza's behest, the foreign minister told me that Mexico would help U-boats to the extent of its powers in certain circumstances."[83] In contrast to the report of his Austrian colleague, Eckardt says nothing of Mexico's own request from Germany.

Zimmermann still considered the closer cooperation between the two countries proposed in the Mexican government's memorandum to be premature. "The current moment, at any rate, does not appear to be the best for the conclusion of new, specific agreements. As soon as peace comes, we would energetically push for them."[84] Several months later, Zimmermann wrote: "I rejected Carranza's suggestion without reservations at the time, as I did not think that the moment for such a move had arrived. I did not yet know whether there would be unlimited U-boat warfare and whether, as a result, our relations with America would be severely strained. Thus I expressed myself with unusual caution."[85]

This caution also appears to have overruled the desire of the Admiralty to establish support installations for U-boats in Mexico. The Reich had immediately seized upon the Mexican offer to provide a base for U-boats. In the middle of November, the Mexican government was informed that German agents in Mexico had made all preparations for the construction of a U-boat support station and that only the approval of the regime was required. The Germans asked what Mexico wanted in exchange "in view of the financial and economic crisis which the country is experiencing."[86] The further course of the negotiations is not known, but it is clear that no German U-boat bases were established in Mexico.

If Germany did not wish to appear too friendly to Carranza, it also feared that Carranza, left to himself, would either seek a rapprochement with the United States or would be quickly toppled by the American armed forces. Thus the German government was prepared to advocate the sale of 20 million rounds of ammunition to Carranza through a German firm in Chile.[87]

### The Zimmermann Telegram

At the beginning of 1917, German-Mexican relations entered a new stage. By the end of 1916 the leadership of the German Reich had become convinced that a complete victory, which alone could make possible the realization of the wide-ranging war aims of Germany,[88] could no longer be achieved on land. Thus, on 7 January 1917, the decision was made for unlimited U-boat warfare. From that point on, any ship found in designated waters, regardless of its flag, was a potential target.

Unlimited U-boat warfare made the probability of a German-American war even greater. Zimmermann thus felt that the moment had come to take decisive steps to tie up the Americans in Mexico. The former Mexico adviser in the Foreign Office, Kemnitz, who was now the East Asian and Latin American expert, explained to him that this goal could best be achieved if a Mexican attack on the United States were to occur immediately after America's declaration of war against Germany. Kemnitz was thinking in this regard of an action similar to the one launched against Columbus by Villa in March 1916. He considered it quite probable that such an attack would create a warlike situation. The failure of the American punitive expedition against Villa was proof to the German leaders of how little American troops could accomplish against Mexican guerrillas.[89]

Zimmermann seized upon the proposal with enthusiasm. In the budget committee of the Reichstag, he stated:

It has often been asserted, and I can only agree, that the Mexicans are extremely courageous soldiers and that the Americans, when they entered Mexico, had no success but were forced to withdraw. It is also known, and has been confirmed to me from many sources, that should America attempt to carry out a mop-up operation in Mexico, it would face a war of long duration and would encounter many difficulties. Mexico's hatred for America is well founded and old. Of course, Mexico has no weapons in the modern sense, but the irregular bands are nonetheless adequately armed to create discomfort and unrest with the border states of America. Moreover, we are in a position to provide weapons and ammunition with U-boats, which should also be taken into account.[90]

The objective situation appeared favorable to Zimmermann's plans. After the Mexican government had rejected an American proposal for a conditional withdrawal from Mexico, renewed tensions had developed between the two countries. Moreover, the memorandum of the Mexican government of November 1916 and Aguilar's offer to provide U-boat bases in Mexico had aroused the hope in Zimmermann that the Mexican government would be prepared to make an alliance with Germany.

German diplomacy now had to solve the problem of how Carranza could be prompted to attack American territory. Kemnitz and Zimmermann saw one sure path: Germany would offer Mexico the return of Texas, New Mexico, and Arizona. Driven by the desire to take over these territories, Carranza would, in their estimation, immediately move against them, like a small child incapable of waiting any longer to claim his toy. "I don't think the Mexicans are in a position to take these areas, but I wanted to hold them out in advance to the Mexicans as a goal, so that they would not be content to inflict damage upon the Americans on their own soil, but would immediately create incidents in the border states forcing the Union to send troops there and not here."[91]

Zimmermann and Kemnitz understood that in the event of an attack on the United States, Carranza could not count on victory and would strike only if he received aid and above all a guarantee that the German Reich would not abandon him and that no peace would be concluded without him. Kemnitz thus offered Carranza a treaty of partnership that would also contain a clause on the joint conclusion of peace.

At the same time, the Foreign Office wanted to address a second problem with the help of Mexico. In the course of 1916, secret peace negotiations had taken place in Stockholm between the local German ambassador Lucius and the Japanese ambassador Ushida. The objective pursued by

German diplomacy in these negotiations was the conclusion of a separate peace with Japan and Tsarist Russia, in order to weaken the Allies decisively.[92] One of the reasons for the failure of these negotiations was Germany's excessive demands on Russia. Was it possible that German-American tensions could now lead to a resumption of the negotiations with Japan? Japan had used the world war in order to achieve a decisive position in China and had thus engendered real hostility in the United States. Would not Japan seize the opportunity of an American-Mexican war in order to dislodge the Americans from their positions in the Far East?

Ten months earlier, Zimmermann's predecessors had considered a Japanese-American war to be quite improbable and Secretary of State Jagow in response to a query in the Reichstag as to whether Japan had built eleven consulates in Mexico had answered: "On the whole, I don't think that Japanese policy is leading to a war with America. The Japanese have better things to do; they don't want to start two things at once."[93] Zimmermann and Kemnitz, at the beginning of 1917, did not share these reservations and decided to urge Mexico to offer an alliance to Japan. In a written justification of this move drafted a year and a half later, Kemnitz characterized it as the one means he had to reopen discussions with Japan, since his superiors had discouraged direct contacts. As "my repeated suggestions to approach Japan once again directly aroused no enthusiasm from my superiors, because they did not want to 'crawl' to Japan, I proposed pushing Mexico, which has had close relations with Japan for over ten years, to the fore."[94] He had not had much hope, he added, that Japan would join a German-Mexican alliance against the United States.

A German-Mexican-Japanese alliance against the United States would have somewhat strengthened Germany's position. What, however, would occur if Japan did not join? In that case, a treaty of partnership with Mexico would have brought Germany serious disadvantages in that the obligation contained in the treaty proposed to Carranza to make peace jointly would have tied the hands of German diplomats in any treaty negotiations with the United States and would have forced Germany to exact concessions for Carranza instead of for itself.

Kemnitz and Zimmermann found a way to avert these difficulties. "When, moreover, I refer in my instruction to 'joint waging of war' or 'joint conclusion of peace,'" Zimmermann explained in the Budget Committee of the Reichstag, "this is, of course, only a proposal, not a fixed agreement. I wanted to give our envoy an opportunity to offer Carranza something attractive, so that he would attack as quickly as possible, thus preventing American troops from being sent to the European continent. Offers and concluded treaties are two different things.

Obviously the representative would have limited himself initially to enticing Carranza and would not have concluded a definitive treaty, but would have initially consulted us, and then I would naturally have considered the specifics very carefully."[95] The German government would have signed such an agreement only "if Mexico had agreed to our suggestion to bring Japan into the alliance and if this three-way alliance had come about."[96]

Such reservations were not to be shared with Carranza. In the proposals which were finally submitted to the Mexican government, there was no mention of them. According to Kemnitz and Zimmermann's plan, Carranza was to attack the United States with complete faith in the German alliance proposal, and Germany would then have simply left him to his fate, except in the unlikely event that Japan entered the alliance. In other words: the alliance proposal was in reality a large-scale deceptive maneuver to incite Carranza to a suicidal attack on the United States.

The alliance proposal to Mexico worked out by Kemnitz met stiff resistance from the department chiefs in the Foreign Office.[97] The causes of their opposition are not fully known, but they were clearly aware of what devastating consequences for the German government could come about if the proposal were made known in the United States. Kemnitz met all objections with the argument that the offer, if it remained secret, "would create only benefits." "Not long ago, Mexico had offered us an alliance," he wrote later, referring to the Mexican memorandum of 3 November. "Assuming that we accepted the alliance, there would be two possible results: either Mexico would change its attitude and would refuse out of fear of the United States. Then our move would in any case strengthen the pro-German mood in Mexico, without having any other consequences. Or else Mexico accepts our proposal; in that case, considerable numbers of American troops would be tied up on the Rio Grande del Norte, without any practical obligations arising for us."[98]

Zimmermann was all enthusiasm. This enthusiasm was probably strengthened by the fact that some time before, the kaiser himself had suggested a German-Mexican alliance to him.[99] Zimmermann did not consider it necessary to consult Eckardt or Bernstorff in the United States. For reasons of time, it would moreover have been difficult for him to do so, since the proposal was to be made in Mexico on the day of the announcement of unlimited U-boat warfare. There is no evidence that he consulted with Chancellor Bethmann-Hollweg before sending his proposal.[100]

On 15 January, six days after the decision to begin unlimited U-boat warfare, the alliance proposal to Mexico, known since then as the "Zimmermann note," was in the Foreign Office ready to be sent. The final text read:

We intend to begin unlimited U-boat warfare on February 1. Attempts will nonetheless be made to keep America neutral.

In the event that we fail in this effort, we propose an alliance with Mexico on the following basis: joint pursuit of the war, joint conclusion of peace. Substantial financial support and an agreement on our part for Mexico to reconquer its former territories in Texas, New Mexico, and Arizona. Settlement on details left to Your Right Honorable Excellency.

Your Excellency shall present the above to the president in the strictest secrecy as soon as war with the United States has broken out, with the additional suggestion of offering Japan immediate entry to the alliance and simultaneously serving as mediators between us and Japan.

Please inform president that unlimited use of our U-boats now offers possibility of forcing England to negotiate peace within few months. *Confirm receipt. Zimmermann.*[101]

German diplomacy was now confronted with the question of how and through what channels the note was to be sent to Mexico. Zimmermann categorically refused to entrust the note to the Mexican envoy in Berlin. Aside from the fact that the envoy was at that time in Switzerland, he had an interpreter whom the Foreign Office did not completely trust. It is possible that Zimmermann no longer completely trusted the envoy himself.

It was initially decided to have the note conveyed to Mexico by the U-boat *Deutschland.* Zimmermann, however, quickly reversed this decision. A U-boat needed thirty days to cross the Atlantic and thus would not have arrived in Mexico before 16 February; it was absolutely necessary, however, that the note arrive in Mexico on 1 February, the day on which unlimited U-boat warfare was to begin.[102] Therefore, Zimmermann decided to send the note by telegram.

Apart from the rare German ships that succeeded in breaking the blockade and reaching America, the German government had only its large radio transmitter at Nauen for transmission of messages to its representatives abroad.[103] There was only one radio station in the United States that could receive messages transmitted from Nauen: the Sayville station, built by German technicians. Until 1915, the American government had permitted the transmission of coded telegrams to Germans in the United States. When it was learned that German U-boats had received instructions from Sayville, these communications were placed under censorship by the American navy. The navy thereafter permitted coded messages only in isolated instances.[104]

The German government had made attempts to find another way to transmit messages. It succeeded in persuading the neutral government of Sweden to send telegrams through its diplomatic representatives to the American continent. The Swedish envoy in Mexico, Cronholm, was very pro-German and an ally of Eckardt and most of the correspondence between Germany and Mexico was transmitted through him. When at the beginning of 1917 the Swedish legation in Mexico was to be closed down and transferred to Chile, the Foreign Office intervened with the Swedish government and actually succeeded in maintaining the mission in Mexico.[105]

At the end of 1916, another possibility for the transmission of messages to America opened up for the German government. Moved by the fear that one of the two belligerent parties in the European war could become too powerful, the American government had begun to mediate between them at the end of 1916.[106] Wilson initially requested that each side announce its war aims. For this purpose, Bernstorff demanded the possibility of being able to communicate directly with the Foreign Office. Wilson granted this request over the opposition of his secretary of state, and Bernstorff was permitted to send coded messages through the State Department and the American diplomatic representatives. The American government asked only for assurance from him and the Foreign Office that the messages were in fact related to Wilson's peace initiative.[107]

The Foreign Office decided to send the Zimmermann note through this channel because it was much faster than the Swedish route. At the same time, however, the Swedish route was to be used as well, for the Foreign Office wanted to proceed with certainty. On 16 January, the coded note was given to the American ambassador in Berlin, Gerard. "When the ambassador inquired," reads the report of the Foreign Office's special investigator on the disclosure of the Zimmermann note, "about the contents of the note, he was told it dealt with the reply of the Allies to President Wilson and that it contained instructions for the personal information of Count Bernstorff."[108] Zimmermann himself cynically remarked several weeks after the telegram had been sent, speaking to the Budget Committee of the Reichstag: "These telegrams dealt ostensibly with questions of general peace efforts. I added the telegram to another telegram of that nature."[109]

On 18 January, the American State Department gave the coded text of the Zimmermann note to Bernstorff, which he transmitted to Eckardt in Mexico one day later.

The Zimmermann note boomeranged. It became one of the biggest defeats of German diplomacy as a result of something with which no one in Berlin had reckoned: the fact that the British secret service was in possession of the German codes.

The story of the interception and deciphering of the Zimmermann telegram has become one of the great spy stories of all time. It is a classic tale which is included in all histories and manuals of espionage. It definitely deserves this reputation, yet the story as it has been told until now contains serious inaccuracies. The "classic" account of the telegram's interception goes as follows:

The intelligence service of the royal navy, which was under the command of one of the most capable men in this field, Admiral Reginald Hall, had great success in obtaining the key to German codes. In August 1914 Russian ships sank the German warship *Magdeburg* and salvaged a copy of the German naval code, which they then passed on to the intelligence service of the royal navy. At the beginning of 1915, the German government had sent an agent named Wassmuss to Persia to win that country over for a war against England. He was, however, captured and was to be handed over to the English. Wassmuss himself was able to escape, but had to leave behind his baggage, which fell into British hands and was sent to London. Hall had it searched, and in it was found a copy of code book 13040, the code used for communications with a large number of locations overseas, including Mexico.[110] Finally, Hall had obtained a copy of an important German code with the help of Alexander Szek, an employee of the Brussels radio transmitter then under German control. (The specific nature of the code in question was never disclosed.) Once he had handed over the code, Szek was murdered by British agents as a precautionary measure.

With the possession of these code books it was possible for the British naval secret service to decipher most German messages. The messages sent from Nauen were received by British stations and passed on to Hall. The American telegraph cable, through which Bernstorff's messages were sent, passed through British territory, and the British secret service was accordingly in a position to intercept these messages as well.

In this way, the Zimmermann note sent in a variation of code 13040 arrived in January 1917 in the hands of Sir Reginald Hall, who immediately recognized the important role the telegram could play in bringing the United States into the war on the side of the Allies. He was, however, confronted with a serious problem: how could he make public the telegram without letting the German authorities know that the British secret service possessed the codebooks and hence causing them to abandon the codes?

Hall decided to release the contents of the telegram only after covering up the fact that the British government had decoded it. To this end, he needed a copy of the telegram Bernstorff had sent from Washington to Eckardt in Mexico and which clearly differed in minor respects from the original. In this way, he hoped to give the impression that the Zimmermann note had been intercepted on the American continent and not en route to America.[111]

Hall quickly obtained a copy of the telegram from Bernstorff to Eckardt. Hall's former associate and later biographer, Sir William James, explains how this was accomplished. Hall had requested one of his agents in Mexico to obtain a copy of the telegram. The agent contacted an employee of the Mexican wire service, who in turn had a friend who owned a publishing company. The latter one day discovered that a worker at his press was producing counterfeit money, an act punishable by death. The owner of the press hid some of the plates which he had found and told the story to his friend, the employee of the wire service, to get his advice. Meanwhile, the worker who was making the counterfeit money had returned to the press. When he realized that he had been discovered, he turned the tables and denounced his employer to the police for counterfeiting. The owner of the press was immediately arrested and sentenced to be shot. His friend then turned to Hall's agent, who brought about an intervention by the British government. The intervention succeeded, and the owner of the press was released. In thanks, the employee of the wire service provided the British agent with a copy of Bernstorff's telegram to Eckardt.[112]

Hall received this copy in the second half of February. Until that time, he had kept the telegram a secret,[113] not only in the desire to conceal his possession of the code, but also in the hope that disclosure of the telegram would not be necessary to prompt U.S. entry into the war. More precisely, the British government hoped that unlimited U-boat warfare by Germany would achieve this objective. That hope, however, was not to be realized. The American government did break off diplomatic relations with the German Reich, but the anticipated declaration of war did not come about.

At this point Hall decided to publish the Zimmermann note, in the hope of bringing about American participation in the war. On 24 February, he gave the text of the note to the Foreign Office, which immediately passed it on to the American ambassador in London, Walter Page.

These accounts are all based on one source: Sir Reginald Hall himself. During the war he told this story to Ambassador Page, and in 1921 he repeated it to Burton J. Hendricks, an American author who was writing a biography of Page.[114]

Edward Bell, the diplomat responsible for security matters in the U.S. embassy in London and for liaison with Hall, characterized Hendrick's account as being "stiff with inaccuracies." According to Bell, the story that the British had been able to decipher the telegram sent by code 13040 from Berlin to Washington in January 1917 was untrue. The British had intercepted a coded message from Berlin at the time but could do nothing with it because it was not sent by code 13040, which they knew, but by a newer cipher they had been unable to crack. It was a new and secret code the Germans had relayed to their embassy in Washington through their U-boat *Deutschland*. "In the preceding summer the Bosh had sent out a new table for the cipher code to B. in Washington by the submarine *Deutschland*. It hadn't been used much and Blinker's [this was Hall's nickname] lads had been able to do little with it, so when this message went through London in this new code it yielded very little to their efforts." Thus the pendants to this story—Hall sitting on the telegram for many weeks from mid-January to the end of February, the special agents sent to Mexico to obtain the text wired by Bernstorff to Eckardt—were also untrue.

What is true is that the telegraph office in Mexico was the source of the telegram. Fortunately for the British, Eckardt in Mexico had not received the new code and Bernstorff "had to decode and recode it in the old book." A British agent working in the telegraph office in Mexico sent it to London, without realizing what he was transmitting.

> Blinker had a plant in the telegraph office in Mexico who sent back copies of all cipher messages which passed through for Eckardt, as opportunity offered. This message was sent in January and a copy of the cipher text, in the form in which B. sent it to Eckardt, reached Blinker towards the end of February. He was able to uncork it, as it was in the old code, and this not only gave him the message itself but also, by comparison with the text that went through London, a start on the new code. It was a kind of Rosetta Stone.

Thus, it was only the Zimmermann telegram that revealed the Germans' most secret code—0075—to the British. Bell continues:

> Blinker was torn between reluctance to give away the fact that he could read the Bosh signals and the desire to pin something good right on them. He took me into his confidence and I pressed for the latter. Finally it was agreed that Mr. Balfour (then Secretary for Foreign Affairs but previously First Lord and consequently acquainted with Reggie's performances) should give a translation to Mr. Page with assurances that it was the goods, as being a stronger move than Reggie's giving it to me. Remember, this was our first offense. Afterwards we dispensed with intermediaries.

The above statements by Bell were contained in a bitter letter he sent to State Department officials in 1921. In that year Hendricks had asked the department's permission to publish his version of the story of the Zimmermann telegram. The department consulted Bell, who pleaded for suppression of the story. He accused "Blinker" of having "spilt the beans," of committing a "breach of confidence." He felt that the main reason for this revelation was British resentment at not getting credit for this espionage feat.

There were two sound reasons why the world should have been led to believe at the time that it was the Americans who had done the trick:

First, to put the Bosh off the scent. It wouldn't have done at all for him to have known how fly the English were as that might have put ideas in his head (of which he remained innocent to the last) about naval radio messages and the Berlin-Madrid W/T. Second, to throw a scare into him about ourselves; to put the wind up him and cramp his style in the U.S. In both these respects the vaccination worked like a charm, and the world rang with the praise of our wonderful Secret Service. Do you remember how for months afterwards the Treasury and Justice each swore that they had done the job and tried to put each other in the Ananias Club? And Pennoyer's hypothesis that Mrs. Warren Robbins must have worked it in B.A.? (this particularly pleased Blinker).

It was always a most jealously guarded secret and now it has been revealed. It makes no difference, perhaps, to Reggie and the F.O. now; and the latter were always furious that we got the (undeserved) credit.[115]

In line with how a good spy should behave, Hall remained deceptive to the end and tried never to reveal to the Germans that in addition to code 13040, their most secret code 0075 had been cracked.

Beyond these facts, Bell wrote, "the resultant sensation is history." "Mr. Page came back from his interview with Balfour with the translation in his hand and blood in his eye, and Eugene and I sat up all night getting off the telegram." Page immediately gave the telegram to the State Department in Washington. He also recounted how the English had acquired the note, but urgently asked that absolutely nothing be revealed. "This system," wrote Page, "has hitherto been a jealously guarded secret and is only divulged now to you by the British Government in view of the extraordinary circumstances and their friendly feeling toward the United States. They earnestly request that you will keep the source of your information and the British Government's method of obtaining it profoundly secret, but they put no prohibition on the publication of Zimmermann's telegram itself."[116]

Secretary of State Lansing had just left on a trip when Page's report with the note arrived. His assistant, Polk, went immediately to Wilson, who showed "great indignation." This indignation increased still more when Lansing told him a day later how the telegram had been conveyed.[117]

The Zimmermann telegram came into Wilson's hands at an opportune moment. He was just in the process of asking Congress for measures against Germany's unlimited U-boat warfare. These involved the arming of merchant vessels and the right "to use every other means and method, which are necessary and appropriate to protect our ships and our people . . . on the seas."[118] The opponents of American entry into the war raised a storm against these measures, and the latter proposal was attacked with particular severity. Wilson thus had the Zimmermann telegram published one day before the planned debate (1 March). Its publication, however, did not take the form of a government communiqué, but of a report from the Associated Press news service.

The note was immediately denounced as a fraud by Wilson's opponents. The leading German propagandist in the United States, the German-American George Sylvester Viereck, wrote to Hearst on the same day:

> The alleged letter of Alfred Zimmermann published today is obviously faked; it is impossible to believe that the German foreign secretary would place his name under such a preposterous document. The letter is unquestionably a brazen forgery planted by British agents to stampede us into an alliance and to justify violations of the Monroe doctrine by Great Britain. This impudent hoax is made public simultaneously with frantic appeals of allied premiers enjoining the United States to enter the war. If Germany were plotting against us she would hardly adopt so clumsy a method. The *realpolitiker* of the Wilhelmstrasse would never offer an alliance based on such ludicrous propositions as the conquest by Mexico of American territory. The creaking of the machinery of the British propaganda is clearly perceptible; the intention is of course to arouse the war spirit of the peace-loving west and to overwhelm the pacifists in every part of the country.

Hearst agreed with this interpretation and characterized the note as "in all probability an absolute fake and forgery, prepared by a very unscrupulous Attorney General's very unscrupulous department. Everybody knows that the secret police are the most conscienceless manufacturers of forged evidence in the world."[119]

To counter these assertions, Republican Senator Lodge, who favored an American declaration of war against Germany, introduced a resolution in the Senate in which the government was called upon to take a position on the note. Wilson and Lansing had foreseen such a development. If the American government was to give an absolute guarantee of its authenticity, the note would have to have been deciphered by American authorities on American territory. To this end, the British government was asked to place the German code book at the disposal of the United States. The English, however, did not wish to comply. "The question," wrote Page, "of our having a copy of the code has been taken up, but there appear to be serious difficulties. I am told actual code would be of no use to us as it was never used straight, but with a great number of variations which are known to only one or two experts here. They cannot be spared to go to America."[120]

A clever solution was found. The American government acquired the coded text sent by Bernstorff to Eckardt from the archives of Western Union and sent it immediately to the American embassy in London. The

British secret service gave the code book on a temporary basis to the United States security official, Bell, who decoded the telegram with the help of British aides. Thus the deciphering had been accomplished by an American and it had been accomplished on American territory, the American embassy.[121]

On 2 March, Wilson confirmed the authenticity of the note and stated that the American government was in possession of the text. This statement, however, did not silence the doubtful, who continued to denounce the note as a falsification. The American government was thus in a difficult position, for it could reveal nothing about the origins of the decoding without revealing British possession of the German code book. Lansing limited himself to the statement that any further information on the origin of the note would endanger human life. In this way, he hoped to confuse the German government and to lead the Germans to believe that the note had been revealed by a traitor.[122]

In spite of this statement, Hearst continued to denounce the note as a fraud, and several senators as well challenged its authenticity.[123] At that moment, the American government's worries were relieved with a single stroke: on 3 March, Zimmermann publicly confirmed the contents of the note. "I had expected," Lansing later wrote in his memoirs, "that Zimmermann would repudiate the message and would challenge us to show proof of its authenticity. That would have been the shrewdest move, because it would always have been possible to raise the accusation that the entire affair had been a fraud aimed at pushing through the law on the arming of merchant ships . . . . Many Americans, both those sympathizing with the Allies and those sympathizing with Germany, would have believed that . . . . With the greatest surprise and tremendous joy I read that Zimmermann . . . had admitted the authenticity of the message."[124] Not only was Zimmermann's confirmation a devastating blow for all those in the United States who had challenged the authenticity of the note, but the note itself became a highly effective propaganda instrument in the hands of those who favored U.S. entry into the war. "As soon as I saw it," wrote Senator Lodge, "I knew that it would arouse the country more than any other event."[125] Lodge was right. The note had its greatest impact in precisely those areas of the United States where isolationism and thus opposition to U.S. involvement in the war were particularly strong: the Southwest. People in this area found the German offer to Mexico of annexation of Texas, Arizona, and New Mexico especially offensive. "The Zimmermann note put an end to all pro-German sentiment in the U.S.," one of Germany's main propagandists in the United States noted.[126]

After the disclosure of the note, the Japanese Foreign Ministry immediately characterized the German proposal as totally unacceptable.

The deputy to the Japanese foreign minister, Baron Shidehara, stated: "We are quite surprised to hear of the German proposal. We don't understand how Germany could think that we would allow ourselves to be drawn into a war against the United States by the mere request of Mexico. It is as ridiculous as that. I hardly need to state that Japan will remain true to its allies."[127] The secretary of the Japanese embassy in Stockholm also told a German agent: "It is quite incomprehensible how Germany could have intended to reach an agreement with Japan through Mexico. It would be out of the realm of possibility for Japan to tolerate the mediation of Mexico in such an agreement."[128]

The Zimmermann note arrived in Mexico at an unfavorable moment for German diplomacy: just as the U.S. punitive expedition began to leave the country and Mexican-American tensions began to subside.

The Mexican government was nonetheless in no way convinced that the danger of an American invasion had vanished; quite the contrary. An Argentine diplomat in Mexico reported that Foreign Minister Aguilar had explained to him several days before the disclosure of the Zimmermann note that the Mexican government "was expecting the outbreak of a war between Germany and the United States, and that such a war would pull in Mexico against the United States. The Mexican government knows that the Germans would attempt to destroy the oil fields. That would have as a consequence the landing of British or American armed forces, whom the Mexican government is determined to resist."[129] These fears were obviously far from being unfounded. After the United States entered the war, the oil companies actually demanded that the American government occupy the oil fields with troops.[130] Carranza neither would nor could have accepted such an occupation.

The fear of the outbreak of a Mexican-American war and the desire to be able to count on German aid in the event of an American invasion of Mexico may have prompted Carranza to tender a series of proposals, which would have greatly favored Germany, to the neutral American states. Thus he proposed that all deliveries of armaments to belligerent parties be forbidden, thereby forcing them to make peace.[131] Since Germany, because of the British blockade, obtained very few goods from neutral countries, such a measure would have harmed her far less than the Allies. Thus Eckardt hailed Carranza's proposals, which were rejected by the United States.

Carranza's efforts show that the Mexican government, both before and after the withdrawal of American troops from Mexico, did not discount the possibility of a Mexican-American war. Thus the Mexican military leaders prepared for such an eventuality, in which they assumed the participation of Japan on the side of Mexico and Germany. On 2 February, or more than two weeks before Eckardt discussed the question of an alliance with Aguilar, José Flores, an agent of the Mexican Ministry of Defense in the United States, reported that after a visit to California, Arizona, New Mexico, and other states, he had come to the conclusion "that the situation is very favorable for us." Japanese and Mexicans had at their disposal three hundred thousand firearms and adequate ammunition. "At the moment when war is declared against Germany, we will be able to count on at least two hundred thousand Germans in the United States and throughout South America."[132]

All these considerations make it understandable that the Mexican government did not dismiss the Zimmermann note out of hand as a phantasm. The response of the Mexicans was based less on the German "promises" than on the very real fear of an American invasion.

Eckardt explained the contents of the note on 20 February to Cándido Aguilar, Mexico's secretary of foreign affairs. In the telegram itself, he had been instructed to do this only in the event of the outbreak of war between Germany and the United States. On 8 February, Zimmermann changed these instructions. "If there is no danger," he wrote to Eckardt, "that the secret will be betrayed to the United States, it would be desirable for you to speak to the president without delay about the question of an alliance. The final conclusion of an alliance would nonetheless depend on the outbreak of a war between Germany and the United States. The president could still sound out Japan now on his own initiative."[133]

After Eckardt had conveyed the offer of an alliance, Aguilar, in the view of the German envoy, appeared to be "not in the least reticent."[134] Eckardt reported that Aguilar, whose attitude he characterized as sympathetic, had discussed this question with the Japanese envoy in Mexico for an hour.[135] Eckardt was nevertheless unable to report any results from that meeting.

The authors of the Zimmermann note, especially Kemnitz, had hoped that the Mexican government would urge Japan to form an alliance with Germany against the United States. But Aguilar was in no way prepared to take such a course of action. In two separate talks with Kintai Arai, a low-level official of the Japanese consulate in Mexico, he broached only the question of how Japan would conduct itself in the event of a German-American war. When the official made it clear to him that Japan had no intention of changing sides and informed him that Japan would maintain its previous attitude toward the Allies, Aguilar backed away from further discussions of this kind, to say nothing of any proposal for an alliance between Japan, Germany, and Mexico.

Arai initially considered this conversation so insignificant that he did not even report it to the Foreign Ministry in Tokyo. Only after the publication of the Zimmermann note did the Japanese representative in Mexico understand Aguilar's intent in these discussions. Two months later, in a discussion with chargé d'affaires Ohta, the Mexican foreign secretary admitted that he had in fact wished to sound out Japan and that he had come to the conclusion that Japan would never come over to the German side.[136]

There are no precise records of the Mexican government's reaction to the Zimmermann note, but some conclusions can be drawn from available sources.

Shortly before his death, Aguilar told a professor of the University of Veracruz, Xavier Tavera, that he had welcomed the proposal, but that Carranza had been opposed; Carranza, however, had told him not to give any final refusal to Eckardt.[137] According to another report, Carranza had commissioned a high-ranking officer, Díaz Babio, to examine the proposal, after which he adopted a negative attitude. Díaz Babio consulted with his friend López Portillo y Weber, and both men came to the conclusion that the alliance was unworkable. Their most important argument was that Germany would never be in a position to insure adequate supplies of arms and ammunition to the Mexican army; Germany had too few merchant U-boats of the *Deutschland* type, the only vessels useful for the transport of arms, quite aside from the fact that the American fleet would prevent the landing of U-boats in Mexico. López Portillo y Weber further pointed out that the repossession of Texas, Arizona, and New Mexico would be a permanent source of conflict with the United States and would have to lead to a new war. Moreover, the power of the Americans living there would be so great that they would quickly acquire a decisive influence in Mexico, so that "I would not know whether we had annexed them or they had annexed us."[138]

An intimate colleague of Secretary of War Obregón told an American secret agent that Carranza had called a cabinet meeting to discuss the problems raised by the note. Obregón had apparently raised strong protests at this meeting against accepting the German proposals. He argued that Mexico's only salvation lay in "preserving the friendship and moral support of the United States." He restated his generally anti-American attitude, but explained at the same time that "Mexico's salvation depends on the Americans."[139]

All these reports show that Carranza did not want to rush into a war with the United States, and certainly not on the basis of a German offer of Texas, Arizona, and New Mexico. But it can also be surmised from these indications that he wanted to keep Germany in reserve for the eventuality, which Carranza considered a probable one, of an American attack on the Mexican oil fields. These considerations also explain his subsequent behavior with regard to the Zimmermann note. He did not immediately reject the proposal for an alliance, but discussed with the German minister the concrete forms of aid which Germany could provide to Mexico in the event of war.[140]

On 26 February, two days before the publication of the note, Fletcher, the American ambassador in Mexico, received instructions to disclose the contents of the note to the Mexican government and to ask the Mexicans to repudiate it unequivocally. He spoke initially with Foreign Minister Aguilar, who explained to him that he knew of no such note. To make his assertion more credible, Aguilar added that Eckardt had impatiently asked him several times about the date of Carranza's return. This took place six days after he had discussed the note with Eckardt![141] Aguilar's ties to the German were, however, hardly so close that he would have told Eckardt that the Americans were aware of the entire affair.

After the publication of the note, the Mexican government continued this policy. Both in the declarations of leading politicians and in the press, it was asserted that Mexico had never been approached by Germany with the offer of an alliance.[142] Eckardt also denied everything. Fletcher was then told to discuss the entire affair with Carranza himself, and to do this precisely on the occasion of the presentation of his credentials.

There are several accounts of this discussion, and at least two of them came from Aguilar himself. Thus, shortly before his death, he told his former colleague Isidro Fabela that upon receipt of the Zimmermann note, he had immediately grasped its pernicious quality and had not even shown it to Carranza. He had then allegedly been informed that Fletcher was going to break off diplomatic relations with Mexico or even threaten Mexico with a declaration of war if Carranza refused to break off diplomatic relations with Germany as proof that he had no intentions of allying with Germany. Aguilar further explained that he had kept Fletcher from presenting his credentials to Carranza as long as possible in order to give tempers a chance to cool. When Fletcher presented his credentials to Carranza in Guadalajara several days later, he gave him the American demands. Carranza explained to him that he had received no offer of an alliance from Germany and that there was no reason for breaking off relations with Germany. Mexico had declared its neutrality and he saw no reason why Mexico's neutral attitude should push the United States to break off relations. Fletcher was convinced and withdrew the demands.[143]

In a report Aguilar gave Eckardt, a completely different version emerges. "'Give me a sincere assurance of friendship, and we will withdraw the troops, which we need in Europe,' Mr. Fletcher told him. The answer was: 'It has not yet been made possible for the Mexican people to have friendly feelings for the United States.'"[144]

Fletcher himself gave a third account in his report to the American government. In a long discussion with the Mexican president, he said, he had attempted to get Carranza to repudiate clearly the German alliance proposal. When Carranza complained that the American government had imposed an arms embargo against Mexico, Fletcher replied that "as long as our people, or a substantial portion of it, had any doubts on this question [Mexico's attitude toward the German alliance proposal], it would be very difficult for the president to permit the export of arms to Mexico."[145] Carranza did not, however, elaborate any further but merely asserted that he had received no proposal for an alliance from Germany and that he therefore needed to take no public stand on such an offer. He stated at the same time that Mexico had no interest in the extension of the war across the Atlantic.[146]

One day later, Fletcher began a new tack. "I drafted a pencil memorandum in Spanish...to be used as the basis of a telegram to the Department, and it concluded with the categorical statement that in case Germany should propose an alliance to Mexico it would be rejected. I gave this memorandum to General Aguilar with the request that he show it to the First Chief. He did so and later, after we had left Mr. Carranza's train, he gave me another draft in his own handwriting changing somewhat the phraseology of my draft but omitting altogether the categorical statement that they would refuse an alliance if proposed by Germany."[147] To Fletcher's question about the omission, Carranza explained that he could take no position on a proposal which had not been made to him. Moreover, his proposals for an embargo against the belligerent powers would have to be discussed first.[148]

Secretary of War Obregón showed himself less restrained than Carranza. He told Fletcher immediately after the disclosure of the note that he "considered the proposal of a Mexican alliance with Germany absurd and believed that the Mexican government should devote itself, after six years of civil war, to reorganizing and satisfying the needs of the country, and that it would be very stupid for Mexico to become involved with a European power which would one day demand payment for services rendered."[149]

Carranza and Aguilar did not repudiate the note. Aguilar even utilized it for a clever propaganda trick by starting the rumor that the entire affair was a fabrication of the Mexican government to put pressure on the United States.[150] After Carranza had become increasingly convinced that there was no immediate danger of an American invasion, he rejected the proposal for an alliance on 14 April in a secret conversation with the German minister. In doing so, he made an effort not to present this rejection as final, so that in the event that war with the United States did break out, he would be able to count on German support. "The president stated," Eckardt wired to Berlin, "that he intended to remain neutral under all circumstances. If Mexico were nevertheless to be dragged into the war, we would have to see." He said, "the alliance has been bungled through its 'premature disclosure,' but would become necessary later."[151]

## The German Reaction to the Zimmermann Telegram

The disclosure of the note led in Germany to sharp attacks on Zimmermann. They came from the right and from the left, and the motivations for them were very different from each other. The right and the majority of the center conducted these attacks on the private level and behind the scenes, while the Social Democrats attacked Zimmermann in the Budget Committee of the Reichstag, in the Reichstag itself, and in the press.

The military and the extreme right, which considered U.S. intervention in the war to be of little significance, repudiated the Zimmermann note for chauvinistic reasons. They attacked Zimmermann for having dealt with Carranza on a basis of equality and not as a leader of bandits. "In the office of the navy," the Austrian ambassador in Berlin reported, "one of the comments to be heard was that no treaties can be made with a Carranza. You merely slip gold into one of his hands and a knife into the other, and he knows what to do."[152]

Even sharper were attacks from protagonists of the "third way," that is the people who were hoping to wage unlimited U-boat warfare without pulling the United States into the war. They were for the most part to be found in the ranks of the center. The Zimmermann note appeared to shatter their hopes effectively. The chairman of the Federal Council, Lerchenfeldt, wrote disapprovingly: "In my opinion, the affair is to be deplored as a symptom that in spite of all their bad experiences, the people in the Foreign Office cannot give up working with obviously worthless and petty methods. How much the agitation in England, Ireland, Morocco, and among the Senussis have cost us in men and in money, without producing any results—how unfavorably the attacks on munitions factories in America have worked for us and how meager was the result. These examples might still have warded them off from an action in Mexico."[153] Matthias Erzberger explained to the Austrian ambassador in Berlin: "If this note had not been sent, the Foreign Office might later have been criticized because of this omission, now it is said that the whole thing had been nonsense, that one makes no alliances with bandits, but at any rate this attempt should never have become publicly known, for that is the final stupidity."[154]

Even sharper was the reaction of the elements who were opposed to U-boat warfare. This included a section of the bourgeoisie which had close economic ties to American capital. Their analysis was expressed quite clearly by Walter Rathenau. "For us to hand Texas and Arizona over to Carranza," he wrote to General von Seeckt, "and to offer Japan an alliance in return for Kiouchou, with the mediation of a brigand to boot, is too sad even to laugh about."[155]

In the Budget Committee of the Reichstag and especially in the Reichstag session of 5 March, these forces held back. Prior to the meeting of the Budget Committee on 5 March, according to reports by Lerchenfeldt, Bavaria's minister to the federal government, they had "agreed to cause Secretary of State Zimmermann no difficulties over the affair, even though no one actually agreed with the secretary's move, which was considered rather unfortunate."[156] In principle, there was support for the note itself, and criticism was aimed only at its disclosure.

The deputy of the National Liberal Party, Prince zu Schöneich-Carolath, explicitly approved the Zimmermann note in the Budget Committee of the Reichstag. "Why," he asked, "should Germany not attempt to create difficulties for the United States with Mexico? The moral qualities of the Mexican president are in such circumstances a matter of indifference to us. It was simply a question of our attempt—strictly in view of the war situation—to tie up the United States and to divert its energies as best we could by creating difficulties for them."[157] He did not take seriously Japanese declarations that Japan had no intention of participating in such an alliance. He stated: "The spoken word has very little value in Japan. The Japanese are the biggest liars in the world. It is considered elegant there never to tell the truth, not even within the family. It is a method of education."[158] He only complained that the note had not been transmitted orally but in writing. Schöneich-Carolath was speaking in the name of the National Liberal faction, "but opinion even in his own party does not appear to support him," Lerchenfeldt reported, "as I was able to glean from a discussion with another National Liberal deputy who was energetically deploring the note as a very clumsy job."[159]

In a similar tone to the remarks of Schöneich-Carolath was the statement of Deputy Gröber of the right wing of the Center Party. "One could scarcely find a better method," he stated, "than sending a clever fox into the enemy's rear to nip at his legs."[160] He pointed out the useless efforts of the American army to capture Villa and asserted: "A modern army capable of defeating Mexico cannot be assembled in America in the foreseeable future." He concluded with the words: "The secretary of state has pursued a proper objective with regard to American policy, even if the form he chose was an unfortunate one. There is no basis for criticizing the Foreign Office."[161]

With the exception of David, who represented the government socialists, and Ledebour as representative of the Social Democratic caucus, the other deputies of the Budget Committee spoke in general on behalf of Zimmermann's move. Gothein criticized only the offer made to Carranza of Texas, Arizona, and New Mexico, which could stir up public opinion against Germany in the United States, whereas Bruhn considered the possibility of winning over Japan through Mexico to be extremely unlikely.[162]

The situation was similar in the press. Most newspapers hailed the German proposal for an alliance. The statement of the *National-Zeitung* was typical: "Mexico is quite capable of mobilizing five hundred thousand men in an emergency, while the United States has previously been incapable of raising even a third of that number." It went on to state that "The mood in Mexico during the war was extremely pro-German. The students, for example, wore emblems with little pictures of Kaiser Wilhelm in their buttonholes to show their sympathies. The mood was such that it can be said that people were generally expecting an alliance with Germany."[163] The *Kölnische Zeitung* sounded a similar note. On 3 March 1917, it wrote: "It was simply self-evident that we would make an effort, in the event of a war with the United States, to bring the natural enemies of the Union over to our side and to prompt them to attack."

The Zimmermann note was opposed above all by those forces that had already opposed unlimited U-boat warfare. These included the groups of the commercial bourgeoisie with links to the United States, the right-wing Socialists who feared that an expansion of the war would cause them to lose control over their supporters, the centrists, and, finally but most of all, the left-wing Socialists, who were fighting against the war as a whole.

The representative of the left-wing Social Democratic caucus in the Budget Committee of the Reichstag, Ledebour, directed sharp attacks against Zimmermann, which were nevertheless more of a tactical than a fundamental nature. He considered it acceptable "for the Foreign Office to look for allies against America," but did not see Carranza as a reliable ally, since he was only "the most successful bandit leader." He noted ironically that the alliance was hardly necessary, in view of the constant assertions by the navy that the United States represented no danger for Germany. "Secretary of State Capelle, on an earlier occasion, did not consider American troop transports crossing the Atlantic to be very dangerous, but noted ironically that they would be excellent targets for our U-boats." Ledebour criticized the offer of Texas, Arizona, and New Mexico, since in his opinion it violated the right of popular self-determination. He expressed the view that Japan had no intention of turning against the United States. "The Secretary of Internal Affairs," he concluded, "has indicated earlier that at this time nothing is to be gained through idealism, but that we must engage in practical politics. However, with the practical politics currently being employed by the government, we will only get more deeply into trouble."[164]

Indignation over the calculated deception of Carranza or a principled repudiation of the dispatch as an extension of the war policy was not to be heard from Ledebour. By contrast, the *Leipziger Volkszeitung,* which represented the radical wing of the Socialists, came out decisively on the same day against the notion put forward by governmental authorities that the note had been a preventive measure. "We cannot accept it. And the effect, which is currently making itself felt in the rapid intensification of a belligerent mood in America and in the possibility of an extension of the world war to the American continent as well, necessarily confirms our opinion, like that of all opponents of the war, that with the methods of state policy used up to now, which are being so drastically illustrated by the German-Mexican affair, only a further intensification of the war and a further extension of the world conflagration is to be attained. The conclusions to be drawn are self-evident."[165] Franz Mehring, a member of the Spartacus group who was campaigning for a by-election to the Reichstag, gave the Zimmermann note an important place in his electoral campaign.[166]

David, who represented the right-wing Social Democrats in the Budget Committee of the Reichstag, was far more moderate in his criticism than Ledebour. He attacked neither the alliance as such nor the general attitude which Zimmermann had manifested. "There is no need," he stated, "to see the affair from the ethical viewpoint, for such a viewpoint is, as we have seen from the war, no longer decisive in such matters."[167] He criticized the clumsiness of the Foreign Office, which he held responsible for the disclosure of the note, and did not believe that Japan would change its orientation toward the world war on Mexico's account. David expressed doubts about Mexico's capabilities as an ally and viewed in particular the proposal to separate Texas, Arizona, and New Mexico from the United States as unrealizable and with regard to public opinion in the United States as harmful. "The outlook for preserving peace with America was not very great after the opening of intensified U-boat warfare in any case. As a result of our activities in Mexico, it has sunk to zero."[168] This criticism won him the gratitude of Zimmermann: "I am thankful to Herr Deputy David for the calm and objective fashion in which he criticized my actions."[169]

The Zimmermann note, which was seen as an additional war provocation, aroused such indignation in a large part of the German working class that two weeks later at a public session of the Reichstag, Scheidemann felt compelled to speak far more energetically against it than his colleagues in the Reichstag had done. He characterized the note on this occasion as "a part of that domain of foreign policy for which the Social Democratic faction disclaims all responsibility."[170]

Aside from the Social Democratic press, only a few newspapers came out against the note. The *Berliner Tageblatt,* which represented the circles of the German bourgeoisie with close ties to the United States, stated on 5 March 1917 that "no gem of statesmanship has been lost between Berlin and Mexico."[171] The only right-wing politician who openly expressed his unease over the note was Count Reventlow, the leading columnist for the conservative *Deutsche Tageszeitung* and close to the Pan-Germanists. Reventlow, a partisan of unlimited U-boat warfare, formulated his criticism in such a way that he could take his distance from it at any moment. "We see in this development and its possible consequences nothing which makes us pessimistic. All those, however, who are placing great hopes on the divided mood in the United States for the preservation of peace, will not be able to avoid deep regret at this turn of events and a sense of injustice that, precisely at this moment, the government is pursuing a policy with regard to Mexico that can only be called a 'match in the powderkeg' policy."[172]

This criticism irked the *Berliner Tagesblatt.* On 5 March 1917, the newspaper wrote sarcastically: "It is a little disconcerting to hear all this from Count Reventlow, who places so little value on German-American relations, and who touched the match to the powderkeg with such boldness. This recalls the scene in *Wallenstein's Death,* where Octavio Piccolomini says to Butler after the murder 'I raise my hand of honor' and assures him painfully 'that I am not guilty of this horrible deed.'"

Reventlow had published his criticism of the Zimmermann note on 3 March, or immediately after its disclosure and before the right-wing parties had settled on their tactics. Their decision to support Zimmermann in this question and the sarcastic criticism of the *Berliner Tageblatt* prompted Reventlow to make the retreat he had left open for himself. As early as 6 March, he wrote in the *Deutsche Tageszeitung* that his criticism had only expressed the opinion of those "who were placing great hopes on the maintenance of peace with the United States," and that he himself nonetheless supported the note completely. Reventlow, in his criticism, had nonetheless only anticipated the standpoint of the navy and of the extreme right. In light of the fiasco of the unlimited U-boat warfare they had advocated, they stated later that it was the Zimmermann note and not the U-boat warfare which bore the brunt of the responsibility for the U.S. entry into the war.[173]

Zimmermann even had to account for himself to the kaiser. "His Majesty Kaiser Wilhelm," reported the Austrian ambassador in Berlin, "has called the secretary of state, who was received today, to account for this affair, and Herr Zimmermann gave the brief report cited above to His

Majesty the Kaiser in a fairly long presentation." In so doing, however, Zimmermann was able to counter some of Wilhelm II's reproaches with the reminder that the alliance proposal was in keeping with the kaiser's own suggestions. "The secretary of state asserted," continued Ambassador Hohenlohe, "that it had been his self-evident duty to attempt to secure Mexican aid for the eventuality of war, which the kaiser himself had previously suggested to him."[174]

In his public defense, Zimmermann could have denied the entire affair and presented it as a fabrication by the enemy. That would undoubtedly have been the most clever maneuver. We have no more detailed information on why he admitted that the note was authentic; he told the kaiser only that "he had initially considered it the best policy to publish the actual contents himself before it was distorted by the enemy and neutral press."[175] Two reasons were probably decisive for his actions. On the one hand, it might be attributed to the fact that he did not know how the note had been intercepted. He thought that it had been divulged in the United States and that the American government would be able to produce handwritten proof in the event of his denial. On the other hand, he had no idea of the potential effect of the note in the United States. On the contrary, in his remarks in the Budget Committee of the Reichstag, he went as far as to find positive aspects to the discovery of the note. He stated there "that it will quickly occur to the American people what a dangerous position they could place themselves in by waging war against us."[176] He was generally inclined, in Lerchenfeldt's words, toward a "vigorous optimism" where the United States was concerned. Characteristic of this is a statement he made immediately before relations with the United States were broken off. "On the very evening before relations were broken off," Lerchenfeldt wrote, "the secretary of state complained about the terrible pessimism of these people who were warning against America's hostility, and said: 'Don't worry, I'll straighten things out with Jimmy [American Ambassador James Gerard].'"[177]

His defense tactic pushed Zimmermann in three directions: he treated the impact of the note lightly, he attempted to place the responsibility for its disclosure on Bernstorff, and he continued to do everything possible to bring about an alliance with Mexico. Zimmermann's attitude and that of the Foreign Office were characterized on 4 March by the Austrian ambassador in Berlin with the words: "In the Foreign Office it was explained to me that the publication of the alliance proposal with Mexico was very irritating, but that on the whole the entire affair was relatively unimportant, because everybody would have to recognize that Germany would attempt to find allies for a possible war with America by whatever means."[178]

Zimmermann also expressed himself in these terms before the Budget Committee of the Reichstag. "Moreover, President Wilson can hardly be surprised," he stated, "that, if he declares war against us, we use every possible means of making difficulties for him." He backed up his argument with the remark that the American journalists in Berlin had shown complete understanding for his viewpoint: "In the statements they had already drawn up, it was noted that no one could find fault with the note, as it was to be delivered after war had broken out."[179]

The tenor of the semi-official press was similar. The question of Texas, Arizona, and New Mexico was avoided. Zimmermann attempted to justify this offer with the explanation that its only goals had been to incite Carranza to attack American territory. He added moreover: "The deputy then said that it would have the effect of a hammer blow on public opinion in America if it is learned that we are offering American territory to the Mexicans. We offered the Mexicans only an *agreement,* which they could take or leave. That is a major difference."[180]

An interview which was prepared beforehand for Bernstorff to be conducted by a journalist upon his arrival in Copenhagen ran along similar lines. According to the draft prepared by the Foreign Office, Bernstorff was to have stated: "One thing is clear, that a terrible act of disloyalty and a violation of trust and good faith in relations among peoples has taken place . . . . I am convinced that if it were the German way to publish correspondence with countries having peaceful relations with us, we would have found things in some of the writings of the American government destined for abroad that would have mixed rather badly with President Wilson's pathetic talk of peace."[181]

These lines even struck Kemnitz as excessive, and he had them omitted.[182] Bernstorff then stated that Germany had never pursued anything but economic goals in Latin America and Mexico. Germany had "often even neglected the needs of the large economic interests which it has in all these countries in order to placate the sensitivities of the United States." Germany had envisioned the note only for a state of war. "This explains the fact that the Mexican government would never have heard anything of our intentions from any German if the United States had not declared war on us. I think it is scarcely possible to act more correctly . . . . That the German government made general plans for measures to parry the blow which America was preparing against us was not only its perfect right, but its duty and obligation to the German people."[183]

Bernstorff was very bitter over this interview, in which he was forced to speak for a policy which he completely opposed. It nevertheless reinforced the Americans' belief that he was one of the main guilty parties in the whole affair. For this reason in Copenhagen he surreptitiously let the

Americans know that he had not prepared the interview, but that it had been worked out by the Foreign Office.[184]

One of the most important ways in which Zimmermann replied to the criticism leveled against him was his attempt to put the blame for the disclosure of the note on Bernstorff. In all his declarations he asserted that the idea of the note itself was a good one and that the damage had occurred only through its disclosure. He repeatedly underlined his innocence in this regard and implied or had it stated by spokesmen of the Foreign Office that the note had been disclosed in Washington through Bernstorff's neglect. Zimmermann told the kaiser: "Count Bernstorff was forced to hire a completely new staff at the embassy, as indiscretions had always taken place there in the past, and he was afraid that this time an employee of the embassy itself had been bribed and had sold the telegram to the American government."[185] In confidential talks with the Austrian ambassador and the envoys of the individual German states in Berlin, spokesmen of the Foreign Office repeated these assertions. They acquired still more weight from the fact that a trunk with Swedish dispatches was confiscated by the English on the same ship that brought Bernstorff back to Europe. The English spread the rumor that the Zimmermann note had been among them. Wilhelm II, probably with the aid of Zimmermann, gave credibility to this rumor; Bernstorff was convinced that the kaiser was giving him the cold shoulder for this reason.[186]

In the Budget Committee of the Reichstag, it was more difficult to present such unverifiable accusations, particularly as Bernstorff had some supporters there. In this instance, Zimmermann acted with much greater refinement. He accused Bernstorff while giving the appearance of defending him. "It is impossible for me to imagine that the kaiser's ambassador, as I read yesterday in a newspaper, handed the note over to a courier who was to take it to Mexico. I cannot believe that Count Bernstorff acted so carelessly. We will be able to give an explanation of this later."[187]

Dozens of rumors concerning the disclosure of the note had appeared in the press, but Zimmermann had considered only this single rumor to be worthy of mention. Deputy Gröber took the bait and then attacked Bernstorff himself. "In Washington," he stated, "something improper has certainly occurred. The 'loss' of a dossier of documents in a streetcar, the theft of a checkbook and so forth are quite striking and require a thorough investigation of the German embassy. It will be necessary for the secretary of state to seek only the truth in this affair. The whole spectacle surrounding the departure of the German ambassador is also not very inspiring. Somewhat more reserve and somewhat less emotion would have been more appropriate."[188]

Zimmermann was pursuing a double objective with these attacks. On the one hand, the blame was to be shifted to Bernstorff; this was all the easier because Bernstorff was very unpopular with the right wing because of his opposition to unlimited U-boat warfare. At the same time, Zimmermann wanted to remove from his path a potential rival and a man who was partially opposed to his policies.

Bernstorff defended himself as well as he could. Immediately after his arrival in Copenhagen, he told the German representative there that he considered a betrayal by employees of the embassy to be out of the question.[189] At the same time, he appears to have turned to the Americans for help. He informed the American ambassador in Copenhagen that he had prospects of becoming vice-chancellor and that the affair of the Zimmermann note had destroyed this possibility. Only if the Americans would make public where they actually had obtained the note, relieving him of the blame, would there still be a chance for him to obtain this post.[190] The Americans, naturally, did not go along with him.

The desire to blame Bernstorff also seems to have predominated in an investigation ordered by Zimmermann. Privy Councillor Goeppert was commissioned to gather information on the disclosure of the note and was empowered to "question those employees whose opinion he considered relevant."[191] Goeppert had to grapple from the beginning with two conflicting versions. There was Zimmermann's assertion that the note had probably been divulged from inside the German embassy in Washington. Although Zimmermann had put forward this interpretation repeatedly, he had also conceded in a conversation with Lerchenfeldt that the code that had been employed, already in use in the prewar period, might have fallen into the hands of another power.[192] Bernstorff's analysis also moved along these lines. Never questioned by Goeppert, Bernstorff stated in Copenhagen "that either the code is known to the English or the Americans, or else the note was divulged in Mexico."[193]

Goeppert appears to have adopted the latter notion of Bernstorff for a short period. "Various factors indicated betrayal by Mexico," the German government wired Eckardt on 21 March, "greatest caution urged, all compromising materials should be burned."[194] Eckardt fiercely opposed this view. "More security than already practiced here impossible," he replied. "Sole existing texts read quietly to me at night by Magnus (non–German-speaking servants asleep in adjoining house); text otherwise only in his hands or in safe which only Magnus can open."[195] With an adroit sideswipe at Bernstorff he concluded: "According to Kunkel, even secret telegrams known to entire embassy in Washington. Routine second copy for embassy counselors. No question here of carbon paper. Please inform immediately as soon as we are exculpated, as will undoubtedly occur;

otherwise both Magnus and I will insist on a legal investigation, possibly by Consul Grunow."[196] This interpretation by Eckardt was gleefully adopted in the Foreign Office. "Following your telegram," read the reply, "it is hardly tenable that the betrayal occurred in Mexico. In view of same, all indicators pointing to such an interpretation lose their significance. Neither you nor Magnus are blamed."[197]

The view widely held in Germany that Carranza himself had sold the note to the Americans proved untenable in light of Eckardt's statement that he had never read aloud the contents of the note to Carranza. Almost all inquiries were now focused on the German embassy in Washington. At the same time, Goeppert had to deal with the most varied reports of the German secret service on the disclosure of the note. These often contained facts which had been intentionally disseminated by Hall to confuse the investigation of the German authorities. Thus, in one report it was stated that the note went by way of Holland and had been divulged there.[198] The head of the code office, from whom a statement was also requested, stated: "No report on the compromise of code 13040 is known to me." He had also attempted to place the blame for the disclosure of the note on the Washington embassy. "That a particularly intense campaign of espionage was being waged in the United States against the embassy and its staff is well known,"[199] he emphasized.

On 4 April, Goeppert presented a preliminary concluding report. Initially he dealt with the question of whether secret code 0075, in which the note had been sent to Washington, or the code 13040, in which it had been forwarded from Washington to Mexico, could have been known to the Americans. As far as code 0075 was concerned, Goeppert fell completely into the trap set by Hall. Hall had made public not the text sent from Berlin to Washington, but the one sent from Washington to Mexico. Goeppert concluded from this that code 0075 could not have been compromised. "If code 0075 was known to the American government, then the Mexican note with the date of the 16th and not of the 19th would have been published."[200] He considered it impossible for the Americans to have known the code, when they handed over the note, for, in his opinion, they would not have then passed the message on to Gerard. Moreover, the German government knew that the Americans had been surprised by the announcement of unlimited U-boat warfare.

Goeppert then considered the possibility that code 13040, which was used by the German operations in most Latin American countries and in the United States, could have fallen into American hands. "The American government," he wrote, "could have acquired the code itself, or could have obtained a copy or photograph of it. This could have happened in any place where the code was in use. The theft of the code has nowhere been reported.''[201] He did not completely exclude the possibility that the code had been betrayed, but added that the only place where such a theft could have occurred was Washington, since there was a safe in the German embassy there whose combination lock had not been changed since 1902.[202]

The only correct analysis, namely, that the English had the German codes, was never mentioned, although it had been pointed out by Bernstorff and Goeppert himself had received a similar suggestion in a communiqué from the German secret service. Among the many reports submitted to him, there was one in which it was stated that ''the German plan regarding Mexico has been discovered by 'the intelligence and enterprising spirit of the English.' The German secret political code is no secret for England (English statement).''[203] Goeppert obviously knew what was expected of him, for he stated: ''It is more probable that the contents of the Mexico note were betrayed.''[204] In Washington, six or seven employees had apparently worked on the deciphering of the dispatch. ''All middle-level employees, with the possible exception of Privy Councillor Sachse, who was sick, and the supernumerary Kühn, knew the contents of the Mexico dispatch, and one of them read through the decoded message again a week later.'' He plaintively added: ''The file in which this document was kept was accessible . . . to all middle-level employees of the embassy.''[205]

After Goeppert had fallen into the trap Hall had set for him, he was led astray by Lansing. ''The idea of a betrayal is also confirmed by Lansing's statement in the Senate, in which he said that he could not reveal more details on the acquisition of the dispatch without endangering the lives of certain persons. This does not necessarily mean someone in Germany or en route to Germany. It is also possible that it had occurred to Lansing that Germany would take its revenge in America as well.''[206] Nonetheless, Goeppert could name no suspects, but concluded with the observation that all employees ''who were questioned considered it impossible that one of their colleagues could have committed such a deed.''

In the aftermath, however, the German government seems to have found a ''suspect.'' Kunkel, a low-level official of the German embassy in Washington, had not returned to Germany, but had gone to Mexico, fearing that he would not receive free transit from the English, because he had escaped from a prisoner-of-war camp in Canada.[207] It was reported in May that Kunkel had been seen in Washington, and the suspicion was raised that ''Kunkel had divulged the note.''[208] Bernstorff himself confirmed that Kunkel was in Washington. He wrote that Kunkel had participated in the deciphering of the note, but considered it improbable that he was responsible for its disclosure.[209] This suspicion was the sole result of

Goeppert's investigation.[210] Eight years later, without any comment, an archivist of the Foreign Office placed in the already closed file a newspaper report that appeared in 1925 with Hall's statement that the English had known the German secret codes from the beginning of the war.

Goeppert's work was, however, not without its importance. With the conjecture that the note had been divulged in Washington, his investigation helped to bury Bernstorff's position. In his memoirs, Bernstorff himself blames the affair of the note for the fact that he had been unable to play any appreciable role in German politics.[211] That was probably not the only reason, however, because his opposition to U-boat warfare already left him little chance to muster support from the military. The main result of Goeppert's report was that German imperialism experienced one of its biggest fiascos of the First World War. Because Goeppert concluded that there was no evidence that the German codes had been compromised, the code 0075 was not changed, even though the most elementary rules of caution warranted such a change to cover all eventualities after an incident of the dimensions of the disclosure of the Zimmermann note. Thus it was possible for the English to intercept and decode almost all radio dispatches between headquarters and the overseas stations and to initiate the appropriate Allied countermeasures.

The attacks on Bernstorff undoubtedly contributed to Zimmermann's ability to deal with the criticisms directed against him in the Reichstag with relative ease. This development surprised many observers. "It is noteworthy," wrote Lerchenfeldt, "that Zimmermann has come out of the affair quite unscathed. Individual Reichstag deputies have, of course, said privately that Jagow would never have done such a thing, but since Zimmermann is popular, he is spared."[212] The deeper reason may lie in the fact that neither the kaiser nor the army nor the parties of the governmental majority, including the Social Democrats, were prepared to do without Zimmermann. His aggressiveness, his energetic actions, and his ambitious plans had won him the kaiser's benevolence. The army and the right-wing parties were impressed by his unqualified support for U-boat warfare, while for the other parties, his status as a nonaristocratic secretary of state offered a "democratic" facade which made it easier to defend an imperialist foreign policy.

### German Policy in Mexico after the Disclosure of the Zimmermann Telegram

In spite of his temporary success, Zimmermann knew that his prestige had been damaged. The most effective way to restore it was to prove that his proposal to Mexico still had some chance of success. As a result, after the disclosure of the note the attempts to achieve an alliance with Mexico, far from being abandoned, were continued on an intensified level.

On 8 March 1917, seven days after the publication of the note in the United States, the Political Section of the General Staff informed the Foreign Office: "After discussions with the chief of the General Staff and the consultation with the Admiral Staff of the Navy, the Military High Command is prepared to provide Mexico with the following arms and ammunition from reserves in Germany: 30,000 modern repeating rifles with 9 million rounds of ammunition, 100 German machine guns together with 6 million rounds, 6 mountain cannon, 7.5 cm. caliber, with 2000 shells each, 4 howitzers suitable for mountain transport, 10.5 cm caliber with 2000 shells each."[213]

These proposals by the General Staff show clearly that the German government had never seriously considered implementing any of the promises implied in its offer of alliance to Mexico, which turns out to have been fraudulent in practically every respect. Had Carranza really attacked the United States on the basis of Zimmermann's proposal, not only would the German government have refused to ratify the alliance, its offer of "plentiful" weapons and ammunition was an illusion. Not only were they not plentiful (it is to say the least difficult to assume that 10 cannon, 100 machine guns and 30,000 rifles would have allowed Mexico to attack the United States) the German government had really conceived of no effective way of sending the arms to Mexico.

Various methods of transportation for these weapons were considered. The General Staff proposed "transport on a freighter equipped by the kaiser's navy and flying under a foreign flag" or—in the hope, not yet abandoned, that Japan would join the planned alliance—"procurement of arms and ammunition from Japan." The General Staff also considered a purchase of arms and ammunition from South America, "with German financial aid, which could be guaranteed from funds of the Foreign Office."[214]

The forms of transportation envisioned represented as much of an adventure as the Zimmermann note itself. The Political Section stated that with the first option, there would be a "danger of sinking by foreign warships." The second option depended essentially on the (quite unlikely) entry of Japan into the war against the United States. If arms were purchased in South America, the transport ships would have to pass through the blockade of the American fleet in order to get to Mexico, which would be extremely difficult. It is interesting that the only way by which arms could have been shipped to Mexico, that is, by merchant submarines, was never considered. It is not clear why this was not done.

Carranza's rejection of the alliance proposal was kept a strict secret not only from the public, but from the Budget Committee of the Reichstag as well. A new attempt was made to win Carranza over to an alliance and to an attack on the United States. In April–May, a new alliance proposal was worked out, which in this instance was not conveyed to Mexico by radio, but was slipped through by Delmar, an agent of the General Staff's Political Section. Carranza was once again to be persuaded to attack the United States, for which he was offered more arms in return; there was no longer any reference to territorial promises. "Should a treaty relationship develop," reported the Austrian envoy in Mexico, "Mexico would be offered without charge several hundred thousand rifles, several hundred cannon, the assignment of experts in munitions production, and so on. The communiqué says nothing of an immediate gold draft or a dispatch of U-boats."[215]

Zimmermann's ideas were even more grandiose on this occasion. All Mexican parties, that is, the revolutionaries Villa and Zapata as well as the Científico forces under Felix Díaz were to ally with Carranza for a joint attack on the United States. The leadership of this army was to be in the hands of Obregón. At the same time, uprisings in the southern United States in support of this attack were planned.[216] In a desperate gamble to regain some of his lost prestige Zimmermann made patently untrue statements in the Reichstag. "Villa appears to be rallying to Carranza," he expounded before the Budget Committee of the Reichstag on 28 April; however, not a single report from Mexico in the German archives bears this out. "The hostility between these two men appears to be diminishing in face of the common American enemy. In Mexico, what we have been expecting has thus come to pass. Mexico's attitude toward Germany is a thoroughly favorable one, and should America actually turn against us, I think it can be assumed that the Mexicans will not miss the opportunity to stir up trouble on the Mexican border and to launch an attack there."[217]

All these plans failed, because the Mexicans had no notion of utilizing these "opportunities." The second alliance proposal was presented to Carranza in August 1917 and was refused by him just as he had refused the first one. "President refused, claiming that the alliance, in view of the military weakness of the country, would mean almost certain ruin, but asked for a guarantee of the aid offered him for the eventuality of an attack by the United States, which he definitely expects. He did, however, accept without reservation the aid Germany promised him for the postwar period. This aid is of both a military-diplomatic and economic nature, and involves the pacification of the country, its economic reconstruction, and the securing of its integrity."[218] These postwar promises included, among other things, the "assignment of military instructors, deliveries of arms, development of the wireless telegraph, settlement of interest payments, loans for the reconstruction of the country, modification of the commercial treaty, diplomatic support in the negotiations on petroleum and mining concessions, and with regard to the two issuing banks in the capital."[219] These promises were intended to strengthen Carranza in his policies of neutrality.

The General Staff appears to have had from the beginning no great optimism about the possibility of an alliance. It had given Delmar a letter for the eventuality of a refusal by Carranza, asking Carranza to "keep alive . . . American fears of a Mexican attack against them,"[220] in return for which interest in Mexico's integrity was promised. Carranza replied that "American troop concentration on the Mexican border constituted proof that Germany's wish had already been fulfilled by Mexico's strictly neutral attitude, the construction of arms factories, and the like."[221]

German hopes for unity against the United States by all parties in the Mexican struggle proved to be just as illusory. German agents actually appear to have attempted to bring about a reconciliation between Carranza and Villa in an anti-American perspective. According to a report to the American consul in Nogales from the German-American Biermann, who had very close ties to German operations in Mexico, German agents had attempted to bring about an agreement between Carranza and Villa; Carranza, however, had refused to go along. Several days later, Carothers, the former American representative with Villa, reported that the German businessman Kettelsen had attempted in vain to bring about a meeting between Villa and Murguía, the commander of the Carranza military forces in Chihuahua.[222]

Hopes for success in these efforts may have prompted German authorities to continue to deliver arms to Villa in March 1917. "The vice-consul in Mazatlán reports that Villa, supported by Germans, is expecting to receive three shipments of ammunition, which are to be landed by sailboats between Mazatlán and Manzanillo," wrote the German military attaché in Mexico. "The vice-consul claims that this information is reliable."[223] When no agreement was worked out between Villa and Carranza, and it was necessary to choose between them, the Germans appeared to have dropped Villa completely. After April–May 1917, there are no reports in either German or American documents about German aid to Villa.

In his reports to Berlin during the whole of 1917 Eckardt continually stressed his confidence in Carranza's pro-German attitude. Such reports were primarily destined to gain Eckardt the goodwill of his chief, Zimmermann, and to induce the German government to back up its promises to Carranza with money and possibly arms.

Eckardt's actions, which he only reported later, belie this confidence.

They came as a result of a growing conviction by the German minister in the months of April to June 1917 that Carranza was contemplating a change of attitude, possibly a turnaround in his attitude toward Germany.

This conviction was not unfounded. There are indications that in those months Carranza was in fact thinking of a reversal of his previous policies. The options he was considering reached from an active pro-American neutrality to a declaration of war against Germany. U.S. pressure, fear of an American intervention as well as the U.S. arms and, in part, food embargo contributed to Carranza's attempts to reverse his policies.

On 24 May 1917, Fletcher had visited Carranza at Wilson's behest and had asked the Mexican government to prevent any German attempt to conduct sabotage operations against the United States from Mexico.[224] Carranza not only agreed to this demand, which was incumbent on a neutral power according to international law, but went on to suggest that the Allies extend peace proposals to Germany. If Germany did not accept, the neutral countries ought to join the Allied camp.[225] This proposal was undoubtedly favorable to the Entente, and Fletcher was quite "encouraged" by it. It is not known whether Carranza made still other proposals. This appears probable, because both American diplomats and the American press were repeatedly stating throughout this period that Carranza was moving increasingly close to the Allies. Thus, according to German reports, the American ambassador in Switzerland had said: "According to reports from Washington, the Mexican danger is ended. Carranza has probably been bought. Contrary to its original intentions, America will now send troops to France."[226] At the end of April, the *New York Times* wrote in a correspondent's report from Monterrey: "It is quite probable that Mexico will break off relations with the Central Powers in the next few days, and will join the Entente."[227] At the beginning of June 1917, the Mexican government went one step further. On 4 June, Mexico's Foreign Secretary Aguilar told Ohta, Japan's envoy in Mexico, that in case Mexico joined the Allied side, it would declare war against Germany as an ally of Japan.[228] Mexico wished to avoid the impression that it was joining the Allies because of U.S. pressure.

The Japanese government immediately instructed Ohta not to get involved in Mexican affairs. The Japanese Foreign Ministry told its representative in Mexico that Aguilar's argument was absolutely ridiculous and motivated simply to use Japan for Mexico's convenience.[229]

While these negotiations went on, several members of the Mexican Congress and Senate were calling for a break with Germany. Eckardt was not unaware of all these efforts. He took them so seriously that he immediately organized a conspiracy, about which he later wrote: "Less than a year ago, I felt it advisable—this was in April—to guarantee our position. Members of the Senate who had been bought off, and delegates in the chamber were urging Carranza to break off relations with Germany in view of the financial squeeze and food shortages. I had nightly meetings with influential generals; twelve of them organized a secret association. They gave me their assurance, potentially compromising themselves with Carranza, that they would take up arms against him if he reached an agreement with the United States at our expense."[230]

Both the Americans and Carranza knew that the assurances of these generals was no empty talk. In October 1917, Fletcher reported that General Treviño and General López had stated that, in the event of a break with Germany, they would attack Tampico and destroy the oil storage dumps there.[231] A month later, the American consul in Frontera de Tabasco reported that the army officers stationed there had openly told him that they would revolt if Mexico entered the war on the side of the Allies.[232] A few weeks later, the American consul in Mazatlán wrote that the Mexican army was preparing to revolt if Mexico gave up its neutrality.[233] In 1933, Justo Acevedo, a close confidant of Carranza's, told the American ambassador in Mexico that during the world war, he had asked Carranza to announce his sympathy for the Allies. Carranza had responded by letter, saying that if he did such a thing he would be overthrown by his generals, particularly Obregón and Calles.[234] What was decisive in determining the attitude of the army leaders, however, was not Eckardt's conspiratorial activities; such activities were successful only because of the openly anti-American sentiment which dominated the army.

A neutrality favoring the United States was rendered impossible for Carranza not only by the army's attitude, but by American policy itself, which for a long time had been formulated with the slogan "All or Nothing." After lengthy negotiations, it was made clear to Carranza that Mexico would get an American loan only by giving up its neutrality. American warships remained in Mexican ports beyond the 24-hour limit set up by international law.[235] Though the ban on arms exports to Mexico was lifted briefly in July 1917, it was reimposed when Carranza took no steps to break with Germany. Mexico was also hard hit by an American ban on the export of food.[236] Fletcher himself described this policy as follows: "The Mexican government is discovering that it is difficult to remain in power and to stay neutral at the same time."[237] Precisely for this reason Carranza decided to seek assistance from the country he thought would exact the lowest price in return: Germany.

**Part 4**

**The Politics of
Brinkmanship: The Carranza
Presidency, 1917–20**

# 10 Germany and Carranza, 1917–18

## Germany's Political, Economic, and Military Aims in Mexico

After Carranza definitely rejected all German proposals for an alliance, there were two possibilities for German policy. First, Germany could simply continue to pursue its main objective of promoting a Mexican-American war. Such a policy would have had little chance of success but would have led inevitably to a break with Carranza and would have made all economic and political expansion in Mexico impossible.

Second, Germany could set as its main objective the attainment of a benevolent neutrality by Mexico. This would mean, in military terms, tying up important American military forces on the Mexican border and the acquisition of bases from which to conduct sabotage; in political terms, it would mean the strengthening of the neutral block in Latin America, whose most important members, in addition to Mexico, were Argentina, Chile, Colombia, and Venezuela; in economic terms, finally, it would mean preventing the exclusion of German capital from the Mexican economy. Benevolent neutrality by Mexico was the necessary basis for an ambitious German expansion in that country. If the German government wished to embark on that path, it would have to cultivate good relations with Carranza, who favored such a policy, and would have to impose substantial limits on sabotage activity in Mexico and in the immediate vicinity of the Mexican-American border.

For Eckardt, Mexico represented primarily an object for the expansion of German imperialism. He appears to have been a supporter of the Pan-German League. Shortly before his departure for Mexico, he met with a representative of the league, Petzold, and asked him to forward all the league's publications—particularly Class's statement on war aims—to Mexico. In a report to Class, Petzold expressed great satisfaction over his discussion with Eckardt.[1] *"Berlin is the center of attraction,"* wrote Eckardt in November 1917. "Mexico is oriented...toward Berlin. The legacy of Hernando Cortez, extended far beyond the equator, is for sale. Humboldt described its value. Let us seize it. To the attack, into the fray, suspending...the operation of the law of strong and weak neighbors...as we did on the Bosporus."[2] Eckardt was quite clear about his objectives in his report to the Reichskanzler on 7 August 1918: "I am assuming, like all Germans, that the war will have a happy ending, and I conclude from this that the German Reich will have to pursue a transatlantic policy toward Latin America, ruling out the thought of an agreement with the United States at Mexico's expense."[3]

It is clear that a Mexican-American war would have made German expansion in Mexico impossible. Thus Eckardt's statement to an American journalist in 1932 that he had opposed the Zimmermann note is credible. When the second German alliance proposal arrived in Mexico in August 1917, Eckardt told the courier Delmar that he considered "the launching of a war to be unlikely at this time, for the country is both militarily and financially quite poorly prepared and a quick defeat would therefore be inevitable, which would be extremely unfavorable for both our current and future interests."[4]

Until August 1917, the Foreign Office in Berlin had pursued as its major objective the unleashing of a Mexican-American war. Nevertheless, it had already considered the possibility of a German postwar expansion in Mexico, in the event that the plans for an alliance did not materialize. The instructions of 8 February, in which Eckardt was told to meet Carranza immediately with the aim of concluding an alliance, stated that "If the president, out of fear of future reprisals, should refuse, you are empowered to offer him a definite alliance for the postwar period, if Mexico is successful in involving Japan in this alliance."[5]

In April–May 1917, this outlook had already changed substantially. As an incentive for the second alliance proposal, Carranza was offered, among other things, military instructors, military supplies, development of the wireless telegraph, settlement of debt service questions, a loan for the reconstruction of the country, modification of the commercial treaty, and diplomatic support in the negotiations on petroleum and mining concessions.[6] There was no longer any discussion of Japan's participation as a precondition for the realization of these plans. It is not clear in any case whether in April–May 1917 the Foreign Office was already envisioning a German expansion in Mexico as its major objective in these proposals or whether it was at that time merely attempting to keep Carranza neutral with promises for the postwar period. In any case, after August 1917 the Foreign Office took no steps to push a Mexican-American war. After the beginning of 1918, it placed a primacy on future efforts at German expansion into Mexico.

Eckardt developed many activities in his efforts to make Mexico a target of German imperialist expansion. Initially he requested a systematic economic report to facilitate an intensified penetration of German capital into Mexico. This report was to concentrate on four areas—mining, petroleum, railroads, and other extensive projects and concessions—and on the "exchange rate on New York and Germany."[7]

Eckardt simultaneously submitted to Berlin a memorandum, framed in extremely aggressive terms, by the German businessman Eugen Motz, who was residing in Mexico. In this memorandum, Motz urged German capital and the government to regard Mexico as a prime target for expansion. "The Tampico oil fields could and actually should be almost completely in German hands.... The main point in such matters is for us to move quickly and to take risks, especially where the interests of the fatherland are at stake, before big English and American capital have taken the situation over for themselves. Then, it will be necessary to buy up quietly some of the larger coastal estates, under the pretext of using the timber or something of the sort, in order to have support stations for our navy in the event of war, international law or not! One or more industries with machine-related activities could be built in such places, so that there would be a reason for a large accumulation of coal and food."[8]

Eckardt proposed the integration of Mexican oil into German war aims to the Reich leadership. "In the event that a significant need for oil arises in Germany after the end of the war, there would be a possibility for meeting it by prompting the English government to give up its rights from the contract with the Doheny concern, or, in the event that it is not itself a partner in the contract, to put the appropriate pressure on those English citizens who are involved."[9] With the energetic collaboration of Eckardt, a Deutsch-Österreichische Petroleum AG was founded, which had as its objective "the emancipation of ... Germany ... from Standard Oil, which already had a monopoly position ...in order to assure for our fatherland its rightful place in the sun in this domain as well."[10] At the same time, Eckardt warmly urged support for a project of De Lima, the director of the Banco de Comercio e Industria. De Lima proposed a takeover of the Banco de Comercio e Industria by the Deutsche Bank. After he had sketched the devastation of the Mexican economy, De Lima wrote: "This difficult situation and the necessity of financial aid, which will soon be seen, ought to favor the branches of strong international banking institutions. If Germany is interested in creating a strong economic position for itself here, the establishment of a strong foreign bank, in the form of a subsidiary, ought to be seen as the centerpiece of overall German interests. Mexico, as you know, has little industry, and is thus a good customer for export countries, but is also extraordinarily rich in raw materials ...petroleum, as well as woods of all kinds."[11]

A second, even more explicit proposal, which Eckardt had his legation secretary formulate, integrated Mexico, if only indirectly, into German war aims. Magnus explained that, without a reorganization loan from abroad, Mexico would never "be able to consider settling its foreign claims, nor even establishing a normal situation internally .... This would obviously mean the establishment of foreign financial control, and this would, moreover, have to be quite extensive, given the habits of Mexican civil servants. The procurement of the credits necessary for such a loan will *not be easy* after a world war which has destroyed so much. *Precisely for this reason, the power which nonetheless is capable of raising this money*—Germany could raise it from war reparations—*will be able to dominate Mexico economically and thus politically.*"[12]

Magnus's proposal was intended for the postwar period. Six months later, Eckardt worked out a plan for reaching this objective even before the war had ended. He referred to the intention of the Mexican government to establish a state bank, and stated: "300 million marks necessary, whoever gives them will rule Mexico. I recommend giving this money in spite of the risks, in case our current political and future commercial policy goals require the attainment of Mexico's independence from the United States, and we decide to bring it about."[13]

Prior to the end of 1917, Eckardt's proposals had only limited success. They had, of course, met with the enthusiastic approval of the German businessmen in Mexico and the managers of the local subsidiaries of German firms. The head offices in Germany, however, proved much less interested. The reasons for this reserve are to be found less in the "burdens of the world war" than in their hopes of obtaining similar concessions for nothing as a result of successes in the world war and of obtaining them in other parts of the world-much safer than Mexico. The war aims of German imperialism extended to annexations in Belgium and France, in the Balkans, in the Middle East, in Russia, and in Africa. Until the United States entered World War I, Latin America was seen by Germany primarily as a region where it should extend its commercial penetration. This was expressed very clearly in a memorandum on German war aims drafted in late 1914 by Otto Hoetzsch. After describing Germany's extensive war aims in other parts of the globe, he became very restrained when speaking of "middle and South America," where "colonial expansion should be limited to trade."[14] After the United States entered the war, Kaiser Wilhelm articulated some German war aims with regard to Latin America. Thus he asked for indemnifications of 12 billion marks from Brazil, from Cuba, and from Bolivia, to be paid not in money but in kind. From the United States he demanded reparations of $30 million.[15] It is possible that he considered collecting part of this sum not only in the form of raw materials, but also in the form of American concessions in Latin America.

Large German capital on the whole showed only limited interest in these plans until the end of 1917. German capital wanted to have its sources of raw materials within easy reach and not on the other side of the ocean, where communications could be interrupted by hostile maritime powers. The obstacles to an extensive German push into Mexico during the First World War, however, also grew out of the situation in Mexico and the policy of the United States.

The acquisition of concessions by German firms was complicated by the fact that the Mexicans who were selling or leasing their property to Germans were discounting the dangers of being boycotted by the United States and all Allied firms. The basis for such a move was the Trading with the Enemy Act passed shortly after the United States entered the war, which forbade commercial and economic relations with businessmen and firms of the Central Powers. To make the ban effective, blacklists had been drawn up.[16] This obstacle could nonetheless be partly circumvented by German acquisition of concessions from the Mexican government.

Much more difficult for German concerns was the question of the practical use of mines and oil concessions. The necessary machinery could be purchased only in the United States, because German suppliers could hardly be expected to break through the British blockade; Mexico itself had no machine tool industry to speak of. Smuggling was, of course, possible, and some things could be obtained through middlemen, but these methods were very expensive and extremely unreliable. There was also the problem of sales. The Mexican market could absorb very little. The bulk of these raw materials thus had to be exported. The only countries to which exports were possible, however, were the United States and the Allied countries, to which most German firms neither could nor wished to export. These circumstances had to affect the Mexican government's willingness to grant concessions. Mexico's most important sources of income were from taxes on oil and mining. Concessions which were not used, however, created no income. This naturally did not prevent the Mexicans from granting a certain number of concessions to Germans as a reserve for the postwar period. A major economic offensive by German firms in 1917, however, would have been very difficult. In view of this, the rapid advance in Mexico of the Merton concern, the Frankfurter Metallgesellschaft, is all the more remarkable.

## The German Metal Trust and Mexico

The Merton concern was one of the German firms with very substantial raw materials operations overseas. A majority of its holdings were located directly in the spheres of control of the other great powers: in Australia, in various British colonies, and in the United States. The constant possibility of tensions or war between these countries and Germany and the desire to have recourse to the aid of the governments of these countries in such an eventuality seem to have prompted the Merton concern to develop, among other measures, a clever system of concealment and camouflage. This system was clearly expressed in the circumstances of ownership of the Frankfurter Metallgesellschaft's subsidiary in the United States, the American Metal Company. Only 49 percent of the stock was directly owned by the Frankfurter Metallgesellschaft; 13 percent was owned by an affiliate of the concern in Australia, and the rest was in the hands of various American capitalists.[17] The same was true for the Mexican enterprises of the Merton concern. The most important of these were the Compañía Minera de Peñoles and the Compañía de Minerales y Metales de México, which owned important copper and lead mines. They belonged in part directly to the Frankfurter Metallgesellschaft and in part to the American Metal Company and American capitalists; they appear to have been registered both as German and American companies.[18] The international masking of the real ownership worked to some extent to the advantage of the Merton concern during the First World War. It did not, however, prevent the English from placing the subsidiaries in Australia and in the British territories under British control.[19] The Frankfurter Metallgesellschaft was nonetheless successful in saving part of its capital and transferring it to Mexico.

In 1916, the Frankfurter Metallgesellschaft began an ambitious program of expansion in Mexico. In the state of Chihuahua alone, $10 million was invested in the purchase of mines.[20] The affiliates began to surpass in breadth and scope the American Guggenheim concern, which had previously exercised a near-monopoly in Mexican mining. The American authorities showed the deepest concern about this development, and both the American consuls and specially selected secret agents of the State Department and the army conducted extensive investigations. In addition, the American government ordered all its consuls in Mexico in areas where the Metallgesellschaft was active to submit detailed reports.[21] The result of these investigations and the reports of the consuls in no way quieted the fears of the American authorities. The consul in Coahuila stated that the Metallgesellschaft wanted to dominate Mexican mining.[22] His colleague in Monterrey spoke of the company's monopoly position in large parts of Mexico.[23] The American customs official Zachary Cobb, who also played an important role in the Secret Service of the State Department, expressed these fears most drastically. "The Mexican policy can change," he wrote, "and Mexican politicians can come and go, but if the metal trust from Germany wins the upper hand in Mexican mining, then the industrial domination of Mexico by the Germans will last forever."[24]

How was the Frankfurter Metallgesellschaft able to enjoy such a rapid rise? The most important factor was undoubtedly the multinational character of the Merton concern. On the one hand, its subsidiaries in the United States and Mexico fulfilled their "patriotic duties." German propaganda reports were wired daily to the German legation in Mexico City through the company's American subsidiary, and these were in turn passed on to the German authorities.[25] The Compañía Minera de Peñoles earned Eckardt's particular praise for its support of a German school.[26] On the other hand, the subsidiaries of the Merton concern were openly selling war-related metals at top prices to the English, who regarded the company as "American." The profits from these transactions went toward the purchase of new enterprises in Mexico.[27]

The U.S. entry into the war complicated the company's situation and led to an intensified surveillance by the American authorities. The Mexican subsidiaries of the firm, whose business offices had up to that time been located in the United States, then transferred to Mexico and presented themselves as neutral Mexican companies.[28] To emphasize this "neutrality," political discussions of the war were forbidden in their plants.[29] The president of the American Metal Company told the American government that his company was purely American and asked the government to send a representative to participate in all meetings.[30] The future growth of the company at that time depended on the actions of the American government. If it placed the American or Mexican subsidiaries of the firm on the blacklist or turned the administration of the American Metal Company over to trustees as enemy property, the American market would be almost completely lost for the Metallgesellschaft.

The Americans, in any case, went about their work with extreme care. The shares of the American Metal Company belonging to the Frankfurter Metallgesellschaft were turned over to a custodian of enemy property, who only appointed some directors to the company's board. The majority of the stock nonetheless remained in the hands of the former owners, who thus continued to control the firm.[31] There were not even any changes in the management of the company. This "mildness" on the part of the American government was no accident. The government knew that if it placed the American Metal Company under government supervision, it would indeed control its American owners but would not dominate the Mexican subsidiaries in which the Merton concern had invested directly and whose shipments were of great importance for the American war industry. The Mexican subsidiaries, for their part, never gave a moment's thought to stopping deliveries to Germany's enemies, but sold them important metals in continually increasing quantities which contributed decisively to the forced pace of American armament.

This silent agreement between the Americans and the Merton concern had its formal confirmation in April 1918, when a director of the American Metal Company received permission to meet with a representative of the Merton concern of Germany in "neutral territory."[32] Agreements were reached, about which, unfortunately, no greater detail is known. One of the results appears to have been the dismissal of many of the German employees of the concern in Mexico.[33] For its support of the American government, moreover, the American Metal Company was officially praised.[34]

However "cooperatively" the Americans generally dealt with the Metallgesellschaft in Mexico, they nevertheless cast aside all moderation when the company attempted to gain a foothold in the Mexican oil fields in 1917 and acquired extensive concessions from private sources. The Huasteca Oil Company made the sharpest protest, and the German petroleum geologists Boese and Pusch were accused of espionage by the American representatives in Tampico and were hindered in their work.[35] The assertion that Boese and Pusch were spies appears to have been a fabrication, for both of them immediately returned to the United States to defend themselves against the charges. In the United States, they were neither brought to trial nor interned. The Metallgesellschaft, nevertheless, had understood the hint and gave up its efforts to move into the oil business.[36]

If the Merton concern obtained advantages from its American "label," it showed its German colors when circumstances demanded it. The industrial enterprises of the Metallgesellschaft in northern Mexico, for example, asserted their German character in 1916 in order to give Villa no pretext for attack at a time when he was causing the greatest difficulties for the American companies.[37] These elements were even more clearly expressed in their relations with Carranza. When, at the beginning of 1917, he had urgent need of financial experts for the reorganization of his administration, he could hardly rely on Germans, for that would have unleashed loud protests in the United States. He did not want Americans or citizens of the Allied countries. What could be of greater use than Americans who maintained close ties with Germany? Thus it was hardly an accident that some of the most important experts he hired were employees of the American Metal Company, such as Henry C. Bruere, a director of the firm. The hiring of Bruere deeply disturbed the American government. "As you will probably remember, Henry C. Bruere went to Mexico to . . . solve the problems of the country," Polk wrote to Secretary of the Interior Lane. "The secret service of the State Department and the army are very disturbed by the activities of the company he is working for."[38] The government had Bruere's correspondence read but could not find anything suspicious. Furthermore, it is unlikely that he was involved in any conspiracies. The hopes of Carranza and the fears of the United States government that Bruere might support Mexican nationalism because of the German connections of his company proved to be completely unfounded.[39]

The American Metal Company was a forerunner of the modern multinational corporation for which national allegiances were of secondary importance. The affiliates of the Merton syndicate worked with equal enthusiasm and determination to supply both sides during World War I; they represented the "internationalist" line of the Metallgesellschaft, which wanted to remain on the best terms with all paying parties. The Frankfurter Metallgesellschaft was, as we have said, the only German company that attempted substantial advances in Mexico. According to American reports, it was heavily financed in these ventures by the Deutsche Bank and the Disconto-Gesellschaft.[40]

## The Activities of German Intelligence in Mexico

In spite of all the obstacles that confronted German economic expansion in Mexico in 1917, Eckardt increased his efforts in this direction. In May 1917, he proposed extensive German economic espionage: "Since the stocks of the major industrial enterprises, cotton, wool, petroleum, metals (iron, gold, copper, lead), cement, dynamite, and the like are almost exclusively in the hands of the Allies, we can obtain reliable information on the development of these industries by acquiring shares and thus gaining access to general stockholders' meetings. In order to avoid the collision of private interests and to be completely nonpartisan, the use of borrowed shares belonging to private persons or banks is ruled out. I thus recommend emphatically, in spite of the novelty of the practice, that I be empowered to acquire gradually small amounts of shares of otherwise inaccessible companies, after consulting with businessmen and bankers."[41]

All these plans of Eckardt's and the Foreign Office stood in sharp contrast to those of the Political Section of the General Staff, the military secret service, which conducted most German sabotage activity abroad. Agents of the Political Section in Mexico had attempted to carry out an extensive program of sabotage and diversion, without taking into account the political consequences—the inevitable break with Carranza. At the beginning of 1917, antagonisms between the Foreign Office and the Political Section assumed increasing importance. In February 1917, the Political Section had asked the Reich Treasury to transfer a large sum of money to Mexico for its activities there. After consulting with the Foreign Office, the Treasury stated its desire "to be informed of the aims and uses of the money by the Foreign Office" in future transfers to Mexico; this would avoid "giving the General Staff a free hand, as previous experiences of this kind had been far from encouraging."[42]

Two months later, these antagonisms erupted in Mexico. One of the most important agents of the Political Section in the United States, Fred R. Hermann, had been instructed to set fire to the oil fields in Tampico. At the beginning of 1917, Hermann went to Mexico to carry out the mission with an agent named Raoul Gerdts, whom he had recruited.

Since Hermann had no money, he called on Eckardt and asked for his help. But Eckardt received him with great mistrust. "Hermann (blond, slender, German with an American accent)," Eckardt wired to Berlin, "claims to have received instructions at the end of last year from the General Staff and again in January of this year from Hilken to set afire the Tampico oil fields and now wants to carry out the project. He asks me if he should do it; should I not reply that I have no communication with Berlin? Herr von Verdy [German envoy to Cuba] thinks he and his companion Raoul Gerdts are American or English spies. Request fast answer by wire."[43]

The Political Section confirmed Hermann's story. "Project of Tampico sabotage militarily important. If arson not possible, at least disrupt loading procedures and capacity to supply Allies oil. Give Hermann money for this." At the same time, the decision on how the plan should be executed was left to Eckardt, "as political impact cannot be assessed from here."[44] Germany was still hoping that Carranza would declare war on the United States, and thus at that time even the representatives of the General Staff wanted to avoid anything that might lead to a rupture with Carranza. The Foreign Office translated the communiqué of the General Staff into diplomatic language. The word "arson," in particular, was replaced by the more elegant term "immobilization." The communiqué was then sent to Eckardt, with the addendum: "Please tolerate nothing which might endanger relations with Mexico."[45] Eckardt took the hint and ordered Hermann to put a stop to his activities. He wired the Foreign Office: "Immobilization must be postponed as long as Mexico not yet ready for war."[46]

On his own initiative, Eckardt also put a stop to another project of Hermann's. Hermann had gone to Sonora with the purpose of chartering a ship there and providing it with a German crew; he probably had in mind sailors from German merchant ships interned in Baja California. This ship was mainly intended to stage raids on American freighters. If Hermann had been able to realize this plan, an immediate American intervention in Mexico would probably have taken place. After the instructions from Berlin gave him the opportunity to control Hermann's activities, Eckardt gave the order to cancel the action and recalled Hermann from Sonora.[47]

With Hermann, who was in the last analysis only an agent subordinate to the General Staff, Eckardt had little difficulty imposing his will. He was confronted with great difficulties in the summer of 1917, when the agents of the Political Section of the General Staff and of the German Admiralty charged with sabotage activities in the United States, Anton Dilger alias Delmar and Kurt Jahnke, set up headquarters in Mexico.[48] Both men were completely independent from Eckardt and were responsible only to their own headquarters. From the beginning Eckardt was on the best of terms with Jahnke, who headed German Naval Intelligence, and remained on such terms throughout. With Delmar, however, conflict soon erupted, though at first there had been an understanding between Delmar and Eckardt.[49]

## The German-Mexican Financial Negotiation

At the end of 1917 all German agents in Mexico temporarily buried their differences when the German government appeared to have lost all interest in Mexico.[50] The German-Mexican loan negotiations of 1917 were an expression of this loss of interest.

Eckardt viewed a loan to Carranza as one of the most important means of strengthening German influence in Mexico. Such a loan was to tie Carranza to Germany and at the same time put him in a position to resist American pressures.

After Eckardt had been informed by the Foreign Office in April 1917 that preparations were underway "to send . . . substantial sums," he offered Carranza a German loan. Carranza, who feared an American invasion after the publication of the Zimmermann note, rejected the offer.[51] The Austrian envoy in Mexico thought that "Financial support offered by Germany in April not accepted, obviously in order not to stir up trouble in the United States. Also shifting views of regime here on outcome of war prevents it from prematurely involving itself to such an extent with Germany."[52] Carranza actually hoped to receive such a loan from the United States. He was, however, compelled to abandon this hope, for the American demands that he give up Mexican neutrality and important articles of the new constitution were unacceptable to him.

Eckardt now felt the time had arrived to bring about the final collapse of the Mexican-American negotiation. On 1 June 1917, he wired to Berlin: "Very complicated situation. . . . Reopening of financial question to be expected in several days. Are 100 million pesos available for founding of state bank? This is most appropriate use of money here; government commission is working out plans for project."[53]

Eckardt's proposals were an unpleasant surprise for the Foreign Office, for it had no plans for a loan to Mexico. The "substantial" financial aid promised to Carranza in the Zimmermann note was to amount to only 30 million marks following discussions between the Foreign Office and the High Command.[54] "Impossible to forward loan or sums adequate for founding of bank during war," the Foreign Office wired Eckardt, "telegrams 29 and 39 involved money for bribes.[55] In event of appropriate political use, suggest confidential offer of similar amount. Offer substantial support for economic purposes for postwar period."[56]

Eckardt did not give up. He understood that in a situation where a loan appeared to be of decisive importance for the existence of the government, bribes would necessarily be ineffective and that only a significant loan could achieve the desired effect. "Money urgent here," he thus wired again. "Washington offering loan of initial $50 million and creating new pressure to break with us. Please empower me to make a specific offer—at least 100 million pesos—with estimation of when a portion of that sum in gold can arrive here."[57] On 18 June, he was even clearer. "My sense of situation is that Mexico's neutrality, because of demonstrated effects on America, so important that 100 million pesos could be taken from war fund if necessary. Since enormous impact of alliance note, all Mexico encouraged, bribery unnecessary."[58]

Eckardt's warning was not without effect in Berlin. A rupture in Mexico's relations with Germany would have completely discredited, among others, Zimmermann, who was still in office at that time. On 16 July, or before the arrival of Eckardt's second warning, he was told "to please assure the president of our complete readiness to support Mexico financially and economically in the best possible fashion. Request that he forward directly to us full proposals for money transfer, possibly through special emissaries."[59]

The Mexican government, however, began no negotiations with Germany. It had not given up hopes of receiving a loan, if not from the American government, at least from private American sources. At the end of June 1917, Finance Minister Luis Cabrera announced the beginning of negotiations to this end with American bankers. He stated that he was not approaching the American government because Mexico wished to preserve its neutrality.[60]

The negotiations dragged on and finally failed, because the American bankers demanded the same conditions as their government. On 1 November 1917, Cabrera announced the failure of the Mexican-American loan negotiations.[61]

Eckardt appears to have contributed to this result with promises to the Mexican government. In doing so, he was basing himself on the Foreign Office's general agreement for loan negotiations of 16 June. Three weeks later, on 9 July, the situation appeared to be developing along more favorable lines for Eckardt. Delmar arrived in Mexico as representative of the General Staff and told Eckardt that the High Command had agreed to a loan of 100 million pesos for Carranza.[62] In September, when the failure of the negotiations with the United States was already evident, the Mexican government appears to have considered a German loan for the first time. On 8 September, Eckardt wired to Berlin: "I could now permanently weaken American influence if I had 100 million pesos here and could offer them for an emergency."[63] But neither the money nor any corresponding communiqué arrived from Berlin. Unfortunately for German diplomacy, communications via Argentina and through the Swedish embassy were also interrupted. Carranza increasingly lost faith in German diplomacy. "The danger, however, is gradually increasing that the president will feel compelled to accept money from America."[64]

In order to save the situation, Eckardt and Delmar, who still had received no answer from Berlin, decided to make new promises to Carranza. On 26 September, Eckardt conveyed to Carranza the proposals of the Foreign Office for cooperation after the war and a letter from Delmar in which—as he himself reported—"I held out the prospect of weapons, German military instructors and so forth in the event of war. Oral reference to likely arrival in near future of money from Argentina."[65]

Carranza made it clear to the German representatives that under no circumstances did he desire a war with the United States. He would "like to have weapons," he reported, "in the event of a war, but he wanted to avoid such a war."[66] He was obviously attempting to avoid anything that could be interpreted by the United States as a pretext for an intervention. Finally he requested fulfillment of the many German promises. Since Eckardt had been stringing him along for months with general promises, while Delmar could call on him with concrete proposals, he got the impression that the High Command, in contrast to the Foreign Office, was really interested in Mexico. Carranza told Delmar that "he had complete trust in the High Command, but no longer in the Foreign Office, aside from the minister personally." He thus began to negotiate with Delmar. Initially he requested from him "plans, and the like for a factory for Mauser rifles, 7mm, with a daily output of 200 rifles . . ., as well as technical personnel and finally specialists for airplane construction."[67] On 10 October, when the negotiations with the United States were at the point of rupture and his position was becoming increasingly difficult, Carranza asked Delmar for "10,000 rifles immediately, 15 machine guns, 4 million rounds of ammunition as a sample addressed to the executive offices of the telegraph company."[68]

After the negotiations with the United States had finally failed, Carranza contacted Delmar and requested "a loan of 50 million pesos for the founding of a state bank. An additional 50 million shall be raised in Mexico itself. In addition, we are being asked for 20 million pesos for pressing current needs."[69]

Delmar regarded this loan as essential for preserving Mexico's neutrality, but also as a means of transforming the country into a military and political semicolony of Germany. He expressed this bluntly in the negotiations with the Mexican finance minister. As a condition for such a loan, he specifically demanded that the government give "assurances that the country will under no circumstances go to war against us, that money will be used for specified purposes and under German control, commercial advantages in the postwar period, and military supplies only from us."[70] In Delmar's words, these demands were "accepted unconditionally, with the additional possibility of future German influence on the conduct of foreign policy."[71]

In view of the importance of these negotiations, Delmar sent to Madrid an agent of the General Staff, Dr. Gehmann, who was to forward an urgent appeal to Berlin. Gehmann reported that Eckardt had lost Carranza's trust; in addition, he brought with him a message from Eckardt in which the latter asserted that a loan of 100 million pesos was inevitable. "We are convinced that we . . . will have permanently exhausted our options if the situation in Mexico is endangered by further delay in the approval of the requested credits."[72] The military attaché in Madrid, Kalle, supported this demand. He indicated the real importance of Mexico as a base of operations for sabotage activity in the United States and as a connection for German agents en route to India. He requested military and political aid for Mexico, because "Mexican troops on American border . . . limit American troop transports to Europe." Moreover, he still hoped that financial and military aid for Mexico would provoke a Mexican-American war, which could lead to a shift in the Japanese attitude. "The rupture with the United States of a Mexico strengthened by us would perhaps have as a result Japan's intervention in America, but certainly its benevolent neutrality toward Mexico. If the United States came to an agreement with Mexico, a similar agreement with Japan would follow."[73]

The Foreign Office's reply was ambiguous. On the one hand, Eckardt was told: "Requested material support for president technically impossible," but on the other hand the Mexican president was "to convey relevant proposals through Almaraz, whose return was desired."[74] The Germans attempted above all to offer Carranza hope for the postwar period. Eckardt was instructed "to assure Mexico of important economic support after peace was concluded in the event that Mexico remained neutral."[75] Until the end of 1917, all attempts to obtain a loan for Mexico were unsuccessful. The secretary of state of the Foreign Office told Count Rödern in a letter "that it is not possible at this time to give Mexico sums even approaching the amount required for our purposes."[76]

How can the ambivalent attitude of the German government regarding a loan for Mexico be explained? To what can one attribute the fact that Germany was initially willing to provide a loan, but later refused?

After the decision to send the Zimmermann note, both the Foreign Office and the Political Section of the General Staff had discussed the various possibilities for sending money and arms to Mexico. In February 1917 the Political Section suggested that the president of the Deutsche Ozeanreederei in Bremen, Lohmann, who had been sent to the United

States prior to the outbreak of the war to sell all holdings belonging to the German government, transfer $9 million to Mexico. The Reichsbank stated that it was able to send $1.9 million to Mexico. The Deutsch-Südamerikanische Bank, for its part, was willing to provide Eckardt with 3 or 4 million marks through its branch in Mexico.[77] Finally, the Deutsche Bank stated that it would transfer 6 or 8 million marks to Eckardt through the Banco de Comercio e Industria in Mexico. However, it could not guarantee this transaction. The Banco de Comercio e Industria belonged to it and to the American banking house Speyer. The director, De Lima, was considered pro-German, but it was not certain whether he "would comply with instructions having an anti-American thrust."[78]

All these plans were rejected by the Foreign Office in favor of what it considered a better plan, which could raise larger credits and which would not affect the currency reserves. In the same way that the Americans had been used to deliver the Zimmermann note, Germany now wanted to maneuver them into paying the money that was to be used primarily against them. This plan was characterized by the same mixture of cynicism, naiveté, presumptuousness, and incompetence that was shown in the affair of the Zimmermann note.

German firms had purchased large amounts of wool, which because of the world war could not be sent to Germany. The wool was being stored in Buenos Aires and was to be shipped to Germany after the war. The plan of the Foreign Office consisted in selling this wool to a neutral bank. The bank was then to obtain a loan in New York, using the wool as security, and to place this money at the disposal of the German secret service. The bank selected for this transaction was the Spanish Banco de Castilla, which had close business ties with the Deutsch-Südamerikanische Bank, whose director, Klimsch, was German.[79] Had this plan succeeded, credits for 15 to 20 million marks would have been available. But this sum did not approach the 100 million pesos Eckardt was demanding. It is therefore not clear on what basis Delmar was talking about the 100 million which was to emerge from the "Argentine transactions."[80] Were there plans to expand the transaction, or had the High Command simply not gotten its bearings? Nothing more specific can be ascertained in this matter.

The plan, at any rate, failed. The Spanish bank stated that it was not in a position to execute such a transaction, since it had already been on the "French blacklist"[81] for a long time. It was clear to Director Klimsch that the Americans would quickly see through such a deal and would never give it their approval.

After the failure of this plan, the possibilities for the procurement of money for Mexico were severely curtailed. To the extent that credits were obtained prior to the end of 1917, they were not intended for the Mexican government but for the legation and the secret services. Thus, on 18 May,

200,000 marks were designated for espionage and intelligence services.[82] In the wake of the U.S. declaration of war and the stiff American measures against German firms, the money transfers that had initially been considered could no longer be made. At that point, only two paths remained open. German businessmen in Mexico and in other Latin American countries could be urged to provide money to the German legation, if they were compensated in Germany with an equivalent in marks. The second option was the transfer of money from neutral countries to Mexico.

The first option was used to cover the legation's considerable expenses for propaganda, sabotage, bribery, and so forth. The constant monetary depreciation in Mexico and the insecure position of the banks had prompted German businessmen in Mexico to deposit much of their money in American banks. When German monies in American banks were confiscated after the United States entered the world war, German businessmen were compelled to seek other means of security for their financial holdings. The German envoy offered to compensate them in marks in Germany for whatever they handed over in Mexican pesos. Many German businessmen immediately turned over large sums, totaling 2,759,679 marks.[83] These monies were in fact sufficient for the ongoing expenditures of the legation, but not for a loan to the government.

The Foreign Office appears to have abandoned completely the idea of a loan for Mexico at the end of 1917. The impractical way chosen for funneling money to Mexico may not have been the only cause for this shift in the attitude of the German government. After Zimmermann had been toppled in August 1917, Kühlmann was named as his successor. Kühlmann advocated, if only hesitantly, a settlement in the west and, in keeping with this, may have called for German moderation in Mexico. This attitude emerged, for example, when, in October 1917, the Foreign Office suddenly characterized the Zimmermann note in a confidential circular as devastating for the mood of the American population. "The press' slanderous activities were tremendously facilitated," read the circular, "by the disclosure of the telegram to the kaiser's legation in Mexico. This telegram did unusual damage to the German cause in the United States, in that it convinced wide strata of the justice of the American government's cause. In German-American circles, the telegram was widely deplored. This attitude, however, was mixed with bitter reproaches against the German authorities who had not concealed this dangerous secret more skillfully."[84]

With regard to Mexico, Kühlmann saw in microcosm what he later came to feel in a general way: the determining role of the armed forces in German foreign policy. When, at the end of 1917, money had still not arrived in Mexico, Delmar himself went to Madrid in order to make one last attempt to obtain a loan for Mexico through the High Command. "Should Carranza fall for lack of funds," he reported to the Political Section, "and should Díaz come to power with the help of the Allies, we will be finished once and for all. The general consensus is that a break with Mexico must be followed by breaks with Argentina and Chile. For this reason, something absolutely must be done for Mexico. Minister and I are making urgent request for rapid reply and finally for lucidity."[85] Delmar's warning did not go unheeded. The General Staff conveyed his communiqué to the Reichskanzler, and added: "A tying up of American troops on the southern border of the United States is also of importance for the High Command. General Ludendorff would thus be grateful if such a development were expedited by us."[86] One day after the arrival of the High Command's decision, the secretary of state in the Foreign Office wired Eckardt that the Mexican government should immediately send a representative to Germany for loan negotiations and sales of raw materials.[87]

## German Plans for the Economic Penetration of Mexico

Ludendorff's instructions set in motion an activation of Germany's Mexico policy. The year 1918 marked the high point of German efforts at expansion in Mexico and of the German-American struggle for hegemony in that country. This struggle was waged in three domains, the economy, espionage and secret service activity, and propaganda.

In the economic sphere, a shift occurred in the attitude of important circles of large German capital. For the first time since the outbreak of the war, German capitalists began to show an active interest in Mexico. It became increasingly clear to many industrialists and bankers that the ambitious German war aims could not be realized in their entirety and that their hope of obtaining all important raw materials from German possessions was destined to remain a chimera. Thus they began to seek sources of raw materials primarily in the neutral countries. In this search, Mexico, which was not only extremely rich in raw materials but which also welcomed German capital, came increasingly to the fore. This shift in the attitude of German capital was also warmly welcomed and encouraged by civil and military authorities. The Foreign Office instructed Eckardt to make all preparations necessary for the purchase of raw materials in Mexico in the postwar period. In view of the difficult communication with the legation in Mexico, the expansion in Mexico was also actively supported through the military-commercial division of the German embassy in Bern. In the spring of 1918, this embassy succeeded in recruiting as an agent the Mexican general consul in Bern, Dominguez, "whose pro-German sympathies and capabilities in dealing with economic problems are indisputable."[88] Dominguez was planning to travel to Mexico in June–August 1918. He stated his willingness "to take care of all questions of an economic nature concerning Germany, in part through his own knowledge, and in part through experiences he would acquire during his next stay in Mexico."[89] In particular he was to investigate possibilities for the purchase of raw materials and for the acquisition of raw materials concessions. The military-commercial division informed the large German concerns of this project and asked them to make their wishes known.

When all preparations had been made for Dominguez's trip, an important meeting took place on 30 July 1918, in the building of the Zentralverband Deutscher Industrieller, in order to make fundamental decisions on German expansion to Mexico and to provide Dominguez with concrete assignments. Thirty-eight representatives of leading German economic associations and enterprises took part in the meeting, which was chaired by President Rötger of the Zentralverband Deutscher Industrieller.

The secretary of state in the Foreign Office and former minister to Mexico, Paul von Hintze, sent a message to the participants. In it he expressed hope that the meeting would make manifest "the willingness of industry and commerce" to establish business ties to Mexico and to expand and solidify those that already existed.[90] The Reich Economic Office and the Ministry of War expressed themselves in similar fashion. The secretary of state in the Reich Economic Office used the occasion to express his particular interest in Mexican oil: "From an economic viewpoint, I would consider it most welcome if Germany could gain a foothold in the tremendous potential of Mexican oil production."[91] The Ministry of War emphasized the importance of this meeting with the statement: "The army administration will consider it of decisive importance for Germany to be provided with raw materials in the period after the war, and thus asks that efforts in this direction be supported in every way possible."[92]

The keynote speech was made by the representative of the military-commercial division at the German embassy in Bern, Nölting. He underlined the willingness of the Carranza government to make concessions and stated: "Energetic economic activity on our part in Mexico would provide Carranza's government with support against the pressing demands for concessions from the north, which, if they were granted, would gradually bring the country completely under American influence."[93] Nölting then indicated the discussion on this question which was in progress in leading financial circles. "Many German circles," he elaborated,

> have the view that there is no point in purchases of raw materials in Mexico, for we will either achieve the kind of peace we need, and will then obtain all the raw materials, or we will get an unsatisfactory peace, and then we will have to turn our attention eastward. Others say that purchases of raw materials would be very good, if they only knew how long the war would last, for otherwise interest, storage, and insurance

costs will make goods far more expensive. Some people think, however, that in all likelihood the lack of raw materials will make itself increasingly felt in the United States and that they will be compelled to turn to the Mexican market. The pressing demands for concessions by the Americans already speak for such a view.[94]

Nölting unequivocally advocated penetration of Mexico. In his view, "the Allies are aiming at the control of all raw materials and will attempt to close off all sources to us. If there is a compromise peace, they may officially let us buy what we need without constraints. In reality, however, all sources of raw materials may already be in firm control. It is, however, doubtful that after the conclusion of peace, the Allies would declare themselves willing to provide us with the necessary raw materials. If our foreign companies do not prevent such a situation by securing all accessible and desirable materials as well as the ongoing production of these materials in time, hardly anything will be left for us after the conclusion of peace."[95] Nölting proposed that Dominguez be provided with a secret code. He was to wire Germany immediately about the concessions and raw materials he could obtain, and the economic circles, for their part, were to wire back their decisions immediately so that he could act without delay.[96]

Rötger summarized the results of the meeting in the following way:

1. The question of cost ought to play no role, in view of the national interest, and as far as individual interests are concerned, the companies involved are to help cover the costs.

2. The government authorities are to be informed that commerce and industry have a greater interest in the resumption of commercial relations with Spain and Mexico.

3. The reestablishment in practice of commercial ties with Mexico, beyond mere announcements and reports, is in the interest of the economic power of the German Reich. The Reich Economic Office and the Board of Directors of the Reichsbank are thus to be informed that regarding the realization of our outstanding liabilities and the exchange rate problem, we recommend a procedure comparable to English practice, that is, acquisition of raw materials without regard for monies committed.

4. The question of the extent to which the Reich Economic Office is willing to give German firms free disposal of the raw material required is to be clarified.[97]

These measures were not adequate for many German businessmen and bankers. Several days after this meeting, on 3 August 1918, leading Hamburg banks and commercial firms submitted a memorandum to the Foreign Office. In this memorandum, they emphasized the great importance of Mexico's neutrality for German companies. If the Americans succeeded in drawing Mexico into the world war, they wrote, "the result would be not only a considerable strengthening of our enemies during the war, but German influence for the postwar period would also be lost in an area whose significance *extends far beyond the framework of the interests of German commerce.*"98 Thus, they demanded that Carranza be granted a loan of 200 to 300 million pesos. "The Carranza government *must* obtain the money in the near future," they asserted in backing up their demand, "in order to be able to bring the country back to a healthy situation; it *can* have such a loan from the Allied countries, and especially from the United States of North America, but at the price of giving up their neutrality toward Germany and the Central Powers." In return for a loan, they proposed, among other things, "*(a)* the supply of local products and minerals essential for Germany on the basis of supplier contracts for the postwar period, guaranteed by the Mexican government and groups close to it; *(b)* customs preferences, for a period to be determined, on important individual exports which, as in the case of guayule, when compared with the low prices for plantation rubber, Mexico will no longer be able to export without a tariff reduction; *(c)* the granting of concessions on oil-producing properties and on mining rights for mineral production of importance to Germany."99

The German financial circles focused their main attention on Mexican oil. The Erdöl AG, closely tied to the Disconto-Gesellschaft, showed, in the words of the state secretary in the Reich Economic Office, "lively interest" in Mexican oil properties and was in the process of privately sending "a reliable Swiss geologist to Mexico for further study of the situation."100 The Reich Economic Office also established contact with the Deutsche Petroleum AG. This company, with ties to the Deutsche Bank, showed less interest; the Deutsche Bank obviously expected to be able to resume its collaboration with American firms after the war. But it did not wish to abandon the field completely to the Disconto-Gesellschaft. Therefore, it held out the prospect of investments of between half a million and one million marks in Mexican oil.101 The Deutsche Bank's attitude prompted the Reich Economic Office to grant the Disconto-Gesellschaft a leading role in investments in Mexican oil. "I am prepared," wrote the secretary of state in the Reich Economic Office, "to grant the Deutsche Erdöl AG a share larger than that of any other participant in the formation of such a group and to see to it that the costs to Deutsche Erdöl AG of sending a geologist or other expenses which I have approved are borne by the group as a whole."102

None of these plans for Germany's expansion were ever realized. Even before its defeat in the First World War, they had been given up, for various reasons. The view of an important section of large capital mentioned by Nölting that "then we will have to turn our attention eastward" was actually put into effect. In the east, the Germans hoped to secure the necessary raw materials for the "transitional period" without having to put up the financing. On 27 August 1918, costly additional treaties were imposed on Soviet Russia, providing for Soviet deliveries to Germany totaling 6 billion marks.[103] The resources necessary for an ambitious expansion in Mexico were no longer available to Germany in the last months of the war. Here as elsewhere, the contradiction between the desires and possibilities of German imperialism was expressed in particularly crass form.

There was also a series of lesser factors. Dominguez's trip was postponed when the suspicion surfaced that he was in the pay of the Allies.[104] The Disconto-Gesellschaft began to doubt Carranza's sympathies for Germany and thus put off its investment plans in Mexico. On 19 October 1918, the secretary of state of the Reich Economic Office wrote: "General Director Nöllenberg has raised doubts, in the wake of reports recently received on the comportment of the Carranza government with regard to American and Japanese oil interests, on the advisability at this time of official moves by the German government regarding the Mexican government. I cannot dismiss these concerns as unfounded out of hand."[105]

The gap, so characteristic for Germany, between its desires and actual possibilities was expressed with particular clarity in the negotiations for a German loan to Mexico in 1918.

The announcement by the Foreign Office at the beginning of January 1918 that the Mexican government was being requested to send a representative to Berlin for loan negotiations gave Eckardt hope that the Reich was finally prepared to go along with his increasingly urgent requests. At the end of 1917, he had once again wired that the situation was "extremely critical." He spoke of an "important shift in public opinion engendered through a clever press campaign by the Allies. As a result of this campaign, the dangerous belief had become widespread that the economic situation, which had deteriorated even further as a result of a bad corn harvest, absolutely required immediate aid from abroad, and that proposed U.S. aid had been thwarted up to the present only by Germany's empty promises."[106]

Eckardt's disappointment must have been all the greater when, at the end of February, he was informed of the sum allotted to Mexico, totaling 10 million Spanish pesetas or 5 million Mexican pesos, one-twentieth of what he had estimated as the most urgent requirements of the country. A Spanish bank held this amount in the account of the Foreign Office. It was not the Foreign Office but Bleichröder who was to make the loan officially and who signed a contract to this effect with the Foreign Office. The loan was to be credited to Mexico's account in Spain; it extended over three years with interest and fees totaling 6.5 percent.[107]

There is no indication in the documents that Eckardt ever informed the

Mexican government of the proposed amount. He was obviously afraid that the Mexicans would then send no representative to Berlin, and he may have hoped that the German government would change its attitude during negotiations in Berlin. His efforts were thus directed both at getting the Mexican government to send a representative and at urging larger concessions from the German government. He was also supported in this enterprise by Delmar, who wrote in mid-March: "Mexican Finance Minister Nieto told me that he could raise 50 million pesos in domestic loans without involving German banking houses. With the inclusion of German houses, in my opinion, this amount could be considerably increased. A radio message to Mexico to this effect would be highly recommended."[108]

When Eckardt, in keeping with his instructions, asked the Mexican government to send a delegate to Germany for negotiations, the Mexicans showed far greater reserve than could have been supposed from the reports of Eckardt and Delmar. "I will probably receive answer to telegram about loan after finance minister's return from Washington," Eckardt reported. "President has already told me that he needs the approval of the Congress for a loan, but not for advances on a loan."[109]

The key to an understanding of the attitude of the Mexican government is probably to be found in the first part of this telegram, in which there is reference to the presence of Mexico's finance minister in Washington. The Mexican government apparently still had hopes of obtaining a loan in the United States. In July 1918, it directed another request along these lines to the American government. According to information from the military commercial division at the German embassy in Bern, the Mexicans asked for a "loan of 300 million gold pesos." The United States was prepared to make a loan of 100 million pesos, but nonetheless posed the following conditions: "immediate break in diplomatic relations with Germany, economic war and later war with Germany."[110] The Mexican government refused. It is not out of the question that the Mexicans viewed the negotiations with Germany as a means of pressure for obtaining an American loan without giving up neutrality and the constitution of 1917.

This factor may also have played a considerable role in the trip made to Spain in the spring of 1918 by Carranza's former foreign minister Isidro Fabela, who was still one of his closest collaborators. According to Eckardt's account, he was "empowered to engage in loan negotiations" with Germany.[111]

Fabela was shadowed throughout his trip by the American secret service. The route to Spain was by way of Havana, where American officials watched all passengers en route from Mexico to Europe who aroused their suspicion. In general, the suspects were held by the Cuban authorities, who then turned them over to the Americans. This procedure could not be used in the case of Fabela, for he carried a diplomatic passport protecting him from such investigations. Fabela himself told the author that from the moment he left the ship, he was watched by American police agents. A European diplomat told him that the Americans had planned an episode which would have given them a pretext to bring him to a police station. There, he was to be physically searched; the Americans hoped to find a draft of an alleged secret treaty between Germany and Mexico. Fabela avoided such an attack by not leaving his hotel. His baggage, however, was stolen. Fabela lodged an energetic protest with the Cuban Foreign Ministry. Shortly before his ship's departure to Europe, the baggage was "found" by Cuban officials, but all the locks had been broken and the suitcases searched.[112]

In May 1918, Fabela arrived in Madrid. Delmar, who was there at the time, wanted to meet with him, but Fabela refused to receive him.[113] The German ambassador wrote to Berlin that Fabela had "special orders for Berlin, where he is to function as a minister. Requests transportation by U-boat."[114] Kühlmann urged the Admiral Staff to accept this request: "because of the Mexican government's previous sympathies for Germany and the importance of these sympathies for us, it would be of the greatest political desirability if the envoy's request could be fulfilled. In doing so, however, the greatest caution with regard to Spanish sensibilities would be called for. More specifically, the execution of the plan can be considered only if it can be arranged, through a secret rendezvous, to have the individual in question picked up from a merchant ship on high seas."[115] The Admiral Staff, however, refused. "Rendezvous with U-boat unfortunately not practicable," read the reply, "without either violation of Spanish terms of neutrality or exposing U-boat to destruction."[116]

Fabela was advised either to go to Scandinavia on a neutral ship and to travel from there to Germany or to conduct his business through the German ambassador in Madrid.[117] Fabela did nothing of the kind, but left Spain soon thereafter for Argentina. His actions raise the question of whether he actually was supposed to carry on loan negotiations. Fabela himself told the author that he had had no instructions to begin loan negotiations with Germany and that he had also never gone to the German embassy. It is possible that the Mexican government only wanted to use Fabela's mission as a further means to pressure the United States and that it was not very interested in actual loan negotiations with Germany.

After Fabela's departure, Delmar decided to enter into direct negotiations with the Mexican envoy in Madrid. He was empowered by Berlin "to take the Mexican envoy into his confidence and to ask him if he knew a safe way for the remittance of monies."[118] The envoy assured Delmar that he had couriers who would transport the money safely. In addition, he stated, he had wired Carranza to come immediately to Madrid to conclude the arrangements.[119]

The loan, however, never materialized. The precise reasons for this cannot, unfortunately, be ascertained. It is probable, however, that the Mexican government was not very interested in a German loan which would destroy all its hopes for a financial agreement with the United States without securing substantial aid. Since Mexico did not wish to flatly refuse Germany, which it still needed as a counterweight against the United States, it is not unlikely that the Mexican government intentionally prolonged the affair.

On 11 October 1918, the German ambassador in Madrid urgently requested 10 million pesetas for the embassy's activities, since, "in view of developments, the procurement of money through Banco de Castilla might encounter insurmountable difficulties."[120] The deputy secretary of state agreed, "since the kaiser's minister apparently does not need the money, or remittance has apparently not been possible, we also have no interest in giving money to Mexico at the present time."[121] Thus the attempt to form links to Mexico with a German loan had finally failed.

The German authorities never showed any willingness in 1918 to exceed the amount of 10 million pesetas. In March 1918, the Foreign Office was informed that a German agent of Swiss citizenship was to travel to Mexico. The Foreign Office told him to inform Carranza "that Germany could not unfortunately provide Mexico with any larger financial support at the moment,"[122] but that it hoped "to be in a position to be able to satisfy Mexico's future financial needs in the postwar period." There is, however, no indication to be found that the Swiss actually went to Mexico.

Delmar's proposal that German firms in Mexico should be enlisted in a loan to Carranza was intentionally misunderstood. Delmar had written: "Thus, in view of general uncertainties, a great deal of money in Mexico, including that of German firms, is being withheld in safes. There are good reasons to believe that if the minister requested it, these firms would be willing to place a significant amount of their money at the disposal of the Mexican government, provided that the Bleichröder bank took over the guarantees."[123] The German government explained that Bleichrörder could only take over a guarantee for 5 million pesos, that is, for the envisioned 10 million pesetas, and added: "Should a loan be raised domestically in Mexico, we would consider it politically advisable for German firms not to be left out, provided that the government puts up worthwhile security."[124]

What was the source of the reticent attitude of the German government toward the requests of the Mexican government and of Eckardt and Delmar and toward the all-embracing proposals of the German firms in Mexico on 3 August? Part of the reason was undoubtedly expressed by the director of the head office of the Deutsch-Südamerikanische Bank, W. Fricke, who had lived in Mexico for years and who came out against the loan proposal of the German businessmen in Mexico in a memorandum to the Foreign Office.[125]

Fricke initially stated that "because of the currency in circulation, the Reichsbank could not spare half a billion in gold." He saw, moreover, no way of transferring the money to Mexico, and "depositing the money in a neutral foreign country would probably not achieve the objective, because the paper money issued against it in Mexico would be badly viewed, since the people have become extremely skeptical toward all paper money after the experiences of recent years." He argued that the Mexican government could hardly grant concessions "as almost everything is already in private hands." He was especially afraid that a German loan for Carranza could lead to his overthrow. "What would be gained politically?" he asked. "I mean: open hostility and unconstrained actions against Carranza by the Allies. This would not even require great exertion on the part of the Allies, which could take some pressure off us, and we would have achieved exactly what should have been prevented." In contrast to the businessmen, Fricke expressed the opinion that Mexico would not capitulate to the United States, even without a loan. "In my opinion, we can expect nothing more than what its most immediate interests require it to do: preserve its independence from the United States.... Carranza knows what tremendous services Germany can render Mexico after the war, if the bill for damages caused during the revolution is presented by the Allies."[126]

The most important factor determining German "reserve" during the period when large German capital was showing interest in Mexico was impotence. The ambitious plans for expansion were made in the shadow of impending defeat. Even if it had wanted to, the government in this period was hardly in a position to provide large sums of money to Mexico.

### The German Secret Service in Mexico

After the United States entered the world war, the German secret service in North America had moved its headquarters to Mexico. When, in October 1917, the German military attaché in Spain, Kalle, was emphasizing Mexico's importance for Germany, he pointed especially to the possibility of "sabotage in the United States."[127] Three state bodies were involved in this activity: the Political Section of the General Staff, the Admiral Staff, and the Foreign Office, whose representatives in Mexico were deeply involved in the work of the secret service.

The representative of the Political Section in Mexico and leader of its agent network there was Delmar, whose real name was Anton Dilger. Dilger (alias Delmar), a German-American—his father had immigrated to the United States shortly before the outbreak of the American Civil War and had risen during the course of the war to the rank of brigadier general in the American army—was born in 1884 in Port Royal, Virginia. He studied medicine, first at Johns Hopkins University in Maryland and later in Heidelberg. After the outbreak of the world war, he officially entered the service of the German Red Cross and worked for a long period as a doctor in a military hospital in Karlsruhe. This "humanitarian" activity was compatible with his status as an American citizen, but his activities as an agent, which he had been performing for the German secret service since 1915, were not. At the behest of the secret service, he had gone to the United States, where he waged "bacteriological warfare": he established laboratories for the cultivation of bacilli with which cattle destined for the Allies were to be infected.

In January 1916, Delmar returned to Germany, officially to continue his "humanitarian" activities with the German Red Cross. But as early as February 1916, he took part in an important conference of the Political Section of the General Staff, at which plans for the intensification of sabotage activity in the United States and Mexico were worked out, and in June 1917, he was sent to Mexico as the leader of the North American division of the Political Section. Because of his American citizenship and his previous caution, he was able to cross the Atlantic unmolested and get to Mexico, where he arrived at the end of August.[128]

The Political Section appointed a certain Hinsch as Delmar's assistant. Hinsch was the captain of the steamship *Neckar*, which was used to supply coal to German warships. At the time of the outbreak of the world war, the *Neckar* found itself on the high seas. Hinsch immediately went to the American port of Baltimore, where he remained. Very quickly, he became a leading member of the German secret service and played a decisive role in the two most important German sabotage actions in the United States during the First World War, helping to set ablaze the Black Tom shipyard in New York and the Kingsland factory in New Jersey.[129] In June 1917, as the situation was becoming more and more difficult for him in the United States—Hinsch was a German citizen and was faced with the prospect of internment or at least surveillance—he moved to Mexico, where he became Delmar's right-hand man.[130]

At roughly the same time, Kurt Jahnke arrived in Mexico to assume the direction of the German navy's secret service for North America. It was German naval intelligence that had carried out most of Germany's covert activities in Mexico. Sommerfeld had been recruited by the German naval attaché in Washington, Boy Edd, and sabotage experts from the navy had planned the destruction of the Mexican oil fields. Long before the outbreak of World War I, the German navy had set up what was apparently the first covert network of agents embracing all of the American continent. In the major port cities and in many capitals of American states an "Etappendienst der Marine" was set up whose main task it was to furnish German warships with coal and other supplies in times of war.[131] This organization constituted the backbone of Germany's naval intelligence organization after the outbreak of World War I.

On the whole the activities of these naval agents were not very successful. Sommerfeld was found to be a German agent and interned by American authorities after the United States declared war on Germany (though his participation in a plot to have Villa attack the United States was never discovered by the Americans). The navy's plans for sabotaging the Mexican oil fields were never implemented and Boy Edd's covert activities in the United States were so obvious that he was declared persona non grata and expelled from the United States.

According to a report submitted by the head of the "Etappendienst" in the United States, Knorr, it suffered a number of similar setbacks mainly through the incompetence of its personnel. The report on the activities of this service in Mexico is characterized by a strange mixture of grotesque descriptions and bureaucratic dryness.[132]

Several weeks after the outbreak of World War I, when the United States was still neutral, the German cruiser *Leipzig* arrived in San Francisco to refuel. In accordance with American neutrality laws U.S. authorities allowed the cruiser to remain only twenty-four hours, and to obtain only a limited amount of coal. At this point German naval agents in San Francisco decided to supply the *Leipzig* surreptitiously with more coal. For this purpose the steamer *Mazatlán* was chartered and loaded with coal without the knowledge of the American authorities. It was a difficult operation since from the first the Americans were extremely hostile to Germany. According to Knorr, this hostility was caused mainly by the appearance of the German consul in San Francisco, Schack, above all his "wearing a monocle and using the clipped tones of the Prussian guard."[133]

Nevertheless, it had been possible to load the *Mazatlán* without attracting the attention of the Americans. For its trip to the port of Guaymas in Mexico, where the *Leipzig* was awaiting the supply ship, the agents had chartered a young German, Captain Jebsen, known to be "daring" and to be on good terms with "dubious elements in the United States and Mexico." "Unfortunately," Knorr remarked, "Jebsen had one weakness, his liking for women." The departure of the *Mazatlán* was delayed because, as Knorr put it, "Jebsen spent the night with girlfriends." While the captain was thus occupied, a fire broke out on board the *Mazatlán*,

American firemen put out the fire, and U.S. authorities discovered the undeclared coal. They warned the German consul that if the coal was delivered to the *Leipzig*, they would impose a heavy fine on him. Jebsen nevertheless sailed for the Mexican port of Guaymas and delivered the coal to the cruiser *Leipzig*. Unfortunately, he had not been very careful about the men he hired, and the telegrapher was an Englishman, with whom he had quarelled. When the *Mazatlán* arrived at its destination in Mexico the telegrapher immediately went to the British consulate, alerted British naval intelligence, which followed the loading of the German cruiser from a hilltop in Guaymas. The Americans, upon hearing of this, were so incensed that they imposed a heavy fine on the German authorities who had hired the *Mazatlán*. But they decided to go further. According to Knorr, Jebsen had taken along on the trip "two ladies of dubious reputation," and, as soon as the ship returned to San Francisco, he was arrested by the vice squad in San Francisco for violating the "white slavery" act. As a result of these activities, the operations of the "Etappendienst" were curtailed for a time in the United States.

Jahnke, the man who in 1918 assumed the direction of the covert activities of the German navy in North America, was of a different caliber. He was probably the most intelligent of all the German agents. Not only was he an extremely able saboteur, but he was also a man whose specialty it was to infiltrate popular organizations and use them for his own purposes. He thus set up sabotage networks in the United States with the help of Irish lodges and trade unions opposed to the war. He was the only one of the German agents in America who was to play a prominent role in Germany after World War I. Jahnke became involved in multiple conspiracies staged by parts of the German army, the so-called Black Reichswehr in the 1920s. After Hitler came to power he became adviser to Rudolf Hess on intelligence matters. After Hess defected to England, Jahnke became a member of the Sicherheitsdienst of the SS and a close collaborator of its most prominent leaders Reinhard Heydrich and Walter Schellenberg.[134] He was captured by Russian troops in 1945 and probably died in Soviet captivity. Officially, he was a private detective in San Francisco but, according to information from American customs officials, appears to have been involved in other ventures, especially the smuggling of arms and opium. He maintained close ties to the German consulate in San Francisco and was recruited to the secret service shortly after the outbreak of the world war by Boy Edd.[135]

Shortly after the arrival of Jahnke and Delmar in Mexico, deep tensions developed between Eckardt and Jahnke on the one hand and between Delmar and Hinsch on the other. The representatives of the individual German secret service in Mexico were independent and were responsible only to their superiors in Berlin. Since communications with Germany were often slow and difficult, sources of conflict easily developed. Political motives, above all, lay at the bottom of these conflicts.

Delmar had traveled to Madrid at the end of 1917 and had left behind instructions with his assistant, Captain Hinsch, for extensive sabotage activity in Mexico, including plans for the Tampico arson and for the organization of bands in northern Mexico for attacks on the United States.[136] At the same time, he had attempted to strengthen his position by seeking to replace Jahnke with Hinsch, who was completely devoted to him. Such a development would have signified a decisive weakening of the position of Eckardt, who was working very closely with Jahnke. Jahnke needed Eckardt's support in his competitive struggle with Delmar, but he shared fully Eckardt's attitude on the curtailment of sabotage activity in Mexico, since he absolutely required a calm political environment for the construction of U-boat bases in Mexico and as a refuge from which to conduct sabotage work in the United States. In December, Delmar was successful in obtaining a directive for himself from Berlin with the support of the German military attaché in Madrid. He had criticized Jahnke's lack of organizational abilities, "his lively fantasy, his American mentality and his dual nationality," but had recommended at the same time that Jahnke not be completely dropped because he knew too much and might otherwise turn against Germany. When Eckardt was informed by Berlin that Jahnke was to be replaced by Hinsch, he responded by joining forces with Jahnke and passing over to the counterattack. Jahnke characterized Hinsch as incompetent in a report to the Admiral Staff. He listed his own achievements, including the sinking of one Japanese, one British, and two American steamers, and the destruction of the DuPont factory in Tacoma, and mentioned that he had built agent networks in the United States, Argentina, Chile, Panama, Japan, the Philippines, Hawaii, and Alaska.[137] Eckardt himself contacted the Foreign Office on 21 February: "Collaboration between Jahnke and Hinsch is impossible because of mutual distrust. Jahnke's successful work cannot be interrupted, and I will continue to support him financially. On the basis of very grave experiences, I request that Dr. Delmar, Hinsch, and Jahnke be formally subordinated to my authority."[138]

This claim arrived in Berlin at a time when the political leadership was dominated in every sphere by the military High Command. Thus neither the Admiral Staff nor the General Staff was willing to subordinate their agents in Mexico to the representative of the Foreign Office. But they were aware of the fact that military personnel, who were hard to control from Berlin because of the difficult communications with Mexico, could easily bring about a break with Mexico through independent actions. Such a break would not have fit in either militarily or economically with the plans of the army or the navy. At the beginning of 1918, Ludendorff had stated that Mexico's most important use for Germany lay in tying up large contingents of American troops on the Mexican border; on the economic level, officials in the Ministry of War began to consider Mexico seriously as a supplier of raw materials for the postwar period at the beginning of 1918.

The reply to Eckardt took these viewpoints into account. The military leadership refused to subordinate their agents to him ('' direct subordination of Jahnke and Delmar to Your Excellency not desired''), but granted him de facto veto power over the activities of the agents, who were to undertake ''nothing in Mexico'' without his approval.[139] In the final directive of the Foreign Office, ''nothing in Mexico'' was shortened simply to ''nothing'' and Eckardt was thus granted a larger scope of action.

Eckardt's most important request, his insistence on retaining Jahnke, was, however, granted: ''Jahnke sole representative of navy.''[140] In practice, Jahnke thus became the most important German secret agent in Mexico, since Delmar was in Spain. He not only took over the direction of the navy's agent network, but also part of the network of the Political Section of the General Staff.[141]

**Attempts to Set up a German Wireless Station in Mexico**

One of the most important requirements for successful activity by the German secret service in Mexico was the maintenance of regular communication with the head offices at home. When all cable communications had been interrupted, some possibilities for communication with Germany still remained open to the German operatives in Mexico. The first option was the German embassy in the United States. In the beginning, the transmission of communiqués through the United States occurred virtually without difficulty. Such transmission became much more difficult, even impossible, when, in the middle of 1915, the American naval authorities placed all communiqués broadcast from the Sayville radio station to Nauen under censorship. In addition, the American government had permitted use of its own overseas cable for the transmission of German ''messages of peace.'' The extent to which the Germans misused this privilege was seen in the events surrounding the Zimmermann note.

The American link was completely closed off after the United States entered the war in April 1917. Even earlier, however, the Germans had developed a new means for the transmission of communiqués to the United States and to Mexico: the Swedish government stated its willingness, in spite of its neutrality, to transmit coded German messages. The Zimmermann note, among others, had arrived at its destination through this route, and Eckardt's reports to Berlin passed through the same channel. In September 1917, however, the Swedish route was also closed down. The Americans had published a German telegram intercepted by the British secret service, in which Eckardt proposed the Swedish minister to Mexico, Folke Cronholm, for a decoration, because he had untiringly forwarded reports for Germany.[142] Cronholm confirmed these allegations to Fletcher, but insisted that he had only been acting on orders from his government.[143] The Allies promptly placed Swedish telegrams under surveillance.

There had been efforts in Germany to prepare for such a development. The American censorship at the Sayville radio station and the growing tensions with the United States had already prompted the German authorities to seek means of communication independent of the United States in 1916. To this end, an extensive radio network in Latin America was planned, mainly to include receiving stations with transmitting capacities of real importance, since these stations were to be used not only for diplomatic communications and instructions to agents, but also for propaganda purposes. These receiving installations, which were "of immediate importance for the war," were to be built in Mexico, Colombia, Ecuador, Peru, Chile, Argentina, Uruguay, Brazil, Surinam, and Venezuela.[144] This project was in keeping with a plan developed even before the war for the creation of a worldwide radio network and was in no way conceived purely for wartime use. It was asserted "that it...is absolutely necessary at least to make an attempt to establish ourselves in those parts of the world which are of significance for our worldwide radio and telegraph network."[145]

The beginning was to be made in Mexico. In May 1916, Eckardt had wired the Foreign Office: "Desire installation of radio and telegraph connection between Mexico and Germany. In Mexico, a high frequency machine with transmitter would be necessary."[146] In letters to the Reich Post Office and to the naval command, the Foreign Office urgently supported this proposal with the argument that such a link "would make us independent of the North American stations."[147]

The Reich Post Office came out against the proposal. It argued in its assessment that the station in Mexico would be almost 3,000 kilometers farther from Nauen than the American Sayville station and that such an installation would cost millions, which the Reich government was hardly willing to provide. The Post Office further argued that it would be very difficult to send the necessary equipment and workers to Mexico.[148] The Admiral Staff was much more positive toward Eckardt's proposals. Initially it expressed doubt about whether it would be right to build the transmitter, because it would not be ready for operations in two years at the earliest. "For the current war, there is thus nothing to be gained from the construction of a second major radio installation on the American continent." The Admiral Staff, however, considered it necessary to view the whole affair "not merely from the viewpoint of our situation in the current war, but in the context of an overall plan for a future German worldwide radio and telegraph." The Admiral Staff totally supported the construction of a simple receiving installation. "A receiver could . . . easily be built at little cost and in a relatively short period, . . . through which the *most urgent* needs (general war reports, instructions of the Reichskanzler) might be taken care of."[149]

The conflicts among the various agencies over this question, however, did not stop. On 15 July, the Reich Post Office once again asserted its opposition to the construction of any kind of radio installation in Mexico. It stated that the equipment for such a station could not be sent to the American continent from Germany and that placing an order with the Telefunken subsidiary in the United States, Atlantic Communication Company, would be pointless, for "shipments from the United States to Mexico cannot be sent in view of the current political relations between those countries."[150] The naval command thereupon consulted the Telefunkengesellschaft, which opposed the viewpoint of the Post Office. Therefore, on 9 July, the naval command intervened vigorously against the Reich Post Office: it would "be possible to obtain the necessary equipment without any particular difficulty, as only receiving amplifiers are required." Nor was it difficult to get such equipment out of the United States. "An attempt, in any case, ought to be made, given the tremendous interest of the minister in Mexico in the direct reception of communiqués from Nauen, unhindered by American censorship, particularly as the costs are minimal."[151]

The Reich Post Office then yielded to the pressure of the Admiral Staff and the Foreign Office. The Post Office justified the shift in its thinking, saying that it had been unaware of the receiving station built by Telefunken prior to the war in Mexico City's Chapultepec, which might require only a few improvements.[152] At the same time, it proposed a meeting of representatives from all relevant ministries.

This meeting took place on 22 July, attended by representatives of the post office, the navy, the Foreign Office, and the Telefunkengesellschaft. The group endorsed the construction of a receiving station in Mexico and pointed out that such a station would allow "the German minister in Mexico to receive communiqués unimpeded by the American censorship" and that "uncensored communiqués for the German embassy in Washington could also be sent under certain circumstances."[153] The Telefunkengesellschaft was given the contract for the work involved.

The realization of this project initially ran up against two difficulties. The first difficulty was the procurement of materials. These were to be obtained in the United States, with recommendations that German intentions be camouflaged "by avoiding any visible involvement of the

German embassy or the Atlantic Communication Company." From Mexico, an order for the materials was to be made to "an individual specified by Telefunken. This individual (a technician) shall get the necessary equipment to Mexico, together with a worker with telegraph experience, through appropriate channels, and set up the receiving station."[154] The second difficulty was of a financial nature. The German government actually hoped that the Mexican government would bear the costs, but was so interested in getting the project underway that it was prepared, if necessary, "to cover the costs with Reich finances."[155] The Reich Treasury stated its willingness to pay up to 60,000 marks for costs incurred in the project.[156]

When the plans for the construction of the radio station had been brought to the United States by merchant U-boat, the Telefunkengesellschaft immediately went to work. Through the Dutch engineer Van de Woude, who aroused less suspicion and had more freedom of movement because of his neutral status, the necessary equipment was ordered from the American firm Frorupp by the Mexican subsidiary of Telefunken.[157] The Mexican government put up $5,000 for the order.[158] Its significant interest in such communications, which would make it independent of the United States, was expressed in its memorandum to the German government in November 1916; the Mexican minister to Germany also spoke on behalf of such a link.

After it had been assembled, the equipment was sent to Mexico, probably on a neutral ship, on 28 February 1917.[159] The shipment was made precisely one day before the publication of the Zimmermann note by the Americans, who probably increased their vigilance as a result. On the way to Veracruz, most of the equipment was confiscated by American warships.[160] Construction work on the installation began immediately with the parts which had not been confiscated and with other parts which were found in Mexico. For technical reasons as well as reasons of security, it was built in the suburb Ixtapalapa instead of the existing government station at Chapultepec. On a technical level, better reception was promised if the transmitter and receiver were separated; in addition, the Germans hoped that the installation would escape notice by the Americans through this change of location.[161]

On 9 March, it was announced in the United States that Mexico City was now in direct wireless contact with Nauen. The Admiral Staff immediately informed the kaiser: "It has been reported that the receiving station built in Mexico on German initiative and with German financial and material aid has begun operations. Confirmation of this report has not yet been received."[162] The announcement appears to have been somewhat ahead of events, for the technician in charge wired from Mexico in April: "Have been attempting reception since April 6 from 4 A.M. through

4 P.M. Central European time. No results."[163] Two weeks later, the first communiqués from Nauen were received and from then on communications were open on a regular basis.[164] The premature American announcement was either the result of false information by the U.S. intelligence agencies or, since the announcement was made one week after the publication of the Zimmermann note, was consciously calculated to intensify the impact of the note by attempting to exaggerate German influence in Mexico.

The German legation and the agents of the secret service henceforth received their instructions through this station, and German propaganda received its war reports. All this was passed along by the Mexican government officials in charge of the station. "Coded telegrams for me and for ambassador are delivered to us...by government station,"[165] reported Delmar on 10 December 1917. "The telegraph director, Mr. Mario Mendez, sends me the Nauen war telegrams by Syrian courier every day,"[166] wrote Eckardt in August 1918. Nevertheless, the Germans did not want to be completely dependent upon the Mexican government in this operation. The Political Section of the General Staff thus appears to have built its own receiving station. "I have a secret radio station which can pick up Nauen,"[167] Delmar reported on 9 December 1917. This report is confirmed by U.S. intelligence, which mentioned a radio installation in the house of Delmar's assistant Hinsch.[168]

In 1916, German officials, citing the costs and the lengthy construction period required by a radio station, had manifested their reserve about such a project. At the beginning of 1917, this attitude changed out of fear that Germany would be completely cut off from neutral countries abroad by the Allies. This concern was expressed on 14 February at a meeting involving the Reich Post Office, the Foreign Office, the Reich Colonial Office, the Reich Treasury, the army, and the navy, dealing with plans "for a worldwide radio and telegraph network." The participants came to the conclusion that the former German cables might not be in German hands after the war; "moreover, we have urgent need of direct radio and telegraph links with certain lands, with whom we could previously communicate only by cables under foreign control. Without this radio and telegraph link, Germany would be cut off from world commerce for a long time." It was also pointed out that the Allies had attempted to take over all concessions for radio installations for themselves. It was decided "that the preparation of machines, equipment, and antennae must immediately be set in motion, for the three major stations to be established in Mexico, in China, and in South America, either in Brazil or in Uruguay, regardless of whether they will be in operation during the war."[169]

An agreement on the establishment of a transmitter in Mexico between the Reich Post Office and the Telefunkengesellschaft was then arranged. The latter proposed setting up a provisional transmitter in Mexico, "so that at least receipts, short signals, and, perhaps in favorable circumstances, telegrams can be sent here." Two ways of reaching this goal were mentioned. The first consisted in setting up "a wireless station of 50 to 80 kilowatts using the system with rotating spark gaps." The advantage of such a station would be "that nothing would have to be supplied from here or from America," for it was hoped that most of the necessary materials could be obtained in Mexico. The second proposal was to send to Mexico by U-boat a high-frequency transmitter that had been built for Austria but had not yet been delivered. In any case, the Reich Post Office was to approve Reuthe's travel to Mexico; Reuthe, a German engineer, had worked at the American Sayville station but had recently been removed from his functions there by the American authorities.[170] The second proposal was rejected because the transmitter was too big for a U-boat; the first option was chosen. Reuthe was immediately instructed to go to Mexico, where he arrived a short time later.[171]

In the meantime, however, new difficulties had arisen in Mexico. In April 1917, the Admiral Staff informed the Reich Post Office that the Mexican government was opposed to the construction of the station for "political reasons."[172] This was in keeping with the noncommittal Mexican policy toward Germany in April–May 1917. Several months later, the construction of the station appears to have resumed, and in July 1918, Chapultepec began to broadcast;[173] in Nauen, however, these broadcasts could not be received until the end of the war. Eckardt could not understand the failure of this transmitter. Agents of the American secret service, who were watching the transmitter very carefully, reported that the broadcasts would never be able to reach Germany because of their wave length.[174] The Germans, however, did not limit themselves to receiving messages from Germany and attempting to transmit them, but also attempted to have a direct and indirect effect on the news media in Latin America. Thus, for example, the war reports arriving regularly from Nauen were broadcast to El Salvador, which had remained neutral in the world war.[175]

Of still greater importance was the plan to assemble a radio transmitter (in all probability a receiver) for Argentina in Mexico.[176] German documents give no specific information on this project. It is not unlikely, however, that it was related to a request from the Mexican to the Argentine government, intercepted by the Americans in 1918, requesting permission from Argentina for technicians on a Mexican warship to enter the country and to equip Argentine radio stations to receive broadcasts from Mexico. The Argentine government approved entry for the technicians but was opposed to their coming on a Mexican warship.[177] The Americans assumed, probably not incorrectly, that the technicians were Germans who were being transported on a warship to escape the control of American blockade ships. It is possible that German plans also involved the shipment of the radio equipment to Argentina in this fashion, thus escaping American naval surveillance.[178] Since no further reports on the project are available, it was probably a failure.

The establishment of the German receiving station in Mexico made it possible for the German authorities to receive regular reports and instructions from Berlin even after the interruption of communications through Sweden. The problem of forwarding reports to Berlin was solved with the help of neutral Spain. The reports arriving there were transmitted to Nauen on a transmitter of the German embassy.[179]

The Political Section of the General Staff, which had taken over responsibility for communications with Germany by all German operatives in Mexico, initially attempted to send coded telegrams from commercial firms in Mexico to businessmen in Spain through the United States. But the project failed because of the vigilance of the American censors.[180] Links were maintained by couriers who traveled on Spanish steamers from Veracruz to Spain. The Americans took corresponding countermeasures: in Havana, where the ships had to call, passengers, crews, and ships were thoroughly searched by American intelligence.[181] When these measures proved to be inadequate, the Americans attempted, not without success, to put pressure on the management of the shipping company. "Communications to Mexico have been badly interrupted in the recent period," Delmar reported in March 1918, "for our contacts among the crew of the steamer *Alfonso XIII* were suddenly transferred to the Mediterranean line just before its departure. As a result, our last reports to Mexico did not get out."[182]

But the Americans appear to have had limited success even with these measures, and thus new steps were taken. In April 1918, the Cuban government was asked not to provide coal to Spanish ships en route to Mexico. The result was initially the interruption of communications between Mexico and Spain.[183] In any case the Mexican government was not willing to accept without protest such an interruption, for this made it completely dependent on communications passing through the United States. When the steamer *Alfonso XIII* was unable to continue its trip to Mexico, the Mexican government sent a warship to Havana to pick up mail and passengers going to Mexico.[184] In spite of its own lack of coal, Mexico stated its willingness to provide Spanish steamers with adequate supplies of coal so that shipping could be resumed. The link with Germany was therefore never completely broken.[185]

## German Espionage and Sabotage Activities

The German secret service in Mexico concentrated its activities on the United States, the Far East, Central America, and Mexico itself.

The military attaché in Madrid, Kalle, had filed the operations in the United States under the heading "sabotage."[186] According to the instructions received in May 1918, Jahnke was supposed to incite a revolt in the American army in the spring of 1918, to carry out sabotage actions in the United States, at the Panama Canal, and in American possessions, and to sabotage Japanese ships.[187] Unfortunately, what was actually undertaken along these lines is not known. There is one report by Jahnke in which he claimed to have destroyed four Allied ships in the year 1917.[188]

There appears to have been a division of labor between Jahnke and Hinsch for sabotage activity in the United States. While Hinsch directed his attention primarily toward the East Coast, Jahnke concentrated his efforts on the West Coast.[189] According to his reports, his agents included "Irishmen, priests, state senators and other political figures."[190] An additional group of agents working with Jahnke, whose members were arrested by the American authorities in 1918, was the so-called Irish Secret Lodge,[191] which was working with the Germans out of hostility to England. Nothing is known about the effectiveness of Jahnke's activities in the United States.

East Asia was another field of operations for German agents stationed in Mexico. Kalle characterized Mexico's importance with regard to Asia with the words: "Only from Mexico can we possibly influence the situation in Asia; only link with Indian nationalists."[192]

Among the German plans for taking advantage of revolutionary movements during the First World War was the use of the Indian independence movement against British colonialism. With German aid, an insurrection was to take place, and to this end the Indian National Committee was constituted in Berlin. One of the main centers of these efforts was the United States, where many Indians who had been forced to flee India were living. An attempt had been made, for example, to send weapons from the United States to Indian revolutionaries on a ship allegedly traveling to Mexico; the attempt, however, was a failure.[193] The Americans arrested most of the Indian revolutionaries for violating the Neutrality Acts and brought them to trial in San Francisco.[194]

Shortly after the United States entered the war, many of the Indians who had been working with German authorities left the United States and went to Mexico. The most important of these exiles was M. N. Roy, alias Martin, who had been living in the United States since 1916 in hopes of obtaining arms for Indian revolutionaries with German aid.[195] In June 1917, Roy had to flee the United States. In Mexico, he immediately resumed contact with the German secret service. At the beginning of 1917, Hilmi, a prominent member of the Indian National Committee who until then had been living in New York, was also called to Mexico. There he was to work out all further details for the conspiracy in India with agents of the General Staff and then to proceed to China, where $50,000 had been deposited for him.[196]

The agents from the Political Section of the General Staff responsible for Asian affairs were a former Krupp representative, Vincenz Kraft, and a Dr. Gehmann.[197] They were successful in maintaining ties with Asia. The results of their activities, however, appear to have been quite minimal. As one reason for this, Roy stated that "many German agents, some of them in high positions, were more interested in making money than in 'helping the fatherland to win the war.' Two of these agents, whom I met in Java, were living the high life in Mexico when I arrived there in the summer of 1917."[198]

Japan also interested the German secret service in Mexico, if only indirectly. Ambitious diplomatic actions to pry Japan away from the Allies with the help of Mexico were not attempted after the failure of the Zimmermann note. In December 1917, Eckardt had inquired "how we are to act regarding Japanese attempts at rapprochement. Carranza supports them and wants to arrange a secret meeting with the Japanese minister for me."[199] He was promptly instructed: "Don't get involved in Japanese affairs, as communication through you is too difficult. If the Japanese are serious about this, they have enough representatives in Europe for these purposes."[200]

The Germans nevertheless hoped to purchase arms in Japan both for the planned insurrection in India and for Mexico. Kraft was entrusted with this task, and to support him a Japanese agent of the German secret service, Nakiao, was also sent to Mexico.[201] In October 1917, Kraft traveled to the Far East to obtain arms for Mexico from Japan.[202] Exactly where Kraft went cannot be ascertained. There is little likelihood that he went to Japan, since Japan was at war with Germany. It seems far more probable that he was somewhere in the Dutch East Indies. He had selected two staff members of the Mexican embassy in Tokyo for the arms deal, the commercial attaché Jimenez and his colleague Vera. But Vera, to whom Kraft had given $100,000 for arms purchases, informed the American embassy of the planned transaction.[203] The British military authorities also learned of it; they even obtained a list of all participants in the transaction.[204] It is quite doubtful whether Japan was at all willing to sell arms to Mexico. In any event, the disclosure of the plans assured the failure of the project. In July 1918, Delmar reported: "Apparently Kraft has not made it to Japan, and thus nothing is to come of the arms shipment so urgently desired by Carranza."[205]

An additional field of activity for the German secret service in Mexico appears to have been Central America. On 21 September 1918, the German ambassador in Madrid wired: "Spanish ambassador to Mexico reports intentions of dissatisfied parties in Central American states of overthrowing their heavily pro-American governments and of asking kaiser's minister to Mexico for aid in this project. German minister apparently willing to go along if parties in question give assurances of support from Mexican government beforehand."[206]

In Mexico itself, the German secret service concentrated on five tasks: the building of U-boat bases, the infiltration of the Mexican civil service and especially of the Mexican army, the preparations of attacks on the United States, contacts with Carranza's opponents and counterespionage against the secret services of the United States and the Allies.

The construction of U-boat bases was one of the major objectives pursued by the German navy in Mexico. As early as the end of 1916, the Mexican government had been approached on this matter, but these efforts were not sustained. In the middle of 1918, Jahnke was instructed to make all necessary preparations for the establishment of a U-boat base on the Gulf of Mexico.[207] In August 1918, Eckardt reported, "preparations have been made for any arriving submarines."[208] He and Delmar repeatedly asked the Reich government to send U-boats to the Gulf of Mexico and to attack the American ships lying off the Mexican coast, for the sinking of American warships would give a particularly powerful boost to German propaganda in Mexico.[209] But U-boats do not appear to have arrived in the Gulf of Mexico, nor does the Admiral Staff appear to have attempted to dispatch U-boats to the base that had been prepared in Mexico.

The reasons for this involved Mexico as much as Germany itself. According to Eckardt, Carranza had agreed to the construction of a U-boat base in Mexico at the end of 1916. This approval was given, however, at a time when Carranza was hoping by such a measure to secure the withdrawal of American troops from Mexico as a result of a German diplomatic move in the United States.[210] It had been granted mainly because the United States was not yet at war with Germany. A German U-boat base in Mexico in 1917 or 1918 could very easily have provoked American intervention. "Should [German] U-boats call at Mexican ports, a situation might result in which the United States would be able to make stringent demands on Mexico for immediate action to maintain its neutrality,"[211] Polk, a State Department adviser, recommended in a memorandum to his superior Lansing in June 1918. Polk proposed as a warning to Mexico the open concentration of 6,000 American marines in the port of Galveston.

Carranza, of course, was unaware of this memorandum, but he was quite aware of the American troop concentrations on the Mexican border and in the Texas ports. If a German U-boat base were built in Mexico, he could expect serious steps to be taken by the Americans.[212] Therefore, it is not likely that Carranza approved a U-boat base for Germany on his own initiative. When Eckardt reported in August 1918 that preparations for U-boats had been made, he did not mention Carranza in this regard, but Minister of Communications Mario Méndez, who oversaw "all preparations he had made."[213] It is quite possible that Eckardt and Jahnke, together with Méndez, who was working for them, had made these preparations without Carranza's knowledge. It is just as possible that the same military figures whom Eckardt had previously urged to opposed Carranza in case of a break with Germany had once again been mobilized to put pressure on him. Such an interpretation is supported by information given to American authorities in Guatemala in September 1918 by a confidant of Carranza. According to this information, a German U-boat base had been approved only with the greatest reluctance and on the condition that attacks be carried out only in the Atlantic and not in the Gulf of Mexico.[214]

The obstacles in Berlin were no less formidable. Out of fear of causing an overreaction in the United States and prompting the neutral countries in Latin America to turn away from Germany, the Wilhelmstrasse was reluctant to declare the American coast under blockade. "The government has decided not to close off American ports with U-boats," reported the Hanseatic minister in Berlin, "in order not to upset the Americans."[215]

The naval and army commands did not agree with this moderation. In two meetings in July 1918, sharp conflicts erupted over this question between the military authorities on the one hand and the kaiser and the Foreign Office on the other. The minutes of the first meeting, which took place on 2 July, report:

> *Hindenburg* brings up question of blockade.
> *His Majesty:* Declaration of a blockade against America was not yet possible for lack of materiel. Our earlier agreements with South America also grounds for moderation. In Argentina and Chile, the atmosphere has not been unfavorable to us up to now. We must prevent them from handing over our ships under pressure from Wilson. Until we have sufficient numbers of U-boats, we should not declare a blockade . . . .
> *Hindenburg and Ludendorff* underline military interest in U-boat warfare.
> *Envoy von Rosenberg:* The Foreign Office is afraid of complications with Spain.

*Ludendorff:* ...I am hoping for important relief as a result of activity by our U-boats in American waters....

*His Majesty:* I don't agree. In my opinion, the anticipated military advantages do not *at this time* outweigh the inevitable political disadvantages.

*Captain von Rastorff:* Admiral Staff for blockade. Allowance should be made for political disadvantages.

*His Majesty:* I am of a different opinion and I have decided differently.[216]

In the second discussion on 27 July, Admiral von Holtzendorff once again raised the question. He advocated U-boat warfare in the most fervent terms: because "the extension of the blockade area would considerably increase the already existing shortage of shipping personnel in America, defense measures would also have to be taken on the American coast, and the convoy system would have to be introduced on the entire ocean."[217] The secretary of state in the Foreign Office, Hintze, argued strongly against this proposal. "American coastal shipping conducted by neutral ships. Inclinations of neutral countries would continue to intensify against Central Powers, and they would move closer to the Allies! The war was lasting too long for the neutral countries. Reason for their antipathy toward Germany: Germany cut off from trade overseas, Allies shaping public opinion even before the war. Fear of deterioration of mood in Scandinavia and of Spain's entry into war. A further realignment of neutral countries would be devastating for Germany. 'As with the enemy, if not perhaps more so, the nerves of our people have suffered.'"[218] It was also asserted that such measures "would be harmful to the attempt to open communications with Wilson."

When Holtzendorff once again came out for the declaration of a blockade, Hintze countered him, asserting that even in wartime, diplomacy had to keep channels open to the enemy. "The forging of a divided public opinion into a united front against us"[219] had to be voided. The kaiser finally decided not to announce a blockade of the American coast. He cited as his reason that "a deterioration in the climate of public opinion in America would be certain. A unified opinion against us in North America would also be a danger because of its effects on South America." He also felt that the atmosphere in Germany was slowly becoming more cautious: "We must also remember that we are not in the second, but the fourth year of war, and that we cannot therefore do everything that we have done in the past. People are getting edgy."[220] Amazing words from the mouth of the kaiser!

Eckardt was also pursuing the objective of infiltrating the Mexican army and of creating his own power apparatus in that institution. In these efforts, no small role was played by more than forty German or German-Mexicans serving in the Mexican army. The best known of these men was General Maximilian Kloss, the son of a Prussian officer, in charge of munitions production.[221] Among the German-Mexicans, Commander Krumm Heller, a doctor, deserves special mention.

Arnoldo Krumm Heller had rallied to Carranza in 1913 and had sent messages to the German authorities then supporting Huerta in which he urged them to back Carranza. The reply was hardly flattering: the German authorities called him a criminal and a madman,[222] but that did not prevent Krumm Heller from making enthusiastic pro-German propaganda speeches immediately after the outbreak of the world war. He translated and distributed, among other things, Bethmann-Hollweg's war speech before the Reichstag. In 1916, he was appointed by Carranza to be Mexican military attaché in Berlin. Immediately after his arrival in Germany, he presented himself at the Foreign Office, where a letter of recommendation from Eckardt had already arrived for him. Krumm Heller, who had written a book in which both Carranza and Germany were extolled, asked the Foreign Office to help him in getting his work published in Germany.

In the Wilhelmstrasse, both this project and Krumm Heller himself were greeted with some mistrust. "Even if, as Herr von Eckardt's report states, Krumm Heller's trip has as its foremost objective to promote the currently dominant pro-German mood in Mexico and to counter the influence of the Allied powers, it is still not to be discounted that Krumm Heller may intend to use Germany in Mexico's interests against the United States, and that the publication of the manuscript in question is intended to further these aims." There were also political reasons to avoid giving the United States any impression that the German government supported Mexico's anti-American tendencies.[223] These hesitations disappeared after the disclosure of the Zimmermann note and the U.S. entry into the war. Krumm Heller's book *Für Freiheit und Recht* [For freedom and justice] was published, and the Foreign Office approved its presentation to the kaiser, in spite of certain "coarse" expressions which the book contained.[224]

Krumm Heller appears to have given only second or third priority to Mexican affairs during his stay in Germany. "One completely loses sight of the fact that he is officially a representative of a neutral power because of his strongly asserted interests in Germany," wrote an official of the Ministry of War who accompanied him on a visit to a prisoner-of-war camp which Krumm Heller was inspecting for propaganda reasons. "The depths of his being express themselves in an almost fanatical hatred of the English and an unlimited enthusiasm for Germany."[225] This attitude was probably also the cause for Krumm Heller's recall to Mexico six months later. In a letter to Zimmermann, he attributed his recall to the fact that the Mexican minister in Berlin, who had initially been pro-German, had now changed his mind. Because of the English blockade, he feared the journey to Mexico and offered his services to Zimmermann as a propagandist.[226] Krumm Heller's fears were not unfounded, since both the English and French authorities were determined not to allow him to return to Mexico.[227] Zimmermann accepted the offer of Krumm Heller's services and placed him in the Intelligence Division of the Foreign Office.[228] He appears to have collaborated actively there in the propaganda destined for Latin America and to have been recruited for the gathering of confidential and secret information on Mexico.

For the realization of Eckardt's goals, the generals Eckardt assembled for a conspiracy in the event that Carranza abandoned his neutrality were of decisive importance. Eckardt did not rely solely on their collaboration, however, but established an extensive network of agents which also could have constituted a reserve force had Carranza changed his position toward Germany. Some of the agents' reports, which Eckardt disclosed in part to Carranza, have remained in the archives of the German legation in Mexico. Thus a Captain Morán of the Mexican army informed Eckardt of a conspiracy against Carranza planned by Alfredo Robles Domínguez; in conclusion, he asked for "fifty pesos, so that I can at least buy some clothes for myself and allow myself to be seen in public."[229] Another report contains a list of French citizens residing in Mexico who were conducting a propaganda campaign on behalf of American intervention in Mexico.[230]

The most important German agent inside the Mexican government, who apparently also kept channels open to Carranza when Eckardt was not meeting with him personally, was Mexico's Minister of Communications Mario Méndez.[231] According to American reports, Méndez received $600 a month from Eckardt.[232] Simultaneously Eckardt attempted to keep communications with Carranza open and to cultivate contacts with his opponents, although only with conservative opponents. Two forces among these currents aroused his special interest: the army of the former Huerta general Higinio Aguilar, which was in the Veracruz region, and the Catholic Church.

Secret negotiations were begun with Higinio Aguilar. An agent of Eckardt assured him that he could count on German aid if Carranza had a rapprochement with the Americans.[233] That by itself, however, would not have been enough to interest Aguilar seriously. What Eckardt wanted from him was much more concrete. The Admiral Staff was thinking of building an additional German radio station in Veracruz, and Eckardt had hopes of having it built in the region controlled by Aguilar and having it guarded by his troops. Eckardt probably wanted a second link to Germany which would be independent from the Mexican government in the event of a shift by Carranza. Aguilar agreed.[234] The further developments of relations with Aguilar are not known, and there are no reports indicating that such a station was actually built. It is hardly likely that Eckardt, given his increasingly close relations with Carranza, wished to deepen his ties with Carranza's opponents, who were, after all, seen only as a reserve force.

With the Catholic Church, however, which opposed Carranza, Eckardt maintained open relations. He considered it to be ideologically the only power that could "save" Mexico; its anti-American stance was also in favor with him. "The Catholic clergy is, as a high-ranking priest recently informed me, completely pro-German."[235] Eckardt had thus attempted to bring about a reconciliation between Carranza and the Church. Anticlerical remarks were forbidden in the newspapers subsidized by the German legation; when offenses occurred, support was withdrawn.

Counterespionage played an important role in the activities of the German secret service. One of the most important projects of this kind was the theft of a plan, allegedly American, for sabotage of oil wells.[236] "In Tampico, Mexicans are being hired to set the oil wells afire, and at the same time others are being hired to say afterwards that the fire was set by Germans. The people are providing me with secret information on the Fletcher plan and are making their statements in notarized documents. Fletcher, receiving reports of this, offers them 5000 pesos for the document, having no idea that in the meantime, I have been handing over all the material proof to the president, to be saved for the *momento oportuno*."[237]

It cannot be determined to what extent these assertions are true. Such a plan is completely within the realm of possibility, for the Americans knew that German sabotage actions in the oil fields could have brought about a break between Germany and Carranza, who was financially dependent on the taxes on oil. One cannot rule out the possibility, however, that the entire affair was concocted by Eckardt himself, precisely as a countermeasure in the event that the agents of the Political Section of the General Staff still carried out their plans to set the Tampico oil fields afire. The allegations Eckardt made to the Mexican government about this American plan were taken very seriously. The Mexican ambassador in Washington informed the American government of them and lodged a sharp protest. The American government immediately denied any such intention.[238]

A second project of German counterespionage was the "confusion" of the Americans with regard to the German radio station. Eckardt reported "that a spy who appears to be working for Mr. Fletcher, but who is actually working for us, told me that he had been ordered to ascertain the location of the wireless station in contact with Nauen. I asked Mr. Aguilar what the spy should tell the Americans, under the guise that the location had been divulged to him by a Mexican official. The minister gave me a location in the state of Hidalgo in an almost inaccessible desert, which the Americans have been looking for ever since."[239] The success, however, was only a relative one, for the Americans knew precisely where the radio station in Mexico City was.[240]

Eckardt's agents informed the Mexican government of talks between American agents and Felix Díaz in Oaxaca.[241] At the same time, Eckardt appears to have succeeded in winning over American and Mexican employees of American offices. One American, Gibsons, who shared his residence with such people as Silliman, Wilson's temporary special agent and later the American consul in Guadalajara, gave regular reports to Eckardt.[242] According to American reports, Eckardt also had bribed a number of employees of the American consulates in Veracruz and Nuevo Laredo.[243] Although no confirmation is available, American authorities also suspected that German agents had stolen one of their secret codes.[244]

There was complete agreement on these activities among the Germans working in Mexico, but not on sabotage in Mexico and border incidents, for these were a source of constant conflict between Eckardt and representatives of the General Staff.

As early as May 1917, Eckardt had expressed his opposition to such actions,[245] but this did not keep Delmar from preparing an attack on the United States in the Mexican border state of Sonora with the aid of General Calles. While it is doubtful whether the figures provided by an agent of the American army corresponded to the facts (900 Germans and 45,000 Mexicans were allegedly prepared for the attack), there is no doubt that German agents were preparing an attack on the U.S. from Sonora.[246] In the summer of 1918, Delmar considered all necessary preparations complete. From Madrid, he wired Berlin on 8 July: "The fact that the American troop transports are arriving in France without any significant U-boat interference prompts me to propose, after conferring with the military attaché, that we give up our previous viewpoint on policy toward Mexico and that we sacrifice this country and push it into a war with America. I believe I can bring this about by having General Calles, the commander in the state of Sonora, attack the States. In the event of agreement in Berlin, I would attempt to get to Mexico in spite of all the difficulties."[247] Six days later, Delmar had doubts. "Carranza has 108 field cannon and 36 mountain cannon. Are additional arms shipments impossible, or should we act in accordance with Telegram 2554 of July 8?"[248]

The Political Section of the General Staff presented Delmar's proposal to the Foreign Office, which rejected it.

First of all it appears questionable whether our agent has enough influence to push Mexico into a war with the United States which would from the outset necessarily seem hopeless to the Mexican government.

Border attacks have occurred regularly until now without causing a war with the United States or provoking major military actions.

Whether Germany is in a position to provide Mexico with the necessary arms for an offensive war cannot be determined from here. Any conceivable financial support for these ends is considered out of the question by all parties involved. To conclude from the agent's own statements, the possibility of waging war is therefore obviated.

In a belligerent conflict between Mexico and America, we would have to provide arms sooner or later. The blame for the conflict, and for its outcome, would in any case be attributed to us. As a result, not only our previous friendship with Mexico would collapse, but we would be giving America itself a reason for occupying Mexico, and with it, one of our important future sources of raw materials. From both the political and economic standpoint, therefore, a war between Mexico and America appears to be against our interests. Whatever military advantages we might gain from such a conflict are best left to the judgment of the military authorities.[249]

These considerations are in fact the opposite of those that had prompted the Zimmermann dispatch. This was not only attributable to the fact that Hintze knew Mexico better than Zimmermann or that he had a better grasp of the realities in question. What was decisive above all in this case was the changed balance of forces. At the beginning of 1917, the Germans had merely cast a glance at the American army, which was small in number, and had mechanically conceived of tying it down in Mexico. Because of the hopes that had been placed in U-boat warfare, the Germans believed that it would suffice to tie up American troops for a few months to win the war against England. In view of the ambitious war aims, whose realization no one doubted, Mexican raw materials appeared purely secondary. In the summer of 1918, however, the situation changed completely. The U-boat warfare had not led to success. In the United States, powerful armed forces had been mobilized, of which only a fraction would have been required in a war with Mexico. Finally, it had been recognized in the Foreign Office that the plans for obtaining all raw materials from conquest and the spoils of war were untenable, and thus great hopes were then placed in Mexico. Moreover, it is questionable if the Foreign Office wanted additional complications in relations with the United States at that precise moment.

The Political Section adopted the views of the Foreign Office. Delmar was instructed to drop his plans in view of Mexico's importance for the "transition period." These negative instructions also represented the final triumph of Eckardt's perspectives over those of Delmar.[250]

To cover the large expenditures of the Political Section in Mexico, 200,000 marks were initially earmarked with the approval of the Foreign Office for "espionage and intelligence activities" in April 1917.[251] It was asserted at the same time that this sum would probably not be sufficient.[252] In response to an inquiry by the secretary of state in the Reich Treasury on the use of this money, Kemnitz wrote that it had been agreed to discuss these matters only orally.[253] At the end of 1917, an additional $300,000 were apparently transferred from Spain to Mexico for these activities.[254] A portion of the 2,759,679 marks that German businessmen had deposited with the embassy in Mexico was probably also used for espionage and sabotage. This is all the more likely inasmuch as the embassy was administering and distributing the funds for the agents of the military secret services in Mexico.[255]

## The Activities of the Allied Intelligence Services in Mexico

The secret services of the United States and its allies went vigorously into action to counter the Germans. Five different American secret services were active in Mexico, the State Department, the army, the navy, the Department of the Treasury, and the Justice Department.[256] Exactly what kind of division of labor existed among these agencies is not ascertainable, and it is possible that they themselves did not know. In any case, the work in Mexico was directed by the American military attaché and was supported effectively by the American censorship authorities, who maintained surveillance of almost all letters, telegrams, and the like to and from Mexico.

Like the Germans, the individual American secret services were in continual conflict. The agent of the State Department, Cobb, who began an investigation of the Mexican subsidiaries of the Frankfurter Metallgesellschaft in 1916, complained constantly about the activities of the agents of the army, who were interfering with his work. He demanded their immediate recall, and after the intervention by the State Department, it was done.[257] The consul in Nuevo Laredo complained bitterly that the secret service of the army was withholding proof from him that a former employee of his consulate had collaborated with the Germans.[258] Like various German agents who used their activities for their own personal enrichment, some American agents appear to have been profiteers. When the American consul in Ensenada, Baja California, was asked to determine whether there was a secret German radio station in his area, he entrusted an American private detective, Erdmann, with the investigation. State Department officials felt that Erdmann was in no way suited for the job, for he did not speak Spanish and he was actually pursuing completely different objectives. With the consul's knowledge, he was simultaneously in the employ of an American businessman and was using his position, the State Department later asserted, to buy up at low cost the German ships interned in Baja California.[259]

Along with the American secret services, English agents were busy in Mexico. The commander of British naval intelligence, Hall, sent one of his best agents, the writer A. E. W. Mason, to Mexico, where Mason developed an extensive agent network. Other British agents were ordered to Mexico from India, to initiate surveillance of the activities of the Indians who had emigrated there and of the channels of communication to India passing through Mexico.[260] French intelligence also appears to have been very active in Mexico.[261]

Among the most important duties of these intelligence operatives were the economic struggle against German firms and the political struggle against the German secret service. While failures outweighed successes in economic activities, the political activities proved more fruitful.

In economic matters, the American secret services in particular were charged, together with the legal authorities of the State Department, with maintaining the blacklists, that is, with pinpointing German firms and fronts as well as the Mexicans and foreigners who were dealing with them.[262] In this endeavor they had to deal with the interference of the Mexican government, which penalized the use of such lists in Mexico. The governor of the state of Sonora, Calles, who was sympathetic to Germany, went so far as to grant tax breaks to German businessmen and firms named on the blacklists.[263]

The Americans, however, were not successful in dislodging German businessmen from Mexico. Eckardt was able to report in 1918 that they were getting through the war without any serious difficulties and that they had even made substantial improvements in their position. This was due in part to the policy of the Mexican government and in part to the Germans' own business experience and multiple connections, which constantly enabled them to find new possibilities for camouflage. But it was also the case that a considerable number of American businessmen were not very interested in pressuring them, since as much as two-thirds of the goods sold by the Germans prior to the war were American. Characteristic of this attitude is a report by the Mexico specialist of the Office of Foreign Trade Adviser. In his report, which was almost a tract in defense of the German businessman, the author advised the authorities to consider the German businessmen as "harmless" and not to equate them with agents.[264] The aim and purpose of this moderation became quite clear after the war, when German businessmen received important franchise offers from Americans.[265]

The struggle against the German secret service, however, was conducted not only with the greatest intensity, but to a large extent with real success. The most important weapon of the Allies was their knowledge of the German secret code. British receiving stations were intercepting the messages sent from Nauen for Mexico and Spain as well as the communiqués coming to Spain from Mexico and broadcast from there to Germany. Some of these reports were turned over to the Americans, although British-American collaboration did not always proceed without incident. On 15 November 1917, when the State Department instructed the American embassy in London to obtain German telegrams destined for Mexico from British intelligence, it was informed that this request had encountered difficulties. No reasons for this were given; nonetheless, the American embassy assured Washington that it would continue to try to obtain the requested reports, which were in fact given to the Americans shortly thereafter.[266]

Further tension developed from the British fear that secret materials might become known to unauthorized persons in the United States. In order to prevent this, the circle of those who had knowledge of these materials was reduced to a minimum. According to the British, neither the British ambassador to the United States nor the British military attaché were to know anything about them. When, in March 1918, the British ambassador in Washington suddenly asked the State Department if the telegrams to be forwarded by his government had actually arrived, he was told that nothing was known of such telegrams.[267] This answer caused great irritation in England. Were the British communiqués to the United States lying unused in some drawer? To a British inquiry, the State Department responded that it had indeed received the telegrams, but that in the conversation with Lord Reading it had only been observing British wishes that its own ambassador be told nothing of the affair.[268] The British mistrust of the United States, however, did not subside. When it was announced at the beginning of 1918 that the Mexico specialist in the State Department, Canova, was to be dismissed because of differences with his superior, Hall asked the American ambassador in London if there was any danger that Canova might divulge the secret of the code. He made it clear to Page that he might have to stop sending reports to the United States.[269] The State Department, however, immediately assured him that Canova knew nothing of the code.[270]

The secret remained well guarded, and the German authorities continued without the slightest suspicion to use the code known to the English. It appears that the Americans themselves acquired one or more German codes in the course of the world war. They were unable to acquire the key to code 0075 which the British consistently refused to divulge to the Allies.[271]

Knowledge of the German telegrams made it possible for the Allied authorities to learn the assignments and names of the most important agents of the German secret services. To obtain an overview on the practical execution of these assignments and a specific knowledge of the agent networks, however, the Allied secret services had to proceed in other ways. To these ends, they employed an extensive system of surveillance of German agents and for the infiltration of informers into their organizations. These efforts proved extremely successful, and the Allies also profited from the lack of cooperation among the various German secret services and the incompetence of some of their agents.

These factors came to the fore in particularly crass fashion in the case of the agents Hermann and Gerdts. Fred L. Hermann was a German-American who had been recruited by the German secret service in June 1915 during a private visit to Germany.[272] His first field of activity was England, where he carried on espionage work for Germany for several months. He later became one of the most important agents of the Political Section in the United States. After he had proved himself in this arena through his involvement in the sabotage of the large Kingland factory in New Jersey in January 1917, he was given the assignment of setting fire to the Tampico oil fields.[273] To carry out this assignment, he left New York in the company of the German-Colombian Raoul Gerdts, whom he had recruited, and got to Veracruz by way of Havana.

The American authorities, whose suspicions had been aroused, had him under constant surveillance by agents of the Justice Department in Havana.[274] It was, however, less the work of these agents than Hermann's own actions that gave his intentions away. As soon as he arrived in Havana, he went directly to the German legation. The minister considered Hermann and Gerdts to be provocateurs assigned by the English or American secret services to carry out acts of sabotage so that the Germans could be blamed for them. He sent a wire to this effect to Eckardt;[275] at the same time, he reported Hermann's and Gerdts's intentions to the Mexican ambassador in Havana, who promptly informed his government, which in turn alerted the chief of police in Tampico.[276] The chief of police, however, had close ties to the Americans, and he provided them with a detailed report.[277] The Americans also obtained details on the action from Gerdts.[278] After Gerdts had refused to participate in sabotage in Tampico, Hermann had fired him and sent him to Colombia with no compensation for his troubles. To take his revenge, Gerdts informed an American consul in Colombia of all the details of the planned action.[279] Hermann's activities in Mexico were henceforth under the strictest surveillance by the Americans.

With one important exception, the Americans were eventually successful in placing all important German agents in Mexico under constant surveillance. As early as July 1917, Cobb had learned of Hinsch's arrival in Mexico.[280] In August 1917, Hinsch went to Chihuahua in northern Mexico in the company of an interpreter (he did not understand Spanish) to register all Germans living there. The interpreter informed an American secret agent who was tailing them of Hinsch's assignments and intentions.[281] In March–April 1918, the Americans also picked up Jahnke's trail and thereafter had him under constant surveillance.[282]

The only important German secret agent who was never traced down in Mexico was Delmar. In July 1917, he officially returned to the United States under his real name. The Americans suspected him of having some kind of relations with Germany and had him questioned by an agent of the Justice Department. They appear, however, to have found no hard evidence for the suspicions, for Delmar was left undisturbed.[283] It was in Spain that Dilger was discovered for the first time to be the long-sought Delmar. Delmar himself noticed very quickly that he had been recognized. On 15 March, he reported to Berlin: "Although I am staying here under the name of Albert Donde, the Allied espionage agent has succeeded in tracing me to the hospital here and identifying me as Delmar. There has obviously been an indiscretion on the part of the Mexican Finance Minister or the Mexican Foreign Ministry."[284] There had, however, been no "indiscretion"; the Mexican consul Barreiro had simply betrayed Delmar's identity.[285] Even though he had been unmasked, Delmar intended to return to Mexico in the fall of 1918, but he caught the Spanish flu and died on 12 November 1918. "I have just received a note from my government about this German spy Delmar," the French ambassador in Washington reported to the American government, "who wanted to travel to Mexico for destructive ends. The note informs me that he has taken another trip, the trip from which no one ever returns. On this occasion, the Spanish flu did not observe neutrality."[286]

There then began a tug-of-war between Germans and Americans over Delmar's body and belongings that was still going on after the armistice. The Political Section had assumed the costs of Delmar's burial, and the German authorities were claiming his belongings.[287] On 25 January 1919, when the Americans confirmed that Delmar and Dilger were the same person, the American embassy in Spain was instructed to request the transfer of his belongings, since he was an American citizen.[288] The Americans then attempted to prove Dilger's American citizenship with a photo and thereby claim his possessions. No one, however, could any longer make an unequivocal identification of Dilger on the basis of the photo.[289]

What were the Americans attempting to do? It was hardly a question of Delmar's belongings. If there were any secret or compromising documents to be found, the German authorities had every occasion to remove them. The Americans were probably interested in an unequivocal, official identification of Delmar, which could have been exploited for propaganda purposes.

Particularly successful in the surveillance of a German agent was the American agent Cobb, who worked as a customs official on the

Mexican-American border. The German consul in Ciudad Juárez had an intimate friend, an American, in whom he confided all his secrets. Cobb succeeded in recruiting this man for the American secret service, so that he learned, down to the smallest deail, everything the trusting consul divulged.[290] In order to be sure that all of the consul's secrets were known, Cobb also bribed an employee of the Mexican telegraph office in Ciudad Juárez, who gave him copies of all telegrams sent and received by the consul.[291]

Along with the surveillance of German agents, the Allies had attempted, again not without success, to infiltrate their own people into the German agent network. The best known of these was an Austrian named Altendorf. He succeeded in gaining Jahnke's confidence and in entering the naval secret service. According to the report of the German Foreign Office, he was able "to learn certain things" in this fashion.[292] He had one of his biggest successes in turning over one of Jahnke's most important agents, Lothar Witzke alias Waberski, to the Americans. Witzke, who already had extensive experience in sabotage in the United States, had been ordered to carry out new actions in the United States together with Altendorf.[293] Altendorf alerted the American authorities, and Witzke was picked up as he crossed the border. He then revealed everything he knew about the German secret service.[294] He was nevertheless condemned to death, then pardoned, and finally freed several years later.[295]

Another agent working for British intelligence, who is identified only with the letter Y, apparently worked for the General Staff and was responsible for relations with Japan. Hall's biographer William James recounts that Eckardt had lost confidence in him. In order to regain it, the British and American intelligence services fed the German authorities reports on Y's alleged sabotage activities in the United States. When Y arrived in Mexico as a steward on a French ship, he was apparently greeted by Eckardt with open arms.[296] Was Y actually Kraft? This question cannot be answered definitely. It is noteworthy, however, that Kraft was responsible for contacts with Japan and that the Americans made special efforts to learn what the German secret service knew about Kraft.[297] The American reports also mention an infiltrator in the German ranks, who is mentioned only as N. Here again it cannot be definitely ascertained if N and Y are the same person.[298] The Allies' success in infiltrating an agent named Monck into the German spy network also remains an open question.[299]

Various Germans offered the Americans their "services" or "documents" for an appropriate sum. Thus a German employee in Nuevo Laredo, Brand, told the American consul there that he was prepared to give information on the German secret service for $25,000.[300] The American authorities, however, were not sure whether valuable information was being offered or whether Brand wanted only to present them with fabricated stories to earn some money. As the simplest solution, the head of the American intelligence service in Laredo suggested that Brand be kidnapped.[301] Unfortunately, nothing is known about the outcome of the affair. The American consul in Veracruz was offered a plan for U-boat bases in Mexico by several Germans which they alleged had been stolen from the German legation in the capital.[302] The Germans asked for a large sum of money. The consul believed the plan to be real but was not willing to pay more than $1,000 for it, since he assumed that the Germans would change their plans after discovering that it had been stolen.[303]

The Allied secret services hardly limited themselves to mere observation of the activities of their German counterparts. One of their most important actions was the attempt to destroy the German receiving station. The initial plan was to sabotage the installation's supply of lamps. On 13 July, Eckardt had contacted Berlin with an urgent request that five dozen audial tubes, which were of great importance for the radio station, be sent to him through Madrid.[304] The Admiral Staff instructed the naval attaché in Madrid to obtain the lamps immediately. The naval attaché, however, reported a month later that he had been unable to obtain any lamps; he would, however, "attempt to obtain them from England or France, which nevertheless takes time."[305]

These reports were intercepted by the British secret service. Hall thereupon sent Mason to Mexico to locate the German radio installation and at the same time buy up all available audial tubes.[306] Under the cover of a scientific researcher, Mason traveled through Mexico, discovered the German radio station in Ixtapalapa, bought up as many audial tubes as possible and returned to England. Hall then assigned him to put the installation out of operation. The way in which he claimed to have achieved this could have been taken from one of his numerous adventure novels. According to this account, he built up an agent network led by "a prominent officer of Madero's private police,...Huerta's chief of police," and a thief. With their help, he invited the commander of the Mexican division guarding the station to a meal and got the soldiers drunk. While this was going on, Mason's men slipped into the radio station and stole the audial tubes.

Mason was convinced that with this action, he had put Ixtapalapa out of operation. After he had observed the station for an extended period, he wired on 12 October to London: "It is now established that no communications have been received in Ixtapalapa since the accident which the authorities, I have heard, are blaming on the United States."[307] The American secret service also reported on 21 July 1918 that Mason had destroyed the station. Four weeks later, Eckardt wrote his final report, in which he not only made no mention that the installation had been put out of operation, but even claimed that he had received the German war telegrams every day.[308] Three questions must be clarified here: was there a second German radio station after all? Did Mason's attack fail? Or was Eckardt telling only part of the truth? There is much to be said for the last hypothesis. A report by Magnus in particular points in this direction. At the beginning of 1919, he informed the Foreign Office that "only sparse, irregular reports from Germany"[309] arrived during the last months of the war.

If one wishes to assess the overall activities of the German secret service in Mexico, the following questions must be asked: to what extent was it successful in keeping its activities secret? To what extent was it able to realize the goals it set for itself?

Allied knowledge of the German secret codes and the infiltration of the German agent network show how seldom the first objective was realized. This is seen most clearly by comparing one of Eckardt's reports on the effectiveness of the German secret service with the reality of the situation. "It remains unknown to the White House," he wrote in August 1918, "in spite of the enormous espionage carried on throughout the republic, for which $200,000 was apparently spent every week, that loan discussions have been carried on with Mr. Carranza, that Fabela was sent to Spain to travel on to Berlin, that we have a wireless connection with Nauen, that preparations have been made for any arriving submarines, that the president receives almost daily written reports which I receive through official channels or otherwise from various parts of the country on the internal situation (rebels, administration, and so forth), and that the Mexicans are being briefed on American espionage activity (to ascertain what weapons, ammunition supplies, and war materiel of all kinds the Mexican army has at its disposal)."[310]

In fact, the United States, because of its knowledge of the German telegrams alone, had been able to follow the loan negotiations in every detail, and every phase of these negotiations was recorded in the American archives.[311] The opening of a radio connection with Nauen was noted and recorded by the Americans, although the Allies temporarily made a series of faulty judgments in this connection. Thus the American military attaché wrote to his ambassador that the Germans could find no parts for a radio station in Mexico (in fact parts had been brought to Mexico by the Germans).[312] Reports of a German transmitter in Mexico whose beams could be picked up in Germany also proved to be false. But Eckardt's most important secret in this regard, the existence of a receiving station at Ixtapalapa and the German involvement in it, had been discovered by the Allies. Fabela was being shadowed everywhere he went throughout his trip. The Americans were also informed of the planned U-boat base, even if they did not know its exact location. The domain in which they probably had the least information, because it had not been discussed in any radio communications to Germany, was the breakdown and the subordinate agents of the German espionage apparatus. But even here, they had made real inroads with the infiltration of their own agents and with the theft of a series of German documents.

The concrete results of the activities of the German secret services are naturally more difficult to assess. In this domain, as in their attempt to keep the location of the radio station a secret, the Germans appear to have suffered one setback after another. Hardly anything is known in this period of uprisings or important sabotage actions in the United States (which by no means rules out such events, as many developments were consciously covered up by American authorities). The same is true for the ambitious sabotage actions at the Panama Canal. The Indian insurrection planned with German inspiration also failed to occur. U-boat bases were not built in Mexico. Communications from Mexico to Germany by radio transmitter never materialized. The German secret service was undoubtedly most successful in its infiltration of the Mexican army, but even there the hopes placed in the enterprise were unrealistic. Germany's notion that it could dominate Mexico was based on a gross overestimation of its own strength, on a similar underestimation of the strength of the Americans, and a complete ignorance of the dynamics of the Mexican revolution.

## German Propaganda in Mexico

One of the most noteworthy characteristics of the First World War was the extremely widespread and distinctive propaganda developed by both sides. This propaganda was aimed at both opponents and neutral states. Each side depicted the imperialist policies of the other in terms that were sometimes exaggerated, but that frequently corresponded to the facts. In the neutral or belligerent countries where the population had had direct experience of one side as an oppressor (as, for example, in the Slavic areas of the Austro-Hungarian monarchy or in Ireland), this propaganda struck an authentic note.

The German authorities placed great importance on the propaganda in the Latin American states. In doing so, they were pursuing two objectives: First, Germany wanted to insure that these countries remained neutral. Particularly after the United States had entered the war, this objective was of great importance for Germany. And, second, the Germans had attempted to solidify or at least to maintain the positions attained by Germany prior to the war. This was all the more important when the English blockade had completely closed off German trade with Latin America, at the same time that the Allies' trade with these countries and the economic penetration of the United States was constantly increasing.

German propaganda work was essentially carried on under the auspices of the Foreign Office, which worked extremely closely in this endeavor with the Reich Office of the Interior and the military authorities, particularly the army intelligence division under Commander Nicolai. Responsibility for overseas propaganda was in the hands of the intelligence division of the Foreign Office under Major Deutelmoser. This was broken down into Section B of embassy adviser Hahn, which was the headquarters for German publication abroad, and the military section under Lt. Col. von Haeften. There was also a foreign news office in the Foreign Office responsible for the transmission of communiqués abroad.

In 1916, the functions of these divisions were defined more precisely. In the Foreign Office, there were three divisions for overseas propaganda: first, the division for political propaganda under General Consul Thiel, who was temporarily managing director of the Central Office for Foreign Service; the division for military propaganda under Lt. Col. von Haeften; the division for economic propaganda, headed by Freiherr von Braun, who was also in charge of the intelligence office of the Reich Office of the Interior.[313]

Two organs were created for propaganda in neutral foreign countries and particularly overseas after the outbreak of the war: the Central Office for Foreign Service was brought into existence on 14 October 1914, at the instigation of the Foreign Office. It was the highest censorship and coordination center for all propaganda publications intended for neutral countries. These publications were produced in part directly under the Central Office, in part by other organizations under its supervision. The Central Office was headed by retired ambassador Mumm von Schwarzenstein, who was advised and assisted by a committee which included representatives of the intelligence service of the Reich Naval Office, the Press Division of the General Staff and the intelligence division of the Foreign Office. Matthias Erzberger, a Reichstag member, who was responsible for Catholic propaganda, also belonged to this committee.[314]

The Central Office issued a series of publications itself, including *A War Chronicle, The War Calendar 1914–15*, a book *The World Looks at Germany*, pamphlets on the German-English antagonism, writings on the theme the German war and Catholicism, and an illustrated magazine *The Great War in Pictures*, aimed primarily at Spanish-speaking countries.[315] At the same time it enlisted the most varied economic and cultural organizations for propaganda in Latin America. These included such groups as the War Committee of German Industry, which sent brochures and communiqués mainly to German firms in Latin America.[316] Also participating in this campaign was the German Economic Association for South and Central America, which published its own newspaper in Spanish and Portuguese.[317]

The Ibero-American Association in Hamburg, founded in January 1916, sent extensive propaganda articles to the Latin American states.[318] In 1918, a special significance was attributed to this group. Its director, Professor Schädel, and one of its leading members, Specht, were called to the German embassy in Bern, where they founded the so-called Specht group. This group became very active in solidifying German positions in Latin America for the "transition period."[319] The Ibero-American Association was also responsible for the information provided to German officials on Latin America. It published a newsletter which evaluated the most important news from Latin America either gathered in Switzerland or arriving through Switzerland.[320] There was a division of labor between this association and the German–South American Institute, founded in 1912 as a "German information service in South America,"[321] which had its headquarters in Aachen and later in Cologne. While the main activity of the Hamburg association was the dissemination abroad of articles written by Germans, the institute concentrated on the publication of Latin American propaganda articles favorable to German imperialism. Thus, for example, the former Peruvian military attaché in Berlin, Commander Guerrero, prepared a war chronicle entitled *La Guerra Europea-mirada por un Sudamericano.*[322]

Another organization enlisted in the propaganda campaign in Latin America was the News Service for Spanish and Portuguese-Speaking Countries, which had its headquarters in Frankfurt am Main; its aim was "to be a link . . . between the vital Germanic homeland and those peoples of Spanish and Portuguese origin who, in keeping with their glorious past, have retained an appreciation for the heroism of an entire nation."[323] The writings of the news agency were aimed especially at clubs and nonpolitical organizations; for this reason, its reports also took on a more "apolitical and objective" quality.[324]

Also viewed as quite important in these activities was the bureau of Matthias Erzberger, which was in charge of Catholic propaganda for Latin America and which was advancing the German cause, not without success, and particularly in Church circles.[325] In addition, special articles on the role of the Catholics in Germany as well as *Katholische Korrespondenz* were put out by Erzberger's bureau.[326]

In addition to general propaganda (extolling the German armies, depicting the war as a "just war of defense," attacks on "perfidious Albion and decadent France" and later on "Wilson's hypocrisy," portraying Germany as a model state), the Germans concentrated on three points with regard to Latin America: First, German industry was praised and its "special qualities" emphasized. With this, Germany hoped to compensate at least partly for the interruption of commercial relations with Latin America. Second, the Allied powers were depicted as expansionist states, at the same time that all German imperialist ambitions in Latin America were disavowed.[327] When the German-Mexican W. Fink called for the installation of German coaling stations in Mexico, Ecuador, and Chile in a brochure on the Germans in Latin America, the Foreign Office had the passage deleted, arguing that it would bring about a manifold increase in anti-German sentiment throughout Latin America.[328] Third, an overall emphasis was placed on the role of German Catholics and of Catholicism in Germany. The Germans hoped in this way to score major successes in Catholic Latin America.[329]

The number, ambitions, and objectives of the German propaganda organizations for Latin America stood in inverse proportion to the possibilities for getting their propaganda material to Latin America. While shipment through neutral states, especially Italy and Scandinavia, was relatively easy in the first months of the war, it soon became much more difficult.[330] Italy's entry into the war, the intensification of the British blockade, which led to an increasingly vigilant monitoring of neutral ships, and finally the U.S. entry into the war brought the shipment of this literature to Latin America to a virtual standstill. Whereas German propaganda materials were still being sent by the thousands in the first months of the war—the Central Office for Foreign Service had a card index totaling 116,000 addresses[331]—their number declined from month to month. Soon it was literally impossible to smuggle anything but individual copies which were then locally reproduced and distributed.

The difficulties of shipping printed matter to Latin America bestowed real importance on another German firm: the Transozean GmbH. The Transozean GmbH had emerged from the German Overseas Service, which had been founded just before the outbreak of the war, in spring 1914, by large German capital. Thirteen industrial firms were involved in it, among them the Vereinigte Stahlwerke Köln-Deutz, the AG für Anilinfabrikation Berlin, and the Deutsche Übersee-Elektrizitätsgesellschaft, and ten other commercial firms and organizations, including the Hamburg and Bremen chambers of commerce, the three major German banks (Deutsche Bank, Dresdner Bank, and Disconto-Gesellschaft), and the shipping companies Norddeutscher Lloyd, Hapag, and the Deutsche Dampfschiffahrts-Gesellschaft Kosmos. The chairman of the board of the German Overseas Service was the secretary of the Central Association of German Industrialists, Rötger.[332] This overseas service, which was conceived primarily for the countries of the American continent and which intended to conduct extensive propaganda there, showed the increasing interest in Latin America on the part of large German capital. The close ties of this project with official German policy can be seen, for example, in the annual subsidy of 250,000 marks which the ostensibly independent German Overseas Service was receiving from the Foreign Office even before the beginning of the war.[333] It was entrusted with the supervision of all of Germany's information outlets, via wire or mail, in the countries of the American hemisphere. The Foreign Office outlined the importance of the work of this enterprise: "The expansion of company activities and the utilization of that expansion for foreign policy requires the constant cooperation and attention of the kaiser's representatives overseas."[334] Members of the board of directors of the Transozean GmbH included the director of the Deutsche Bank, Arthur von Gwinner, the director of the Dresdner Bank, Hjalmar Schacht, as well as the directors of Hapag and AEG.[335]

Transozean received an annual contribution of one million marks through a secret contract with the government, which was paid out of the 40 million marks placed at the disposal of the Foreign Office for secret purposes by the Reich Treasury.[336] In exchange, the Foreign Office was allowed to monitor Transozean's telegrams.[337] The daily dispatches of the Transozean were transmitted from Nauen to Sayville and Tuckerton in the United States. Messages destined for Latin America were either wired directly from the Transozean office in the United States to neighboring countries, primarily Mexico, or were sent to a distribution point in Panama, which then sent them on to Latin America.[338]

As the English blockade increased its effectiveness and the shipment of German publications to the American continent became more difficult, the significance of the Transozean service increased. The U.S. entry into the war, however, which put an end to the Nauen–U.S. communication links, was a devastating blow for Transozean. After the break in German-American relations in February 1917, Bernstorff had continued to hope that Transozean could be preserved in "purely commercial form." "During earlier periods in our relations with the United States," he wrote, "I had already made contact with all organizations to which the Transozean service was distributed from Washington, in order to prevent an interruption of our information service in the event of a rupture with America. It had been agreed that, should such a situation arise, these organizations would order a specific number of words on a daily basis for Herr Klaessig, the representative of the Wolff office in New York. To keep the affair on a purely commercial basis not connected with any propaganda work, it was necessary that the recipients pay Herr Klaessig for the information and that they cover the costs of the telegrams themselves."[339] To finance this news service, Bernstorff had transferred large sums to the German embassies in Latin America, including Buenos Aires

($400,000), Guatemala ($64,000), Bogota ($48,000), Mexico ($96,000), and Havana ($32,000).[340] When the United States entered the war, however, most Latin American countries no longer could receive news directly from Germany. One exception was Mexico.

In Mexico, German propaganda had initially gotten underway in mid-1915, after Eckardt's arrival. Three stages are to be distinguished in this process. The first stage lasted from mid-1915 until the summer of 1916, the second from the summer of 1916 until the United States entered the war, and the third from April 1917 until the war came to an end.

During the first phase, German propaganda had a very limited impact. Its disseminators were almost all members of the German colony in Mexico, who had formed the German Reich Citizens' Association in 1915. From this association emerged the German Information Service, which devoted itself to German propaganda.[341] The most important propaganda functionary in this phase was the editor of the German newspaper, Dr. Schumacher, the Transozean agency's representative in Mexico.[342] Both in the large and in the secondary cities of Mexico, he was assisted by collaborators, principally the acting consuls of the German Reich; in Torreón this function was taken over by the manager of the Deutsch-Südamerikanische Bank's subsidiary.[343]

German propaganda activities in Mexico in this period consisted essentially in the distribution of propaganda materials arriving from Germany, the publication of locally prepared propaganda materials, and finally attempts to conduct German propaganda through the Mexican press. After the solidification of the British blockade, very few German publications arrived in Mexico. After Italy entered the war, the propaganda material coming from abroad was partly printed in the United States and partly (to the extent that it could penetrate the blockade) obtained from Spain. In Mexico itself, the publication of locally prepared materials intensified. The local German newspaper published a weekly Spanish edition.[344] At the same time, additional newsletters were created, such as the *Noticias Inalámbricas,* which published German army reports,[345] and a special newspaper in the oil city of Tampico, *El Noticiero Europeo,* which enjoyed special subsidies from Transozean. Transozean explained that it would be important, in view of "the significance of the city, which in all probability has a great future in the development of Mexican crude oil . . . if something could be done there now for the promotion of German interests by this kind of support for the newspaper."[346] In Merida, the Germany colony published the *Boletín de la Guerra.*[347]

The publication of material in the Mexican press was eagerly promoted. This included both telegrams of the Transozean and articles on topics ranging from the situation in Germany to German achievements, cultural ideals, and political objectives. "The public," wrote Schumacher, "which greets pure propaganda literature with justified skepticism, will be all the more quickly and easily won over by the merits of the German intellect."[348] Similarly, in German stores and offices, war reports were posted almost daily. This propaganda, however, could only reach those who were able to read and write, or only a minority of the population. The Germans thus resorted to other means. In October 1915, Schumacher recommended "the distribution of informative photographs to illustrated newspapers, displays of good German illustrations, and the like."[349] He also proposed the organization of regular showings for German films.[350] Among the poorest strata of the population, much success was also expected from the construction of a German hospital. "Its deep significance, precisely for propaganda purposes, needs no elaboration."[351] For the intellectuals, German courses were organized and were attended by about two hundred people.[352] "Anyone who learns German," wrote the Julio Albert firm to Eckardt, "is a gain for us, not only in the ideological sense, but also because such a person will be interested in German goods, will visit Germany, spend money there."[353]

The successes of German propaganda were relatively small until the middle of 1916, since, according to Eckardt's report, the Mexican press was inclined to favor the Allies;[354] there was the additional problem that the Transozean service was quite expensive. Since they had a high opinion of the significance of their propaganda productions and of the demand for them, the Germans were convinced that the Mexican press would continue to pay for such reports. Eckardt even proposed "that a code be used for the dispatches, so that their content is known only to the local representative. Otherwise, the local newspaper will obtain the reports with bribes and publish them."[355] It appears, however, that the newspapers initially showed little interest in either the free propaganda distributed by the Germans or in the telegrams offered for sale.

This situation changed somewhat when, according to Eckardt, the press was instructed to remain neutral.[356] Such instructions, however, do not always appear to have been followed by the press. In the Mexican files, there are constant protests from the German legation from the years 1915–16 against reporting alleged to be overly favorable to the Allies. Thus, on 26 September 1916, Eckardt protested against an article in the semiofficial *El Pueblo*, according to which 150 German Social Democrats, many of them old and sick, had been sent to the front line on orders from the kaiser.[357] Foreign Minister Aguilar thereupon asked *El Pueblo* to exercise the greatest "caution" in the publication of war reports, in view of Mexico's neutrality.[358] A day later the newspaper apologized to the government and claimed to have taken over the story unread from an American news agency. It promised to exercise greater vigilance in the future.[359]

The decisive shift occurred in June 1916, after the Mexican-American tensions had reached a high point in the wake of the American punitive expedition and Carranza's attempt to find backing from imperial Germany. Eckardt reported at that time that Carranza had instructed the largest newspapers to take a pro-German stance.[360] The editor of the newspaper *El Demócrata*, Rafael ("Rip Rip") Martínez, recounts that Carranza called him to his office and asked him to adopt a pro-German attitude in the interests of neutrality.[361] *El Demócrata* was to counter the influence of the newspapers that had opted for the Allies.

*El Demócrata* became the organ of the German legation, which gave the newspaper powerful support. "Most important independent newspaper *Demócrata*, previously sympathetic to the Allies, has been won over to our side. As it immediately lost all its quite lucrative French advertising, without the prospect of obtaining German ads, and as paper prices are increasing enormously, paper is requesting a monthly subsidy of 800 American dollars. I request authorization for payment for duration of war."[362] Approval appears to have been granted, for two months later Eckardt expressed great satisfaction over the dissemination of *El Demócrata*, which "is working reliably on our side. The paper is currently the cheapest major daily, is operating without financial support from the government, and thus has to fight for financing. I have taken steps to gain an even larger distribution for the paper, mainly in the interior, and I am providing it with the necessary supplies of paper, which are extremely hard to come by."[363] With the government newspapers *El Pueblo, El Nacional, El Occidental,* and *La Vida Nueva* in Puebla, agreements were made for purchase of Transozean cables.[364]

In 1917, American agents succeeded in stealing a report from the German propaganda office.[365] According to this report, which was probably authentic, *El Demócrata* was receiving paper and 8,000 pesos a month, the newspaper *Minerva* in Puebla 200 pesos a month, *El Día* in Monterrey 2,000 pesos, *La Opinión* in Veracruz 750 pesos, *La Reforma* in Tampico 3,500 pesos, and *La Gaceta* in Guaymas 750 pesos a month. *La Opinión, La Reforma,* and *La Gaceta* were also receiving paper. The propaganda apparatus was also showing a corresponding growth, as were the sums requested from Germany by Eckardt. A new propaganda chief, Lt. Col. Stapelfeld, was appointed and paid by the legation.[366] Schumacher was provided with a monthly salary of 200 pesos in addition to costs incurred as a representative.[367] In January 1917, Eckardt had asked for $2,000 a month from Germany for propaganda purposes.[368] This sum appears to have increased significantly in a very short time; the Americans estimated the Germans' monthly expenditures for propaganda and intelligence work at $25,000.[369] This estimate does not differ greatly from the estimate made by German businessmen in Mexico.

The Germans attempted to shift part of the costs to the Austrians. "Please inform by wire if I may spend $2500 to participate in extensive German propaganda beginning 7.1.16,"[370] the Austrian minister in Mexico wired to Vienna. The Austrian Foreign Ministry immediately had its ambassador in Berlin gather information on German propaganda in Mexico; he also presented a complete picture of the German propaganda network there. Officials in Vienna understood quite correctly the deeper goals of this propaganda and refused to participate, since "German propaganda is pursuing exclusively German interests. Financial support of German propaganda by us does not seem opportune."[371] Since the telegram was transmitted through Sweden and the Austrians feared that the first, anti-German section might fall into the hands of the Germans, it was deleted and only the refusal itself was sent to Mexico.[372]

The contents of German propaganda consisted mainly in the trumpeting of German "victories" and of German "excellence" in attacks against England and France. Anti-American reports could, of course, be found in the newspapers, in keeping with the policies of the Carranza government, but the Germans, for their part, took pains not to do very much in this regard until 1917.[373] In 1916, on the contrary, when the Mexican-American conflict was becoming sharper and sharper, the Germans had every interest in countering the impression in the United States that Germany had a hand in these tensions.

When the United States entered the war, the situation of German propaganda changed in many respects. Its task became much larger, and the obstacles it had to confront grew enormously. Its major objectives became the prevention of Mexico's alignment with the Allies and the preparation of the groundwork for later expansion. Efforts to woo the press were greatly intensified. "Over the press in the capital and in the provinces," Eckardt reported, "we increasingly won influence through large expenditures of money and effort—in the most important cities newspapers took on a pro-German attitude, pro-Allied papers were prompted to adopt a neutral attitude or at least not to attack us."[374]

Eckardt was undoubtedly proceeding quite skillfully in his propaganda when he attempted to use the anti-American sentiments of the Mexican people for his own ends.

Whereas we initially adopted only a defensive posture, countering the lies of the enemy, since the American declaration of war, I have been aggressively attacking the United States and the Allies, especially Great Britain. We could not merely promote the already existing sympathy of the Mexicans for a German policy barely known to them beforehand, nor could we content ourselves with keeping alive a mood that was momentarily favorable, but which could shift all too quickly. No, the policy of neutrality prescribed by Carranza for his government had to be placed on the one solid basis of the 'odio de los gringos,' of the hatred for the traditional enemy from the north which burns in the heart of every Mexican. The friendship felt for Germany, which even the rebel leaders communicated to me through couriers in spite of my hostile attitude toward them, could only develop, and did develop, as a secondary result of this hatred. Ruthless attacks on President Wilson in articles we consistently placed in the press, and brochures, of which I should single out for special praise those of legation secretary Freiherr von Schoen, had the desired effect; the Mexican people curses the enemy which robbed it of wealthy provinces 70 years ago, and which to this day will not leave Mexico in peace; it considers every German victory as its own and rejoices at each setback of the 'punitivos,' that is, members of the 'punitive expedition,' as it calls the Pershing troops sent to Europe, referring to his Villa expedition of 1916.[375]

Eckardt mixed his anti-American propaganda with a glorification of German imperialism. The German armies were portrayed as unbeatable, German industry as the best in the world, German welfare measures for workers as a culmination of human development.[376] This kind of propaganda, however, was so crude that it sometimes achieved the opposite of what was desired. Occasionally these reports were repudiated by the German propagandists themselves. In July 1915, the Transozean representative in Argentina, Schmersow, had written to Berlin that on the basis of the publication of Transozean dispatches "various errors had come to fore . . . which were immediately recognized as incorrect and which are being referred to here with the expression 'plancha.'" He stated that "something of this kind should not get by an official agency, for otherwise . . . the damage will be irreparable," and warned against "too much of a tendency to trumpet German successes."[377] In Mexico, articles appeared announcing such events as the destruction of New York, an insurrection in the American army, and the capitulation of England.[378]

Eckardt also organized an extensive program of lectures. "In Mexico City and in the interior, I am scheduling lectures by good speakers. In theatres and lecture halls filled to capacity, they have been speaking on the neutrality question, welfare measures for workers, German industry (Krupp, Zeiss) accompanied by slides we have produced here. At the end of the lecture, we have been showing the photos of His Majesty the Kaiser and his most famous commanders; there is stormy applause."[379] The Americans considered the director of *Noticias Inalámbricas,* Manuel León Sánchez, to be the most successful of these speakers.[380] The Argentine writer Ugarte played a special role in the German propaganda, asserting during a visit to Mexico "that the Germans have never attempted to intervene arrogantly in the fate of Spanish America, but have restricted themselves to peaceful activity," in contrast to British and American imperialism. The purpose of such propaganda was to "counter the belief" that Germany "was attempting to win influence in the South American republics through its propaganda."[381] In the army, the generals who had committed themselves to a coup against Carranza in the event that Mexico abandoned its neutrality were making "propaganda for us, distributing pamphlets which I had written for this purpose."[382]

Eckardt reported that in 1917, a total of 56,000 propaganda publications had been sold. The propaganda was so "effective" that its distributors in Mexico believed it themselves. As late as August 1918, Eckardt wrote: "I am expecting, like every German, a happy ending to the war."[383] When the first news of an armistice arrived on 11 November, Eckardt had a denial published in the newspapers: "Germany has rejected the Allied proposals for an armistice."[384]

To preserve the favor of the Mexican government, the newspapers were instructed to support Carranza unconditionally. "The national sensibility had to be appeased. The complaints with which the Allies inundated the Foreign Ministry were to be avoided wherever possible, all criticism was to be avoided as meddling in internal affairs. Carranza had to be convinced that we believe in the sincerity of his patriotism, that we fully appreciate the value of his pro-German policy, that we see in him a statesman superior to the presidents of the other Latin American countries. For one article along these lines printed at my behest in our organ, the *Informaciones Inalámbricas*, I twice received emphatic thanks."[385]

There was nonetheless one point on which Eckardt's support for the policy of the government came to a halt: the question of the Church. This came to the fore quite clearly in the case of the German-subsidized newspaper *El Occidental* in Guadalajara. The paper, heavily supported by the advertising of various German firms, had opened a sharp anticlerical campaign, in keeping with the domestic political line of the Carranza government. The Church, which was on a solid footing in Guadalajara, reacted extremely violently. Its organ, *La Época*, not only attacked *El Occidental*, but began to publish a blacklist designating all firms that advertised in *El Occidental*, calling on Guadalajara's Catholics to boycott these businesses.[386]

While this action was a heavy blow for the German businessmen in Guadalajara, it was even harder in political terms. The Guadalajara clergy was distinguished by an exceptional sympathy for Germany. German attempts to persuade the editors of *El Occidental* to put an end to their anticlerical propaganda appear to have met with no success. Eckardt then turned to the German consul in Guadalajara, asking why the Germans had not also advertised in *La Época*, and instructed the consul to take steps to this effect.[387] The consul replied that *La Época* was completely uninterested in advertising, a situation which probably resulted from its subsidization by the Church.[388]

Eckardt then instructed the consul to confer "with the editors of *La*

*Época* on the question of the blacklists, or if this should prove impossible for whatever reason, with influential people in the Catholic party which backs *La Época*." The consul was to make it clear in these discussions that *El Occidental* was pro-German in its international political perspective, but that it was not expressing German opinion in its radical domestic orientation.

> We have nothing to do with the internal politics of Mexico, and we want to have nothing to do with them. We must therefore energetically oppose the attempts of the Catholics to use domestic politics to undermine the advertising revenues of a pro-German newspaper which happens to be anti-Catholic. If the Catholics of Guadalajara wish to conclude from the support for *El Occidental* that the businesses which advertise in that newspaper are anti-Catholic, then we can conclude, with far greater justification, judging from the methods of *Época* and its backers which bear such resemblance to the methods of our Anglo-Saxon enemies, that they are anti-German. Under the circumstances, we must therefore regard the boycott of the *Época* as *unfriendly and ungrateful.*[389]

Should the Catholics persist in their campaign, the consul was to threaten to intervene with the Mexican government.[390]

The "gratitude" of the Catholics was not as great as Eckardt had expected. *La Época* would not be persuaded, and German businessmen were compelled to withdraw their advertising from *El Occidental,* which folded shortly thereafter.[391] "*El Occidental* is dead, may its counterparts die a similar death,"[392] the American consul in Guadalajara reported triumphantly. *El Demócrata* then attempted to distance itself from the struggle against the Church and held the Allied boycott measures responsible for the demise of *El Occidental.*[393]

There is some indication that within the Mexican government, there were differences of opinion concerning German propaganda in the Mexican press. On 13 April 1918, Aguilar sent a note to all Mexican newspapers in which he requested, in the name of the president, that pains be taken to avoid unnecessary attacks on leading functionaries or citizens of those countries having "friendly relations" with Mexico. He justified this request, citing the "sensitivities of foreign governments . . . and very tense international relations."[394] On 24 April, Manuel Andrade, editor of the pro-Allied *El Universal,* replied that bulletins were prepared on a daily basis in the Ministry of the Interior for publication in the press which contained pro-German articles. Some of these articles, he wrote, were by the minister's private secretary.[395] Whether the distribution of this bulletin to the press was halted after this incident cannot be ascertained. It is quite possible that Aguilar's report was only a propagandistic assertion of Mexico's neutrality. It may also have been an attempt by Carranza to restrain to some degree the extensive German propaganda.

To influence the upper classes and the intellectuals, Eckardt had Goethe's *Werther* and *Faust* and *Kapitän Königs Fahrt der "Deutschland"*—he mentions them all in the same breath—translated into Spanish.[396] German courses were introduced in the universities, and the German schools were expanded.[397] On the whole, German propaganda was able to record considerable successes in Mexico because of its anti-American orientation. In Coahuila, the American consul estimated that 72 percent of the population was friendly to Germany.[398] In the opinion of the American consul in Piedras Negras, 80 percent of the local population was considered to be inclined toward Germany.[399] The War Department was even more pessimistic, estimating 90 percent of the Mexican population to have anti-American views.[400] Similar reports came from Tabasco and Baja California.[401] The consul in Piedras Negras articulated quite clearly the reasons for these German successes. He explained that *El Demócrata* was the most widely distributed newspaper in Mexico. "*El Demócrata*'s editor has been able to exercise a major influence in this part of Mexico, especially among the lower classes.... The hostility to America which this newspaper has evoked in its readers is steadily growing and cannot be overestimated. Among the lower classes, which make up the majority of the population, every word is taken as good coin and their bitterest feelings against the U.S. are aroused."[402]

## Allied Countermeasures against German Propaganda in Mexico

Until the United States entered the war, the measures taken by the Allies to neutralize German propaganda had only a limited effect. They were restricted to interference with the shipment of German propaganda materials from Germany to Mexico and occasional protests lodged with the Mexican government against pro-German articles in Mexican newspapers. After the United States entered the war, tremendous efforts were set in motion to put an end to German propaganda. The Allies used five methods in this campaign: the flow of information was interrupted; imports of necessary materials, especially paper supplies of pro-German newspapers, were cut off; the shipment and sale of pro-German papers was prevented where possible; pressure was brought to bear on Mexican officials; and finally, pressure was also applied to businessmen who advertised in pro-German newspapers.

It had been hoped in the United States that after the outbreak of the war with Germany that the pro-German newspapers in Mexico would no longer be able to obtain information. The radio contact with Nauen had been broken and the German propaganda bureaus in the United States were closed. In addition, the Allied news agencies refused to give their dispatches to pro-German newspapers. These hopes nonetheless revealed themselves to be illusory, for German propaganda circumvented the Allied countermeasures, especially with the construction of a radio receiving station in Mexico. "The director of the telegraph company," Eckardt explains, "sends me the war telegrams from Nauen every day through a Syrian courier."[403] These reports were then printed in the pro-German newspapers as dispatches coming from the United States. It also appears that the dispatches of the Allied press agencies were being passed along, at least temporarily, to the pro-German newspapers by the Minister of Communications Mario Méndez.[404] Méndez, however, denied this energetically when *El Universal* published an article to this effect, but in view of his connections to the German secret service, the accusation may not have been a complete fabrication. Ways were apparently also found for smuggling American newspapers over the Mexican border, cribbing their stories, and publishing them in rewritten form.[405]

The American attempt to deprive the Germans of paper represented a much greater danger for German propaganda. Nonetheless, because it endangered the interests of a large American company, the National Type and Paper Company, this plan took a long time to be put into effect. As early as 19 April 1917, the American consul in Veracruz was complaining that pro-German newspapers were receiving American paper. The State Department did not react to this complaint, but informed him that there was no law prohibiting the export of paper from the United States.[406] A month later, the British embassy in Washington protested to the State Department. It confirmed that the National Type and Paper Company was selling paper originating in Canada to pro-German newspapers.[407]

Seven weeks later, Fletcher also intervened in this discussion, requesting that the sale of American paper to pro-German newspapers be stopped.[408] He had already spoken with the Mexican representative of the National Type and Paper Company, who, however, had refused to cooperate. He argued that other companies were doing the same thing and that the Mexican government, moreover, had large reserves of paper at its disposal which it could give to the Germans in an emergency.[409] The paper company, which was afraid of losing its large profits in Mexico because of Fletcher's stance—there had been a significant increase in paper prices—defended its viewpoint in a petition to the State Department. This petition showed that there were enough paper mills in Mexico to produce newsprint locally in the event of an American paper embargo. These mills were not producing any paper at the time because their products were more expensive than American paper and hence were not competitive.

In this petition, the National Type and Paper Company expressed the deeper reasons for its stubborn resistance to an embargo on paper supplies to German newspapers. In the event of such a ban, the company feared that it would lose not only its pro-German customers, but the entire Mexican market as well. The Mexican government had abolished its import duties on paper to promote the circulation of books and newspapers and had thus made it possible for the National Type and Paper Company to push the Mexican paper mills, which operated at higher cost, out of the market. "There is no doubt," wrote the company, "that the government will consider it necessary, in the event of an embargo, to place a new and increased import duty on newsprint in order to protect the domestic industry. And this duty would stay in effect for years."[410]

The National Type and Paper Company proposed to the American government that the sale of paper to Mexico be centralized. In this way, the pro-German newspapers would not be completely cut off from paper, but would be supplied "for their immediate needs." It should, however, be made clear "that they conduct no agitation for the production of newsprint in Mexican mills"![411] The Americans should therefore not ask them to desist from further anti-American statements. In the company's view, the entire power of the American economy and of American diplomacy in Mexico ought to be used, not against German propaganda, but against the emergence of a Mexican newsprint industry.

Eleven days later, Lansing also came out against a paper embargo, though he used other arguments. "Such an embargo," he wrote to Fletcher, could easily "be attacked in Mexico and throughout Latin America" as an attempt by the American government "autocratically to control public opinion."[412] As an alternative, Lansing proposed to bring concrete economic pressures to bear against the pro-German newspapers by having the businessmen of the Allied nations advertise extensively in these newspapers so that they could then force them to abandon their pro-German stance with the threat to withdraw their advertisements. Lansing himself appears to have had certain doubts about the practicality of this plan, however, for he asked if the pro-German newspapers had adequate financial support to minimize the possible influence of other businessmen.[413]

Fletcher strongly opposed his superior's suggestions. He viewed Lansing's idea as impractical, given the subsidies they received from the Germans. He once again urged a paper embargo and stated: "I do not share [the State] Department's fears that restricted shipments would have [the consequences in Mexico and Latin America which you mention.]" Neutral papers such as *El Pueblo* should continue to receive newsprint, and only the aggressively pro-German publications would receive none. He was opposed to hesitant and hyperscrupulous concern for Latin American sensibilities. "The choice, as I see it," he concluded, consists on the one hand in aid and support for anti-American propaganda, which would at the same time facilitate certain limited advantages for American exports, and on the other hand in the monitoring of American paper shipments to Mexico, which would render more difficult slanderous and hostile attacks on the U.S.[414]

Because of these far-reaching differences of opinion, the question was referred to Wilson, who unequivocally supported Fletcher's viewpoint. "It seems to me," he wrote to Lansing on 3 August, "that [Fletcher's proposals are] more than interesting. They are important, and so far as I can judge from this single presentation of the matter I should think they ought to be acted on."[415] As a result, Lansing imposed a paper embargo on all pro-German newspapers a week later. The decision concerning who would still be able to buy paper was left to the American embassy in Mexico.[416] The National Type and Paper Company had no alternative but to submit to this decision along with all other American paper companies.[417]

It quickly became clear that the National Type and Paper Company had not been completely wrong about the limited effectiveness of an embargo. A series of German-owned paper mills immediately began to produce newsprint.[418] This production, however, did not cover the requirements of the pro-German newspapers. There was thus an attempt to get the French-owned paper mills to supply newsprint to the pro-German papers, and the Norwegian director of the factory, whom the Americans viewed as having pro-German sympathies, also announced his willingness to do so. Fletcher thereupon asked the French authorities to do everything possible to mobilize the mill's stockholders in France and to put an end to these sales.[419] It cannot be ascertained to what extent these efforts were successful.

The Mexican government energetically resisted this external control of the Mexican press. It made its reserves of paper available to the pro-German newspapers; at the same time it imposed a customs duty on paper which was to be paid, not in money, but in paper. Part of this paper was given to the pro-German newspapers.[420] These newspapers either wrote nothing on the sources of their newsprint, or followed the lead of *La Reforma* in Tampico, which spoke of a regular supply of newsprint delivered by German U-boats. The Mexican government also attempted to buy newsprint in Japan. Initial efforts to do so were opposed by Japanese authorities. An attempt later in the summer, tied to the assurance that the paper was for government newspapers, initially had more success, for a Japanese firm was granted a permit to supply paper. The project, however, was to some extent the object of serious attack in the Japanese press.[421] It is not known whether the paper was actually delivered.

On the whole, the American paper boycott was only a partial success. Some pro-German papers in the provinces had to close down either permanently or temporarily, but the main organ of German propaganda, *El*

*Demócrata,* was not affected. "Many German businessmen," wrote Eckardt in August 1918, "are still secretly obtaining goods from their old Spanish friends; this, however, becomes more difficult every day, particularly the procurement of paper for the needs of our press and of our journalistic friends. The government, which is being increasingly harassed on this question, is helping as much as it can, and two local German paper manufacturers are producing the minimum necessities with improvised domestic raw materials."[422]

The other American countermeasures had similarly limited effectiveness. When the American-owned Sonora News Company, which had a contract with the Mexican railway authorities for the exclusive sale of newspapers in the railway stations of the state of Sonora, refused to sell *El Demócrata,* the contract was cancelled by the Mexican government.[423] Somewhat more effective were American measures to paralyze the shipment of pro-German newspapers through American territory. Many Mexican provinces in the western part of the country and particularly in Baja California were extremely difficult to reach from the capital. Some mail arrived there through the United States, and some came by sea, where American ships had a virtual monopoly. This situation permitted the Americans to limit the shipment of pro-German newspapers to such locations.

Allied economic sanctions were equally effective, even if within the very limited framework represented by certain provincial papers. In Progreso (Yucatán) the Germans published *Boletín de Guerra,* which was distributed free of charge. "As a result of ongoing persecution to which the *Boletín* has been subjected for many months by the American consul in Progreso," wrote the German consul in Yucatán, "the advertising is slowly being withdrawn; and through systematic pressure on the various presses threatened with a blacklist, the Americans are getting them to refuse to continue the *Boletín.*"[424] The American consul in Yucatán triumphantly reported the disappearance of the paper.[425] In Torreón, in the state of Coahuila, whose governor was pro-Allied, the English in particular were successful in using pressure and offers of money to turn the pro-German newspaper *La Opinión* into a pro-Allied paper.[426]

The State Department itself had proposed that the paper's outlook be changed through advertising (possibly with money from the American government),[427] but rejected proposals to bribe the paper's editors directly. In those cases where American representatives did use such methods successfully, they were not reprimanded. The use of bribery would have had only limited success where the press was concerned, since in the last analysis the papers were not independent and—with the exception of some provincial newspapers—had adopted their stance essentially at the government's behest. The editor in question would have simply been fired in such a case, and the bribery attempt used as propaganda against the Americans.[428]

The cinema was the arena of a struggle similar to that waged for the press. In 1916, Bernstorff had concluded a contract with a German businessman named Camus to show German war films in Mexico and in the United States. Bernstorff proposed to send the films to the United States on merchant U-boats and to forward them from there to Latin America. Zimmermann agreed to this and promised to send the films destined for Mexico to the German consulate in New York.[429] It is not known how many films were shipped in this fashion; in any case, when the United States entered the war, this project as well was interrupted.

Camus, however, did not abandon his efforts. Through Spanish middlemen he attempted to get German war films to Mexico through Spain; in addition, a series of anti-Allied films produced in the United States before the Americans entered the war were ordered and shown in Mexico.[430] The American reaction to this endeavor was very sharp and probably effective as well. The American secret service succeeded in tracking down Camus's Spanish middlemen and in paralyzing German film shipments through Spain. It was even easier to prevent the delivery of American films to Camus. The most effective method proved to be the threat of a boycott against all theaters showing pro-German films; they were informed that they would no longer receive American comedies, which would practically have put them out of business.[431]

The Allies, for their part, also developed an extremely active propaganda system. After the United States entered the war, a major propaganda offensive was launched all over the world. The main organ of this campaign was the Committee of Public Information, headed by Georges Creel. This institution published extensive, richly documented, and illustrated materials and, together with the American press services and their affiliates in Mexico, provided the pro-Allied press in Mexico with information. The most important pro-Allied paper was *El Universal,* a daily, which was edited by a temporary collaborator and comrade-in-arms of Carranza, Felix Palavicini. It was supported by the Allies with ads and cheap paper.[432]

*El Universal* initially faced no explicit measures of hostility from the Mexican government, although the paper had published sharp attacks on German imperialism and spoke in glowing terms of the Americans. Carranza wanted to show proof of his neutrality through the existence of two newspapers as opposed to one another as *El Universal* and *El Demócrata.* Moreover, in spite of his cooperation with the Germans, he may not have wanted a German monopoly of the press. In matters of domestic politics, *El Universal* generally supported Carranza. As Mexican-American relations deteriorated, however, the paper took an increasingly pronounced stance against the government. This stance, together with Eckardt's pressure, prompted the Mexican Ministry of the Interior to expel Palavicini from Mexico. Eckardt noted triumphantly: "The secretary of the Interior, Aguirre Berlanga, a politician completely devoted to Carranza but who is very ambitious and hence not too reliable, has performed the excellent service of forcing Felix Palavicini, the American-paid editor of *El Universal,* to leave the country. This paper, which was slandering us in the most vulgar fashion on a daily basis and which had been demanding my expulsion for months, has since lost its importance."[433] *El Universal* did not, in fact, abandon its pro-Allied stance, but the intensity of its attacks on the Germans subsided.

Propaganda was undoubtedly the terrain on which German imperialism achieved one of its greatest successes in Mexico. "With the possible exception of Spain," the Committee of Public Information retrospectively concluded, "German propaganda has proceeded in no other country with such resolve and malicious aggressiveness, as in Mexico."[434] The basis for this success was the Mexican people's deep-rooted antipathy toward the United States and its lack of direct experience of German imperialism, which up to that time it had come to know only in camouflaged form.

# 11 The Allies and Carranza

After the United States entered World War I heated controversies developed in Germany over the question of what policies should be pursued in Mexico. The intelligence service of the General Staff advocated an aggressive policy aimed at provoking U.S. intervention, while German business interests, with the increasing support of the Foreign Office, pursued the opposite aim of keeping the United States out of Mexico in the hope of converting Mexico into an object of German economic expansion.

In spite of their intensity, these controversies were limited in scope in that they were restricted to Germany. Germany's allies were not interested in Mexico and were not involved in the controversies Germany's policies in Mexico had generated.

The situation of the Allies was quite different. In addition to internal policy controversies, the Allies—particularly the United States and England—became embroiled in clashes with one another which gave rise to several tense situations. Prior to 1917 England and the United States had been open rivals in Mexico, and their rivalry had not ended with the U.S declaration of war and the resulting alliance between the two countries. This rivalry was reflected in the very different—and often opposed—objectives the two nations pursued.

After a brief, vain attempt to bring about Carranza's downfall, many of the British firms in Mexico began to pursue a defensive policy of solidifying and defending positions already acquired and of seeking a rapprochement with Carranza to this end. This orientation was opposed by most English military leaders as well as many politicians. They advocated instead a ruthless, offensive orientation which they hoped would serve to intensify Mexico's internal conflicts and ultimately result in the overthrow of Carranza's government.

The policy of the United States was moving in the opposite direction. While a number of American companies with interests in Mexico were attempting, through the overthrow of Carranza, to consolidate and preserve the acquisitions they had made in Mexico during the revolutionary period, the vast majority of the U.S. military and political leadership was opposed to any intervention in Mexico so long as World War I lasted. Their main objective during the war was to keep Mexico "quiet" so as to remain free to concentrate their energies overseas.

460

## British Policy in Mexico during the First World War

Of the three major Allied powers with important interests in Mexico, it was England that pursued the sharpest and most aggressive policy in that country during the First World War. This policy was in no way limited to countermeasures against the activities of the German secret service and German propaganda in Mexico, but was aimed, almost until the end of the war, at the violent overthrow of the Carranza government. The unconcealed aggressiveness of British policy arose out of fear of growing German and American influence and concern about the serious setbacks that the entire British position had undergone in Latin America during the years 1914–18.[1]

England's troubled relations with the Carranza regime had their origins in the period before the world war when England maintained very close relations with Huerta and Sir Lionel Carden had been Huerta's most important supporter and closest adviser. For a time it seemed that British-Mexican relations had shaken off the burden of Carden's legacy. Shortly after Huerta's defeat, Carden left Mexico and relations between Carranza and England improved briefly, even achieving the dimensions of a rapprochement, in 1914–15.

Although Carranza declared his neutrality in the world war, he assured English representatives that his sympathies lay with the Allies, an assertion thoroughly confirmed by Eckardt's tirades of hatred against Carranza in 1915. Carranza's attitude was undoubtedly influenced by German plots on Huerta's behalf, about which he was quite well informed.

Relations with England began to deteriorate in 1916, when Carranza, confronted with the advance of the Pershing expedition, felt compelled to seek a rapprochement with Germany. During this period the English secret service intercepted messages in which Carranza offered Germany U-boat bases in the event that German diplomats succeeded in persuading the Americans to withdraw their troops from Mexico. Eckardt's reports, confirming Mexico's benevolent attitude toward Germany's alliance proposal, were also intercepted by the British secret service.[2] As a result, Great Britain began to turn against Carranza with increasing vehemence.

Until the United States entered the war, however, England's opportunities for intervening in Mexican affairs were quite limited. The landing of troops in Mexico was precluded, from a military point of view, by the situation in Europe; and direct English involvement would have provoked serious tensions with the United States at a time when England was hoping that the United States would enter the war on the Allied side.

In the eyes of the British, the situation was completely transformed once the United States entered the war. At that point, the relations of all Allied countries with Carranza came to a head, and the British government felt it could entertain legitimate hopes for joint Anglo-American actions against Carranza.

England's trouble with Carranza was due in part to its dependence on Mexico's petroleum and to the fear born of that dependence that Germany would succeed in sabotaging oil production. Both the British government and the British oil interests were also concerned over efforts by the Mexican government to increase national control over its greatest natural wealth. To forestall such policies the British oil companies had attempted to buy the services of revolutionary politicians. When it seemed that the Convention would triumph, Lord Cowdray's oil company showed great interest in attempting to suborn Miguel Díaz Lombardo, one of Pancho Villa's highest civilian officials. His name had been suggested to Cowdray's representative in Mexico by Ernesto Madero, the uncle of the murdered Mexican president. Cowdray's representative, J. B. Body, told Madero that he wanted Díaz Lombardo to be more than just a legal representative. "I told him (Madero) that we should not want him to act in a legal capacity but in an ambassadorial one. He said that he believed that the candidate he had mentioned would be a satisfactory one."[3] Having received this assurance, Body wrote one of his associates about Díaz Lombardo. "Of course you know him and when the time comes and if I am not back in Mexico I wish you would take the matter up with Mr. Ryder and you, or both of you, approach him and tell him that we want him to see everything we have, be convinced of the truth of our statements and then to act with whoever is in authority to nullify as far as possible the misstatements that have been made against us."[4]

Body was obviously worried that it would become known that his company was attempting to purchase the services of Villa's associate. In the final paragraph of his letter he instructed, "In any cables you may send to me regarding Lic. Díaz Lombardo I suggest that you refer to him by the name of Morgan."

It cannot be ascertained whether Díaz Lombardo was ever approached, but it is known that when the Carranza faction became the dominant force in Mexico, Cowdray made an explicit approach to Carranza's most important and intelligent civilian adviser, Luis Cabrera. A conversation took place between Cowdray's representative in Mexico, Ryder, and Cabrera that had all the earmarks of a classic bribery attempt. "We decided that it would be more advisable for Mr. Ryder to attend the interview yesterday without me," Cowdray's main representative in Mexico, J. B. Body, reported to his chief. "As we intended asking his advice and recommendations for someone of his party to represent us before the new government, which we meant to convey should be himself through a third party and we thought it would be less embarrassing to him if I were not present."[5] Cabrera refused to go along, though he expressed no anger or indignation at the attempt.

After this failure British oil companies joined American oil interests in turning more toward Carranza's enemies. The main object of their interest and support was General Manuel Pelaez, a landowner from Mexico's oil region who had taken up arms to fight against Huerta and in the ensuing split of the revolutionary forces had declared for the Revolutionary Convention. It is not clear what kind of relations Pelaez had with the Conventionist government but after his troops occupied the oil fields he established very close relations with the American and British oil companies who supported him with arms and money. He never recognized Carranza's authority and the Mexican president accused him of being a tool of the oil companies. The companies never denied that they were supplying Pelaez with money but stated that they were doing so under duress since his troops occupied their fields and installations and insisted that he was certainly not working for them.[6] As this book will attempt to show, the oil companies were by no means unwilling victims of Pelaez.

The British government not only approved the oil companies' actions but secretly provided Pelaez with arms.[7] Thus the oil fields were under the control of a relatively strong Mexican army which in turn was quite dependent on England. Not surprisingly, Pelaez and his army were soon at the center of English plans for a coup in Mexico.

As a result of these activities, tensions between the Carranza government and the oil companies as well as between the Mexican government and the British government were constantly on the increase. These tensions were further heightened by the Carranza government's confiscation of large English companies, particularly the railroads.[8]

The causes of Carranza's actions have not been investigated in depth. Mexican government officials told English representatives that they had seized the British railways because information on government troop movements had been given to the revolutionaries opposing Carranza by railway employees.[9] This was, in all probability, something more than a pretext. At the beginning of 1917, Cummins, who was in charge of the British legation in Mexico, had worked out plans for a coup against Carranza and had discussed these plans in the British Club, so that, according to the English consul, Grahame Richards, Mexican government officials were aware of them.[10] Under these circumstances, the Carranza government was understandably not disposed to leave a sector with the strategic importance of railroads under the control of a hostile power.

Financial considerations may also have played a role in these expropriations, which were explicitly designated as provisional by the Mexican government. Carranza was in a difficult economic situation, because im-

portant political and economic groups in both Great Britain and the
United States were preventing him from obtaining a loan in those countries. The expropriations were at once a source of income and a means of
pressuring the British government and British interests to raise no further
obstacles to a loan. Moreover, the Mexican government could confiscate
English companies more easily than American ones since it was much
more difficult for England to carry out effective reprisals while engaged in
the world war. Carranza could therefore deal calmly with the harsh but
ineffective English response to these expropriations. Britain not only
protested but also withheld appointment of a minister to Mexico and even
recalled Thurstan, its chargé d'affaires, leaving only a low-ranking diplomat, Cummins, to carry on the affairs of the British legation.

In the years 1917–18 the British were attempting to fight a three-front
war in Mexico directed against Germany, the United States, and the
Mexican nationalists. The difficulties British diplomacy faced in attempting to reconcile these aims are clearly expressed in a memorandum written by Thurstan in early 1917. The British official attempted to assess the
potential results of "Carranza's throwing in his lot with the Central Powers and the possibility of his joining the United States and the Allies."[11]
That he was afraid of the first alternative comes as no surprise. "Carranza's alliance with Germany," he wrote, "would in all probability result
in the total destruction of British property in Mexico and there is no doubt
whatsoever that the oil fields would be fired if a means to accomplish it
could be found." What at first seems surprising is that Thurstan was no
less afraid of the second alternative he had mentioned; that Carranza
might join the Allies. "On the other hand we should hardly be in a more
enviable position were Carranza to espouse our cause," he stated. "He
would in such an event throw dust in the eyes of the United States and be
constantly plotting against us behind the scenes." What the British
diplomat feared above all was that the Mexican president "could seize
British properties while making loud protests of friendship." In a veiled
form Thurstan was expressing a fear that British diplomats would voice
much more openly and bluntly in months to come, the fear that an alliance
between Carranza and the United States would be forged at Britain's
expense.

Were such an alliance formed, Thurstan felt that Britain would have to
give up what he appeared to consider its trump card in Mexico, its close
relations with General Pelaez and his relatively powerful fighting force.

The Thurstan memorandum illustrates the persistent fear of British
officials that the United States intended to utilize its new-found strength
to dominate Mexico. One of the most explicit expressions of this fear was
a memorandum by Grahame Richards, Britain's consul general in Mexico, which stated that a new aggressiveness toward Mexico and a new anti-

European attitude was emerging in the United States as a result of America's participation in World War I. Before the United States entered the war, Richards wrote, armed British intervention in Mexico might have provoked protest in the United States but he felt that American pacifists would probably have prevented American actions against Britain.

Whether this statement be accurate or not regarding past times, it most certainly is not applicable to the present condition of things, nor will it prove to be so in the future. For America's entry into the European war sounded the death-knell of the do-nothing parties and, already pre-occupied as she is with preparations for the tremendous overseas con-flict, America's attitude towards the Mexican question has assumed a complete volte face; the American press is being inundated with articles urging geographical and military justifications for the annexation of Mexico; Monroism, weakened at first by reason of entrance into the European war and the moral considerations involved, is now daily finding converts amongst those who for years were its most obstinate opponents, and it is those converts who are urging the annexation and application of an advanced Monroism to Mexico.[12]

How might England best achieve its objectives of halting American expansion, frustrating German plans in Mexico, and restraining Mexican nationalism in order to restore the political and economic influence it had enjoyed prior to 1914? English diplomats, companies with interests in Mexico, and military figures had sharply divergent views on this question.

The English were in agreement on only one thing: that American mili-tary intervention in Mexico had to be avoided at all costs, not only be-cause it would jeopardize American aid for the Allies in Europe, but because, from a political and economic point of view, an American occu-pation of Mexico would result in a significant decline in English influence.

Apart from this area of consensus, two competing views as to what England's course of action should be predominated—one view favored a coup against Carranza and the other favored an agreement with the Mexi-can president.

## Early British Plans for a Coup in Mexico

The first British plans for a coup appear to have developed in the minds of British diplomats in Mexico and to have had the immediate support of the largest British company in Mexico, the Cowdray concern. Between March and June 1917 three such plans against Carranza were worked out and presented to the Foreign Office. The architects of these plans were the British chargé d'affaires in Mexico, Thurstan, who had just been recalled from Mexico to London, his representative in Mexico, Cummins, and the Cowdray representative, Body.

Thurstan's memorandum to the Foreign Office contained a plan to overthrow Carranza's government and an analysis of recent developments in Mexico. This analysis expressed exactly the same racist opinions that had been set forth earlier by the German minister. Mexico was not a "white" country, but an Indian one, and could not, therefore, be ruled in the same fashion as the "white countries."[13] The only appropriate way to rule Mexico had been found by Porfirio Díaz. "If such a thing as a popular vote were possible in Mexico (it is of course inconceivable), the Díaz regime would hold 95 percent of the votes. It was and is the only form of government possible for this country . . . . It fell, not owing to any faults in the system but owing to the inadequacy of the material." According to Thurstan, the problem with the Carranza regime and the source of its hostility to foreigners was that "the gigantic experiment is being tried of ruling the country by the agency of Indians, and if experience counts for anything the experiment is foredoomed to disastrous failure."

Thus the sole way to save Mexico was to bring to power "white men by blood and education." To this end, Thurstan proposed that money and arms be provided by the United States and the Allies to Carranza's opponents. Pelaez's army was to be the driving force of the anti-Carranza elements. The leaders of the coup should be assured that, as soon as they have demonstrated reasonable success, they will have the practical support of the United States and the Allied powers. In this way, declared Thurstan, "we might have the entrance into power of the white men of Mexico, of the decent elements who alone are capable of giving the country any real form of government, men who would be acceptable to the Mexican people at large, who would owe their existence as a Government to us and who could be relied upon to be friendly." Thurstan saw the support of the United States as the sine qua non for the success of such a coup. The British government was to discuss this project with the Americans.

A plan similar to Thurstan's was developed by Cummins, but, in contrast to his superior, Cummins dispensed with all historical analysis. He justified his plan simply: "A resolute policy will save our properties, lives and prestige, and will not cost one drop of our blood."[14]

Under the Cummins plan the United States and the Allies were to give their support to a coalition consisting of supporters of Villa, led by Felipe Ángeles and Roque González Garza, of conservatives, led by Eduardo Iturbide, and Zapatists, led by Francisco Vásquez Gomez. In exchange for support from the Allies, the new rulers would have to state their willingness to grant special privileges to foreigners. Cummins was convinced they would be willing to do so.

The exiled Mexicans and those opposed to the Carrancistas are so reduced by hopelessness that they will accept any terms imposed upon them.

The following conditions should be imposed:

Foreigners in the Commission handling all Government funds—to give confidence and protect lending banks.

The foreigners must enjoy the same rights as Mexicans abroad. Foreign claims must be examined and acknowledged when just.

All foreigners and foreign corporations must have the right of appeal to their respective governments' diplomatic representatives, notwithstanding that they may have waived such rights.

In contrast to Thurstan, who obviously had in mind a return to the Díaz era, Cummins called for some modest reforms by which the government would heavily tax uncultivated land and would give every peasant in Mexico the right to cultivate previously uncultivated land for a year. This, however, was the extent of Cummins's "concession" to the agrarian revolutionaries whom he was trying to win over to the Allies.

The most comprehensive plan for a coup was worked out by Cowdray's representative in Mexico, Body. He advocated an ultimatum to Mexico by the Allies and the United States calling for the immediate reinstatement of the contractually guaranteed rights of foreigners. In addition, all expropriated foreign property—particularly the railroads—was to be returned to its previous owners, all laws regulating the petroleum industry were to be repealed, and the amount of the royalties required from the oil concerns was to be reconsidered.[15]

Should the Mexican government not go along with these demands, all Allied governments would break off diplomatic relations with Carranza and dispatch their armed forces to occupy all ports. Carranza, Obregón, González, and certain other Mexican generals were to be made personally liable for any excesses against foreign life or property during this period. In addition, the plan called for the recognition as president of Pedro Lascuráin, Madero's foreign minister and a participant in Huerta's seizure of power, and for the money and arms he would need to rule.

Body also felt it would greatly enhance the plan's chances for success if all of Carranza's opponents participated—to varying degrees. The conservative armies of Pelaez and Felix Díaz were to be the driving force. Body was far more cautious about including the revolutionaries who were fighting Carranza. He saw the Zapatistas as "incapable of forming an organized and disciplined force." Consequently, the sole purpose of the negotiations with their representative in San Antonio was to use them to tie up Carranza's army. Body did not mention what was to be done with them after the victory of the "revolution."

Body had a similar mistrust of Villa, and initially he did not want to involve him in the objectives of the new movement, but he arrived at the conclusion that Villa, who, he said, would "seek and listen to good advice," would eventually offer full support to the plan for Carranza's overthrow. In that case, there would be no problem in providing him with arms—while carefully preventing him from assembling a larger army— and then buying him off after the victory by making him a regional chief of the *rurales*, the rural police. Villa would, of course, first have to apologize for the murder of Benton and "go through the formality of saluting the British flag."

Body formulated these plans on a trip from Mexico to Washington and discussed them there with Frank Polk, an important State Department official concerned with Mexican affairs. "We discussed the question of Señor Lascuráin 'blazing the trail,' as Mr. Polk expressed it, for a new party. Mr. Polk explained they could not immediately appear to change their course, but they could later help him with arms and money, and that they would give the matter further consideration. I explained how Pelaez was guarding the oil properties, who said he would continue to do so until Foreign forces appeared, when he would discretely retire and leave the situation in their hands, which news Mr. Polk was pleased to have."[16]

A memorandum from the then-English General Consul in Mexico, Grahame Richards, gives evidence of a tendency within the world of English diplomacy running counter to that of the adherents of a coup, namely, the belief that a coup would be pointless and condemned to failure. Because the United States had joined the war and had thus strengthened itself militarily, Richards assumed that "Monroeism" had undergone a rebirth and that the advocates of the annexation of Mexico were on the rise. Such an annexation would be tantamount to the complete elimination of any non-American foreign influence in Mexico that might pose a threat to America's security. British firms would hardly be in a position to handle the merciless tax pressure of the Americans and would thus quickly collapse. Even if the United States felt compelled by pressure from the Great Powers to give up its annexation plans, it would still attempt to impose a government of its choosing on Mexico.

In view of its large investments in Mexico, Richards argued, England could not tolerate such American action in Mexico, and the United States for its part would never allow England to intervene militarily in Mexico, to say nothing of attaining hegemony there. "Bluntly," he stated, "Britain is no more in the position to remain quiescent and permit America to absorb Mexico, than is America to sit with folded hands should Britain seek to acquire the dominant position."[17] Thus, Richards concluded, there remained only the possibility of persuading France and the United States to act jointly with England in Mexico.

Richards shared his views with Thurstan, Cummins, and Body, who also envisioned joint action with the United States in their plans for a coup. In Richards's opinion, however, the Allies should not solidify their influence through a coup, but through a loan to Carranza. The Carranza government, according to Richards, was Mexico's most stable regime in years and would in all likelihood remain so for some time. Therefore, England, France, and the United States should make a loan to Mexico on an equal basis. "If Mexico, having received such a loan, finally defaults, intervention, military or otherwise, must be the common work of the three powers named, as must be the subsequent administration of the country which would be established." Richards backed his memorandum by citing full support for his proposals by one of the richest British bankers in Mexico, Honey, president of the Central and International Mortgage Bank, the Hidalgo Bank, and many state banks and the owner of the Pachuca-Tampico railway line, then under construction, as well as several haciendas. Since the Mexican government had already confiscated a considerable portion of his assets, Honey proposed to avoid further confiscation of his property by making the Mexican government a loan. The British government would of course have to guarantee the repayment of this loan in the event that the Mexican government was unable to keep its commitments. Richards saw such a loan as the first step toward strengthening English financial influence in Mexico.

Richards also attempted to undermine the credibility of his opponents in the diplomatic service, reporting in his memorandum some of the rumors about Thurstan, Cummins, and Hohler circulating in the British colony in Mexico, which in his view cast these British officials in an unflattering light. Thurstan had apparently made no attempt to meet directly with Carranza, but conducted all negotiations by phone, while the American ambassador, Fletcher, had always cultivated good personal relations with the Mexican president. During his stay in Torreón, where he managed a boot factory, Cummins's cohabitation with an unmarried woman had provoked a scandal. Cummins was also associated with a series of failures: his boot factory had gone bankrupt, and he was dismissed from his position with the United Boot Company in Mexico. Richards went on to write that Hohler, for his part, had business ties with Cummins and had thus proposed that he be the commercial attaché to the British legation in Mexico.

Neither Cummins nor Hohler had been able to preserve their "dignity" as British diplomats. Hohler did not want to deal with Carranza, but had also once waited for hours to see the Mexican president. Cummins had occupied without payment the house of a wealthy Mexican in the capital to save it from confiscation by the government. Thus the British chargé d'affaires had essentially become the doorman for a wealthy Mexican.[18]

## The Foreign Office and the Plans for a Coup

In the Foreign Office in London the initial reaction to the machinations of both groups of plotters was one of reserve. While some officials, especially the expert on U.S. affairs Rowland Sperling, were sympathetic to Thurstan's coup plans—Sperling called Thurstan's plan the only "coherent proposal"[19] for a solution to the Mexican problem—no immediate decision was contemplated. It was clear to the members of the Foreign Office that it would be impossible to carry out plans for a coup against Carranza without the participation of the United States. While the British ambassador to the United States, Spring Rice, was instructed to seize any opportunity that presented itself to persuade the United States that such a coup would constitute the best solution in Mexico, the Foreign Office hoped that the growing strength of the United States, which was assembling a large army for the war effort, would intimidate Carranza and prompt him to alter his policy.[20]

The concrete actions of the Foreign Office were at first relatively restrained and amounted to little more than an increase in the money and arms provided Pelaez. Grahame Richards's plan was never seriously considered. But the reaction of the Foreign Office was far less calm in the summer of 1917 when rumors of a unilateral agreement between the United States and Carranza began to circulate.

In June 1917 Cummins reported that because of financial difficulties, Carranza might be willing to reach an agreement with the United States and that the Americans themselves were pushing for an accord "in which British interests might be forgotten."[22] Therefore, Cummins urged that England and France attempt to conclude an agreement with Carranza in order to prevent an accord between the Americans and the de facto government, "inimical to British interests." As a precondition for such an agreement, Carranza would have to commit himself to returning all expropriated British property. Cummins, however, characterized such an agreement as an emergency solution which he thoroughly opposed and which should be applied only if the Americans reached an agreement with Carranza.

For Hohler, the former chargé d'affaires in Mexico who was now responsible for Mexican affairs in the British embassy in Washington, even Cummins's proposals went too far. He submitted a memorandum to the Foreign Office written by an Englishman whom he did not name but with whose views he identified himself completely. The memorandum rejected the abandonment of Mexican neutrality demanded by important American officials as a precondition for a loan to Carranza. Recognition of Mexico as an ally meant that the Mexican government would have to be treated accordingly. The author of the memorandum wanted to avoid that at any cost. "If it is a matter of a loan to save the country, then it is better for everyone that they stay neutral, but accept the crudest and even most humiliating form of financial tutelage—but *they should not be allowed* to declare themselves officially as an ally."[23]

Similar fears that the United States was outmaneuvering England were expressed by British diplomats in the fall of 1917, when rumors surfaced that Eduardo Iturbide, a conservative, was planning a coup with American support. Iturbide was on good terms with the British authorities—during his exile in the United States, the British embassy had even helped him to obtain work—but Britain did not want an Iturbide government brought to power by the United States alone. Cummins thus advised the Foreign Office, in the event that the United States actually intended to support such a coup, to make it a joint Allied operation in which England and France were also involved.[24]

The mistrust of the United States on the part of British diplomats was not entirely unfounded. In a confidential file assembled by Secretary of State Lansing on Canova, there is a secret agreement between Canova and Iturbide.[25] In exchange for considerable financial support, Canova promised to assist Iturbide, who, for his part, stated that if his movement was victorious, all English control over the Tehuantepec Railway, which was partially owned by the British Cowdray concern, would be eliminated.

The fears of the English diplomats proved groundless when the loan negotiations between the United States and Carranza broke down and when the State Department became aware of and flatly rejected Canova's plans.[26]

## Cowdray's Turnabout

In November 1917, the Mexican question once again loomed large in the thinking of the Foreign Office and led to conflicts between the financial circles with interests in Mexico and the British military leadership.

By October–November 1917—despite the fact that in June Cowdray's representative had worked out a plan for the overthrow of Carranza—Cowdray had made a radical turnabout and was advocating full recognition of Carranza and the sending of a British minister to Mexico.[27] Cowdray's attitude reflected the outlook of other large British concerns with interests in Mexico; for example, Vincent Yorke, representative of the British railway companies, also advocated recognition.[28] Cowdray's sudden policy shift, as well as pressure for the recognition of Carranza by other large British firms in Mexico, was undoubtedly linked to the American government's attitude toward Carranza. Because of the de jure recognition of the Carranza government by the United States in September 1917, Body's plans for a coup, worked out in May–June 1917, were clearly without any prospect of success.

Another factor was that Carranza had indicated his willingness to return property confiscated from British companies, with the exception of the railways, to their earlier owners.[29]

Various other factors must be considered as well in order to explain Cowdray's surprising about-face. The unfolding of the Mexican revolution, the nationalism openly proclaimed in the 1917 constitution, and England's increasing inability because of the war to intervene in Mexico, prompted Cowdray to make arrangements to sell some of his Mexican properties. In May 1917 he proposed to the British government that it invest 5 million pounds sterling in his oil company.[30] At the same time Cowdray's agent in Mexico and the British representative there were moving ahead with plans for a coup.

Cowdray's hope for financial participation in his companies by the British government was not fulfilled, and he began to seek other buyers for his property. In the fall of 1917, he began negotiations with the Mexican government and with the Standard Oil Company; he wanted to sell his share of the Tehuantepec railway to the former and his oil interests to the latter.[31]

The sale of the Tehuantepec railway to the Mexican government was an extremely complex financial transaction. The line which belonged to both Cowdray and the Mexican government owned a considerable quantity of stock in the extremely profitable Mexican-American Steamship Company, an American firm. In return for Cowdray's share in the Tehuantepec line, worth $10,000,000, the Mexican government was prepared to turn over its stock in the Mexican-American Steamship Company. It was a profitable arrangement for both sides. Instead of the Tehuantepec line, which had been losing money for years and which was already administered by the Mexican government, Cowdray obtained an important investment in a prosperous North American shipping company. The financially plagued Carranza, on the other hand, obtained $10,000,000, which he could hardly have raised anywhere else.[32]

Cowdray made clear to the Foreign Office that this deal had one prerequisite: Carranza had to remain in power, at least for a time. A regime that emerged from a coup against Carranza might accuse Cowdray of having supported its opponent and carry out reprisals against him. In spite of the serious reservations of certain figures in the Foreign Office, an agreement was worked out between Cowdray and the Carranza government along these lines.

The British authorities, however, prevented Cowdray's other and much larger sales project. The Board of Trade vetoed his plan to sell his oil operations to the Standard Oil Company, noting that Great Britain was already dependent on American oil imports for 84 percent of its needs and that such dependency should not be increased.[33]

Cowdray's effort to get England to recognize Carranza may also have been prompted in part by his desire to sell his oil fields to the Standard Oil Company. He was no longer contemplating an expansion of British ownership and thus was no longer interested in the plans for a coup being considered by England. He was much more concerned with bringing his policies into harmony with those of the United States, and at the end of 1917, U.S. policy was clearly oriented toward keeping Carranza in power.

In early November Cowdray and his allies succeeded in rallying the Foreign Office to their viewpoint. The Foreign Office cabled the British embassy in Washington: "Notwithstanding possibility of a movement on behalf of Iturbide, and reports of Carranza's intrigues with the Germans, Messrs. Pearson supported by other interested British firms continue their pressure upon His Majesty's Government to recognize Carranza and appoint a Minister. We desire to proceed in entire agreement with United States Government and propose to adopt the policy advocated by the interested firms unless United States Government have been moved by the latest accounts from Mexico to drop Carranza and support his opponents, in which case it is obvious that recognition by His Majesty's Government would be inopportune."[34]

### The Intervention of the Armed Forces

At the end of November, there was another reversal in British policy, when important military figures protested the recognition of Carranza and called for the overthrow of his government. British military leaders were convinced that the attitude of the Mexican government had changed in October–November 1917 and that Carranza was now willing to enter an alliance with Germany and to launch an attack against the United States. The basis for this new interpretation of Carranza's policy was Germany's second alliance proposal to Mexico, about which British intelligence was well informed. The British secret service believed that while Carranza had refused to consider the offer communicated to him on 26 September by Delmar, the representative of the German General Staff, he had in fact stated his willingness to attack the United States eight days later. Further, the secret service believed it had uncovered a German strategy to win over Felix Díaz and Pelaez, with Delmar buying arms in Japan and bringing them to Mexico in four ships which would break the Allied blockade. Meanwhile, Germany was thought to be giving a number of German officers and soldiers marching orders for Mexico.[35]

A spokesman of British military intelligence implored the Foreign

Office in an urgent letter to recognize Carranza only after he had eschewed participation in all German conspiracies and had expelled Delmar from Mexico. The intelligence officer did not mention what was to occur in the event that Carranza did not meet England's conditions.[36]

The author of a memorandum from naval intelligence to the Foreign Office expressed himself somewhat more clearly. This memorandum argued that Carranza, who was in great financial difficulty, would be willing to attack the United States in January 1918 in exchange for German funding. British naval intelligence recommended that Carranza be pushed aside in a coup centered on Pelaez and Felix Díaz. Villa and Zapata, who were considered unreliable bandits, were not to be involved in this coup nor informed of the plans. Only the foreign powers—the United States, England, and France—and the circles around Pelaez and Díaz were involved in the plan, which aimed at the accession of Felix Díaz and his immediate recognition as the legitimate president by the Allied powers. The author of the memorandum was thoughtful enough to add that an effort should be made to avoid bloodshed with appropriate "bonuses" for the Mexican troops. He also noted that, if necessary, the Allies would have to provide military aid to Pelaez by occupying the ports of Tuxpan and Tampico.[37]

The Admiralty's plan contained various anti-American elements, such as the use of non-American, or more precisely English and French, ships for the occupation of Tuxpan and Tampico. "If possible the Mexicans should be assured that France and Great Britain were acting genuinely in defence of their interests, and would not be subservient to U.S. dictation."[38]

The fears of the English military leaders were highly exaggerated. Carranza had already rejected Delmar's alliance proposal in August 1917, and Germany considered a Mexican attack on the United States to be so improbable, if not impossible, that Carranza's acceptance of such a plan was not demanded as a precondition for a loan. In return for the relatively small sum of ten million Spanish pesetas which was offered to Mexico, the German authorities demanded only a benevolent neutrality on the part of Mexico, toleration for the activities of the German secret services, and economic concessions for the postwar period. In November 1917 the German military attaché in Madrid, Calle, emphasized the importance of Mexico for Germany in a memorandum arguing for significant financial aid to Carranza, but there was no mention of any impending attack on the United States.[39] The basis for the British conviction that Carranza was prepared to accede to German plans is not known, but the telegrams sent by German agents from Mexico to Berlin and deciphered by England were clearly not the source. The English had succeeded in slipping an agent into German military intelligence, and it is possible that this agent passed on reports of this nature to London.[40] What British intelligence considered an accomplished fact may have been Delmar's project—a project which had failed to win the support of Carranza, of the German Foreign Office, or of German naval intelligence.

Even if Carranza had approved such plans, it was highly unlikely, as Sir Maurice de Bunsen pointed out, that Japan would change sides and supply arms to Mexico; it was even more unlikely that Germany would be able to break the blockade.[41]

The preoccupation of the British military leadership may have been due primarily to the depressing position of the Allies in late 1917 and early 1918. In November 1917, the Bolsheviks had triumphed and were pulling Russia out of the war. The Allies expected Germany to intensify its efforts on the Western front and feared that such an intensification, in light of the still minimal presence of American troops, would create tremendous difficulties for them. In this dire situation, the military leaders were obviously afraid of the catastropic consequences that could occur if the United States were diverted from the European theater by a Mexican-American war. And even if Carranza did not agree to an alliance with Germany, there was reason to fear the successes of the German secret service in Mexico.

In spite of the coolness of the British ambassador in Washington, who did not take the possibility of a Mexican coup very seriously, the Foreign Office was already eagerly grappling with the question of how to make the overthrow of Carranza a reality. The preparations for a coup continued into the late summer of 1918. Repeated difficulties and increasingly bitter controversy between the United States and Mexico gave the English confidence that the United States would ultimately agree to such a joint Allied plan in Mexico.

Throughout the war America's policy toward Mexico was oriented toward two objectives that seemed essentially incompatible: to keep Mexico "quiet," and thus to free American forces for other arenas, while at the same time preventing the implementation of the clauses contained in the 1917 constitution. Both the American government and American companies attempted to achieve the latter goal with economic pressures and promises (prospects for loans, the threat of embargos on food, arms, money, and the like). The American government and American companies repeatedly held negotiations for the same purpose with Carranza's representatives, but these negotiations, with few exceptions, failed because of the demands made by the Americans.

As a result of the failed negotiations, Carranza raised the royalties and taxes for foreign companies in an effort to alleviate his frightening financial situation and at the same time took steps to bring the oil fields under his control and to push aside Pelaez. American companies, whose displeasure Carranza had incurred with these measures, demanded an intervention by the American government. This prompted Carranza to seek a temporary rapprochement with Germany in an effort to pressure the United States to be more flexible in negotiations. Negotiations were resumed but soon proved unsuccessful. Whenever the cycle of Mexican-American relations reached its nadir, the enthusiasm for a coup peaked in the Foreign Office; British diplomacy was again haunted by the nightmare of a Mexican-American war as well as the fear that Carranza would move against Pelaez and thereby cut off British oil supplies. Thus, when crisis erupted between Washington and Mexico, the English saw their chance.

The British diplomats' initial approach to the United States after the armed forces had pushed so forcefully for a coup in Mexico was a conversation between Sir Maurice de Bunsen and Wilson's closest associate, Colonel House. De Bunsen approached this encounter with extreme "diplomatic flexibility" and attempted to sound out and influence House in a low-key fashion. Instead of asking for American assistance in England's plans for a coup, he told House that England was on the verge of sending a minister to Mexico to bring England's policy in Mexico into step with United States policy. The British government, he continued, had had reservations on this question, because of "ominous reports which reached us from Mexico of German intrigues with Carranza aimed at creating internal disturbances and even active hostile measures against the United States of a nature if successful, would compel employment of very considerable American forces along the frontier to the detriment pro tanto of the supreme joint effort of the United States and the Allies in the war."[42] Moreover, de Bunsen told House, Carranza would have access to 2 million pounds sterling from Anglo-American property as a result of his recognition by the Allied powers. (De Bunsen was alluding to the anticipated agreement on the Tehuantepec railway between Cowdray and Carranza.)

De Bunsen probably calculated that if the Americans had plans for a coup in Mexico, House would give him some indication of this to keep England from recognizing Carranza and to prevent Carranza from obtaining $10,000,000. If the United States had no such plans, de Bunsen hoped to bring about a shift in American policy with his revelations of a conspiracy between Carranza and Germany.

De Bunsen's efforts were unsuccessful. House was cool and unimpressed. The question had so little interest for him that he limited the meeting to fifteen minutes. He reacted to de Bunsen's revelations with the noncommittal remark that he was pleased to find "a happy understanding" between England and the United States on the Mexican question "as on all other questions."

In spite of this discouraging development, the British diplomats did not abandon their efforts. Between October 1917 and March 1918, the English authorities presented to the American embassy in London seven memoranda "collected from our secret sources of information, and containing a complete exposé of German plans in Mexico."[43] At the same time, the Mexico expert at the British embassy in Washington several times approached American military officials to warn them of a Mexican attack on the United States inspired by Germany and to seek support for British plans for a coup.

In spite of the indifference they encountered on the part of the Americans, the English diplomats continued to elaborate plans for a coup. Almost without exception, these plans shared three main ingredients. First, it was felt that a coup carried out by England and France alone was impossible, while one executed by the United States alone was undesirable. All three powers had to coordinate their plans and agree on a single leader for a new "revolution." Second, the armies of Pelaez and Felix Díaz were to play an important role. And, third, the new, victorious government was to return all confiscated British property, particularly the railroads, to their English owners and was also to commit itself to dealing "in good faith" with all claims on Mexico by foreign companies.

Closer examination of the various English coup plans reveals a striking divergence of opinion on two essential questions. The differences centered on *(a)* whether the Allies should actively intervene in the military aspects of the coup, and *(b)* what role the revolutionary forces hostile to Carranza, especially Villa and Zapata, were to play. The disagreements these questions provoked among the various "conspirators" were matters of tactics rather than principle. They arose primarily because the British diplomats and businessmen in Mexico, who fancied themselves "old hands" in Mexican politics, considered the British military plans, elaborated from afar, to be impractical and unrealizable.

Thus, for example, Thurstan energetically opposed the occupation of the oil fields by Allied armies which had been proposed in a memorandum by British military intelligence. Such an occupation, he argued, would give new life to nationalism in Mexico and would create broad popular support for Carranza. The pragmatically-oriented military men put forward the opposing viewpoint that it was essential to bring the Científicos to power, that the combined military power of Felix Díaz and General Pelaez could win easily with Allied support, and that this was reason enough for the Allies to intervene.[44]

Although the British diplomats and businessmen were as sympathetic as the military leaders to Felix Díaz and Pelaez, they nevertheless did not believe that these movements were capable of winning by themselves. Without support from the revolutionary movements of Villa and Zapata, it was felt, the plans would simply fail.

These views are presented in a particularly blunt fashion by an English businessman named Bouchier.[45] That Bouchier's plan actually attracted attention is confirmed by a note passed on to the Foreign Office from the British embassy in Washington referring to it as a particularly "interesting" plan which ought to be considered more carefully.[46] In his plan, Bouchier advocated "infusing new blood into the reactionary party so that the latter could oust Carranza and his crowd."[47] To this end, Bouchier recommended that help be obtained from the revolutionaries, albeit with caution. Villa, he wrote, "should be used for a specific purpose and if he abused the position that was given him it would be exceedingly easy for him to accidentally disappear." Zapata, Bouchier explained, "is a bad man and his troops unprincipled but would serve their purposes until they were either subsequently brought into line or practically wiped out through concentration methods, which is about the only manner in which to tackle these men owing to the extraordinarily accidental nature of their territory."

In April 1918, Thurstan was still explaining the failure of British efforts to enlist the United States in a joint attempt in Mexico by reference to Wilson's peculiar "devotion" to Carranza.[48] But by then, the British Foreign Office began to give credence to a very different explanation, namely, that the United States itself was attempting to organize a coup in Mexico. These fears were exacerbated by various reports received by the Foreign Office in April 1918. The British embassy in Washington had obtained a secret memorandum from the American military intelligence in Fort Sam Houston analyzing the strength of the various contending forces in Mexico, as well as the possibility of a coup against Carranza.[49] British authorities believed they could get some sense of American intentions from this memorandum. It was stated near the end of the memorandum that the appropriate stance toward the Felix Díaz group and other forces fighting against Carranza could produce a friendly orientation toward the United States and the Allies, that the proper use of the embargo would further this, and that if they were permitted to secure arms and ammunition from the United States, the combined forces of the various factions were capable of bringing about the immediate downfall of the Carranza government.

Ambassador Fletcher, who up to that time had always opposed coup attempts, advised the British government in March against recognizing Carranza because he might have concluded a secret agreement with Germany. Fletcher also hinted that a coup against Carranza might occur in the near future. He explained "that Doheny would conclude it was cheaper to throw Carranza out through supporting a new revolution than to pay his share of Carranza's taxation." It is easy to see from Fletcher's attitude that he was in no way opposed to these efforts. "The ambassador,'' reported Cummins, "seemed desirous to convey more than he put in words. I told him I had certain knowledge that one camp of revolutionaries had received ammunition from New Orleans. He laughed and replied that he knew that and more and that they were getting it from Galveston."[50]

Fletcher's actions must be seen in the context of a Mexican-American crisis which had broken out in February 1918 when Carranza had announced an increase in the royalties payable by foreign oil companies and registration of all foreign property in Mexico. At the same time, Carranza had attempted, albeit unsuccessfully, to bring the area ruled by Pelaez under his control by means of a military offensive.[51]

Both the oil companies and the American government had sharply protested these actions. Fletcher wrote to Secretary of State Lansing in April 1918 that he could no longer "keep the Mexican question from distracting our attention and efforts from the Great War."[52]

The Foreign Office in London felt it had discovered the key to American plans in Mexico after a meeting in Washington between Hohler and an attorney named Carranco, who presented himself as the representative of Alfredo Robles Domínguez. Alfredo Robles Domínguez was an old comrade-in-arms of Madero, who had continued to occupy high government posts under Carranza. He had been governor of Mexico City and, until the end of 1914, commander of the Carranza forces in the state of Guerrero, a position he had given up after conflicts of an unknown nature with leaders of the Carranza movement. Robles Domínguez nonetheless had never completely broken with Carranza, but had remained a Querétaro delegate to the Constitutional Assembly, where he acted as a spokesman for the conservative wing of the assembly.[53]

Carranco sought out Hohler in Washington in April 1918 and told him that preparations were underway for an uprising which was to overthrow Carranza and bring Robles Domínguez to power. Carranco assured Hohler that all groups hostile to Carranza and oppositionists of all shadings stood behind Robles Domínguez, including Pelaez, Zapata, Villa, and Gutiérrez. As proof, Carranco showed the English representative a letter from Zapata to Villa in which Zapata gave Robles Domínguez his support.[54] (Carranco had no reliable information on Villa's current attitude, however.) According to Carranco, the "Domínguez project" was being financed by the International Harvester Company, the St. Louis Car Company, and special oil interests "which are represented by Mr. Helm."[55]

Carranco gave Hohler the impression that the American authorities were quite favorably disposed to his movement and that the customs officials in Laredo "were keeping quiet about his project" and had looked the other way when he smuggled 50,000 rounds of ammunition over the border. Carranco cited as further evidence of the American authorities' "friendly assistance" a warning he had received from a New York employee of the American secret service not to stay in a hotel frequented by Carranza agents. But Hohler must have been most struck by Carranco's insinuation that Colonel House in a personal conversation with him had given his approval to the Robles Domínguez plan.

The reason for Carranco's visit to the British embassy may have been his fear, which he also expressed to Hohler, that the Americans would demand too much from his movement in return. He was obviously hoping England would serve as a counterweight to the United States. He explicitly told Hohler several times that he had sought him out without the knowledge of his American supporters and that the United States would withdraw its support for Robles Domínguez if Carranco's visit to the English embassy ever became known.

At the end of the conversation, Carranco gave Hohler the draft of a proclamation in which the new movement announced the reinstatement of the 1857 constitution, the appointment of Robles Domínguez as provisional president and the scheduling of new elections.[56] There was no attempt to propitiate the Americans in this proclamation. Carranco, however, in a confidential discussion with Cummins, the English chargé d'affaires in Mexico, described the concessions his movement was prepared to make to the Allies.

There was to be established a " 'Bank of Mexico,' the Consultive Board of which, composed of British, Americans, French and Mexicans, two of each, will handle and check the receipts and expenditure of the Government. It will practically be the Ministry of Finance though for appearances sake a Mexican Minister, an obedient dummy will be appointed."[57]

Magdalena Bay in Baja California, which was of strategic interest to both the United States and Japan, was to be turned over to the League of Nations. Carranco assumed that the league "would place this strategic point in the hands of the United States for use as a naval base on the Pacific."

Carranco promised that Robles Domínguez intended to settle all controversial questions confronting Mexico and the United States, that is, the Chamizal problem, the difficulties with the Tlahualilo Company, and the like, in a "spirit favorably disposed towards the foreign interests." Carranco also assured Cummins that the new government would be especially attentive to England's interests and that it had already been decided to entrust England's Marconi Company with the administration of Mexico's radio network.

This information gave Cummins a certain optimism; he was convinced that America intended to set up, "secretly, and unknown to us, a new party and that they may select, without outside suggestion, the man who is peculiarly well disposed towards us."

## The Conflicts over Mexico in the British Cabinet

London did not share Cummins's optimism. On the contrary, reports from Washington and Mexico to the effect that the American government was supporting the coup planned by Robles Domínguez brought to a head the heated debate on Mexican policy which had been underway since the outbreak of the world war. In May 1918, this debate flared into an open conflict between the General Staff and the Foreign Office.

After the arrival of the reports of a coup planned by Robles Domínguez with American support, the question arose of why the United States was refusing to organize a coup in Mexico in concert with England and why the American government was so obstinately denying its intention of staging a coup, though that intention seemed transparently obvious to the British authorities. It was assumed that the United States was attempting to use the war to dislodge England from its economic positions in Mexico and throughout Latin America. Hohler's report to the British embassy in Washington on the American feeling that "only the U.S. has the right to exercise authority on the American continent"[58] correlated remarkably well with the information received by the Foreign Office on America's advance knowledge of the Robles Domínguez plan. Hohler warned in his report that well over half of British overseas investment was concentrated in Latin America and that it was threatened by United States policy. "There is marked jealousy of our commerce and our enterprise, and there is at the present moment a definite attempt to occupy our place in trade."

While the prospect of American hegemony in Mexico certainly disturbed the Foreign Office, this fear by itself would not have been enough to cause the mood of alarm that seized both the Foreign Office and the British armed forces in May 1918. This panicked atmosphere resulted much more from suspicion that the United States was in the process of planning a military intervention in Mexico, probably in connection with the Robles Domínguez coup. The British military leaders in particular felt this to be the reason that the American government had made such a secret of its support of the coup planned by Robles Domínguez. According to calculations by both Thurstan and the British General Staff, 500,000 American troops would be necessary for a successful intervention in Mexico.[59] In view of the military situation of the Allied powers in the spring of 1918, the British General Staff found such a prospect frightening.

At the beginning of 1918 Germany seemed in a very strong position. In February it had signed the treaty of Brest-Litovsk with revolutionary

Russia, from which it emerged both economically and militarily strengthened. It gained control of an extensive territory, which included both the Ukraine and the Baltic states, and was hence in a position to transfer a significant number of troops from the Eastern front and to concentrate them in the West. In March the surrender of Rumania further strengthened Germany. And in the spring the German High Command withdrew large numbers of troops from the East and launched one of the most aggressive German offensives of the war. During that period the Germans were able to register certain successes, and the Allies found themselves quite hard pressed. German troop strength was superior to that of the Allies, and in both England and France the army and the civil populations were increasingly expressing war weariness. Several months earlier, in 1917, several rebellions had shaken the fighting power of the French army from within, even though they had been bloodily and ruthlessly crushed by General Petain. In this depressing situation, the Allied leadership had placed its hopes on troops and arms from the United States. But as of May 1918, only nine American divisions had arrived in Europe.[60] An American intervention in Mexico would have long delayed the arrival of the American reinforcements so desperately needed by the Allies at this critical juncture in the war.

These fears prompted British Foreign Secretary Balfour on 7 May 1918 to wire the British ambassador in Washington, ordering him to hold discussions on the Mexican question as quickly as possible with President Wilson. Lord Reading was to inform Wilson of Balfour's "great agitation" over developments in Mexico, and to warn him of increasing German influence on Carranza, and of German attempts to persuade Carranza to attack the United States. Reading was also to call Wilson's attention to the dangers posed to Allied oil supplies and to warn him against involving American troops in an American-Mexican war. Even if Carranza were not prepared to risk an open attack on America, there was nonetheless always the possibility of a German provocation aimed at getting the United States to move into Mexico.

Balfour wanted Reading to inform Wilson of the best methods for moving against Carranza: "to give active support to the revolutionary leaders and possibly to encourage a diversion on the part of Guatemala. He did not, however, want to take any steps which conflicted with Wilson's policy."[61] Reading was to ask Wilson for an immediate response.

The timid moves of the Foreign Office hardly satisfied the British military leaders. They demanded a clear invitation to the American president to intervene in Mexican politics in concert with England. On 9 May 1918, a memorandum was delivered to the British war cabinet on the situation in Mexico, in which the General Staff no longer concealed its criticisms of the American government.[62] The memorandum stated that as a consequence of the American policy "of drift, the situation in Mexico had developed in a critical, and perhaps even dangerous direction," and "requires immediate action" to avert a serious crippling of Allied war operations. The memorandum accused the American government of having disregarded all English warnings of German intrigues and of having been dishonest and disloyal to Great Britain. The United States had denied the existence of the negotiations which according to the General Staff, it had secretly conducted with Iturbide and Robles Domínguez in pursuit of its objectives of on the one hand gaining material advantages for itself and on the other hand launching an American intervention in Mexico. "The American government," the British General Staff stated indignantly, appears "to view with complacency the possibility of open hostilities with Mexico as likely to furnish excellent opportunities for the training of their troops."

In the proposal intended for Wilson, the General Staff planned to offer him two alternatives, both of which involved joint action with France and England. If Carranza would declare his willingness to side with the Allies and expel all Germans from Mexico, he would receive recognition. If he refused to do so, the General Staff proposed "definite repudiation of Carranza, followed or accompanied by his overthrow"; this alternative was the admitted preference of the General Staff. "The Mexican leaders should then be invited to select a President known to be persona grata to the three Allied Governments, and a definite guarantee should be given that he will be supported in every way provided his Government acts in the interests of the Entente." The General Staff concluded its memorandum with an attack on both the British Foreign Office and the United States Department of State for having paid too much attention to "vested interests" (i.e., the interests of the large companies) and too little attention to military considerations. Balfour replied to the memorandum of the military leaders in his own sharply worded memorandum, which was given to the king and to the war cabinet. "The General Staff," he wrote, "have taken advantage of the leisure provided for them by the German Offensive to circulate a paper telling the Cabinet how the State Department at Washington and the Foreign Office in London are mismanaging our relations with the Republic of Mexico."[63] Balfour was primarily concerned with defending the rights of the Foreign Office against encroachment. By submitting a memorandum on foreign policy to the war cabinet without first consulting the Foreign Office, the General Staff had not only preempted the Foreign Office's rights, but had attempted to prescribe foreign policy for Great Britain unilaterally.

The differences between the Foreign Office and the General Staff concerned not merely the content, but also the timing of English foreign policy. Both camps agreed on the ultimate objective of ousting Carranza by means of a coup jointly engineered with the United States; the differences of opinion focused on the pacing of the necessary steps and on the question of how best to win Wilson over to such a project. Balfour considered the military leaders' fears that war between Mexico and the United States was imminent and that the United States would employ twenty divisions in such a war to be "quite exaggerated."

The note Balfour had sent to Reading on 7 May asking him to sound out Wilson on U.S. policy in Mexico shows that he considered it quite impossible to pressure Wilson into changing his Mexico policy.[64] He was undoubtedly thinking of British experiences several years earlier, especially in 1913–14. At the height of Britain's power, before the country had been weakened by the world war and had become dependent on American aid, the British government had attempted in vain to get Wilson to change his Mexican policy. Given England's situation in 1918, such an enterprise was even more hopeless.

The war cabinet came to no decision on the Mexican question but asked the representatives of the General Staff and the Foreign Office to hold discussions and to reach an agreement on a Mexican strategy.[65]

Meanwhile, President Wilson had assured Lord Reading that no coup or intervention preparations were in progress[66]; Carranza had informed him that he was delaying implementation of the decrees that had been issued against the oil companies; and on 26 May Cummins received word from Carranco that Domínguez had received less support for his plans to overthrow Carranza than he had expected.[67] This allayed to some degree the fears of the military leaders. But it took the failure of the last major German offensive, the landing of several hundred thousand American troops, and the successful Allied offensive in July 1918 fully to restore the confidence of the General Staff.

While the General Staff criticized the Foreign Office for being too lax toward Carranza and too attentive to the desires of the "vested interests," these interests—particularly Lord Cowdray—replied that the Foreign Office by refusing to appoint a minister and to recognize Carranza had not taken adequate account of the requirements of the "major" companies active in Mexico. Early in 1918, in spite of Carranza's hard line against foreign oil companies, a rapprochement between the Cowdray firms and Carranza had taken place. Cowdray had flatly refused to go along with the Foreign Office's proposals to organize a coup against Carranza in collaboration with Doheny, the representative of the largest American oil company in Mexico.[68]

Cowdray's efforts, as well as those of other English companies with investments in Mexico, went squarely against those of the General Staff. The unbridgeable gap between the two camps can be seen in a letter sent to England by one of Cowdray's colleagues on the same day that the

General Staff presented its memorandum to the war cabinet. The analysis of the political situation in Mexico contained in the letter did not contradict that of the military leadership; Cowdray too was expecting a German-inspired attack on the United States by Mexico. He wanted, however, to exploit such a war instead of preventing it. England, in his view, should not take any steps to overthrow Carranza before he could launch such an attack, as the military leadership had urged in May 1918 and as Cowdray's colleague Body had done in June 1917. In spite of the existing Anglo-American alliance, Cowdray's associate wrote: "I do not see any particular reason why England, or any other of the Allies, should be drawn into this coming conflict and there are many reasons why they should not."[69] He also articulated that reason quite clearly: "Apparently the strong pro-German sympathy of the Mexican Government would indicate an anti-Ally policy, but the pro-Germanism is really anti-Americanism and there is no strong feeling against the other Allied nations. Consequently, in the event of an outbreak of hostilities between Mexico and the United States, by the other Allied Nations keeping out of it, it would not only greatly lessen the material losses of the war, but would reduce the resources at the disposal of the Mexican Government, as they would not be at liberty to seize the property of friendly, or at least neutral nations."

It is thus obvious that Cowdray's colleagues were entertaining the idea of exploiting a Mexican-American war to strengthen the economic position of British firms.

### British and German Policy in Mexico: A Perspective

A comparison of English and German policy in Mexico in the months between the U.S. declaration of war and the armistice reveals some interesting parallels. The top diplomats and military leaders of both countries viewed the political situation in Mexico through the same racist lens and both were hostile to the goals of the Mexican revolution. With equal ineptitude, the political leaders of both countries developed, tested, and discarded plans characterized by the same lack of realism and aimed at pushing Mexico into a war—the conflict with the United States which the German leaders desired, or the civil war which important groups in England wanted to provoke. The English authorities were similarly incapable of realistically assessing the disposition, interests, and objectives of their potential ally, and the English plans to win Wilson over to a jointly inspired coup in Mexico seem almost as unworkable as Zimmermann's daydreams of getting Carranza to attack the United States. Illusion reigned on both sides.

However much the ultimate objectives of England and Germany

contradicted each other, the minimal objectives of the two governments converged. Mexico was to remain neutral in the war—even if England and Germany had different notions of that neutrality, and brought different expectations to it—and the American influence in Mexico was to be kept to a minimum.

The Mexican policy of each country was colored by the tensions that existed between the armed forces and the business communities. While the armed forces wanted to make Mexico into a war theater, the business community sought stability and rapprochement with Carranza. Instead of provoking conflict in Mexico, however, the military authorities were forced to fight their own foreign policy makers.

The essential difference in the Mexican policy of the two countries resides in the way the rival foreign ministries of England and Germany pursued their objectives. The German foreign ministry at first carried out a relentlessly offensive policy, which led to the Zimmermann note and numerous other plans by the secret service. Germany's Mexican policy, however, quickly underwent a shift, and the Foreign Office began to counter the extravagant plans of the armed forces for launching sabotage actions in the oil fields or a border attack on the United States.

The policy of the British Foreign Office evolved in the opposite direction. At first it practiced a policy of conciliation and in November 1917 seemed ready to recognize Carranza. A short time later, however, the Foreign Office made a complete turnabout and went to great lengths to overthrow the Mexican government.

In the conflict between the companies with interests in Mexico and the armed forces, the German Foreign Office took the side of the companies, while the British Foreign Office sided with the armed forces. Because British companies had a far greater presence in Mexico than German firms, this seems at first glance more difficult to understand. The foreign ministries' divergent attitudes toward the proposals of the armed forces have multiple causes and cannot be reduced to a common denominator.

In Germany, there was no agreement among the military authorities on a Mexican strategy. Thus, the German navy wanted only a neutral Mexico and opposed the ideas of the General Staff, which argued for border attacks on the United States and sabotage actions in the oil fields aimed at provoking American intervention. German naval authorities hoped to find in Mexico a launching ground for German sabotage actions in North and Central America. The upshot of the disagreements within the armed forces was that the Foreign Office was able to impose its own views on Mexican policy while acceding to the desires of the military leaders on every other question.

In Great Britain, however, the army and the navy were in complete agreement on the necessity of offensive action against the Mexican government.

A second factor explaining the divergent attitudes of the German and British foreign ministries toward the policies of their respective armed forces was the fact that the German companies and the German military leaders were confronting the same enemies in Mexico: the Allies, in particular the United States and Great Britain.

The British companies and the British military leadership, on the contrary, had to deal with two different opponents. For the military leaders, Germany was the main enemy, while for British companies, it was the United States. In this conflict, the Foreign Office sided with the armed forces, even if it showed a certain reserve in doing so, but it was precisely this reserve that incurred the wrath of the General Staff.

Perhaps the differing attitudes of the foreign ministries of both countries toward the projects of their respective armed forces can best be explained by the consequences that would have followed from realization of their plans. The outbreak of a Mexican-American war, as desired by the German General Staff, would have meant the end of all German plans for expansion in Mexico. Eckardt's dream that Germany could partially claim the "legacy of Cortez" would be over.

Successful execution of the coup plans of the British army and naval authorities, by contrast, would have achieved three objectives at once: Germany would have been pushed back or even expelled from Mexico; American intervention would have been averted; and England would have been assured of a role in any future settlement of the Mexican question. In addition, Mexican nationalism would have been checked.

Compared with these ambitious aims, the concrete results of British policy were modest. It was not British policy, but the outlook of Carranza and the victorious Mexican revolutionaries around him that assured Mexico's neutrality and its refusal to go to war on Germany's side. Yet British policy in Mexico did record some impressive successes in the 1917–18 period.

The first success involved control of the oil fields. Through active support of Pelaez, the British government, along with English and American companies, succeeded in keeping the Mexican oil fields, if not the ports of Tuxpan and Tampico, out of government control.

The most spectacular British success was in the area of espionage. The deciphering of the Zimmermann note and the English authorities' success in feigning ignorance of the German secret codes thus permitting them to decode all German secret service notes through the end of the war, remain notable in the history of espionage. British naval intelligence also showed great ability to slip British agents into the German secret service network in Mexico.

In light of these successes, the British secret services' enormous errors of judgment concerning German, American, and Mexican intentions are all the more surprising. In seven memoranda from November 1917 to June

1918, British intelligence reported an agreement between Carranza and Germany for a Mexican attack on the United States.[70] Such an attack, however, never took place, and this information, as we have shown above, was totally inaccurate. After Carranza had rejected the second German alliance proposal, as transmitted by Delmar in August 1917, the German authorities had abandoned the hope of a Mexican attack on the United States and had concentrated on economic expansion in Mexico. It was clear from all of Carranza's actions (and the American diplomats understood this) that he was considering military cooperation with Germany only in the event of an American attack on Mexico. British claims that the American government was planning a unilateral coup in Mexico prior to the end of the world war proved equally false.

The British secret service's expectations and calculations, of course, were not completely unfounded. Delmar and a whole series of agents of the German General Staff were hoping to promote a Mexican attack on the United States and sabotage actions in the Mexican oil fields. Some Mexican generals had told German agents of their willingness to organize incursions into the United States. Some State Department officials, particularly the head of the Mexico desk, Canova, along with certain American oil companies, were planning a coup in Mexico.[71] But each of these cases involved activities that contravened the policies of the German, American, and Mexican governments during the November 1917–June 1918 period.

As long as the archives of the British secret service are not accessible to researchers, and perhaps even after they become available, one will only be able to guess at the causes of these erroneous analyses by British intelligence. It is possible that a certain role was played in the British armed forces' analysis by the opinions of the three second-level British diplomats responsible for Mexico: Cummins, the administrator of the British legation in Mexico; Hohler, the Mexico expert at the British embassy in Washington; and Thurstan, the recalled chargé d'affaires. All three of these men advocated violent overthrow of Carranza, and in their reports they consistently exaggerated the possibility of a plot between Carranza and Germany. It is thus not surprising that local French diplomats viewed the British legation as "alarmist."[72]

Another cause of the erroneous analysis of the British secret service may be found in the special relationship between English authorities and the Southern Military Command of the United States. In the archives of the British foreign ministry, there are some highly confidential reports on Mexico from the intelligence division of this Southern Military Command.[73] It is noted on some of these reports that they were in no circumstances to be shown to American officials; this means that the British had obtained them against the will, or at least without the knowledge, of the

American government. These reports, which appeared to be the only ones emanating from the United States which were directly in line with British anxieties, contradicted the analyses of Fletcher, the American ambassador to Mexico, and the officials of the State Department. At the beginning of 1918, at the same time that Fletcher was arguing that Germany was primarily interested in economic expansion in Mexico, the Intelligence Division of the Southern Military Command was reporting that German agents and Carranza were planning an attack on the United States. The Southern Military Command was also developing plans for a coup in Mexico promoted by the United States.

A third cause of the numerous errors of analysis by the British may, paradoxically, have been the smooth functioning of the British secret service. The British agents had been very successful at infiltrating the ranks of German military intelligence in Mexico, which means the Political Section of the General Staff, the most vociferous advocate of an attack on the United States. As a result, the agents' reports to the Foreign Office may have presented a false picture of the actual situation.

There exists, nevertheless, an unexplained discrepancy between the successful gathering of intelligence on German activities in Mexico and its evaluation in the Foreign Office and the British intelligence agencies.

## French Policy in Mexico, 1917–18

Among the great powers in Mexico, France was the odd man out. In the 1860s France had attempted a single-handed, single-minded penetration into Mexico, but during the Mexican Revolution it was the only one of the great powers that never attempted to carry out an independent policy with respect to Mexico. It was also the only power whose policies never had a serious impact on that country.

Until 1917 the French essentially aligned their policies with those of their closest ally, Great Britain. They supported two of the basic tendencies of Britain's Mexican policy in that period: its unrelenting opposition to every faction among the Mexican revolutionaries and its growing fear of German intrigues in Mexico. In those two fields the interests of both powers completely coincided. Like the British, the French had been beneficiaries of Porfirio Díaz's domestic and foreign policies and they dreamed of the return of a Díaz-like regime. Like the British, the French, after the outbreak of World War I had every reason to fear German-inspired provocations in Mexico which might result in curtailed U.S. arms deliveries to the Allies and prevent the United States from intervening in the war.

Unlike the British, the French did not want to carry out an anti-American policy in Mexico. This was by no means because of any great appreciation of Woodrow Wilson's Mexican policies. On the contrary, analysts in the French foreign ministry denounced U.S. policy in Mexico in even more vitriolic terms than their British counterparts. They had considered Wilson's attitude to be motivated primarily by "a desire to maintain U.S. preponderance in Mexico; fear that Huerta could become, with the help of Europe, an effective instrument against American influence in Central America."[74]

French diplomats in Mexico had viewed Woodrow Wilson's special agents to the different revolutionary factions with unrestrained contempt. In a description of the role played by the four principal agents of the United States to the revolutionary factions—Silliman, Carothers, Canova, and Hall—the French representative in Mexico characterized them as "men without culture," corrupt men who instead of trying to implement some kind of U.S. policy were constantly fighting among themselves in order to further the interests of one of the revolutionary leaders whose fortunes they had personally embraced:

> all of them have only one aim—the victory of the chief to whom they are accredited. They are similar to election managers going from door to door and from legation to legation to canvass in favor of their candidates.
>
> They have all signed secret pacts with the chieftains to whom they are accredited, which in case of his victory would provide them with substantial profits.
>
> They did not even belong to the second set of the United States political world. Mr. Silliman at the same time that he was U.S. consul in Saltillo had a dairy business. Mr. Carothers was an agent for an express company, Mr. Canova was probably a station master at some railway station, Mr. Hall was a hotel manager in Cuernavaca.
>
> Their intellectual capacities did not prepare them for these tasks. They have all the defaults of Americans of their class: lack of culture, lack of delicacy, narrowness of views, excessive pretentiousness and above all a lack of tact, comprehension for finer feelings and suppleness which could be explained by some Germanic origin.
>
> Thus Mr. Wilson's confidential agents could perhaps have been good salesmen for a Chicago canning factory, but they are out of place as diplomats in the great drama taking place in Mexico.[75]

In spite of these feelings about Wilson and his agents, the French did not want to be drawn into an anti-American policy in Mexico from which they would not benefit. They had on the whole far less reason to fear U.S. supremacy in Mexico than did their British allies. They had few concessions they could lose to the Americans. There were few French investments in mining (the Compania del Boleo in Baja California was one of the outstanding exceptions) and even fewer in oil. French investments were concentrated in bonds and banking. American control or even supremacy in Mexico might have limited French possibilities to acquire new loans or to extend their banking system in Mexico but it would at least have guaranteed the value of their existing holdings. It is thus not surprising that in September 1914 the French chargé d'affaires in Mexico wrote to his foreign ministry: "as far as the lives and properties of our compatriots are concerned, they have more to lose from the continuation of the present anarchy than from American intervention.

"Under present circumstances, I believe I can say that armed American intervention would be welcome, if, as I assume, it would be possible to obtain a guarantee of economic equality and an open-door policy."[76]

For a brief period the French seemed to be in the extremely uncomfortable position of having to choose between angering their British allies or participating in a policy of opposition to U.S. penetration in Mexico which they did not want to carry out. They were thus extremely relieved when the British retreated in 1913–14 and gave up their opposition to Wilson's Mexican policy.

After the United States entered World War I French policy vacillated between aligning its Mexican policy primarily with Britain or with the United States. On the one hand, the French shared British fears of German intrigues in Mexico which might lead to an American intervention in that country. But, on the other hand, they refused to participate in Britain's attempts to prevent U.S. hegemony in Mexico. The vacillations in French policy in Mexico reached a high point in November and December 1917, when the British warned them that Delmar had persuaded Carranza to wage war against the United States.

Two very distinct viewpoints emerged among French diplomats. The French representative to Mexico, Couzet, took the British warnings very seriously and proposed a project to his foreign minister calling for apocalyptic reprisals against Mexico. In his opinion, the French government should suggest to the United States that they send emissaries to Mexico to buy or "corrupt" Mexican politicians. If these measures proved unsuccessful, then the United States should "starve Mexico and bring it to its ruin." At the same time, the United States should contemplate, instead of preventing the growth of internal troubles in Mexico, provoking "such troubles, even at the peril of endangering the property of foreigners, so that this country find itself in such an anarchy that Germany itself could do nothing there. I am so convinced of the necessity of subordinating everything to the needs of the European war, that even this extreme remedy should not be discarded in my opinion."[77]

The French ambassador in Washington, Jusserand, was far more skeptical about the British warnings concerning Mexico. At the same time the French representative in Mexico was contemplating extreme measures against Carranza, the ambassador in Washington wrote, "all these fears and vacillations are due to Mr. Hohler, former British chargé d'affaires, in Mexico and now second counselor of the British embassy in Washington, for whom the fall of Carranza, which he had already announced some time ago, is a sort of panacea."[78] The ambassador not only discounted British fears that Carranza, together with the Germans, would attack the United States, but he supported the U.S. attitude of maintaining Carranza in power. "The American government, which, after all, is the one mainly interested in the situation in Mexico and which has good means of information about that country, has, as I have repeatedly stated, no illusion about Carranza, but is attempting, with all the means at its disposal, to maintain him in power, preferring the presence at Mexico's helm, of a personality badly disposed toward the United States to that of so-called better candidates whose success would lead to eternal troubles, possibly requiring armed U.S. intervention. Preventing such intervention is the primary aim of U.S. policy in Mexico at this time."

French skepticism about British reports of a German-Mexican alliance reflected in part the skepticism of the United States about such reports. Also, the British never informed the French that they had cracked the German codes and so they never knew how their allies came by their information. As a result they tended to be even more skeptical of British revelations about Mexico.[79] As time passed and repeated British warnings about an imminent attack by Carranza on the United States were not confirmed, French pessimism about their ally's intentions and reliability as far as Mexico was concerned increased.

When, in March 1918, the British suggested to the French that they jointly bring pressure on Wilson to reverse his Mexican policies and to either send an ultimatum to Carranza to break with Germany or to help his enemies to topple him, the French were not willing to go along with Great Britain. In a report prepared for the French foreign minister, analysts at the Quai d'Orsay concluded, "it must be noted that in accordance with the opinion of Mr. Paul Cambon the measures suggested by England seem hard to accept. Our ambassador indicates that the relations of Carranza and Germany are by no means clear but these reports are based on allegations by German agents obtained under conditions which cannot be determined."[80]

From this point on, French policies in Mexico were limited to supporting in a secondary capacity both British and American intelligence as well as propaganda agencies in their fight against the Germans. They definitely refused to participate in any of Britain's attempts either to topple Carranza or to have the United States do so jointly with the Allies.

French resentment against the United States' attitude in Mexico did not cease. It was expressed in full force again after the end of World War I. In

December 1919 the French chargé d'affaires stated "that it must be said that the Americans tend to consider themselves here not only in their own country but in a conquered country. Instead of treating Mexico as a free and sovereign country the Americans consider it as a country of negroes and inferior beings; as a result, there is constant disagreement between them and the Mexican authorities."[81]

## U.S. Policy in Mexico, 1917–18

In contrast to the policies of the European powers, United States attitudes toward its southern neighbor in 1917–18 have been the subject of so many studies[82] that there is no need to subject them to detailed study once again. Nevertheless, a survey of the policies of the United States and of American companies in Mexico, at least in broad outline, is indispensable for an understanding of the attitudes of the European powers.

In the United States there existed a divergence of opinion on Mexico similar to that in Great Britain, but the roles were reversed. Whereas American companies aimed at the violent overthrow of the government, the Wilson administration was resigned to the fact that Carranza would remain in power until the end of the war. The most important task that Wilson assigned to his ambassador in Mexico, Henry F. Fletcher, was to keep Mexico "quiet" as long as the United States was engaged in the European war.

At first glance American policy differences with England seem baffling. The American government did not want to intervene in Mexico at the time, for its attention was focused on the European war. And England had gone to great lengths to prevent an American move into Mexico. But even though both governments seemed to be pursuing virtually identical objectives, it could hardly be said that their Mexican policies were convergent or even complementary. The British government was working for a coup against Carranza, while the American government did not want to attempt any violent actions against the Mexican president until the end of the war. In February 1917, Colonel House instructed Fletcher "to do everything to avoid a break with Carranza."[83]

These instructions remained the leitmotiv of American policy in Mexico until the end of 1918, and Fletcher could state with satisfaction at the end of the war: "During the war, it was my task to keep Mexico quiet, and this task was accomplished."[84]

How can the different orientations of the American and the British governments be explained? The divergent historical experiences of the two countries in Mexico undoubtedly played an important role. Wilson had initially supported Villa and then Carranza, but his support had not prevented either of them from opposing any domination by the American president. What guarantee did the American authorities have that another Mexican government would act any differently?

The American government must have had great doubts about the reliability of any potential allies in Mexico, for there was scarcely a party opposed to Carranza which, at some point in its history, had not stood up to the United States. Villa's attack on Columbus and Zapata's extremely sharp condemnation of U.S. recognition of Carranza scarcely provided the basis for the American government to conclude that it was dealing with a reliable potential ally. But even the conservative forces Great Britain wished to rely on were hardly trustworthy allies in the eyes of the Americans. Almost all members of the old federal army had fought on the side of Wilson's enemy, Huerta. Even those leaders who clearly supported the Allies in their proclamations had in fact acted far more dubiously than their promises might have indicated. Felix Díaz had temporarily established contact with German agents. Similarly, American and British agents had reported threats by Pelaez to seek German aid if Carranza received active support from the Allies.

The only way the United States could be sure that it would be able to maintain the support of a new Mexican government, at least to some degree, was with the threat of military intervention. As long as the world war continued, however, such a threat could only be problematic.

This explains why almost all important American politicians and officials, in spite of their various notions of the "solution" to the Mexican question, were unanimous in their belief that the problem should be put off until after the war. They knew that time was working for them and that their army was becoming stronger by the day, and they hoped to be in a position to impose their policy on Mexico in the postwar period without European help and without any great effort.

The experiences of the United States in Mexico led most American leaders to believe that a coup would not be as simple as the English military strategists assumed from their vantage point in London. If the Allies turned against Carranza, what would prevent him from attacking the oil fields, making an alliance with Germany, and destroying American property? Such action by Carranza would then lead to American intervention in Mexico. But this was precisely what the United States wanted to avoid as long as the war continued. Such fears were expressed by Frank Polk, the man in the State Department centrally concerned with Mexican affairs, during a discussion of England's plans for a coup with the French ambassador in Washington.[85]

If the American government had accepted the view of the British military leaders that Carranza had consented to an alliance with Germany and that an attack on the United States and the destruction of the oil fields were imminent, it might have acted differently. But the American government did not accept this view; it had a much more realistic grasp of both Mexican policy and German objectives in Mexico in 1918.

Indeed, Fletcher developed a perfectly accurate analysis of Carranza's objectives with regard to Germany and of current German intentions in Mexico. "In my opinion," wrote Fletcher in 1918, "the key to Mexico's attitude in the world war is its fear of a general extension of American influence here. I am convinced that President Carranza—and that, today, means Mexico—seeks correct rather than intimate relations with the U.S., and hopes that German victory or at least a stalemate in the world war will create a bulwark or counterweight to the moral and economic influence of the United States in Mexico."[86]

Concerning Germany's intentions, Fletcher argued: "As far as the State Department knows, there is reason to believe that Germany has offered Mexico financial aid for the future, and perhaps even for the present. Germany's goal is not merely to keep Mexico neutral in the war, but to constantly incite it against the Allies and particularly against the U.S. in the hope of making it a profitable source of commercial, economic and political exploitation in the postwar period. This policy is proving successful under Carranza."

In a memorandum on collaboration between Germany and Carranza dated 4 June 1918, Polk did not even mention the possibility that Carranza might be considering a declaration of war against the United States at that time.[87]

What was the cause of these divergent assessments of Carranza's policies and intentions by the American and British governments? This question cannot be answered with any certainty, but one factor may have been the two governments' different sources of information. England, on the one hand, relied primarily on the messages between the Berlin government and its agents in Mexico, which it intercepted and which often contained an optimism having little basis in reality. The United States, on the other hand, had an extensive network of spies and observers throughout Mexico, especially along the border, who would have immediately reported any concentrations of Mexican troops.

The qualities of the representatives of the two countries may also have contributed to the divergent assessments. England's low-ranking officials in Mexico lacked both the personal contacts and the necessary political savoir faire to make a correct analysis of the situation in that country. Fletcher was quite a different sort of diplomat from the British representatives Cummins, Thurstan, and Hohler; however repugnant the Mexican Revolution may have been to him personally, he cultivated normal relations with Carranza and his government.

Finally, the different military positions of England and the United States no doubt affected their perceptions of events in Mexico. In

November 1917 and in the spring of 1918—the very period when the idea of a coup in Mexico was steadily gaining currency in London—Great Britain was in a precarious situation. A victorious German offensive and revolutionary unrest at home were within the realm of possibility. England's main line of defense against such hazards was the arrival of American reinforcements as soon as possible. The British military leaders were therefore quite nervous; they feared America's entanglement in a war with its southern neighbor and a consequent delay in the transport of American troops. The British were thus inclined to see Carranza's pro-German sympathies as more of a threat than they actually were. The United States felt less threatened by Germany than England did and did not fear massive internal unrest. The Americans had just entered the war, had not yet suffered any serious losses, and the war-weariness apparent in Europe was scarcely visible in the United States. As a result, the Americans were more inclined to see the situation as it was.

### Economic Relations between Mexico and the United States

The confident American assessment of the Mexican situation also reflected economic circumstances. The United States had at its disposal important means of economic pressure by which it hoped to make Mexico more favorably disposed toward its interests without a coup or intervention. This economic leverage derived from profound changes in the relationship between the United States and Latin America as a result of the European war.

During the First World War the economy of Latin America entered a completely new phase of development. On the one hand, trade to and from Europe declined rapidly because of the war, and hence the United States began to assume an increasingly large place in Latin America's trade. On the other hand, the United States was not in a position to absorb all the goods previously sold to Europe, nor could it provide all the imports previously obtained from Europe. As a result, very different trends in U.S.–Latin American economic relations emerged. One trend led to an enormous increase in American economic influence on its southern neighbors. In addition to the expansion of U.S. trade, American firms intensified their investment activity in Latin America. Many American firms used part of the profits they obtained from war production to expand their investments in Latin America. The second trend ran counter to the first and signified increasing economic development and independence. It resulted from the fact that the world war was also a period in which the prices of raw materials increased dramatically and resulted in increased foreign exchange holdings for the countries of Latin America. These holdings helped to finance industrialization which was intended to compensate for the loss of imports from the advanced industrial countries. As a result, a new surge of nationalism manifested itself throughout Latin America.

Among the countries of Latin America, Mexico found itself in perhaps a unique position. As a result of the revolution, it had one of the most nationalistic governments in the area. But in economic terms, its dependence on the United States was perhaps greater than that of any country of comparable size in Latin America. Above all, the country was more dependent than ever before on the support of its powerful northern neighbor for arms, ammunition, food, and gold.

Mexico had no munitions industry of its own and had to import arms and ammunition from abroad. Since the outbreak of the revolution, the American government had used the right to purchase arms and ammunition in the United States as a means of political pressure. Governments and parties acceptable to the United States were able to acquire arms; those that were unacceptable could not. Prior to the outbreak of the First World War, these actions by the American government had only a limited effect, because arms could be obtained in Europe or Japan. It was also not very difficult to obtain arms from American munitions firms seeking customers and then to smuggle them over the poorly guarded Mexican-American border.

After July 1914, however, the situation suddenly changed. The Allied demand for American arms and ammunition far exceeded the supply, and it became much more difficult for the Mexican government and Mexican revolutionaries to obtain them. When the United States entered the war in 1917, the demand for arms increased once again and the domestic arms industry was swamped with orders. As the Allied and U.S. government demand for arms increased, greater constraints were placed on arms smuggling into Mexico; security on the Mexican-American border became so tight that contraband arms shipments became virtually impossible. Thus, Carranza and his armies were more dependent on legal arms purchases from the United States than any Mexican regime in history.

In 1917 the United States government introduced official controls on the export of food, industrial goods and gold similar to the controls it had imposed on arms exports since 1910.[88] This action was taken at a time when Mexico's food and industrial production had already been badly diminished by seven years of revolution. Mexico thus became dependent on its northern neighbor in these areas as well.

The financial situation of the government was no less precarious. A deepening state of financial emergency prevailed, resulting from enormous war expenditures and the lack of much needed foreign investment and loans. Even industrial production, which was accelerated in every possible way, and the increasing revenues from higher petroleum and sisal prices were not enough to reverse this state of affairs. In this situation, the American government assumed that it could impose its demands on Carranza through economic pressures. In this connection it is significant that the United States was less concerned by Carranza's collaboration with Germany than by the nationalistic elements of his policy.

In comparison with measures taken by other third-world revolutionary governments in the second half of the twentieth century, Carranza's policies seem quite mild and restrained, though representatives of foreign business interests clearly did not regard them in this way.

The Carranza government had taken no radical measures against foreign enterprises. There had been no nationalizations, and before 1920 very little foreign-owned land was distributed to the peasants. In contrast to other countries where revolutions with a markedly nationalistic character have occurred during the twentieth century, the Mexican Revolution did not reduce the power of foreign firms. On the contrary, the value of American investments in Mexico increased between 1910 and 1920.[89] As one official of a large American mining company put it, "Disorder consequently suits us; mining claims are cheap, competition scarce."[90]

Carranza's goals were far more modest than nationalization of foreign property, although in principle such nationalizations were provided for in the 1917 constitution. His ideas were set forth in a series of pronouncements which came to be known as the Carranza doctrine.[91] In these statements he anticipated some of the principles of the Bandung conference in the 1950s, which stressed the solidarity of the underdeveloped countries and called on the great powers not to interfere in their domestic affairs. The forms of interference that the Mexican president repeatedly condemned were the claims of large foreign interests in Mexico to protection by the governments of their home countries. He strongly opposed the Monroe Doctrine, which he considered as a direct claim by the United States for hegemony in Latin America. He repeatedly called on Latin American countries to counterbalance U.S. influence by alliances with each other as well as closer relations with outside powers.

In practical terms Carranza's policies with regard to foreign enterprises had three immediate objectives: forcing foreign companies to pay higher taxes and royalties, limiting the political and economic power of these companies, and asserting Mexico's sovereignty over its raw materials and all firms active in the country. Decrees of this kind had been issued by Carranza and some of his governors as early as 1915–16, and in 1917 these efforts were written into the Querétaro constitution. In order to increase the revenues from the foreign companies, Carranza issued a series of laws imposing increased taxes on petroleum.[92] At the same time, the Carranzist governor of Yucatán, Salvador Alvarado, created a state monopoly on the sale of sisal fibers, resulting in a sharp increase in the price of that product in the United States. Laws were passed which made the sale of Mexican property to foreigners subject to official approval. Other measures by Carranza required foreign companies planning to acquire new property to register as Mexican corporations, to prevent diplomatic intervention by foreign powers. Mining companies were to be compelled, under the threat of closure or sale, to resume production at their closed mines.

The most heated conflicts with the United States began in January and February 1918 as the result of a series of measures on the petroleum question by the Mexican government. In February 1918, a tax increase was imposed on petroleum and in the same month Carranza's troops attempted to occupy the oil fields and to disperse Pelaez's troops.

In February the Mexican government issued a decree requiring all foreign companies to reregister their property titles. This reregistration effectively meant a recognition of the constitution of 1917, particularly on the question of Mexico's sovereignty over its natural resources. Failure to register their property in accordance with the new laws would result in the loss of all ownership rights, and the property would become subject to sale or lease.

Carranza was successful in only two areas. After making loud protests, the oil companies paid part of the increase in royalties, which was hardly a tremendous burden for them in view of their wartime profits. And the sales monopoly on sisal also proved an impressive success for the Mexican government until the end of the war.

All of Carranza's other efforts, however, ended in failure. Foreign companies paid no attention to the official controls on the sale of Mexican property, but continued to make new acquisitions. No mining companies were expropriated for refusing to resume operations. Carranza was also unable to keep foreign companies from applying diplomatic pressure through their embassies. Finally, the foreign oil companies refused to reregister their titles in keeping with the law of February 1918, and while Carranza did not withdraw his reform decree, he did delay the date of its application from month to month.

The American government moved on several levels to prevent the Mexican government from actually implementing its laws against foreign companies. The United States threatened to intervene and plans were elaborated for an occupation of the Mexican oil fields. At the same time, American authorities attempted to use economic inducements in order to get Carranza to retreat. Arms shipments to the Mexican government were halted, resumed, and then halted again. The same procedure was used for shipments of food and industrial goods.

Also, American authorities either actively supported Carranza's opponents or quietly tolerated the activities of groups in the United States which supported them. Thus the State Department endorsed the oil companies' financial and military support for Pelaez. The strict American embargo rules were lifted on behalf of Esteban Cantu, formerly an officer in Huerta's army, who controlled the state of Baja California. The American government did nothing to block the aid that it knew through intelligence reports that Felix Díaz was receiving from the Catholic Church in the United States, from well-to-do Científicos living in the United States, and from large U.S. interests.[93] Finally, it cannot be ascertained to what extent the American government attempted to accommodate Obregón, but the embargo on the export of gold and industrial goods was loosened on his behalf, a move which was also seen as an attempt to strengthen a potential opponent of Carranza.

Carranza's revolutionary opponents Villa and Zapata, on the other hand, received no aid whatsoever from the United States. In March 1917, Senator Fall, the most committed supporter of American intervention in Mexico, had attempted to use the Villa movement, which was then scoring important military successes in Chihuahua, for his own purposes. To this end, he had one of his colleagues, Charles Hunt, write a letter to Villa, asking him to meet with Fall. Hunt wrote:

> Having talked to Senator A. B. Fall and many prominent operators in the state of Chihuahua, and understanding the extreme disgust with which they look on Carranza and his mal-administration of affairs in the Republic of Mexico, I write to ask you to write an invitation, fixing a time and place where Senator Fall and friends may meet you at any place you desire to confer upon a plan by which we can assist you in any legal manner, and in my opinion, the parties of whom I write will be the means of bringing you large revenues from the country which you dominate, and will ask you only one favor in return, and that is that you will guarantee the protection of all foreign properties within your jurisdiction.

The letter was later intercepted by American agents and printed in the *New York Times*. Its authenticity was confirmed by Fall.[94]

The real objectives of this plan were much more ambitious than mere "protection" of American property in the area controlled by Villa. Seven years later, Charles Hunt stated that Villa had been urged to form a northern republic in Mexico made up of Baja California, Sonora, Chihuahua, Coahuila, Nuevo León, Tamaulipas, and the northern portion of Veracruz. According to Hunt, Villa had rejected this proposal out of hand.[95]

Villa's refusal to participate in plans devised by foreign companies was also confirmed by a report from American military intelligence submitted in spring 1918, which stated that Villa was receiving no financial aid from abroad and that he was financing his movement exclusively from the region he controlled.[96]

The American government succeeded in one of its most important objectives, which was to prevent application of the clauses of the 1917 constitution affecting foreign companies while the world war continued. Carranza gave in to American demands by repeatedly delaying the application of the oil legislation of February 1918 and finally by modifying it. With the exception of tax increases for foreign companies, none of Carranza's decrees limiting the power of foreign companies and preventing expansion by these firms during the revolution were ever applied.

The Americans, however, did fail to achieve their main objective, which was to use the prospect of loans and economic aid, along with pressure and threats, to get Carranza to repudiate the constitution of 1917, to reach an agreement on the Mexican debt question, and to accede to U.S. demands for compensation payments to foreign companies for damages inflicted during the revolution. The American government also failed in its attempt to win Carranza away from his benevolent neutrality toward Germany.

The "successes" of U.S. diplomacy were not enough for a number of American companies who wanted to organize a coup against Carranza during the war, or failing that, to force U.S. military intervention in Mexico. In this respect the English were quite correct to suspect the existence of a plot involving American companies in Mexico in collaboration with Iturbide and Robles Domínguez. In December 1917, American agents seized a secret agreement being transmitted from unnamed American companies to Mexican partners, which contained plans for the overthrow of Carranza. In this agreement, Mexican conservatives, in return for aid from the American companies, agreed to precipitate a break between Mexico and Germany. The Mexican participants in the agreement also stated their willingness to float a bond abroad and to give preference in placing this bond to the American financial group that signed the agreement.[97]

Important points in the agreement stipulated "that the offices of foreign and finance minister will be occupied only by men capable of restoring harmony between the governments of Mexico and the United States, and who also enjoy the confidence of you and your backers." The agreement also provided "that the Mexican government will appoint your backers as financial consultants and financial agents to carry on all financial negotiations which must be conducted in the United States." In an additional clause of the agreement, it was agreed that the British Pearson firm would be forced to cede its control of the Tehuantepec railway to the Mexican government. The Mexican government, for its part, would sell 49 percent of these shares to the American financial group that signed the agreement. Furthermore, all properties taken from the Mexican politician Iturbide were to be returned to him. The agreement, which was mailed from New York to Canova, the State Department's Mexico specialist, contained no names, but Secretary of State Lansing quickly succeeded in uncovering the plotters. Cecil Ira McReynolds, an attorney involved in the plot, told one of Lansing's colleagues

> that the primary goal of the revolution we planned was to obtain control of the oil in Tampico and the German ships in Mexican waters; an agreement had been made with the participation of Corwin, Swain and Helm of the Standard Oil Company and the State Department. They met in New York and discussed the plan.
>
> McReynolds also said that the Standard Oil Company had initially contributed $5 million to the plan. $2.5 million were to be used to buy the ships, $1.5 million to finance the revolutionaries, and the remaining $1 million was to be used to pay the supporters of the movement. S. told X. that it was his impression that V. was to be paid out of this money.

In this report from Lansing, which was of an extremely confidential nature, V. referred to Canova.[98]

One of the Mexican conspirators, whom Lansing referred to solely by the letter S, wanted to be certain that the American government would back the plan completely before he proceeded with the anticipated coup in Mexico. To this end, he approached a close friend of the secretary of state, who in turn met with Lansing. Lansing kept his distance from the plot, immediately informed Woodrow Wilson, and later dismissed Canova, who nonetheless maintained ties with the State Department.[99] The American financiers did not, however, abandon their plans for a coup, and several months later the English, as we have seen, uncovered a similar plot involving not Iturbide but the Mexican politician Robles Domínguez.

The American oil companies, the International Harvester Corporation, and other participating American companies in no way limited their political actions to this kind of conspiracy, but repeatedly called on the American government to take decisive action in Mexico. In mid-1918, the International Harvester Corporation demanded that the American government immediately occupy the Yucatán peninsula to force a reduction of the price of sisal. In August 1918, oil companies supported by important American officials such as Mark Requa, general director of the oil division of the American Fuel Administration, attempted to bring about U.S. military intervention in Mexico. It is not clear whether they planned to occupy the oil fields or all of Mexico.[100]

In contrast to the suspicions of the British military leaders and diplomats, most officials in the American government took a negative view of these conspiracies and threats to intervene so long as the war continued. Lansing and Wilson were reinforced in their attitude by a number of companies led by the Morgan banking house, which wanted to avoid armed intervention in Mexico at any cost. Morgan's Thomas Lamont refused to participate in a pressure group composed of American companies favoring intervention.[101] The Morgan bank, which was heavily involved in the British bond market, had every intention of avoiding American intervention in Mexico, which would have called into question or at least delayed an Allied victory in the world war. Also, the banks wanted above all to assure repayment of their debts and to win control of the Mexican financial market. They hoped to obtain both objectives through pressure on Carranza.

Although the American government, and particularly Wilson himself, wanted no conspiracies or interventions in Mexico before the war ended, the attitudes of important American officials on this question began to change during the final months of the war. Interventionism became more attractive to important American diplomats and officials as tensions with Carranza increased and as victory in Europe became a tangible prospect.[102]

## Japan and Carranza

On the whole, the leaders of the great powers were far more accurate in assessing each other's intentions and policies in Mexico than many contemporary observers and later historians have given them credit for. Where these leaders erred was in their assessment of the Mexican revolutionaries and their policies. When European and American politicians did make mistakes about each other's intentions in Mexico (as the British did with respect to a German-Mexican attack on the United States in 1917–18), these errors were nearly always linked to faulty interpretations of Mexican attitudes and aims.

Was Japan the one exception to this rule? Was it the one great power whose policies toward Mexico its adversaries and even its allies were unable to assess correctly? Certainly Zimmermann committed a great error of judgment when he assumed that Japan would join Germany and Mexico in an alliance against the United States.

In the United States itself, both within and outside the administration, strong suspicions were expressed about Japan's intentions in Mexico. These were basically of three kinds: first, that Japan was seriously considering an attack on the United States, and that for such an eventuality it was exploring the option of securing bases in Mexico and making alliances with some faction in that country. Second, that Japan wanted to achieve what Germany had been attempting to do since the end of 1914: embroil the United States in a war with Mexico and thus prevent it from interfering with Japan's designs in China. And, third, that Japan hoped to use Mexico as a bargaining chip to secure American concessions in the Far East.

These suspicions were not wholly unfounded. Japan was exploring these three options but it was doing so in such small, tentative doses that they constituted a warning but not a serious irritant to the United States.

In 1914, Japan entered World War I on the side of the Allies and immediately proceeded to occupy the German base in China. This was only the first step in a grand design to assure Japanese supremacy there.

In January 1915, Japan secretly presented twenty-one demands to President Yuan Shih Kai of China. These demands were divided into five groups. The first four were mainly economic; Japan asked China for wide-ranging concessions, especially in Inner Mongolia and Manchuria. The fifth group of demands would have established a quasi protectorate of Japan over China. Among other things Japan demanded that both countries jointly administer the police in China's leading cities, that joint military technical commissions by both countries be set up, and that China procure its ammunition in Japan (a demand which would have led to a far-reaching dependence of the Chinese armed forces upon Japan).[103]

The governments of Great Britain, France, and Russia were anything but enthusiastic about this threat to the rights and prerogatives they had exercised in China for so long, but they had no effective means of resisting Japan's claims. They had become more and more embroiled in the European war and the weakest member of the Allies, Russia, had become more and more dependent on Japanese arms.

The Japanese government had underscored this state of affairs by undertaking secret negotiations with Germany for a separate peace and a possible switch of alliances.[104] In 1915–16 Germany suggested to Japan that it abandon the Allies, switch to the German side, and induce Russia to do the same or at the very least to seek a policy of neutrality. In return Germany would relinquish all its possessions in the Far East to Japan and agree to important concessions for that country in China. The Japanese government leaked these negotiations to the Allies, who thereupon agreed to most of Japan's demands in China in order to keep the Japanese on their side.

One power nevertheless remained unalterably opposed to Japan's assuming a preponderant role in China and since it was not yet involved in World War I it also had at least some means of pressing its opposition. This was the United States. Shortly after Japan had made its twenty-one demands on China, the United States government declared in May 1915 that it could not recognize any agreement between China and Japan that threatened the treaty rights of the United States, the territorial integrity of

China or the Open Door policy.[105] As a result tensions between the United States and Japan increased and Mexico began to assume a definite, albeit secondary, role in Japan's efforts to reverse or counteract U.S. opposition to its expansionist policies in China.

In two ways Mexico constituted a highly favorable setting for Japanese intrigues: Unlike the United States or the European powers, Japan had very little to lose in Mexico. There were practically no Japanese investments in that country, Japanese-Mexican trade was minimal, and there were few Japanese in Mexico (most of whom were of lower class origin and hence of secondary interest to the Japanese government).[106] Thus Japan never had to face the kind of dilemma that constantly confronted Germany: how to maintain its large economic interests in Mexico and at the same time to utilize that country as a means of influencing U.S. policy and possibly provoking an American military intervention there.

In addition most Mexican governments in the years 1910–20, and especially the Carranza administration, showed great interest in establishing closer ties to Japan. What attracted them was precisely the fact that Japan had no large investments in Mexico, and therefore no conflicts between Japanese business interests and Mexican nationalism could arise.

Another distinct advantage of Japan over Germany, from Mexico's point of view, was the fact that it was the only power which could sell arms to Mexico and thus undermine if not break the American arms embargo.

What role, if any, racial factors, that is, Japan's Asian and non-European status played in Mexico's attitude is far more difficult to determine.

The Japanese Foreign Office seems to have attempted to use these circumstances, though only in a very minimal way, to convey a mild warning to the United States.

Japan, however, could not escape the contradiction that afflicted the policies of all the great powers toward Mexico: the conflict between the attitudes of the civilian and military authorities with regard to policy toward Mexico. Like its counterparts in Germany, Great Britain, and the United States, the Japanese navy was in favor of a much more aggressive policy in Mexico than the civilian authorities.

With regard to the Japanese Foreign Office there is no evidence that it responded to repeated overtures by both the Huerta and the Carranza governments by showing substantial interest in Mexico. It was obviously afraid of irritating the United States and kept in mind "the Japanese scares" that had erupted in the United States during the Japanese-American tensions in 1907–8 and as a result of the Magadalena Bay rumors of 1911–12.

With one possible exception in 1916 the Foreign Office in Tokyo repeatedly rebuffed all Mexican advances. It firmly rejected the proposals for closer cooperation between Japan and the Carranza government submitted by Fukutaro Terasawa, a Japanese in the service of the Mexican government to the Japanese Foreign Office in late 1915 (see chap. 9). Japan's diplomats were equally adamant in refusing to consider a new proposal made by the Carranza government in the spring of 1917 for Mexico to enter World War I against Germany but to do so not as an ally of the United States but as an ally of Japan.

Nevertheless, this reserved attitude by the Foreign Office in Tokyo does not mean that it did not want to utilize United States–Mexican conflicts for its own ends. Japanese diplomats, generally in very subtle terms, attempted to convince American officials that Japan should enjoy the same kind of preeminence in East Asia that the United States was claiming for itself on the American continent.

In a far less subtle manner propagandists closely linked to Japan, such as James S. Abbott, wrote, "If we insisted on a Monroe Doctrine for America, why should Japan not have a Monroe Doctrine for Asia."[107] Japanese diplomats soon lost their reticence and openly expressed the same kind of ideas in negotiations with the United States. In late 1917 Japan sent a special envoy, Viscount Kikujiro Ishii, to the United States to negotiate a United States–Japanese agreement in view of the fact that both were now allies in the war against Germany. Kikujiro Ishii now openly demanded American recognition of an Asian Monroe Doctrine. "From our point of view" he told his American counterparts, "Japan in the whole of China and especially in regions of that country adjacent to Japan has interests greater than those of other countries. Such a condition is a reality resulting from the arrangements of nature. Just as the reason for the Monroe Doctrine exists whether or not it is recognized by other powers, so does the position of Japan with respect to China exist regardless of the recognition of other nations."[108]

Ishii used the example of Mexico to counter American arguments that recognition of Japan's paramount interest in China would jeopardize the Open Door policy. "America had paramount interest in Mexico," he said, "but it was not believed on that account restrictions of any sort were placed on the Open Door in Mexican foreign relations."[109]

The subtle diplomacy of the Japanese Foreign Office toward Mexico did not satisfy the Japanese navy, which by 1917 "formally adopted a policy of viewing the United States as the most likely enemy."[110] From 1913 onward Japanese naval strategists had begun to consider the possibilities of a Japanese-American conflict. Thus reports of the Japanese navy's great interest in Mexico should come as no surprise though some of these reports cannot be substantiated from Japanese sources.

In early 1915 Pancho Villa told the American diplomatic envoy George

Carothers that a Japanese admiral had come to see him and told him that Japan had been planning for three years on a conflict with the United States. Villa reported that the Japanese admiral asked him what attitude he would assume if such a conflict broke out.[111] Villa stated that he would side with the Americans.

Around the same time a highly publicized incident occurred in San Bartolomé Bay in Baja California. In November 1914 a Japanese cruiser, the *Asama,* ran aground in San Bartolomé Bay, or Turtle Bay, as it was known in the United States. It refused any help by American warships in the area and remained in the bay for more than six months while other Japanese cruisers, repair ships, and colliers came to assist it.[112] The Hearst press in the United States wrote articles stating that in reality this was only a pretext for establishing a Japanese naval base in Baja California and that it constituted part of Japanese preparations for a military conflict with the United States. These rumors were laid to rest when the *Asama* finally left San Bartolomé Bay several months later. While these rumors were obviously exaggerated and there is no substantiation for these activities from Japanese sources, American fears were not entirely devoid of substance. Both incidents occurred at a time when the Japanese navy was more and more seriously envisioning the possibility of a conflict with the United States and they took place precisely at the moment when Japan was voicing its controversial twenty-one demands with respect to China. In all probability the conversation of the Japanese admiral with Pancho Villa as well as the *Asama*'s trip to Turtle Bay were part of a policy of exploration by the Japanese navy of the possibilities of utilizing Mexico in case of a Japanese-American war. At the time the Japanese admiral spoke to Villa the latter was frequently referred to as the Mexican Napoleon, the invincible and charismatic dictator who would soon rule the whole of the country. It is thus not inconceivable that the Japanese were seriously attempting to sound out his attitude toward the United States. In the same vein the *Asama*'s original trip to Turtle Bay may have been made with the aim of exploring whatever strategic possibilities this part of Baja California offered in case of a Japanese-American war. Whether the lengthy repairs of the *Asama* were part of a plan to explore Baja California or were simply due to technical difficulties is still open to speculation.

The high point of the Japanese navy's interest in Mexico occurred in May 1916 when the American punitive expedition had penetrated into Mexico and the United States and its southern neighbor seemed on the verge of war. It was also the period in which the sharpest conflict over Mexico occurred between the Japanese Foreign Office and the Japanese navy.

In May 1916 when Mexican-American tensions had reached a high point, Mexico's Foreign Secretary Cándido Aguilar met with Tamikuchi Ohta, the Japanese chargé d'affaires in Mexico, and requested that Japan mediate between Mexico and the United States.[113] At the same time he told Ohta of Mexico's desire to purchase arms and ammunition from Japan. The Japanese Foreign Office, which Ohta had consulted, bluntly rejected Aguilar's suggestions; it refused to mediate in this Mexican-American dispute and stated that Japan could not sell arms to Mexico since all of its arms sales were destined for its allies. Nevertheless, Mexico did not give up and a few weeks later Secretary of War Álvaro Obregón had a meeting with Ohta in which he requested that Japan meet with a Mexican delegation sent to that country to buy arms.[114] Ohta at first refused to accede to that request but, for reasons that are not clear, he changed his mind and allowed the delegation to proceed to Japan although in his report to the Foreign Office he said that its mission would certainly be fruitless.[115] The secret military mission from Mexico finally proceeded to Japan in the early summer of 1916.

The Japanese Foreign Office in Tokyo, like its representatives in Mexico, did everything in its power to discourage the Mexican delegation. Vice-minister for Foreign Affairs Shidehara told the Mexican minister in Tokyo that Japan was treaty-bound to supply arms only to its allies—it could not sell anything to Mexico. At this point the Japanese navy suddenly intervened. The Japanese minister of the navy told the Mexican representatives that the navy was in favor of selling arms to Mexico.[116] In fact the navy even criticized the Mexicans for not having asked the Japanese government for help and support sooner. The navy soon showed itself to be more powerful than the Foreign Ministry, and Mexico acquired 30 million cartridges, and the machinery to install a gunpowder and a cartridge factory in Mexico. Also, Mexico appears to have acquired an indeterminate quantity of rifles and other arms in Japan.[117]

The actions of the Japanese navy are significant, for they occurred at a time when Mexico stood practically alone in its conflict with the United States. The Germans at that time refused to support Mexico, hoping that even without their intervention Mexico would be drawn into a war with its northern neighbor. Latin America gave Mexico mainly moral support. Japan was thus practically the only country supplying help to Mexico. While the arms and factories coming from Japan were obviously not of decisive importance, they certainly encouraged Carranza in his policy of absolute refusal to grant any concessions to Woodrow Wilson in return for the evacuation of the punitive expedition from Mexico.

When that evacuation finally did occur it seemed to put an end to the Japanese navy's interest in Mexico. The reasons for this loss of interest in Mexican affairs are not clear. It certainly was not because the Japanese navy had abandoned the idea that a conflict with the United States might occur. On the contrary, this idea was becoming more and more widely shared within the navy. It is possible, however, that the withdrawal of the punitive expedition convinced the navy that a Mexican-American war would not take place for some time to come. It may also have hoped that the growing conflict between the United States and Germany would divert America's attention from the Far East and make another diversion in Mexico unnecessary.

As the Japanese navy lost interest in Mexico, the control of Japan's Mexican policy once again reverted to the Foreign Office in Tokyo. The latter did not completely abandon the policy of selling arms to Mexico. Sporadic deliveries of Japanese arms to the Carranza government continued until September 1917. The Foreign Office, however, was not primarily interested in goading Mexico into resisting American pressure with the expectation of triggering a Mexican-American war, as the navy seems to have hoped. Its aim continued to be to utilize Mexico as a bargaining chip in its complex negotiations with the United States. This is precisely what occurred when Japan sent its special envoy, Viscount Ishii, to the United States in September 1917 to negotiate some kind of agreement on China with the Wilson administration. Ishii's attempt during these negotiations to compare the United States' relationship to Mexico with Japan's relationship to China was more than a mere historical parallel.[118] It was also a warning that if the United States continued to ignore Japan's special rights in China, Japan might ignore America's special rights in Mexico. It is not clear to what degree this inference exerted influence on the long and convoluted negotiations between Ishii and Secretary of State Robert Lansing. At any rate after Lansing and Ishii signed the agreement in which Japan and the United States reiterated the Open Door policy in China, while at the same time the Americans conceded that Japan had special interests in that country,[119] Japan seems to have followed a policy of complete restraint in Mexico. Although the agreement by no means settled the conflicts between the United States and Japan and new contradictions with respect not only to China but also to Siberia emerged between the two countries, Japan seems to have given up any involvement in Mexican affairs.

It is difficult to assess the importance of Japan's Mexican policies in the Carranza years. With one significant exception they were of an exploratory nature with no concrete consequences. The exception was the decision taken at the instigation of the Japanese navy in 1916 to supply arms to Mexico at a time when American-Mexican tensions had reached their peak. It is not easy to assess the military consequences of this decision. The ammunition and powder factories that Carranza bought from the Japanese would not have made any difference in a possible war with the United States. In the continuing internal struggle that Carranza was waging with his rivals, however, they doubtless helped him to maintain his precarious supremacy over the country. This Japanese help, coming at a time when Mexico stood alone against the United States, probably also had some psychological impact on the Carranza leadership (the mass of the population knew little about these dealings and was not influenced or impressed by them). This impact cannot, however, have been too great, for only five months after the negotiations between the Japanese and Mexican representatives had begun in May 1916, Carranza turned to Germany. Since Japan and Germany were at war and the Mexican president had no way of knowing that secret negotiations had been going on between the two countries, Carranza's overtures to Germany were a tacit admission that Japanese help could never be substantial. If the Mexicans had any doubts on that score, Japan's refusal to join Zimmermann's plans for an alliance and its equally sharp rebuff in May 1917 of Mexico's offer to declare war on Germany as an ally of Japan must have convinced the Mexicans that the Japanese card was played out for them.

It is interesting to speculate (no concrete evidence is available to do more) why the Japanese refused Mexico's offer of an alliance. An obvious reason for such a refusal would have existed if Mexico's offer had been directed against the United States and if the Carranza government had asked Japan to guarantee Mexican independence. There is no evidence that this was what the Mexicans had suggested. It seems that what they wanted primarily was a pretext to declare war on Germany without seeming to do so at the instigation of the Americans. But even this kind of an offer was something the Japanese had no reason to accept, for it offered them no concrete advantage. The United States and not Japan would have been the main beneficiary had Mexico joined the Allies. It might have been able to withdraw many of the troops stationed along the Mexican border. This was precisely what the Japanese, whose rivalry with the United States was continuing, did not want. Since Japan was not interested in securing economic concessions in Mexico, the Mexicans really had nothing to offer Japan in return for an eventual alliance.

Did Japan have any impact on the internal or external course of the Mexican Revolution? Its hesitant and at times contradictory policies toward Mexico, with the possible exception of the arms sales to the Carranza government in 1916, probably did not. But Japan's overall policies, its rivalry with the United States, and the ever present possibility of an armed conflict with the Americans did have consequences for the United States' attitude toward Mexico. It contributed substantially to the hesitations of the Wilson administration to extend its intervention in Mexico and to its decision to withdraw its troops from that country in spite of Carranza's refusal to accede to American demands.

# 12 Carranza and World War I

When the end of the First World War finally made it possible for the United States to concentrate its attention on Mexico, an ambitious interventionist campaign was set in motion. The originators and promoters of this campaign were primarily the front men and attorneys for the American oil companies. In order to create the psychological atmosphere for an intervention, they depicted the Mexican government as pro-German and called Carranza a German agent. They focused on three basic accusations, that Carranza was in the pay of Germany, that Carranza had prepared an attack on the United States,[1] and that Mexico was financed and controlled by Germany. It was said that every important decision in domestic politics made in Mexico during the period 1916–18 was the result of German initiative and that the Mexican constitution of 1917 had been drafted and worked out by German jurists.[2]

Our entire exposition, as well as the documents we have cited, show that such accusations are completely false. There is no proof that Carranza was bribed by Germany; Eckardt's remark "bribery unnecessary" proves precisely the opposite. Carranza's reactions to the Zimmermann note and the second German alliance proposal are clear evidence of his opposition to German suggestions that he attack the United States. Germany made no loans to Mexico during the world war (the only specific American allegation, that Mexico received an advance of 800,000 pesos, remains unsubstantiated; such a sum, moreover, would have been insignificant).[3]

The Mexican government's decisions in domestic policy were not only made independently, but quite often in opposition to the desires of the German representatives. There is no evidence whatsoever that German jurists wrote the 1917 constitution. Eckardt actually had a very negative reaction to this document. He characterized the members of the constitutional assembly in Queretaro as "primarily Catilinarian figures." As for the constitution itself, he wrote that it was "the result of two months' labor by men of whom only a handful, by general consensus, are really up to the task. The new constitution obviously lacks a thorough legal foundation, which was already precluded by the short period in which it had to be drafted. It is obvious from its most serious innovations—the articles dealing with church and school, acquisition and ownership of land, and

social security—that the law is tailored for the masses and gives them
rights which derive at least in part from a completely incoherent and false
view of serious social questions."[4] Eckardt's proposal that he ally with
the church[5] was also rejected by Carranza.

All this reveals the utter groundlessness of the charge that Germany
was controlling Mexico and of the assertion that the Carranza government
was made up of German agents. It is nevertheless a fact that the sympathies and hopes of the Mexican government in the course of the world
war were strongly oriented toward Germany. In August 1918, Eckardt
wrote with his usual melodramatic pathos:

> General Obregón, then minister of war and later the winner of the battle
> of Celaya which was so crucial for Carranza, told me well before the
> United States had declared war that "no one is neutral in this war; one is
> either for Germany or against her." Both the clarity of thought and the
> pregnant formulation were striking. They showed how much this man
> was caught up, above and beyond his own concerns, in the great clash of
> peoples on the other side of the ocean, and how unambiguously he took
> our side . . . Mexico was *for* Germany in the world war, and that will be to
> its glory in the German history books. This was no secondary factor, but,
> in my opinion, one of primary importance. Because of its impact on Latin
> America, and its open sympathies for us, who were the enemies of the
> United States, Mexico forced the U.S. to keep 200,000–500,000 armed
> men on the Mexican border. In May 1917, Carranza had promised me
> that he would support us in this way.[6]

How did this attitude come about? How far did this "pro-German"
sentiment really go? Were essential interests of Mexico compromised?
These are the decisive questions which must be posed in this connection.

At the outbreak of the world war, Carranza declared his neutrality,
expressing a deep mistrust of both England and imperial Germany, which
had supported Huerta almost to the end. In the first months of the war,
this neutrality even showed a certain pro-Allied orientation. The German
plots to provoke a Mexican-American war with the aid of Huerta were
hardly a secret to Carranza; his intelligence service appears to have even
had a hand in uncovering them. His relations with the German representatives, initially with the German consuls in the areas he controlled and
later with Eckardt, were extremely cool. Characteristic of this orientation
was the Mexican government's unfriendly reaction to an inquiry of the
German consul in Veracruz, who implied that oil shipments to England
constituted a violation of Mexican neutrality. In March 1915, the Carranza government informed him that such shipments could in no way be
seen as a violation of neutrality, "as we do not view petroleum as war
contraband. Oil has many uses which are absolutely unrelated to war. To
view it as an essential war material would constitute a tremendous blow to

important commercial interests having nothing to do with the belligerent nations.''[7]

Eckardt's attitude toward the Carranza government, and his attacks on Carranza himself, to whom he initially referred in his reports in the crudest fashion, are eloquent testimony to the state of German-Mexican relations at that time. When relations deteriorated with the United States and Carranza sought support from a major power, he turned not to Germany but to Japan. The Japanese government, however, was not very accommodating. Japan's attitude, the Allies' preoccupation with Europe, their increasingly intimate relations with the United States, and their growing dependency on American imports all created a situation in which there remained only one major power that Carranza could play off against the United States: Germany. Carranza sought a rapprochement with Germany only after the advance of the American punitive expedition into Mexico had brought him to the brink of a war with the United States. "Since 1916 Wilson has been driving him into our camp with his frivolous games and finally with Pershing's punitive expedition,"[8] Eckardt wrote at the end of 1917. The first of Carranza's real pro-German actions worth mentioning occurred in this period: reorientation of the press toward the Central Powers; the appointment of Krumm Heller, an open supporter of German imperialism, as Mexican military attaché in Berlin; the transmission to the German government of a memorandum proposing closer economic and political relations between the two countries; and, finally, the offer of a U-boat base in Mexico.

Carranza was seeking two advantages in these attempts at rapprochement. Initially, and rather naively, he expected a German diplomatic move in Washington demanding U.S. withdrawal from Mexico. Such a move, had it ever been attempted, would have had no prospect of success, quite aside from the fact that it had nothing to do with the interests of German diplomacy, which of course deeply desired an American intervention in Mexico. The fact that Eckardt did not even transmit this request to Berlin indicates how lightly he viewed it. Was Carranza overestimating the importance of German interests in Mexico? Was he overestimating the power of Germany? There is no unequivocal answer to these questions. It seems likely, however, that he did overestimate Germany's power. Carranza's lack of experience in world affairs and Eckardt's propaganda were not unimportant in this regard.

Carranza's second, far more concrete hope, was for arms from Germany. The Mexican-American tensions resulting from the advance of the American punitive expedition into Mexico had led to the imposition of an American arms embargo. For Carranza, however, arms were a vital necessity, given the possibility of a Mexican-American war and his need to hold his domestic enemies, who were on the rise again, in check. The successful visits to the United States by German cargo-carrying U-boats seemed to hold open the possibility of arms shipments to Mexico. Carranza's initiative at first encountered only hesitation and reserve at the German Foreign Office. The Mexican-American war so desired in Berlin seemed imminent without any further German involvement. An open German rapprochement with Carranza might have had the opposite effect and once again drawn American attention to Germany. Thus Zimmermann treated the Mexican memorandum as an issue for the postwar period, and German arms shipments to Carranza were not even considered at first. However, in order not to discourage him excessively but to keep him from being driven into the hands of the Americans, the Germans arranged an arms shipment from South America. The eventual American withdrawal from Mexico was in no small way due to Germany's actions, if only indirectly. The undesirable prospect of being tied down in Mexico during a period of increasing tensions with Germany prompted the Americans to withdraw their troops.

Germany's declaration of unlimited U-boat warfare, the rupture in German-American relations, the U.S. declaration of war, and finally the American withdrawal from Mexico created a situation in which the initiative passed from Carranza to the German government.

Was the Mexican government really interested in Zimmermann's proposal for an alliance against the United States, except as a defensive measure in case of a renewed U.S. invasion? There are two scenarios for which there are indications, though no positive proof, that Carranza might have contemplated accepting Germany's offer of an offensive alliance resulting in a Mexican attack on the United States. One such scenario would have been an about-face by Japan and its direct participation in a German-Mexican alliance against the United States. A second scenario, which Carranza was not entirely discounting, was a civil war in the United States. In his memoirs Adolfo de la Huerta recounts that Carranza was fascinated by the possibility of reincorporating Texas, Arizona, and New Mexico for Mexico.[9] This is borne out by the support he gave the San Diego plan movement. In February 1917, after the punitive expedition withdrew from Mexico, he seems to have ended his support for the Mexican-Americans. Nevertheless, as the previously mentioned report by one of his secret agents in the United States indicates, some Mexican military men believed that in case of a German-American war, hundreds of thousands of German-Americans in the United States would rise and that they might spearhead a revolt by blacks and Mexican-Americans against the U.S. government. Had such a contingency occurred, Carranza might have attacked the United States. When he became convinced that Japan would not change sides in the war and that no uprising would take place in the United States, he stubbornly rejected all subsequent German offers for an attack on the United States.

Mexico's international policies in the years 1917–18 were essentially a reaction to five main dangers which the Carranza government felt threatened its survival and Mexico's sovereignty.

1. Renewed military intervention by the United States was a threat that plagued Mexico. While a complete military occupation of Mexico seemed improbable as long as World War I lasted (though the Mexican government never completely ruled it out), limited intervention seemed not at all out of the question. Oil and sisal interests as well as high U.S. administration officials were privately and publicly advocating the occupation of the Mexican oil fields and Yucatán. In view of the military importance of the oil fields Wilson did not completely discard such a possibility, though he wanted to avoid it as much as possible.[10] Carranza was constantly receiving reports that such options were being seriously considered in the United States.

There is no evidence that he had informants close to the White House or to the highest levels of the State Department but reports of deliberations taking place there, or of plots by United States business interests did filter through to him. Carranza had an excellent intelligence service along the border and his agents had succeeded in penetrating almost every group of Mexican exiles in the United States. As soon as agents of U.S. corporations, or even the U.S. government, informed real or potential Mexican allies of their plans, Carranza heard of them. The files of the Mexican Foreign Office are full of such reports. At the same time the German secret service handed him similar reports. Since they were mostly corroborated by information reported by his own agents this increased the credibility of the Germans in the Mexican president's eyes.

2. Carranza's government expected an Allied-inspired coup in Mexico in which Britain and the United States would support Carranza's conservative foes as well as emerging opposition groups within his own movement with arms and money. Carranza was quite aware that plans for such options were being worked out by U.S. interests and by British diplomats. Cummins had discussed plans for a coup so openly in the British club that, according to statements from the British consul in Mexico, the Mexican government knew them in detail. German intelligence had also informed Carranza of the Robles Domínguez conspiracy.[11]

3. United States economic policies toward Mexico assumed more and more the form of a near-total blockade against Mexico as the war progressed. Until the United States entered World War I, restrictions imposed by its northern neighbor upon Mexico were limited to two fields: since 1911, with some interruption, the U.S. government had to approve

shipments of arms to its southern neighbor. At the same time, Carranza had been unable to secure any loan in the United States. While the financial restrictions were easy to enforce, the arms embargo was far more difficult for the United States to implement. It was very difficult to control the long border between the two countries and substantial arms smuggling went on constantly between 1910 and 1917. After the United States entered the war on the side of the Allies, the administration received new powers and new authority which it could impose upon Mexico. In view of German threats, border controls were strengthened even more. For the first time in the history of the two countries smuggling of arms could effectively be prevented. At the same time, export controls, which until March 1917 had been limited to ammunition, were extended to a wide variety of products. In September 1917 the United States Treasury imposed a general embargo on the export of bullion to any country in order to stabilize the dollar and keep gold in the United States. A short time later the government issued a decree controlling and preventing the export of food to Mexico.[12]

4. A German-inspired coup in Mexico—Eckardt's plot of leading Mexican generals to topple Carranza in case he broke with Germany—was considered a very serious danger by the Mexican president.

5. If Germany decided to carry out large-scale sabotage actions in the Mexican oil fields, Wilson might be forced to intervene against his will. Should such an intervention occur, Carranza, apart from the substantial loss of oil revenue, would have faced an impossible dilemma. If he resisted, he would have on his hands a war with the United States which he could not win. If he did not resist, domestic resentment against his passivity might lead to his fall.

From March to about September 1917 Carranza sought to allay these dangers by a policy of rapprochement with the United States. Except for one new tax on oil and limited restrictions on new concessions, which would make it mandatory for those seeking to obtain such concessions to renounce diplomatic intervention by their governments, Carranza made no attempt to implement Article 27 of the Constitution. American reports that, between March and May 1917, the Mexican government was seriously considering a break in relations with Germany were confirmed by Eckardt's intrigue with the generals. When it became clear that such a measure would provoke serious domestic repercussions, Carranza considered another option he hoped would allow him to break with Germany and still maintain his nationalistic posture and the support of his generals. Aguilar suggested to the Japanese minister a special alliance between Japan and Mexico by which Mexico would enter the war on the Allies' side, but ostensibly as an ally of Japan rather than the United States. Obviously the Mexican government hoped that such an agreement would dispel the fears of its own military that it was selling out to the United States and at the same time provide Mexico with a protector, Japan, which in the postwar years and even during the war it could play off against the United States. Even when the Japanese rejected these proposals and this apparently easier way of joining the Allies was closed to Mexico, Carranza did not give up his hope of seeking rapprochement with the United States.

The administration in Washington reacted to these overtures by the Mexican government by temporarily lifting the embargo on arms and ammunition and extending de jure recognition to the Mexican government in September 1917.

Carranza's rapprochement with the United States failed, not so much because of the plot of the generals and Eckardt's machinations, but because it became clear to the Mexican president that the United States would lift its economic restrictions only if he consented to serious infringements of his country's sovereignty. He acquired this conviction as a result of lengthy financial negotiations with the United States.

In June 1917 the Carranza government had come to an agreement with an American firm, Inselin and Company, for a loan to Mexico. The company was to mint Mexican gold coins in the United States, which would then be used to stabilize the Mexican currency. The United States Treasury vetoed this arrangement, giving as a reason in part Inselin's links to Germany and in part the fear that stabilization of the Mexican currency would depreciate the American dollar.

In August 1917 loan negotiations between representatives of Carranza and large American banks failed when the banks refused to extend credit to the Mexican government. After smaller American banks told the Mexican government that they would be willing to make a loan to Mexico if the U.S. government would be ready to guarantee it, Carranza began negotiations wth the representatives of the Washington administration. The administration told Carranza that it did not oppose a loan in principle, but that guarantees concerning "valid vested interests" would have to be made by the Mexican government. Carranza obviously felt that this condition seriously infringed on Mexico's sovereignty and refused to accept it.[13] The breakdown of these loan negotiations was followed by U.S. embargoes on gold and food exports to Mexico.

It was around this time that Delmar arrived in Mexico as a representative of the German General Staff and presented Mexico with Germany's new offer of an alliance against the United States. Unlike the Zimmermann telegram Delmar's offer was not an all-or-nothing proposal. Even if Carranza refused the offer of alliance, which he did, Delmar offered close postwar cooperation which might help to break the American blockade over Mexico and he raised the possibility of a loan extended to Mexico during the war. With the help of German money Carranza might be able to circumvent some of the consequences of the American embargo by buying food and other essentials in the neutral countries of South America with which Mexico was establishing increasingly close relations. Delmar's alliance proposal also showed Carranza that Germany, in spite of his refusal to accept Zimmermann's offer, had not lost interest in Mexico.

It was at this point that Carranza took the decision of establishing the closest possible links to Germany short of an alliance. With his policies he was pursuing both short-term and long-term objectives.

His most important short-term objective was undoubtedly to obtain German aid in the eventuality, which he seemed to consider quite likely, of armed intervention by the United States or an Allied-inspired coup. He also hoped to obtain from Germany some kind of loan which would tide him over until World War I ended and Germany would have the means to help him substantially. Another essential short-term objective of Carranza's rapprochement with Germany was to prevent German agents from carrying out sabotage actions in the oil fields, since such actions were the one sure way of insuring U.S. intervention in Mexico.

Carranza may also have hoped that collaboration with the German secret service would dissuade the Allies from supporting his domestic opponents and from intervening in Mexico. Both England and the United States feared that a conflict with Carranza could result in a debacle for the Allies' companies in Mexico. They may have had doubts about Carranza's willingness or ability in an emergency to carry out the massive destruction of the Allies' property. They had no doubts, however, that a strong German secret service in Mexico, given a free hand by Carranza, would concentrate its efforts primarily on the destruction of the Allies' companies.

It is probable that the promise of German support stiffened Carranza's resolve to counter U.S. economic warfare against his government by reprisals of his own. These consisted essentially of trying to force American interests to make increased payments in the form of taxes or royalties to compensate for the losses Mexico suffered as a result of the U.S. economic blockade against the country.

In September 1917, after the United States imposed its embargo on gold exports to Mexico, Carranza issued decrees trying to force American mining companies to pay in gold a part of their exports from the country. At the beginning of 1918 new decrees increasing the taxes and imposing new regulations on the oil companies were imposed by the Mexican government.[14] These decrees led to sharp State Department protests against the policies of the Mexican government and vociferous calls for intervention in Mexico by the affected American interests. At this point the prospect of German help undoubtedly strengthened Carranza's desire to resist.

In April 1918 the Mexican ambassador in Washington had submitted reports indicating the Americans' intentions of blockading the Mexican ports of Veracruz and Tampico; "the foreign minister told me," Eckardt wrote, "that in the event of a blockade the president would not negotiate but would have to strike back. When he asked me if I had the power to conclude an alliance I answered in the affirmative, even though this is not the case."[15]

Another goal of Carranza's short-term as well as long-term collaboration with Germany was his Latin American policy. He wanted to create a Latin American bloc led by Mexico and Argentina, which could collectively defend itself against the United States. In pursuing this goal, his desires momentarily converged with those of German diplomats. Both countries wanted to preserve the neutrality of as many Latin American countries as possible. Carranza thus proposed to Eckardt that Germany step up its propaganda in Colombia against that country's entry into the war.[16] There appears to have been collaboration in Central America as well during the same period. In addition to these foreign policy moves, an important factor of domestic policy also played a role: the maintenance of the unity of the Carranza movement. The conspiracy of the generals was a clear warning for Carranza. The population as a whole was so anti-American that if Carranza made any serious concessions to the Americans, the generals would have had mass support.

Carranza's most important long-range goal was undoubtedly his desire to have strong support from Germany in the postwar period, when the United States would once again be able to turn its attention to Mexico. The American consul in Mazatlán stated this quite clearly and succinctly:

That the Mexican government and...the Mexican people are disposed to hazard a lively friendship with the Germans there can be no doubt.... This sentiment I believe to be materially fostered by the disposition on the part of the Mexican people ever since the Mexican War to refuse to look upon the United States as a friend, but rather considering our country as a permanent enemy, and upon their desire to seek the friendship...of some powerful European country other than England or France, in order that Mexico may not stand alone in international matters upon which she may hold a view different from that of the United States. This inclination towards friendship with Germany seems to have arisen since the outbreak of the European War and to have been due largely to the admiration the Mexican people...have for the power of German arms on land and under the sea.

Carranza was probably also hoping for financial aid, as a result of countless German promises. "We are moving forward," he told Eckardt, "but there are still great difficulties to overcome. We will continue fighting until, as I hope, we receive aid from Germany."[18]

Carranza's second long-term goal shows that he had certain illusions about the character of German imperialism. He was hoping to industrialize Mexico with German aid. He was already expressing such wishes in a memorandum of November 1916. The military-commercial section of the German embassy in Bern reported similar hopes on the part of the Mexicans. "The United States, in their view, is exploiting the country, taking money but giving none in return in order to keep the country under its control. Mexico is therefore looking for other trading partners to break free of the United States."[19] As late as 1919, Carranza told Jahnke of his hope that Germany would industrialize Mexico.

Carranza's pro-German policy was aimed at thwarting German sabotage action, at maintaining the loyalty of his generals, and at frightening the Allies. He also hoped to receive German aid if the United States carried out armed intervention.

Carranza may also have hoped that he would be able to exploit America's fears of a deeper German involvement in Mexico and force the Americans to give him a loan without demanding as a condition that he repudiate the 1917 constitution or Mexican neutrality. Repeated negotiations for such a loan were conducted by Mexico and the United States in 1917–18.

To the extent that Carranza's own guidelines were sometimes transgressed in those negotiations, this was done without his knowledge or against his will.

In 1917–18, none of the plans that the German military leadership, English governmental circles, or American companies developed for the Mexican situation were ever realized. German agents carried out no sabotage action in the oil fields. Carranza's opponents never received any of the serious aid or official recognition from the Allies they would have needed to become a serious threat to the Mexican government. Nor, finally, did any foreign military intervention occur in Mexico. To what extent can this "moderation" on the part of the great powers be attributed to Carranza's foreign policy? What actual effect did the pro-German attitude of the Mexican president during the First World War have on the policies of the great powers with interests in Mexico?

From the American viewpoint, it was Carranza's domestic and economic policies, and his orientation toward American companies, oil companies in particular, which were decisive. Carranza's sympathies for Germany were never taken seriously in Washington and had only limited effect on Wilson's Mexican policy.

The attitude of the European powers was quite different. England's plans for a coup were primarily a response to Carranza's collaboration with Germany and the British military leadership's resulting fear of a German-Mexican attack on the United States. The English plans, however, had no impact, for the United States was not willing to participate in them.

In reality, Carranza's pro-German orientation had its most important effect on Germany's Mexico policies. As a result of Carranza's attitude, the German government decided to forego the one effective form of action—major sabotage operations in the oil fields—which was open to it. A threat to the Allied oil supply might have been the one basis on which Wilson would have considered intervention in Mexico during the world war. By countering the sabotage plans of the German military leadership with limited concessions, Carranza may actually have prevented foreign intervention in Mexico.

To what extent did Carranza accommodate the Germans in order to achieve his goals? Two documents provide extensive information on this question. One is a confidential memorandum of Polk, the State Department adviser in charge of Mexico, to Lansing, written in June 1918. Polk stated that Carranza had adopted a clear pro-German stance, which was expressed in the following measures:

1. Material aid from Germany in the form of money, officers to educate the army, radio equipment, etc.;
2. Fabela's official trip, ostensibly to Argentina, but in reality to Germany by way of Spain;
3. Repression against pro-Allied newspapers and support for anti-Allied newspapers such as El Demócrata, for which paper was even purchased in Japan;
4. Toleration of the use of Mexico as a base of operations for espionage by Germany;
5. Breakoff of relations with Cuba.[20]

Of these five points, the first two must be corrected or restricted to the extent that German financial aid for Carranza never materialized, and insofar as there is no proof for the allegations about Fabela. Aside from these problems, Polk's memorandum is quite similar to Eckardt's final report to the Reichskanzler of 7 August. After stating "that the portrait of our kaiser decorates Carranza's office and the president follows the movements of the German army with the closest attention, seeing in every victory a confirmation of his own policies," Eckardt cited almost the same points: loan negotiations with Carranza; wireless connection to Nauen; preparation for U-boats. He also mentioned "that the president receives almost daily written reports which I gather through official or other channels from various parts of the country . . . on the domestic situation," and added that Carranza was being kept abreast of espionage activity directed against him by the Allies. Fabela's trip was also mentioned here; Eckardt's information on this question, however, cannot be substantiated, as we have already pointed out. Eckardt also praised Secretary of the Interior Aguirre Berlanga for deporting Felix Palavicini, the editor of the pro-Allied newspaper *El Universal*.[21]

Both reports therefore converged on the central points. With two exceptions, Carranza's actions did not constitute a threat to Mexico's sovereignty, nor did they pose any serious possibility of American intervention. The two exceptions were the granting of a U-boat base for Germany and toleration of the activities of the German secret services. The U-boat base could easily have led to American intervention. All evidence indicates, however, that Carranza either knew nothing of such an offer or that the support station was built against his will.

The problem posed by the activities of the German secret service were somewhat different. Carranza knew both Delmar and Jahnke and received regular reports from them on the activities of the Americans. He obviously had hopes of using these agencies for his own ends. He had made it quite clear that he opposed both sabotage activity in Tampico and border attacks launched from his territory. The German secret services, however, did not limit their activities to preparing reports for the Mexican government. Saboteurs were sent into the United States from Mexico, and in Sonora Delmar prepared an attack on the United States. Either of these developments could have triggered American intervention. The secret services became even more involved in Mexican internal politics with the generals' plot. One gets the impression that the German apparatus in Mexico to some extent overwhelmed Carranza and that some actions were taken by Mexican authorities without his consent.

There appeared to be no unanimity within the Mexican government or army leadership on what stance to adopt toward Germany. The supporters of the Allies advocated a break with Germany and in some cases even an active intervention in the world war on the side of the Allies. The most prominent member of this group was General Pablo González, commander of the troops fighting against Zapata and member of the French circle in Mexico which in October 1917 wanted Mexico to break off diplomatic relations with Germany.[22] This group also included the governor of Coahuila and members of the Mexican senate. Thirteen senators, including Alonso, Reynoso, and Cepeda, introduced a resolution at a secret meeting of the senate on 20 October calling for a break in diplomatic relations with Germany. In the vote, which took place on 18 December, the resolution was voted down, 35–13.[23]

This group was opposed by an extreme pro-German wing. Among the most enthusiastic supporters of imperial Germany, Eckardt included Mario Mendez, the minister of communications, Breceda, the chief of police of the Federal District, and Aguirre Berlanda, the minister of the interior, whom Eckardt, albeit with a trace of mistrust, praised highly; in addition to these men, he also included generals Calles, Dieguez, Murguía, and, probably incorrectly, Obregón.[24]

Between these groups, there was a center consisting of Aguilar, Carranza, and probably Obregón. Before America entered the war, Obregón had spoken of Germany in very positive terms to Eckardt. After the disclosure of the Zimmermann note, he immediately told the Americans that such a proposal was unthinkable. In 1917 he traveled to the United States on business. "Through a special envoy," wrote Eckardt, "he told me I should not be led astray if he were enthusiastically received by the 'gringos'; he would always be on our side." Obregón's journey was an occasion for one of Eckardt's numerous chauvinist utterances about the Mexican people: "One can say as a general rule that 'A Mexican may not be able to bear the Yankee, but he is always happy to take his dollar.' "[25]

In the United States, Obregón made an unambiguous anti-German declaration. In a conversation with the American correspondent of a French newspaper, the general stated:

1. Mexico cannot survive without the grain shipments and finished goods of the United States. The United States, however, makes its shipments contingent on the political stance of the neutral countries toward the powers of the Allies.
2. Mexico must float a bond to pay compensation for damages incurred during the last revolution.
3. The United States is becoming a strong military power, and there is reason to fear that after the war, its officers will be reluctant to lay down the sword....
4. We love France, and England rules the seas.[26]

Obregón's statements show that he was skillfully exploiting the great powers' contradictions without taking one side or the other.

What was at stake in the struggle between this center group and the extreme pro-German elements in the Mexican government and army was not the desire to collaborate with Germany, but the limits of such cooperation. For Carranza, Aguilar, and Obregón, the limits were fixed at the point where American intervention became a danger. Both Mario Mendez—as it became apparent over the U-boat question—and, judging from Delmar's remarks, Calles were apparently willing to exceed these limits.

One must ask to what extent Carranza was aware of the dangers which the activities of the German representatives in Mexico might pose for him. Did he perceive only the danger of being pulled into a war with the United States? Or was he also aware of the danger of opening the door to a new imperialist power no less ruthless than the United States?

Neither the archives of the Mexican foreign ministry nor the memoirs of politicians close to Carranza contain any material which sheds further light on these questions. Mexico's foreign and interior ministries' different views on the relationship between propaganda and neutrality indicate that objections were raised at certain points to pro-German moves.

Something more than this can be gleaned from German and Austrian archives: the dismissal of Krumm Heller shows that attempts were made to keep excessively pro-German elements out of the Mexican diplomatic service. One conversation between Schwabach, representative of the Bankhaus Bleichröder, and Ortiz, the Mexican minister in Berlin, clearly shows that the Mexican government did not completely trust Germany. Ortiz had asked if Germany would provide Mexico with a loan after the war. "We have always had people," Schwabach reported, "who were fundamentally opposed to foreign loans . . . . The position of a government wishing to loan money to Mexico would be greatly strengthened for future discussions in parliament or in the press if Mexico granted us some important economic advantages, such as oil concessions. Mr. Ortiz thought it would be difficult to obtain such concessions and had reason to believe that the recent negotiations between Mexico and the United States had collapsed over similar demands by America."[27] Pablo González's endorsement of the Allies was clearly no accident, for he was closer to Carranza than any other military leader. His stance was not only intended to emphasize Mexico's neutrality to the outside world; it was in all likelihood conceived as a counterweight to the influence of the pro-German generals in domestic politics.

The reports of Kania, the Austrian minister to Mexico, are far more sanguine about Carranza's pro-German sympathies than those of Eckardt; this was due to some extent to Eckardt's desire to exaggerate his successes to Berlin. "President up to now committed to preservation of neutrality, as armed forces would otherwise abandon him,"[28] Kania wired to Vienna on 17 July. Nine days later, he reported that "Mexican government's fluctuating opinion on outcome of war is for the moment causing it to keep Germany at arms length."[29]

One gets the impression that Carranza was clearly keeping his distance from German plans and provocations which might lead to a Mexican-American war. He undoubtedly underestimated the dangers German imperialism could have posed for Mexico, but he was not blind to them. Carranza had set clear and firm limits to German activity in Mexico. The occasional violation of these limits occurred either without his knowledge or against his will. In conclusion, it can be said that the Mexican government, which the major powers viewed solely as a malleable instrument for their own policies, had succeeded in turning the tables and in exploiting their rivalry for its own ends. Neither the American, nor the British, nor the German plans came to fruition. Carranza, however, was able to obtain American withdrawal, German abstention from sabotage activity, and, finally, neutrality for his own country.

**Part 5**                    **Epilogue**

# 13 Carranza and the Great Powers, 1919–20

"We will continue fighting until, as I hope, we receive aid from Germany,"[1] Carranza had told the German minister in Mexico in 1917. He had obviously hoped that after the end of the First World War a victorious or at least undefeated Germany would give him the means to break the American economic blockade and to defeat his domestic enemies. When the war ended in November 1918 with Germany's defeat, his hopes were shattered. He now faced an immeasurably greater external threat than ever before, accompanied by a strong resurgence of domestic opposition.

The United States emerged from the First World War as the strongest power in the world, both in economic and military terms. Instead of the small U.S. regular army Carranza had faced in 1916, he now found his country threatened by a huge American force of several million men. In economic terms during the war, the United States had replaced the European powers as the most important investor and trading partner of most Latin American countries. Mexico was no exception to this trend and during the war, in spite of all Mexican efforts to the contrary, the United States had succeeded in gaining an economic preponderance it had never enjoyed before. While European investments in Mexico sharply declined during the most violent phases of the Mexican revolution, U.S. investments continued to increase.[2]

In bitterly worded descriptions European diplomats in Mexico showed how U.S. corporations in conjunction with the American government had succeeded in weakening European economic power in Mexico:

The Americans made use of censorship to carry on economic espionage to put pressure not merely on German companies, but also on English and French ones. On 13 August 1919, the German minister to Mexico wrote:

In the same way that the English censorship used surveillance of mail to conduct widespread commercial sabotage during the first years of the war, the American censorship is now doing the same thing. A whole series of cases have come to light in which business offers or orders arrived at their destinations after months of delay, and where the sample materials enclosed in these letters had simply been confiscated. Here again, the Americans were only applying the English model of using espionage not only against the companies of enemy countries, but against the companies of neutral powers and their own allies as well. The English and French business communities complained bitterly when they learned that their rivalries were being exploited by the American firms and their price bids being undercut.

In Mexico, the American attempt to monopolize the import and export trade was directed not only against the blacklisted firms, which included all German, many Mexican, certain Spanish, and even some French companies, but simply against all non-American businessmen, meaning the British, French, and Japanese in general. Commercial espionage was carried on quite openly by the American consulates, which maintained a network of paid informants for this purpose, and by the newly founded "Chambers of Commerce," which were intimately linked to political propaganda activities.[3]

Through financial manipulations, American companies were able to create a situation at various firms in Mexico where the capital stock was in Europe, while the debt, which was secured by mortgages, was held in the United States. As early as 25 December 1915, Eckardt had reported from Mexico:

> The author of a confidential report I have received, a German-Swiss well informed on economic questions, claims that even the Mexico Tramway Company, the Light and Power Company, and the National Railways of Mexico, which were all created with foreign capital, will be easy prey for the capitalists of Wall Street... Their [the American bankers'] methods for a systematic implementation of this plan are illustrated by two examples among many parallel cases: the experiences of the Mexican Tramway Company, of the Mexican Power Company, and further along, the experience of the Mexican railways. In these cases, according to the balance sheets available to my informant, both the capital stock sold abroad and that belonging to the Mexican government has been lost, primarily as a result of the revolution, but the factories will apparently pass into the hands of the debt holders, who are American bankers and private investors. With the use of substantial new credits, they will proceed to create profitable companies under American control. My informant makes it clear that this is the result desired by the American financiers.[4]

As a result of the constant struggles in Mexico, many middle-level Mexican and European companies had found it preferable to sell their assets, which were acquired by Americans.

The balance of power had also shifted in the area of oil, even if the change was not as dramatic as it was in other areas. The Pearson company's share of Mexican oil production had declined. Several times during the course of the war, Pearson had conducted negotiations with Standard Oil for the sale of his oil company; one cannot rule out the possibility that the temporary suspension of his supplier's contract with the British Admiralty played a role in these efforts. In February 1917, when everything had been prepared for Standard Oil's absorption of the Pearson company, the British government vetoed the sale. In October 1918, Pearson began negotiations with Royal Dutch Shell, the large Anglo-Dutch oil company, which acquired Pearson's interests in the spring of 1919.[5] Although the El Aguila company, now under new control, was weaker than the American oil companies, it nevertheless remained the strongest British company in Mexico.

At the beginning of 1919 American and European bankers, spurred on by the hope that Carranza's deteriorating domestic and international situation would force him to accept their proposals, suggested an agreement that would in effect have neutralized the 1917 constitution, allowed U.S. interests unrestricted access to Mexico's natural resources, settled the Mexican debt on conditions favorable to foreign interests, and restricted Mexico's sovereignty. The bankers' proposals were submitted to Mexico's acting minister of finance Rafael Nieto in March 1919. The Mexican debt was to be refinanced into a single comprehensive issue and the indebtedness of the National Railways was also to be settled. To do this Mexico was to receive a large loan and in return to submit to a series of restrictions on its sovereignty. The customs revenues were to be pledged as security under some form of international supervision, a new federal bank with an international directorate would be set up, and a treaty of amity and commerce which would ''provide a satisfactory basis for the operation of business enterprises in Mexico by the nationals of the countries'' would be signed.

Carranza had shown several times that he was open to compromise as far as the application of the constitution of 1917, which he had never fully endorsed, was concerned. But he had throughout his career refused to accept any limitation of Mexico's sovereignty and he refused to do so again in 1919, thus rejecting the proposed agreement.[6]

From this point on the campaign and demands for military intervention in Mexico grew by leaps and bounds in the United States. Two organizations in the United States spearheaded these demands. They were the National Association for the Protection of American Rights in Mexico and the Organization of Oil Producers in Mexico. The former included the representatives of almost all companies that had invested capital in Mexico; the latter was a group within the first organization, chaired by E. L. Doheny and bringing together all oil companies in Mexico. Both of these organizations launched a major press and propaganda campaign which culminated in a call for military intervention in Mexico.[7]

The Organization of Oil Producers in Mexico sent a delegation, headed by Doheny, to the peace negotiations in Paris. On 1 February 1919, the German ambassador in The Hague reported: ''Representatives of the English and American oil companies want to travel to France to urge the peace conference to adopt a specific position on English and American mining rights in Mexico. . . . It can hardly be surprising that the American financiers, who have been pushing for intervention in Mexico for years, are now attempting to utilize the current hegemonic position of the United States once again to promote serious action against their southern neighbor.''[8] Doheny himself described the objectives of his trip as follows: ''We merely go to ask a big question. We have hopes that the Peace Conference may see fit to answer it: How far may new governments go in ignoring or confiscating the vested rights of foreign inhabitants and of foreigners in the lands where the new governments are established.''[9]

Nothing was initially known about the results of the delegation's visit. Professor Starr, of the University of Chicago, wrote in the *Los Angeles Times:* ''War with Mexico was planned and fixed up at the peace conference in Paris. Of this I am positive.''[10] Secretary of State Lansing, however, asserted that the peace conference did not deal with this question at all.[11] An influential member of the Republican party outlined what may actually have been decided in a conversation with the head of the German secret service in Mexico: ''The peace conference agreed that the current situation in Mexico could not remain as it was much longer, and either an understanding must be reached between the United States and Mexico, or other means will be used, such as the violent overthrow of Carranza through blockade, intervention, or war.''[12]

Whatever the peace conference may have decided, interventionists in the United States felt that, with or without international sanctions, they should proceed with their plans concerning Mexico.

In the Senate these efforts were spearheaded by Senator Albert B. Fall from New Mexico, who maintained close relations to oil interests. He set up a subcommittee to investigate Mexican affairs in order to mobilize public opinion for intervention and to exert pressure on Wilson to that effect. To this end, numerous Americans living in Mexico were summoned to testify and were urged to recount their sufferings and losses at the hands of Mexican revolutionaries.[13]

An important role was played in this inquiry by Doheny, who called for energetic measures in the name of ''the United States' national interests'' in Mexican oil. He stated: ''The future welfare and prosperity of the United States, both during and after the present great world war, may be said to be largely dependent upon or at least affected by the uninterrupted operation and control of the oil fields in Mexico now owned by American companies. . . . Without this legitimately acquired supply, and with the certainty that the other great oil pools of the world are or will be placed at the service of the other great commercial powers, the hope for an American ocean transportation system which will serve the purposes of this country in its extension of trade and influence over the seven seas cannot be realized."[14]

"Traditional" interventionists such as Fall found increasing support among administration members, especially Lansing, Polk, and Fletcher, who had been adamantly opposed to military intervention in Mexico as long as World War I lasted;[15] military men, such as Leonard Wood, hoped that U.S. intervention in Mexico might postpone the demobilization of U.S. armed forces.

The end of World War I not only led to increased foreign pressure but also to increased domestic pressure on the Carranza government. He had kept his domestic foes at bay but had not succeeded in defeating them and as the world war ended and the specter of American intervention loomed on the horizon they increased their efforts to topple the Mexican president. Their movements were fueled by increasing popular dissatisfaction with Carranza's domestic policies. In 1918/19 food production was only 65 percent of what it had been in 1910.[16] There was widespread hunger which was compounded by the corruption of Carranzist officials who cornered large amounts of food and exported it or sold it at inflated prices.

Carranza had been unable to reestablish peace and large parts of the country were ravaged by warring factions. Above all, as Zapata bitterly stated in an open letter to Carranza, the reforms the president had promised had not been carried out. Zapata declared "that the land has not been returned to the villages and that, as a result, most of them remain landless. No land is being distributed to the working population, the truly poor and needy peasants." Zapata's condemnation of the dissolution of the trade unions, and of the control exercised over them by the government, was no less harsh. He accused Carranza of having destroyed the democratic freedoms that he had previously proclaimed. "Give the people their freedom, give up your dictatorial power, let youth take the helm!"[17] Zapata's intensified efforts to fight Carranza were matched by similar efforts from Villa. In the latter part of 1918, the Villa movement was on the upswing again. In Chihuahua Carranza's conservative policies had produced profound disillusionment. Up to 1919 no land at all had been given to the peasantry of Chihuahua. In fact no agrarian commission was operating in the state.

A profound split had developed between the military commanders of the state and the Carranzist civilian authorities who controlled the Defensas Sociales, the home guard. As a result some of these units had been disarmed, and others were attacked by government troops. Convinced that Carranza would be unable to restore peace to the state, carry out any kind of reform, or stabilize the situation there, many of its inhabitants again turned to Villa. The latter had acquired new respectability in their eyes when in December 1918 his old companion in arms, Felipe Ángeles, returned from exile in the United States to rejoin him. Ángeles offered Villa the support of a powerful group of Mexican exiles in the United States, the Alianza Liberal Mexicana, which comprised both revolutionaries and conservatives.[18]

Ángeles also hoped that he would be able to carry out some kind of reconciliation between Villa and the United States, which, though it might not lead to American support, would at least bring about American neutrality toward Villa.

In all his speeches Ángeles emphasized the need for friendship between Mexico and the United States.

An even more serious situation for Carranza was created by the fact that for the first time the movements opposed to him were seriously considering the possibility of coordinating and even uniting their efforts against the Mexican president.

Such unity had seemed inconceivable for a long time. The gap separating conservatives such as Felix Díaz and Pelaez from radicals such as Villa and Zapata was greater than the gap separating each of them from Carranza. Nevertheless, by 1919 these forces were attempting to reach some kind of agreement. On the one hand the negotiations were based on the conviction that only if they all combined their forces would they be able to topple Carranza and to prevent intervention by the United States. On the other hand, regionalism presented a basis of agreement for these movements. None of the revolutionary factions opposed to Carranza had been able to gather a national constituency after 1915. The Zapata movement was essentially restricted to Morelos and some adjacent regions. Villa's influence did not extend beyond the confines of Chihuahua and Durango, Felix Díaz's troops limited their operations essentially to Veracruz, Oaxaca, and Chiapas while Pelaez only operated in the oil region. A solution giving each faction control of its own territory with a "neutral" president with limited powers, acceptable to all of them and to the United States seemed a viable compromise to most of the factions.

Both Zapata and Pelaez considered Francisco Madero's former running mate in the presidential election of 1910, Francisco Vázquez Gómez, as an acceptable candidate.[19] Felipe Ángeles thought that he himself would be an ideal candidate for such a compromise function. He was highly regarded by both Villa and many former officers of the old federal army fighting in the ranks of Felix Díaz. Of all of Carranza's opponents he seemed to be the one most acceptable to the Americans. In 1915 Wilson had seriously considered supporting him as candidate for the Mexican presidency, but there was no evidence of similar support in 1918/19.

An opposition which was far more dangerous to Carranza than that of his traditional foes was a movement developing within his own ranks. In June 1919 Alvaro Obregón announced that he would be a candidate to succeed Carranza as president in the election of 1920. Obregón's presidential bid found strong support among the military, part of the new bourgeoisie (essentially from Sonora) which had emerged as a result of the revolution and among most of the radicals within the Carranza movement. Carranza was strongly opposed to Obregón's candidacy, but he had no intention of violating the constitution and of succeeding himself as president. Instead he initiated and supported the candidacy of an associate, Ignacio Bonillas, who was Mexico's ambassador to the United States. Carranza expected that when Bonillas, who was scarely known in Mexico and had no constituency in the country, became president, he would depend so strongly on Carranza's support that the latter would continue to wield power in Mexico.

By mid-1919 Carranza had three formidable opponents to contend with: the United States, his traditional domestic enemies, and Obregón and his supporters. In order to preclude such a three-front war, some of Carranza's supporters urged him to make peace with one of his foes. They were not thinking of Villa or Zapata but of either the Americans or Obregón. Carranza thought in different terms. He was not ready to make any compromises with his domestic foes. Nor was he prepared to accept any American terms that would have endangered Mexico's sovereignty. But he did hope to prevent American intervention and perhaps come to some arrangement with the Americans on his own terms.

First, he tried to convince the Americans, as well as Mexico's traditional upper classes, that he represented the only viable alternative to both anarchy and radicalism. In line with this policy he intensified his campaign against both Zapata and Villa and in April 1919 scored his first significant success. At the beginning of 1919 Pablo González commissioned one of his subordinates, Jesus Guajardo, to kill Zapata. Guajardo thereupon "deserted" to Zapata with his entire unit and asked to be taken into his army. Such a development represented welcome reinforcements for Zapata, who desperately needed soldiers and, above all, arms. Nonetheless, he was skeptical, and he ordered Guajardo to attack a Carranzist garrison to prove his revolutionary commitment. Guajardo provided his "proof." He not only carried out the attack, but even executed the Carranzist soldiers he captured. After that, Zapata felt he could trust Guajardo and agreed to a meeting at the Chinameca hacienda. On 10 April 1919 he proceeded there with several companions. Guajardo received him with an honor guard standing at attention. When Zapata approached, a "salute of honor" was fired and Zapata was killed instantly. For this murder, Guajardo received a large reward from González. Even though they were badly weakened by the death of their leader, the Zapatistas continued to fight.[20]

This "success" on the southern front was matched by another success in the North. Felipe Ángeles fell into the hands of Carranza's troops after his escort had betrayed him. After a military trial he was sentenced to death and shot on 26 November 1919. In spite of demands from many quarters that he commute Ángeles's sentence, Carranza refused to do so.

This hard-line domestic policy of the Mexican president seemed to strengthen his regime to some degree. Zapata's assassination weakened the Zapatista movement though it did not destroy it. The killing of Ángeles constituted a serious blow to the hopes of Mexican exiles in the United States to set up a broad coalition of anti-Carranza factions in Mexico.

These policies were linked to Carranza's attempts to rally the country's upper classes to his banner more than he ever had before. Some of the most controversial cases, involving the return of estates to their former owners, were decided in the latter's favor in 1919. Above all, Carranza now attempted to take a step he had hesitated to take earlier: namely, to carry out a policy of reconciliation not only with the mass of hacendados but with the leading members of the Científico oligarchy. Just as Porfirio Díaz had in 1903, Carranza now hoped to strengthen his regime by granting widespread concessions to Mexico's wealthiest landowner, a man who for many Mexicans had come to epitomize the term *hacendado*, Chihuahua's former ruler and governor, Luis Terrazas. In 1917, the Mexican president had ordered that the Terrazas's properties not be returned to their former owners but placed under state supervision.[21] He obviously felt that opposition to the former governor and to his own regime in the state was so strong that a return of Terrazas could seriously jeopardize his position.

Ever since Carranza's victory over Villa, Luis Terrazas had indicated that he wished to make his peace with the victorious constitutionalists and would be willing to throw his support to them if they returned his properties to him. In August 1918, he obviously felt that the time had come to make an open bid for Carranza's support. That month he wrote a long letter to the Mexican government in which he called for the return of his expropriated holdings and attempted to refute all the charges which, in the long course of the Mexican Revolution, revolutionaries of very different persuasions had leveled against him.[22] His large holdings, he insisted, had not been obtained by despoiling peasants and poor people of their lands but by buying estates from wealthy landowners at a time when their value was minimal because of repeated Apache raids and lack of communications and railways in the state. His fortune, he wrote, was essentially the result of the increase in value of these properties once the Apaches were defeated, railways had been built, and economic conditions generally began to improve. Terrazas gave a lengthy description of those aspects of his political activities in which he had cooperated with Benito Juárez in fighting the conservatives and the French and he insisted on the fact that he had fought against Porfirio Díaz in the latter's attempts to seize power in 1872 and 1876. But the Chihuahuan leader only briefly glossed over the periods during the Porfirian era, when he had been governor of the state. He insisted on the fact that after the revolution had broken out in 1910, he never took any active role in fighting it and as a matter of fact had completely withdrawn from politics in that period. He claimed that he was essentially a victim of Pancho Villa, who had expropriated his properties and imprisoned his son Luis for two years and that the latter, after coming to the United States, died as a result of the suffering which he endured during his imprisonment. The proceeds from his estates, Terrazas insisted, had contributed to the military victory of the Division of the North and later of the Carranza forces in the state. "From all I have shown it can be clearly concluded that I have always fulfilled my duty as a citizen and as a public official by supporting the general constitution of the country as well as its autonomy and its legitimate government; in the last years of my life I have had nothing to do with politics and for that reason there is absolutely no motive for which I have been prevented for so long from taking control of my legitimately acquired properties and for that reason I ask and request that the confiscation of my properties in the state of Chihuahua be ended and that all of them be returned."

Carranza submitted Luis Terrazas's letter to state governor Andres Ortíz for consideration. In the reply Ortíz sent to Carranza he proceeded to refute each of Terrazas's arguments.[23] He sharply attacked the latter's contention that his vast empire had been acquired solely by sales of rich landowners and not at anyone's expense. "In the majority of cases," Ortíz stated, the Terrazas's haciendas had been acquired from a "surveying company that obtained these lands by surveying the lands of the state. The state then gave them great amounts of land which in many cases had belonged to owners who through negligence or ignorance did not have their titles in order and many others did have them in order but they were not respected by the authorities." Ortíz stressed the fact that during the Porfirian period Terrazas's main aim was "the absolute control of the government of the state for the protection and broadening of his interests for which purpose he never hesitated to use proceedings well known in the Porfirian period. He did not limit himself to this but the tax laws of the state were protectionist laws for the Terrazas interest." Ortíz stated that these properties were systematically undervalued so that their tax bracket would be extremely low.

Ortíz sharply refuted the former governor's contention that since the beginning of the revolution he had not intervened in politics. Ortíz insisted that the family had acted as a whole and that the elder Luis Terrazas remained in the background letting his sons carry the brunt of political activities. Thus after the revolution broke out in 1910, Luis's son Alberto organized a corps of a thousand men to fight the revolution while his brother Juan proceeded in other parts of the state to levy forces of a similar size.

After Orozco rebelled in 1912, the Orozco movement proceeded to levy a voluntary loan of 1,200,000 pesos; "a large amount of the bonds were taken over by the Terrazas family to the amount of $500,000 (as well as by local banks which the family controlled almost totally)." After Huerta's victory, he enjoyed the full support of the Terrazas family. Luis's son Alberto organized a new corps of volunteers which until 1914 fought for the Huerta government. In 1914 the Banco Minero, which was controlled by the Terrazas interests, issued special bonds to finance the Huerta government.

"In the period between 1910 and 1915 Luis Terrazas the elder essentially worked through his sons, thus succeeding in apparently remaining aloof from public affairs."

Ortíz discussed the huge size of the holdings, stating that Terrazas controlled about a tenth of the lands in the state of Chihuahua and, above all, its richest and most valuable agricultural land. He stressed that a return of these lands to their former owner would have a tremendous impact on the state. Perhaps because he knew the opinions of his chief, Governor Ortíz did not rule out the possible return of the Terrazas estates to their former owner, but he insisted that if this were done the state should at least obtain some guarantees, such as the right to buy them any time at their tax assessed price.

Neither the objections nor the suggestions of the governor had any influence on Carranza and in March 1919 he decided to make a major overture to the Terrazas clan. In that month, he decreed the return of the properties of a number of Terrazas's sons and relatives and the return of all nonagricultural properties to Luis Terrazas the elder.[24] The haciendas were at first excluded from this settlement. Perhaps before returning all his properties to the northern caudillo, Carranza hoped for some tangible sign of his support. Carranza may even have hoped that Terrazas would persuade his American lawyer, New Mexico's Senator Albert Fall, who was leading the campaign in the U.S. Senate for intervention in Mexico to moderate his policies. If so, he was mistaken for Fall continued his interventionist policies at full scale. Nevertheless, Carranza, in what was perhaps the last important measure of a social nature he took before being forced out of office, completed what he had begun one year before. After a lengthy interview with Carlos Cuilty, Terrazas's lawyer, Carranza, in May 1920, decreed the unconditional return of all of Terrazas's properties.[25] He had obviously now come full circle and had decided to make his final peace with Mexico's traditional oligarchy. If with this measure he had hoped to stave off disaster and prevent his overthrow, he was bound to be disappointed. When the Sonoran military revolted against him, the hacendados made no move to help the man who had brought them back from exile and returned their holdings to them. For Terrazas, Carranza's overthrow was to have profound effects. The new government did not ratify the measures Carranza had taken and which he had not yet had time to implement.[26]

In Washington Carranza's conservative policies and his harsh measures against his domestic foes brought about favorable reactions. In April 1919 Frank Polk congratulated Carranza's General Jacinto Treviño for the killing of Zapata and expressed the hope that Villa would be next. In May 1919 the State Department asked the governors of Texas, Arizona, and New Mexico to permit the Mexican army to cross their states in pursuit of Villistas.[27]

In June 1919 Villa and Ángeles staged an attack on Ciudad Juárez. By capturing this Mexican border city, they probably hoped to reestablish some kind of modus vivendi with the Americans, such as had existed before 1915. Whatever hopes the two Mexican leaders may have entertained for American neutrality were shattered when U.S. troops crossed the border and (without either permission or sanction from the Carranza government) expelled Villa's troops from Ciudad Juárez.

A clear expression of the success of Carranza's domestic policies was the testimony Frank Polk gave around that time to the Senate Foreign Relations Committee. He made it clear that the United States would refuse to cooperate with Carranza's traditional foes. He stated that the United States had a choice between Carranza and intervention since one opposition leader was "dissolute" (Felix Díaz) and another was a "ruffian" (Villa).[28]

Carranza's strategy to blunt the edges of American opposition to his regime was by no means limited to his domestic policies. He did everything he could to encourage anti-interventionism in the United States and to recreate some kind of cooperation if not alliance with the great European powers against American supremacy in Mexico.

In the United States Carranza not only vied for the support of groups traditionally opposed to interventionism, labor, progressives, liberals, and protestants, but also attempted to find support among some business groups. His attitude toward mining interests was so conciliatory that representatives of the latter did not testify at the Fall Committee Hearings and refused to participate in the U.S. campaign for intervention in Mexico. With less success Carranza also attempted to gain backing among smaller oil companies to offset the influence of the largest petroleum producers.

Carranza's efforts to gain British and French support against the United

States were in many respects similar to Porfirian policies. Like Díaz before him, Carranza believed that the best way to achieve this aim was to grant significant concessions to British and French companies. In some respects such a policy seemed to offer even more possibilities of success in 1919 than it did before 1910. Mexican oil production had increased dramatically between 1910 and 1919 so that Mexico was now considered one of the world's most important oil-exporting countries. The war had enormously expanded the strategic importance of oil. The Russian Revolution, which had led to the expropriation and nationalization of oil production, had constituted a particularly sharp blow for the British and French companies with very heavy investments in Russian petroleum. It was not unreasonable for Carranza to assume that they would try to compensate for their losses in Russia by expanding their holdings in Mexico.

Carranza first attempted to conciliate Britain. In 1919 confiscated British property was returned to its former owners and Carranza gave preference to British oil companies over their American counterparts.[29]

When the British did not respond to Carranza's overtures, he turned to France. On 17 March 1920, Mexico's Minister Pani gave the French government a memorandum[30] in many ways reminiscent of the one the Mexican government had given the German government four years earlier. The memorandum began with an affirmation of the Mexican people's sympathies for the French. This was followed by a warning that France was on the verge of losing its economic position in Mexico to the United States. The memorandum stated "that Mexican petroleum could be of use to French industry" and offered oil concessions to France. The French government not only refused to consider these proposals, but even attempted, at the behest of the United States, to persuade Carranza to accede to the American demands.

The reasons for Great Britain's and France's refusal to resume the traditional policies they followed during the Porfirian era are varied. In part they simply reflected the fact that at that time they felt too weak to challenge the newly developed power of the United States in a country many considered as its "home ground."

They probably felt that Wilson's arrangement to have European bankers constitute 50 percent of an international banker's committee to supervise Mexico's finances, thus giving them a veto power to prevent further U.S. encroachment on their interests in Mexico, was a better way of protecting their interests than an alliance with Carranza. They did not trust the Mexican president and did not regard him as a serious potential ally capable of restoring order to Mexico.

Perhaps some Europeans were also seeing the Monroe Doctrine in a new and more favorable light. Until the outbreak of the First World War they had only taken the first part of the doctrine, which demanded European nonintervention in American affairs, into consideration. After the end of the war, when the United States was interfering in European affairs on a massive scale, the second part of the doctrine, which pledged U.S. nonintervention in Europe, gained new relevance. Many Europeans were now disposed to recognize U.S. supremacy on the American continent in return for American noninterference in Europe.

In the first months of 1920 Carranza could point to impressive successes on two of the three fronts where he was fighting. He had decimated his traditional foes and prevented them from unifying against him. In spite of the intense and vociferous activities of interventionist groups in the U.S., no intervention had taken place. It is doubtful, however, that Carranza's political activities in 1919/20 had been very important in bringing about this turn of events. His conservative domestic policies had gained him some sympathies in the State Department by mid-1919.

This sympathy disappeared very rapidly once Carranza attempted to impose new controls on the oil companies and Lansing, Polk, and Fletcher rejoined the interventionist camp. It was Woodrow Wilson's opposition that prevented U.S. intervention in Mexico.[31] Such intervention might have weakened Wilson's efforts to have the United States join the League of Nations and play a larger role overseas. Above all, Wilson did not consider Carranza a dangerous radical. Carranza's conservative policies in 1919/20 may have strengthened Wilson's convictions in this respect but he needed no supplementary proof to show him that Carranza was no Lenin, threatening the free enterprise system, which Wilson considered the foundation of western civilization.

As the end of his term of office approached, Wilson was even more reticent about getting involved in Mexico. "If there is war, let the Republicans wage it," he told his secretary.[32]

It was the third group Carranza was fighting, his former allies led by Obregón, which brought about his undoing. As the electoral campaign progressed, Obregón and his supporters became the objects of increasing harrassment by the Carranza authorities. In the first months of 1920 the Mexican president attempted to deal his foe a decisive blow by undercutting his power in his native state of Sonora. Carranza decided to send federal troops to occupy the state. At that point the governor, Adolfo de la Huerta, a supporter of Obregón's presidential bid, rebelled against Carranza. On 23 April 1920 the rebels issued the plan of Agua Prieta, which accused Carranza of having betrayed the revolution, called for his removal from office, and named Adolfo de la Huerta provisional president of the country. After the overwhelming majority of the revolutionary army had joined the movement, Carranza attempted to flee from Mexico City to Veracruz with his government. Attacks by rebels on the presidential train led him to flee into the mountains in the Puebla region. Rebels caught up with him and his party in the remote village of San Antonio Tlaxcalantongo, where he was spending the night, and killed him. Obregón's victory was in line with what has frequently been called a Bonapartist solution and is common to the history of many revolutions, beginning with the French Revolution: a takeover by the military after the most radical phase of the revolution has passed.

It was also an expression of Carranza's increasing isolation. The Mexican president had lost the support not only of large segments of labor and the peasantry who were disillusioned by his opposition to reform but also of substantial groups of the middle class and the new bourgeoisie who were the revolution's main beneficiaries. In their eyes Carranza had proven incapable of stabilizing the country and reestablishing peace.

With the victory of the men of Sonora a new and different evolution began in Mexico.

### Germany and Mexico, 1919–20

The clearer it became that Great Britain and France were not going to support him against the United States, the more Carranza was interested in strengthening his relations with Germany in the hope that in spite of its defeat it could still help him against the United States.

These hopes of the Mexican president were frustrated more and more as the Americans went on the offensive against Germany's influence in Mexico as soon as the Armistice, which put an end to World War I, went into effect.

As early as 22 November, the American government transmitted a note through the Swiss foreign ministry to the German government in which it stated "that the German minister in Mexico is continuing to foment anti-American propaganda in that country, and this will no longer be tolerated by the American government." It was categorically asserted that if the American government "were to take in good faith the German government's recent request for aid, it must request that the agitation in question cease and the German minister to Mexico be recalled immediately."[33]

The Foreign Office fulfilled this request; Eckardt was immediately recalled.[34] Some months went by before all the formalities were carried out, but Eckardt finally went back to Germany. He traveled by way of the United States, where he was accompanied throughout his trip by an official of the Justice Department. Eckardt told the official that he had harbored no aggressive intentions against the United States, but his claims were ignored because the Americans were blaming him for certain actions taken by his superiors. Thus, according to the Justice Department official, Eckardt had been behind the Zimmermann note. To the charge that he had attempted to provoke a war between Mexico and the United States, Eckardt replied that such a war would have been pointless: "Mexico would have quickly been defeated and the hatred of the people would have turned against Germany." This reply was undoubtedly in keeping with his attitude in 1918, but had little to do with his actions during the period of the Zimmermann note. He made no detailed reply to the charge that "he had carried on intrigues through agents (general staff, admiral staff)." "I have never done anything, or ordered anything to be done," he stated indignantly, "which needs to be concealed from the light of day."[35]

The Foreign Office's change of policy toward Mexico was by no means limited to the recall of Eckardt. On the same day that the American note arrived in Berlin, a discussion took place between Kemnitz and Solf, the new secretary of state in the Foreign Office. Although the precise contents of this discussion are not known, Solf apparently accused Kemnitz of authoring the Zimmermann note, for two days later Kemnitz wrote him a lengthy letter dealing with their discussion.[36] In his letter, Kemnitz admitted having been the first to suggest the telegram, but denied responsibility for it, for at the time he had been the Foreign Office adviser on East Asian not Mexican, affairs. His main assertion, however, was that he had nothing to do with the alliance proposal, and that if he had been in charge, the telegram would never have been sent by way of Washington. This was the core of his argument, which culminated in the following: "Had the telegram remained . . . a secret, it could only have been to our advantage"; if Mexico had accepted the alliance proposal, "important American forces would have been tied down on the Rio Grande del Norte." If Mexico had refused, pro-German sympathies would nevertheless have been reinforced there. Moreover, Kemnitz stated, he had hoped in this way to open the dialogue between his superiors and Japan. He tried to put the entire blame and responsibility for the negative consequences of the Zimmermann note on Montgelas, the expert on Mexico who had argued for the alliance proposal.

In an assessment by Rhomberg prepared for the secretary of state, Kemnitz's arguments were refuted. On the basis of the archives, Rhomberg proved that he had not only suggested sending the note, but he had written the original draft. Moreover, it was pointed out that the alternative route, by way of Sweden, which he had proposed for the transmission of the alliance proposal also went through Washington.[37] Shortly thereafter, Kemnitz was no longer working for the Foreign Office. The precise conditions of his departure are not known. His rival, Montgelas, however, was appointed minister to Mexico.

The causes of this development are not completely clear. Did Germany want to make a gesture of goodwill for Wilson? This is possible, but there is no indication that the Americans were informed of Kemnitz's role or of his dismissal. Was Kemnitz made a scapegoat for domestic political reasons?

The propagandistic, economic, and political apparatus Eckardt had built up in Mexico now began to crumble like a house of cards. A section of the pro-German press went over to the Allies;[38] thus, for example, the director of the *Reforma* in Tampico offered his services to the Americans. Other papers, such as *El Demócrata,* followed. Many German businessmen tried to establish ties with the Americans. Magnus railed bitterly against "the heads of some of Germany's most powerful houses who did well, and sometimes extremely well, during both the revolution and the war," and who now could not wait "until they could fill their half empty warehouses with goods from German factories." He quoted Fletcher, who had apparently spoken of the "undignified servility of certain German businessmen," and expressed the fear that "prior to the conclusion of peace and the restoration of world trade . . . and with the aid of the intelligence, the business acumen, and the connections of the German businessmen," the Americans would succeed "in driving English, French, but also German companies out of the Mexican market and in strengthening their own position there."[39]

As in the 1919–20 period, Germany's Mexico policy fluctuated between two contradictory tendencies. On the one hand, the Carranza government was one of the few that continued to seek German support and was willing to grant concessions to German firms. Carranza had also underlined his position by rejecting an official French proposal that Mexican securities and business enterprises owned by Germans be placed under far-reaching Allied control, in keeping with the terms of the Armistice.[40] In addition, Carranza appointed Isidro Fabela, one of his most important and influential collaborators, to serve as his minister in Germany.

When the defeat temporarily put an end to all German plans for expansion, Mexican raw materials appeared all the more valuable. Thus Germany attempted, even if only in a limited way, to maintain its connections in Mexico. Emigration societies were set up. Eckardt made speeches to Hamburg businessmen underlining the importance of German trade with Mexico. In a discussion at the Reich Post Office, he suggested that the radio link to Mexico be expanded.[41] In September 1919, when the Mexican Foreign Minister Cándido Aguilar visited Europe, the German representatives in Bern and Madrid, where he planned to visit, were instructed: "Treat him with attentiveness if situation presents itself; also, present him with best wishes for the Mexican national holiday on September 16."[42]

These desires, however, continued to be subordinated to Germany's efforts to provoke no tensions with the United States, whose support was being sought against England and France. In January 1919, when the Foreign Office learned of the intentions of some German officers to accept positions in the Mexican army, it raised "serious political objections." "We must be particularly careful in Mexico," said the Hanseatic representative in Berlin in outlining the Foreign Office's position, "particularly after we fulfilled Wilson's unjustified demand to recall our minister, Eckardt.... Carranza obviously does not have Wilson's sympathies, especially because he was able to maintain his neutrality throughout the entire world war."[43] At the end of 1919, when German businessmen attempted to supply arms to Mexico, the American military attaché in Stockholm immediately lodged a protest with the local German representatives. He informed Ambassador Lucius that "he was expecting an understanding between Germany and America in the near future if we are able to treat his compatriots with openness and honesty. The attempt of private individuals to smuggle arms through Holland to Mexico, some of which have made it as far as Amsterdam, has a very negative effect on the shaping of future relations."[44]

These contradictory tendencies were expressed with particular acuteness in a final attempt, made just before the overthrow of Carranza, to gain a foothold in Mexico and to use Mexico as a lever of influence on the United States. After Eckardt's departure from Mexico, Jahnke had stayed on. The admiral staff had instructed him to put an end to his activities. He acknowledged this order and informed the admiral staff that he would remain in Mexico until he received further orders.[45]

In the middle of 1919, Jahnke met with "a representative of the Republican party and of high finance, at his repeated request." This "representative," a certain Keedy, who presented himself as a cousin of Lansing, approached Jahnke with some far-reaching proposals. Keedy suggested that the Germans persuade the Mexican government to soften its laws dealing with petroleum and labor, mine operations, and land acquisition. "Mexico's public debt had to be brought under control, the railroads and other foreign enterprises in Mexico had to be compensated for damages incurred during the revolution. A New York bank heading a consortium wanted to lend Mexico a billion pesos for that purpose, guaranteed by the U.S. government (and approved by Lansing) on terms to be negotiated.... A political and economic understanding with Mexico is infinitely more valuable for the United States for obvious reasons, as a war to achieve the same ends would be quite costly—a war with Mexico would destroy the U.S.'s relations with almost all of Latin America." Keedy was effectively demanding the liquidation of the 1917 constitution and of everything that had been won during the revolution. If the German authorities could get Carranza to carry out such measures, Keedy was prepared "to move toward political, economic, and military support for Germany."[46]

In return, Jahnke demanded that the Republicans intervene to change the terms of Germany's postwar settlement. Keedy had no objections in principle to such a tradeoff and asked Jahnke for more precise proposals, which the latter was unable to provide since he was no longer in contact with the German authorities. Jahnke did not make this clear to Keedy, but told him instead that he would have to travel to Berlin for consultation. According to Jahnke's report, Keedy spoke "of the increasing hatred in America for England's capitalistic plans and for the completely pro-English President Wilson, who is using America's power to do England's dirty work." He went on to say

> that the entire world now owes America money and that in Republican circles it is obvious that England and France want America out of European politics—the Moor has done his duty, now he can leave—that Wilson is helping to keep American influence as minimal as possible, and that they, the Republicans, will attempt to influence European politics through Germany and Russia. The League of Nations in its present form is an English plaything which they will not ratify. The same holds for the Franco-American treaty. France must give up its harassment of Germany or it will receive no American aid, and it is also possible that a separate peace will be concluded with Germany in which Congress will simply declare the state of war with Germany to no longer exist.[47]

Jahnke briefed Carranza, whom he had already informed of Keedy's attempts at rapprochement, on some of Keedy's wishes. He wrote to him "that the Americans desire changes in various laws, a political understanding, settlement of Mexico's public debt, etc. They wish to lend Mexico a billion pesos to rebuild its international relations and obligations. They want to support Germany economically, politically, and militarily." He characterized Carranza's reaction as quite positive. "As far as I can see, Carranza is going along and is happy to have done us a new favor, and hoped that Germany could get something for itself out of all this." He asked Carranza to give Keedy an audience, which was in fact granted. In this discussion, Carranza limited himself to some general statements ("his finance minister would take charge of the problem, and he would think about the economic agreement and its conditions"). "On my advice, the Republican did not speak to Carranza about the German-Mexican-American program for cooperation, and Carranza would not have told him anything in any case."

Carranza had never been enthusiastic about the revolutionary portions of the 1917 constitution, and much of it had been accepted against his will. Nevertheless, he was unwilling to give up the constitution, particularly in the areas which most interested the Americans. Yet he still hoped to reach an agreement with the Americans which required no important concessions from Mexico. In view of growing American pressure and the isolation in which Mexico generally found itself, he might have been prepared to make some concessions. With German mediation, he was probably hoping for better terms, or at least a series of quite specific advantages, which he made known to Jahnke. During Jahnke's last visit to the president prior to his return to Germany, Carranza spoke of "the necessity to build industry in Mexico." In his instructions, Méndez articulated these wishes to Jahnke: "Mexico wishes to establish a factory for agricultural equipment, an airplane and automobile plant, an arms and ammunition factory, a steel works and a shipyard. The construction of a cyanide plant for the production of cyanide is of utmost urgency for the processing of ores.... in this area, Mexico is totally dependent on the United States at the moment. The establishment of any German industries whatever will be supported by the Mexican government, for exports from Mexico to South and Central America, or wherever they wish."

Upon his arrival in Berlin, Jahnke immediately delivered his proposals, which were thoroughly discussed in the Foreign Office by Eckardt, von Storer, a high official of the Foreign Office, Privy Councillor Trautmann, Under Secretary of State Haniel, and Foreign Minister Muller. Jahnke mentioned, as members of the Republican group represented by Keedy, "Senator Johnson, the governor of California, Congressman Khan, Senator MacConville, and Reed. This group also includes the attorney Wilson, who has ties to the Standard Oil Company, and a major banking firm in New York."[48]

Jahnke proposed that the group's offer be accepted and that their pro-German activities in the United States be supported with the aid of his contacts, which included various trade union leaders, various congressmen whom he did not mention explicitly, as well as certain Irishmen and priests. Eckardt was to conduct the negotiations in Mexico. The latter was quite enthusiastic about Jahnke's proposals and took "full responsibility ...for the person, the honesty, and the information of Herr J."[49]

In the view of Eckardt and Jahnke, these proposals would once again assure Germany of an important position in Mexico, while simultaneously cementing ties to the Republican party, whose victory was confidently expected in 1920, and winning better terms for Germany in the peace agreement. In addition, they were certainly quite aware that they were helping to dismantle the most advanced aspects of the Mexican constitution, which were also those most apt to frustrate Germany's plans.

All of these arguments persuaded Trautmann to give his assent to Jahnke's proposals, even if he did so far more cautiously than Eckardt.

He expressed doubts about "whether we really want to establish ties with the Republicans at all, since they are not yet in power, and thus expose ourselves to the danger that the current American government will view this as an action against itself and as interference in internal American affairs."[50] He nevertheless accepted Jahnke's arguments and felt "that Lansing's attitude is . . . proof that this danger does not exist." Moreover, he expressed the conviction shared by so many German diplomats since Zimmermann that it would be easy to keep such actions a secret in the United States. "It seems to me," concluded Trautmann, "that we should not dismiss out of hand the possibility of establishing contact with the Republicans. Initially, we can simply sound out the terrain with these people and find out what we really can expect from them. If our doubts are relieved by the statements we receive, we can proceed carefully. Our actions in Mexico can moreover be limited to sending a chargé d'affaires and opening up economic negotiations in Mexico (construction of industries, etc.) until we can see our way more clearly."

In contrast to Trautmann, Fuehr, who had been heavily involved in German propaganda in the United States, made a devastating condemnation of Jahnke's proposals. He initially expressed doubts on the importance of the people whom Jahnke had mentioned. He had never heard of Keedy. "As for his relationship to Lansing, it is well known that the family of the secretary of state, who began as an insignificant country lawyer from Watertown, New York, is of no political importance and that Lansing owes his rise exclusively to the family of his wife."[51] He indicated that the sole important man in this group was Johnson, the Republican senator from California, but he doubted Jahnke's assertion that Johnson would be the Republican presidential candidate. He dismissed the other politicians as either unknown or without influence.

Fuehr had lived in the United States during the first years of the war and had experienced the collapse and discovery of one German conspiracy after another; he expressed serious doubts that Jahnke's activities could actually be kept secret. His most important argument, however, was that Germany should make absolutely no accommodation in Mexico to the politicians mentioned by Jahnke for the sake of a rapprochement. "In the United States, quite independently of our actions," he wrote, "everything possible is being done to prevent the ratification of the peace treaty or, more importantly, the creation of an effective League of Nations. Involved in this effort are the Irish, the German-Americans, the powerful Hearst press, as well as the anti-Wilson current consisting of Johnson, Borah, and the like, on the one hand, and Knox, on the other. An attempt by us to influence these senators—which would inevitably be seen as interference in internal American affairs—is thus quite superfluous."

Foreign Minister Muller agreed with this analysis and told Jahnke "that he would have nothing to do with such a program, as this government no longer wishes to involve itself in secret policy, but only in open policy of an official kind."[52] Nevertheless, he did not completely drop the plans developed for Mexico: "The Mexican side of the proposal (desire for industry) has been accepted and will be implemented."

Jahnke, however, did not give up, but presented his program to Kapp. He told him "that the current cabinet is unable or unwilling to engage in politics and is calling for the aid of the 'national circles in Germany.'"[53] The results of the negotiations with Kapp are not known, but they were probably positive, for shortly thereafter Jahnke returned to Mexico. The Americans were quite aware of his arrival. The American consul general sent an alarming report to Washington expressing fear that Jahnke had been sent to Mexico to organize sabotage against oil fields and factories in the United States.[54]

In the interim, however, the ground had collapsed under Jahnke's feet. In Germany, the Kapp putsch had come to an inglorious end, and in Mexico, Carranza, in whom he had placed his hopes, was overthrown. The American military attaché told his government that Jahnke, who at the time of his departure had hoped to obtain an official position with the German delegation in Mexico, had abandoned these hopes and had taken a job as an administrator on a hacienda. The military attaché even went so far as to praise him, having received plans from Jahnke which envisioned a joint German-American action against England and France.[55]

There was, nonetheless, concern in Washington. The American representative in Berlin was instructed to lodge a complaint over the Jahnke affair. Under Secretary of State Haniel told him in the course of a long discussion that Jahnke had applied for a passport, not under his own name, but under the name of Steffens and had presented himself as the secretary of Professor Hellmanns, who wanted to conduct agricultural research in Mexico. Haniel went on to say that the Foreign Office had asked Jahnke to return his passport as soon as his true identity had been discovered, but that Jahnke had refused. The under secretary of state then made the official declaration "that the German government has given him [Jahnke] no instructions whatsoever, and will have nothing more to do with him."[56]

In the assessment of these plans, certain questions arise: Who was Keedy? What were the objectives of the Republicans? What did Jahnke want?

J. M. Keedy (or Keady) was an American businessman whom U.S. customs official Zachary Cobb, stationed at the United States–Mexican border, considered part of an "infernal stream of impostors and grafters who do no good for the government and who at best confuse the Mexican mind."[57] Cobb voiced these accusations in a letter written in 1916 to the

Justice Department in which he expressed the suspicion that Keedy was misrepresenting himself as an agent of that department.

Cobb was right. Keedy was not a Justice Department official (though he had been a U.S. attorney in Puerto Rico during the administration of Theodore Roosevelt) and he was part of the army of lobbyists and businessmen who attempted to enrich themselves through the Mexican Revolution.[58] In 1914 he had gone to Mexico, gained the confidence of Pancho Villa, and engaged in business in northern Mexico. That same year Keedy attempted to convince Martin Falomir, one of the wealthiest landowners in Chihuahua whose holdings had been confiscated by Villa, that for a sufficient fee he might convince Villa to return his estates. Falomir had no confidence in Keedy and refused.[59]

Villa never learned that Keedy had established contact with his enemies, continued to trust him, and sent Keedy on a confidential mission to Washington in the summer of 1915. He was to tell the State Department that Villa, in return for recognition, would recognize a non-Villista as president of Mexico.[60] This was not enough for Leon Canova, who was in charge of the Mexican desk at the State Department. He sent Keedy back to Mexico with a list of all cabinet officials Villa was to appoint in return for recognition. Villa, refusing to sacrifice his country's independence refused Canova's terms and broke off all relations with Keedy.[61] The latter now established new contacts.

On 2 October 1917, Cobb reported that Keedy, who had also conducted business with the Villa government, wanted money from the Germans to help free German citizens interned in the United States. Cobb called him a traitor and stated: "Keedy has impressed the Germans with the idea that he speaks with real authority."[62] The State Department reacted with surprising mildness to these accusations. It was obviously suspicious of Keedy since it refused him a passport,[63] but no other actions were taken against him. The cautious attitude of the department may have been influenced by the fact that Keedy had established links to some of the largest American banks. In 1919 he went to Mexico to negotiate a loan of $600,000,000 with the Carranza government. According to an American consular report Keedy represented a bank consortium that included Morgan and the National City Bank.[64]

Since American bankers had never been able to persuade Carranza to agree to their terms, Keedy (with or without the knowledge of the banks he represented) probably hoped that the Germans would be able to convince Carranza to accede to the banks' terms.

Keedy had obviously overestimated Germany's influence on Carranza and underestimated the Mexican president's nationalism. The latter received Keedy at Jahnke's insistence but refused his terms which included the abandonment of the constitution of 1917 and Carranza's agreement to have two representatives of the bankers "in Department of Hacienda to exercise control over expenditures."[65]

Keedy thus had the perhaps unique experience of being rebuffed by both Villa and Carranza when he suggested to them that they sacrifice Mexico's sovereignty to U.S. interests. No evidence clarifies Keedy's exact position, whether he was only speaking for the banks he represented, whether he also was an agent for the Republicans in whose name he spoke, or whether he was engaged in a gigantic bluff. He may very well have misrepresented the scope of his political influence to the Germans in order to gain their support and then be able to present himself to the Republicans as the one man capable of pacifying Mexico.

Whatever the case, a Republican rapprochement with the Germans absolutely cannot be ruled out. They had nothing to lose from such a connection, for they consistently opposed the League of Nations and the ratification of the Treaty of Versailles. They were, however, extremely interested in bringing the revolution in Mexico to an end and in forcing Carranza to make concessions. Since, according to Jahnke's own information, they had vastly overestimated German influence in Mexico, it is quite possible that the Republicans wanted to deprive Carranza of his last hope that he would be able to rely on any other power against the United States. To Jahnke, moreover, the entire project appeared to present an opportunity to rebuild his devastated intelligence network in the United States. In the last analysis, German diplomacy denied support for this effort because there was nothing to be gained from it. The Germans were quite correct in relying on the anti-English and anti-French policies of the Republicans and saw no reason to put any strain on these efforts by secret agreements with groups in the United States who were not in power and whose credentials were in doubt.

# *14* Conclusion

The Mexican Revolution began in the waning days of what has often been called the classic period of imperialism, when the great powers were jockeying for position in the conflict they all anticipated. The revolution reached its highest pitch in the course of World War I. When the armed phase of the revolution subsided with the fall of Carranza in 1920, the international scene had changed beyond recognition. The power of the United States had increased to an unprecedented degree. Politically and economically the United States had established its hegemony on the American continent and now exercised an influence on the Old World it had never had before.

The face of the Old World had also changed beyond recognition. Germany was defeated. The Austro-Hungarian empire had dissolved. In spite of their victory Great Britain and France emerged greatly weakened from the slaughter and devastation of World War I. The Bolshevik revolution had exercised an influence far beyond the Russian borders.

What effect did this international turmoil have on the policies of the great powers toward the Mexican Revolution before and during World War I and in its immediate aftermath? How did they affect the course of the revolution itself? These are the main questions this book has sought to answer. Closely related to them is a second set of questions. What influence did business interests concerned with Mexico exercise on the policies of their respective governments and on the Mexican revolutionaries?

These questions are easiest to answer for the Madero revolution and his administration but become more complex for the period following his fall. When the Madero revolution broke out in 1910, it was considered by the governments of all the great powers and by foreign financial interests in Mexico as nothing more than a coup in the classic Latin American mold, with no profound social implications. Their attitude toward the revolution essentially depended on the relationship they had maintained with the Díaz government and the ruling Científicos. The British and French governments and their respective financial interests deeply resented the Madero revolution, fearing that they would lose the preeminence they had enjoyed in Porfirian Mexico. The attitudes toward Madero in both the United States and Germany were far more contradictory. While some

550

American and German interests considered Díaz the only dependable guarantor of peace and order in Mexico, others established links to the Madero movement. With Madero's help American oil companies hoped to upset Porfirio Díaz's pro-British policies. Germany's Deutsch Süd-amerikanische Bank in particular had established close economic ties with the Madero family and expected to capitalize on a revolutionary victory. On the whole, both the Taft administration in Washington and the government of imperial Germany at first saw the Madero revolution in a much more favorable light than their British and French counterparts.

By 1912 it had become clear that Madero had unleashed social forces he could not control. The governments of the great powers and the vast majority of foreign business interests then supported the coup that toppled the Madero government. Differences emerged only on who should replace Madero. Europeans favored Huerta while U.S. Ambassador Henry Lane Wilson preferred Felix Díaz. On the whole, however, this was the only time in the course of the Mexican Revolution when all the great powers and their respective business interests displayed unanimity in their attitudes toward Mexico's internal conflicts.

When the second phase of the Mexican Revolution erupted in the spring of 1913, profound differences emerged between the European powers and the newly inaugurated U.S. president, Woodrow Wilson. This time the Europeans realized they were dealing with a social revolution and they wanted to crush it with Huerta's military government, which they had helped to install. By contrast, Woodrow Wilson, after some hesitation, wanted to use the revolution to mold Mexico into a model for Latin America and perhaps for all underdeveloped countries; he wanted Mexico to have a parliamentary democracy with free elections and an orderly transfer of government. Wilson opposed social upheavals, which might threaten the system of free enterprise, but he advocated some kind of agrarian reform, never specifying at whose expense and in what way it should take place. He wanted the holdings of American investors to be guaranteed and for Mexico to limit the influence of European governments and European business interests, which he considered imperialistic. Wilson wanted Mexico to turn to the United States for guidance and counseling.

The European powers in Mexico were so inhibited by their fear of antagonizing the United States and by their increasing mutual rivalries that their policies failed completely. After the outbreak of World War I in July 1914, the policies of all great powers in Mexico became subordinated to the imperatives of the war. At that point a profound change in the attitudes of European powers toward revolutionary movements began to occur.

In the course of the First World War, spurred by their intense conflict with each other, the European powers finally began to do what the United States had already been doing for more than a decade and a half. They attempted to draft nationalist and revolutionary movements of every color and persuasion into the service of their own global strategies. The United States' intervention in Cuba in 1898 had revealed the great potential of such attempts. Through its ingenious support of the Cuban independence movement against Spain, the United States had been able, without major sacrifices in men and material, to convert the island into a semicolonial appendage of its own. In 1914 the European powers followed suit: Germany lent its support to nationalist and/or revolutionary movements in Ireland, India, and the Caucasus, and even extended a helping hand to the Russian revolutionaries when it permitted Lenin to pass through Germany on his return from exile. Similarly, the Allies gave assistance to nationalist movements in Austria-Hungary and the Ottoman Empire and even sent one of their own, Lawrence of Arabia, to organize the Arab uprising against the Turks. The rebels and dissenters whom the great powers aided were not for the most part agents of these powers, but rather dedicated leaders committed to causes of their own, who were simply trying to accomplish on a smaller scale what the great powers were trying to accomplish on a somewhat larger one. No mere ignorant pawns of power politics, they were themselves as eager to exploit the conflict between the great powers as these in turn were eager to exploit conflicts between the rebels and their enemies.

Mexico is an especially notable case in point, because it was experiencing an intense internal conflict at the time that much of the rest of the world was fighting the First World War. As a result of the world war, most of the major powers attempted to capitalize on Mexico's internal conflict, while both revolutionary and counterrevolutionary leaders in Mexico sought to capitalize on the global conflict.

Between the fall of Madero and the end of World War I, three powers attempted to influence events in Mexico on a massive scale: Great Britain, Germany, and the United States. Britain's policies had the most important repercussions in Mexico in 1913–14 and those of Germany from 1915 to 1919. United States policy was of decisive importance for events in Mexico during the whole course of the revolution.

The interventions of Britain and Germany in Mexican affairs were largely indirect and covert, those of the United States more direct and overt. Britain and Germany managed to maintain consistently good relations with the factions they supported (Britain with Huerta throughout his regime, the Germans with Carranza from mid-1916 until his overthrow), but the Americans did not. For short periods of time, the Europeans exercised considerable influence on the factions they favored. In the long run, however, only the United States decisively influenced the course of the Mexican Revolution.

Among the great powers Britain pursued the most consistent policy in Mexico between 1910 and 1920. Not even remotely considering the option of sending a Lawrence to influence the Mexican revolutionaries, it opposed every revolutionary faction in those ten years and consistently supported counterrevolutionary groups. The conviction expressed by the British envoy Thurstan that what Mexico needed was "a government of white men," was shared by most responsible officials in the British Foreign Office. Racism, however, was not the main determinant of Britain's policies. The close relationship of British interests with Porfirian forces as well as the fluctuating alliances of the revolutionaries with both the United States and Germany strongly influenced the British role. On the whole, the consistency of British policy was matched by its ineffectiveness.

For a short period of time, between March and November 1913, it seemed as if Britain, by supporting Huerta, had achieved an influence in Mexico even greater than it had exercised in the time of Porfirio Díaz. Britain's relations with Huerta have been the object of dispute and conflicting interpretations among both politicians and historians. In 1913 Woodrow Wilson and his closest advisers were convinced that British diplomats in Mexico and above all the British minister, Sir Lionel Carden, were exercising a decisive influence on Huerta, encouraging him to resist United States pressure and to remain in office and doing so with the full accord of the Foreign Office in London as well as British business interests. Some historians have tended to discount these interpretations, since no conclusive evidence for them was found among the papers of Woodrow Wilson or his advisers. The records of the British Foreign Office proved to be inconclusive in this regard.

Evidence from both German and French sources not only confirm Wilson's suspicions with regard to British policies and intentions but shows that British policy in Mexico was even more anti-American than the president had thought. According to Germany's representative in Mexico, Paul von Hintze, probably the best-informed and most intelligent diplomat in Mexico, the influence of Sir Lionel Carden over Huerta was so great that Huerta did nothing without consulting the British minister. Hintze felt that his British colleague was almost pathologically anti-American.

According to analysts of the foreign ministry of Britain's closest ally, France, Carden's attitude was by no means an isolated phenomenon. It enjoyed the backing of powerful British business interests as well as important sectors of the British government. In fact both Hintze and the French foreign ministry officials believed that the British were working to precipitate a war between the Huerta regime and the United States in 1913. Britain's alliance with Huerta not only constituted a failure; it was counterproductive. The United States retaliated by preventing British

economic penetration into other Latin American countries such as Colombia. Above all Huerta's stubbornness, which the British had encouraged, drove Wilson to embrace his revolutionary opponents. Between
March and October 1913 Wilson had showed himself ready to accept a
solution that would have allowed one of Huerta's collaborators, such as
Federico Gamboa, to become president of Mexico. Such a solution might
have salvaged a Huertista regime without Huerta. After October 1913,
when Huerta dissolved the Mexican parliament and had himself reelected,
Wilson threw his full-fledged support to the Constitutionalists, thus making their victory practically inevitable.

After the outbreak of World War I, Britain's capacity for influencing
events in Mexico was sharply curtailed because it had to concentrate all
its efforts and resources on the war. At the same time the number and
strength of its adversaries in Mexico sharply increased. Deeply incensed
at British support of Huerta, Mexican revolutionaries of all persuasions
showed little respect for either British diplomats or British properties in
Mexico. Both U.S. business interests and the U.S. government attempted
to make use of World War I to weaken British economic and political
influence in Mexico. At the same time Britain had to contend with Germany's rising influence in that country.

In the three-front war the British were waging in Mexico from 1914 to
1918 against the Mexican revolutionaries, the United States, and the
Germans, they suffered a series of defeats, with but one conspicuous
exception. They were unable to prevent the Carranza government from
making British properties the only target of massive confiscations of
foreign holdings in Mexico. Although British oil fields were not affected,
 British-held banks and railways were seized by the Mexican government
and the British government was unable to retaliate in any way. Repeatedly formulated plans by both the British military and the Foreign
Office to topple Carranza through a coup based on conservative military
elements in the country came to nothing when the United States refused
to endorse them. As in all of Latin America, during World War I, the
United States encroached on British economic influence in Mexico in
every possible way.

It was against the Germans that the British scored one of their few
major successes in Mexico, by deciphering the Zimmermann telegram and
by reading the secret messages the Germans sent to their agents. These
British successes had a major impact on U.S. policies toward the European war. But in Mexico, in spite of their extensive knowledge of German
activities, the British were not able to prevent the Germans from exercising an ever increasing influence in the press, the army, and the government.

One of the most baffling aspects of British policy in Mexico is the
question why, in spite of their enormous successes in the field of intelli-

gence (their knowledge of the German secret codes in Mexico was supplemented by their penetration of the German clandestine services in that country), they were unable to assess German intentions correctly between August 1917 and April 1918. At a time when the Germans had given up their aim of provoking a Mexican-American war and were concentrating instead on an economic and political penetration of Mexico, the British repeatedly predicted an imminent German-Mexican attack on the United States which always failed to materialize, and because of that, their credibility in the eyes of the U.S. government suffered badly.

The British military were so convinced of the erroneous interpretations of their secret services that in May 1918 they brought the matter to the attention of the war cabinet and formulated projects that were absolutely impossible to carry out. These errors of interpretation had other consequences. They prevented the British government from accepting compromise proposals from Carranza which their own oil interests were strongly supporting and which would have slowed down, though probably not prevented, the erosion of Britain's economic strength in Mexico.

In November 1913, Sir William Tyrell, a close associate of Foreign Secretary Edward Grey, visited the United States and conferred with Wilson and Bryan on the Mexican question. Bryan accused British policymakers of bowing to the dictates of British oil companies. Tyrell vehemently rejected these allegations, but the British government never denied the fact that it considered its primary duty in underdeveloped countries to defend British economic interests. The European powers were not ready to accept the concept of missionary diplomacy as advocated by Woodrow Wilson.

British policymakers were faced with serious problems when conflicting interests emerged among British companies or when the interests of these companies conflicted with Britain's overall strategy. Between March and November 1913, no such conflict had emerged. British interests in Mexico supported Huerta unanimously and he seemed so strong that Wilson might sooner or later be forced to recognize him.

By the end of 1913, when it became clear that Huerta could not pacify the country, British banking and railway interests called for a reversal of Britain's policy of support for Huerta. This pressure came just as the Foreign Office was becoming more worried at the prospect of a split between the United States and Great Britain at a time of rising tensions in Europe. At this point the British government withdrew its support for Huerta and seemed to capitulate to U.S. pressure. This capitulation was only halfhearted. British diplomats actually tried to play both ends against the middle. While the Foreign Office called on Huerta to resign and told the Americans that they would stop supporting him, Sir Lionel Carden encouraged Huerta to stay in power. At the same time a British consortium headed by future prime minister Neville Chamberlain surreptitiously sent Huerta the arms he needed on German ships. This policy essentially benefited British oil interests, which had suffered far less from the civil war in Mexico than British railway companies and banks. The oil companies' main aim, as the well-informed German minister Hintze saw it, was to protect the concessions and holdings they had acquired. One possible option that Carden seriously considered was to divide the country, with Huerta remaining in control of the South and of the oil fields. A more realistic possibility consisted in supporting Huerta until the United States officially agreed to guarantee British oil concessions. This policy was successful and in June 1914 the U.S. government declared that it would not recognize any changes in the pattern of oil properties in Mexico which might result from the policies of the victorious revolutionaries.

This harmonious relationship between the British government and its most important business interests suffered its first sharp break in late 1917 and the resulting divergences continued throughout 1918. A strong conflict emerged between the interests of British oil companies in Mexico and what the British government considered to be its overall strategic interests. Faced with increasing Mexican and American pressure, Lord Cowdray sought either to sell his properties to Standard Oil or to effect a British rapprochement with Carranza. The British government vetoed both options, for strategic reasons. This conflict was only resolved after the end of World War I, when Cowdray was able to sell his oil properties to a powerful Anglo-Dutch company, the Royal Dutch Shell.

Britain managed to hold on to its main positions—above all the oil fields—and to obtain from the United States a limited recognition of some of its principal interests. In 1914 the United States agreed not to profit from an eventual expropriation of British oil interests and in 1918 Wilson agreed to give British and French interests 50 percent of the votes and thus veto power, in a prospective international committee of bankers formed to negotiate with Mexico. Nevertheless, the traditional power Britain had enjoyed in Mexico before the revolution, its special links to the rulers of the country, and its perceived role as a bulwark against U.S. expansionism were gone forever.

The second power that had enjoyed special relations with the Porfirian elite was France. Like its British ally, France was unable to influence events in Mexico in any important way during the revolution. Unlike Britain, it never attempted to do so. The French government and French financial interests were as violently opposed to the Mexican revolution as their British counterparts. They had profited as much if not more from their close links to the Porfirian oligarchy. They welcomed Huerta's coup and supported him in the first months of his rule, hoping for a return to a Díazlike dictatorship and stability. When these hopes proved to be futile, they, unlike the British, decided that the best solution for their interests .

would be complete U.S. hegemony in Mexico. Having few investments in raw materials, they did not fear American competition.

What France's government and financiers wanted above all was a government willing and able to repay the huge loans the French had made to the Díaz government. A Mexican government dominated by the United States would have had both the means and the desire to meet all of Mexico's financial obligations. The greatest problem French diplomacy faced in the years of the Mexican Revolution was not how to influence Mexico's development, but how to keep out of the increasing United States–British conflict over Mexico. On the one hand, the French could not openly voice their quite real support for U.S. supremacy in Mexico without creating grave conflicts with their closest ally, Great Britain. On the other hand, they saw no reason to support Britain's anti-American designs. As a result, French diplomacy's efforts alternated between attempts to conciliate British and American policies in Mexico and retreats into passivity when such endeavors proved impossible.

Only when it came to fighting German expansion in Mexico in the years between 1916 and 1918 did the French attempt to implement an active policy. Lacking the intelligence network and, in particular, the access to the German codes their British and American allies had, the French were able to play only a subordinate role in this struggle.

In view of the obvious impotence of the French government to influence events in Mexico, France was the only one of the great powers in which no serious conflicts over Mexican policy occurred between the government and business interests and among the business interests themselves.

Unlike Britain, for whom Mexico was an end unto itself, Germany formulated its Mexican policy to serve global aims reaching far beyond Mexico. Unlike the British, the Germans carried out a basic change of tactics in the course of the revolution. They switched from a policy of total opposition to all revolutionary movements to one that attempted to use these movements for their own ends. As a result, their impact on the Mexican revolutionaries was far greater than that of any other European power. But it was a short-range impact. In the long run the Germans had no more influence on the course of the revolution than Britain or France.

Germany's involvement with Mexico has been the least understood. Both its role as a major exploiter of that revolution and its efforts to achieve that role have for a long time been shrouded in mystery. For this reason German activities in Mexico have been a special concern of this book. Germany's involvement with Mexico both during the Porfirian era and the Mexican Revolution can be divided into four distinct eras. Up to 1898 Germany's policy was one of active economic expansion without political aims. Between 1898 and 1914 Germany began to include Mexico to an ever increasing extent in its various global strategies. Between 1914 and 1917 it did everything in its power to utilize both the revolutionary and counterrevolutionary groups to provoke a war between the United States and Mexico. Finally, after 1917 it set out to use its influence with the revolutionaries to make of Mexico a German quasi protectorate.

Until 1898 the process of German expansion in Mexico was none too different from its expansion into other parts of Latin America with the exception of Argentina, Brazil, and Chile, where massive immigration of Germans had taken place. The first impulse for it was provided by German merchants, but the real momentum came from German banks. In this period German entrepreneurs twice succeeded in gaining supremacy in vital sectors of Mexico's economy: during the late 1870s in foreign trade, and between 1888 and 1898 in public finance. No lasting political advantage could be gained, however, from this temporary supremacy. The hopes German bankers and diplomats may have entertained that Mexico would become dependent on Germany in the same way that many Asian and African countries had were disappointed. The cause of this disappointment was the United States. Its proximity and its overwhelming economic presence in Mexico set very firm limits to Germany's ambitions.

This does not mean, however, that Germany during this period found itself in any direct antagonism with the United States. Quite the contrary, for in fact German and American economic developments did not clash but progressed along parallel lines. While America's direct antagonist in Mexico was England, Germany's direct antagonist was France. Wherever German enterprises had important interests at stake, they clashed head on with those of a French challenger: German merchants vied with French merchants, German weapons producers with French weapons producers, German banks with French banks.

The year 1898 marked a turning point for German affairs in Mexico, because it was then that Mexico was transformed from a mere investment project into an instrument of power politics. Until 1898, German policy had been dictated primarily by the economic interests of German entrepreneurs. After that date, it came to be controlled by Germany's larger political interests. The consequence of this transformation for German entrepreneurs was by no means clear-cut. Germany's larger political interests now determined whether its diplomatic efforts resulted in restraining or in promoting Germany's business interests in Mexico.

Conditions in Mexico after 1898 began to seem opportune for the accomplishment of one of Germany's long-range political goals: that of challenging American supremacy in Latin America. On the face of it, Mexico did not seem to be a propitious place at all for such an endeavor since U.S. interests were more powerful there than almost anywhere else in Latin America. Economically, Mexico was almost an appendage of the United States: 40 percent of all American foreign investments were placed there. Politically, Mexico was at the heart of the American sphere of influence, almost a cornerstone of the Monroe Doctrine: the United States had not taken lightly the French invasion of 1861–67 and tolerated it only because its hands were tied by its own Civil War.

What made the circumstances in Mexico so much more advantageous for a European challenge of the Monroe Doctrine than might at first appear was that England had a prominent economic interest in the area. While Germany had always been alert for an opportunity to subvert the Monroe Doctrine, it did not, despite frequent and insistent demands by Pan-Germans and by the navy, dare to challenge it alone. Any such venture had to be a joint Anglo-German operation, because Germany did not want to invite a single-handed showdown with the United States and because it hoped for an Anglo-American rift. Venezuela in 1902 had offered the first opportunity for a joint Anglo-German challenge to the Americans. It failed because of the sharp American rebuff. Since then England had been reluctant to court another such rebuff. In Mexico, however, England's economic interests seemed to Germany too substantial for this reluctance to prevail. What seemed to make circumstances in Mexico even more opportune was the desire of the Mexican government to strengthen European investment as a counterweight to the United States. And what seemed to make them more propitious yet was the deepening American-Japanese antagonism in which the Germans hoped to involve Mexico. Germany's rulers advocated wide-ranging plans in this respect which contemplated either a German-American alliance with a possible joint occupation of Mexico or as an instrument to provoke a Japanese-American conflict.

The outbreak of the Mexican Revolution was as much a surprise for German diplomats and businessmen as it was for their counterparts from all other great powers. At first they considered the Mexican Revolution as nothing more than a coup, with some popular backing, which would strengthen the existing political and economic system. Like the British and French diplomats in Mexico, the German representatives in that country were worried that Madero might defer more to American demands than Porfirio Díaz had done. Unlike the British and French, however, some German businessmen and diplomats felt they had much to gain from the Científicos' fall from political power. The new rulers of Mexico had fewer links to British and French business and closer links to German financiers than their Porfirian predecessors. They could thus be expected to, and actually did, favor German interests more than their predecessors had.

The interests of German bankers, financiers, and other businessmen did not prevent Germany's representatives from attempting to use the Mexican Revolution for global aims which, in the last instance, might have proved harmful to them. An intensive, covert propaganda campaign was launched by German representatives, calling for a German-American alliance against Japan and a resulting occupation of Mexico by the United States.

Many of these considerations, though, became secondary for Germany when its diplomats became convinced that Madero could not control the popular forces he had mobilized in the first stages of the revolution. Germany's minister, Paul von Hintze, turned against Madero and participated in his overthrow. When Hintze perceived that his action had mainly benefited the United States and that the Huerta regime was "a tool of the American embassy," he attempted to reverse his role and made an unsuccessful attempt to save Madero's life.

It was in the period of Huerta's rule, from March 1913 to June 1914, that German diplomacy displayed an unprecedented activity in Mexico and attempted to use that country for its global purposes. During this period, for the first time since the Venezuelan crisis, serious efforts were mounted to challenge the supremacy of the Monroe Doctrine by promoting a joint intervention in Mexico on the part of Germany, the United States, England, and possibly even France and Japan. Hintze's proposal for "friendly cooperation," already approved by the German Foreign Office, would have converted Mexico into a European-American protectorate and would have created a precedent for all of Latin America. This policy, however, with its utterly mistaken conception of American objectives and of the significance of the Mexican Revolution and its awkward meddling with Mexico's internal affairs failed completely.

Germany's rulers also hoped that cooperation with Britain in Mexico and in other minor questions could offset the profound hostility that Germany's aggressive foreign policy and especially its naval rearmament program were causing in Britain. This hope failed. German hopes that Huerta would be able to crush the revolutionary movement floundered as well.

The ill-fated policy revealed in the Zimmermann telegram has been described as a wartime improvisation, entirely unrelated to Germany's prewar diplomacy in Mexico. The efforts of German diplomats between 1905 and 1913 to utilize Mexico to create hostilities between Japan and the United States, the converse attempts to have the United States invade Mexico as part of such a conflict, the hopes of utilizing Mexico to strengthen United States–British tensions, and German proposals for a joint invasion of the country by the great powers show that Zimmermann's later schemes had deep-seated roots in Germany's previous policies.

In the years from mid-1914 until 1917, Mexico was seen by Germany's rulers as no more than an instrument with which to influence American policies, a noose, as it were, with which to tie the United States to the American continent. Germany's already prominent involvement in Mexico's internal affairs since the beginning of the twentieth century paled by comparison with its intense involvement during the first three years of World War I: the conspiracy with Huerta, the sabotage activities in a neutral country, the attempted conspiracy with Villa to incite American intervention, countless armed provocations on the border, military plots against Carranza, and especially the Zimmermann telegram. What is most striking about German policy in this period is that while it was based on coldblooded *realpolitik,* there was nothing very realistic about it. Germany grossly misjudged both its potential ally, Mexico, and its enemy, the United States. In return for Mexico's attack on the United States, Germany promised Mexico three American states. When that offer did not persuade the buyer, the price tag was simply changed on the premise that ultimately Carranza could not "deny himself the chance" of striking at the United States.

The Zimmermann telegram, insofar as it is considered at all in German historiography, is either dismissed as an aberration in German policy, a personal whim of Zimmermann's, or it is judged to be a legitimate attempt on the part of Germany to gain allies in case of war with the United States. Neither of these views is correct. As for the first, the German records reveal quite clearly that Zimmermann's telegram was in fact the culmination of a long series of concerted attempts on the part of Germany's leading decision makers to involve Mexico in a war with the United States. Jagow issued instructions to prod Villa into an attack on the United States. Falkenhayn approved a conspiracy with Huerta. The kaiser himself recommended sending the Zimmermann telegram and Ludendorff added his consent. As for the second view, Zimmermann's declarations to the German Reichstag subsequent to the publication of his telegram show unequivocally that his was not a genuine offer of alliance to Carranza. Carranza was to be goaded into a war with the United States and then to be left to his own devices—except in the extremely unlikely case that Japan should enter the German-Mexican alliance as a third partner.

After 1917 Germany once more significantly altered its policy toward Mexico. No longer was tying the United States down in a border war with Mexico the primary objective. After unlimited submarine warfare and the offer of alliance to Carranza had failed, new strategies were contemplated toward Mexico. The new objective was Mexico's subjugation to Germany, its conversion into a kind of German protectorate. In his reports Eckardt speaks in very candid terms of "taking control of Mexico." By forging a far-flung network of spies to pervade both the Mexican army and government, by taking charge of large sections of the Mexican press, by smuggling agents into the boards of directors of non-German foreign companies in Mexico, Germany hoped to set the stage for a kind of "conquista" of Mexico, to be completed through extensive German loans and investments after the conclusion of the world war.

In spite of such hopes by Germany's rulers the relations which Germany established with Mexico in the years 1917–18 were not those of subjugation and domination. Germany simply did not have the power to implement such relations. In practical terms cooperation resembling an unofficial alliance existed between both governments. On the one hand it was based on both sides' future expectations. Carranza hoped for German economic and diplomatic help in the postwar period (and in the eventuality of a conflict with the United States at an earlier period). Germany hoped in the postwar period to dominate Mexico or at least secure important concessions for raw materials from that country. On the other hand, this alliance was also based on very immediate considerations. In return for Mexican neutrality and for Carranza's willingness to allow the German secret service agents to use Mexico as a base of operations against the United States, the Mexican government expected economic help, and military restraint with respect to sabotage activities in Mexico from Germany.

Mexico never received any economic help. Germany was not willing to grant more than a loan of ten million Spanish pesetas to Mexico in the course of the war, and even this paltry sum could not be sent across the Atlantic. Germany's military reticence, though, was vital for Mexico. The German government, against the advice of the agents of the German General Staff in Mexico, decided to forego the one effective means it still possessed to damage the Allied war effort and to bring about U.S. military intervention in Mexico: large-scale and effective sabotage operations in the oil fields.

What influence did Germany exercise on the course of the Mexican Revolution? While German propaganda was extremely effective in creating pro-German sympathies among the Mexican population, Germany exercised very little influence on the domestic policies of the Mexican government. In the few cases in which it attempted to do so, by opposing the constitution of 1917 or by trying to effect a reconciliation between the Carranza government and the Catholic Church, it failed. Mexico's neutrality in World War I was not primarily a result of German pressures (though Eckardt's plot with the generals was not without effect), but of the nationalism of Mexico's new elite.

While hopes of a German victory certainly stiffened Carranza's opposition to the United States, his policies did not significantly change after Germany was defeated.

The most important way in which Germany affected the course of events in Mexico was not through its Mexican policy, but as a result of its involvement in World War I. It was the increasing probability of war with Germany that persuaded Woodrow Wilson to withdraw the punitive expedition unconditionally from Mexico and helped to prevent any subsequent armed intervention in the affairs of its southern neighbor until the end of 1918.

Like their British counterparts, German policymakers were faced with recurring conflicts over what policies they should carry out in Mexico. In the case of Britain conflicts arose between those who considered Germany as Britain's main foe and others, like Carden and later Cowdray, who, while never openly saying so, were far more afraid of U.S. expansion than of German expansion.

In the case of Germany the conflict over Mexican policy was basically between those who saw Mexico as an end in itself and those who considered it as a means of achieving global aims. In 1914 German merchants and bankers were in favor of an American occupation of Mexico as the only means to stabilize the country and allow it to pay its foreign debt. The German Foreign Office strongly opposed such an objective for reasons of general policy and strategy. In 1917–18 the General Staff advocated large-scale sabotage operations in Mexico. Both the German civilian authorities and German business interests who hoped for a postwar policy of large-scale economic expansion into Mexico prevented these plans from being carried out.

Germany's defeat in World War I temporarily dampened its expansionist aims in Mexico. Some years later, however, the Nazis revived the projects of imperial Germany, but their accomplishments were far less "impressive" than those of the kaiser's representatives.

Would a different outcome of World War I have made it possible for Germany to achieve some of the aims it had set itself in Mexico and to subjugate that country at least to a limited degree? This possibility cannot be entirely discarded in view of the enormous power that Germany had in fact accumulated in Mexico. Its control of the Mexican press, its covert influence on the Mexican army, and the sympathy it had cultivated among the population could have been used as instruments to strengthen Germany's power in that country. Eckardt's exaggerated hope, which he expressed in 1917 when he wrote, "the inheritance of Cortez is for sale, let us buy it," could not have been implemented under any circumstances.

Among all the great powers the policies of the United States toward the Mexican Revolution seemed the most contradictory. Every victorious faction in Mexico between 1910 and 1919 enjoyed the sympathy, and in most cases the direct support of U.S. authorities in its struggle for power. In each case, the administration in Washington soon turned on its new friends with the same vehemence it had initially expressed in supporting them.

The Taft administration at first viewed the Madero revolution with great sympathy. Some historians maintain that Taft even gave it covert support.

One year later that same administration sharply reversed its stand concerning Madero and in February 1913 Ambassador Henry Lane Wilson played a decisive role in the coup that toppled Madero and brought Huerta to power.

Woodrow Wilson took even more energetic measures and interfered even more drastically in Mexico's affairs in order to force Huerta from the office to which H. Lane Wilson had aided in elevating him. In the process of fighting Huerta, Woodrow Wilson threw his support to both Pancho Villa and Venustiano Carranza. A short time later he turned against Villa and helped Carranza to inflict a decisive defeat upon the latter. Subsequently he nearly went to war with Carranza.

This consistent American inconsistency had one common denominator: the fact that every Mexican faction, once it assumed power, carried out policies considered detrimental by both the administration in Washington and U.S. business interests.

This common denominator was not of equal importance in all cases. It was decisive, though, as far as the Taft administration was concerned. Taft looked with sympathy upon the Madero revolution and considered it nothing more than a coup in the classic Latin American tradition. He hoped that Mexico's new ruler would put an end to Díaz's pro-European policies. When Madero began to tax U.S. properties, failed to give U.S. business interests the kind of support they had expected, and seemed incapable of controlling the social forces he had aroused, the Taft administration turned against him.

There is little doubt that Woodrow Wilson's opposition to Huerta was heightened by Huerta's close links to Britain. Nevertheless, this was not the primary motive for Wilson's opposition to the Mexican dictator, or for his alliance with the Mexican revolutionaries. Wilson's concept of missionary diplomacy led him to embrace the revolutionaries and in the process to attempt to mold them in his image.

By the end of 1915 Wilson seemed to have achieved a large measure of success: he had decisively contributed to the defeat of both Huerta and of the most radical wing of the revolutionaries.

While rejecting the American president's tutelage and U.S. supremacy, Carranza in 1915 and 1916, nevertheless, seemed to carry out policies that in many ways conformed to the wishes and aspirations of the American president. Carranza showed himself as committed as Woodrow Wilson to the system of free enterprise and private property. Not only did he voice no socialist aspirations, but he began returning confiscated properties to their former owners on a large scale. His administration seemed to be the first in Mexico's history since the 1880s to have established no close relations to European powers, whose support for Huerta he deeply resented. Of all the European powers, the Mexican leader was especially wary of Germany in view of its intrigues with Huerta and Villa officials with the aim of provoking American intervention in Mexico.

While Carranza's government in 1915 and early 1916 had imposed some new taxes and restrictions on U.S. companies, these were not yet severe. Wilson hoped that successful loan negotiations between Carranza and U.S. banks would put an end to these restrictions and establish close economic ties between the new Mexican government and the United States.

Villa's attack on Columbus, New Mexico, on 8 March 1916, based on the guerrilla leader's conviction that Carranza was surrendering Mexico's independence to the United States, concluded the second honeymoon in the relationship between Carranza and Wilson. The punitive expedition Wilson sent to Mexico not only brought Mexico and the United States to the brink of war, but it put an end to Wilson's policy of aligning himself with revolutionaries. The punitive expedition sparked such a strong wave of anti-American nationalism that, when it withdrew from Mexico in February 1917, it left behind a country where not one of the revolutionary factions, however much they might have hated each other, was willing or able to resume the old policy of alliance with the United States. Wilson never seriously considered the option, advocated by the British government, of aligning himself with Mexico's counterrevolutionaries in the years 1916–18. Not only had they been defeated and discredited, but, more important, he did not trust them. There was not one conservative leader who had not at some time supported Huerta and opposed the American president in the years 1913–14. Wilson thus felt he had no potential ally left in Mexico. In this period U.S. policy in Mexico reverted to traditional methods and aims and Wilson transferred his missionary zeal to other parts of the globe. The quasi-economic blockade Wilson now imposed on Mexico only contributed to fanning the fires of anti-American resentment and to pushing the Carranza government and most of its generals into the arms of Germany.

From 1916 to the end of 1918 the aims of U.S. policy essentially consisted in keeping Mexico quiet for the duration of World War I and in protecting American business interests. For this purpose both military intervention (the punitive expedition, which the Wilson administration attempted to utilize not only to destroy Villa but also to secure guarantees for American interests from the Carranza administration) and economic sanctions were applied. The U.S. government now expressed opposition to the kinds of social reforms in Mexico that Wilson and Bryan had advocated so strongly in 1913–14.

One of the few legacies of Wilson's earlier "idealistic" diplomacy in Mexico was his refusal to carry out military intervention in that country after the withdrawal of the punitive expedition. But this policy was by no means due only to his attitude toward Mexico; it was at least as much a product of the increasing global commitments of the United States. Intervention in Mexico in 1917–18 would have seriously hampered American participation in the European war. Later it might have dealt an even greater blow to the uphill fight Wilson waged in the postwar period to maintain and strengthen American overseas commitments.

As in Britain and Germany, the problem of what policy to carry out toward Mexico led to sharp conflicts within the administration, between civilian and military authorities, between the administration and some business interests, and among the business interests themselves. These conflicts had already emerged during the Madero revolution. While U.S. agricultural interests as well as most medium-sized businesses had been in favor of backing Díaz to the hilt, the oil interests seemed to be supporting Madero. Whether Taft's increasing coolness toward Díaz was the product of the pressure exercised by oil interests or simply the result of Díaz's pro-European policy is still an unresolved question.

In the United States, as in Europe, the last months of the Madero government constituted the one period in the course of the Mexican Revolution when a consensus on Mexican policy was achieved. Ambassador Henry Lane Wilson, practically all major and minor U.S. business interests in Mexico, as well as Taft and Knox hoped for Madero's fall. Consensus foundered only on the question of what should be done to implement these hopes. In contrast to U.S. business interests neither Taft nor Knox wanted the United States to intervene in Mexico.

Woodrow Wilson's dramatic policy reversal toward Mexico and his refusal to recognize Huerta, let alone support him, seemed to challenge the Mexican policy of large American interests. But it was only a brief challenge, and the portrait of Woodrow Wilson as a kind of lone fighter in a solitary battle against both Huerta and all U.S. business interests in Mexico is misleading. In March and April 1913 the largest U.S. companies interested in Mexico had attempted to convince Wilson to recognize Huerta. By the summer of that same year most of them began to support their president's policies fully and to align themselves with different revolutionary factions.

The reason for this shift of policy was not that American oil or mining men had suddenly become converts to Wilson's concept of missionary diplomacy, though they had no quarrel with many of the aims that Wilson proclaimed, such as cementing the system of free enterprise in Mexico or protecting American investments. The reversal of the attitude of the business interests was induced by a wide variety of other factors. In part it was simply an adaptation and a reaction to existing conditions. Once the revolutionaries controlled most of northern Mexico, the mining companies whose most important investments were located in that part of the country had no choice but to reach some kind of agreement with them. Huerta's increasing cooperation with European, above all British interests, no doubt contributed to the increasing hostility of U.S. oil companies toward his regime. Nevertheless the support American business interests gave to Woodrow Wilson and Mexican revolutionaries was also due to other considerations: while the fighting brought losses to U.S. mining and agricultural interests (though the oil companies scarcely suffered from the effects of the civil war in Mexico), it allowed the largest of these companies to acquire land and resources at very low prices from panic-stricken Mexican owners who feared that their holdings would be expropriated by revolutionaries or from middle-sized foreign companies who did not have the financial resources to weather the storm. The oil companies hoped that Huerta's defeat would lead Cowdray to sell his holdings in Mexico. Above all, the large U.S. companies saw Wilson's policies as a prelude to the establishment of some kind of American protectorate over Mexico. Some advocated military intervention in Mexico, while others hoped for a division of Mexico between north and south, with the northern revolutionaries playing a similar role to the Panamanian "revolutionaries" of 1903 who separated Panama from Colombia. All expected that at the very least the United States would impose a kind of Platt amendment on Mexico, as it had in Cuba. By the end of 1914 Woodrow Wilson's reluctance to carry out such policies led to a considerable cooling of relations between his administration and U.S. business interests in Mexico.

Between 1915 and 1918 relations between Wilson and American interests led by the oil companies were far more complex. There was consensus on both sides on certain minimum demands of these interests. With every means at its disposal, short of intervention, the State Department protested against the implementation of the constitution of 1917 and the imposition of taxes on U.S. businesses. It also opposed Carranza's attempts to wrest control of the oil region from Pelaez. In 1916 the U.S. government attempted to utilize the presence of the punitive expedition in Mexico to obtain from the Mexican government guarantees for U.S. business interests.

The Wilson administration nevertheless strongly opposed what could be called the maximum aims of the large corporations, especially of the oil companies. In contrast to some officials of his administration Wilson refused to support the plots of American companies to replace the Mexican government by Mexican officials with whom they had reached secret agreements. Wilson opposed the Canova-Iturbide plot of 1915, the Canova–Felix Díaz plot of 1916, the Canova-Iturbide conspiracy of 1917, and the Robles Domínguez plot of 1918, in all of which some of the largest American corporations in Mexico were involved. The U.S. president also rejected all demands by these companies for total or partial occupation of Mexico between 1917 and 1920. This attitude was due as much to Woodrow Wilson's opposition to converting Mexico into a U.S. protectorate as to considerations of strategy. Any involvement in Mexico as long as World War I lasted would have detracted from America's overseas war effort. This position was shared by large U.S. interests, especially the banks whose primary interests were centered on Europe.

When assessing the complex relationship between Woodrow Wilson's policies and U.S. corporations in Mexico, it should be stressed that the American president was never faced with unanimous opposition from "big business" toward his Mexican policies. Even in 1919, after the end of the European war, when large American corporations organized an unprecedented campaign for U.S. intervention in Mexico in which they enjoyed the support of powerful groups in the Senate, led by Albert B. Fall, and of members of the administration including Secretary of State Lansing, very important business interests remained opposed to U.S. intervention in Mexico. American mining companies had come to an agreement with Carranza, while some of the largest bankers, whose overseas commitments were increasing, did not want the United States to get bogged down in Mexico. This favorable attitude of some business groups toward Wilson's Mexican policies was bolstered by the fact that, short of intervention, the administration in Washington was doing everything that it, or for that matter, any other administration, could do to protect American interests from Mexican nationalists.

Like his counterparts in Europe, Wilson was faced with a military establishment demanding an aggressive policy in Mexico. After the U.S. intervention in Veracruz, in 1914, Secretary of War Garrison called for the occupation of all of Mexico, and in 1916, while unsuccessfully chasing Villa through the arid vastness of Chihuahua, in the midst of an increasingly hostile population, Pershing had advocated similar policies. In view of the traditionally less important role the military played in the United States than in Europe, it was far easier for Wilson to control them than for the civilian governments of Europe to do so. Once the United States became involved in World War I, the military's interest drastically shifted from Mexico to overseas and Wilson's conflicts with his military chiefs with regard to Mexico all but ceased.

What influence did the policies of Woodrow Wilson have on the course of the Mexican Revolution? There is little doubt that the direct, and more important the indirect, help the United States gave the Mexican revolutionaries in 1914–15 contributed to their victory, but to what degree did it also shape their social policies?

In ideological terms, this was certainly not the case. The constitution of 1917 challenged basic principles and assumptions held not only by large

American corporations, but by the State Department and Woodrow Wilson as well. It drastically restricted the rights of foreigners in Mexico and under certain circumstances made their holdings subject to confiscation. It declared that the state had the right to expropriate large estates in order to carry out agrarian reform.

In practice though, the Mexican Revolution up to 1920 produced results very different from other great upheavals in the twentieth century. Not only was there no large-scale expropriation of foreign property, but American investments by 1920 were more important than they had been at the beginning of the revolution in 1910. By displacing European interests, American capital had assumed an economic supremacy in Mexico it had never enjoyed before.

In contrast to other social upheavals in which peasants participated, the agrarian structure of Mexico remained fundamentally unchanged. The large estates and the majority of their owners frequently survived the revolutionary period far better than the peasants.

Were these developments linked to U.S. policies?

To answer this question one must examine the character of the forces that emerged as victors from the civil war of 1914–15.

As I have tried to show, what is generally known as the Mexican Revolution in the years 1910–20 did not constitute one revolution, but a series of very different revolutions and revolts that were centered in the states of Morelos, Chihuahua, Coahuila, and Sonora. Outside of these states the revolutionary movements were on the whole less important and were subordinated to the leadership from one of these four core states. A peasant revolution took place in Morelos. There was a populist revolution in Chihuahua in which the lower and the middle classes of the state united to fight its upper classes and expropriated the latter's holdings. Members of the lower classes played a decisive, but by no means exclusive role, in its leadership. In Coahuila, a far more conservative revolt of revolutionary hacendados with middle class participation and some lower class support had emerged. In Sonora, a similar revolt had occurred, but here the influence of the revolutionary hacendados was weaker and that of the middle classes stronger than in Coahuila. As these movements transcended their states of origin, they began to seek allies in other parts of Mexico, frequently with very different social ideas and of very different social origin. At this point, some of the movements began to be transformed and some of their aims and purposes changed. The least affected by such changes was the Zapata movement, since it scarcely extended beyond the confines of Morelos and its surroundings.

But even the Zapata movement had to compromise some of its basic tenets when it ventured outside its agrarian mainstay and attempted to occupy some larger cities. Its peasant troops were not disposed to garrison the city of Puebla, and Zapata had to resort to an uneasy alliance with former federal troops to accomplish this purpose.

The Villa movement entered into alliances with heterogeneous forces outside the state of Chihuahua ranging from Zapata's radical peasants to Maytorena and his conservative allies and even to the former federal officers that had assembled a fighting force made up of remnants of the federal army in Baja California. The Coahuilan and Sonoran revolutionaries sought to broaden their base by gaining support not only from the upper classes of central Mexico but from the free peasants and urban workers of that region as well. In southern and southeastern Mexico they actively courted and captured the support of peons from large haciendas who lived in conditions of semislavery.

Naturally enough the process of canvassing for a wider base of support and catering to a different set of desires significantly modified the original character and objectives of these movements, blurring many of the important differences that had existed between them previously. Not, however, to the point of completely erasing them. Certain basic differences still remained. In spite of the opposition of its conservative wing the great majority of the Conventionist leadership remained committed to the expropriation of Mexico's large estates. By contrast in spite of the radical tendencies of some of its members the Constitutionalist movement was able to carry out, with little opposition, the massive return of expropriated estates to their former owners.

The core of the Constitutionalist movement, which ruled most of Mexico after the defeat of the Convention in 1914/15, was essentially made up of two groups. The first were the revolutionary members of the Porfirian hacendado class. Their role and importance steadily diminished between 1915 and 1920. Their most important leader and spokesman was Venustiano Carranza. The second group whose influence was on the rise consisted essentially of members of what, for want of a better name, could be called the middle class, predominantly from the North, many of whose leaders had in the course of the revolution been transformed into a new bourgeoisie. The most prominent among them, Alvaro Obregón, was by no means the only one who secured large agricultural holdings and great commercial interests as a result of revolutionary changes.

Both of these groups had wanted to eliminate the economic and political supremacy of the old oligarchy in Mexico, but had no irreconcilable antagonism to that oligarchy such as the one that separated the triumphant bourgeoisie in France from the traditional landowners in that country. The French revolutionaries including their Napoleonic successors never returned lands to traditional estate owners as the triumphant Constitutionalists did in Mexico.

In fact, in spite of the radical nature of the constitution, Mexico's rulers until 1920, among whom the revolutionary hacendados still played an essential role, sought to emulate many of the policies that Porfirio Díaz had implemented after taking power in 1876.

The problems Díaz faced at that time were not so different from those faced by Carranza after securing victory in 1915. The country Díaz had to rule was disunited, and large parts of it were dominated by powerful local caudillos. Thousands of former soldiers who had fought against the French roamed the Mexican countryside and had to be brought under some kind of control. Many members of Mexico's traditional upper class who had been linked to Díaz's predecessors rejected his coup and felt that he would not be able to guarantee them the new holdings many had acquired as a result of the civil war against the Church. Mexico was isolated in international terms as rarely before. The United States had refused to recognize the new government and demanded important political concessions from it. As a result of the war against Maximilian, Mexico's traditional relationships with the great European powers had been broken and at first the latter had not recognized the Díaz regime.

In spite of these obstacles Porfirio Díaz within a few years succeeded not only in consolidating but in strengthening the state tremendously and gaining the support of Mexico's upper classes and of all important foreign powers.

Although he did not bow to political pressures from the United States, he managed to secure at first American recognition, and later U.S. support by large-scale economic concessions to American capitalists and investors. The new revenues Díaz managed to obtain from increasing foreign investment allowed him to strengthen the Mexican state and thus to give better guarantees than ever before to Mexican landowners and to other members of the upper class with regard to their property and traditional rights. This newly strengthened state was also an instrument by which Díaz managed to bring the local caudillos under control. He was able to remove them from political power and dissolve their private armies. He bought their acquiescence to this by allowing them almost unlimited opportunities for self-enrichment. By transforming the traditional caudillos into capitalists, Díaz had given them a greater stake in keeping Mexico stable: the value of their property and the availability of overseas loans depended on it!

Díaz attempted to forestall unilateral American control by making overtures to European governments and European investors and attracting them by all possible means to Mexico.

Thanks to these methods the Mexican dictator obtained the support of foreign governments and of foreign capital within a relatively short time.

The majority of Mexico's upper classes rallied to him, and until the end of the nineteenth century even dissatisfied members of these classes, with very few exceptions, refused to revolt or to challenge his rule directly.

There was one group toward whom Díaz remained intransigent and showed no readiness to make any kind of concessions: the lower classes of society. A policy of repression was applied uniformly toward any protest movements by either the peasantry or the industrial working class.

There are strong indications that Carranza, after securing both military victory and American recognition in October 1915, attempted to apply a similar policy toward Mexico.

Like Díaz, he remained intransigent toward the United States as far as any kind of political concession was concerned. But in economic terms he was quite ready to undertake loan negotiations with the United States which would have secured not only existing American rights and holdings, but probably would have led to increasing American influence in Mexico. Like Díaz, Carranza hoped to counter American economic influence by inviting other powers into Mexico, but with different powers than Díaz had. He concentrated his efforts first on Japan and then on Germany. Like Díaz, Carranza was faced with the problem of controlling the huge military forces the revolution had spawned and the local and regional caudillos who led them.

Carranza attempted to solve these problems in a way similar to that of the former dictator, by strengthening the state and by playing off one caudillo against the other. He also allowed these caudillos to enrich themselves by whatever means they wanted in the hope that by transforming them into capitalists he would prevent them from carrying out coups and revolts.

Finally, like Díaz, he did everything in his power to attract the upper classes and especially hacendados to his cause.

Carranza's main means of achieving this purpose was to return the confiscated estates to their former owners. To achieve a maximum gain from this operation he made sure that only Mexico's central government and not the local military chieftains would have a right to do this. He also made this a process lasting between two and three years, which increased the dependency of the estate owners upon the goodwill of the Carranza administration.

In contrast to Díaz, Carranza was prepared to do in words what neither of them was prepared to implement in deeds: concessions to the lower classes of society. But in practical terms Carranza's flamboyant revolutionary rhetoric stood in sharp contrast to the strongly repressive measures he took against the lower classes in the early part of 1916, soon after having been victorious in Mexico's civil war.

And yet Carranza, by implementing these policies, never achieved

Díaz's success in stabilizing and consolidating his hold over the whole of the country. One reason Díaz's policies failed to work for Carranza was the fact that he never managed to secure the economic support from the  United States he had hoped for in late 1915 and early 1916. Villa's attack on Columbus in March 1916 and the resulting penetration of Pershing's punitive expedition into Mexico had spoilt that prospect. The expedition, by bringing Mexico to the brink of war with the United States created a legacy of hostility and mistrust that made it impossible, in the short run, for any Mexican leader to seek a rapprochement with the United States. Carranza's attempted rapprochement with both Japan and Germany brought no economic benefits or revenue to compensate for the loss of American support.

Another reason Díaz's policies failed to work for Carranza was of course the strength and magnitude of the popular movements that they  had to contend with. While Villa and Zapata had been defeated in their attempts to seize national power, they were still potent regional leaders to be reckoned with. In the Carranza movement itself, as a result of its social promises in 1915 and of the constitution it drafted in 1917, radical movements had sprung up among both the peasantry and the industrial workers. In spite of attempted government repression, they grew greatly in combativeness and strength between 1915 and 1920.

It was in the final account the failure of his Porfirian strategy which led to Carranza's fall. The new leaders who took over the country and who essentially consisted of the new bourgeoisie which had come from the northern middle class did not entirely break with Carranza's policies as far as the hacendados and Mexico's upper classes were concerned. They carried out no massive attempt at destroying the latter's economic power. But they did endeavor to remedy what they considered the two main weaknesses of the Carranza regime. They achieved a compromise, at least on a temporary basis, with the United States. And they expressed a genuine willingness to yield to at least some of the demands for social reform where strong and important popular movements existed. Thus they finally made their peace with the remnants of the Zapata movement and with Villa and granted far more lands to peasants than Carranza had ever done.

Were Carranza's conservative economic and social policies and especially his stubborn refusal to implement more than token agrarian reform due to outside pressure? Was his victory and conversely the defeat of the Conventionist faction the result of action by either the Wilson administration or large U.S. interests?

There is little doubt that without American pressure more taxes and more restrictions would have been imposed on American properties.  American investors would have had to relinquish their rights as foreigners and submit to a wide variety of controls. Nevertheless, there is no evidence that either Carranza or the other leaders of the victorious factions contemplated any large program of nationalization or had any socialist aspirations. Apart from the restrictions and taxes they imposed on foreign holdings they would probably have tried to diversify investments and attract investors from other countries, especially from Germany and possibly from Japan and Mexico.

With regard to agrarian reform there is no evidence that either Carranza or the main leaders of his movement were prevented from carrying out such reforms by outside pressure. They simply had no wish to change the agrarian structure of the country. But the fact that Carranza could carry out such a policy and gain supremacy without having had to make significant concessions to the peasantry was related, though only indirectly, to U.S. policies. A short time after the outbreak of the Constitutionalist revolt, in May 1913, Delbert G. Haff, in a memorandum on the Mexican situation, submitted to Woodrow Wilson in the name of some of the largest U.S. interests in Mexico, had noted: "The Constitutionalists are practically ... without resources, that is without funds and have exhausted, for the most part, their sources to obtain funds." A few months later, because of their alliance with the Wilson administration and some U.S. business interests, this problem was solved for the Constitutionalists. They not only received substantial contributions from U.S. interests but were allowed to sell their products and buy arms across the U.S. border (this was the case even before Wilson removed the embargo on arms sales to Mexico).

Without these funds the northern revolutionaries would have had to do what Zapata did in the South—resort to guerrilla warfare. This in turn would have implied, as it did in Morelos, such a degree of peasant participation and control that agrarian reform would have become inevitable. Instead, Carranza, because of his alliance with the United States, secured the means to wage conventional warfare and to set up a regular army, which soon lost its popular basis and became a professional army with no compunctions about fighting against the peasantry.

The situation might have been very different if the Convention had won Mexico's civil war. While there were strong forces inside the Conventionist faction opposed to agrarian changes, its main leaders, Zapata and Villa, were in favor of profound social reforms and were strongly opposed to the return of large estates that Carranza was carrying out. The essential problem, then, is whether the defeat of the Convention was directly or indirectly the result of foreign pressure, foreign intervention, or foreign opposition. There is little doubt that Carranza received important American help. The withdrawal of American occupation forces from Veracruz at a time when he was able to occupy the city gave him an essential base from which to operate. Taxes paid by oil companies were also a great financial help to his movement. By allowing Carranza's troops to cross the United States in order to attack Villa at Agua Prieta, Woodrow Wilson no doubt helped the Mexican president to inflict his last great defeat on Villa. Nevertheless, this help was not decisive. The occupation of Veracruz helped Carranza to survive, but it did not insure his victory.  Financial contributions from the oil companies were important for his movement, but other American companies, especially mining enterprises, were helping Villa at the same time. While there is little doubt that the battle of Agua Prieta meant final defeat for Villa, the decisive battles in which he lost his military supremacy, Celaya and León, were fought before the United States had recognized and aided his enemy. It was not the direct, but rather the indirect influence of the United States that was decisive in the internal conflict sweeping Mexico. Unlike American help for Carranza, the United States' embrace of Villa proved to be deadly for its recipient. The fact that Villa was able to sell the products of confiscated estates in the United States and thus acquire arms from his northern neighbor prevented him from carrying out any large-scale agrarian reform in the first stages of his movement. As a result a chain of events was set in motion which ultimately isolated Villa from the peasantry, which constituted the basis of his movement. The administrators Villa named for the confiscated estates had a vested interest in preventing reform and constituted one of the bases for the conservative faction of the Villista movement. Villa's increasing dependence on arms from the United States made it more and more imperative for him to gain American recognition and thus not to antagonize the Americans by radical social changes. The financial backing of American companies allowed him to print large amounts of paper money whose value depended more and more on the attitude of these companies. This had a double effect. On the one hand, it made him extremely vulnerable to any loss of confidence of American financial interests. On the other hand, it gave him the necessary means to transform his army from a popular into a professional military force. This in turn made it less imperative for him to carry out immediate social reforms. The result of all these factors, the decision to postpone agrarian reform, not only spelled Villa's defeat by making him lose the support of the peasantry but also meant the postponement of agrarian reform in most of Mexico for many years to come. In this respect Woodrow Wilson's policies of aligning himself with the revolutionaries had in fact achieved far-reaching results.

To what degree was the victorious faction among the Mexican revolutionaries able to utilize contradictions between and the struggle among the great powers for its own ends?

While less divided among themselves than their Conventionist opponents, the victorious Constitutionalists were anything but a homogeneous group. In spite of their divergences the vast majority of the Constitutionalists agreed on certain basic aims of their domestic and international policy. They all wanted to break the power monopoly the Porfirian elite had exercised and to broaden the bases of political power in Mexico. They all wanted to replace the federal army with the new army which had emerged from the revolution. The vast majority of the victors wanted to retain the system of free enterprise and were against immediate radical social reforms such as a sweeping program of land division. There is no evidence of any great opposition by the overwhelming majority of the victorious revolutionaries to the return of confiscated estates to their former owners.

In international terms most groups within the Constitutionalist movement wanted to limit both the economic and political influence of foreign (especially United States) governments and foreign companies.

The Constitutionalists were successful in securing their domestic aims. They destroyed the political (but not the economic) power of the old Científicos. They disbanded the federal army and replaced it with one that had emerged from the revolution, though to a large degree, it soon ceased to be a revolutionary army. They maintained the system of free enterprise and defeated their Conventionist rivals whose leaders advocated immediate and profound agrarian reforms.

To achieve these aims they were able to make use of the direct and indirect help of both the Wilson administration and of large American companies operating in Mexico.

They were far less successful in achieving some of their international aims. United States economic influence in Mexico had increased rather than decreased in the course of the revolution. American corporations, especially the oil companies, achieved a preeminence in Mexico they had never enjoyed before in spite of the provisions of the constitution of 1917. British and French interests, which had been greatly weakened as a result of both World War I and the Mexican Revolution, were unwilling and to a large degree unable to resume the role they had played prior to 1910 as a counterweight to U.S. influence. Mexican efforts to persuade the Japanese to carry out large-scale investments in their country failed, and the German gamble did not succeed in economic terms. Nevertheless, in another related field, Mexico's rulers were eminently successful. They were able to maintain Mexico's political independence at a time when it was in greater danger than it had been since the Mexican-American War of 1846–48 and the French intervention. United States business interests and military men called for wide-ranging forms of intervention in Mexico. The Wilson administration intervened repeatedly in the internal affairs of its southern neighbor. In 1913, Wilson proposed to Carranza sending U.S. troops to northern Mexico. In 1914 he ordered the occupation of Veracruz. In 1915 he played with the idea of imposing a president on Mexico chosen by the United States, and in 1916 he sent the punitive expedition into Chihuahua and attempted to make its withdrawal contingent upon political concessions by the Carranza government. Had any of these interventions been successful, the results would doubtless have been what Britain's high-level diplomat and Wilson's sympathizer William Tyrrell had predicted: a virtual American protectorate.

During this period the Germans were either attempting to provoke a United States–Mexican war, which would have led inevitably to a foreign occupation of Mexico, or, to quote the German minister von Eckardt, "to buy the heritage of Cortez" and convert Mexico into a German colony. French diplomats contemplated starving Mexico into submission, while the British General Staff called a special meeting of the war cabinet to propose the overthrow of the revolutionary government and the restoration of the Porfirian oligarchy to power.

In this complex and extremely dangerous situation for Mexico, Carranza's stubbornness, his willingness to go to the brink of war, his subtle utilization of the contradictions within and between the great powers achieved considerable results. He objected to American troops being sent to Mexico in 1913 and to the occupation of Veracruz in 1914 though both measures were designed to speed his victory. Three times he brought his country to the brink of war with the United States. In the summer of 1916 he ordered his troops to resist by force any further advance of the Pershing expedition into Mexico. In the fall of 1916, against the advice of his most important military men, including Obregón, he refused to ratify a United States-Mexican agreement which would have led to the withdrawal of the punitive expedition from Mexico but would have imposed clear-cut restrictions on his country's independence. His final act of boldness was to allow the German secret services to operate in and from Mexico in the summer of 1917. This could easily have led to sharp U.S. reprisals.

Carranza was successful in all three phases. As a result of his stubbornness in 1916, the United States withdrew its punitive expedition unconditionally in February 1917.

The permission the Mexican president granted German intelligence to operate in his country in 1917–18 conjured up the danger of a possible U.S.  intervention. It prevented the much greater danger of massive German sabotage actions in the oil fields, which would almost inevitably have led to U.S. occupation of the oil region.

Carranza doubtless made wide-ranging promises to U.S. business interests and to the Wilson administration in 1913–14 as well as to the Germans in 1917–18 in return for their support. He never carried them out nor did he seem to want to.

When he was driven from office in 1920, the record he left behind was extremely ambiguous. He had been instrumental in preventing the implementation of social changes for which so many Mexicans had fought in the stormy years between 1910 and 1920. But he had also done at least as much to maintain his country's independence in the face of a rising tide of interventionism among the world's great powers.

# Notes

## Chapter 1

1. Politisches Archiv des Auswärtigen Amtes Bonn (hereafter referred to as AA Bonn), Mexico 1, vol. 23, Bünz to Bethmann-Hollweg, 17 September 1909, and vol. 25, Bünz to Bethmann-Hollweg, 4 December 1910.

2. United Nations, Department of Economic and Social Affairs, Economic Commission for Latin America, *External Financing in Latin America* (New York, 1965), p. 17.

3. The most comprehensive work on the Díaz regime is the monumental multivolume *Historia Moderna de Mexico, El Porfiriato,* ed. Daniel Cosío Villegas (Mexico, D.F., 1963–74). See also José C. Valadés, *Breve Historia del Porfirismo* (Mexico, D.F., 1971). For a very different analysis of the Porfirian period, see Juan Felipe Leal, *La Burguesía y el Estado Mexicano* (Mexico, D.F., 1972).

4. An excellent description of the history, organization, and structure of the free villages is to be found in Frank Tannenbaum, *The Mexican Agrarian Revolution* (Washington, D.C., 1930).

Contrary to the long-held assumption that the nineteenth century represented a period of uninterrupted decline in the status of the free villages, John Coatsworth ("From Backwardness to Underdevelopment: The Mexican Economy, 1810–1910" [unpublished], chap. 7) has shown that in the first part of the nineteenth century these villages managed not only to maintain their lands and rights but to consolidate them.

5. See Tannenbaum, *The Mexican Agrarian Revolution,* chaps. 1 and 2; John Womack, Jr., *Zapata and the Mexican Revolution* (New York, 1969), chap. 2; Friedrich Katz, "Peasants in the Mexican Revolution of 1910," in *Forging Nations,* ed. Joseph Spielberg and Scott Whiteford (East Lansing, 1976).

6. See Walter V. Scholes, *Mexican Politics during the Juarez Regime* (Columbus, Mo., 1969), pp. 102–5.

7. Luis Nicholas d'Olwer, "Las Inversiones Extranjeras," in Daniel Cosío Villegas, ed., *Historia Moderna de Mexico, El Porfiriato: Vida Economica,* p. 1134.

8. These rights were clearly spelled out in a proclamation by the *intendante* of the Spanish province of Nueva Vizcaya (which included the territory of the present state of Chihuahua) setting up the first military colonies in that state in 1778. See Archivo del Departamento Agrario, Dirección de Terrenos Nacionales, Chihuahua, Exp. 161. See also Katz, "Peasants in the Mexican Revolution of 1910."

9. Departamento Agrario, Dirección de Terrenos Nacionales, Diversos, Chihuahua, Exp. 178, Letter of the inhabitants of Namiquipa to President Porfirio Díaz, 20 July 1908.

10. Ibid., Exp. 75–1407, Letter of Porfirio Talamantes representing the inhabitants of Janos to President Porfirio Díaz, 22 August 1908.

11. Francisco R. Almada, *La Revolución en el Estado de Chihuahua,* 2 vols. (Mexico, D.F., 1964–69), 1:23–25.

12. Francisco P. Ontiveros, *Toribio Ortega y la Brigada González Ortega* (Chihuahua, 1914).

13. Heliodoro Arías Olea, *Apuntes Históricos de la Revolución de 1910–1911* (Bachíniva, 1960).

14. See Francisco R. Almada, *La Rebelión de Tomochic* (Chihuahua, 1938).

15. See Evelyn Hu Dehart, "Pacification of the Yaquis in the Late Porfiriato: Development and Implications," *Hispanic American Historical Review* 54 (February 1974): 72–94.

16. See Francisco R. Almada, *Resúmen de Historia del Estado de Chihuahua* (Mexico, D.F., 1955), p. 350.

17. Hector Aguilar Camín, *La Frontera Nómada: Sonora y la Revolución Mexicana* (Mexico, D.F., 1977), pp. 83–85.

18. El Colegio de México, *Estadísticas Económicas del Porfiriato: Fuerza de Trabajo y Actividad Económica por Sectores* (Mexico, D.F., n.d.), pp. 147–55.

19. See d'Olwer, "Las Inversiones Extranjeras," pp. 1154 and 1161.

20. Pablo Martínez del Río, *El Suplicio del Hacendado* (Mexico, D.F., 1939), p. 15.

21. See Friedrich Katz, "Labor Conditions on Haciendas in Porfirian Mexico: Some Trends and Tendencies," *Hispanic American Historical Review* 54 (February 1979): 30–37.

22. Ibid.

23. See Laura Helguera Reséndiz, "Tenango: Metamórfosis Campesina," in Laura Helguera, Sinecio López, and Ramón Ramírez, *Los Campesinos de la Tierra de Zapata*, 3 vols. (Mexico, D.F., 1974), 1:108–9, 135–36.

24. José Fuentes Mares, *Y México se Refugió en el Desierto: Luis Terrazas, Historia y Destino* (Mexico, D.F., 1954), p. 244.

25. Ibid., pp. 166, 171.

26. Aguilar Camín, *La Frontera Nómada*, p. 153.

27. William K. Meyers, "Interest Conflicts and Popular Discontent: The Origins of the Revolution in the Laguna, 1880–1910" (Ph.D. diss., University of Chicago, 1979), chap. 3.

28. Richard Estrada, "Liderazgo, Local y Regional en la Revolución Norteña" (unpublished).

29. Ibid.

30. Meyers, "Interest Conflicts and Popular Discontent," chap. 3.

31. Ibid.

32. Katz, "Labor Conditions on Haciendas," pp. 45–47.

33. Ibid.

34. For the rise of the Terrazas clan, see Fuentes Mares, *Y México se Refugió en el Desierto;* Mark Wasserman, "Oligarchy and Foreign Enterprise in Chihuahua" (Ph.D. diss., University of Chicago, 1975), pp. 14–59; Harold D. Sims, "Espejo de Caciques: Los Terrazas de Chihuahua," *Historia Mexicana* 18 (January–March 1969): 379–99.

35. See Francisco R. Almada, *La Revolución en el Estado de Sonora* (Mexico, D.F., 1971), pp. 11–15. During most of the Porfiriato these two men together with two allies, Ramón Corral and Rafael Izábal, alternately ruled the state of Sonora as governors.

36. See Wassermann, "Oligarchy," chap. 4.

37. Ibid., chap. 6; Aguilar Camín, *La Frontera Nómada*, chap. 1.

38. See Anthony T. Bryan, "Mexican Politics in Transition, 1900–1913: The Role of General Bernardo Reyes" (Ph.D. diss., University of Nebraska, 1970).

39. For a description and analysis of the ideology of the Científicos, see Leopoldo Zea, *El Positivismo en México* (Mexico, D.F., 1968); William D. Raat, *El Positivismo Durante el Porfiriato* (Mexico, D.F., 1975).

40. Meyers, "Interest Conflicts and Popular Discontent," chap. 3.

41. Madero's conflicts with American interests are described in Stanley R. Ross, *Francisco I. Madero: Apostle of Mexican Democracy* (New York, 1955), p. 53, and William K. Meyers, "Politics, Vested Rights, and Economic Growth in Porfirian Mexico: The Company Tlahualilo in the Comarca Lagunera," *Hispanic American Historical Review* 57 (August 1977): 425.

42. See Channing Arnold and J. Tabor Frost, "Esclavitud en las Haciendas," and Henry Baerlein, "Los esclavos de Yucatán," in Friedrich Katz, ed., *La Servidumbre agraria en México en la Época Porfiriana* (Mexico, D.F., 1976), pp. 95–123.

43. Ross, *Francisco I. Madero*, pp. 11–14.

44. Deutsches Zentralarchiv, Potsdam (hereafter referred to as DZA Potsdam), Reichschatzamt no. 2476, Wangenheim to Bülow, 29 October 1904.

45. United States Senate Documents, Foreign Relations Committee, *Investigation of Mexican Affairs, Report and Hearings* (2 vols.), 66th Congress, 1st Session, Senate Document no. 62 (Washington, D.C., 1919), 1:217.

46. Haus, Hof und Staatsarchiv Wien, Politisches Archiv (hereafter referred to as HHSta Wien, PA), Mexico Reports, 1902, Auersthal to Goluchowsky, 24 November 1902.

47. Archives du Ministère des Affaires Etrangères, Correspondance Commerciale, Paris (hereafter referred to as AMAE, Paris, CC), Mexique, vol. 17, Blondel to Delcassé, 20 July 1901.

48. AA Bonn, Mexico 1, vol. 17, Wangenheim to Bülow, 7 January 1907.

49. AMAE, Paris, CC, Mexique, vol. 17, Blondel to Delcassé, 28 April 1901.

50. El Colegio de Mexico, *Estadísticas Económicas del Porfiriato: Comercio Exterior de Mexico* (Mexico, D.F., 1960), pp. 524, 546.

51. This was reported by the German minister to Mexico in July and November 1905 (DZA Potsdam, AA II, no. 12297, Wangenheim to Bülow, 17 May 1905; AA II, no. 1746, Wangenheim to Bülow, 29 November 1905).

52. There are two biographies of Weetman Pearson: J. A. Spender, *Weetman Pearson, First Viscount Cowdray* (London, 1930); Desmond Young, *Viscount Cowdray: Member for Mexico* (London, 1955).

53. See Alfred Vagts, *Mexiko, Europa und Amerika unter besonderer Berücksichtigung der Petroleumpolitik* (Berlin, 1928), p. 153.

54. DZA Merseburg, Rep. 120, CX III, 17, no. 2, vol. 8, Heyking to Bülow, 29 August 1903.

55. Ibid., Heyking to Bülow, 2 November 1906.

56. DZA Potsdam, AA II, no. 4457, Wangenheim to Bülow, 2 November 1906.

57. Ibid., no. 4491, Consul in Chihuahua to Bethmann-Hollweg, 31 March 1910.

58. *Investigation of Mexican Affairs*, 2:2559.

59. Ibid., 1:215.

60. DZA Potsdam, AA II, no. 4459, Bünz to Bülow, 29 May 1909.

61. Ibid., no. 4460, Hintze to Bethmann-Hollweg, 13 January 1912.

62. M. S. Alperovich and B. T. Rudenko, *La Revolución Mexicana de 1910–1917 y la Politica de los Estados Unidos* (Mexico, D.F., 1960).

63. Spender, *Weetman Pearson*, pp. 151–53; Young, *Viscount Cowdray*, pp. 129–30.

64. AA Bonn, Mexico 1, vol. 40, Herwarth von Bittenfeld to Minister of War, 11 November 1913.

65. See Edwin Lieuwen, *Mexican Militarism, 1910–1940* (New Mexico, 1968), pp. 1–5; James W. Wilkie, *The Mexican Revolution, Federal Expenditure and Social Change since 1910* (Berkeley and Los Angeles, 1970), p. 102.

66. Paul J. Vanderwood, "The 'Rurales': Mexico's Rural Police Force, 1861–1914" (Ph.D. diss., University of Texas at Austin, 1970).

67. For an analysis and history of the Liberal party, see especially, James D. Cockcroft, *Intellectual Precursors of the Mexican Revolution* (Austin, Tex., 1968).

68. For the most extensive description and analysis of the Reyes movement, see Anthony Bryan, "Mexican Politics in Transition."

69. AA Bonn, Mexico 1, vol. 19, Wangenheim to Bülow, 1 November 1907.

70. Ibid., Wangenheim to Bülow, 14 January 1907.

71. Manuel González Ramírez, *La Huelga de Cananea* (Mexico, D.F., 1956).

72. DZA Potsdam, AA II, no. 4491, Consul in Chihuahua to Bülow, 10 May 1909.
73. Ibid.
74. See Robert Lynn Sandels, "Silvestre Terrazas: The Press and the Origins of the Mexican Revolution in Chihuahua" (Ph.D. diss., University of Oregon, 1967), pp. 137–55.
75. Ibid., p. 162.
76. See Cosío Villegas, *Historia Moderna de Mexico, El Porfiriato: Vida Política Exterior* (Mexico, D.F., 1960), vol. 7, part 1, pp. 629–733; part 2, pp. 298–320.
77. AA Bonn, Mexico 1, vol. 23, Bünz to Bülow, 30 July 1909.
78. For the election in Morelos see Womack, *Zapata*, pp. 10–36.
79. Ross, *Francisco I. Madero*, pp. 57–64.
80. The full text of the plan can be found in Jesús Silva Herzog, *Breve Historia de la Revolución Mexicana*, 2 vols. (Mexico, D.F., 1960), 1:133–43.
81. Ross, *Francisco I. Madero*, p. 126.
82. The history of the revolution in Coahuila is described in Ildefonso Villarello Vélez, *Historia de la Revolución Mexicana en Coahuila* (Mexico, D.F., 1970). For the most comprehensive analysis of the revolution in the state of Sonora, see Aguilar Camín, *La Frontera Nómada*.
83. See Womack, *Zapata*, pp. 67–96.
84. For a description of the vast Terrazas family network in Chihuahua, see Wasserman, "Oligarchy," chaps. 5 and 6.
85. There are two biographies of Abraham González; see Francisco R. Almada, *Vida, Proceso y Muerte de Abraham González* (Mexico, D.F., 1967) and William H. Beezley, *Insurgent Governor: Abraham González and the Mexican Revolution in Chihuahua* (Lincoln, Neb., 1973).
86. See Michael C. Meyer, *Mexican Rebel: Pascual Orozco and the Mexican Revolution* (Lincoln, Neb., 1967).
87. See Sandels, "Silvestre Terrazas," pp. 126–209.
88. Ontiveros, *Toribio Ortega*.
89. Arías Olea, *Apúntes Históricos*.
90. For a description of Pancho Villa's origins and his early years, see especially Martin Luis Guzmán, *Memorias de Pancho Villa* (Mexico, D.F., 1938); Ramón Puente, *Villa en Pie* (Mexico, D.F., 1937); John Reed, *Insurgent Mexico* (New York, 1969), pp. 95–121.
91. Elías Torres, *Vida y Hazañas de Pancho Villa* (Mexico, D.F., 1975), p. 11.
92. There is as yet no comprehensive study of the social composition of Villa's army. For the role of peasants in that army, see Katz, "Peasants in the Mexican Revolution of 1910." John Reed, in *Insurgent Mexico*, pp. 21–86, gives a clear impression of the heterogeneous composition of the Villista army.
93. Gildardo Magaña, *Emiliano Zapata y el Agrarismo en México*, 3 vols. (Mexico, D.F., 1934–41), 2:141.
94. AA Bonn, Mexico 1, vol. 30, Hintze to Bethmann-Hollweg, 2 October 1911.
95. Ross, *Francisco I. Madero*, p. 220.
96. See Womack, *Zapata*, chaps. 4 and 5.
97. Ibid.
98. Silva Herzog, *Breve Historia*, 1:267.
99. Ross, *Francisco I. Madero*, p. 235.
100. Ibid., p. 277.
101. Michael C. Meyer (*Mexican Rebel*, pp. 56–57, 65–66) found that Orozco enjoyed the support of Chihuahua's prerevolutionary oligarchy. The Austrian minister to Mexico believed that large American business interests, especially those involved in mining, the railways, and rubber were backing Orozco (Minister in Mexico to Austrian Foreign Office, HHSta Wien, PA, Mexico Reports, 1912, 12 December 1912).
102. AA Bonn, Mexico 1, vol. 31, Hintze to Bethmann-Hollweg, 24 October 1912.
103. Ibid., Hintze to Bethmann-Hollweg, 20 December 1912.

104. In 1911 and 1912 both American and Mexican politicians and journalists repeatedly accused Standard Oil of having supported and financed the Madero revolution. These accusations were the target of a Senate investigation in 1912. See *Revolutions in Mexico*, Hearings before a Subcommittee of the Committee on Foreign Relations, United States Senate, Sixty-second Congress, second session (Washington, D.C., 1913), pp. 458–72. In a private letter to President Taft and in his memoirs U.S. ambassador to Mexico, Henry Lane Wilson, expressed similar convictions (Taft Papers, Box 448, no. 1662, H. L. Wilson to Taft, 17 July 1911; Henry Lane Wilson, *Diplomatic Episodes in Mexico, Belgium and Chile* [Garden City, 1927], p. 206). The Austrian minister to Mexico was equally convinced that such a relationship existed (see Minister to Mexico to Austrian Foreign Office, HHSta Wien, PA, Mexico Reports, 1912, 12 December 1912). In 1912 a German company, Bach, interested in oil lands, wrote a confidential letter to the German minister in Mexico stating that there was close cooperation between the Maderos and the Standard Oil Company (see DZA Potsdam, AA II, no. 21600, Petroleum Produktion und Handel in Amerika, p. 147). The German minister to Mexico Paul von Hintze was convinced of the fact that the Standard Oil Company had backed Madero (see DZA Potsdam, AA II, no. 4461, Hintze to Bethmann-Hollweg, 16 March 1912). For an extensive examination and discussion of this issue, see Kenneth J. Grieb, "Standard Oil and the Financing of the Mexican Revolution," *California Historical Society Quarterly* 40 (March 1971): 59–71.

105. Quoted in Ross, *Francisco I. Madero*, p. 237.

106. Ernest Gruening, *Mexico and Its Heritage* (New York, 1928), p. 561.

107. *Papers Relating to Foreign Relations of the United States 1912* (hereafter cited as FR) (Washington, D.C., 1918), H. L. Wilson to Knox, 22 August 1912, Lascuráin to Knox, 22 October 1912.

108. Edgar Turlington, *Mexico and Her Foreign Creditors* (New York, 1930), p. 247.

109. DZA Potsdam, AA II, no. 4461, Hintze to Bethmann-Hollweg, 16 March 1912.

110. HHSta Wien, PA, Mexico Reports 1912, Minister to Mexico to Austrian Foreign Office, 12 December 1912.

111. Papers of Leonard Wood, Library of Congress, Washington, D.C., Box 60, Brooks to Wood, 4 January 1912.

112. AA Bonn, Mexico 1, vol. 52, Hintze to Bethmann-Hollweg, 24 October 1912.

113. Ibid.


# Chapter 2

1. Moisés González Navarro, *La Colonización en Mexico* (Mexico, D.F., 1960), p. 90.

2. This figure is based on a statement by German Foreign Secretary Gottlieb von Jagow to the German Reichstag in April 1914 in which he estimated German holdings in Mexico at 500 million marks (AA Bonn, Mexico 1, vol. 45, speech by Jagow to Reichstag, 29 April 1914). These estimates were for 1913, but there is no evidence of any significant new German investments or losses in Mexico between 1910 and 1913.

3. El Colegio de Mexico, *Estadísticas Económicas del Porfiriato, Comercio Exterior de México, 1877–1911* (Mexico, D.F., 1960), pp. 524, 546.

4. *Der Export*, 1889, p. 218.

5. Chester Lloyd Jones, *Mexico and Its Reconstruction* (New York, 1922), p. 199.

6. AMAE, Paris, CC, Mexique, vol. 16, Signoret to Millerand, 6 October 1900.

7. *Der Export*, 1889, p. 218.

8. DZA Potsdam, AA II, no. 12288, Zedwitz to Bismarck, 30 December 1889.

9. DZA Potsdam, AA II, no. 12299, Wangenheim to Bülow, 10 March 1906.

10. DZA Potsdam, AA II, no. 1741/1, Bruchhausen to Bethmann-Hollweg, 5 November 1911.

11. Rudolph Darius, "Die Entwicklung der deutsch-mexikanischen Handelsbeziehungen von 1870 bis 1914" (Ph.D. diss., University of Cologne, 1927), p. 20.

12. Edgar Turlington, *Mexico and Her Foreign Creditors* (New York, 1930), p. 212.

13. DZA Potsdam, AA II, no. 1727, Zedwitz to Bismarck, 24 February 1889.

14. Ibid.

15. AMAE, Paris, Correspondance Politique (CP), Mexique, vol. 75, Sainte Foix to Spuller, 10 September 1889.

16. Ibid.

17. Ibid., 9 September 1889.

18. Ibid., Spuller to Sainte Foix, 8 October 1889.

19. In a conversation with Romero Rubio, who was Mexico's minister of the interior and Díaz's father-in-law, the French minister to Mexico expressed surprise that Mexico should have agreed to sign such a secret clause. Rubio told the minister that Díaz had not known about it when he signed the loan agreement. The secret clause was the strategy of Finance Minister Dublán, who had close financial ties to Bleichröder (ibid., vol. 76, Sainte Foix to Spuller, 10 February 1890). In view of the tremendous power that Díaz already exercised at that time it is very dubious that the finance minister would have agreed to such a far-reaching clause on his own.

20. DZA Potsdam, AA II, no. 1727, Zedwitz to Bismarck, 13 December 1889.

21. AMAE, Paris, CP, Mexique, vol. 76, Sainte Foix to Ribot, 21 April 1890. The German archives contain no record of such a conversation or of Zedwitz's threats. This could indicate that Romero Rubio had made up the whole conversation in order to impress the French government with Mexico's determination to resist any German attempt to secure financial hegemony in Mexico. It could also indicate that Zedwitz, having failed to intimidate the Mexican government, preferred not to report his failure to Berlin.

22. Turlington, *Mexico and Her Foreign Creditors*, p. 218. AMAE, Paris, CP, Mexique, vol. 77, Wiener to Hanotaux, 10 April 1895.

23. AA Bonn, Mexico 1, vol. 14, Wangenheim to Bülow, 2 November 1904.

24. DZA Potsdam, Reichschatzamt, no. 2476, Wangenheim to Bülow, 29 October 1904.

25. DZA Potsdam, AA II, no. 1746, Bressler to Bülow, 27 June 1906.

26. Ibid., no. 4460, Hintze to Bethmann-Hollweg, 13 January 1912.

27. Ibid.

28. Bernhard Huldermann, *Albert Ballin* (Berlin, 1922), p. 61.

29. DZA Potsdam, AA II, no. 12298, Wangenheim to Bülow, 27 August 1905.

30. Ibid., no. 1748, Bruchhausen to Auswärtiges Amt, 8 August 1910.

31. Ibid., no. 12298, Wangenheim to Bülow, 27 August 1905.

32. Carl Fürstenberg, *Die Lebensgeschichte eines deutschen Bankiers 1870–1919* (Berlin, 1931), p. 525.

33. DZA Potsdam, AA II, no. 4457, Wangenheim to Bülow, 7 December 1906.

34. Ibid., no. 4459, Bünz to Bülow, 29 May 1909.

35. Ibid.

36. Ibid., no 4491, Consul in Chihuahua to Bethmann-Hollweg, 31 March 1910.

37. Ibid., no. 15393, Bruchhausen to Bethmann-Hollweg, 21 January 1911.

38. Ibid., no. 1748, Bruchhausen to Auswärtiges Amt, 1 July 1910.

39. Ibid., no. 1748, Bruchhausen to Bethmann-Hollweg, 23 November 1911.

40. Ibid., no. 4457, Bruchhausen to Bülow, 30 May 1907.

41. Ibid., no. 1748, Bünz to Bethmann-Hollweg, 25 March 1910.

42. Ibid.

43. Ibid., no. 1748, Bruchhausen to Auswärtiges Amt, 1 July 1910.

44. Ibid., no. 1741/1, Bruchhausen to Bethmann-Hollweg, 11 October 1911.

45. Ibid.

46. Ibid., no. 1748, Bruchhausen to Bethmann-Hollweg, 1 August 1910.

47. Ibid., no. 1741/1, Bruchhausen to Bethmann-Hollweg, 16 May 1911.

48. El Colegio de Mexico, *Estadísticas Económicas del Porfiriato, Comercio Exterior*, p. 524.

49. Alfred Vagts, *Deutschland und die Vereinigten Staaten in der Weltpolitik* (London and New York, 1935), 2:1666.

50. AA Bonn, Mexico 1, vol. 10, Heyking to Bülow, 28 May 1902.

51. Ibid., Heyking to Bülow, 2 June 1902.

52. DZA Potsdam, AA II, no. 8462, Krupp to Mühlberg, 1 January 1894.

53. AMAE, Paris, CP, Mexique, vol. 75, Sainte Foix to Spuller, 9 September 1889.

54. DZA Potsdam, AA II, no. 8462, Winckler to Caprivi, 6 December 1893.

55. AA Bonn, Mexico 1, vol. 11, Flöcker to Bülow, 10 May 1903; vol. 12, Flöcker to Bülow, 26 August 1903; vol. 23, Bünz to Bülow, 3 May 1909.

56. AA Bonn, Mexico 1, vol. 11, Bülow to Heyking, 5 October 1902.

57. Ibid., vol. 11, Flöcker to Bülow, 10 May 1903.

58. Ibid., vol. 23, Bünz to Bülow, 3 May 1909.

59. *Statistisches Jahrbuch für das Deutsche Reich* (Berlin, 1910).

60. Barbara W. Tuchman, *The Zimmermann Telegram* (London, 1959), p. 27.

61. Archivo Nacional de Cuba (hereafter referred to as AN Cuba), Secretaría de Estado Leg. 336–655, Minister in Mexico to Zaldo, 2 February 1904.

62. AA Bonn, Mexico 1, vol. 12, Secretary of State to Flöcker, 20 November 1903.

63. Ibid.

64. Ibid., vol. 13, Secretary of State to Flöcker, 24 January 1904.

65. Ibid., Flöcker to Bülow, 27 Janaury 1904.

66. Ibid., Flöcker to Bülow, 15 February 1904.

67. AN Cuba, Secretaría de Estado Leg. 336–655, Minister to Mexico to Zaldo, 2 February 1904.

68. AA Bonn, Mexico 1, vol. 19, Wangenheim to Bülow, 22 December 1906.

69. Ibid., comments of Wilhelm II about the foregoing report.

70. Ibid., Wangenheim to Bülow, 10 November 1907.

71. Ibid.

72. Ibid., Wangenheim to Bülow, 7 January 1907.

73. Ibid., Tschirsky to Wangenheim, 2 February 1907.

74. AA Bonn, Mexico 1, vol. 20, Speck von Sternburg to Bülow, 22 August 1907.

75. Ibid., Wangenheim to Bülow, 19 March 1907.

76. Ibid.

77. Ibid., comments of Wilhelm II.

78. Ibid., Radowitz to Bülow, 16 April 1907.

79. Ibid., vol. 21, Radowitz to Bülow, 27 June 1908.

80. V. J. Lepsius, A. Mendelsohn-Bartholdy, and F. Thimme, eds., *Die grosse Politik der europäischen Kabinette, 1871–1914*, 40 vols. (Berlin, 1922–27), vol. 26, part 1, no. 8553, Sternburg to Auswärtiges Amt, 8 November 1911.

81. Bernhard von Bülow, *Denkwürdigkeiten*, 4 vols. (Berlin, 1930–31), 2:352, 374.

82. AA Bonn, Mexico 10, vol. 1, Wangenheim to Bülow, 25 May 1907.

83. Ibid., Wangenheim to Consul in Guadalajara, 8 April 1907.

84. Ibid.

85. Ibid., Consul in Guadalajara to Wangenheim, 1 May 1907.

86. Ibid., Consul in Chihuahua to Wangenheim, 3 May 1907.

87. Ibid., Wangenheim to Bülow, 15 July 1907.

88. Ibid., Mumm von Schwarzenstein to Bülow, 27 December 1907.

89. AA Bonn, Archive of German Legation in Mexico, Folder 13, Kritzler to German Legation in Mexico, 27 July and 7 October 1907.

90. HHSta Wien, PA, Mexico Reports 1907, Minister to Mexico to Ärenthal, 14 October 1907.

91. Ibid.

92. AA Bonn, Mexico 10, vol. I, Wangenheim to Bülow, 26 October 1907.

93. *Die grosse Politik*, vol. 26, part 1, no. 8553, Sternburg to Auswärtiges Amt, 8 November 1907.

94. Tuchman, *The Zimmermann Telegram*, p. 32.

95. W. Goetz, ed., *Briefe Wilhelms II an den Zaren Nikolaus II, 1894–1914* (Berlin, 1920), p. 236, letter of 28 December 1907.

96. AA Bonn, Mexico 10, vol. I, Mumm von Schwarzenstein to Bülow, 18 February 1908.

97. Elizabeth von Heyking, *Tagebücher aus vier Weltteilen* (Berlin and Leipzig, 1926), p. 324.

98. Ibid., p. 364.

99. AA Bonn, Mexico 1, vol. 52, Bünz to Bethmann-Hollweg, 17 September 1909.

100. Ibid.

101. DZA Potsdam, AA II, no. 4460, Bruchhausen to Bethmann-Hollweg, 22 February 1911.

102. AA Bonn, Mexico 1, vol. 28, Hintze to Bethmann-Hollweg, 19 May 1911.

103. Ibid., Hintze to Bethmann-Hollweg, 12 April 1911.

104. DZA Potsdam, AA II, no. 1741/1, Hintze to Bethmann-Hollweg, 22 July 1911.

105. Archivo de Relaciones Exteriores de Mexico (hereafter referred to as AREM), 619 R, Mexican Minister in Berlin to Secretary of Foreign Affairs, 20 December 1910.

106. Ibid., 623 R, Consul in Hamburg to Secretary of Foreign Affairs, 22 December 1910.

107. Henry Lane Wilson, *Diplomatic Episodes in Mexico, Belgium and Chile* (Garden City, 1927), p. 205.

108. Alfred Vagts, *Mexiko, Europa und Amerika unter besonderer Berücksichtigung der Petroleumpolitik* (Berlin, 1928), p. 191.

109. Staatsarchiv Hamburg (hereafter referred to as Sta Hamburg), CId26 Waffen-schmuggel Hic 21/11, Waffenausfuhr nach Mexiko, Record of a conversation that took place on 25 March 1911.

110. Ibid., Reichschancellor to Hamburg Senate, 6 April 1911.

111. *Deutsche Zeitung in Mexiko*, 24 April 1911.

112. Bülow, *Denkwürdigkeiten*, 2:352, 374.

113. AA Bonn, Mexico 1, vol. 57, Minister in Tokyo to German Foreign Office, 24 March 1911; Bernstorff to Bethmann-Hollweg, 4 April 1911.

114. *Kölnische Zeitung*, 4 April 1911.

115. Tuchman, *The Zimmermann Telegram*, p. 37.

116. AA Bonn, Mexico 1, vol. 27, Bernstorff to Bethmann-Hollweg, 4 April 1911.

117. Ibid., Bernstorff to Bethmann-Hollweg, 20 March 1911.

118. Horst von der Goltz, *My Adventures as a German Spy* (New York, 1917), p. 40. While many of Goltz's statements cannot be proven and seem exaggerated, his claim that he worked for German intelligence is confirmed by German sources. See DZA Potsdam, Auswärtiges Amt, Nachrichten und Presseabteilung, Commentary to Horst von der Goltz's book.

119. AREM, Mexico, Le 796 R, Minister in Tokyo to Mexican Foreign Secretary, 23 March 1911.

120. AA Bonn, Mexico 1, vol. 27, Bernstorff to Bethmann-Hollweg, 4 April 1911.

121. Ibid., Mexico 10, vol. 1, Minister in Tokyo to Bethmann-Hollweg, 23 March 1911.

122. Henry Lane Wilson wrote a letter to Knox in February 1918 to deny the allegations of Horst von der Goltz, whose book had just been published in the United States. Knox forwarded Wilson's statement to Secretary of State Robert Lansing and in a letter to Lansing expressed his full agreement with Lane Wilson's claim. Lansing fully agreed with Knox's letter and wrote the latter that the search of records of the department failed to disclose any mention of such a treaty. See Iyo Kunimoto, "Japan and Mexico, 1888–1917" (Ph.D. diss., University of Texas at Austin, 1975), pp. 107–10.

123. DZA Potsdam, Reichstag no. 1311, Proceedings of the Budget Committee, 5 March 1917.

124. Microfilm of captured Japanese Foreign Office documents, Mexico MT 1133 02 397, Consul in Portland to Minister of Foreign Affairs in Tokyo, 17 March 1911.

125. *Atlantic Monthly*, February 1912.

126. DZA Potsdam, Papers of Herwarth von Bittenfeld, Bittenfeld to Minister of War, 13 March 1912; *New York Sun*, 6 April 1912.

127. AA Bonn, Mexico 1, vol. 30, Hintze to Bethmann-Hollweg, 24 March 1912.

128. Ibid.

129. Ibid., vol. 40, Bernstorff to Bethmann-Hollweg, 25 November 1913.

130. Ibid., vol. 28, Bernstorff to Bethmann-Hollweg, 10 June 1911.

131. Vagts, *Deutschland und die Vereinigten Staaten*, 2:1478.

132. AA Bonn, Mexico 1, vol. 27, Hintze to Bethmann-Hollweg, 10 June 1911.

133. Ibid., vol. 34, Hintze to Bethmann-Hollweg, 20 February 1913.

134. Ibid., vol. 29, Hintze to Bethmann-Hollweg, 29 July 1911.

135. This letter is quoted by Hintze in AA Bonn, Mexico 1, vol. 28, Hintze to Bethmann-Hollweg, 10 June 1911.

136. Ibid., vol. 29, Hintze to Bethmann-Hollweg, 29 July 1911.

137. Ibid., vol. 30, Kiderlen-Wächter to Hintze, 15 August 1911.

138. DZA Potsdam, AA II, no. 1747/1, Bruchhausen to Bethmann-Hollweg, 11 October 1911.

139. Ibid.

140. Ibid., Körner to Hintze, 13 January 1912.

141. Ibid., Jüdell to Lehmann, 16 November 1911.

142. Ibid., Report by Kemnitz, 4 December 1911.

143. Turlington, *Mexico and Her Foreign Creditors*, p. 247.

144. Archivo de Madero, Secretaría de Hacienda, Mexico (hereafter referred to as ASM), Mardus to Madero, 7 June 1911.

145. DZA Potsdam, AA II, no. 29071, Report of Foreign Office to Ministry of War, 15 October 1912.

146. Archivo General de la Nación (hereafter referred to as AGN Mexico), C 54, Luna to Madero, no date.

147. AA Bonn, Mexico 1, vol. 32, Hintze to Bethmann-Hollweg, 10 October 1912.

148. DZA Potsdam, AA II, no. 1741/1, Hintze to Bethmann-Hollweg, 22 July 1911.

149. Ibid., no. 1748, Consul in Antwerp to Bethmann-Hollweg, 2 September 1911.

150. Ibid., no. 1741/1, Hintze to Bethmann-Hollweg, 22 July 1911.

151. Ibid., no. 1748, Hintze to Bethmann-Hollweg, 23 November 1911.

152. DZA Potsdam, Section 7 of the Political Department, Governor General of Belgium, Report no. 9, Belgian Economic Interests in Mexico.

153. Turlington, *Mexico and Her Foreign Creditors*, p. 247.

154. AA Bonn, Mexico 1, vol. 27, Bernstorff to Bethmann-Hollweg, 12 April 1911.

155. *Kölnische Zeitung*, 11 April 1911.

156. AA Bonn, Mexico 1, vol. 28, Hintze to Bethmann-Hollweg, 3 May 1911.

157. Ibid.

158. Ibid.

159. Darius, "Die Entwicklung der deutsch-mexikanischen Handelsbeziehungen von 1870 bis 1914," p. 43.

160. AA Bonn, Mexico 1, vol. 29, Hintze to Bethmann-Hollweg, 7 December 1911.

161. Ibid., vol. 32, Hintze to Bethmann-Hollweg, 4 December 1912.

162. Ernest Gruening, *Mexico and Its Heritage* (New York, 1940), p. 560.

163. HHSta Wien, PA, Mexico Reports 1913, Minister in Mexico to Berchtold, 12 February 1913.

164. AA Bonn, Mexico 1, vol. 30, Hintze to Bethmann-Hollweg, 12 March 1913.
165. Ibid., Hintze to Bethmann-Hollweg, 13 March 1912.
166. Ibid., vol. 30, Secretary of State to Hintze, 1 April 1912.
167. Ibid.
168. Ibid.
169. Ibid., vol. 33, Hintze to Bethmann-Hollweg, 21 January 1913.
170. Ibid.
171. Ibid., vol. 32, Hintze to Bethmann-Hollweg, 24 October 1912.
172. Ibid.

## Chapter 3

1. AA Bonn, Mexico 1, vol. 32, Hintze to Bethmann-Hollweg, 24 October 1912.
2. Gildardo Magaña, *Emiliano Zapata y el Agrarismo en México*, 3 vols. (Mexico, D.F., 1934–41), 2:363–64.
3. Stanley R. Ross, *Francisco I. Madero: Apostle of Mexican Democracy* (New York, 1955), p. 278.
4. In a sharply worded reply, the Mexican government dismissed these accusations. It declared that the oil tax designated as "confiscatory" by Lane Wilson was lower than the corresponding tax in California and that the American employees of the National Railways had been dismissed because they were unwilling to learn Spanish. It was further asserted that four of the thirteen cases of murder alluded to in the American note had occurred under Díaz. Lascuráin drew up a list of Mexicans who had been lynched in the United States without any action by the American government against the guilty parties. FR, 1912, Lascuráin to Wilson, 22 October 1912.
5. AA Bonn, Mexico 1, vol. 34, Hintze to Bethmann-Hollweg, 29 February 1913.
6. Ibid., vol. 33, Hintze to Bethmann-Hollweg, 21 January 1913.
7. Henry Lane Wilson, *Diplomatic Episodes in Mexico, Belgium and Chile* (Garden City, 1927), p. 343.
8. National Archives, Washington, D.C., State Dept. Files (hereafter referred to as NA StDF) 812.00/5697, Taft to Knox, 16 December 1912.
9. Ibid., 812.00/7229A, Knox to Taft, 27 January 1913.
10. Ross, *Francisco I. Madero*, pp. 280–81.
11. Manuel Marqués Sterling, *Los ultimos Días del presidente Madero* (Havana, 1917), p. 336.
12. AA Bonn, Mexico 1, vol. 33, Hintze to Bethmann-Hollweg, 21 January 1913.
13. Ross, *Francisco I. Madero*, pp. 281–82.
14. Ibid., pp. 276–77.
15. Ibid.
16. Ross, *Francisco I. Madero*, pp. 191–202; Michael C. Meyer, *Huerta: A Political Portrait* (Lincoln, Neb., 1972), pp. 21–30.
17. Francisco R. Almada, *La Revolución en el Estado de Chihuahua*, 2 vols. (Mexico, D.F., 1964–69), 1:341–43.
18. Meyer, *Huerta*, pp. 41–42.
19. Ibid., p. 43.
20. Public Record Office, London, Foreign Office Files (hereafter referred to as PRO FO) 371 1677 6102, Hohler to Grey, 24 September 1913.
21. Meyer, *Huerta*, p. 47.
22. PRO FO 371 1677 6402, Hohler to Grey, 24 September 1913.
23. Ross, *Francisco I. Madero*, p. 291.
24. PRO FO 371 1677 6402, Hohler to Grey, 24 September 1913.

25. Ross, *Francisco I. Madero*, p. 281.
26. FR, 1913, Wilson to Knox, 10 February 1913.
27. AA Bonn, Mexico 1, vol. 34, Hintze Diary, 16 February 1913.
28. Marqués Sterling, *Los ultimos Días del presidente Madero*, pp. 379–80.
29. Hintze Diary, 16 February 1913.
30. Ibid.
31. Wilson, *Diplomatic Episodes*, p. 183.
32. Hintze made known his attitude toward Madero by refusing asylum to the latter's parents in the German legation (HHSta Wien, PA, Mexico Reports, Minister to Mexico to Berchtold, 12 February 1913).
33. AA Bonn, Mexico 1, vol. 34, Hintze to Bethmann-Hollweg, 25 February 1913.
34. HHSta Wien, PA, Mexico Reports, 1913, Minister in Mexico to Berchtold, 12 February 1913.
35. FR, 1913, Wilson to Secretary of State, 9 February 1913.
36. Ibid., Wilson to Knox, 11 February 1913.
37. Ibid., Knox to Wilson, 12 February 1913.
38. Hintze Diary, 12 February 1913.
39. Wilson, *Diplomatic Episodes*, p. 258.
40. Hintze Diary, 12 February 1913.
41. Marqués Sterling, *Los ultimos Días del presidente Madero*, pp. 375–76.
42. Hintze Diary, 14 February 1913.
43. Ibid., 15 February 1913.
44. FR, 1913, Wilson to Secretary of State, 15 February 1913.
45. Ross, *Francisco I. Madero*, p. 300.
46. FR, 1913, Knox to Ambassador in Mexico, 15 February 1913.
47. Hintze Diary, 15 February 1913.
48. AA Bonn, Mexico 1, vol. 34, Hintze to Auswärtiges Amt, 17 February 1913.
49. Cólogan's description of his role during the Decena Trágica is contained in his report to the Spanish Foreign Minister (Spanish Foreign Ministry Archives, Madrid, Cólogan to Spanish Foreign Minister, 2 March 1913).
50. Peter Calvert, *The Mexican Revolution, 1910–1914: The Diplomacy of Anglo-American Conflict* (Cambridge, 1968), p. 150. Stronge's role during the Decena Trágica has been analyzed by Calvert (pp. 131–58).
51. Hintze Diary, 17 February 1913.
52. Ibid., 18 February 1913. Taft had as little desire as Knox to claim public responsibility for the coup. Nonetheless, he interfered in no way with the activities of Lane Wilson.
53. Ibid.
54. Ross, *Francisco I. Madero*, pp. 304–5.
55. Hintze Diary, 18 February 1913.
56. Ross, *Francisco I. Madero*, p. 305.
57. Hintze Diary, 18 February 1913.
58. AA Bonn, Mexico 1, vol. 34, Hintze to Bethmann-Hollweg, 28 February 1913.
59. Hintze Diary, 18 February 1913.
60. Ibid.
61. PRO FO 371 1677, 6402; Hohler to Grey, 24 September 1913.
62. Ibid.
63. Ibid.
64. FR, 1913, Wilson to Secretary of State, 18 February 1913.
65. Ernest Gruening, *Mexico and Its Heritage* (New York, 1928), p. 568.
66. Ross, *Francisco I. Madero*, p. 326.
67. Ibid., pp. 315–16.
68. AA Bonn, Mexico 1, vol. 34, Hintze to Bethmann-Hollweg, 25 February 1913.

69. FR, 1913, Wilson to Knox, 19 February 1913.

70. AA Bonn, Mexico 1, vol. 34, Hintze to Bethmann-Hollweg, 25 February 1913.

71. Hintze Diary, 20 February 1913.

72. Ross, *Francisco I. Madero*, p. 322.

73. Gruening, *Mexico and Its Heritage*, p. 570.

74. FR, 1913, Knox to Wilson, 20 February 1913.

75. For very different points of view concerning the murder of Madero, see Jesús Silva Herzog, *Breve Historia de la Revolución Mexicana*, 2 vols. (Mexico, D.F., 1960), vol. 1, chap. 8; Isidro Fabela and Josefina E. de Fabela, eds., *Documentos Históricos de la Revolución Mexicana, Revolución y Régimen Maderista*, vol. 5 (Mexico, D.F., 1960); Ross, *Francisco I. Madero*, chaps. 18 and 19; and Meyer, *Huerta*, chap. 4.

76. Private Archive of Martin Luis Guzmán, undated letter from Fernández y Arteaga to Martin Luis Guzmán. The letter has not been available to historians before but statements by Madero's murderer Francisco Cárdenas have. On 6 June 1915 the El Paso *Morning Times* published a confession by Cárdenas quite similar to the Fernández statement. This confession was one of the major incriminating pieces of evidence implicating Huerta in the murder of Madero. While not discarding the possibility that Huerta was responsible for Madero's assassination, Michael C. Meyer feels that Cárdenas's confession is not reliable because on two previous occasions he had given interviews about the murder of Madero which ran counter to his later confessions (Meyer, *Huerta*, pp. 79–81). Many historians seem to believe that no one would have carried out such an assassination without Huerta's agreement and that the many killings he later ordered while president of Mexico bear out his readiness to resort to political assassinations. Officially all representatives of the United States and the more important European powers accepted the government's version that Madero and Pino Suárez had been killed during a rescue attempt by their supporters. Unofficially, however, many had strong doubts which they did not wish to express because they all thought that the Huerta government should be recognized and supported. Such doubts were expressed by the British minister, Sir Francis Stronge, who had written, "I fear there can be no doubt that the Ex-president and Vice-president were executed by order of military revolutionary chiefs and that story of attempted rescue is an invention. The crime is regarded as a necessary and inevitable measure which is likely to facilitate the pacification of the country" (Calvert, *The Mexican Revolution*, p. 169). In a report to the Spanish government, Minister Cólogan stated: "I have not heard a single person (this opinion was even expressed to me privately at the American embassy) who was not convinced that they [Madero and Pino Suárez] were simply murdered." While saying that he would find it inconvenient to reject the official version, he "clearly informed" his foreign minister about what was "being openly said by everyone. In Mexico executions have always been considered a political solution destined to destroy a faction and prevent future uprisings. It is said that this was the way in which Porfirio Díaz imposed his government from 1876 onward. The maintenance of peace for thirty years resulted from the fear he inspired" (Archivo de Relaciones Exteriores Madrid, Cólogan to Spanish Minister of State, 5 March 1913).

There is an interesting and significant discrepancy between this first account by Cólogan sent to his superiors in Madrid and another version of his report which has been found in the Foreign Ministry Archives in Mexico (it has been published in Isidro Fabela and Josefina E. de Fabela, *Documentos Históricos de la Revolución Mexicana, Revolución y Régimen Maderista* [Mexico 1965], 5:225–37). It seems to be an attempt to justify his role during the Decena Trágica. Significantly the text from "In Mexico . . ." to the end of the quotation has been omitted from this report.

77. Every statement that Ambassador Henry Lane Wilson attempted to save Madero's life during his interview with Huerta is based on a letter from the only other participant in that conversation, Paul von Hintze. In a letter written in China on 8 January 1916 Hintze stated: "I remember the time of poor Madero, an idealist, reformer, and a courageous man. I

remember very well Wednesday, the 19th of February, 1913, when early in the morning I called on you and found you and Mrs. Wilson, after a short dialogue, enthusiastic over the necessity of saving the life of the unfortunate Madero. We went together to the Palace and saw General Huerta and we got from him his word of honour as a caballero and a soldier to protect the life of his defeated opponent. We got some more promises. Do you remember that I told you when we reached your Embassy, 'in future days you will realize that by today's action you have added a laurel wreath to the Crown of the United States'? You have—and I am sure you and every American are proud of it" (Wilson, *Diplomatic Episodes,* p. 281).

There is a very clear discrepancy between the favorable description of Henry Lane Wilson's attitude that Hintze gives in his letter and the far less favorable image of the American ambassador that emerges from Hintze's diary, which I have quoted extensively. The diary, written during the events of February 1913 in Mexico, is obviously far more trustworthy than the letter Hintze wrote three years later. The letter, written in the winter of 1916 during the U.S. presidential campaign, was probably political in nature. By strengthening Henry Lane Wilson's position, Hintze may have hoped to encourage those within the Republican party who were advocating U.S. military intervention in Mexico.

78. Library of Congress, Washington, D.C., Papers of Leonard Wood, Diary, 7 April 1913.

79. AA Bonn, Mexico 1, vol. 34, Bernstorff to Auswärtiges Amt, 25 February 1913.

80. Jerry W. Knudson, "When Did Francisco I. Madero Decide on Revolution?" *The Americas,* 30 (April 1974): 532–34.

## Chapter 4

1. AA Bonn, Mexico 1, vol. 37, Hintze to Bethmann-Hollweg, 24 September 1913.

2. Ibid., vol. 45, Hintze to Bethmann-Hollweg, 19 March 1914.

3. Ibid., Hintze to Bethmann-Hollweg, 25 March 1914.

4. "Since my return I have seen the president three times. On two of these three occasions he was under the influence of alcohol," Hintze reported. "Like most heavy drinkers his physical appearance is not affected by alcohol anymore. His alcoholism expresses itself above all in senseless talk" (ibid., vol. 37, Hintze to Bethmann-Hollweg, 29 September 1913).

5. Ibid., vol. 41, Hintze to Bethmann-Hollweg, 22 January 1914.

6. Ibid.

7. Ibid., vol. 45, Hintze to Bethmann-Hollweg, 24 March 1914.

8. There are not many studies of Victoriano Huerta. The most recent and thorough book on him is Michael C. Meyer's *Huerta: A Political Portrait* (Lincoln, Neb., 1972).

9. Luis Liceaga, *Felix Díaz* (Mexico, D.F., 1958), pp. 300–305.

10. Marjorie Clark, *Organized Labor in Mexico* (Chapel Hill, 1934), p. 24.

11. Jesús Silva Herzog, *Breve Historia de la Revolución Mexicana,* 2 vols (Mexico, D.F., 1960), 2:13.

12. AA Bonn, Mexico 1, vol. 39, Hintze to Bethmann-Hollweg, 11 October 1913.

13. Ibid.

14. Ibid., Hintze to Bethmann-Hollweg, 29 October 1913.

15. Ibid.

16. John Womack, Jr., *Zapata and the Mexican Revolution* (New York, 1969), p. 172. Besides Womack's fundamental book on the Zapata movement, see Jesús Sotelo Inclán, *Raíz y Razón de Zapata* (Mexico, D.F., 1943); Gildardo Magaña, *Emiliano Zapata y el Agrarismo en Mexico,* 3 vols. (Mexico, D.F., 1934–41); Antonio Díaz Soto y Gama, *La Revolución Agraria del sur y Emiliano Zapata, su Caudillo* (Mexico, D.F., 1960); and

François Chevalier, "Le Soulèvement de Zapata, 1911–1919," *Annales, Economies, Sociétés, Civilisations* 16 (1961): 66–83. For the situation in Morelos before, during, and after the revolution, see Arturo Warman, *Y Venimos a Contradecir: Los Campesinos de Morelos y el Estado Nacional* (Mexico, D.F., 1976) and Laura Helguera Reséndiz, Sinecio Lopez, and Ramón Ramírez, *Los Campesinos de la Tierra de Zapata*, 3 vols. (Mexico, D.F., 1974).

17. José Mancisidor, *Historia de la Revolución Mexicana* (Mexico, D.F., 1976), pp. 286–87.

18. For an estimate of the number of free villages in Chihuahua, see Frank Tannenbaum, *The Mexican Agrarian Revolution* (Washington, D.C., 1930), p. 56. For a description of the structure of these villages see Friedrich Katz, "Peasants in the Mexican Revolution of 1910," in *Forging Nations*, ed. Joseph Spielberg and Scott Whiteford (East Lansing, 1976).

19. See Paul J. Vanderwood, "The 'Rurales': Mexico's Rural Police Force, 1861–1914" (Ph.D. diss., University of Texas at Austin, 1970).

20. See Isidro Fabela and Josefina E. de Fabela, eds., *Documentos Históricos de la Revolución Mexicana, Revolución y Régimen Maderista*, vol. 3 (Mexico, 1965), Carranza to Madero, 23 February 1912, p. 129; vol. 5, Pablo González to Carranza, 5 February 1913, p. 19; Carranza to Madero, 8 February 1913, p. 32.

21. Roberto Guzmán Esparza, *Memorias de Don Adolfo de la Huerta* (Mexico, D.F., n.d.), p. 34.

22. For some very different assessments of this question, see Barry Carr, "Las Peculiaridades del Norte Mexicano, 1880–1927: Ensayo de Interpretación," *Historia Mexicana* 22 (1973): 320–46; and Alan Knight, "Nationalism, Xenophobia, and Revolution: The Place of Foreigners and Foreign Interests in Mexico" (Ph.D. diss., Oxford University, 1974).

23. There is as yet no comprehensive biography of Carranza based on all the new archival sources, especially Mexican archives that have been made available to researchers in the last few years. See Alfredo Breceda, *Don Venustiano Carranza* (Mexico, D.F., 1930); Alfonso Junco, *Carranza y Los Orígenes de su Rebelión* (Mexico, D.F., 1935); Douglas Richmond, "First Chief of Revolutionary Mexico: The Presidency of Venustiano Carranza" (Ph.D. diss., University of Washington, 1976); and Alfonso Teracena, *Carranza* (Mexico, D.F., 1963). Richmond is the only one of these authors to have used the Carranza papers.

24. Silva Herzog, *Breve Historia*, 2:24.

25. Hector Aguilar Camín, *La Frontera Nómada: Sonora y la Revolución Mexicana* (Mexico, D.F., 1977), p. 279.

26. Francisco R. Almada, *La Revolución en el Estado de Sonora* (Mexico, D.F., 1971), p. 89.

27. Aguilar Camín, *La Frontera Nomada*, pp. 180–86, 222–32.

28. Antonio Uroz, *Hombres de la Revolución* (Mexico, D.F., 1969), pp. 130–31. PRO FO 371 3836 2658, Cummins to Foreign Office, 20 June 1919.

29. Daniel Moreno, *Hombres de la Revolución* (Mexico, D.F., 1971), p. 224.

30. Uroz, *Hombres*, pp. 113–16.

31. Justo Manzur Ocaña, *La Revolución Permanente, Vida y Obra de Cándido Aguilar* (Mexico, D.F., 1972), pp. 37–38. PRO FO 371 3836 2658, Cummins to Foreign Office, 20 June 1919.

32. Guzmán Esparza, *Memorias de Don Adolfo*, p. 11.

33. Ibid., p. 27.

34. Silva Herzog, *Breve Historia*, 2:24.

35. Armando de María y Campos, *La Vida del General Lucio Blanco* (Mexico, D.F., 1963), pp. 55–65.

36. *Investigation of Mexican Affairs*, 1:278.

37. DZA Potsdam, AA II, no. 4461, Hintze to Bethmann-Hollweg, 16 March 1912.

38. *Revolutions in Mexico,* Hearing before a subcommittee of the Committee on Foreign Relations, United States Senate, 62d Congress (Washington, D.C., 1913), p. 748.

39. *New York Herald,* 18 June 1914. Lázaro de la Garza papers, Nettie Lee Benson Collection, University of Texas at Austin, Wallet G. Felix Sommerfeld to Lázaro de la Garza, April 1914.

40. *New York Herald,* 18 June 1914.

41. Ibid.

42. Ibid.

43. There is as yet no comprehensive biography of Pancho Villa. The most revealing works that have been written about him are in Luis Aguirre Benavides, *De Francisco I. Madero a Francisco Villa: Memorias de un Revolucionario* (Mexico, D.F., 1966); Martin Luis Guzmán, *Memorias de Pancho Villa* (Mexico, D.F., 1938); Ramón Puente, *Villa en Pie* (Mexico, D.F., 1937); John Reed, *Insurgent Mexico* (New York, 1969); Silvestre Terrazas, "El Verdadero Pancho Villa," *Boletin de la Sociedad Chihuahuense de Estudíos Históricos,* vols. 5–8 (1944–55). For a description and an assessment of the voluminous literature on Pancho Villa, see Guadalupe Villa Guerrero, "Francisco Villa: Historia, Leyenda y Mito" (Thesis, University of Mexico, 1976).

44. Francisco P. Ontiveros, *Toribio Ortega y la Brigada Gonzales Ortega* (Chihuahua, 1914).

45. Reed, *Insurgent Mexico,* p. 158.

46. For Talamantes's role in the Díaz period, see Archivo del Departamento Agrario, Mexico, Dirección de Terrenos Nacionales, Diversos. Exp. 75 – 1407; for his role during the revolution, see Armanda B. Chávez M., *Diccionario de Hombres de la Revolución en Chihuahua* (Ciudad Juárez, n.d.).

47. For the best portrait of Fierro, see Martin Luis Guzmán, *El Aguila y la Serpiente* (Mexico, D.F., 1941), pp. 191–203, and Patrick O'Hea, *Reminiscences of the Mexican Revolution* (Mexico, D.F., 1966), pp. 161–63.

48. For Silvestre Terrazas's origins and activities during the Díaz period, see Robert Lynn Sandels, "Silvestre Terrazas: The Press and the Origins of the Mexican Revolution in Chihuahua" (Ph.D. diss., University of Oregon, 1967). Silvestre Terrazas described his activities as a close collaborator of Pancho Villa in what are essentially his memoirs of that period, "El Verdadero Pancho Villa," which from 1944 onward were serialized in *Boletín de la Sociedad Chihuahuense de Estudíos Históricos,* vols. 5–8 (1944–55).

49. Very little has been published on the role of Federico González Garza during the Villa period. My information is based on the unpublished answers to a questionnaire which Martin Luis Guzmán had sent out to Federico González Garza (private papers of Martin Luis Guzmán, Mexico City; I wish to express my thanks to the family of Martin Luis Guzmán for allowing me to consult his papers).

50. Ermilo Coello Salazar, "El Comercio Interior," in Daniel Cosío Villegas, ed., *Historia Moderna de Mexico, El Porfiriato, Vida Económica* (Mexico, D.F., 1965) 3:746.

51. Friedrich Katz, *Agrarian Changes in Northern Mexico in the Period of Villista Rule, 1913–1915, in Contemporary Mexico* (Los Angeles, 1976), pp. 259–73.

52. *Crónicas y Debates de las Sesiones de la Soberana Convención Revolucionaria* (Mexico, D.F., 1965) 2:237.

53. Katz, *Agrarian Changes,* p. 261.

54. *El Paso Times,* 17 January 1914.

55. Terrazas, "El Verdadero Pancho Villa," *Boletín de la Sociedad Chihuahuense de Estudíos Históricos* 7:473.

56. *El Paso Times,* 27 December 1913.

57. Katz, *Agrarian Changes,* pp. 259–73.

58. Reed, *Insurgent Mexico,* pp. 133–34.

59. Francisco R. Almada, *La Rebelión de Tomochic* (Chihuahua, 1938).

60. Francisco R. Almada, *La Revolución en el Estado de Chihuahua* (Mexico, D.F., 1969), 1:116–18.

61. Departamento Agrario, Mexico, Dirección de Terrenos Nacionales, Diversos, Exp. 178, Letter of the inhabitants of Namiquipa to President Porfirio Díaz, 20 July 1908.

62. Ibid. This file contains the text of the original concession granted by the Spanish *intendante* of the province of Nueva Vizcaya, Teodoro de Croix, to the first six military colonies that were founded in that territory.

63. Katz, *Agrarian Changes*, pp. 261–62.

64. Papers of Roque González Garza, Mexico City, undated memorandum by Roque González Garza on the causes for the break between Villa and Carranza.

65. Venustiano Carranza, *Informe del C. Venustiano Carranza, Primer Jefe del Ejército Constitucionalista Encargado del Poder Ejectivo de la República, Leído ante el Congreso de la Unión en la sesión del 15 de Abril de 1917* (Mexico, D.F., 1917).

66. Silvestre Terrazas Collection, Bancroft Library, Berkeley, California, Silvestre Terrazas to Luis Caballero, 2 July 1914.

67. Reed, *Insurgent Mexico*, p. 57.

68. See NA Washington, D.C., StDF 812.00/12741, Zach E. Cobb to Boaz W. Long, 3 July 1914.

69. Lázaro de la Garza's role and activities came out in a somewhat strange trial that took place before a Los Angeles court in March 1919. At the trial Alberto Madero in representation of Pancho Villa accused Lázaro de la Garza of having stolen $200,000 that Villa had given him to buy ammunition with and asked for the money to be returned to Villa. The charge was dismissed by the judge, but in view of the facts that Villa was considered one of the top enemies of the United States and that a U.S. punitive expedition had only a short time ago gone to Mexico to hunt him down, it is remarkable that such a trial could take place at all. See *Los Angeles Express*, 27 March 1919.

70. For very contradictory views of Ángeles, see Federico M. Cervantes, *Felipe Ángeles en la Revolución, 1896–1919* (Mexico, D.F., 1964); Byron Jackson, "The Political and Military Role of General Felipe Ángeles in the Mexican Revolution, 1914–1915" (Ph.D. diss., Georgetown University, 1976); and Bernadino Mena Brito, *Felipe Ángeles, Federal* (Mexico, D.F., 1956).

71. See speeches of Ángeles and proceedings of his trial, quoted in Cervantes, *Felipe Ángeles*, pp. 303–65.

72. NA Washington, D.C., StDF Record Group 59, File 812.00/14622, undated report by Duval West to the Secretary of State.

73. AMAE, Paris, CP, nouvelle série, Mexique vol. 9, Jusserand to Doumergues, 27 January 1914.

74. Archives du Ministère de la Guerre, Vincennes, France, 7 in 1716, French military attaché in the United States Bertrand to Deuxième Bureau, 30 December 1914.

75. Address of 27 August 1913, *A Compilation of the Messages and Papers of the Presidents*, 20 vols. (New York, 1922), 16:7888.

76. George M. Stephenson, *John Lind of Minnesota* (Minneapolis, 1935), p. 246.

77. NA Washington, D.C., StDF Record Group 59, File 812.00/14622, undated report by Duval West to the Secretary of State.

78. *Papers Relating to the Foreign Relations of the United States; The Lansing Papers* (Washington, D.C., 1920), Wilson to Lansing, 8 July 1915, 812.00/15412 1/2.

79. Clifford W. Trow, "Senator Albert B. Fall and Mexican Affairs, 1912–1921" (Ph.D. diss., University of Colorado, 1966), p. 96.

80. Harvey O'Connor, *The Guggenheims: The Making of an American Dynasty* (New York, 1937), pp. 336–37.

81. Private Archive of Carlos Reyes Avilés in possession of Salvador Reyes, Ensenada, Baja California, Zapata to Villa, 19 January 1914.

82. Silvestre Terrazas, "El Verdadero Pancho Villa," *Boletín de la Sociedad Chihuahuense de Estudios Históricos* 7 (1950): 362–65.
83. Aguilar Camín, *La Frontera Nómada*, chap. 4.
84. Silvestre Terrazas, "El Verdadero Pancho Villa," *Boletín de la Sociedad Chihuahuense de Estudios Históricos* 8:674–76.

## Chapter 5

1. AA Bonn, Mexico 1, vol. 34, Hintze to Bethmann-Hollweg, 28 February 1913.
2. Richard Hofstadter, *The American Political Tradition* (New York, 1959), p. 257.
3. Robert Freeman Smith, *The United States and Revolutionary Nationalism in Mexico, 1916–1932* (Chicago, 1972), pp. 31–32.
4. Ibid., pp. 31–33.
5. Burton J. Hendrick, *The Life and Letters of Walter H. Page*, 3 vols. (New York, 1922–25), 1:204–5.
6. AMAE, Mexique, Pol. Int. Mex. 6, Direction Affaires Politiques et Commerciales to Ministre des Affaires Etrangères, 20 April 1914.
7. PRO FO 371/1678 6269, Tyrrell to Grey, Private and Personal, 14 November 1913.
8. HHSta Wien, PA, Mexico Reports 1912, Minister in Mexico to Berchtold, 31 December 1912.
9. The opinions of such men were expressed very clearly at the hearing of the Fall Committee in 1919. One of the most characteristic is the testimony of Sewell Emery (*Investigation of Mexican Affairs*, 2:2222).
10. Arthur S. Link, *Woodrow Wilson and the Progressive Era, 1910–1917* (New York, 1954), p. 108.
11. Ray Stannard Baker, *Woodrow Wilson: Life and Letters*, 4 vols. (London, 1932), 4:247.
12. Ibid.
13. Link, *Woodrow Wilson*, p. 112.
14. *Investigation of Mexican Affairs*, 1:278.
15. Ibid.
16. AA Bonn, Mexico 1, vol. 40, Herwarth von Bittenfeld to Minister of War, 11 October 1913.
17. Ibid.
18. Alfred Vagts, *Mexiko, Europa und Amerika unter besonderer Berücksichtigung der Petroleumpolitik* (Berlin, 1928), p. 194.
19. Ibid.
20. AA Bonn, Mexico 1, vol. 40, Herwarth von Bittenfeld to Minister of War, 11 October 1913.
21. J. A. Spender, *Weetman Pearson, First Viscount Cowdray* (London, 1930), p. 169.
22. AA Bonn, Mexico 1, vol. 35, Kardorff to Bethmann-Hollweg, 3 May 1913.
23. AA Bonn, Archive of German Legation in Mexico, Folder 10, Huerta to Holste, 22 January 1914.
24. Weetman Pearson (Lord Cowdray) Papers, British Science Museum, London (hereafter referred to as Pearson Papers), Body to Cowdray, 22 February 1913.
25. Ibid.
26. Ibid.
27. Ibid., Body to Cowdray, 28 February 1913.
28. Ibid.
29. Ibid.
30. Ibid., Cowdray to Body, 28 March 1913.

31. Peter Calvert, *The Mexican Revolution, 1910–1914: The Diplomacy of Anglo-American Conflict* (Cambridge, 1968), p. 162.

32. Pearson Papers, Body to Cowdray, 1 March 1913.

33. Calvert, *The Mexican Revolution*, p. 164.

34. Pearson Papers, Body to Cowdray, 6 March 1913.

35. AMAE, Pol. Int., Mexique 5, Section Amérique to Foreign Minister, 20 November 1913.

36. Pearson Papers, Cowdray to Body, 28 March 1913; Body to Cowdray, 9 April 1913.

37. AA Bonn, Mexico 1, vol. 37, Hintze to Bethmann-Hollweg, 24 September 1913.

38. Yale University Library, Diary of Colonel House, entry of 24 October 1913.

39. AA Bonn, Mexico 1, vol. 35, Beheim-Schwarzbach to Auswärtiges Amt, July 1913.

40. Link, *Woodrow Wilson*, p. 132.

41. Ibid.

42. Ibid., pp. 112–14.

43. Ibid., p. 115.

44. Isidro Fabela, *Historia Diplomática de la Revolución Mexicana*, 2 vols. (Mexico, D.F., 1952), 1:244.

45. AA Bonn, Mexico 1, vol. 37, Hintze to Bethmann-Hollweg, 16 September 1913.

46. Ibid., Hintze to Bethmann-Hollweg, 10 September 1913.

47. Japanese Foreign Office Documents, Mexico, MT 1133 02 402, Tanabe to Makino, 19 July 1913 (microfilm, Library of Congress).

48. Ibid., Adatchi to Makino, 25 July 1913.

49. AA Bonn, Mexico 1, vol. 37, Hintze to Bethmann-Hollweg, 10 September 1913.

50. Spender, *Weetman Pearson*, p. 202.

51. For a detailed description of British recognition of Huerta, see Calvert, *The Mexican Revolution*, pp. 156–66.

52. HHSta Wien, PA, Mexico Reports 1913, Minister in Mexico to Berchtold, 7 July 1913.

53. AA Bonn, Mexico 1, vol. 37, Hintze to Bethmann-Hollweg, 11 September 1913.

54. Vagts, *Mexiko, Europa und Amerika*, p. 192.

55. AMAE, Mexique, CP, vol. 73, Couthouly to Foreign Minister, 3 July 1885.

56. Ibid., Couthouly to Foreign Minister, 20 September 1885.

57. AA Bonn, Mexico 1, vol. 40, Hintze to Bethmann-Hollweg, 4 November 1913.

58. Vagts, *Mexiko, Europa und Amerika*, p. 192.

59. AA Bonn, Mexico 1, vol. 40, Hintze to Bethmann-Hollweg, 24 January 1914, and comment by Kemnitz. Both John Lind and the French minister Lefaivre told Hintze they were convinced Carden was working for Cowdray (ibid.).

60. Ibid., Hintze to Bethmann-Hollweg, 18 November 1913.

61. HHSta Wien, PA, Mexico Reports 1913, Minister in Mexico to Berchtold, 1 December 1913.

62. See also the analysis by the French foreign office staff (note 77 below); AA Bonn, Mexico 1, vol. 40, Hintze to Bethmann-Hollweg, 18 November 1913.

63. Link, *Woodrow Wilson*, p. 112.

64. Hendrick, *Life and Letters*, 1:206.

65. Arthur S. Link, ed., *The Papers of Woodrow Wilson* (Princeton, 1978), 28:448–52.

66. Link, *Woodrow Wilson*, p. 118.

67. Calvert, *The Mexican Revolution*, pp. 269–71.

68. Hendrick, *Life and Letters*, 1:203.

69. Desmond Young, *Member for Mexico: A Biography of Weetman Pearson* (London, 1966), p. 165.

70. Vagts, *Mexiko, Europa und Amerika*, p. 280.

71. Calvert, *The Mexican Revolution*, p. 162.

72. Ibid., p. 163.

73. Ibid.
74. PRO FO 371 1676 6269, Carden to Grey, 12 September 1913.
75. Calvert, *The Mexican Revolution*, p. 224.
76. Ibid.
77. AMAE, Mexique, Pol. Int. Mex. 6, Direction Affaires Politiques et Commerciales to Ministre des Affaires Etrangères, 20 April 1914.
78. Ibid.
79. HHSta Wien, PA, Mexico Reports 1913, Minister in Mexico to Berchtold, 1 December 1913.
80. Ibid.
81. Hendrick, *Life and Letters*, 1:209.
82. Arthur S. Link, *Wilson: The New Freedom* (Princeton, 1956), p. 376.
83. HHSta Wien, PA, Mexico Reports 1914, Austrian Ambassador in Washington, D.C., to Berchtold, 19 January 1914.
84. DZA Potsdam, AA II, no. 21605, Consul in Tampico to Auswärtiges Amt, 24 March 1915.
85. Ibid., Consul in Tampico to Auswärtiges Amt, 2 June 1915.
86. AA Bonn, Mexico 1, vol. 35, Beheim-Schwarzbach to Auswärtiges Amt, July 1913.
87. Ibid., vol. 42, Lichnowsky to Bethmann-Hollweg, 28 January 1914.
88. AMAE, Mexique, Pol. Int. Mex. 6, Direction Affaires Politiques et Commerciales to Ministre des Affaires Etrangères, 20 April 1914.
89. Vagts, *Mexiko, Europa und Amerika*, p. 213.
90. DZA Merseburg, Rep. 120 CXIII 17, no. 2, vol. 12, Hintze to Bethmann-Hollweg, 24 January 1914.
91. Charles Seymour, *The Intimate Papers of Colonel House*, 4 vols. (New York, 1926–28), 1:205.
92. Spender, *Weetman Pearson*, p. 210.
93. Hendrick, *Life and Letters*, 1:217.
94. Ibid., 3:112.
95. Vagts, *Mexiko, Europa und Amerika*, p. 204.
96. Hendrick, *Life and Letters*, 1:203.
97. Link, *Woodrow Wilson*, p. 120.
98. Ibid.
99. HHSta Wien, PA, Mexico Reports 1914, Austrian Ambassador in Washington, D.C., to Berchtold, 19 January 1914.
100. AA Bonn, Mexico 1, vol. 40, Hintze to Bethmann-Hollweg, 18 November 1913.
101. Ibid., Hintze to Bethmann-Hollweg, 6 November 1913.
102. Ibid., Hintze to Bethmann-Hollweg, 18 November 1913.
103. Ibid., vol. 43, Captain of *Nürnberg* to Wilhelm II, 26 December 1913.
104. Ibid., Hintze to Bethmann-Hollweg, 28 January 1914.
105. Link, *Woodrow Wilson*, p. 121.
106. Ibid.
107. Jesús Silva Herzog, *Breve Historia de la Revolución Mexicana*, 2 vols. (Mexico, D.F., 1960), 2:70–71.
108. PRO FO 371 4496 3228, Cummins to Foreign Office, 13 August 1920.
109. Silva Herzog, *Breve Historia*, 2:70–71.
110. Link, *Woodrow Wilson*.
111. AA Bonn, Mexico 1, vol. 45, Hintze to Bethmann-Hollweg, 4 April 1914.
112. Ibid., vol. 41, Hintze to Bethmann-Hollweg, 9 December 1913.
113. Ibid., vol. 40, Hintze to Bethmann-Hollweg, 18 November 1913.
114. Ibid., vol. 43, Hintze to Bethmann-Hollweg, 3 February 1914.
115. Ibid., vol. 42, Hintze to Bethmann-Hollweg, 16 December 1913.

116. Ibid., vol. 43, Hintze to Bethmann-Hollweg, 24 January 1914.
117. Ibid., vol. 44, Hintze to Bethmann-Hollweg, 10 February 1914.
118. Ibid.
119. Ibid., vol. 41, Hintze to Bethmann-Hollweg, 10 December 1913.
120. FR (1914), Page to Bryan, 28 January 1914.
121. Ibid.
122. AA Bonn, Mexico 1, vol. 44, Hintze to Bethmann-Hollweg, 22 February 1914.
123. H. G. Römer, *Amerikanische Interessen und Prinzipienpolitik in Mexiko* (Hamburg, 1929), p. 198.
124. Quoted from ibid., p. 108.
125. Ibid., pp. 108–9.
126. Ibid., p. 110.
127. AA Bonn, Mexico 1, vol. 44, Hintze to Bethmann-Hollweg, 5 March 1914.
128. Ibid., Hintze to Bethmann-Hollweg, 10 March 1914.
129. Pearson Papers, Cowdray Memorandum, 9 January 1914.
130. Seymour, *The Intimate Papers of Colonel House*, 1:196.
131. Pearson Papers, Cowdray Memorandum, 9 January 1914.
132. Ibid., Cowdray to Body, 14 March 1914.
133. HHSta Wien, PA, Mexico Reports, Austrian Ambassador in Washington, D.C., to Berchtold, 5 May 1914.
134. Pearson Papers, Cowdray to Body, 14 March 1914.
135. Edgar Turlington, *Mexico and Her Foreign Creditors* (New York, 1930), p. 258.
136. Link, *Woodrow Wilson,* pp. 122–23; Isidro Fabela and Josefina E. de Fabela, eds., *Documentos Históricos: Período Constitucionalista,* 1:311–15.
137. Fabela and Fabela, eds., *Documentos Históricos: Período Constitucionalista,* 1:311–15.
138. For a description and an analysis of the Veracruz landing and its origins, see Robert E. Quirk, *An Affair of Honor: Woodrow Wilson and the Occupation of Veracruz* (New York, 1967).
139. Fabela and Fabela, eds., *Documentos Históricos: Período Constitucionalista,* 2:357.
140. Link, *Woodrow Wilson,* p. 125.
141. Ibid.
142. HHSta Wien, PA, U.S. Reports 1914, Ambassador to Washington, D.C., to Berchtold, 19 January 1914.
143. AA Bonn, Mexico 1, vol. 41, Herwarth von Bittenfeld to Minister of War, 28 November 1913.
144. Link, *Woodrow Wilson,* pp. 124–25.
145. HHSta Wien, PA, Mexico Reports 1914, Mexican envoy to Berchtold, 20 May 1914.
146. Fabela and Fabela, eds., *Documentos Históricos: Período Constitucionalista,* 2:10–11; Link, *Woodrow Wilson,* pp. 127–28.
147. FR, 1914, pp. 551–52.
148. Hendrick, *Life and Letters,* 1:223–24.
149. AA Bonn, Mexico 1, vol. 34, Hintze Diary, 18 May 1914.
150. Ibid.
151. Ibid., 25 May 1914.
152. Ibid., 2 June 1914.
153. FR, 1914, pp. 718–19.
154. Ibid.
155. Fabela and Fabela, eds., *Documentos Históricos: Período Constitucionalista,* 2:44.
156. Ibid., p. 27.
157. Ibid.
158. Link, *Woodrow Wilson,* p. 127.
159. Fabela and Fabela, eds., *Documentos Históricos: Período Constitucionalista,* 2:75.

## Chapter 6

1. See especially those by the consuls in Chihuahua and Colima; DZA Potsdam, AA II, nos. 4491 and 4492.
2. Edgar Turlington, *Mexico and Her Foreign Creditors* (New York, 1930), pp. 249-50.
3. Ibid., pp. 250-51.
4. DZA Potsdam, AA II, nos. 21, 600, Hintze to Auswärtiges Amt, 10 November 1912.
5. Ibid., Bach to Hintze, 5 November 1912.
6. HHSta Wien, Verwaltungsarchiv (VA), Petroleum 97, Minister in Mexico to Berchtold, 12 September 1913.
7. Ibid.
8. DZA Potsdam, AA II, nos. 21, 601, Minister for Trade and Commerce to Auswärtiges Amt, 10 April 1913.
9. Ibid., nos. 21, 602, Hintze to Bethmann-Hollweg, 9 November 1913.
10. Ibid., Deutsche Petroleum AG to Auswärtiges Amt, 6 March 1914.
11. HHSta Wien, VA, Petroleum 97, Minister in Mexico to Berchtold, 12 June 1914.
12. AA Bonn, Mexico 1, vol. 42, Schwabach to Zimmermann, 22 January 1914.
13. Ibid.
14. Ibid., vol. 35, Kardorff to Bethmann-Hollweg, 18 June 1913.
15. Ibid., Mexico 13, vol. 1, Hintze to Bethmann-Hollweg, 12 April 1913.
16. Ibid., Hintze to Bethmann-Hollweg, 18 December 1913.
17. Ibid., Bach to Hintze, 18 September 1913.
18. Ibid., Hintze to Bethmann-Hollweg, 12 March 1914.
19. Ibid., Bernstorff to Auswärtiges Amt, 12 February 1914.
20. Ibid., Kemnitz's observation, 24 February 1914.
21. Ibid., Mexico 1, vol. 36, Beheim-Schwarzbach to Jagow, 12 August 1913.
22. Ibid.
23. Ibid.
24. Ibid, vol. 34, Secretary of State to Reichskanzler, 27 March 1913.
25. Ibid., Kardorff to Bethmann-Hollweg, 2 April 1913.
26. Ibid.
27. Ibid., Kardorff to Bethmann-Hollweg, 9 April 1913.
28. Ibid., Kardorff to Bethmann-Hollweg, 26 March 1913.
29. Ibid., vol. 35, Kardorff to Bethmann-Hollweg, 3 May 1913.
30. Ibid., vol. 34, Kardorff to Bethmann-Hollweg, 26 March 1913.
31. DZA Potsdam, Reichsamt des Innern, no. 4384, Kardorff to Bethmann-Hollweg, 30 April 1913.
32. AA Bonn, Mexico 1, vol. 34, Secretary of State to Kardorff, 15 May 1913.
33. Ibid., vol. 35, Kardorff to Bethmann-Hollweg, 11 June 1913.
34. Ibid., Captain of the *Bremen* to Wilhelm II, 24 June 1913.
35. Ibid., Kardorff to Auswärtiges Amt, 5 July 1913.
36. Ibid., Kardorff to Bethmann-Hollweg, 5 July 1913.
37. Ibid.
38. Ibid., vol. 37, Hintze to Bethmann-Hollweg, 10 September 1913.
39. Ibid., vol. 42, Hintze to Bethmann-Hollweg, 5 January 1914.
40. Ibid., vol. 43, Hintze to Bethmann-Hollweg, 2 February 1914.
41. A. M. Pooley, *Japan's Foreign Policies* (London, 1920), p. 130.
42. AA Bonn, Mexico 1, vol. 37, Undersecretary of State to Hintze, 7 October 1913.
43. Ibid., vol. 36, Haniel to Auswärtiges Amt, 10 August 1913.
44. Ibid., Kardorff to Auswärtiges Amt, 10 August 1914.
45. Ibid., Jagow to Kardorff, 14 August 1913.
46. Ibid., Jagow to Kardorff, 12 August 1913.
47. Ibid., vol. 37, Kardorff to Bethmann-Hollweg, 19 August 1913.
48. Ibid.

49. Ibid., vol. 36, Jagow to Kardorff, 21 August 1913.
50. Ibid., Kardorff to Bethmann-Hollweg, 10 August 1913.
51. Ibid., Kardorff to Bethmann-Hollweg, 26 August 1913.
52. Ibid.
53. Ibid., vol. 37, Kardorff to Bethmann-Hollweg, 20 August 1913.
54. Ibid., Hintze to Bethmann-Hollweg, 24 August 1913.
55. Ibid., Hintze to Bethmann-Hollweg, 15 September 1913.
56. Ibid., Montgelas to Hintze, 7 October 1913.
57. Ibid., Montgelas to Bernstorff, 7 October 1913.
58. Ibid., Hintze to Bethmann-Hollweg, 16 September 1913.
59. Ibid., vol. 38, Hintze to Bethmann-Hollweg, 30 September 1913.
60. Ibid., vol. 39, Hintze to Bethmann-Hollweg, 14 October 1913.
61. Ibid., vol. 40, Hintze to Bethmann-Hollweg, 4 November 1913.
62. Ibid., Bernstorff to Bethmann-Hollweg, 25 November 1913.
63. Ibid., vol. 38, Jagow to Hintze, 16 October 1913.
64. Ibid., Hintze to Auswärtiges Amt, 19 October 1913.
65. Ibid., vol. 39, Schön to Bethmann-Hollweg, 6 November 1913.
66. Ibid., vol. 40, Hintze to Bethmann-Hollweg, 11 November 1913.
67. Ibid., Hintze to Bethmann-Hollweg, 4 November 1913.
68. Ibid., vol. 39, Undersecretary of State to Bernstorff, 11 November 1913.
69. Ibid., Undersecretary of State to Schön, 16 November 1913.
70. Ibid., vol. 38, Undersecretary of State to Hintze, 25 October 1913.
71. Ibid., vol. 39, Undersecretary of State to Bernstorff, 11 November 1913.
72. Ibid., Bernstorff to Auswärtiges Amt, 11 November 1913.
73. Peter Calvert, *The Mexican Revolution, 1910–1914: The Diplomacy of Anglo-American Conflict* (Cambridge, 1968), p. 122.
74. Burton J. Hendrick, *The Life and Letters of Walter H. Page,* 3 vols. (New York, 1922–25) 1:230–31.
75. AA Bonn, Mexico 1, vol. 40, Bernstorff to Bethmann-Hollweg, 25 November 1913.
76. Ibid.
77. Ibid., vol. 41, Remarks of the Kaiser on the margin of Hintze to Bethmann-Hollweg, 26 November 1913.
78. Ibid., Hintze to Bethmann-Hollweg, 9 December 1913.
79. Ibid.
80. Ibid., vol. 39, Hintze to Bethmann-Hollweg, 21 October 1913.
81. Ibid., vol. 41, Hintze to Bethmann-Hollweg, 26 November 1913.
82. Ibid., vol. 38, Hintze to Auswärtiges Amt, 25 October 1913.
83. Ibid., vol. 39, Hintze to Bethmann-Hollweg, 10 November 1913.
84. Ibid., Hintze to Auswärtiges Amt, 13 November 1913.
85. Ibid.
86. Ibid., Hintze to Auswärtiges Amt, 9 November 1913. Hintze's idea of "half a war" was by no means a misguided one. On 30 November 1913, Wilson actually made such a proposal to Carranza, but the latter rejected it. (See Arthur S. Link, *Woodrow Wilson and the Progressive Era, 1910–1917* [New York, 1954], p. 120.)
87. Ibid., vol. 40, Hintze to Bethmann-Hollweg, 18 November 1913.
88. Ibid., vol. 39, Undersecretary of State to Bernstorff, November 1913.
89. Ibid., vol. 42, Hintze to Bethmann-Hollweg, 16 December 1913.
90. Ibid., vol. 41, Hintze to Bethmann-Hollweg, 26 November 1913.
91. Alfred Vagts, *Mexiko, Europa und Amerika unter besonderer Berücksichtigung der Petroleumpolitik* (Berlin, 1928), pp. 223–24.
92. AA Bonn, Mexico 1, vol. 40, Wilhelm II's marginal notation to Hintze's reports of 4 October and 18 November 1913.
93. Ibid., vol. 38, Bernstorff to Auswärtiges Amt, 16 October 1913.

94. Ibid., Auswärtiges Amt to Hintze, 20 October 1913.
95. FR, 1913, Gerard to Bryan, 8 November 1913.
96. Ibid., Gerard to Bryan, 27 November 1913.
97. AA Bonn, Mexico 1, vol. 38, Hintze to Bethmann-Hollweg, 26 September 1913.
98. Ibid., vol. 41, Hintze to Bethmann-Hollweg, 27 November 1913.
99. Ibid., vol. 40, Hintze to Auswärtiges Amt, 22 December 1913.
100. Ibid., Jagow to Hintze, 2 December 1913.
101. Ibid., Hintze to Bethmann-Hollweg, 9 December 1913.
102. Ibid., vol. 38, Hintze to Auswärtiges Amt, 10 October 1913.
103. Ibid., Bernstorff to Auswärtiges Amt, 23 October 1913.
104. Ibid., Hintze to Auswärtiges Amt, 11 October 1913.
105. Ibid.
106. Ibid., Admiral Staff to Auswärtiges Amt, 14 October 1913.
107. Ibid., Bernstorff to Bethmann-Hollweg, 16 October 1913.
108. Ibid.
109. Ibid., Auswärtiges Amt to Bernstorff, 27 October 1913.
110. Ibid., Zimmermann to Tirpitz, 25 October 1913.
111. Ibid., vol. 40, Hintze to Captain of the *Hertha*, 5 November 1913.
112. Ibid.
113. Ibid., vol. 41, Captain of the *Bremen* to Wilhelm II, 12 December 1913.
114. Vagts, *Mexiko, Europa und Amerika*, pp. 224–25.
115. AA Bonn, Mexico 1, vol. 43, Hintze to Bethmann-Hollweg, 25 January 1914.
116. Ibid., vol. 44, Hintze to Bethmann-Hollweg, 9 February 1914.
117. Ibid., vol. 45, Hintze to Bethmann-Hollweg, 24 March 1914. "Through middlemen trusted by Huerta, I have repeatedly made clear to him the inevitability of an agreement. I have for the present given up discussing it with him directly, because I have noticed that with foreigners he immediately begins to play the fool and the buffoon. My middlemen assure me that Huerta is well prepared and well disposed."
118. Ibid., vol. 44, Hintze to Bethmann-Hollweg, 21 February 1914.
119. Ibid., vol. 45, Hintze to Bethmann-Hollweg, 17 March 1914.
120. Ibid.
121. Ibid., vol. 44, Hintze to Bethmann-Hollweg, 10 March 1914.
122. Ibid.
123. Ibid., Bernstorff to Bethmann-Hollweg, 23 February 1914.
124. *Schulthess europaischer Geschichteskalender, 1914,* 17 February 1914.
125. AA Bonn, Mexico 1, vol. 44, Kemnitz to Montgelas, 4 March 1914.
126. Ibid., vol. 42, Marginal comment of the Kaiser on Lichnowsky to Bethmann-Hollweg, 28 January 1914.
127. Ibid.
128. Ibid., vol. 44, Bernstorff to Bethmann-Hollweg, 23 March 1914.
129. Ibid., Lichnowsky to Bethmann-Hollweg, 1 March 1914.
130. Ibid., Marginal notations by Wilhelm II on Schön to Bethmann-Hollweg, 5 March 1914.
131. Ibid., vol. 42, Bernstorff to Auswärtiges Amt, 28 January 1914.
132. Ibid.
133. The Americans rewarded this effort. On 16 April Lind emphasized to Bernstorff "the excellent relations with Mr. Hintze and the sympathetic attitude of the kaiser's government. If Carden had acted in a similar fashion, Huerta would have already resigned last fall" (AA Bonn, Mexico 1, vol. 45, Bernstorff to Auswärtiges Amt, 18 April 1914).
134. AA Bonn, Mexico 1, vol. 45, Bernstorff to Auswärtiges Amt, 18 April 1914.
135. Ibid., Eckert to Auswärtiges Amt, 18 April 1914.
136. Ibid., Auswärtiges Amt to Eckert, 21 April 1914.
137. Vagts, *Mexiko, Europa und Amerika,* pp. 205–6.

138. AA Bonn, Mexico 7, vol. 1, Ambassador in Madrid to Auswärtiges Amt, 21 March 1917.
139. DZA Potsdam, AA II, no. 4459, Bünz to Auswärtiges Amt, 10 July 1909.
140. Turlington, *Mexico and Her Foreign Creditors*, pp. 258–59.
141. AA Bonn, Mexico 1, vol. 44, Rhomberg to Bethmann-Hollweg, 24 March 1914.
142. Ibid., Mexico 7, vol. 1, Ambassador in Madrid to Auswärtiges Amt, 21 March 1917.
143. Ibid.
144. Michael Meyer, "The Arms of the *Ypiranga*," *Hispanic American Historical Review* 50 (August 1970): 543–55.
145. AA Bonn, Mexico 7, vol. 16, Minister in Madrid to Auswärtiges Amt, 21 March 1917.
146. AA Bonn, Mexico 1, vol. 45, Bülow to Bethmann-Hollweg, 23 April 1914.
147. Ibid., vol. 48, Captain of the *Dresden* to Wilhelm II, 28 April 1914.
148. Barbara W. Tuchman, *The Zimmermann Telegram* (London, 1959), pp. 51–52.
149. AA Bonn, Mexico 1, vol. 45, Bernstorff to Auswärtiges Amt, 21 April 1914.
150. Ibid., vol. 46, Knege Report, 5 May 1914.
151. Ibid., vol. 45, Bernstorff to Auswärtiges Amt, 24 April 1914.
152. Ibid., Bülow to Bethmann-Hollweg, 23 April 1914.
153. Ibid., vol. 46, Bryan to Bernstorff, 28 April 1914.
154. Ibid., vol. 48, Bernstorff to Auswärtiges Amt, 10 June 1914.
155. Ibid., vol. 49, Hintze to Bethmann-Hollweg, 3 May 1914.
156. Ibid., Hintze to Bethmann-Hollweg, 3 June 1914.
157. Ibid., vol. 47, Hintze to Bethmann-Hollweg, 17 May 1914.
158. Ibid.
159. Ibid., vol. 49, Hintze to Bethmann-Hollweg, 3 June 1914.
160. Ibid.
161. Hintze Diary, 23 May 1914.
162. AA Bonn, Mexico 1, vol. 49, Hintze to Bethmann-Hollweg, 3 June 1914.
163. Ibid.
164. Thomas Baecker, *Die deutsche Mexiko Politik, 1913/1914* (Berlin, 1971), p. 185.
165. AA Bonn, Mexico 1, vol. 48, Bernstorff to Auswärtiges Amt, 10 June 1914.
166. Ibid.
167. Hintze Diary, 23 May 1914.
168. AA Bonn, Mexico 1, vol. 47, Bülow to Bethmann-Hollweg, 30 May 1914.
169. AA Bonn, Mexico 1, vol. 49, Hintze to Bethmann-Hollweg, 3 June 1914.
170. Ibid., vol. 48, Consul in New York to Bethmann-Hollweg, 3 June 1914.
171. Ibid., vol. 49, Hintze to Bethmann-Hollweg, 3 June 1914.
172. Ibid., Boy Edd to Reichsmarineamt, 2 June 1914.
173. Ibid., vol. 48, Bernstorff to Auswärtiges Amt, 10 June 1914.
174. Ibid.
175. Ibid., Kemnitz's comment, 10 June 1914.
176. Ibid., vol. 49, Hintze to Auswärtiges Amt, 31 June 1914.
177. Ibid., Boy Edd to Reichsmarineamt, 11 June 1914.
178. Ibid., Hintze to Bethmann-Hollweg, 29 June 1914.
179. Nemesio García Naranjo, *Memorias*, 8 vols. (Mexico, D.F., n.d.), 7:293.
180. Ibid., pp. 240–41.
181. HHSta Wien, VA, Petroleum 97, Pet. 46, Ambassador in Mexico to Berchtold, 12 September 1913.
182. García Naranjo, *Memorias*, 7:247.
183. Ibid., p. 251.
184. AA Bonn, Mexico 1, vol. 49, Hintze to Bethmann-Hollweg, 29 May 1914.
185. Hintze Diary, 22 May 1914.
186. AA Bonn, Mexico 1, vol. 49, Hintze to Bethmann-Hollweg, 29 May 1914.

187. Hintze Diary, 9 June 1914.
188. Ibid.
189. Ibid., 30 April 1914.
190. Ibid., 4 May 1914.
191. Ibid., 1 May 1914.
192. Ibid.
193. Ibid.
194. Ibid., 3 May 1914.
195. Ibid., 25 May 1914.
196. Ibid., 13 June 1914.
197. Ibid., 4 May 1914.
198. Ibid.
199. Ibid.
200. Ibid., 8 May 1914.
201. Ibid., 25 June 1914.
202. Ibid.
203. Ibid., 28 June 1914.
204. AA Bonn, Mexico 1, vol. 50, Hintze to Auswärtiges Amt, 15 July 1914.
205. Ibid., Hintze to Captain of the *Dresden,* 12 July 1914.
206. Ibid., vol. 51, Jagow to Wilhelm II, 16 July 1914.
207. Ibid.
208. Ibid.
209. Ibid., Hintze to Captain of *Dresden,* 11 July 1914.
210. Ibid., Hintze to Captain of *Dresden,* 19 July 1914.
211. Ibid., vol. 52, Captain of *Dresden* to Wilhelm II, 26 July 1914.
212. Ibid., vol. 49, Bernstorff to Bethmann-Hollweg, 24 June 1914.
213. Tuchman, *The Zimmermann Telegram,* p. 53.
214. Ibid.
215. Thomas B. Bailey, *The Policy of the United States toward the Neutrals* (Baltimore, 1942), pp. 263–64.

# Chapter 7

1. *Crónicas y Debates de las Sesiones de la Soberana Convención Revolucionaria* (Mexico, D.F., 1965), 2:178–79.
2. *Investigation of Mexican Affairs* 2:2326.
3. Ibid., 2:221–27.
4. PRO FO 371 3836 2658 Cummins to Foreign Office, 20 June 1919.
5. Barry Carr, "Las Peculiaridades del Norte Mexicano, 1880–1927: Ensayo de Interpretación," *Historia Mexicana* 22 (1973): 320–46.
6. In a confidential report to Venustiano Carranza, which was intercepted by U.S. military intelligence, the Mexican consul in El Paso, Andrés García, reported that Murguía had deposits totaling $248,000 in an El Paso bank in his name and in the names of relatives (Andrés García to Carranza, 20 July 1918, reported by U.S. Intelligence Officer Laredo, 12 March 1919, Military Intelligence Files, National Archives, Washington, D.C.).
7. Raymond T. U. Buve, "Peasant Movements, Caudillos and Land Reform during the Revolution (1910–1917) in Tlaxcala, Mexico," *Boletín de Estudios Latin-Americanos y del Caribe* 18 (June 1975): 112–53.
8. Hector Aguilar Camín, *La Frontera Nómada: Sonora y la Revolución Mexicana* (Mexico, D.F., 1977), pp. 428–40.

9. One of the reasons for this is that there are only few printed documents on this subject, though even those have not been sufficiently analyzed. See especially Venustiano Carranza, *Informe del C. Venustiano Carranza* (Mexico, D.F., 1917) and the debates of the revolutionary convention on 2 and 6 February 1915, in *Crónicas y Debates* 2:149–287. The most important information on the confiscated properties and their return is contained in the Carranza Archives in the Fundación Condumex in Mexico City and particularly in the newly discovered files of the Secretaría de Gobernación in the Archivo General de la Nación for the years 1910 to 1920.

10. *Crónicas y Debates* 2:184.

11. Rosalie Evans, *The Rosalie Evans Letters from Mexico* (Indianapolis, 1926), pp. 46–66.

Not all radicals who supported Carranza agreed with this policy though. Francisco Múgica, one of the most radical reformers at the Constitutional Convention in Querétaro, bitterly opposed the return of properties to their former owners (Armando de María y Campos, *Múgica: Crónica Biográfica* [Mexico, D.F., 1939], pp. 98–103).

12. John Womack, Jr., *Zapata and the Mexican Revolution* (New York, 1969), pp. 196–212; Robert E. Quirk, *The Mexican Revolution, 1914–1915* (New York, 1960), pp. 63–68.

13. Quirk, *The Mexican Revolution*, p. 66.

14. Adolfo Gilly, *La Revolución Interrumpida* (Mexico, D.F., 1972), pp. 98–99.

15. Enrique Beltrán, "Fantasía y Realidad de Pancho Villa," *Historia Mexicana* 16 (1966): 71–84.

16. Bancroft Library, Berkeley, Silvestre Terrazas Papers, Silvestre Terrazas to Luis Caballero, 2 July 1914.

17. Archivo Roque González Garza, Mexico, D.F., undated memorandum by Roque González Garza on the causes for the Villa-Carranza split.

18. Friedrich Katz, *Agrarian Changes in Northern Mexico in the Period of Villista Rule, 1913–1915*, in *Contemporary Mexico* (Los Angeles, 1976), pp. 259–71.

19. NA Washington, D.C., StDF Record Group 59, File 812.00/14622, undated report by Duval West to the Secretary of State.

20. Pablo Machula Macías, *La Revolución en una Ciudad del Norte* (Mexico, D.F., 1977), p. 68.

21. Aguilar Camín, *La Frontera Nómada*, pp. 364–67.

22. Quirk, *The Mexican Revolution*, pp. 33–34.

23. Federico Cervantes, *Francisco Villa y la Revolución* (Mexico, D.F., 1960), pp. 196–201.

24. Quirk, *The Mexican Revolution*, pp. 87–100; Luis Fernando Amaya, *La Soberana Convención Revolucionaria, 1914–1916* (Mexico, D.F., 1966), pp. 75–102.

25. Amaya, *La Soberana Convención*, pp. 106–7.

For a detailed description of events at the convention, see Quirk, *The Mexican Revolution*, pp. 87–131, and Amaya, *La Soberana Convención*, pp. 103–73.

26. Tannenbaum, *The Mexican Agrarian Revolution* (Washington, D.C., 1930), pp. 500–501.

27. PRO FO 371 2961 3167, Harrison to Cummins, 12 May 1917.

28. Salvador Alvarado, *Mi Actuación Revolucionaria en Yucatán* (Mexico, D.F., 1918); Francisco J. Paoli and Enrique Montalvo, *El Socialismo Olvidado de Yucatán* (Mexico, D.F., 1977), pp. 32–49.

29. Rosendo Salazar, *La Casa del Obrero Mundial* (Mexico, D.F., 1962), p. 129. For an analysis of the role of the Red Battalions, see Barry Carr, *El Movimiento Obrero y la Política en Mexico, 1910–1929* (Mexico, D.F., 1978) 1:77–94, and Jean Meyer, "Les Ouvriers dans la Revolution Mexicaine, les Bataillons Rouges," *Annales, Economies, Sociétés, Civilisations* 25 (1970): 30–56.

30. Womack, *Zapata*, pp. 224–55.

31. *Crónicas y Debates*, 2:248.
32. José Mancisidor, *Historia de la Revolución Mexicana* (Mexico, D.F., 1976), p. 250.
33. Quirk, *The Mexican Revolution*, p. 246.
34. Aguilar Camín, *La Frontera Nómada*, pp. 364–67.
35. Private Archive of Roque González Garza, Mexico City, Federico González Garza to Roque González Garza, September 1915.
36. Cervantes, *Felipe Ángeles*, p. 298.
37. Ibid.
38. NA Washington, D.C., StDF Record Group 59, File 812.00/14622, undated report by Duval West to the Secretary of State.
39. *Crónicas y Debates*, 2:159–67, 178–96.
40. Ibid., pp. 226–28.
41. Ibid., p. 237.
42. Private Archive of Roque González Garza, Mexico City, Federico González Garza to Roque González Garza, September 1915.
43. Ibid.
44. Cervantes, *Francisco Villa y la Revolución*, p. 364.
45. Guadalupe Villa Guerrero, "Francisco Villa: Historia, Leyenda y Mito" (Thesis, University of Mexico, 1976), p. 263. For some reason, Martin Luis Guzmán did not include these parts in his publication of Villa's memoirs (*Memorias de Pancho Villa* [Mexico, D.F., 1951]).
46. Marte R. Goméz, *La Reforma Agraria en las Filas Villistas: Años 1913 a 1915* (Mexico, D.F., 1966), pp. 101–31.
47. See Alberto Calzadíaz Barrera, *Anatomía de un Guerrero, el General Martin Lopez* (Mexico, D.F., 1968).
48. Aguilar Camín, *La Frontera Nómada*, p. 416.
49. Francisco Almada, *La Revolución en el Estado de Chihuahua*, 2 vols. (Mexico, D.F., 1964–69), 2:212.
50. Antonio Díaz Soto y Gama, *La Cuestión Agraria en Mexico* (Mexico, D.F., 1959), pp. 29–36.
51. Byron Jackson, "The Political and Military Role of General Felipe Ángeles in the Mexican Revolution 1914–1915" (Ph.D. diss., Georgetown University, 1976), pp. 300–320.
52. Aguilar Camín, *La Frontera Nómada*, p. 416.
53. Library of Claremont College, Claremont, California, papers of José María Maytorena, undated memorandum by Maytorena entitled "Reasons for My Estrangement from General Villa."
54. Ibid.
55. Ibid., Maytorena to Acosta and Urbalejo, 18 October 1915.
56. See Spanish Foreign Ministry Archives, Madrid, reports by Special Agent Emilio Zapico to Secretary of State, 23 August 1915.
In March 1915 U.S. Consul Marion Letcher reported that since the occupation of the state of Chihuahua by Villa forces 444,000,000 pesos in paper money had been issued and that at this stage 1,000,000 a day of Villa pesos were being printed (NA Washington, D.C., StDF Record Group 59, File 812.5157/68, Marion Letcher to Secretary of State, 10 March 1915).
57. Spanish Foreign Ministry Archives, Madrid, Emilio Zapico to Secretary of State, 23 August 1915.
58. Francisco R. Almada, *La Revolución en el Estado de Sonora* (Mexico, D.F., 1971), pp. 172–75.
59. Papers of Roque González Garza, Mexico, Federico González Garza to Roque González Garza, September 1915.
60. AGN, Mexico, Ramo Gobernación Box 30, Exp. 162, Librado González and José Torres to Carranza, 1 November 1917.

61. Ibid.
62. These documents are located in the AGN, Ramo Gobernación.
63. Carranza, *Informe del C. Venustiano Carranza* (Mexico, D.F., 1917), pp. 2–3.
64. I have found no official decree establishing a procedure for the return of expropriated estates. Nevertheless, the hundreds of cases described in the archives of the Secretaría de Gobernación Ramo 1910–1920 in the Archivo General de la Nación all follow a pattern. See, for instance, the case of a Chihuahua hacendado, Castulo R. Chávez, whose properties had been confiscated by Pancho Villa (AGN, Ramo Gobernación, Box 255, Exp. 66).
65. Condumex Foundation, Mexico, Archivo de Carranza (subsequently referred to as Carranza Archives Condumex), Gobernación, Exp. 125, Escobar to Carranza, 13 August 1914.
66. AGN, Gobernación, Box 5, Exp. 19, Guillermo Muñoz to Carranza, 10 May 1916.
67. Ibid., Provisional Governor to Carranza, 1 July 1916.
68. AGN, Gobernación, Box 211, Exp. 57, Rodolfo Cruz to Carranza, 8 February 1917.
69. Carranza Archives, Condumex, vol. 65, J. G. Nava to Carranza, 1 December 1915.
70. AGN, Gobernación, Box 5, Exp. 19, Decree of Carranza, 31 March 1919.
71. AGN, Gobernación, Box 24, Exp. 111, State Governor to Carranza, 11 April 1917.
72. Guy Weddington McCreary, *From Glory to Oblivion: The Real Truth about the Mexican Revolution* (New York, 1974), pp. 201–17.
73. Carranza Archives, Condumex, vol. 66, J. G. Nava to Carranza, 15 December 1915.
74. María y Campos, *Múgica: Crónica Biográfica*, pp. 87–94.
75. Ibid., pp. 95–103.
76. Ibid., pp. 101–103.
77. Pearson Papers, Limantour to Body, 8 November 1915.
78. Pearson Papers, A. E. Worswick to Body, 29 June 1917.
79. Salazar, *La Casa del Obrero Mundial*, p. 216.
80. Ibid.
81. HHSta Wien, PA, Mexico Reports (Mexico, 1916), Minister in Mexico to Foreign Minister, 3 March 1916.
82. Womack, *Zapata*, pp. 253–60.
83. Francisco Almada, *La Revolución en el Estado de Chihuahua*, 2:140–70.

## Chapter 8

1. Arthur S. Link, *Woodrow Wilson and the Progressive Era, 1910–1917* (New York, 1954), p. 131.
2. Robert E. Quirk, *The Mexican Revolution, 1914–1915* (New York, 1960), pp. 256–57.
3. Ibid., p. 258.
4. Ibid., p. 259.
5. Federico Cervantes, *Francisco Villa y la Revolución* (Mexico, D.F., 1960), p. 504.
6. Quirk, *The Mexican Revolution*, pp. 279–81.
7. Ibid.
8. Ibid., p. 285.
9. Arthur S. Link, *Wilson: The Struggle for Neutrality, 1914–1915* (Princeton, 1960), p. 467.
10. Pearson Papers, Limantour to Body, 9 November 1915.
11. Larry P. Hill, *Emissaries to a Revolution: Woodrow Wilson's Executive Agents in Mexico* (Baton Rouge, 1973), pp. 334–36.
12. Friedrich Katz, "Pancho Villa and the Attack on Columbus, New Mexico," *American Historical Review* 83 (February 1978): 101–30.
13. Pearson Papers, Memorandum Cowdray, 7 October 1915.

14. Pearson Papers, Memorandum Cowdray, 12 October 1915.

15. Pearson Papers, Memorandum Cowdray, 7 October 1915.

16. Link, *Woodrow Wilson*, p. 134.

17. *Documentos Relacionados con la Legislación Petrolera Mexicana* (Mexico, D.F., 1919), p. 147.

18. Thomas B. Bailey, *The Policy of the United States toward the Neutrals* (Baltimore, 1942), p. 326.

19. See Katz, "Pancho Villa and the Attack on Columbus, New Mexico"; also Charles Harris III and Louis R. Sadler, "Pancho Villa and the Columbus Raid: The Missing Documents," *New Mexico Historical Review* 50 (1975): 335–47; Larry A. Harris, *Pancho Villa and the Columbus Raid* (El Paso, 1949); Friedrich Katz, "Alemania y Francisco Villa," *Historia Mexicana* 12 (1962): 83–103; Francis J. Munch, "Villa's Columbus Raid: Practical Politics or German Design?" *New Mexico Historical Review* 44 (1969): 189–214; James A. Sandos, "German Involvement in Northern Mexico, 1915–1916: A New Look at the Columbus Raid," *Hispanic American Historical Review* 50 (1970): 70–89; Barbara W. Tuchman, *The Zimmermann Telegram* (London, 1959); and E. Bruce White, "The Muddied Waters of Columbus, New Mexico," *The Americas* 32 (1975): 72–92.

20. There is a very large body of literature on the punitive expedition into Mexico. For some of the main works written by Americans, see Haldeen Braddy, *Pershing's Expedition in Mexico* (El Paso, 1966); Clarence Clendenen, *The United States and Pancho Villa* (Port Washington, N.Y., 1971); Arthur S. Link, *Wilson: Confusions and Crises, 1915–1916* (Princeton, 1964), and *Wilson: Campaigns for Progressivism and Peace, 1916–1917* (Princeton, 1965); Herbert Molloy Mason, Jr., *The Great Pursuit* (New York, 1970); Donald Smythe, *Guerrilla Warrior* (New York, 1963); Michael L. Tate, "Pershing's Punitive Expedition: Pursuer of Bandits or Presidential Panacea?" *The Americas* 32 (1975): 46–72; and Frank Tompkins, *Chasing Villa* (Harrisburg, Pa., 1939). For two Mexican works, one a monograph and the other a collection of documents by authors sympathetic to Carranza, see Alberto Salinas Carranza, *La Expedición Punitiva* (Mexico, D.F., 1936), and Isidro Fabela and Josefina E. de Fabela, eds., *Documentos Históricos de la Revolución Mexicana, Expedición Punitiva,* 2 vols. (Mexico, D.F., 1967–68). For works by Mexican authors sympathetic to Villa, see Alberto Calzadíaz Barrera, *Porque Villa atacó a Columbus* (Mexico, D.F., 1972); Nellie Campobello, *Apuntes sobre la vida militar de Francisco Villa* (Mexico, D.F., 1940); and Cervantes, *Francisco Villa y la Revolución.*

21. NA Washington, D.C., StDF Record Group 59, File 812.00 1-55311/2, Canova to the Secretary of State, 29 May 1915.

22. Diary of Chandler Anderson, 28 May 1915, Library of Congress. The State Department papers contain only the barest outline of Canova's plot. Most of the available information is contained in Anderson's diary, especially the entries for 23 April, 14 May, 19 May, 28 May, 1 June, 29 June, 23 July, and 30 July 1915. Very apparent is the conservatives' desire to apply a strategy in 1915 similar to that they applied in 1911. They were willing to agree to some "compromises" as far as the composition of the government was concerned. Iturbide was quite willing, for example, to include Manuel Bonilla as a representative of the pro-Villa forces and Alvaro Obregón as a representative of the pro-Carranza forces. To insure conservative control of the Mexican army similar to that in 1911, "Iturbide himself would have no part in the new Government, but would act as the leader of the military forces supporting it, which he regarded as essential, in order that he might be in a position to compel the new government to carry out the pledges which it would have to make it order to secure the support of the United States" (Anderson Diary, 22 July 1915).

23. For Anderson's role as lobbyist for American mining, oil, and other interests, see Robert Freeman Smith, *The United States and Revolutionary Nationalism in Mexico, 1916–1932* (Chicago, 1972), p. 95.

24. See Katz, "Pancho Villa and the Attack on Columbus, New Mexico," pp. 119–23.

25. Smith, *The United States and Revolutionary Nationalism,* p. 95.
26. As quoted in David F. Houston, *Eight Years with Wilson's Cabinet, 1913 to 1920* (New York, 1926), 1:133.
27. Link, *Wilson: The Struggle for Neutrality,* pp. 475–76.
28. NA Washington, D.C., StDF Record Group 59, File 812.00 15531/2, Canova to the Secretary of State, 17 July 1915.
29. Katz, "Pancho Villa and the Attack on Columbus, New Mexico," p. 125.
30. González Garza archive, Roque González Garza to Villa, 26 October 1915.
31. *Vida Nueva* (Chihuahua), 21 November 1915. Although it has been ignored by U.S. historians, Francisco Almada printed this manifesto in the appendix to his *Revolución en el Estado de Chihuahua,* 2 vols. (Mexico, D.F., 1964–69), 2:382.
32. Francisco Villa to Jefe de la Columna Expedicionaria del Norte y a los demas Generales que forman parte de ella: Carmargo o en donde se encuentran, 16 December 1915, University of California at Berkeley, Bancroft Library, Silvestre Terrazas Papers, vol. 78, pt. 1.
33. This letter was part of a collection of documents found on a dead Villista after the Columbus attack. They never reached the State Department files but are contained in the Adjutant General's Office, File 2384662, Record Group 94, along with File 2377632. The complete text of this letter was first published in E. Bruce White, "The Muddied Waters of Columbus, New Mexico," pp. 72–92. A complete list of the documents and an attempt to analyze them was published at the same time in Harris and Sadler, "Pancho Villa and the Columbus Raid: The Missing Documents," pp. 335–47.
34. Private archive of Max Weber, El Paso, Texas, Max Weber to Major Britton Davis, 5 December 1916.
35. Link, *Woodrow Wilson,* p. 137.
36. Pearson Papers, Wordswick to Cowdray, 15 April 1916.
37. Isidro Fabela and Josefina E. de Fabela, eds., *Documentos Históricos de la Revolución Mexicana, Expedición Punitiva* 1:270–71.
38. Ibid. 2:283.
39. NA Washington, D.C., StDF Record Group 59, File 812.00/19898, Carothers to State Dept., 27 October 1916.
40. Mason, *The Great Pursuit,* p. 145.
41. Martin Blumenson, *The Patton Papers,* 2 vols. (Boston, 1972), 1:350.
42. Ibid., p. 344.
43. Link, *Woodrow Wilson,* p. 127.
44. See P. Edward Haley, *Revolution and Intervention: The Diplomacy of Taft and Wilson with Mexico, 1910–1917* (Cambridge, Mass., 1970), pp. 195–214.
45. Ibid., pp. 214–23.
46. Joseph P. Tumulty, *Woodrow Wilson as I Knew Him* (New York, 1921), p. 159.
47. Haley, *Revolution and Intervention,* p. 235.
48. Dennis J. O'Brien, "Petroleo e Intervención: Relaciones entre los Estados Unidos y Mexico, 1917–1918," *Historia Mexicana* 27 (1977): 103–41.
49. Link, *Wilson: Campaigns for Progressivism and Peace,* p. 331.
50. Ibid., p. 332.
51. NA Washington, D.C., StDF Record Group 59, File 812.00/24733, Lane to Lansing, 4 January 1917.
52. Peter Henderson, "Counterrevolution in Mexico: Felix Díaz and the Struggle for National Supremacy" (Ph.D. diss., University of Nebraska, 1973), pp. 257–300. See also Luis Liceaga, *Felix Díaz* (Mexico, D.F., 1958), pp. 361–70.
53. NA Washington, D.C., StDF, Office of the Counselor, Report by Justice Dept., 21 September 1916.
54. Peter Henderson, "Counterrevolution," pp. 285–95.

55. For the role of Alfredo Robles Domínguez, see chap. 11, below.

56. Porfirio Palacios, *Emiliano Zapata: Datos Biográfico-Históricos* (Mexico, D.F., 1960), p. 261.

57. Raymond T. U. Buve, "Peasant Movements, Caudillos and Land Reform during the Revolution (1910–1917), in Tlaxcala, Mexico," *Boletín de Estudios Latino-Americanos y del Caribe* 18 (June 1975): 112–53.

58. Clark W. Reynolds, *The Mexican Economy* (New Haven, 1970), pp. 26–36; Joseph E. Sterrett and Joseph S. Davis, "The Fiscal and Economic Condition of Mexico" (Report submitted to the International Committee of Bankers on Mexico, New York, 25 May 1928), pp. 227–30.

59. Marvin D. Bernstein, *The Mexican Mining Industry, 1890–1950* (Albany, N.Y., 1964), p. 101.

60. Smith, *The United States and Revolutionary Nationalism*, pp. 105–26.

61. PRO FO 371 2964, Patrick O'Hea to Foreign Office, 12 November 1917.

62. Charles Cumberland, *Mexican Revolution: The Constitutionalist Years* (Austin, 1972), pp. 324–25.

63. PRO FO 371 3244 2658, undated memorandum by Charles K. Furber.

64. Little has been written up to now on the *defensas sociales*. For their role in Chihuahua, see Almada, *La Revolución en el Estado de Chihuahua*, vol. 2, chap. 9.

65. Cervantes, *Francisco Villa y La Revolución*, pp. 592–95.

## Chapter 9

1. Graf Max von Montgelas and Walter Schücking, *Die deutschen Dokumente zum Kriegsausbruch, 1914*, 4 vols., 2d ed. (Berlin, 1922), vol. 4, no. 876, Moltke to Auswärtiges Amt, 5 August 1914.

2. Franz von Papen, *Der Wahrheit eine Gasse* (Munich, 1952), pp. 69–70.

3. United Nations, *Reports of International Arbitral Awards*, vol. 8, *Decisions of Mixed Claims Commission United States–Germany*, vol. 2 (New York, 1958), p. 354.

4. For the best overall account of the activity of German agents in the U.S., see Barbara W. Tuchman, *The Zimmermann Telegram* (London, 1959), pp. 66–87.

5. AA Bonn, Mexico 16, vol. 2, Eckardt to Hertling, 30 October 1917.

6. Franz von Rintelen, *The Dark Invader* (London, 1933), p. 179.

7. Tuchman, *The Zimmermann Telegram*, p. 79.

8. Ibid., pp. 80 ff.

9. William M. James, *The Eyes of the Navy: A Biographical Study of Admiral Sir Reginald Hall* (London, 1956), p. 101.

10. AA Bonn, Mexico 1, vol. 52, Ratibor to Auswärtiges Amt, 7 December 1914; NA Washington, D.C., StDF 862.202 12/42, MC 336, Roll 55, Stokes to Secretary of State, 28 June 1916.

11. AA Bonn, Mexico 1, vol. 56, Ambassador to Bern in Auswärtiges Amt, 18 February 1916.

12. AREM Mexico, Le 798 R, Consul in Havana to Foreign Minister, 20 January 1916.

13. AA Bonn, Mexico 1, vol. 57, Secretary of State in Auswärtigem Amt to Minister of War, 8 January 1916.

14. Ibid., vol. 56, Memorandum of 23 February 1916.

15. Ibid., Enrile memorandum, 19 April 1916.

16. Ibid., Montgelas's memorandum, 27 June 1916.

17. Ibid.

18. Ibid., Criminal Police Report on Enrile, 17 June 1916.

19. Ibid., vol. 57, Minister of War to Auswärtiges Amt, 3 September 1916.

20. Ibid., Mexico 1 secr., vol. 1, Dernburg to Holtzendorff, May 1915.
21. Ibid.
22. NA Washington, D.C., Department of Justice, Felix A. Sommerfeld file, no. 5305-9, Special Assistant to the Attorney General to Attorney General, 9 July 1918.
23. Ibid.
24. NA Washington, D.C., StDF 812.00/13232, Letcher to Bryan, 25 August 1914.
25. NA Washington, D.C., Department of Justice File, no. 5305-9, Special Assistant to the Attorney General to Attorney General, 9 July 1918.
26. NA Washington, D.C., StDF 812.00/13232, Letcher to Bryan, 25 August 1914.
27. AA Bonn, Mexico 1, vol. 33, Hintze to Auswärtiges Amt, 23 February 1913.
28. DZA Potsdam, AA II, no. 4461, Hintze to Bethmann-Hollweg, 16 March 1912.
29. NA Washington, D.C., Department of Justice, Felix A. Sommerfeld file, no. 5305-9, Statement of S. G. Hopkins.
30. Ibid., hearing of Felix Sommerfeld, 24 June 1918.
31. Ibid.
32. Ibid.
33. Ibid.; see also NA Washington, D.C., StDF 812.00/13232, Letcher to Bryan, 25 August 1914.
34. NA Washington, D.C., StDF 812.00/12706, Cobb to Bryan, 1 August 1914.
35. U.S. Senate Judiciary Committee, *Hearings on Brewing and Liquor Interests and German and Bolshevik Propaganda*, 2 vols., 66th Congress, 1st Session, Senate Document No. 62 (Washington, D.C., 1919), 2:2168.
36. Library of Congress, Washington, D.C., Scott Papers, Box 21, Sommerfeld to Scott, 1 January 1916.
37. AREM Mexico, Le 803 R, Monteverde to Consul in Los Angeles, 7 March 1917.
38. AA Bonn, Mexico 1, vol. 56, Bernstorff to Auswärtiges Amt, 28 March 1916.
39. It must be said here in all fairness that the work related to Mexico was at this time mainly in the hands of the military commands, i.e., the Admiralty and the Political Section of the General Staff, which quite often did not inform the Auswärtiges Amt of their plans.
40. AA Bonn, Mexico 1, vol. 56, Bernstorff to Bethmann-Hollweg, 4 April 1916.
41. HHSta Wien, PA, Mexico Reports 1916, Ambassador in Washington to Foreign Minister, 17 April 1916.
42. AA Bonn, Mexico 1, vol. 56, Bernstorff to Auswärtiges Amt, 24 June 1916.
43. As soon as there began to be talk of withdrawing American troops from Mexico, Texas' Congressman McLemore introduced a resolution in Congress on the initiative of the Irishman Shaemas O'Sheel, a member of the German propaganda section in the United States, calling for troops to remain in Mexico. The resolution, however, did not receive the required majority. George Sylvester Viereck, *Spreading Germs of Hate* (New York and London, 1930), p. 105.
44. AA Bonn, Mexico 1, vol. 56, Montgelas's memorandum, 23 March 1916.
45. Emanuel Viktor Voska and Will Irwin, *Spy and Counterspy* (New York, 1940), p. 917.
46. Ibid.
47. Juan B. Vargas, "Alemania propone a Villa el control de la Zona Petrolera," in *Novedades* (Mexico, D.F.), 10 October 1939.
48. There are several studies of the plan of San Diego. See, for example, Michael Meyer, "The Mexican-German Conspiracy of 1915," *The Americas* 23 (July 1966): 76–89; Allen Gerlach, "Conditions along the Border, 1915: The Plan de San Diego," *New Mexico Historical Review* 43 (July 1968): 195–212; James A. Sandos, "The Plan of San Diego: War and Diplomacy on the Texas Border, 1915–16," *Arizona and the West* 14 (Spring 1972): 5–24; Charles C. Cumberland, "Border Raid in the Lower Rio Grande Valley, 1915," *Southwestern Historical Quarterly* 57 (January 1954): 285–311.
The latest and in my opinion most thorough study of the plan of San Diego is Charles H. Harris III and Louis R. Sadler's "The Plan of San Diego and the Mexican–United States

War Crisis of 1916: A Reexamination," *Hispanic American Historical Review* 58 (August 1978): 381–408.

49. Harris and Sadler, "The Plan of San Diego."

50. NA Washington, D.C., Department of State, Office of the Counselor, Affidavit sworn by John Kvaka Forseck, 3 October 1919.

51. See chap. 10.

52. Archivo de la Secretaría de la Defensa Nacional (Mexico, D.F.), XI, 481.5/100f, 301 Flores to Carranza, 2 February 1917.

53. DZA Potsdam, Reichskanzler, no. 2410, Pudor's Indictment of Reichskanzler Bethmann-Hollweg (Leipzig, 3 July 1916).

54. AA Bonn, Mexico 1, vol. 53, Eckardt to Bethmann-Hollweg, 30 July 1915.

55. Ibid., Admiralty to Boy Edd, 11 March 1915.

56. Ibid., Papen to General Staff, 17 March 1915. This report stands in gross contradiction to Papen's later assertions. In his memoirs he writes: "My decision was from the beginning that such methods [sabotage actions] should not be tolerated. For: after the Battle of the Marne, it was certain that a long war was to be expected. British propaganda had the obvious goal of forcing the decision through America's entry into the war. Acts of sabotage were illegal. They could only have the effect of giving enemy propaganda rich material for bringing opinion against the Central Powers to the boiling point.

"Naturally, I was not in a position to prevent individual acts of sabotage staged by people out of 'patriotic feeling.' But I could and had to prevent such plans from being carried out with state support" (Papen, *Der Wahrheit eine Gasse*, p. 69).

57. DZA Potsdam, AA II, no. 3657, Ratibor to Auswärtiges Amt, 11 February 1915.

58. Ibid., no. 21 605, Consul in Tampico to Auswärtiges Amt, 2 June 1915.

59. AA Bonn, Mexico 1, vol. 53, Eckardt to Bethmann-Hollweg, 30 July 1915.

60. Ibid., vol. 52, Magnus to Bethmann-Hollweg, 25 August 1914.

61. Ibid., vol. 53, Magnus to Bethmann-Hollweg, 24 January 1915.

62. Ibid., Eckardt to Bethmann-Hollweg, 15 June 1915.

63. Ibid., Magnus to Barnstorff, 2 July 1915.

64. Ibid., Eckardt to Bethmann-Hollweg, 15 June 1915.

65. Ibid., vol. 58, Eckardt to Hertling, 30 November 1917.

66. Ibid., vol. 53, Magnus to Bethmann-Hollweg, 16 February 1915.

67. Tuchman, *The Zimmermann Telegram*, p. 79.

68. Japanese Foreign Office Documents, Mexico, MT 1133 02 479-02 481, Terasawa to Kusakabe, 9 September 1915.

69. Ibid., MT 1133 02 484-02 485, Iwasaki to Koike, 10 March 1916.

70. AA Bonn, Mexico 1, vol. 53, Eckardt to Bethmann-Hollweg, 21 June 1915.

71. Ibid., vol. 58, Eckardt to Hertling, 20 November 1917.

72. Ibid., vol. 57, Eckardt to Bethmann-Hollweg, 24 January 1916.

73. Ibid.

74. Ibid.

75. Ibid.

76. DZA Potsdam, AA Nachrichten- und Presseabteilung (NAP), no. 57 679, Eckardt to Bethmann-Hollweg, 19 June 1916.

77. Ibid.

78. HHSta Wien, PA, Mexico Reports, 1916, Mexican Envoy to Foreign Minister, 28 October 1916.

79. Ibid.

80. The text of the memorandum is in DZA Potsdam, AA II, no. 4462; see also Zimmermann's remarks to the Budget Committee of the Reichstag, 5 March 1917 (ibid., Reichstag, no. 1307, Minutes of Budget Committee of 5 May 1917).

81. AA Bonn, Mexico 1, vol. 57, Eckardt to Bethmann-Hollweg, 28 June 1917.

82. Ibid., vol. 56, Bernstorff to Bethmann-Hollweg, 22 June 1916.

83. Ibid., vol. 57, Eckardt to Bethmann-Hollweg, 8 November 1916.

84. DZA Potsdam, AA II, no. 4462, Zimmermann to Bethmann-Hollweg, 10 November 1916.

85. Ibid., Reichstag, no. 1307, Minutes of the Budget Committee, 5 March 1917.

86. Robert Lansing, *War Memoirs of Robert Lansing, Secretary of State* (1935), p. 310.

87. AA Bonn, Mexico 1, vol. 57, Eckardt to Auswärtiges Amt, 4 October 1916.

88. See Fritz Fischer, *Griff Nach der Weltmacht* (Düsseldorf, 1964), p. 383.

89. For the role of Kemnitz in the elaboration of the note, see AA Bonn, Mexico 20, vol. 2, Kemnitz to Solf, 29 November 1918, and vol. 1, Jordan to Lersner, 5 March 1917.

90. DZA Potsdam, Reichstag, no. 1307, Minutes of the Budget Committee, 5 March 1917.

91. Ibid.

92. Fischer, *Griff Nach der Weltmacht*, p. 278; Erwin Hölzle, "Deutschland und die Wegscheide des ersten Weltkrieges," in *Geschichtliche Kräfte und Entscheidungen* (Berlin, 1951), p. 272.

93. DZA Potsdam, Reichstag, no. 1295, Minutes of the Budget Committee, 30 March 1916.

94. AA Bonn, Mexico 16, vol. 2, Kemnitz to Solf, 24 November 1918.

95. DZA Potsdam, Reichstag, no. 1307, Minutes of the Budget Committee, 5 March 1917.

96. AA Bonn, Mexico 16, vol. 2, Kemnitz to Solf, 24 November 1918.

97. HHSta Wien, PA, Krieg 7, Mexico, Ambassador in Berlin to Foreign Minister, 2 April 1917.

98. AA Bonn, Mexico 16, vol. 2, Kemnitz to Solf, 24 November 1918.

99. See report of the Austrian ambassador in Berlin, HHSta Wien, PA Krieg 7, Mexico, Ambassador in Berlin to Minister of Foreign Affairs, 3 March 1917.

100. There is no evidence that Chancellor Bethmann-Hollweg was consulted by Zimmermann. In an anonymous article published in the *Nürnberger Nachrichten*, the author (who seems to have been well informed since he identified Kemnitz as the author of the telegram) wrote that the chancellor was only informed of the matter after the alliance proposal had been sent off. In his diary, Bethmann-Hollweg's close collaborator, Kurt Rietzler, gives no indication that the chancellor had known of the proposal or approved it. On the contrary, Rietzler was highly critical of the whole undertaking for which he blamed the "fantastic idiot" Kemnitz (Kurt Rietzler, *Tagebücher, Aufsätze, Dokumente* [Göttingen, 1972], p. 412).

101. Verfassungsgebende deutsche Nationalversammlung, 15. Ausschuss, *Bericht des zweiten Unterausschusses des Untersuchungsausschusses über die Friedensaktion Wilsons 1916/17* (Berlin, 1920), p. 355.

102. DZA Potsdam, Reichstag, no. 1307, Minutes of the Budget Committee, 5 March 1917.

103. The war had enormously increased the difficulties in communication between the German government and its representatives on the American continent. Two days after the outbreak of the war, the British warship *Telconia* had, with one exception, cut all telegraph cables linking Germany with the rest of the world. The only cable that remained in operation for several months was owned partly by Americans, but it, too, was soon cut. (Tuchman, *The Zimmermann Telegram*, p. 103).

104. Burton J. Hendrick, *The Life and Letters of Walter H. Page*, 3 vols. (New York, 1923–25), 3:335–36.

105. AA Bonn, Mexico 16, vol. 1, Eckardt to Auswärtiges Amt, 13 February 1917, and Lucius to Bethmann-Hollweg, 14 March 1917.

106. Ernest R. May, *The World War and American Isolation, 1914–1917* (Chicago, 1966), pp. 347–70.

107. Hendrick, *Life and Letters*, 3:340.

108. AA Bonn, Mexico 16 secr., vol. 1, Goeppert's Final Report of 4 April 1917.

109. DZA Potsdam, Reichstag, no. 1307, Minutes of the Budget Committee, 5 March 1917.

110. Tuchman, *The Zimmermann Telegram*, p. 17; James, *The Eyes of the Navy*, p. 56; Samuel R. Spencer, *Decision for War* (Ridge, N.H., 1953), p. 55.

111. James, *The Eyes of the Navy*, p. 138; Tuchman, *The Zimmermann Telegram*, p. 156.

112. James, *The Eyes of the Navy*, p. 134.

113. Spencer, *Decision for War*, p. 66.

114. NA Washington, D.C., StDF, Office of the Counselor, Leland Harrison Files, Box 208, Walter Hines Page, publication of his biography including the then secret Zimmermann telegram; documents 1921/1922; Edward Bell to William Hurley, 13 July 1921.

115. Ibid.

What is the reason for these errors in Hall's account, which have misled generations of historians who based their analysis of the Zimmermann affair on Hendrick's findings? I first came upon this discrepancy when I contrasted the Hendrick account and the books of William James and Barbara Tuchman, which are based on Hendrick with the minutes of the Goeppert Commission. Goeppert specifically mentioned code 0075 as the one by which the dispatch was sent to Washington and code 13040 in which the dispatch was then transmitted to Eckardt, who was not in possession of 0075. At the time I felt that the main reason for this discrepancy was that Hall wanted to conceal the fact from the Germans that British Intelligence possessed code 0075. Probably, the Germans were still utilizing that code or a derivative of it. This was certainly one of the motives for the inaccuracies in Hall's statement but not the only one. In 1938, two American cryptographers, William F. Friedman and Charles J. Mendelsohn, wrote a book entitled *The Zimmermann Telegram of January 16, 1917, and Its Cryptographic Background*. It was published by the U.S. Government Printing Office in 1938, which shows the importance attributed to this question by the U.S. government. The significance of the book was underlined by the fact that although more than twenty years had passed since the affairs of the Zimmermann telegram, the matter was considered so sensitive that the book was classified and remained so until 1965.

On the basis of highly classified American documents Friedman and Mendelsohn for the first time revealed the existence of code 0075 (which they labeled 7500). Above all, they felt that from 1917 onward Hall was trying to conceal the fact that "the British Intelligence Service was intercepting and solving not only German code messages but also intercepting and perhaps solving diplomatic messages of the American Government" (William F. Friedman and Charles J. Mendelsohn, *The Zimmermann Telegram of January 16, 1917, and Its Cryptographic Background* [Laguna Hills, Calif., 1976], p. 26).

In the era after World War I, when anti-British feelings were on the rise in the United States, this kind of revelation would have contributed to fueling such resentments. Finally another motivation for Hall's "errors," not mentioned by Friedman and Mendelsohn, was Hall's fear that once Britain's ability to decode cipher 0075 had been revealed, it would only be a matter of time until the fact came out that, in spite of the Anglo-American alliance, the British never gave the key to this cipher to U.S. intelligence. Even in January of 1919 after the European war had ended, the British continued to withhold code 0075 from the Americans. "There must be some reason or other behind the constant refusal to let us have this code," U.S. security expert Bell bitterly complained about the British (NA Washington, D.C., StDF, Office of the Counselor, Box 200, Bell to Harrison, 30 January 1919).

The Hendrick account which was based both on Hall's revelations to him and Ambassador Page's telegrams to Washington (also based on information furnished by Hall) showed the British in a much more generous light. While for technical reasons they had not sent the cipher books for code 13040 to Washington, they had allowed U.S. security expert Bell to decode them in London. Hall thus implied that Britain had, in fact, given access to U.S. intelligence of the key for code 13040. This was true. But a few weeks after the exposure of the Zimmermann telegram, code 13040 became worthless. On 23 March 1917 the Foreign Office in Berlin instructed Eckardt to discontinue use of code 13040 which it considered compromised (a copy of this telegram is located in the files of the State Dept., NA Washington, D.C., Office of the Counselor, Box 203).

In contrast the Germans continued to transmit their messages through code 0075, which the British continued to intercept and decipher and whose key they continued to withhold from the Americans.

116. Hendrick, *Life and Letters*, 3:334.
117. Lansing, *War Memoirs*, p. 226.
118. Link, *Woodrow Wilson*, p. 271.
119. *Hearings on Brewing*, 2:1611.
120. Hendrick, *Life and Letters*, 3:344.
121. Ibid., p. 347.
122. Lansing, *War Memoirs*, p. 230.
123. *Hearings on Brewing*, 2:1611.
124. Lansing, *War Memoirs*, p. 230.
125. Tuchman, *The Zimmermann Telegram*, p. 176.
126. Viereck, *Spreading Germs of Hate*, p. 112.
127. Hendrick, *Life and Letters*, 3:352.
128. AA Bonn, Mexico 16, vol. 1, Lucius to Bethmann-Hollweg, 11 March 1917.
129. NA Washington, D.C., StDF 862.202 12/173a, MC 336, Roll 55, Lansing to Embassy in Mexico, 2 April 1917, and Fletcher to Secretary of State, 4 March 1917.
130. Bernard Baruch, *My Own Story*, 2 vols. (New York, 1957–60), 1:213.
131. FR, 1917, Supplement, DeNegri to Secretary of State, 12 February 1917.
132. Archivo del Ministerio de la Defensa Nacional, XI, 481.5/100f, 301, Flores to Carranza, 2 February 1917.
133. Verfassungsgebende deutsche Nationalversammlung Bericht, p. 356.
134. HHSta Wien, PA, War 7, Mexico, Ambassador in Berlin to Foreign Minister, 3 May 1917.
135. Hendrick, *Life and Letters*, 3:351.
136. Iyo Kunimoto, "Japan and Mexico, 1888–1917" (Ph.D. diss., University of Texas at Austin, 1975), pp. 241–43.
137. Author's interview with Mr. Xavier Tavera.
138. José López Portillo y Weber, "Como perdió Carranza el apoyo de los Estados Unidos y como se relacionó esto con la proposición que a México presentó Alemania en 1917," in *Memorias de la Academia Mexicana de la Historia* 19 (1960), no. 1.
139. NA Washington, D.C., StDF 862.202 12/173a, MC 336, Roll 55, Lansing to Embassy in Mexico, 2 April 1917.
140. On 26 February Eckardt asked Berlin: "Could we provide munitions?" Hendrick, *Life and Letters*, 3:350.
141. NA Washington, D.C., StDF 862.202 12/70, MC 336, Roll 55, Fletcher to Secretary of State, 26 February 1917.
142. Ibid., StDF 862.202 12/89, MC 336, Roll 55, Fletcher to Secretary of State, 10 March 1917.
143. Isidro Fabela and Josefina E. de Fabela, eds., *Documentos Históricos de la Revolucion Mexicana: Revolución y Régimen Constitucionalista*, 6 vols. (Mexico, D.F., 1960–62), 3:284ff.
144. AA Bonn, Mexico 16, vol. 3, Eckardt to Reichskanzler, 7 August 1918.
145. NA Washington, D.C., StDF 862.202 12/89, MC 336, Roll 55, Fletcher to Secretary of State, 10 March 1917.
146. Ibid., StDF 862.202 12/119, MC 336, Roll 55, Fletcher to Secretary of State, 13 March 1917.

147. Ibid.
148. Ibid.
149. Ibid., StDF 862.202 12/177, MC 336, Roll 55, Fletcher to Secretary of State, 4 March 1917.
150. Rickarday, "Como salio de Mexico la expedicion Punitiva," in *Jueves de Excelsior* (Mexico, D.F.), 22 July 1956.
151. Hendrick, *Life and Letters,* 3:354.
152. HHSta Wien, PA, War 7, Mexico, Ambassador in Berlin to Foreign Minister, 4 April 1917.
153. Bayerisches Hauptstaatsarchiv München (hereafter referred to as HSta Munich), Politische Berichte (PB), Berlin Embassy, Lerchenfeldt to Foreign Minister, 5 March 1917.
154. HHSta Wien, PA, Krieg 7, Mexico, Ambassador in Berlin to Foreign Minister, 4 March 1917.
155. Walter Rathenau, *Politische Briefe* (Dresden, 1929), p. 108.
156. HSta Munich, PB, Berlin Embassy, Lerchenfeldt to Foreign Minister, 6 March 1917.
157. DZA Potsdam, Reichstag, no. 1307, Minutes of the Budget Committee, 5 March 1917.
158. Ibid.
159. HSta Munich, PB, Berlin Embassy, Lerchenfeldt to Foreign Minister, 5 March 1917.
160. DZA Potsdam, Reichstag, no. 1307, Minutes of the Budget Committee, 5 March 1917.
161. Ibid.
162. Ibid.
163. *National-Zeitung,* 6 March 1917.
164. DZA Potsdam, Reichstag, no. 1307, Minutes of the Budget Committee, 5 March 1917.
165. *Leipziger Volkszeitung,* 5 March 1917.
166. From the *Leipziger Volkszeitung,* 8 March 1917, one learns only that Mehring's statements on the Zimmermann note played an important role in the election. What Mehring actually said about the Zimmermann note is unfortunately not reported.
167. DZA Potsdam, Reichstag, no. 1307, Minutes of the Budget Committee, 5 March 1917.
168. Ibid.
169. Ibid.
170. *Vorwärts,* 4 April 1917.
171. *Berliner Tageblatt,* 5 March 1917.
172. *Deutsche Tagezeitung,* 3 March 1917.
173. Alfred V. Tirpitz, *Erinnerungen* (Leipzig, 1919), p. 384.
174. HHSta Wien, PA, Krieg 7, Mexico, Ambassador in Berlin to Foreign Minister, 3 March 1917.
175. Ibid.
176. DZA Potsdam, Reichstag, no. 1307, Minutes of the Budget Committee, 5 March 1917.
177. HSta Munich, PB, Gesandschaft Berlin, Lerchenfeldt to Foreign Minister, 4 March 1917.
178. HHSta Wien, PA, Krieg 7, Mexico, Ambassador in Berlin to Foreign Minister, 4 March 1917.
179. DZA Potsdam, Reichstag, no. 1307, Minutes of the Budget Committee, 5 March 1917.
180. Ibid.
181. AA Bonn, Mexico 16, vol. 1, Draft of 7 March 1917.
182. Ibid.

183. *Deutsche Tageszeitung,* 13 March 1917.
184. NA Washington, D.C., StDF 862.202 12/108, MC 336, Roll 55, Egan to Secretary of State, 18 March 1917.
185. HHSta Wien, PA, Krieg 7, Mexico, Ambassador in Berlin to Foreign Minister, 3 March 1917.
186. J. H. Bernstorff, *Erinnerungen und Briefe* (Zurich, 1936), p. 406.
187. DZA Potsdam, Reichstag, no. 1307, Minutes of the Budget Committee, 5 March 1917.
188. Ibid.
189. AA Bonn, Mexico 16 secr., vol. 1, Representative in Copenhagen to Auswärtiges Amt, 12 March 1917.
190. NA Washington, D.C., StDF 862.202 12/108, MC 336, Roll 55, Egan to Secretary of State, 18 March 1917.
191. AA Bonn, Mexico 16 secr., vol. 1, Zimmermann's memorandum, 17 March 1917.
192. HSta Munich, PB, Berlin Embassy, Lerchenfeldt to Foreign Minister, 20 March 1917.
193. AA Bonn, Mexico 16 secr., vol. 1, Envoy in Copenhagen to Auswärtiges Amt, 12 March 1917.
194. Ibid., Secretary of State to Eckardt, 22 March 1917.
195. Ibid., Eckardt to Auswärtiges Amt, 31 March 1917.
196. Ibid.
197. Hendrick, *Life and Letters,* 3:360.
198. AA Bonn, Mexico secr., vol. 1, General Staff to Auswärtiges Amt, 13 March 1917.
199. Ibid., Note of Chief of Code Office, 12 March 1917.
200. Ibid., Goeppert Final Report, 4 April 1917.
201. Ibid.
202. Ibid.
203. Ibid., General Staff to Auswärtiges Amt, 27 March 1917.
204. Ibid., Goeppert Final Report, 4 April 1917.
205. Ibid.
206. Ibid.
207. Ibid., Goeppert's note, 28 May 1917.
208. Ibid.
209. Ibid., Bernstorff to Haniel, 19 June 1917.
210. It is undoubtedly an irony of fate that this same Kunkel was seen as a very important German agent by the Americans, who supposedly had inspired Carranza's proposals for an embargo (NA Washington, D.C., StDF 862.202 12/76, MC 336, Roll 55, Lansing to Embassy in Mexico, 23 February 1917).
211. Bernstorff, *Erinnerungen und Briefe,* p. 406.
212. HSta Munich, PB, Berlin Embassy, Lerchenfeldt to Foreign Minister, 20 March 1917.
213. AA Bonn, Mexico 16, vol. 1, Political Section of General Staff to Auswärtiges Amt, 8 March 1917.
214. Ibid.
215. HHSta Wien, PA, Krieg 7, Mexico, Minister in Mexico to Foreign Minister, 19 December 1917.
216. NA Washington, D.C., StDF 862.202 12/730, MC 336, Roll 56, Lansing to Embassy in Mexico, 30 October 1917.
217. DZA Potsdam, Reichstag, no. 1307, Minutes of the Budget Committee, 28 April 1917.
218. HHSta Wien, PA, Krieg 7, Mexico, Minister in Mexico to Foreign Minister, 22 April 1917.
219. Ibid., Minister in Mexico to Foreign Minister, 19 December 1917.

220. Ibid.
221. Ibid.
222. NA Washington, D.C., StDF 862.202 12/227, MC 336, Roll 55, Consul in Nogales to Secretary of State, 9 April 1917.
223. Hendrick, *Life and Letters*, 2:175.
224. NA Washington, D.C., StDF 862.202 12/270, MC 336, Roll 55, Wilson to Fletcher, 21 April 1917.
225. Ibid., 12/272, Fletcher to Secretary of State, 24 May 1917.
226. Staatsarchiv Bremen, Krieg 1914–1918 M 2 h No. 1, Acta X, Sieveking to Donath, 8 May 1917.
227. *New York Times*, 30 April 1917.
228. Kunimoto, "Japan and Mexico," pp. 296–97.
229. Ibid.
230. AA Bonn, Mexico 16, vol. 3, Eckardt to Reichskanzler, 7 August 1918.
231. NA Washington, D.C., StDF 862.202 12/729, MC 336, Roll 55, Fletcher to Secretary of State, 22 October 1917.
232. Ibid., 12/811, Roll 56, Consul in Frontera de Tabasco to Secretary of State, 22 October 1917.
233. Ibid., 12/860, Consul in Mazatlán to Secretary of State, 25 December 1917.
234. El Colegio de Mexico, Copies of papers of Josephus Daniels, Box 7, Daniels Diary, 4 May 1933.
235. Thomas B. Bailey, *The Policy of the United States toward the Neutrals* (Baltimore, 1942), pp. 319–22.
236. Ibid., pp. 317–19.
237. NA Washington, D.C., StDF 862.202 12/729, MC 336, Roll 55, Fletcher to Secretary of State, 22 October 1917.

## Chapter 10

1. DZA Potsdam, Alldeutscher Verband, Hauptleitung, no. 241, Petzold to Class, 27 November 1914.
2. AA Bonn, Mexico 1, vol. 58, Eckardt to Hertling, 30 November 1917.
3. Ibid., Mexico 16, vol. 3, Eckardt to Reichskanzler, 7 August 1918.
4. Ibid., vol. 2, Delmar to Political Section of General Staff, 4 December 1917. When an American correspondent interviewed Eckardt in 1932, he also asked him: "'What did you think, Doctor, when you read that [Zimmermann] note?' 'This is foolishness, I thought' was the laconic reply" (David W. Hazen, *Giants and Ghosts of Central Europe* [Portland, 1933], p. 51).
5. Burton J. Hendrick, *The Life and Letters of Walter H. Page*, 3 vols. (New York, 1922–25), 2:266.
6. HHSta Wien, Krieg 7, Mexico, Envoy in Mexico to Foreign Minister, 4 September 1917.
7. DZA Potsdam, AA NPA, no. 27,679, Eckardt to Bethmann-Hollweg, 12 October 1915.
8. Ibid., Memorandum of Eugen Motz, 11 January 1915.
9. Ibid., AA II, no. 1742, Eckardt to Bethmann-Hollweg, 2 May 1916.
10. Ibid., no. 21,605, Founding Manifesto of the Deutsch-Österreichischen Petroleum AG (undated); ibid., Eckardt to Bethmann-Hollweg, 19 February 1916.
11. Ibid., no. 1742, Addendum to Eckardt's report, 19 February 1916.
12. AA Bonn, Gesandtschaftarchiv Mexico, Bundle 3, Magnus to Bethmann-Hollweg, 12 September 1916.
13. Ibid., Mexico 16, vol. 1, Eckardt to Auswärtiges Amt, 20 March 1917.

14. DZA Potsdam, Reichskanzlei, no. 2476, Hoetzsch's memorandum, December 1914.

15. Fritz Fischer, *Griff Nach der Weltmach* (Düsseldorf, 1964), p. 467.

16. AA Bonn, Mexico 16, vol. 3, Eckardt to Reichskanzler, 7 August 1918.

17. *Investigation of Mexican Affairs*, 1:673.

18. In reality, the German Heberlein, representative of the Frankfurter Metallgesellschaft, was chairman of the board of both the American Metal Company and the Mexican firms. NA Washington, D.C., StDF 862.202 12/325, MC 336, Roll 55, Vice-Consul in Monterrey to Secretary of State, 2 May 1917.

19. *Investigation of Mexican Affairs*, 1:672.

20. NA Washington, D.C., StDF 862.202 12/661, MC 336, Roll 56, Consul in Ciudad Juárez to Secretary of State, 15 September 1917.

21. Ibid., StDF 862.202 12/858, MC 336, Roll 57, Cobb to Secretary of State, 12 December 1917.

22. Ibid., StDF 862.202 12/309, MC 336, Roll 55, Consul in Coahuila to Secretary of State, 3 May 1917.

23. Ibid., StDF 862.202 12/325, MC 336, Roll 55, Vice-Consul in Monterrey to Secretary of State, 2 May 1917.

24. Ibid., StDF 862.202 12/1743, MC 336, Roll 59, Cobb to Secretary of State, 29 December 1916.

25. DZA Potsdam, AA NPA, no. 57,866, Transozean Gesellschaft to Foreign News Office of Auswärtiges Amt, 20 November 1915.

26. Ibid., no. 57,679, Eckardt to Bethmann-Hollweg, 29 November 1915.

27. NA Washington, D.C., StDF 862.202 12/1741, MC 336, Roll 59, Cobb to Secretary of State, 20 December 1916.

28. Ibid., StDF 862.202 12/341, MC 336, Roll 55, Report from San Antonio to Secretary of State, 20 May 1917.

29. Ibid., StDF 862.202 12/579, MC 336, Roll 56, Consul in Piedras Negras to Secretary of State, 20 August 1917.

30. Ibid., StDF 862.202 12/299, MC 336, Roll 55, General Consul to Secretary of State, 1 May 1917.

31. *Investigation of Mexican Affairs*, 1:672.

32. Ibid., p. 673.

33. Ibid.

34. Ibid., p. 672.

35. NA Washington, D.C., StDF 862.202 12/463, MC 336, Roll 56, Agent Report to Secretary of State, 15 June 1917.

36. Ibid., StDF 862.202 12/464, MC 336, Roll 56, Boese to Secretary of State, 2 June 1917.

37. Ibid., StDF 862.202 12/488, MC 336, Roll 56, Consul in Durango to Secretary of State, 19 July 1917.

38. Yale University Library, Polk Papers, Box 81, Folder 61, Polk to Lane, 7 May 1917.

39. For the close cooperation between Bruere and U.S. banks as well as the U.S. government, see Robert Freeman Smith, *The United States and Revolutionary Nationalism in Mexico, 1916–1932* (Chicago, 1972), pp. 127–28, 130–31.

40. NA Washington, D.C., StDF 862.202 12/89, MC 336, Roll 55, Consul in Piedras Negras to Secretary of State, 8 June 1917.

41. DZA Potsdam, AA II, no. 3289, Eckardt to Bethmann-Hollweg, 9 May 1917.

42. AA Bonn, Mexico 16, vol. 1, Montgelas's note, 20 February 1917.

43. Ibid., Eckardt to Auswärtiges Amt, 16 April 1917.

44. Ibid., Hülsen to Auswärtiges Amt, 19 April 1917.

45. Ibid.

46. Ibid., Eckardt to Auswärtiges Amt, 15 May 1917.

47. United Nations, *Reports of International Arbitral Awards: Decisions of Mixed Claims Commission, United States and Germany* (New York, 1958), 8:383.

48. DZA Merseburg, Rep. 92, E I, no. 13, Kapp Papers, unsigned report, October 1919.

49. AA Bonn, Mexico 16, vol. 2, Delmar to Political Section of General Staff, 4 December 1917.

50. See below, pp. 402–11.

51. Hendrick, *Life and Letters*, 2:268.

52. HHSta Wien, PA, Krieg 7, Mexico, Envoy in Mexico to Foreign Minister on 17 July 1917.

53. AA Bonn, Mexico 16, vol. 1, Eckardt to Auswärtiges Amt, 1 June 1917.

54. Ibid., vol. 2, Zimmermann to Political Section of General Staff, 28 March 1917.

55. The word "bribes" was replaced with "provision of support for influential politicians" before the cable was sent to Eckardt.

56. AA Bonn, Mexico 16, vol. 2, Auswärtiges Amt to Eckardt, 8 June 1917.

57. Ibid., vol. 1, Eckardt to Auswärtiges Amt, 12 June 1917.

58. HHSta Wien, PA, Krieg 7, Mexico, Eckardt to Auswärtiges Amt, 18 June 1917, transmitted by Austrians.

59. AA Bonn, Mexico 16, vol. 1, Auswärtiges Amt to Eckardt, 16 June 1917.

60. Edgar Turlington, *Mexico and Her Foreign Creditors* (New York, 1930), p. 271.

61. Ibid., pp. 273–74.

62. AA Bonn, Mexico 16, vol. 2, Delmar to Political Section of General Staff, 4 December 1917.

63. Ibid., vol. 1, Eckardt to Auswärtiges Amt, 8 September 1917.

64. Ibid., vol. 2, Delmar to Political Section of General Staff, 4 December 1917.

65. Ibid.

66. Ibid.

67. Ibid., Delmar to Political Section of General Staff, 8 December 1917.

68. Ibid.

69. Ibid.

70. Ibid.

71. Ibid.

72. Ibid., Gehmann to Political Section of General Staff, 29 October 1917.

73. Ibid., Kalle to Political Section of General Staff, 28 October 1917.

74. Ibid., Auswärtiges Amt to Eckardt, October 1917.

75. Ibid.

76. Ibid., Secretary of State in Auswärtiges Amt to Rödern, 26 November 1917.

77. Ibid., vol. 1, Minutes of Kemnitz's meeting with Blaschegg, Gwinner, and Fricke, 18 March 1917.

78. Ibid.

79. Ibid., and see also Deutsch-Südamerikanische Bank to Hardt, 12 March 1917; Ratibor to Auswärtiges Amt, 15 April 1917.

80. Ibid., vol. 2, Delmar to Political Section of General Staff, 4 December and 7 December 1917.

81. Ibid., vol. 1, Envoy in Madrid to Auswärtiges Amt, 18 May 1917.

82. Ibid., Proposal of Political Section of General Staff, 18 May 1917.

83. Commerzbibliothek Hamburg, Handelskammer Hamburg, no. 1747, Deposits by German firms in Mexico with the Auswärtiges Amt, 12 April 1920.

84. Staatsarchiv Bremen, Informational Notes of the Auswärtiges Amt, no. 31, 31 October 1917.

85. AA Bonn, Mexico 16, vol. 2, Delmar to Political Section of General Staff, 9 December 1917.

86. Ibid., Representative of the Auswärtiges Amt in General Headquarters to Reichskanzler, 12 January 1918.

87. Ibid., Auswärtiges Amt to Eckardt, 13 January 1918.

88. DZA Potsdam, Reichswirtschaftsamt, no. 1006, War Office to Reich Economic Office, 22 June 1918.

89. Ibid.

90. Ibid., AA II, no. 4462, Hintze to Conference Participants, 28 July 1918.
91. Ibid., Secretary of State in Reich Economic Office to Auswärtiges Amt, 26 August 1918.
92. Ibid., Ministry of War to Auswärtiges Amt, 7 August 1918.
93. Ibid., Minutes of the Meeting, 30 July 1918.
94. Ibid.
95. Ibid.
96. Ibid.
97. Ibid.
98. AA Bonn, Mexico 16, vol. 2, Memo of Hamburg firms to Auswärtiges Amt, 3 August 1918.
99. Ibid.
100. DZA Potsdam, AA II, no. 4462, Secretary of State in Reich Economic Office to Auswärtiges Amt, 26 August 1918.
101. Ibid., Reich Economic Office, no. 1430, Secretary of State in Reich Economic Office to Auswärtiges Amt, 30 August 1918.
102. Ibid., Secretary of State in Reich Economic Office to Deutsche Erdöl AG, 5 September 1918.
103. W. G. Truchanowski, ed., *Geschichte der internationalen Beziehungen* (Berlin, 1963), pp. 48–49.
104. AA Bonn, Mexico 16, vol. 2, General Staff to Auswärtiges Amt, 10 October 1918.
105. DZA Potsdam, AA II, no. 4462, State Secretary in Reich Economic Office to Auswärtiges Amt, 19 October 1918.
106. AA Bonn, Mexico 16, vol. 2, Eckardt to Auswärtiges Amt, December 1917, transmitted through Madrid, 9 January 1918.
107. Ibid., Bleichröder to Haniel, 26 February 1918.
108. Ibid., Delmar to Political Section of General Staff, 15 March 1918.
109. Ibid., Eckardt to Auswärtiges Amt, 5 April 1918.
110. Ibid., Report of the Military Commercial Division of Bern Embassy, 5 July 1918.
111. Ibid., vol. 3, Eckardt to Reichskanzler, 7 August 1918.
112. The American secret service verified that Fabela's luggage had been searched (NA Washington, D.C., StDF 862.202 12/1160, MC 336, Roll 58, Havana Embassy to Secretary of State, 26 April 1918; Appendix: Military Attaché in Havana to Chief of Military Intelligence Branch, Executive Division, 22 April 1918).
113. AA Bonn, Mexico 16, vol. 2, Ambassador in Madrid to Auswärtiges Amt, 13 May 1918.
114. Ibid.
115. Ibid., Kühlmann to Admiral Staff, 21 May 1918.
116. Ibid., Auswärtiges Amt to Ambassador in Madrid, 31 May 1918.
117. Ibid.
118. Ibid., Auswärtiges Amt to Political Section of General Staff, 13 July 1918.
119. Ibid., Delmar to Political Section of General Staff, 9 August 1918.
120. Ibid., Ambassador in Madrid to Auswärtiges Amt, 11 October 1918.
121. Ibid., Deputy State Secretary in Auswärtiges Amt to Political Section of General Staff, 15 October 1918.
122. Ibid., Note of Auswärtiges Amt, 24 March 1918.
123. Ibid., Delmar to Political Section of General Staff, 15 March 1918.
124. Ibid., Auswärtiges Amt to Delmar, 15 March 1918, Appendix.
125. Ibid., Fricke to Hintze, 20 August 1918.
126. Ibid.
127. Ibid., Kalle to Political Section of General Staff, 28 October 1917.
128. *Mixed Claims Commission, United States and Germany,* Lehigh Valley Railroad

Company, Agency of Canadian Car and Foundry Company, Limited, Final Report of the American Agent (Washington, D.C., 1939), p. 58.

129. United Nations, *Reports of International Arbitral Awards,* 8:300–330.

130. AA Bonn, Mexico 16, vol. 2, Busche to Eckardt, 30 April 1917.

131. Bundesarchiv, Militärarchiv Freiburg, Reichsmarineamt, Report by Knorr: Über die Etappentätigkeit in den Vereinigten Staaten von Nordamerika, 3 March 1919.

132. Ibid.

133. Ibid.

134. Alfred Kruck, *Geschichte des Alldeutschen Verbandes* (Wiesbaden, 1954), p. 144; Harold J. Gordon, *Die Reichswehr und die Weimarer Republik* (Frankfurt, 1959), p. 338; Walter Schellenberg, *Memoirs* (London, 1956), pp. 158–60; Ladislas Farago, *The Game of the Foxes* (New York, 1971), pp. 716–21.

135. NA Washington, D.C., StDF 862.202 12/1101, MC 336, Roll 58, Lansing to embassy in London, 11 April 1918.

136. DZA Merseburg, Rep. 92, E I, no. 13, Kapp papers, unsigned report, October 1919.

137. NA Washington, D.C., StDF 862.202 12/1101, MC 336, Roll 58, Lansing to embassy in London, 11 April 1918.

138. AA Bonn, Mexico 16, vol. 2, Eckardt to Auswärtiges Amt, 21 February 1918.

139. Ibid., Telegram draft of the Political Section of General Staff, 29 April 1918.

140. Ibid.

141. This emerges from Jahnke's report to Kapp (DZA Merseburg, Rep. 92, E I, no. 13, Kapp Papers, Jahnke's Report of October 1919); see also NA Washington, D.C., StDF 862.202 12/1430, MC 336, Roll 59, Military Attaché to Chief of Military Intelligence Branch, Executive Division, 31 July 1918.

142. Ibid., StDF 862.202 12/642, MC 336, Roll 56, Lansing to Fletcher, 13 September 1917.

143. Ibid., StDF 862.202 12/669, MC 336, Roll 56, Fletcher to Secretary of State, 26 September 1917.

144. DZA Potsdam, Reichspostamt, Geheime Registratur Z, no. 15 043/1, Minutes of discussion of 23 November 1916 held by representatives of the Reich Post Office, the Auswärtiges Amt, the Reich Colonial Office, the army and the navy.

145. Ibid.

146. Ibid., Eckardt to Auswärtiges Amt, May 1916.

147. Ibid., Auswärtiges Amt to Reich Post Office and Admiral Staff, 20 May 1916.

148. Ibid., Reich Post Office to Admiral Staff, 30 May 1916.

149. Ibid., Admiral Staff to Reich Post Office, 15 June 1916.

150. Ibid., Reich Post Office to Auswärtiges Amt and Admiral Staff, 15 July 1916.

151. Ibid., Admiral Staff to Reich Post Office, 9 July 1916.

152. Ibid., Reich Post Office to Admiral Staff, 19 July 1916.

153. Ibid., Minutes of Meeting Results, 22 July 1916.

154. Ibid.

155. Ibid.

156. Ibid., Reich Treasury to Auswärtiges Amt, 28 August 1916.

157. Ibid., Note on the Discussion in Reich Post Office, 26 February 1920.

158. Ibid.

159. Ibid., Telefunkengesellschaft to Reich Post Office, 28 March 1917.

160. Ibid., Rusch's Report at meeting in Reich Post Office, 26 February 1920.

161. Ibid.

162. Ibid., Admiral Staff to Wilhelm II, 10 March 1917.

163. Ibid., Auswärtiges Amt to Reich Post Office, 20 April 1917.

164. Ibid.

165. AA Bonn, Mexico 16, vol. 2, Delmar to Political Section of General Staff, 10 December 1917.
166. Ibid., vol. 3, Eckardt to Reichskanzler, 7 August 1918.
167. Ibid., vol. 2, Delmar to Political Section of General Staff, 9 December 1917.
168. NA Washington, D.C., StDF 862.202 12/1374, MC 336, Roll 59, Consul Marsh to General Consul in Mexico, 9 July 1918.
169. DZA Potsdam, Reichspostamt, Geheime Registratur Z, no. 15043/1, Report on Results of a meeting in Reich Post Office, 14 February 1917.
170. Ibid., Telefunkengesellschaft to Reich Post Office, 9 February 1917.
171. Ibid., Reich Post Office to Telefunkengesellschaft, 12 February 1917.
172. Ibid., Marginal notations on Report of Auswärtiges Amt to Reich Post Office, 20 April 1917.
173. Ibid., Admiral Staff to Reich Post Office, 28 September 1918.
174. NA Washington, D.C., StDF 862.202 12/1480, MC 336, Roll 59, Lansing to Page, 31 August 1918.
175. DZA Potsdam, Reichspostamt, Geheime Registratur Z, no. 15 043/1, note on conversation with Eckardt in Reich Post Office, 20 February 1920.
176. Ibid., Admiral Staff to Auswärtiges Amt and Reich Post Office, 27 and 28 September 1918.
177. NA Washington, D.C., StDF 862.202 12/1606, MC 336, Roll 59, Lansing to Fletcher, 9 October 1918.
178. Ibid.
179. Ibid., StDF 862.202 12/184, MC 336, Roll 59, Ambassador in Bern to Secretary of State, March 1917.
180. Ibid., StDF 862.202 12/348, MC 336, Roll 55, Fletcher to Secretary of State, 29 May 1917.
181. Ibid., StDF 862.202 12/436, MC 336, Roll 56, Page to Secretary of State, 7 July 1917.
182. AA Bonn, Mexico 16, vol. 2, Delmar to Political Section of General Staff, 15 March 1918.
183. NA Washington, D.C., StDF 862.202 12/1150, MC 336, Roll 58, Consul in Veracruz to Secretary of State, 13 April 1918.
184. Ibid., StDF 862.202 12/1264, MC 336, Roll 58, Fletcher to Secretary of State, 5 June 1918.
185. DZA Potsdam, AA II, no. 4462, Embassy in Bern to Reichskanzler, 5 July 1918.
186. AA Bonn, Mexico 16, vol. 2, Kalle to Political Section of General Staff, 28 October 1917.
187. NA Washington, D.C., StDF 862.202 12/1167, MC 336, Roll 58, Page to Secretary of State, 3 May 1918. This, as in the case of later reports, was a German instruction intercepted by the British secret service.
188. Ibid., StDF 862.202 12/1101, MC 336, Roll 58, Embassy in London to Lansing, 9 April 1918.
189. William M. James, The Eyes of the Navy: A Biographical Study of Admiral Sir Reginald Hall (London, 1956), p. 190.
190. DZA Merseburg, Rep. 92, E I, Kapp Papers, Jahnke's report of October 1919.
191. NA Washington, D.C., StDF 862.202 12/1408, MC 336, Roll 59, Page to Secretary of State, 21 October 1918; ibid., StDF 862.202 12/1621, MC 336, Roll 59, Page to Secretary of State, 21 October 1918; ibid., StDF 862.202 12/1626, MC 336, Roll 59, Page to Secretary of State, 24 October 1918.
192. AA Bonn, Mexico 16, vol. 2, Kalle to Political Section of General Staff, 28 October 1917.
193. M. N. Roy, "Memoirs," Amrita Bazar Patrica, Calcutta, 11 March 1951.
194. Ibid., 25 February 1951.
195. Ibid., 11 March 1951.

196. AA Bonn, Krieg II, Actions and Subversion against Our Enemies, in India, vol. 36, Indian Independence Committee to Hilmi, 23 March 1917.
197. Ibid., vol. 37, Eckardt to Auswärtiges Amt, 23 April 1917.
198. Roy, "Memoirs," *Amrita Bazar Patrica,* Calcutta, 11 March 1951.
199. AA Bonn, Mexico 16, vol. 2, Eckardt to Auswärtiges Amt on 10 December 1917.
200. Ibid., Auswärtiges Amt to Eckardt, 13 January 1918.
201. NA Washington, D.C., StDF 862.202 12/547, MC 336, Roll 56, Lansing to Fletcher, 12 August 1917.
202. AA Bonn, Mexico 16, vol. 2, Delmar to Political Section of General Staff, 8 December 1917.
203. NA Washington, D.C., StDF 862.202 12/885, MC 336, Roll 57, Ambassador in Tokyo to Secretary of State, 6 January 1918.
204. Ibid., StDF 862.202 12/1236, MC 336, Roll 58, Consul in Hong Kong to Secretary of State, 30 May 1918.
205. AA Bonn, Mexico 16, vol. 2, Delmar to Political Section of General Staff, 14 July 1918.
206. Ibid., Ambassador in Madrid to Auswärtiges Amt, 21 March 1918.
207. NA Washington, D.C., StDF 862.202 12/1404, MC 336, Roll 59, Page to Secretary of State, 31 July 1918.
208. AA Bonn, Mexico 16, vol. 3, Eckardt to Reichskanzler, 7 August 1918.
209. NA Washington, D.C., StDF 862.202 12/1619, MC 336, Roll 59, Page to Secretary of State, 21 October 1918.
210. See above, chap. 9.
211. Yale University Library, Polk Papers, Box 34, Folder 20, Polk to Lansing, 4 June 1918.
212. Ibid.
213. AA Bonn, Mexico 16, vol. 3, Eckardt to Reichskanzler, 7 August 1918.
214. NA Washington, D.C., StDF 862.202 12/1645, MC 336, Roll 59, Ambassador in Guatemala to Secretary of State, 4 November 1918.
215. StA Bremen, Krieg 1914–1918, M 2 h 2 no. 1, Acta X, Sieveking to Donath, 4 July 1917.
216. DZA Potsdam, Reichskanzlei, no. 2477, Note on the discussion in spa, 2/3 July 1918, on blockade of North America.
217. Ibid., Note on the discussion in spa, 27 July 1918, on extension of blockade.
218. Ibid.
219. Ibid.
220. Ibid.
221. NA Washington, D.C., StDF 862.202 12/371, MC 336, Roll 56, Fletcher to Secretary of State, 30 May 1917.
222. AA Bonn, Mexico 1, vol. 37, Kardorff to Bethmann-Hollweg, 19 August 1913.
223. Ibid., Mexico 16, vol. 2, Note of Secretary of State in Auswärtiges Amt, 9 September 1916.
224. DZA Potsdam, AA II, Nachrichten und Presseabteilung, Commentary to Arnoldo Krumm Heller, *Für Freiheit und Recht: Meine Erlebnisse aus dem mexikanischen Bürgerkrieg* (Halle and Berlin, 1917).
225. AA Bonn, Mexico 1, vol. 57, Commerell to Ministry of War, 22 January 1917.
226. Ibid., Mexico 16, vol. 1, Krumm Heller to Zimmermann, 25 July 1917.
227. NA Washington, D.C., StDF 862.202 12/470, MC 336, Roll 56, Jusserand to Secretary of State, 30 May 1917.
228. AA Bonn, Mexico 16, vol. 1, Zimmermann to Krumm Heller, 29 July 1917.
229. Ibid., Archive of German Legation in Mexico, Bundle 10, Morán to Eckardt, 6 June 1918.
230. Ibid., File 3183, anonymous report, 20 October 1917.

231. Ibid., Bundle 17, Eckardt to Auswärtiges Amt, 18 December 1917; DZA Merseburg, Rep. 92, E I, no. 13, Kapp Papers, report of October 1919.

232. *Investigation of Mexican Affairs,* 1:1230.

233. AA Bonn, Archives of German Legation in Mexico, Bundle 10, Aguilar's letter to Agente Confidencial, 15 November 1917.

234. Ibid.

235. Ibid., Mexico 16, vol. 3, Eckardt to Reichskanzler, 7 August 1918.

236. AA Bonn, Mexico 1, vol. 58, Eckardt to Reichskanzler, 30 April 1917.

237. Ibid.

238. NA Washington, D.C., StDF 862.202 12/974, MC 336, Roll 57, Assistant Secretary of State to Polk, 15 February 1918.

239. AA Bonn, Mexico 16, vol. 3, Eckardt to Reichskanzler, 7 August 1918.

240. NA Washington, D.C., StDF 862.202 12/1480, MC 336, Roll 59, Page to Secretary of State, 23 August 1918.

241. AA Bonn, Archives of German Legation in Mexico, Bundle 10, Agent Report on Felix Díaz, 18 December 1917.

242. Ibid., Gibsons to General Consul in Mexico on 24 January and 5 February 1916.

243. NA Washington, D.C., StDF 862.202 12/663, MC 336, Roll 56, Consul in Veracruz to Secretary of State, 1 October 1917; ibid., StDF 862.202 12/1292, MC 336, Roll 58, Consul in Nuevo Laredo to Secretary of State, 11 June 1918.

244. Ibid., StDF 862.202 12/647, MC 336, Roll 56, Page to Secretary of State, 24 September 1917.

245. AA Bonn, Mexico 16, vol. 1, Eckardt to Auswärtiges Amt, 1 June 1917.

246. *Investigation of Mexican Affairs,* 1:460.

247. AA Bonn, Mexico 16, vol. 2, Delmar to Political Section of General Staff, 8 July 1918.

248. Ibid., Delmar to Political Section of General Staff, 14 July 1918.

249. Ibid., Under Secretary of State in the Auswärtiges Amt to Political Section of General Staff, 6 August 1918.

250. NA Washington, D.C., StDF 862.202 12/1493, MC 336, Roll 59, Page to Secretary of State, 28 August 1918.

251. AA Bonn, Mexico 16, vol. 1, note of 19 April 1917.

252. Ibid.

253. Ibid., Kemnitz to Secretary of State in the Auswärtiges Amt, 25 May 1917.

254. United Nations, *Reports of International Arbitral Awards,* 8:347.

255. AA Bonn, Mexico 16, vol. 2, Eckardt to Auswärtiges Amt, 21 February 1918.

256. On the American secret services, see Robert Lansing, *War Memoirs of Robert Lansing, Secretary of State* (1935), p. 84.

257. NA Washington, D.C., StDF 862.202 12/51, MC 336, Roll 55, Cobb to Secretary of State, 28 December 1916; ibid., StDF 862.202 12/55, MC 336, Roll 55, Cobb to Secretary of State, 13 January 1917.

258. Ibid., StDF 862.202 12/1334, MC 336, Roll 58, Consul in Nuevo Laredo to Secretary of State, 2 July 1918.

259. Ibid., StDF 862.202 12/1683a, MC 336, Roll 59, Carr to General Consul Eberhardt, 6 February 1919.

260. M. N. Roy, "Memoirs," *Amrita Bazar Patrica,* Calcutta, 25 February 1951.

261. This is established beyond any doubt by the numerous confidential reports on German machinations sent by the French to the State Department; see, among other sources, NA Washington, D.C., StDF 862.202, MC 336, Roll 57, Jusserand to Secretary of State, 21 November 1917.

262. Ibid., StDF 862.202 12/1247, MC 336, Roll 58, Consul in Tampico to Secretary of State, 21 May 1918.

263. Ibid., StDF 862.202 12/1099, MC 336, Roll 57, Consul in Sonora to Secretary of State, 3 April 1918.

264. Ibid., StDF 862.202 12/1099, MC 336, Roll 57, Mexico Specialist of the Office of the Foreign Trade Adviser to Canova, September 1917.

265. DZA Potsdam, AA II, no. 16945, Magnus to Auswärtiges Amt, 14 February 1919.

266. NA Washington, D.C., StDF 862.202 12/794, MC 336, Roll 57, Lansing to Page, 15 November 1917; ibid., Page to Secretary of State, 17 November 1917.

267. Ibid., StDF 862.202 12/1025, MC 336, Roll 57, Page to Secretary of State, 12 March 1918.

268. Ibid., StDF 862.202 12/1035, MC 336, Roll 57, Lansing to Page, 15 March 1918.

269. Ibid., StDF 862.202 12/1732, MC 336, Roll 59, Page to Secretary of State, 17 January 1918.

270. Ibid., StDF 862.202 12/1734, MC 336, Roll 59, Polk to Page, 18 January 1918.

271. Herberto Yardley, "La Criptografia y los Mensajes de Alemania a Mexico," *Sintesis*, Mexico, D.F., January 1940.

272. United Nations, *Reports of International Arbitral Awards*, 8:351.

273. Ibid.

274. Ibid., p. 354.

275. AA Bonn, Mexico 16, vol. 1, Eckardt to Auswärtiges Amt, 16 April 1917.

276. NA Washington, D.C., StDF 862.202 12/274, MC 336, Roll 55, Consul in Tampico to Secretary of State, 15 April 1917, Appendix: Mexican Consul in Havana to Foreign Minister, 29 and 30 March 1917.

277. Ibid.

278. Ibid.

279. Ibid., p. 364.

280. NA Washington, D.C., StDF 862.202 12/451, MC 336, Roll 56, Cobb to Secretary of State, 31 July 1917.

281. Ibid., StDF 862.202 12/657, MC 336, Roll 56, Agent Report of 15 August 1917.

282. Ibid., StDF 862.202 12/1123, MC 336, Roll 58, Fletcher to Secretary of State, 16 April 1918.

283. *Mixed Claims Commission, United States and Germany*, Final Reports of the American Agent, p. 60.

284. AA Bonn, Mexico 16, vol. 2, Delmar to Political Section of General Staff, 15 March 1918.

285. NA Washington, D.C., StDF 862.202 12/1647, MC 336, Roll 59, Jusserand to Secretary of State, 16 November 1918.

286. Ibid.

287. *Mixed Claims Commission, United States and Germany*, Final Report of the American Agent, p. 61.

288. NA Washington, D.C., StDF 862.202 12/1621, MC 336, Roll 59, Lansing to Embassy in Madrid, 23 October 1918.

289. Ibid., StDF 862.202 12/1755, MC 336, Roll 59, Military Attaché in Madrid to Secretary of State, 14 December 1919.

290. Ibid., StDF 862.202 12/451, MC 336, Roll 56, Cobb to Secretary of State, 31 July 1917.

291. Ibid., StDF 862.202 12/790, MC 336, Roll 57, Cobb to Secretary of State, 22 September 1917.

292. On Altendorf, see AA Bonn, Mexico 16, vol. 3, Stohrer's note of 7 October 1919; NA Washington, D.C., StDF 862.202 12/1210, MC 336, Roll 58, Consul in Guaymas to Secretary of State, 13 May 1918; *Investigation of Mexican Affairs*, 1:468 and 1229.

293. *Investigation of Mexican Affairs*, p. 468. Mason in any case asserts that it was he who handed Witzke over to the Americans.

294. Ibid., 2:3255.
295. Roger L. Green, *A. E. W. Mason, The Adventure of a Story Teller* (London 1952), p. 148.
296. Ibid.
297. NA Washington, D.C., StDF 862.202 12/1387a, MC 336, Roll 59, Harrison to Embassy in Mexico, 11 July 1918.
298. Ibid.
299. Ibid., StDF 862.202 12/1387, MC 336, Roll 59, Harrison to Embassy in Mexico, 22 August 1918.
300. Ibid., StDF 862.202 12/600, MC 336, Roll 56, Consul in Nuevo Laredo to Secretary of State, 1 September 1917.
301. Ibid.
302. Ibid., StDF 862.202 12/1509, MC 336, Roll 59, Consul in Veracruz to Secretary of State, 2 September 1918; ibid., StDF 862.202 12/1520, MC 336, Roll 59, Consul in Veracruz to Secretary of State, 5 September 1918; ibid., StDF 862.202 12/1568, MC 336, Roll 59, Consul in Veracruz to Secretary of State, 30 September 1918.
303. Ibid., StDF 862.202 12/1520, MC 336, Roll 59, Consul in Veracruz to Secretary of State, 5 September 1918.
304. DZA Potsdam, Reichspostamt, Geheime Registratur Z, no. 15 043/1, Eckardt to Auswärtiges Amt, 13 July 1917.
305. Ibid., AA NPA, no. 56 679, Admiral Staff to Auswärtiges Amt, 28 August 1917.
306. Green, *A. E. W. Mason, The Adventures of a Story Teller*, p. 148.
307. Ibid., p. 154.
308. AA Bonn, Mexico 16, vol. 3, Eckardt to Reichskanzler, 7 August 1918.
309. Ibid., vol. 2, Magnus to Auswärtiges Amt, 17 January 1919.
310. Ibid., vol. 3, Eckardt to Reichskanzler, 7 August 1918.
311. Yale University Library, Polk Papers, Box 34, Folder 20, Polk to Lansing, 4 June 1918.
312. NA Washington, D.C., StDF 862.202 12/331, MC 336, Roll 55, McCoy to Fletcher, 3 May 1917.
313. DZA Potsdam, Reichsamt des Innern, no. 14 430, Auswärtiges Amt to Intelligence Bureau of the Reich Office of the Interior, 8 July 1916.
314. Ibid., AA Zentralstelle für Auslandsdienst (ZfA), no. 1653, Memorandum on the First Year of the Central Office for Foreign Service.
315. Ibid., Reichsamt des Innern, no. 12 322, Report on Activities of the Central Office for Foreign Service in the Period 15 February–31 March 1915.
316. Ibid.
317. Ibid., AA NPA, no. 57 867, Deutscher Wirtschaftsverband für Süd- und Mittelamerika to Auswärtiges Amt, 20 December 1915.
318. Ibid., no. 57 698, Schädel to Auswärtiges Amt, 23 May 1917.
319. Ibid., no. 57 699, Embassy in Bern to Auswärtiges Amt, September 1918.
320. Ibid., no. 57 698, Schädel to Auswärtiges Amt, 23 May 1917.
321. Ibid., AA ZfA, no. 1359, Deutsch-Südamerikanisches Institut to Bethmann-Hollweg, 10 November 1914.
322. Ibid.
323. Ibid., Reichsamt des Innern, no. 12 319, 1914–15 Annual Report of the News Service for Spanish and Portuguese-Speaking Countries.
324. Ibid.
325. Ibid., AA NPA, no. 57 866, Transozean GmbH to Auswärtiges Amt, 22 September 1915.
326. Ibid.
327. Ibid., Reichsamt des Innern, no. 12 319, News Bulletin no. 56, Article by Gustav Stetzenbach, "The English Danger for South America."

328. Ibid., AA ZfA, no. 1453, Auswärtiges Amt to Luxburg, May 1917.
329. Ibid., AA NPA, no. 57 866, Transozean GmbH to Auswärtiges Amt, 22 September 1915.
330. Ibid., Reichsamt des Innern, no. 12 322, Activities Report of the Central Office for Foreign Service for August 1915.
331. Ibid., Annual Report for 1915 of the Central Office for Foreign Service.
332. Ibid., AA NPA, no. 57 866, Membership List of the German Overseas Services.
333. Ibid., AA II, no. 4032, Memorandum "Grundlagen und Ziele des Deutschen Überseedienstes."
334. Ibid., AA NPA, no. 57 866, Statement of the Auswärtiges Amt, 24 July 1915.
335. Ibid., no. 57 867, List of Board Members of the Transozean GmbH.
336. Ibid., no. 57 681, Auswärtiges Amt to Reich Treasury, 30 March 1917.
337. Ibid.
338. Ibid., no. 57 866, Bernstorff to Bethmann-Hollweg, 2 April 1915.
339. Ibid., no. 57 676, Bernstorff to Auswärtiges Amt, 6 March 1917.
340. Ibid.
341. Ibid., no. 57 697, Introduction to *Der Verband Deutscher Reichsangehöriger in Mexico,* April 1916.
342. Ibid., no. 57 679, Eckardt to Bethmann-Hollweg, 29 November 1915.
343. Ibid.
344. AA Bonn, Mexico 16, vol. 3, Eckardt to Reichskanzler, 7 August 1918.
345. Ibid.
346. DZA Potsdam, AA NPA, no. 57 866, Transozean GmbH to Auswärtiges Amt, 13 November 1915.
347. Ibid., AA II, no. 4032, Confidential Report of the Transozean GmbH to Auswärtiges Amt, March 1916.
348. Ibid., AA NPA, no. 57 679, Schumacher to Auswärtiges Amt, 21 October 1915.
349. Ibid.
350. Ibid.
351. Eckardt to Bethmann-Hollweg, 29 November 1915.
352. Ibid.
353. Ibid., Albert to Eckardt, 20 November 1915.
354. Ibid., Eckardt to Bethmann-Hollweg, 3 May 1916.
355. Ibid., Eckardt to Reichskanzler, 10 December 1915.
356. Ibid., Eckardt to Bethmann-Hollweg, 3 May 1916.
357. AREM Mexico, Guerra Europea 1914–1918, German Legation to Mexican Foreign Ministry, 22 September 1916.
358. Ibid., Aguilar to Editorial Board of *El Pueblo,* 24 September 1916.
359. Ibid., Editorial Board of *El Pueblo* to Aguilar, 26 September 1916.
360. DZA Potsdam, AA NPA, no. 57 679, Eckardt to Bethmann-Hollweg, 19 June 1916.
361. Rafael Martinez, "El Nacionalismo del Presidente Carranza," *El Universal Grafico,* Mexico, D.F., 15 February 1919.
362. AA Bonn, Mexico 1, vol. 57, Eckardt to Auswärtiges Amt, 2 August 1916.
363. DZA Potsdam, AA NPA, no. 57 679, Eckardt to Bethmann-Hollweg, 26 October 1916.
364. Ibid.
365. NA Washington, D.C., StDF 862.202 12/1180, MC 336, Roll 58, Fletcher to Secretary of State, 1 May 1918.
366. AA Bonn, Mexico 16, vol. 1, Political Section of General Staff to Auswärtiges Amt, 25 June 1917; ibid., Auswärtiges Amt to Political Section of General Staff, 29 June 1917.
367. DZA Potsdam, AA NPA, no. 57 679, Eckardt to Bethmann-Hollweg, 29 November 1915.
368. AA Bonn, Mexico 16, vol. 1, Eckardt to Auswärtiges Amt, 25 January 1917.

369. NA Washington, D.C., StDF 862.202 12/1084, MC 336, Roll 57, Campbell to Secretary of State, 5 March 1918.

370. HHSta Wien, PA, Krieg 7, Mexico, Minister in Mexico to Foreign Minister, 20 October 1916.

371. Ibid., Foreign Minister to Minister in Mexico, 26 October 1916.

372. Ibid.

373. AA Bonn, Mexico 16, vol. 3, Eckardt to Reichskanzler, 7 August 1918.

374. Ibid.

375. Ibid.

376. Ibid.

377. DZA Potsdam, AA NPA, no. 57 867, Schmersow to Firma Bromberg & Co., 7 July 1915.

378. NA Washington, D.C., StDF 862.202 12/1428, MC 336, Roll 59, General Consul Hanna to Secretary of State, 30 July 1918.

379. AA Bonn, Mexico 16, vol. 3, Eckardt to Reichskanzler, 7 August 1918.

380. NA Washington, D.C., StDF 862.202 12/1430, MC 336, Roll 59, Fletcher to Secretary of State, 31 July 1918.

381. AA Bonn, Archive of German Legation in Mexico, Bundle 6, Report on interview with Ugarte.

382. Ibid., Mexico 16, vol. 3, Eckardt to Reichskanzler, 7 August 1918.

383. Ibid.

384. NA Washington, D.C., StDF 862.202 12/1638, MC 336, Roll 59, Fletcher to Secretary of State, 13 December 1918.

385. AA Bonn, Mexico 16, vol. 3, Eckardt to Reichskanzler, 7 August 1918.

386. Ibid., Archive of German Legation in Mexico, Bundle 11, Consul in Guadalajara to Eckardt, 5 August 1918.

387. Ibid., Eckardt to Consul in Guadalajara, 13 August 1918.

388. Ibid., Consul in Guadalajara to Eckardt, 15 August 1918.

389. Ibid., Eckardt to Consul in Guadalajara, 20 August 1918.

390. Ibid.

391. NA Washington, D.C., StDF 862.202 12/1545, MC 336, Roll 59, Consul in Guadalajara to Secretary of State, 5 September 1918.

392. Ibid.

393. Ibid.

394. AREM Mexico, III/250 (34..00) (72) 1, Aguilar to Mexican press, 13 April 1918.

395. Ibid., Andrade to Foreign Minister, 24 April 1918.

396. AA Bonn, Mexico 16, vol. 3, Eckardt to Reichskanzler, 7 August 1918.

397. Ibid.

398. NA Washington, D.C., StDF 862.202 12/159, MC 336, Roll 55, Consul in Coahuila to Secretary of State, 27 March 1917.

399. Ibid., StDF 862.202 12/552, MC 336, Roll 57, Consul in Piedras Negras to Secretary of State, 13 August 1917.

400. Ibid., StDF 862.202 12/810, MC 336, Roll 57, War Department to Secretary of State, 28 November 1917.

401. Ibid., StDF 862.202 12/811, MC 336, Roll 57, Consul in Frontera de Tabasco to Secretary of State, 22 November 1917.

402. Ibid., StDF 862.202 12/1126, MC 336, Roll 58, Consul in Piedras Negras to Secretary of State, 13 April 1918.

403. AA Bonn, Mexico 16, vol. 3, Eckardt to Reichskanzler, 7 August 1918.

404. NA Washington, D.C., StDF 862.202 12/953, MC 336, Roll 57, Scorille to Fletcher, 6 February 1918; ibid., StDF 862.202 12/968, MC 336, Roll 57, Fletcher to Secretary of State, 13 April 1918.

405. Ibid., StDF 862.202 12/1064, MC 336, Roll 57, Cobb to Secretary of State, 28 March 1918.

406. Ibid., StDF 862.202 12/262, MC 336, Roll 55, Consul in Veracruz to Secretary of State, 19 April 1917; ibid., Secretary of State to Consul in Veracruz, 4 May 1917.

407. Ibid., StDF 862.202 12/481, MC 336, Roll 55, Memorandum of British Embassy in Washington, 24 July 1917.

408. Ibid., StDF 862.202 12/516, MC 336, Roll 56, Fletcher to Secretary of State, 7 August 1917.

409. Ibid., StDF 862.202 12/529, MC 336, Roll 56, Fletcher to Secretary of State, 14 August 1917.

410. Ibid., StDF 862.202 12/562, MC 336, Roll 56, National Type and Paper Co. to State Department, 25 August 1917.

411. Ibid.

412. Ibid., StDF 862.202 12/580, MC 336, Roll 57, Lansing to Fletcher, 22 August 1917.

413. Ibid.

414. Ibid., StDF 862.202 12/581, MC 336, Roll 57, Fletcher to Secretary of State, 28 August 1917.

415. Ibid., StDF 862.202 12/639, MC 336, Roll 57, Wilson to Lansing, 3 August 1917.

416. Ibid., StDF 862.202 12/581, MC 336, Roll 57, Lansing to Fletcher, 6 September 1917.

417. Ibid., StDF 862.202 12/616, MC 336, Roll 57, Fletcher to Secretary of State, 11 September 1917.

418. AA Bonn, Mexico 16, vol. 3, Eckardt to Reichskanzler, 7 August 1918.

419. NA Washington, D.C., StDF 862.202 12/1054, MC 336, Roll 58, Fletcher to Secretary of State, 23 March 1918.

420. AA Bonn, Mexico 16, vol. 3, Eckardt to Reichskanzler, 7 August 1918; NA Washington, D.C., StDF 862.202 12/1128, MC 336, Roll 58, Consul in Guadalajara to Secretary of State, 12 April 1918.

421. Ibid., StDF 862.202 12/1624, MC 336, Roll 59, Ambassador in Tokyo to Secretary of State, 17 July 1918.

422. AA Bonn, Mexico 16, vol. 3, Eckardt to Reichskanzler, 7 August 1918.

423. NA Washington, D.C., StDF 862.202 12/1197, MC 336, Roll 58, Secretary of State to Fletcher, 9 May 1918.

424. AA Bonn, Archive of German Legation in Mexico, Bundle 11, Consul in Yucatán to Eckardt, 16 March 1918.

425. NA Washington, D.C., StDF 862.202 12/780, MC 336, Roll 57, Consul in Progreso to Secretary of State, 22 September 1918.

426. Ibid., StDF 862.202 12/1004, MC 336, Roll 57, Vice Consul in Piedras Negras to Secretary of State, 27 February 1917.

427. Lansing even recommended these methods quite openly (ibid., StDF 862.202 12/580, MC 336, Roll 56, Lansing to Fletcher, 22 August 1917).

428. Ibid., StDF 862.202 12/924, MC 336, Roll 57, Summerlin to Secretary of State, 23 January 1918; ibid., Lansing to Embassy in Mexico, 28 January 1918; ibid., StDF 862.202 12/1306, MC 336, Roll 58, Consul General in Guayaquil to Secretary of State, 3 May 1918; ibid., StDF 862.202 12/1308, MC 336, Roll 58, Carr to Consul General in Guayaquil, 12 July 1918.

429. DZA Potsdam, AA ZFA, no. 947, Bernstorff to Auswärtiges Amt, 4 October 1916; ibid., Zimmermann to Bernstorff, 13 November 1916.

430. NA Washington, D.C., StDF 862.202 12/1337, MC 336, Roll 58, Committee of Public Information to Fletcher, 24 June 1918; ibid., StDF 862.202 12/1448, MC 336, Roll 59, Lansing to Embassy in Mexico, 15 August 1918.

431. Ibid., StDF 862.202 12/1337, MC 336, Roll 58, Committee of Public Information to Fletcher, 24 June 1918.

432. Ibid., StDF 862.202 12/481, MC 336, Roll 56, memorandum of British Embassy in Washington, 24 July 1917.
433. AA Bonn, Mexico 16, vol. 3, Eckardt to Reichskanzler, 7 August 1918.
434. Thomas A. Bailey, *The Policy of the United States toward'the Neutrals* (Gloucester, 1966), p. 313.

## Chapter 11

1. Between 1915 and 1920 the U.S. share of all goods imported into Latin America grew from less than 16 percent to almost 42 percent (Edward B. Parsons, *Wilsonian Diplomacy: Allied-American Rivalries in War and Peace* [St. Louis, 1978], pp. 47–48).
See also Joseph S. Tulchin, *The Aftermath of War: World War I and U.S. Policy toward Latin America* (New York, 1971), and Jeffrey J. Safford, *Wilsonian Maritime Diplomacy* (New Brunswick, 1978).
2. PRO FO 371 3244 3904, Memorandum by Thurstan, 30 April 1918.
3. Pearson Papers, Body to Riba, 24 September 1914.
4. Ibid.
5. Pearson Papers, Body to Cowdray, 30 December 1915.
6. Robert Freeman Smith, *The United States and Revolutionary Nationalism in Mexico, 1916–1932* (Chicago, 1972), pp. 101–4; Lorenzo Meyer, *Mexico y Estados Unidos en el Conflicto Petrolero, 1917–1942* (Mexico, D.F., 1968), pp. 94–103.
7. PRO FO 371 3961 3167, Foreign Office Minutes, 29 June 1917.
8. PRO FO 371 3244 3904, Memorandum by Thurstan, 30 April 1918.
9. PRO FO 371 2961 3167, unsigned memorandum from the British Embassy in Washington, 18 May 1917.
10. PRO FO 371 2962 3167, Grahame Richards to Foreign Office, July 1917.
11. PRO FO 371 2961 3167, Memorandum by Thurstan, 23 May 1917.
12. PRO FO 371 2962 3167, Grahame Richards to Foreign Office, June 1917.
13. PRO FO 371 2961 3167, Memorandum by Thurstan, 23 June 1917.
14. PRO FO 371 2961 3167, undated memorandum by Cummins.
15. PRO FO 371 2961 3167, undated memorandum by Body, and letter by Body, 29 April 1917.
16. PRO FO 371 2961 3167, notes by Body, 4–9 May 1917.
17. PRO FO 371 2962 3167, Grahame Richards to Foreign Office, June 1917.
18. Ibid.
19. PRO FO 371 2961 3167, Foreign Office Minutes, Comments by Rowland Sperling, 5 July 1917.
20. PRO FO 371 2961 3167, Foreign Office Memorandum, 6 July 1917.
21. PRO FO 371 2961 3167, Foreign Office Minutes, 29 June 1917.
22. PRO FO 371 2962 3167, Cummins to Balfour, 22 June 1917.
23. PRO FO 371 2962 3167, Colville Barclay to Balfour, 23 August 1917, and attached unsigned memorandum.
24. PRO FO 371 2963 3204, Cummins to Foreign Office, 5 November 1917.
25. NA Washington, D.C., StDF, Office of the Counselor, Leland Harrison File, Box 208 (Mexican Intrigue), Secret Memoranda of Secretary of State Lansing, 6, 12 December 1917.
26. Ibid.
27. PRO FO 371 2963 3204, Cowdray to Maurice de Bunsen, 12 November 1917.
28. PRO FO 371 2963 3204, Foreign Office Minutes, 14 November 1917.
29. PRO FO 371 2962 3167, Cummins to Foreign Office, 12 July 1917.
30. See Desmond Young, *Viscount Cowdray: Member for Mexico* (London, 1955), pp. 183–84.
31. Ibid.; PRO FO 371 2963 3204, Cowdray to Maurice de Bunsen, 12 November 1917.

32. Ibid.

33. Young, *Viscount Cowdray*, p. 184. In February 1917, when Cowdray had attempted to sell his holdings to Standard Oil, the British Admiralty had strenuously objected. See PRO FO 800/204 X P.O./6380, Balfour Papers, Graham Greene to Balfour, 13 February 1917.

34. PRO FO 371 2963 3204, Foreign Office to Barclay, 7 November 1917.

35. PRO FO 371 2864 3204 221012, Memorandum by Military Intelligence, 22 November 1917.

36. Ibid., Foreign Office Minutes, 23 November 1917.

37. PRO FO 371 2964 3204, Memorandum by Intelligence Division, Naval Staff, 10 December 1917.

38. Ibid.

39. See chap. 10.

40. PRO FO 371 2962 3167, undated report on British agent in German legation in Mexico.

41. PRO FO 371 2963 3204, Foreign Office Minutes, 27 October 1917.

42. PRO FO 371 2964 3204. Report of Sir Maurice de Bunsen on his meeting with Colonel House, 19 November 1917.

43. NA Washington, D.C., StDF 862.202 12/1025, MC 336, Roll 57, Page to Secretary of State, 12 March 1918.

PRO FO 371 3243 2744, Hohler to Foreign Office, 6 March 1918.

44. PRO FO 371 3244 2658, Memorandum by Thurstan, 9 May 1918.

PRO FO 371 2964 3204, Memorandum of the Intelligence Divison of the Naval Staff, 10 December 1917.

45. PRO FO 371 2964 3204, Bouchier to Roberts, 27 October 1917.

46. Ibid., Barclay to Balfour, 1 November 1917.

47. Ibid., Memorandum from Bouchier, 29 October 1917.

48. PRO FO 371 3244 3204, Memorandum by Thurstan, 30 April 1918.

49. PRO FO 371 3243 2744, Barclay to Foreign Office, 12 March 1918.

50. PRO FO 371 3242 2744, Cummins to Foreign Office, 11 March 1918.

51. Emily S. Rosenberg, "Economic Pressures in Anglo-American Diplomacy in Mexico, 1917–1918," *Journal of Inter-American Studies and World Affairs* 17 (May 1975): 123–52.

52. Smith, *The United States and Revolutionary Nationalism*, p. 119.

53. For an official biography of Alfredo Robles Domínguez, see Diego Arenas Guzmán, Mario Ronzón, and Manuel B. Trens, *Elogio de Alfredo Robles Domínguez* (Mexico, D.F., 1955).

54. PRO FO 371 3244 2651, Memorandum by Hohler, 11 April 1918.

55. Ibid.

56. Ibid.

57. PRO FO 371 3836 2658, Cummins to Foreign Office, April 1918.

58. PRO FO 371 3244 2658, Despatch from 152, Hohler to Foreign Office, 20 March 1918.

59. PRO FO 371 3244 2658, Secret Memorandum by General Staff, 9 May 1918.

60. Ibid.

61. PRO FO 371 3244 2658, Balfour to Reading, 7 May 1918.

62. PRO FO 371 3244 2658, Secret Memorandum by General Staff, 9 May 1918.

63. PRO FO 371 3244 2658, Memorandum by Balfour, 13 May 1918.

64. PRO FO 371 3244 2658, Balfour to Reading, 7 May 1918.

65. PRO FO 371 3244 2658, Proceedings of War Cabinet, 10 May 1918.

66. PRO FO 371 3244 2658, Reading to Foreign Office, 23 May 1918.

67. PRO FO 371 3244 2658, Cummins to Foreign Office, 24 May 1918.

68. Pearson Papers, Memo to Lord Cowdray, Interview between Lord Cowdray and Sir Maurice de Bunsen at Foreign Office, 25 March 1918.

69. PRO FO 371 3244 2658, Letter of collaborator of Cowdray, 9 May 1918.

70. PRO FO 371 3242 2658, Hohler to Foreign Office. These memoranda led to great

tensions between the United States and Great Britain. When questioned by British officials about these memoranda, Wilson, Lansing, and Gordon Auchincloss stated that they knew nothing about them and Hohler reported that Auchincloss "thinks that the telegram containing it must be in the Secret Service Department, but the secretary in charge of this Department tells me he cannot find them and he considers they have been mislaid" (ibid.). I have in fact found these messages in the confidential files of Leland Harrison in the papers of the Office of the Counselor.

Did they become lost there? Did Harrison feel that the British had exaggerated and that these communications were not serious enough to be communicated to Wilson and Lansing? Had Polk (who was not questioned by Hohler), who seems to have been an anti-interventionist, seen them and refused to pass them on because he felt they would fan the fire of interventionism? There is as yet no definite answer to these questions.

71. See Friedrich Katz, "Pancho Villa and the Attack on Columbus, New Mexico," *American Historical Review* 83 (February 1978): 117–23.

72. AMAE, n.s., CP, Guerre 1914–1918, Mexique, vol. 2, Jusserand to Foreign Minister, 14 December 1917.

73. PRO FO 371 3243 2743. See Report of Department Intelligence Officer Headquarters, Southern Military Command, submitted to the Chief of the Military Intelligence Section, Army War College, Washington, D.C., 22 February 1918.

74. AMAE, n.s., CP, Mexique, Pol. Int. 5, Jusserand to Foreign Minister, 16 November 1913.

75. AMAE, n.s., CP, Mexique, Pol. Int. 9, Ayguesparre to Foreign Minister, 26 December 1914.

76. Ibid., Ayguesparre to Foreign Minister, 20 September 1914.

77. AMAE, n.s., CP, Guerre 1914–1918, Mexique, vol. 2, Couzet to Foreign Minister, 7 December 1917.

78. AMAE, n.s., CP, Mexique, 1914–1918, Mexique, vol. 2, Jusserand to Foreign Minister, 14 December 1917.

79. AMAE, n.s., CP, Mexique, Pol. Int. 15, Note for Foreign Minister, 3 March 1918.

80. Ibid.

81. AMAE, n.s., CP, Etats Unis, vol. 75, B103, Relations avec le Mexique, 1919, Ayguesparre to Foreign Minister, 1 December 1919.

82. See Smith, *The United States and Revolutionary Nationalism*, chaps. 4 and 5; Rosenberg, "Economic Pressures in Anglo-American Diplomacy"; Mark T. Gilderhus, *Diplomacy and Revolution: United States–Mexican Relations under Wilson and Carranza* (Tucson, Ariz., 1977); Lorenzo Meyer, *Mexico y Estados Unidos*, pp. 94–103.

83. Smith, *The United States and Revolutionary Nationalism*, p. 93.

84. Ibid.

85. AMAE, n.s., CP, Guerre 1914–1918, Mexique, Jusserand to Minister of Foreign Affairs, 12 March 1918.

86. Smith, *The United States and Revolutionary Nationalism*, p. 93.

87. Yale University Library, Polk Papers, Folder 20, Polk to Lansing, 4 June 1918.

88. Rosenberg, "Economic Pressures in Anglo-American Diplomacy," pp. 129–33.

89. Smith, *The United States and Revolutionary Nationalism*, pp. 144–47.

90. Marvin D. Bernstein, *The Mexican Mining Industry* (Albany, 1964), p. 105.

91. See Isidro Fabela, *La Politica Interior y Exterior de Carranza* (Mexico, D.F., 1979), pp. 217–26.

92. For a detailed description of United States–Mexican economic, political, and diplomatic conflicts in the years 1917–18, see Gilderhus, *Diplomacy and Revolution*, pp. 72–106; Smith, *The United States and Revolutionary Nationalism*, pp. 93–133; Rosenberg, "Economic Pressures in Anglo-American Diplomacy," pp. 123–50; Meyer, *Mexico y Estados Unidos*, pp. 62–106.

93. PRO FO 371 3243 2743, Report of Department Intelligence Office Headquarters, Southern Military Command, submitted to the Chief of the Military Intelligence Section, Army War College, Washington, D.C., 22 February 1918.

94. Clifford W. Trow, "Senator Albert B. Fall and Mexican Affairs, 1912–1921" (Ph.D. diss., University of Colorado, 1966), pp. 184–92.

95. Meyer, *Mexico y Estados Unidos*, p. 101.

96. See note 93 above.

97. NA Washington, D.C., StDF, Office of the Counselor, Leland Harrison File, Box 208 (Mexican intrigue), Secret Memoranda of Secretary of State Lansing, 6 and 12 December 1917.

98. Ibid.

99. Friedrich Katz, "Pancho Villa and the Attack on Columbus, New Mexico," p. 121.

100. Bernard Baruch, *My Own Story*, 2 vols. (New York, 1957–60), 1:213; Thomas B. Bailey, *The Policy of the United States toward the Neutrals* (Baltimore, 1942), pp. 326–28.

101. Smith, *The United States and Revolutionary Nationalism*, pp. 112–13, 129–30.

102. Ibid., p. 132.

103. Julius W. Pratt, *A History of United States Foreign Policy* (Englewood Cliffs, N.J., 1972), p. 306.

104. Frank W. Iklé, "Japanese-German Peace Negotiations During World War I," *American Historical Review*.

105. Pratt, *A History of United States Foreign Policy*, pp. 306–7.

106. Iyo Kunimoto, "Japan and Mexico, 1888–1917" (Ph.D. diss., University of Texas at Austin, 1975), pp. 54–98.

107. Jessie C. Lyon, "Diplomatic Relations between the United States, Mexico and Japan 1913–1917" (Ph.D. diss., Claremont College, 1975), p. 98.

108. Ibid., p. 171.

109. Ibid., p. 173.

110. Akira Iriye, *Across the Pacific: An Inner History of American–East Asian Relations* (New York, 1967), p. 131.

111. Hugh L. Scott, *Some Memories of a Soldier* (New York, 1928), p. 512.

112. See William Reynolds Braisted, *The United States Navy in the Pacific* (Austin, 1971), pp. 164–65; Lyon, "Diplomatic Relations," pp. 93–97.

113. Kunimoto, "Japan and Mexico," p. 210.

114. Ibid., p. 211.

115. Ibid.

116. Ibid., pp. 215–16.

117. Ibid., p. 217.

118. Lyon, "Diplomatic Relations," p. 173.

119. Iriye, *Across the Pacific*, pp. 133, 136.

## Chapter 12

1. *Investigation of Mexican Affairs*, 1:458.

2. George A. Blakeslee, *Mexico and the Carribbean* (New York, 1920), p. 58.

3. Yale University Library, Polk Papers, Box 34, Folder 20, Polk to Lansing, 4 June 1918.

4. AA Bonn, Mexico 1, vol. 58, Eckardt to Bethmann-Hollweg, 19 February 1917.

5. Ibid., vol. 57, Eckardt to Bethmann-Hollweg, 8 January 1917.

6. AA Bonn, Mexico 16, vol. 3, Eckardt to Chancellor, 7 August 1918. Like many other statements by Eckardt, this one contained a great deal of exaggeration. The number of American troops deployed along the Mexican border was not 200,000 to 500,000 men but

only 40,000 soldiers (Yale University Library, Polk Papers, Box 34, Folder 20, Polk to Lansing, 4 June 1918).

7. AREM Mexico, Guerra Europea 1914–1918, Mexican Government to German Consul in Veracruz, 6 March 1915.

8. AA Bonn, Mexico 1, vol. 58, Eckardt to Hertling, 30 November 1917.

9. Roberto Guzmán Esparza, *Memorias de Don Adolfo de la Huerta* (Mexico, D.F., n.d.), p. 184.

10. Robert Freeman Smith, *The United States and Revolutionary Nationalism in Mexico, 1916–1932* (Chicago, 1972), p. 94.

11. AA Bonn, Archive of the German Legation in Mexico, Folder 10, Moran to Eckardt, 6 June 1918.

12. See Emily S. Rosenberg, "Economic Pressures in Anglo-American Diplomacy in Mexico, 1917–1918," *Journal of Inter-American Studies and World Affairs* 17 (May 1975): 123–52.

13. See Rosenberg, "Economic Pressures" and Smith, *The United States and Revolutionary Nationalism*, chap. 5.

14. Smith, *The United States and Revolutionary Nationalism*, chap. 5.

15. AA Bonn, Mexico 16, vol. 2, Eckardt to Auswärtiges Amt, 5 April 1918.

16. AA Bonn, Mexico 16, vol. 2, Delmar to Sektion Politik, 10 October 1917.

17. NA Washington, D.C., StDF 862.202 12/773, MC 336, Roll 57, Consul in Mazatlán to Secretary of State, 31 October 1917.

18. AA Bonn, Mexico 16, vol. 3, Eckardt to Chancellor, 7 August 1918.

19. DZA Potsdam, AA II, no. 4462, Military-Commercial Section of German Embassy in Bern to Chancellor, 5 July 1918.

20. Yale University Library, Polk Papers, Box 34, Folder 20, Polk to Lansing, 4 June 1918.

21. AA Bonn, Mexico 16, vol. 3, Eckardt to Chancellor, 7 August 1918.

22. Percy A. Martin, *Latin America and the War* (Baltimore, 1925), p. 538.

23. Foreign Relations 1917, Supplement, Fletcher to Secretary of State, 20 October 1917, p. 349.

24. AA Bonn, Mexico 16, vol. 3, Eckardt to Chancellor, 7 August 1918.

25. Ibid.

26. *Die Post,* 18 March 1917.

27. AA Bonn, Mexico 18, Schwabach to Auswärtiges Amt, 13 March 1918.

28. HHSta Wien, PA, Krieg 7, Mexico, Minister in Mexico to Foreign Minister, 17 July 1917.

29. Ibid., Minister in Mexico to Foreign Minister, 26 July 1917.

## Chapter 13

1. AA Bonn, Mexico 16, vol. 3, Eckardt to Reichskanzler, 7 August 1918.

2. Robert Freeman Smith, *The United States and Revolutionary Nationalism in Mexico, 1916–1932* (Chicago, 1972), p. 145.

3. DZA Potsdam, AA II, no. 4462, Magnus to Auswärtiges Amt, 13 August 1919.

4. DZA Potsdam, Reichsschatzamt, no. 2478, Eckardt to Bethmann-Hollweg, 25 September 1915.

5. J. A. Spender, *Weetman Pearson, First Viscount Cowdray* (London, 1930), pp. 203–4.

6. Smith, *The United States and Revolutionary Nationalism*, pp. 131–32.

7. Alfred Vagts, *Mexiko, Europa und Amerika unter besonderer Berücksichtegung der Petroleumpolitik* (Berlin, 1928), p. 292.

8. DZA Potsdam, AA II, no. 21605, German Ambassador in The Hague to Auswärtiges Amt, 1 February 1919.

9. Vagts, *Mexiko, Europa und Amerika*, p. 283.

10. *Investigation of Mexican Affairs*, 2:2096.

11. Ibid., p. 2097.

12. DZA Merseburg, Rep. 92, E 1, no. 13, Kapp Papers, Report from Mexico, October 1919.

13. Vagts, *Mexiko, Europa und Amerika*, p. 305.

14. *Investigation of Mexican Affairs*, 1:250.

15. Smith, *The United States and Revolutionary Nationalism*, pp. 157–59.

16. Charles Cumberland, *The Mexican Revolution: The Constitutionalist Years* (Austin, 1972), pp. 397–98.

17. Porfirio Palacios, *Emiliano Zapata: Datos Biográfico-Históricos* (Mexico, D.F., 1960), p. 261.

18. Federico Cervantes, *Francisco Villa y la Revolución* (Mexico, D.F., 1960), pp. 588–600.

19. John Womack, Jr., *Zapata and the Mexican Revolution* (New York, 1969), pp. 316–17.

20. Ibid., pp. 324–27.

21. AGN, Ramo Gobernación Box 88, Exp. 32, Carranza to Aguirre Berlanga, 9 January 1917.

22. Ibid., Luis Terrazas to Secretario de Gobernación, 10 August 1918.

23. Ibid., Andres Ortiz to Aguirre Berlanga, 24 February 1919.

24. Ibid., Subsecretario de Hacienda to Luis Terrazas, 18 March 1919.

25. Ibid., Carlos Cuilty to Carranza, 6 February 1920; Aguirre Berlanga to Cuilty, 17 March 1920.

26. Carranza was overthrown before his decree could be implemented and his successors refused to return the Terrazas's estates to their former owner. Instead, much of the Terrazas's land was distributed to peasants in the early 1920s. See AGN, Ramo Gobernación Box 88, Exp. 32, as well as Francisco R. Almada, *Resúmen de Historia del Estado de Chihuahua* (Mexico, D.F., 1955), pp. 427–33.

27. Smith, *The United States and Revolutionary Nationalism*, p. 153.

28. Ibid.

29. Edward B. Parsons, *Wilsonian Diplomacy: Allied-American Rivalries in War and Peace* (St. Louis, Mo., 1978), p. 169.

30. Alberto J. Pani, *Cuestiones Diversas* (Mexico, D.F., 1922), p. 356.

31. Smith, *The United States and Revolutionary Nationalism*, pp. 158–79.

32. Josephus Daniels, *The Wilson Era: Years of War and After* (Chapel Hill, 1946), p. 522.

33. AA Bonn, Mexico 16, vol. 2, Rhomberg to Auswärtiges Amt, 22 November 1918.

34. Ibid., Auswärtiges Amt to Rhomberg, 22 November 1918.

35. Ibid.

36. Ibid., Kemnitz to Solf, 24 November 1918.

37. Ibid., Memorandum of Rhomberg, 29 November 1918.

38. Ibid., vol. 3, Magnus to Auswärtiges Amt, 23 May 1919.

39. DZA Potsdam, AA II, no. 16945, Magnus to Auswärtiges Amt, 14 February 1919.

40. AA Bonn, Mexico 16, vol. 3, Magnus to Auswärtiges Amt, 23 May 1919.

41. DZA Potsdam, Reichspostamt Geheime Registratur Z, no. 15043/1, Minutes of conference held in mid-1919 (no exact date provided).

42. AA Bonn, Mexico 16, vol. 3, Auswärtiges Amt to Ambassador in Madrid, September 1919.

43. Staats Archiv, Bremen, Krieg, 1914–18, M2h2 no. 1, Sieveking to Donath, 27 January 1919.

44. AA Bonn, Mexico 16, vol. 3, Lucius to Auswärtiges Amt, 16 January 1920.

45. Ibid., vol. 2, Jahnke to Admiralty, 4 February 1919.

46. DZA Merseburg, Rep. 2 E, no. 13, Kapp Papers, unsigned report, October 1919. Although this report is unsigned, there is no doubt that it was written by Jahnke since it contains the same proposals that Jahnke had submitted to the Foreign Office.

47. Ibid.

48. AA Bonn, Vereingte Staaten von Nordamerika, 16 secr., unsigned and undated memorandum.

49. Ibid., undated memorandum by Eckardt.

50. Ibid., undated comments of Trautmann.

51. Fuehr to Under Secretary of State, 16 August 1919.

52. DZA Merseburg, Rep. 92, El, no. 1, Kapp Papers, unsigned reprort of October 1919.

53. Ibid.

54. National Archives, Washington, D.C., StDF 862.202 12/1759, MC 336, Roll 59, U.S. Consul General to Secretary of State, 18 September 1920.

55. Ibid., Military Attaché in Mexico to Secretary of State, 29 September 1920.

56. Ibid., Ambassador in Berlin to Secretary of State, 11 October 1920.

57. Ibid., Cobb to Secretary of State, 26 October 1917.

57. NA Washington, D.C., Justice Department File 180178, Cobb to Attorney General Gregory, 7 March 1916.

58. See NA Washington, D.C., StDF, Office of the Counselor, Box 208. It contains a confidential report on Keady's activities in Mexico by a Justice Department official, E. B. Stone, written in March 1916.

59. Ibid., Stone to Justice Department, 14 March 1916.

60. NA Washington, D.C., StDF 812.00/23 138, Canova to Lansing, 20 July 1915.

61. NA Washington, D.C., StDF, Office of the Counselor, E. B. Stone to Justice Department, 14 March 1916.

62. NA Washington, D.C., StDF 862.202 12/1759, MC 336, Cobb to Secretary of State, 26 October 1917.

63. NA Washington, D.C., StDF, Office of the Counselor, Box 219. Leland Harrison to Flournoy, 16 September 1918.

64. NA Washington, D.C., StDF 862.5/529, Summerlin to Secretary of State, 19 September 1919.

65. Ibid.

# Note on Archival Sources

This book is based on a multiplicity of archival sources in countries of Europe, North America, Latin America, and Japan. One of the main problems I have had to deal with was a certain discrepancy in the nature of the sources. Within the great powers, three types of agencies or institutions dealt with Mexico: The foreign offices, military intelligence services, and large corporations. The papers of the foreign offices of all large countries have been well preserved and are now available to researchers almost without restrictions.

The same cannot be said of intelligence files. Most of the German and Austrian intelligence files (with some significant exceptions) have been destroyed, whereas the papers of British intelligence are not yet available to researchers. By contrast most United States intelligence files have been preserved and have now been largely declassified. There are few available reports on Mexican intelligence activities in Mexican archives, but Mexican consulates in the United States utilized American private detectives to spy on exiles and enemies and their reports are available in the papers of the Mexican Foreign Office.

The unavailability of the papers, some of them destroyed, of European intelligence agencies working in Mexico is not as serious as it might seem at first glance. Three types of sources at least partially make up for these deficiencies. The most important are the correspondence between the intelligence services and the different foreign offices which are preserved in the foreign office files in both Great Britain and Germany.

A second source on German intelligence activities are the telegrams by headquarters in Berlin to German agents on the American continent which were deciphered by British intelligence and are located in the Foreign Office files in London.

The peace treaty which the United States signed with Germany after World War I created a mixed claims commission to examine damages suffered by American citizens at the hands of German agents in the years 1914–17 as long as the United States remained neutral in the war. Lawyers for both sides meticulously examined the activities of the German Secret Service in both the United States and Mexico and came up with much revealing information.

Trials of German agents caught in Great Britain and the United States (especially that of Franz Rintelen) also provide interesting information on the covert activities of intelligence agents.

The papers of the large corporations active in Mexico at the time of the revolution have been even more difficult to examine than those of the intelligence agencies. Only one such major corporation, the Pearson Trust, has made its papers available to researchers without any restrictions. The political activities of the large corporations essentially focused on two different types of aims: to influence the policies of their home governments and to exercise some influence on the different Mexican factions.

The first type of activity is easiest to document since the papers of the foreign offices and those of influential lobbyists (such as Chandler Anderson in the United States) have been preserved and contain important information on this subject. What I found most difficult to document is the second type of activity of business interests: their relation with the Mexican revolutionaries. The Pearson papers contain the most extensive and important description of this kind of activity. The correspondence between lobbyist S. Hopkins and Mexican revolutionaries, stolen from Hopkins's office in 1914 and published in the *New York Herald*, constitutes another revealing source. Another type of source which I have generally found to be reliable are reports in the foreign office files of rival countries on activities of corporations from another country. Thus, the papers of the German Foreign Office provide revealing insights into the activities of American and British business interests.

Press reports and hearings of United States Congressional Committees constitute important but far less reliable types of sources.

The countries whose archives I have used are listed alphabetically and not by the importance of the sources they provide.

*Austria.* Three archives in Austria contain sources on Mexico. The most important is the Politisches Archiv in the Haus, Hof, und Staats Archiv, Vienna. It contains the reports of the Austrian diplomatic representatives in Mexico and Washington. The information on Mexico's internal situation contained in these reports is not very revealing. Austria sent only second-rate diplomats to Mexico; for a long time after the execution of Maximilian it had refused to have any relations. Nevertheless, the reports reveal much about the activities of the other great powers in Mexico and especially about the policies of Austria's closest ally, Germany. I had hoped to find some information on the covert activities of German and possibly Austrian agents in Mexico and the United States in the files of Austria's military intelligence service, the Evidenzburo des Generalstabes. The results were extremely disappointing. The last head of the Evidenzburo had destroyed all essential information contained in its files before the end of World War I, leaving behind only some newspaper clippings and copies of Foreign Office reports.

The third relevant Austrian archive, the Verwaltungs Archiv Wien contains data on trade between Austria and Mexico.

*Cuba.* The papers of the Archivo Nacional de Cuba, Comisión de Estado, contain reports by Cuba's diplomatic representatives in Mexico for the years 1903–11. The most interesting of these reports describes the Porfirian government's attempts to weaken U.S. influence in Mexico and to strengthen Mexico's ties to Europe. In the Cuban archives I had hoped to find the correspondence of Marqués Sterling, Cuba's minister to Mexico during the Madero period, who had been a close friend of the Mexican president and had attempted to save his life after the coup that toppled him. These reports were missing from the archives as were other reports concerning the break of diplomatic relations between Cuba and Mexico in 1918.

*France.* France played a crucial role in Mexico during the Porfirian period but was of less importance for the revolutionary period. Nonetheless, French sources do constitute very revealing documents, not only as far as the policies of France were concerned but also in relation to those of its closest ally, Great Britain, as well as to those of the United States and Germany.

The most important information is contained in the files of the Archives du Ministère des Affaires Etrangères in Paris. It is divided into two sections: Correspondance Politique and Correspondance Commerciale.

The Archives du Ministère de la Guerre at Vincennes contain some revealing reports by the French military attaché in both the United States and Mexico.

A large amount of commercial and financial information on Mexico can be found in the files of the Ministère du Commerce (F 12) and the Ministère des Finances (F 14) at the Archives Nationales in Paris.

*German Democratic Republic.* The two most important archives, which contain very extensive and important information on Mexico, are the Deutsches Zentralarchiv Potsdam and the Deutsches Zentralarchiv Merseburg.

The most important sources I have located in Potsdam are those of three sections of the imperial German Foreign Ministry: its Trade and Commerce Section and its Legal Section as well as its News and Press Division.

The Trade and Commerce Section contains most reports from German consuls in many parts of Mexico up to 1910. It also contains extensive reports on German economic activities in Mexico as well as surveys of economic activities in practically all fields of Mexico's economic life.

The Legal Section of the German Foreign Ministry Archives constitutes a rich source of information on social conditions in Mexico. Detailed descriptions of Germany's propaganda activities in Mexico during World War I are located in the files of the News and Press Division of the Foreign Ministry.

The papers of most other German government agencies of the imperial period are also stored in Potsdam. The most revealing have been the papers of the Ministry of the Interior, the Reichsbank, the Budget Committee of the Reichstag and, to my surprise, the files of the secret section of the Reich Post Office, which describe Germany's covert efforts to set up radio communications with Mexico. The minutes of the secret meetings of the Budget Committee of the Reichstag contain the most extensive information on the origins and the meaning of the Zimmermann telegram.

The papers of different Prussian ministries are stored in the Deutsches Zentralarchiv Merseburg. They contain economic and political reports on Mexico which at times are not contained in the files of the imperial ministries.

The Prussian papers contain extensive information on German emigration to Mexico. Perhaps the most important document I have found in Merseburg is a detailed report by Kurt Jahnke, head of Germany's Naval Intelligence Service for North America in 1917–18 on his activities in Mexico. This report is located in the papers of Wolfgang Kapp.

Some information on Mexico, essentially of an economic nature, can be found in the Saxon Regional Archives in Dresden and the papers of the Deutsches Wirtschaftsinstitut in Berlin.

*German Federal Republic.* The vast collection of the political section (section 1) of the German Foreign Office files located at the Archiv der Auswärtigen Amtes Bonn constitutes the most important German source on Mexico. They deal with both the activities of the German Foreign Office as well as some German Intelligence agencies in Mexico. They also contain the political diaries the German minister in Mexico, Paul von Hintze, kept for the years 1913–14.

The papers of the German Legation in Mexico, also stored in Bonn, contain reports on local and regional conditions in Mexico not considered important enough to be included in the Foreign Office files.

The papers of the German navy are stored in the Bundesarchiv, Abteilung Militärgeschichte in Freiburg im Breisgau. Some of the most sensitive files on covert sabotage and intelligence activities by German agents in Mexico were destroyed at the end of World War I. Nevertheless, the archive does contain interesting and revealing sources. The reports by the captains of German warships sent to Mexican ports are frequently more interesting for their revelations about the ideology of the German navy than for the information they provide about Mexico. At times, however, the captains managed to reveal valuable information on the activities of other powers in Mexico (especially the United States and Great Britain) as well as on the personalities of the Mexican commanders of their ports of call.

The files of one German intelligence agency which had some bearing on Mexico have been preserved in the German naval archives. They are the papers of the Etappendienst der Marine which was responsible for supplying fuel and food for German warships docking in American ports.

Because the states that formed the German Empire in 1870 continued to maintain a large degree of autonomy—they kept their own foreign offices with ambassadors in Berlin—their records constitute an important source of information not only on commercial but also on diplomatic activities. The most important of these regional archives are the collections of the Staatsarchiv Hamburg, the Staatsarchiv Bremen, and the Hauptstaatsarchiv München.

*Great Britain.* The Foreign Office papers, which are located in the Public Record Office in London, constitute an essential source not only for Britain's Mexican policy but for internal Mexican developments as well. In view of the close links between the Foreign Office and British Intelligence agencies these papers provide important information on the activities of these agencies in Mexico.

The papers of Sir Weetman Pearson (Lord Cowdray), which are located in the British Science Museum in London, constitute a unique source for understanding the policies of Cowdray and of all large corporations active in Mexico. The political reports by Cowdray's lieutenants in Mexico are of great interest in assessing the political changes brought about during the revolution.

*Japan.* Some years ago I secured some copies of confiscated Japanese foreign office archives on Mexico of which the Library of Congress has a copy. They contain information on Japanese activities in that country but I found no mention there of the Zimmermann telegram. This gap was filled when I was able to consult the unpublished dissertation of Iyo Kunimoto, "Japan and Mexico, 1888–1917" (University of Texas, 1975), which has made use of entirely new materials.

*Mexico.* The papers of the Mexican Foreign Office (Secretaría de Relaciones Exteriores) are disappointing for historians seeking records of high-level decision making. Most important officials of the Secretaría de Relaciones in the revolutionary period seem to have destroyed the records of their activities or they took the records upon leaving office. Nevertheless, the Foreign Office papers constitute an extremely valuable source with respect to the activities of revolutionaries, exiles, and foreign business groups in the Mexican-American border region. There is an extremely well compiled index on these papers by Berta Ulloa (Archivo Histórico Diplomático Mexicano; Guias para la Historia Diplomática de México, Revolución Méxicana 1910–1920, México 1963). The most important records of high-level decision making in Mexico are contained in the papers of Isidro Fabela, one of Carranza's closest collaborators, who occupied an important position in Mexico's Foreign Office. These papers have, to a large extent, been published by Fabela and his wife, Josefina, in their extensive *Documentos Históricos de la Revolución Mexicana* (28 vols.; Mexico, D.F., 1961–78).

The Archivo General de la Nación is Mexico's largest archive, but for a long time only very few documents for the 1910–20 period were made accessible to researchers. In recent years profound changes took place in the organization of the archives and large amounts of new sources were discovered in its repositories and are now available to researchers. The most important of these are the papers of the Secretaría de Gobernación. They contain above all records of large estates which were confiscated and then returned to their former owners.

The files of the Secretaría de la Defensa Nacional, part of which I was able to consult, contain only limited information on Mexico's foreign relations. They constitute an important source for biographical data on the military leaders of the revolution and for the military and social history of the revolution.

In both Mexican and United States archives I was able to consult the papers of leading Mexican personalities of the revolutionary period. The most important of these records are:

1. The papers of Venustiano Carranza in the Condumex archives, Mexico City.
2. The papers of Roque González Garza in a private archive in Mexico City.
3. The papers of Lázaro de la Garza in the Nettie Lee Benson Collection in the Library of the University of Texas at Austin.
4. The papers of Martin Luis Guzmán in a private collection in Mexico City.
5. The papers of Francisco Madero in the Museo de Antropología Library and those located in the Biblioteca Nacional and those which had been stored at the time I consulted them in the Secretaría de Hacienda.
6. The papers of José María Maytorena in the Library of Claremont College, California.
7. The papers of Silvestre Terrazas in the Bancroft Library at Berkeley.
8. The papers of Emiliano Zapata located at the Archivo Histórico de la Universidad Nacional Autonoma de Mexico, Colección Magaña, and at Archivo General de la Nación.

The Hemeroteca Nacional in Mexico City contains a vast collection of Mexican newspapers and a magnificent multivolume index edited by Stanley Ross provides a complete guide to all articles on the revolution to be found there (Stanley R. Ross, *Introducción, Ordenamiento y Compilación: Fuentes de la Historia Contemporánea de México, Periódicos y Revistas*, 2 vols. [Mexico, D.F., 1965–78]).

*Spain.* For a long time, the only Spanish sources available to researchers were the papers of the Spanish Legation in Mexico. They had remained in possession of the government in exile of the Spanish Republic which allowed the Colegio de Mexico to microfilm them. While they do constitute a valuable source, they are incomplete. The papers of the Spanish Foreign Office in Madrid, which have now been opened to researchers, contain extremely interesting data on social and economic conditions in practically all parts of Mexico since Spaniards were active throughout the country.

*United States.* American sources for the Mexican Revolution (1910–20) have been available longer than those of any other country. They are also, in general, better ordered, more accessible, and more voluminous. As a result United States sources may have played a disproportionate role in assessments of the Mexican Revolution, and one of the aims of this book has been to create a more equitable balance between United States sources and those of other countries.

For many years now the voluminous collection of State Department papers on Mexico (Series 812.00) have been accessible to researchers not only in the National Archives in Washington but also as a microfilm publication. I have consulted them together with the papers of the most important United States politicians involved in Mexican affairs. The most relevant of these papers are those of William Howard Taft, Woodrow Wilson, Colonel Edward House, William Jennings Bryan, Robert Lansing, Leonard Wood, Hugh Scott, Woodrow Wilson's special representative in Mexico John Lind, and his ambassador to Mexico Henry P. Fletcher. With the exception of the House and Lind papers, which are located at the Yale University Library and at the Minnesota State Historical Society Library, respectively, all papers can be consulted in the Library of Congress, Manuscript Division.

Among lesser political figures whose activities were nevertheless very important with respect to Mexico are those of Frank Polk, counselor of the State Department, stored in the Yale University Library and the diaries of Chandler Anderson and James Garfield who acted as lobbyists for American interests and which are held by the Library of Congress.

I have also found the papers of Senator Albert B. Fall, microfilms of which I was able to obtain from the libraries of the Universities of Nebraska and New Mexico, of great importance.

For a long time the main gap in American sources for this period, related to United States intelligence activities in Mexico. In the last years some of the most important files dealing with this kind of activity have been declassified. Some of the most revealing reports concerning United States intelligence and counterintelligence agents are contained in Foreign Affairs Branch, State Department Decimal file, 1910–20; File No. 862.202 12 German military activities in Mexico, microcopy No. 336, Rolls 55–59. The military intelligence files which are among the last to have been declassified contain a complex mixture of essential and absolutely irrelevant information.

The papers of the office of the counselor for the State Department contain information on intrigues by American business interests and State Department officials with respect to Mexico and information with regard to German activities in Mexico which were considered extremely confidential at the time.

While the gap concerning United States intelligence activities in Mexico thus has been partially closed, the same cannot be said with respect to the activities of the largest United States corporations in Mexico. No American corporation has allowed researchers to utilize its files in the same way as Lord Cowdray's heirs have done in Great Britain. These gaps are only partially compensated for by the extensive correspondence of representatives of these corporations with their lobbyists and with high United States officials which are available to researchers.

# List of Archival Sources

**German Democratic Republic**
German Central Archive, Potsdam
a) Foreign Ministry, Trade Policy Division

| Nos. 1724–1726 | Mexico's Economic Situation (1887–1920) |
|---|---|
| 1727–1743 | Mexico's Financial Management (1887–1922) |
| 1744 | Newspaper excerpts |
| 1745–1746 | Banks and Banking in Mexico (1889–1916) |
| 1747–1748 | Economic Undertakings in Mexico (1907–19) |
| 2395–2397 | Conditions of the Coal Market (1907–19) |
| 2894 | Shipments to Mexico (1909–19) |
| 2950–2952 | Arms Shipments from German Firms to Foreign Governments—America (1907–19) |
| 2975–2979 | Collection of Reports on Foreign Trade Conditions—Overseas (1907–19) |
| 3061–3067 | Petroleum Production and Trade (1905–20) |
| 3289 | Trade Experts in Mexico (1906–17) |
| 4032 | German Overseas Service GmbH (1915–18) |
| 4457–4462 | Trade Relations with Mexico (1906–20) |
| 4478 | Complaints of German Citizens with Regard to the Mexican Board of Customs (1907–10) |
| 4481 | Trademark Protection and Patents in Mexico (1904–13) |
| | Yearly Reports of the Consulate |
| 4491 | Chihuahua (1907–14) |
| 4492 | Colima (1907–13) |
| 4493 | Durango (1907–15) |
| 4494 | Guadalajara (1907–10) |
| 4495 | Mazatlán (1907–14) |
| 4496 | Merida (1907–10) |
| 4497 | Mexico (1907–11) |
| 4498 | Tampico (1915) |
| 4510 | Veracruz (1907–12) |
| 4557–4652 | United States Trade Relations with Other Countries of Continental America |
| 4804–4806 | German Banks in Middle and South America (1895–1910) |
| 4838 | Consulate in Monterrey (1907–8) |
| 4839 | Vice Consulate in Oaxaca (1907–13) |

| | |
|---|---|
| 12277–12299 | Trade and Shipping Relations with Mexico and Reports on Trade and Other Matters Concerning This State (1868–1906) |
| 12300 | Wishes Regarding the Reorganization of Trade Contracts with Mexico (1903–6) |
| 12567–12568 | Complaints concerning Mexican Customs |
| 13343 | Yearly Reports of the Consulate in Tapachula (1907–12) |
| 13344 | Yearly Reports of the Consulate in Tepic (1907–14) |
| 13721 | Agriculture in Mexico (1913–16) |
| 15322–15344 | Railroads in Central and South America (1877–1913) |
| 15590 | Reports on the Nature of Foreign Railroads (1887–1911) |
| | Trade and Shipping Relations |
| 16804, 63475 | Italy and Mexico (1857–1919) |
| 16943–16945 | Mexico and the United States (1887–1911) |
| 16963 | Portugal and Mexico (1880) |
| 17039 | Mexico and Guatemala (1887–95) |
| 17048 | Ecuador and Mexico (1888–91) |
| 17051 | Mexico and Japan (1889–1913) |
| 17075 | Mexico and Switzerland (1890–1906) |
| 17094 | Santo Domingo and Mexico (1891) |
| 17106 | San Salvador and Mexico (1893–94) |
| 17144 | Mexico and China (1899–1901) |
| 17167 | Mexico and Nicaragua (1901–4) |
| 17178 | Persia and Mexico (1903) |
| 17189 | Mexico and Cuba (1903–4) |
| 17202 | Chile and Mexico (1904) |
| 17280 | Canada and Mexico (1908) |
| 17302 | Honduras and Mexico (1908–14) |
| 17306 | Russia and Mexico (1909–11) |
| 17353 | Mexico and Australia (1911–12) |
| 17947 | Mexico's Shipping Relations |
| 18954 | Lawful and Administrative Decisions Regarding Customs and Taxes in Mexico (1912–20) |
| 18955 | German Complaints over Mexican Customs |
| 21599–21606 | Petroleum Production and Trade in America (1903–20) |
| 50903/1–50907 | The Legation of the Republic of Mexico at the Kaiser's Court Here |
| 50908–50912 | Mission at the Republic of Mexico (1868–98) |
| 50913 | Foreign Embassies in Mexico (1880–82) |
| | Consulate |
| 52728–52730 | Mexico (1867–91) |
| 52731 | Campeche (1869–87) |
| 52732 | Colima and Manzanillo (1869–76) |
| 52733 | Cordova (1869–71) |

| 52734 | Durango (1871–87) |
| 52735 & 52335/1 | Guadalajara (1869–86) |
| 52736 | Guanajuato (1894) |
| 52737 | Huatusec (1869–72) |
| 52738 | San Louis Potosí (1869–92) |
| 52739 | Matamoros (1869–81) |
| 52740 | Mazatlán (1869–86) |
| 52741 | Mexico (1869–85) |
| 52742 | Puebla (1860–91) |
| 52743 | Tampico (1869–88) |
| 52744 | Tepic (1869–88) |
| 52745–52746 | Veracruz (1869–87) |
| 52747 | Laguna de Términos (1871–89) |
| 52748 | Monterrey (1872–94) |
| | Vice Consulate |
| 52749 | Guaymas (1887–1903) |
| 52750–52751 | Acapulco (1872–89, 1895–1906) |
| 52752 | Frontera de Tabasco (1875–78) |
| 52753 | Merida (1879–87) |
| 52754 | Ciudad Porfirio Díaz (1893–97) |
| | Yearly Reports of the Consulate |
| 54043 | Colima (1887–1905) |
| 54044 | Durango (1887–1906) |
| 54045–54046 | Guadalajara (1887–1904, 1895–1906) |
| 54047 | Guanajuato (1887–1906) |
| 54048 | San Luis Potosí (1894) |
| 54049–54050 | Mazatlán (1887–1901, 1902–6) |
| 54051–54055 | Mexico (1887–1906) |
| 54056 | Tampico (1887–1906) |
| 54057–54058 | Tepic (1887–1904, 1904–6) |
| 54059 | Veracruz (1900–1906) |
| 54060 | Laguna (1887–1906) |
| 54061 | Monterrey (1889–1906) |
| 54062 | Guaymas (1887–1903) |
| 54063 | Acapulco (1890) |
| 54064 | Chihuahua (1900–1906) |
| 54065 | Merida (1887–1906) |
| 54066 | Oaxaca (1900–1906) |
| 54067 | Morelia (1887–91) |
| 54068 | Tehuantepec (1887–1905) |
| 54069 | Ciudad Juárez (1895–1904) |
| 54070 | Tapachula (1900–1906) |
| 54229 | Mexican Consulate in Prussia (1887–1895) |

b) Foreign Ministry, Legal Division

| Nos. 21885–21888 | Postal Relations with Mexico (1866–1910) |
| 29071 | German Military Instruction in Mexico (1912) |

| 34066 | Police in Central America, Mexico (1904–13) |
| 34116 | Complaints against Police in Foreign Lands, Mexico (1912) |
| 34146 | Complaints against the Treatment of Germans in Foreign Lands, Mexico (1911–14) |
| 34187 | Cases of Murder and Robbery in Foreign Lands, Mexico (1913–15) |
| 34694 | The Question of the Worker in Central America (1903–31) |

c) Foreign Ministry, News and Press Division

| No. 57679 | Transocean Society (1916–17) |
| 57681 | Transocean Society |
| 57697 | German Overseas Service (1916–17) |
| 57698–57699 | Iberian-American Federation (1917–18) |
| 57866–57867 | Transocean Society (1915–16) |

Commentary to

Horst von der Goltz, *My Adventures as a German Spy* (New York, 1917)
Arnoldo Krum Heller, *For Freedom and Justice: My Experiences during the Mexican Civil War* (Halle and Berlin, 1917)

d) Foreign Ministry, Central Agency for Foreign Service

| Nos. 1274–1275 | War Committee of German Industry |
| 1497 | Distribution of the Monthly War Journal and Other Materials to the Members of the Hamburg-America Line, Passenger Traffic Division, in Brussels (1915–17) |
| 1653 | Organization of the Central Agency for Foreign Service (1914–17) |

e) Foreign Ministry, Embassy Archive

| No. 1571 | German Legation in China, Emigration to Mexico (1909–10) |

f) Department of the Interior

| No. 1648 | Legislation on Emigration in Mexico (1909–28) |
| 1808 | Emigration to Mexico (1874–1919) |
| 3705–3708 | Yearly Trade Reports of the British Consuls and Ambassadors (1870–1914) |
| 4374 | Germany's Trade Agreement with Mexico (1902–8) |
| 4375–4377 | Commercial Affairs |
| 4378–4379 | Statistical Information on Mexico (1877–1914) |
| 4380–4381 | Customs and Tax Councils (1906–9) |
| 4382 | Complaints in Customs and Tax Councils (1906–9) |
| 4383–4384 | Finance Conditions (1898–1917) |
| 6113 | Secret Matters (1917) |

| | |
|---|---|
| 7039 | Work Stoppages in Foreign Countries (1903) |
| 7761 | Petroleum and Gasoline Trade in Germany (1914–17) |
| 7762–7765 | Petroleum Trade (1903–14) |
| 12266 | The Nature of the Press and of News Reports (1911–19) |
| 12319 | Press and News Service for Spanish and Portuguese-speaking Countries (1914–17) |
| 14430 | Propaganda in Germany and Abroad (1916–23) |

g) German Reichsbank

| | |
|---|---|
| C II 41, Field 137 | Banking Practices in Mexico (1896–1914) |
| C II 41, Field 164 | Finance Practices in Mexico (1898–1914) |
| H II B 41 | Mexico's Economic Situation: Trade, Industry, Business |

h) Department of the Treasury

| | |
|---|---|
| Nos. 1850–1851 | The International Monetary Conference in Berlin, 1903 (American-Mexican Silver Commission) (1903–5) |
| 2476–2478 | Finance Conditions of Foreign Countries, Mexico (1902–19) |

i) Department of the Economy

| | |
|---|---|
| No. 1006 | Commercial Affairs in Mexico (1910–19) |

j) Chancellery of the Reich

| | |
|---|---|
| No. 12 | The United States of America |
| 1979 | The Hamburg-America Line |
| 1980 | German Shipping Firms |
| 2398/10 | General Comments |
| 2403–2405 | The Chancellor's Dealings with Main Headquarters |
| 2410 | Submarine Warfare |
| 2476–2477 | Preparations for the Conclusion of Peace (1914–15), Annex Documents Concerning Fundamental Discussion of War Goals |

k) Postal Department, Privy Registry Z

| | |
|---|---|
| No. 15043/1 | Radio and Telegraph Connections with Mexico (1916–21) |
| 15072 | Radio and Telegraph Connections, Germany and South America (North America) (1914–16) |

l) Reichstag, Protocol of the Reich's Budget Committee

| | |
|---|---|
| No. 1286 | March–April 1914 |
| 1295 | March 1916 |
| 1307 | January–March 1917 |
| 1311–1312 | March–May 1917 |
| 1314–1315 | July–August 1917 |

m) Legacies
  Legacy of Herwarth von Bittenfeld
German Central Archive, Merseburg

| | |
|---|---|
| Rep. 6, No. 756 | Surveillance of Emigrants from Germany to Mexico, vol. 1 (1852–82) |
| 1979 | Trade and Shipping Relations between the Netherlands and Mexico (1825–99) |
| 1982 | Trade and Shipping Relations between France and Mexico (1825–1918) |
| 2009 | Trade and Shipping Relations between Denmark and Mexico |
| 2015 | Trade Relations between Sweden and the Republic of Mexico |
| 2017 | Trade and Shipping Relations between England and Mexico (1854–1919) |
| 2039 | The Peace Treaty and Shipping and Trade Relations between Spain and Mexico (1838–1919) |
| 2082 | Trade and Shipping Relations between Austria and Mexico (1843–1913) |
| 2139 | Trade Relations between Belgium and Mexico (1851–1911) |
| Rep. 89, H VI, America, No. 2, 2a | Documents of the Civil Committee on Mexico |
| Rep. 92, E I, No. 13 | Legacy of Kapp |
| CXIII, 17, | |
| No. 2 | Trade Relations with Mexico (1900–1920) |
| 3 | Trade Relations with the Former Spanish Lands in South America (Mexico, Colombia, Buenos Aires, Chile, Peru) (1831–1934) |
| 7 | The Appointment of Prussian Consuls in the Spanish South American Lands, vol. 7 (1817–1920) |
| 26 | Trade Treaty between the German Reich and Mexico (1869–1931) |
| 81 | Conditions Regarding Patent and Trademark Protection in Mexico (1890–1906) |
| 93 | The Reports of Experts in Mexican Agriculture and Forestry |

Saxon Chief Regional Archive, Dresden
  a) Ministry of Foreign Affairs

| | |
|---|---|
| No. 2030 | Political Conditions in Mexico (1905–23) |
| 2031 | Newspaper Excerpts |
| 6918 | Trade and Shipping Contracts with Mexico (1854–1934) |

b) Ministry of the Interior

| | |
|---|---|
| Nos. 16515–16516 | Reports of Agricultural Experts in Mexico (1899–1902) |

German Economic Institute, Berlin

| No. 0978 | Mexican Light–Power Company, Mexico |
|----------|-------------------------------------|
| 01643 | Mexican Eagle Co., Ltd., London |
| 02025 | National Railways of Mexico |
| 04287 | Mexican Corporation, Ltd., London |
| 05248 | Mexican Central Railways, Co., Ltd., Boston |
| 05469 | Mexican Tramway Co., Toronto |
| 06418 | Mexican Southern Railway, Ltd., London |
| 06427 | Mexikanskaya Telefon Aktiobolaget Erikson, Stockholm |
| 07720 | Mexican Petroleum Co., Ltd., Los Angeles |

**German Federal Republic**
Archive of the Foreign Ministry, Bonn
a) Mexico

| Mexico 1 | Written Exchanges with the Royal Ministerial Ambassador to Mexico as well as with other missions and foreign cabinets concerning the internal affairs and relations of Mexico. From 8 January 1882 the heading reads "General Affairs of Mexico, 58 volumes (1879–1920)" |
|----------|---|
| 1 secr. | General Affairs of Mexico, vol. 1 (1915) |
| 1 add | Information about Private Persons and Protection of Their Interests in Case of Unrest, 8 volumes (1913–19) |
| 2 | Relations between Mexico and Guatemala (Border Conflicts), 4 volumes (1881–1917) |
| 3 | Ministries, 1 volume |
| 5 | Diplomatic Corps in Mexico and Mexican Diplomatic Representatives in Foreign Lands, 2 volumes (1887, 1914–19) |
| 6 | Mexican Presidents, 1 volume (1887–1909) |
| 7 | Relations with North America, 5 volumes (1889–1920) |
| 8 | Mexico's Relations with Russia, 1 volume (1889–1909) |
| 9 | Mexico's Relations with Austria, 1 volume (1890–1901) |
| 10 | Mexico's Relations with Japan, 1 volume (1892–1920) |
| 11 | Mexico's Relations with the Vatican (1895–1905) |
| 12 | Mexico's Relations with Belgium (1890–1913) |
| 13 | Military and Navy, 1 volume (1912–19) |
| 14 | Finances, 3 volumes (1912–19) |
| 15 | Press, 1 volume (1914–16) |
| 16 | Germany's Relations with Mexico, 3 volumes (1917–20) |
| 16 secr. | Private Documents of Privy Councillor Dr. Goeppert, 1 volume (1917) |

b) Germany

| | |
|---|---|
| 122, No. m | Undersecretary Zimmermann (1911–17) |
| 2n | Parlimentary Addresses (1916–17) |
| 127, No. 21 | The Mexican Mission in Berlin (1888–1918) |

c) Legation Archive, Mexico, Bundle 1–20

German Federal Archives, Section of Military History, Freiburg im Breisgau
Archives of the German Navy
Chief Office of Public Record, Munich

| | | |
|---|---|---|
| Mexico MH 53 73 | | Trade and Shipping Relations with South America (Venezuela, Buenos Aires, Havana), Mexico B.A., Chile (1846–1908) |
| | 11598 | Petition by the Moritz Magnus Firm in Hamburg for the Release of Infantry Rifles for Export to America, then Sale of Munitions and Rifles to Mexico (1909–10) |
| | 11668 | Data about Mexican Companies (1899) |
| | 12198 | Mexico's Goodwill, Trade, and Shipping Treaties with the United States (1870–89) |
| | 12199 | Mexico's Trade and Shipping Treaties with the United States (1854–1904) |
| | 12200 | Excerpts from the Reports of the Trade Treaty Union; Information on Trade and Industry, Mexico (1912–14) |
| MK 11790 | | The International School for. Ethnography and Archeology in Mexico (1902–13) |

Office of Public Record, Hamburg
a) Berlin Embassy

| | |
|---|---|
| IIIf | Trade Treaty with Mexico 1870–83 |

b) Senate Commission for Governmental and Foreign Affairs

| | | |
|---|---|---|
| A III | c21 | German Consular Representation in Mexico (1891–1920) |
| A CI | d26 | Weapon Smuggling (1907–20) |
| | 27 | Sale of War Materiel from German Governmental Supplies to Nicaragua, Mexico, and China |
| | 158 | Economic Conditions in, and Exports to, Mexico (1897–1913) |
| A CII | d28 | Export of War Contraband, Especially Weapons, during a war in which Germany remained neutral; American Weapon Trade during Her Neutrality (1915–17) |
| A CIII | c39 | Immigration to Mexico (1900–1911) |

c) Senate Records Concerning Mexico

C1 VI, No. 16h, vol. 2   The German Embassy in Mexico
Vol. 3, fasc. 15         The German Consulate in Mexico
Vol. 3a, fasc. 14        The German Embassy in Mexico
Vol. 3b                  Hamburg Consulate in Tampico (1871–90)
Vol. 3c, fasc. 12        Consulate of the North German Alliance; Kaiser's
                         Consulate in Veracruz (1869–92)

    d) Deputation for Trade, Shipping, and Industry
      II Special File, 21 Mexico, XIX c 21 (1874–1912)
    e) Office of Emigration

II A V 10                Emigration to Mexico
II C XI 12               Immigration into Mexico

    Commerce Library, Hamburg
      Protocol of the Hamburg Chamber of Commerce (1871–1920)
    Office of Public Record, Bremen
      a) Hanseatica

C 13 c 1 b               Consulate General to Mexico
C 13 c 2                 Mexicans in Hanseatica and Bremen

      b) Senate Committee for Foreign Affairs

D d 11 c 2 M 3           Mexico
R 11 pp 1 No. 9          Yearly Reports of the North German Lloyd (1857–
                         1936)

      c) War Files, 1914–18

M 2 h 2 No. 1            Files I–XIII

**Austria**
    House, Court, and Government Archives, Vienna
      a) Political Archives
      Mexican Reports (1904–18)
      Washington Reports (1904–17)
      Embassy Archive Mexico (1904–18)
      War 7, Mexico, Mexico's Position Regarding the World War
      b) Administration Archives
      Trade Relations with Mexico
    War Archives, Vienna
      Files of the Evidence Bureau of the General Staff
**Cuba**
    Archivo Nacional de Cuba, Havana
      Comisión de Estado
      Informes diplomáticós y consulares de México, Leg 38 (1904), 266 (1907),
        313 (1903), 324 (1904), 331 (1904), 341 (1905), 355, 375 (1907), 377 (1903),
        378 (1903), 843 (1911)
      Guerra Mundial, Leg 1148–1155 (1914–18)
**France**
    Archives du Ministère des Affaires Étrangères, Paris
    Correspondance Politique et Commerciale

Correspondance Politique, Mexique, vols. 69–81 (1876–1896)
Correspondance Commerciale, Mexique, vols. 10–30 (1876–1902)
Nouvelle Série, Mexique
1. Politique Intérieure. Révolution. Attitude des Puissances, vols. 1–15 (1897–1918)
2. Armée. Marine, vols. 16–17 (1897–1917)
3. Politique Étrangère. Dossier Général, vols. 18–20 (1896–1913)
4. Relations avec la France, 2 vols. (1891–1917)
5. Finances, vols. 23–32 (1895–1918)
6. Travaux Publics—Mines, vols. 33–40 (1902–18)
7. Guerre 1914–1918, 2 vols. (1914–18)
Archives Nationales, Paris
Série F12. Ministère du Commerce
Archives du Ministère de la Guerre, Vincennes
Reports by the Military Attachés in Mexico and the U.S.

**Great Britain**
Public Record Office, London
Foreign Office Papers
Balfour Papers
British Science Museum, London
Papers of Sir Weetman Pearson (Lord Cowdray)

**Japan**
Microfilm Library of Congress, Washington, D.C.
Microfilm, Japanese Foreign Office Documents, Nichi Bokukan. Mexico, MT 28, Dic No. M.T. 1.1.33., PPs 2291–2590.

**Mexico**
Archivo General de la Nación, Mexico, D.F.
Ramo Gobernación
Ramo Revolución
Ramo Presidentes
Archivo de Madero
Archivo de la Secretaría de Relacione Enteriores, Mexico, D.F.
Ramo Revolución Mexicana
Ramo Guerra Europea, 1914–1918
Archivo del Departamento Agrario, Mexico, D.F.
Ramo Terrenos Nacionales
Archivo de la Secretaría de Hacienda, Mexico, D.F.
Archivo de Madero
Museo Nacional de Antropología e Historia, Mexico, D.F.
Microfilm, Archivo de Madero
Universidad Nacional Autónoma de Mexico, Facultad de Filosofía y Letras
Archivo de Gildardo Magaña
Fundación Condumex, Mexico, D.F.
Archivo de Carranza
Archivo Francisco Léon de la Barra
El Colegio de Mexico, Mexico, D.F.
Muro Collection of the Archivo Histórico de la Defensa Nacional (Microfilm of records of the Spanish legation in Mexico, D.F.)

Private archives
  Papers of Roque González Garza, Mexico, D.F.
  Papers of Martin Luis Guzmán, Mexico, D.F.
**Spain**
  Archivo del Ministerio de Relaciones Exteriores, Madrid
**United States**
  National Archives, Washington, D.C.
    Records of the Department of State
      1. Foreign Affairs Branch, State Department Decimal File, 1910–29, File
         812.00, Political Affairs, Mexico. Record Group 59 (on microfilm)
      2. File 862. 202 12 German Military Activities in Mexico, Microcopy 336,
         Rolls 55–59
      3. Files of the Office of the Counselor
    Records of the Department of Justice. Felix Sommerfeld File
    Records of the Adjutant General's Office
    Records of Military Intelligence
  Library of Congress
    Papers of Chandler Anderson
    Papers of Henry F. Fletcher
    Papers of John J. Pershing
    Papers of Hugh Scott
    Papers of William Howard Taft
    Papers of Woodrow Wilson
  Yale Library
    Papers of Col. Edward House
    Papers of Frank L. Polk
  University of Nebraska
    Microfilm of the papers of Sen. Albert B. Fall
  University of California at Berkeley
    Silvestre Terrazas Collection
  Claremont Colleges
    Papers of José María Maytorena
  Southern Illinois University at Carbondale
    Papers of Francisco Vazquez Gómez
  University of Texas at Austin
    Papers of Lázaro de la Garza
  University of Texas at El Paso
    Microfilm of the papers of John Lind
    Papers of Reyes Avilés

# Index